THE ART OF THE FLOWER

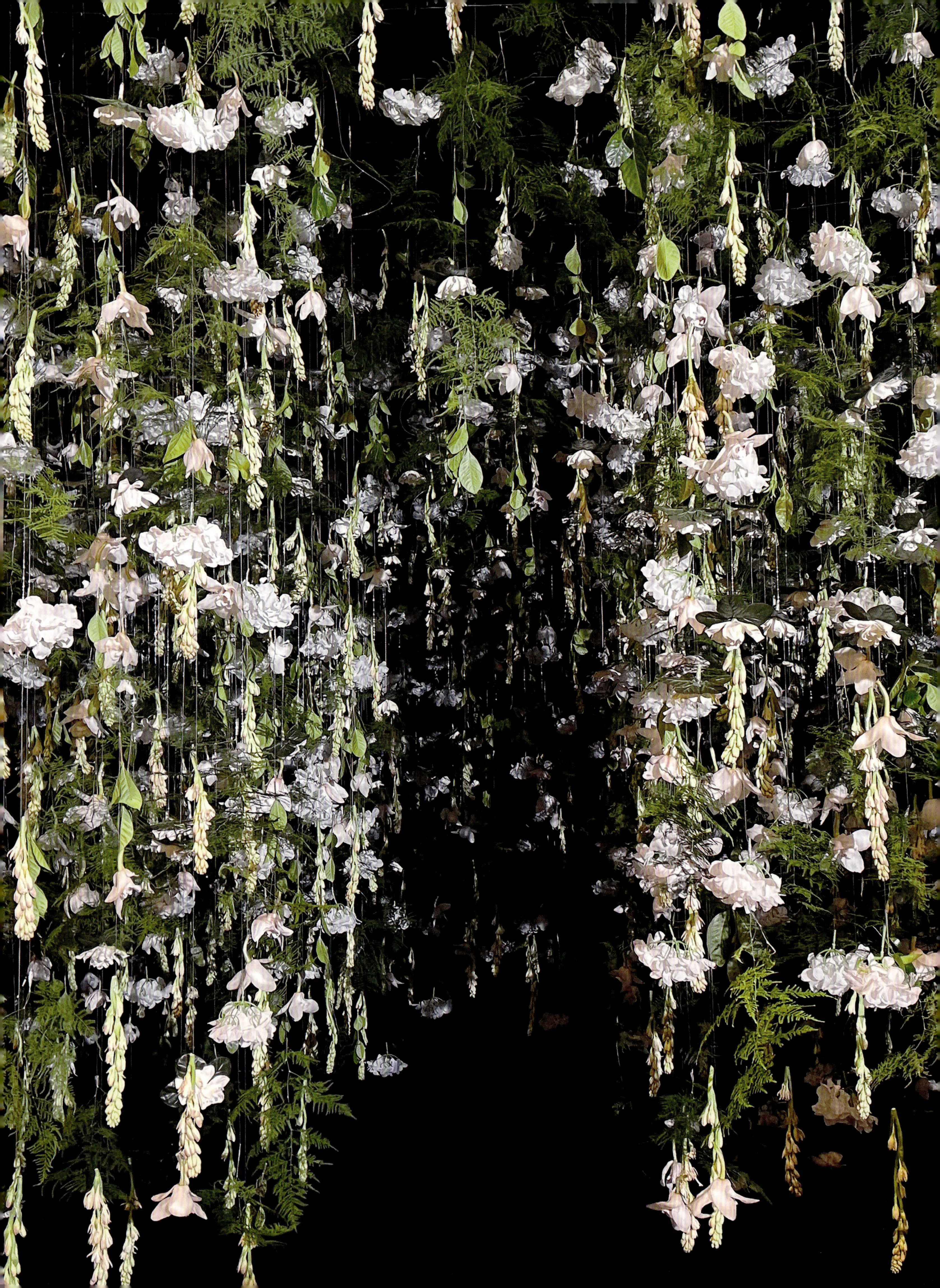

THE ART OF THE FLOWER

A Photographic Collection of Iconic Floral
Installations by Celebrity Florist Jeff Leatham

JEFF LEATHAM

FOREWORD BY Kim Kardashian

weldon**owen**

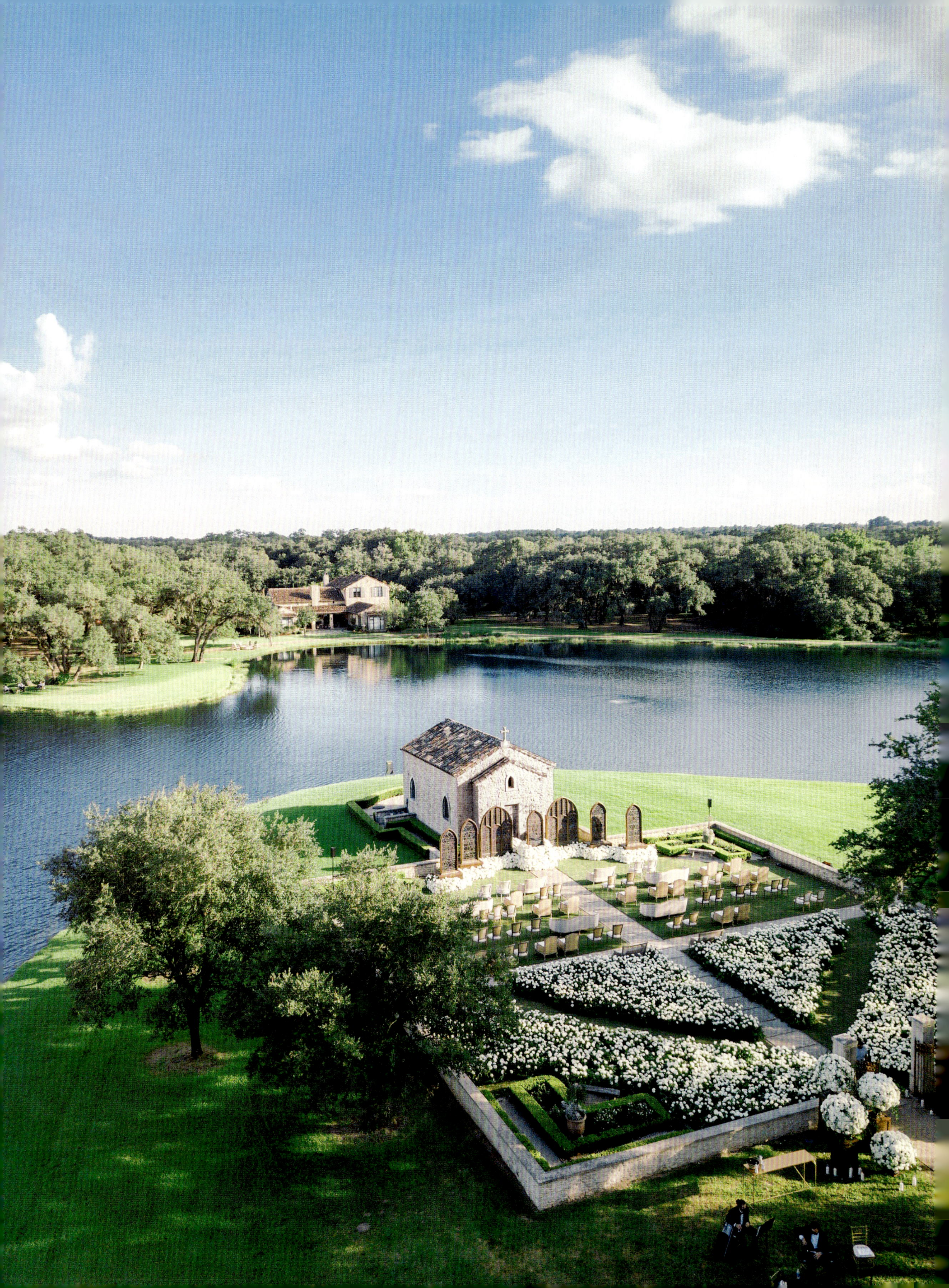

CONTENTS

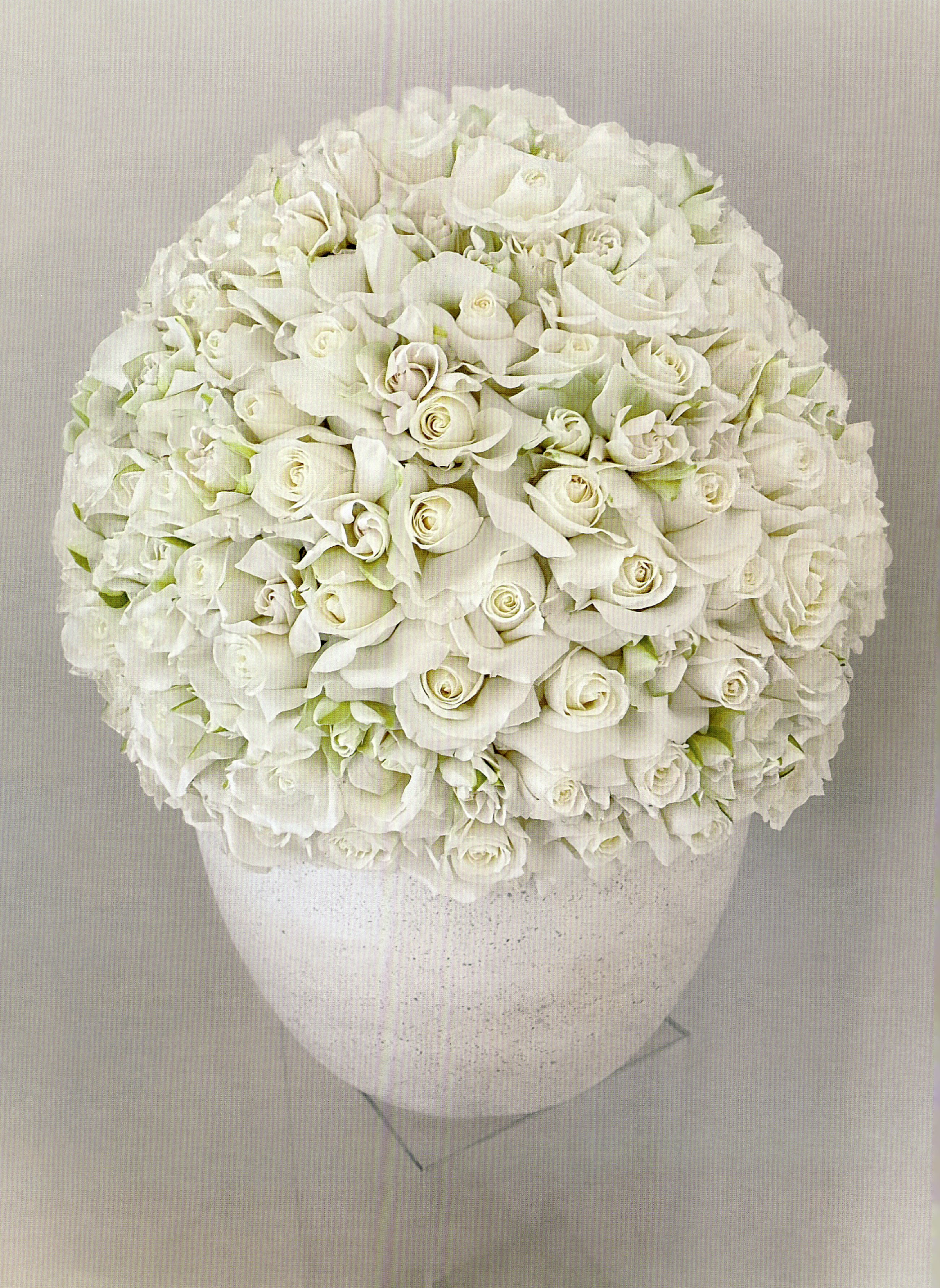

FOREWORD

BY KIM KARDASHIAN

The first time I learned about Jeff and his signature floral designs was from my mom, Kris, who raved about the incredible arrangements she would see inside the lobby at the Four Seasons Hotel George V in Paris, France.

Fast forward many years later, Jeff has become a part of our family, a true friend and collaborator. Every milestone, special event, holiday, and celebration, Jeff has been there to help us create lasting memories with the most beautiful designs to remember them by.

Jeff and I even launched two fragrance collections together, where we introduced six different bottled scents that brought both of our worlds together. From the bottle design to the fragrance notes—as well as the jaw-dropping, fully immersive set designs that Jeff created for our campaign shoots—it was one of the most memorable collections I've ever worked on.

What makes Jeff so special is his ability to personalize and tailor each and every one of his creations with the most thoughtful details, personalized just for you. He is a true master of his craft, not just because of his artistic talents, but because he gives his whole heart into everything that he does.

It's been a pleasure, as Jeff's friend and client, to see him evolve as an artist, using flowers as his medium to always *wow* year after year. As you dive into *The Art of the Flower*, you'll immediately see how flowers, in all shapes and sizes, have the ability to place us in a mood. Flowers do not live forever, so we have to cherish them while they are alive, here in the present. Flowers have the power to lift our spirits and remind us to live in the moment . . . since that is all we really have.

Welcome to the world of flowers, viewed through the eyes of my dear friend, Jeff Leatham.

—KIM KARDASHIAN

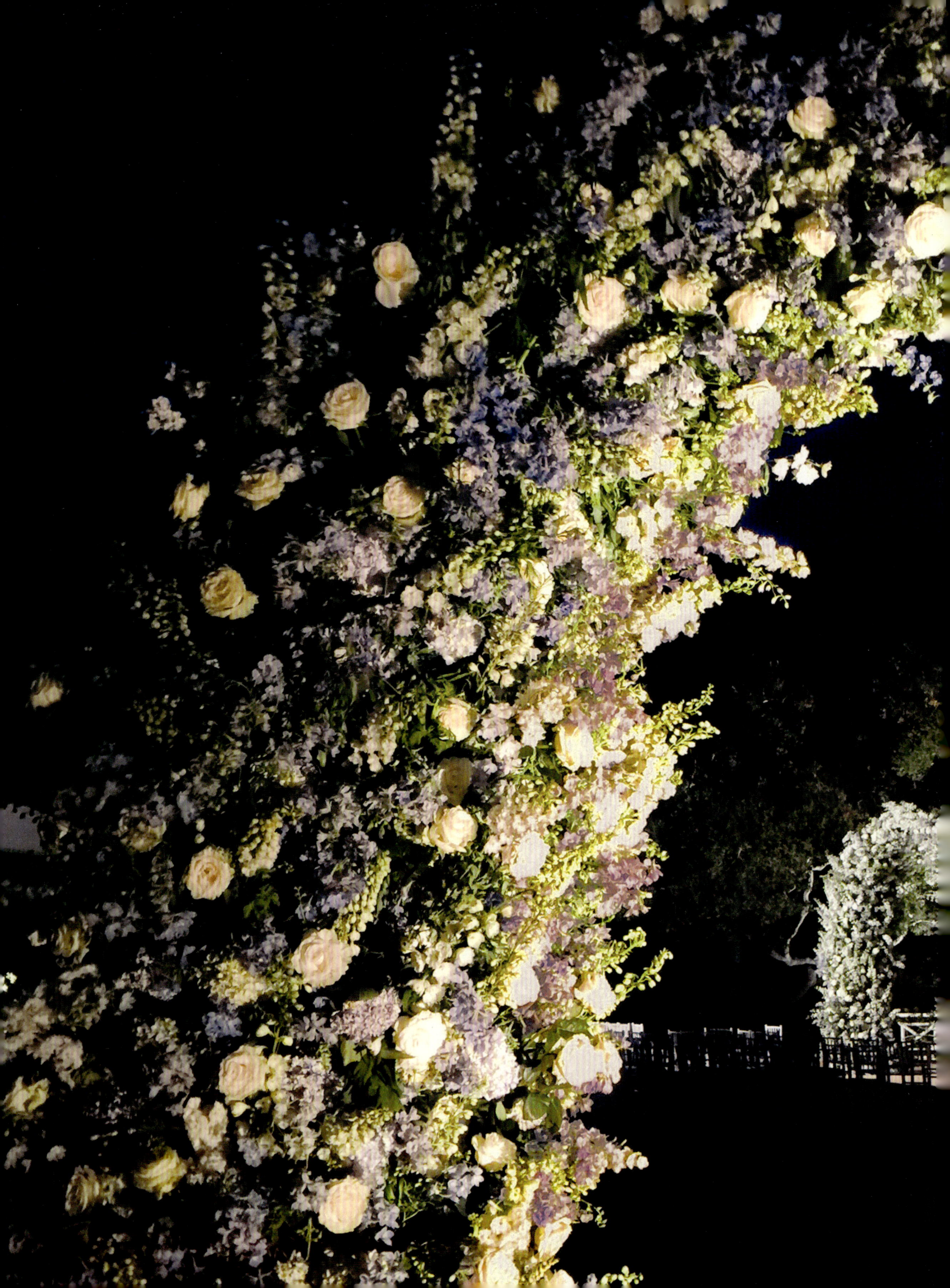

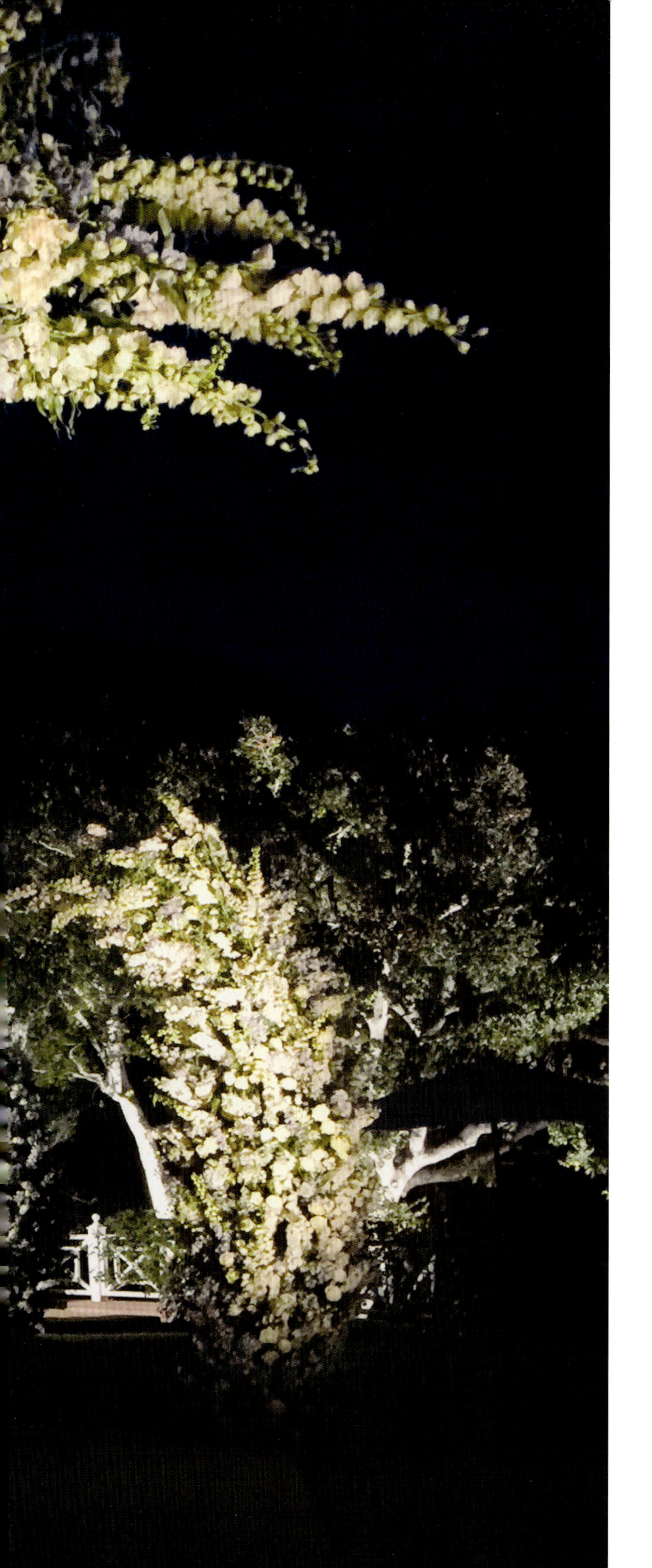

INTRODUCTION

*To my mother, and all of the beautiful women
who have inspired and enriched my life.*

As I sat down to gather my thoughts for the contents of the following pages, the underlying theme immediately sprang to mind: *This book is a love letter to all flower lovers.* It has been several years since I last published a book of my work, and although it feels like only yesterday when I moved to Paris to begin my tenure as the artistic director at the Four Seasons Hotel George V, so much has happened in these past years. I've created floral arrangements, installations, and themes for weddings—not only in the United States but around the world— designed the New York City Botanical Garden Orchid Show (twice!), but most importantly, I have evolved as an artist. In fact, in the past eight years my entire design process has changed and is completely different. Whereas before I used to design for *myself* and the vision inside my head, today I design for people and clients and interpret through my floral art what *they* see.

I have been fortunate to continue working with many of the same clients whom I have in the past—for me, loyalty is the best quality a person can have. Blending and weaving their lives, personal stories, moments of brilliance, and individual artistry together is one of the very components of my artistic process of creation that always brings me so much joy. I never could have dreamed that I would have the clients that I do—and it never ceases to amaze me. My clients and friends are more beautiful than anything I could have dreamed, and I'm so grateful to be allowed into their lives. We have laughed, sung, danced, and seen the world together. It has been a pleasure and an honor to build and design my dreams— and have people appreciate the world in the way that I see it. I'm happy to share it, and always have been. I never imagined when I was modeling in Europe that I would work with flowers . . . or that they would turn me into the world-renowned artist that I am today.

I want viewers to experience and enjoy my work, and there are few things I love more than standing behind the beautifully crafted columns at the George V in Paris and witnessing the reaction of people who see my work for the first time. Truthfully, I never look back at the past very much—repetition is every artist's worst enemy—and have learned throughout my life that I was meant to be the person I am and destined to do what I do, *today.*

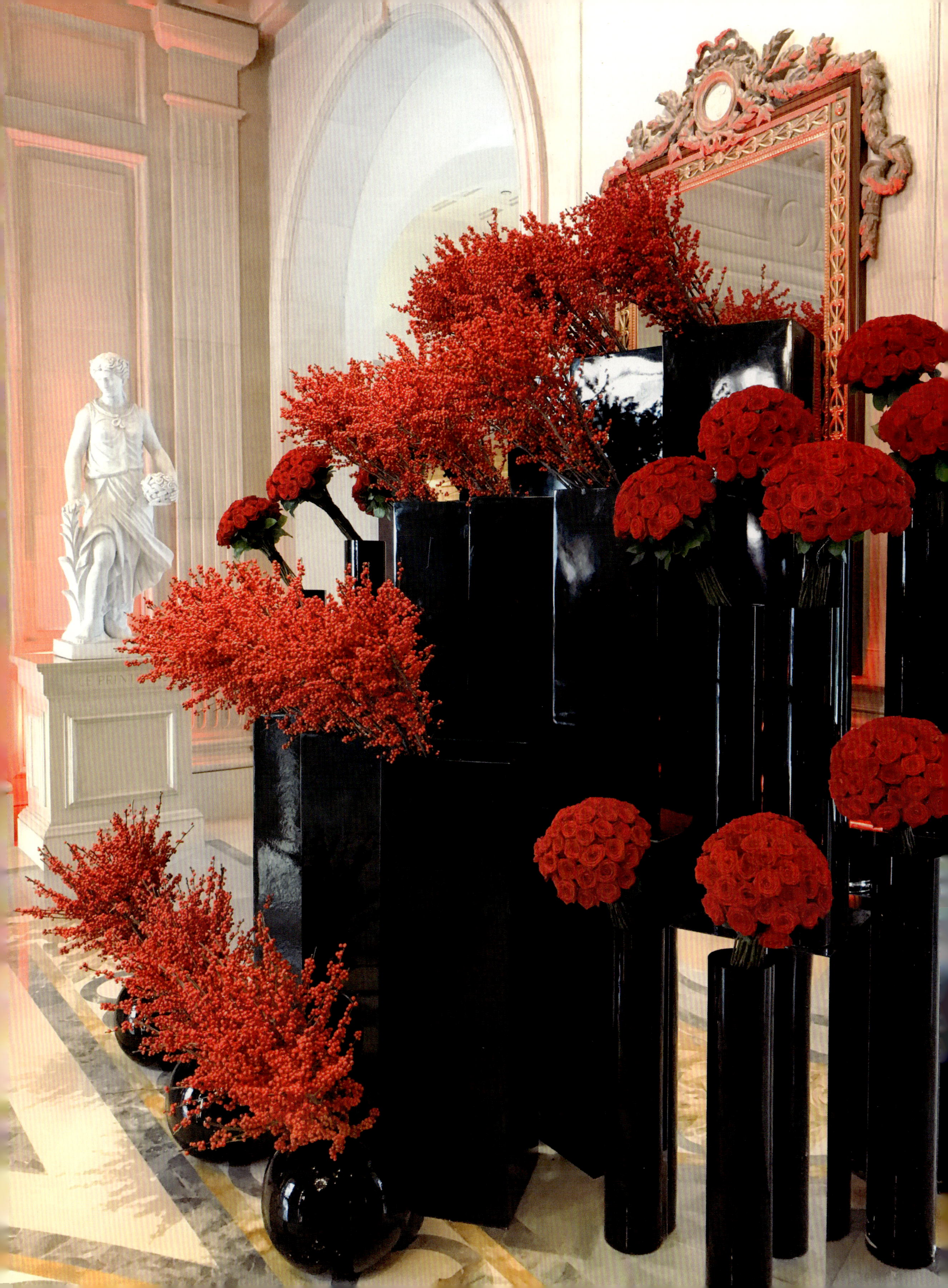

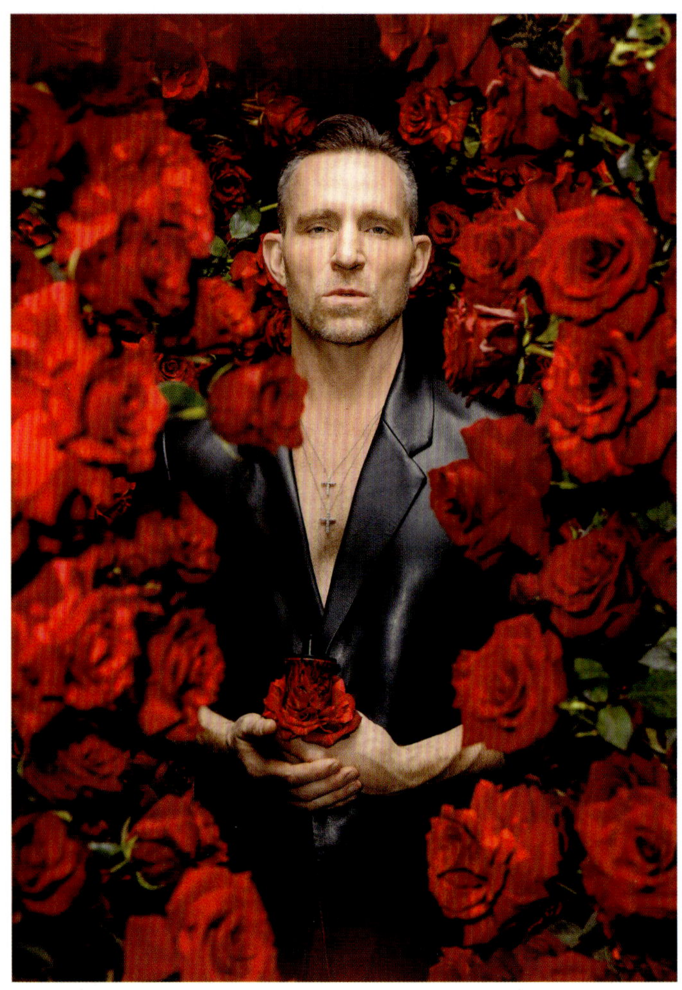

In case we haven't met before, there are a few things to understand about me and my early career. I had a lot of help from some lovely teachers and people, who somehow managed to coalesce around me at the perfect time and give me opportunities I needed to explore every corner of my imagination. You never get to where you are in life because you are simply fabulous; you get to where you are because people help you on your journey and give you support. I'm so deeply grateful to so many because I was not an overnight success. I paid my dues, and I still do. I fundamentally believe it's essential to get your hands dirty—not to mention it's a lot more fun that way. I also think it's important to work with your team and not just finger point. You need to work together and mentor. I don't know how I could simply place my name on a piece and say, "That's a Jeff Leatham floral design" and not have Jeff Leatham help with its creation.

When I stop to think about flowers and the magic they conjure within us, I am immediately drawn to how they excite and play with our senses. Whenever I smell a lilac, I am transported back to my five-year-old self sitting in my grandmother's front yard, surrounded by the sweet spring aroma of my youth. From a visual perspective, flowers have the ability to inspire creativity through their captivating display of hues across the color spectrum. All the master painters were flower enthusiasts—Vincent van Gogh, Claude Monet, and Georgia O'Keeffe—and all studied flowers in minutiae. Monet, in particular, is special to me. When I moved to Paris, I used to travel to his gardens in Giverny on most weekends to be inspired by his famous water lilies. When we look at the art of the flower through the lens of these legendary painters, we're looking at history, life, art, and love captured in a beautiful caught-in-a-moment experience. To me, it's their visual poetry that I try to create in my work today: creating timeless and everlasting memories in the present through my floral works.

Although it might sound a bit strange, flowers can enhance our sense of hearing, which is why I like to listen to music when I'm designing. Flowers also reach us through touch. They are alive and tactile, and we need to feel and work with them—at least I do. These beautiful, kind, and unique objects need a personal touch and passion given to them, and I don't think that's too much to ask. Flowers nourish and feed us in more ways than we can ever really know.

On a more personal level, flowers have always created déjà vu illusions for me that are both memorable and romantic. Whether to celebrate or grieve, flowers are the perfect complements for every life event; they are always present. It has been said that it's very important to gift people flowers while they're still alive. It doesn't matter whether it's one stem or a thousand; flowers have the power to elevate a moment with elegance. Being both traditional and modern, they possess the ability to be both classic and avant-garde—and yet always appropriate and tasteful.

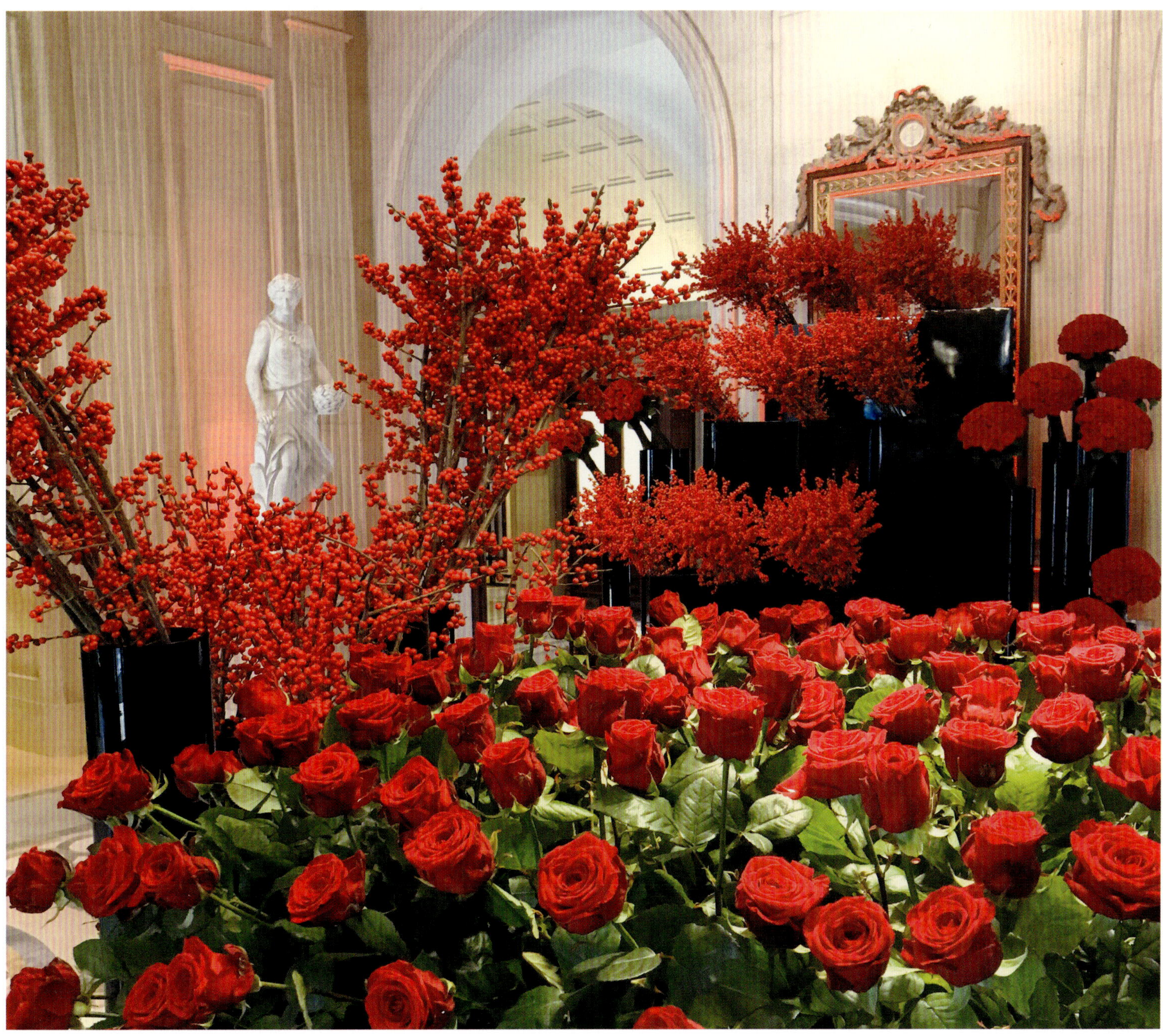

The world of floral and event design has changed so much since I started. Social-media outlets showcase countless talented people all over the world. I'm so proud and happy to see all the participants in the floral industry, many of whom I consider my colleagues and friends, working themselves to the bone to make every single detail about the art of floral design as beautiful as it is. Whether floral designers, growers, or distributors, all are doing such great work, and being a part of the evolution is a matter of great warmth to me.

Because we are one global community now, we must each do our share to conserve our planet and be sustainably responsible. Although I do realize it is necessary in some designs to use floral foam, I am not a supporter of overusing this product. Please design with sustainable alternatives as much as possible. Love and respect Mother Earth . . . she is all we have.

As you might have already guessed, flowers are the *star* of my work and are my muse; they are the real showstoppers, which is why this book is titled *The Art of the Flower*. Every single one is an art form in its own way, even before I touch it. In the following pages, each chapter is dedicated to my unique relationship with flowers via a different venue. From the Art of the Hotel Lobby to the Art of the Holidays, and from the Art of the Event to the Art of the Wedding, each piece was designed with a different theme in mind.

This, to me, is what the art of the flower means, but all you flower lovers already knew that. Thank you for taking part in this journey with me, and thank you for enjoying my work and what I do. My joy wouldn't be the same without you with me every step of the way.

XX
—JEFF LEATHAM

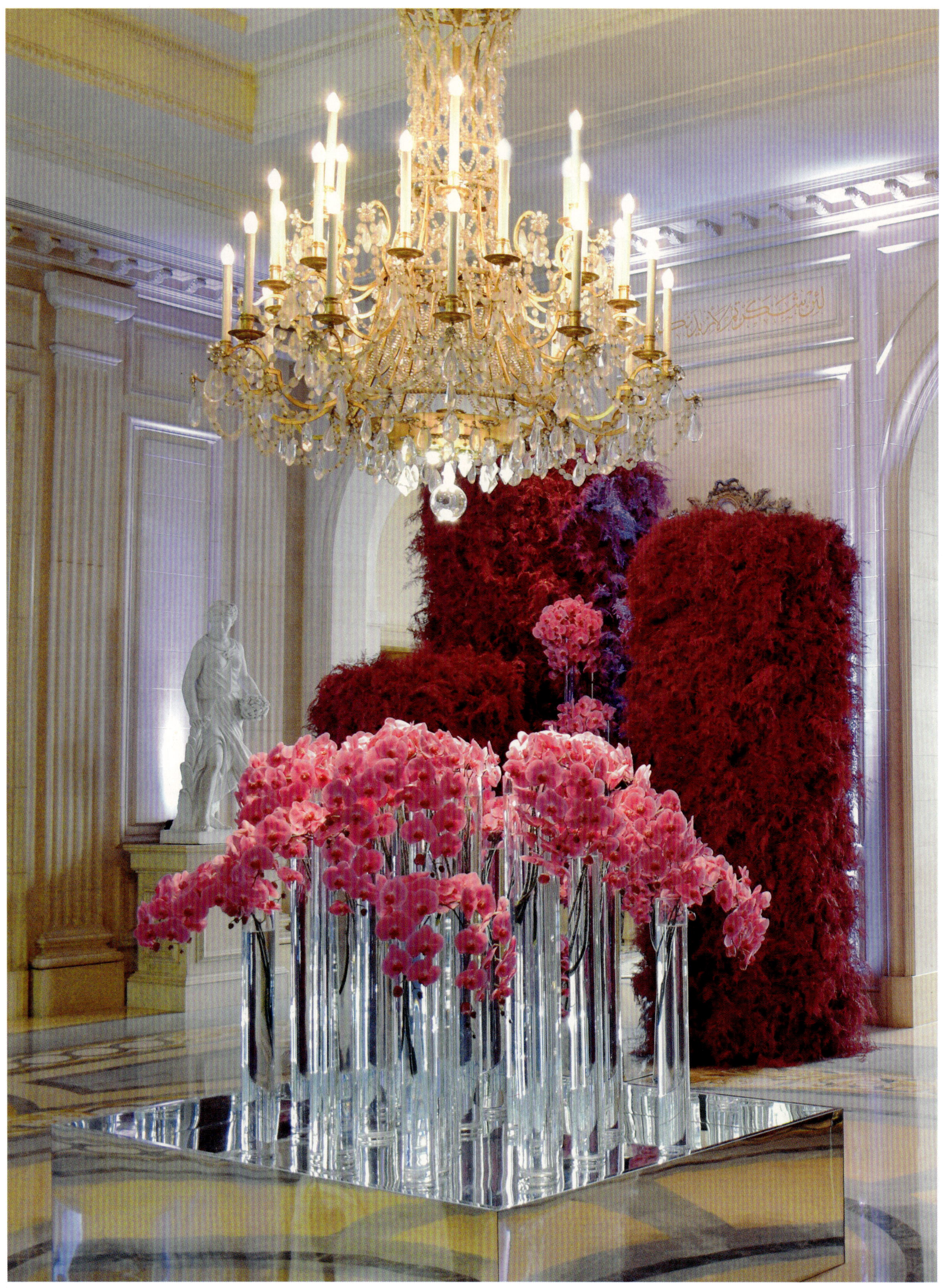

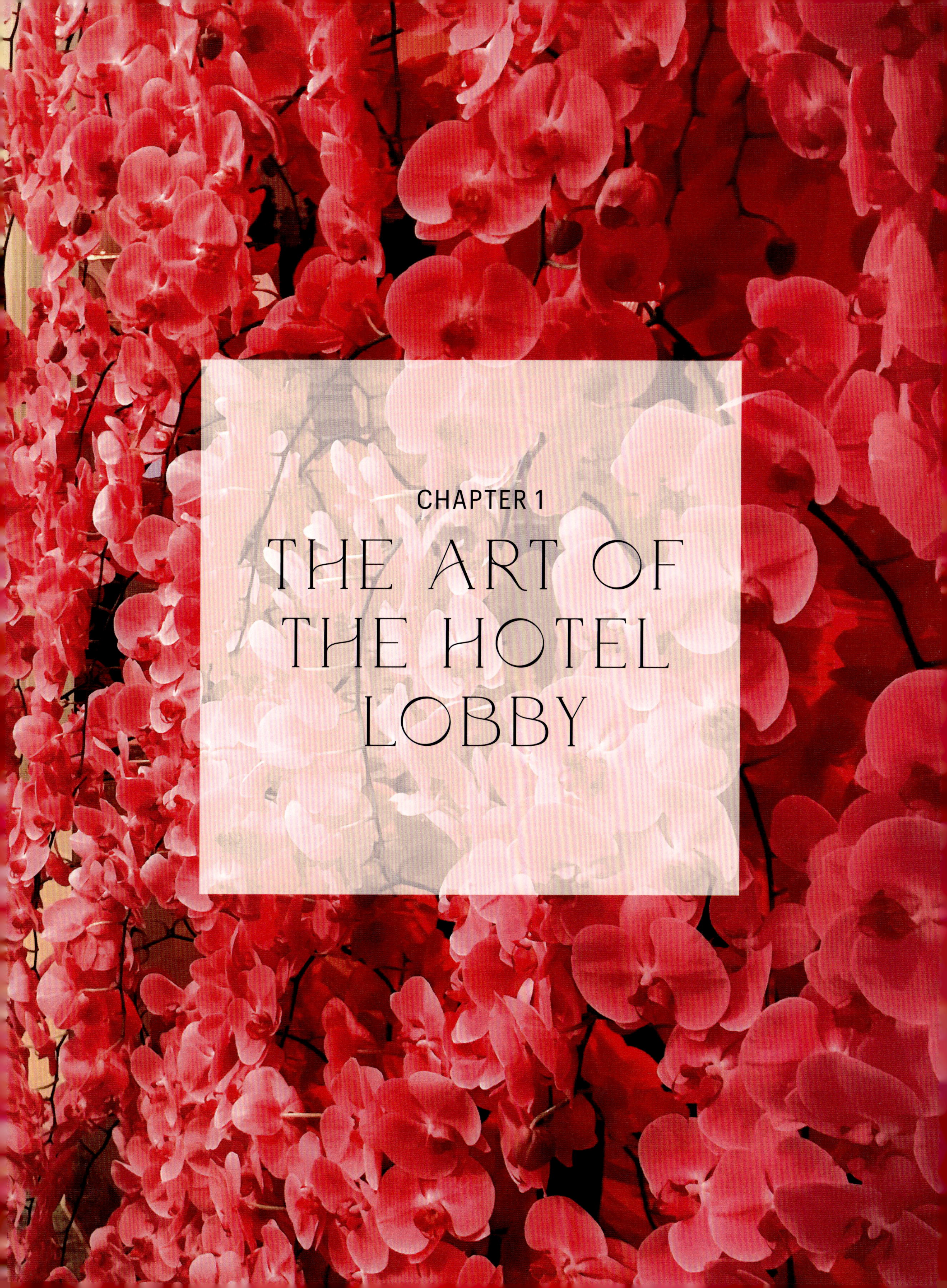

CHAPTER 1
THE ART OF
THE HOTEL
LOBBY

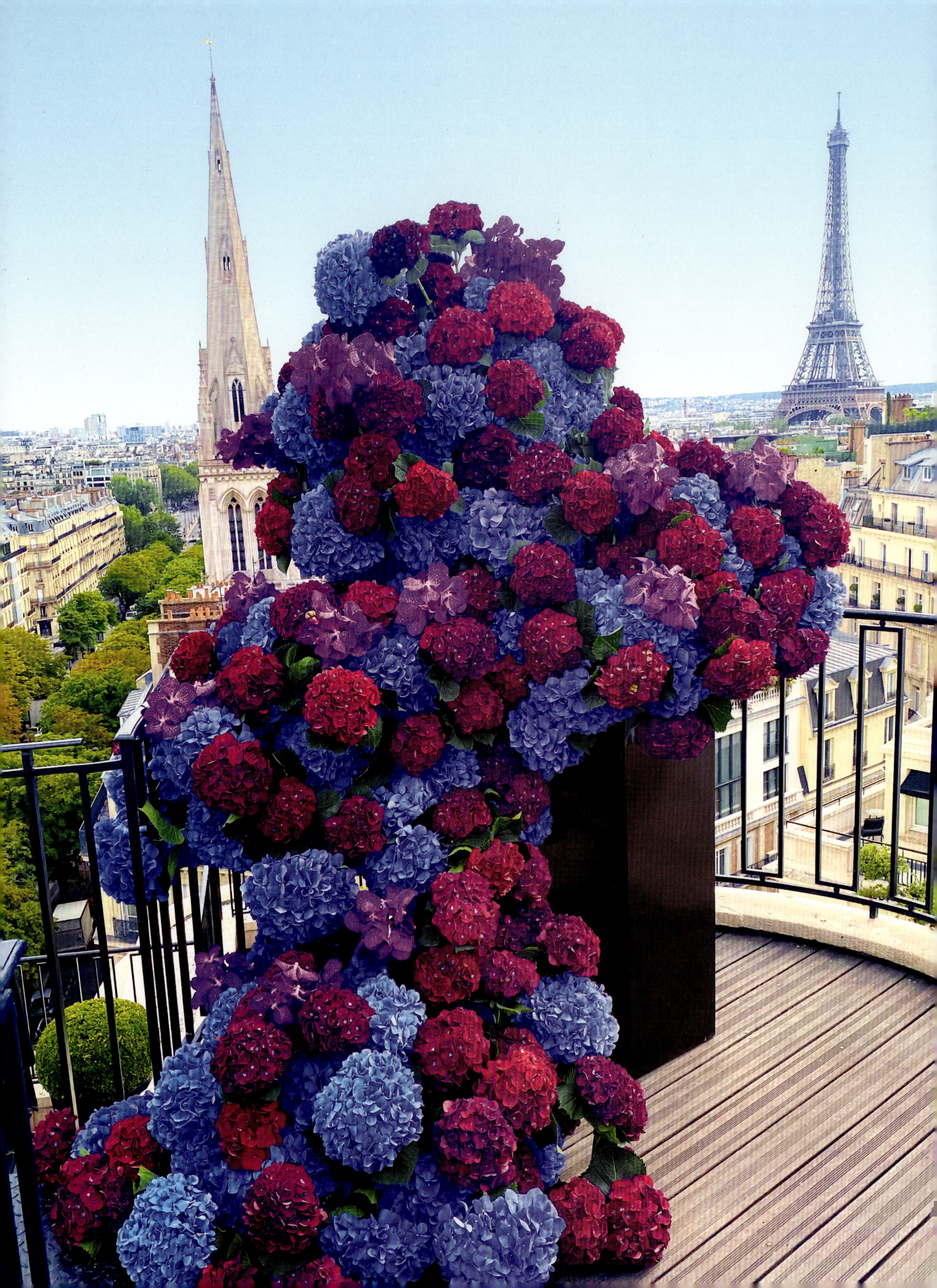

I want to be very clear. I would not be the famed florist Jeff Leatham if it were not for a hotel lobby. Every single major career milestone of mine can be traced to the Four Seasons Hotel empire. In fact, people may not know my name, but they will know me as the "guy who creates the flower arrangements in the lobby." The other thing you must know about me is that I'm obsessed with movies, especially classic films, which possess the magical element to take viewers on a trip to a faraway time and place, yet at the same time make them feel like they never left their homes. Classic movies offer an escape to live a dream for a few moments at your pleasure and present a bygone era that was more idealistic, elegant, and chic. These are the emotions I strive to invoke when I begin any type of floral artwork and that I want people to feel through my medium. To me, hotel lobbies are like giant movie sets for guests. They should feel grand, playful, stylish, sexy, and a little bit like you're getting away with something.

To say a hotel's lobby entrance is one of the most important features is an understatement. Being that the lobby is a hotel's first impression for guests, they *need* to make a bold statement. First impressions matter, and hotel lobbies set a guest's experience, which is why I aim to create a sense of anticipation, a momentary escape from reality, and a hint of what guests will encounter during their stay. This has always been my goal for my floral creations at the Four Seasons Hotels. If I have said it once, I've said it a thousand times: every great relationship has started for me in the lobby of a Four Seasons Hotel!

The Four Seasons Los Angeles at Beverly Hills was the first location I put my floral-arranging skills to the test, and where I was given the chance to begin my career. (Thank you, Paige!) It was here that I began perfecting my floral skills while also designing for my own clients out of my garage—after shopping at the flower markets at 4 a.m. multiple times a week. I was working in the lobby of the Four Seasons Los Angeles at Beverly Hills when I received a call to come upstairs and was offered the position of artistic director at the Four Seasons George V in Paris after they saw my work in person.

When I started my position at the George V and arrived in Paris that first month, I was fortunate to collaborate with the famed French florist Christian Tortu, whose floral works I'd spent years studying and was in awe of his incredible work. I always refer to this period of my life when I arrived in Paris as "the Golden Years." Legendary fashion icons, such as Yves Saint Laurent (with whom I would regularly drink his famous White Lily cocktail at the George V bar), Alexander McQueen, and Karl Lagerfeld were frequent guests during this glamorous period of Tom Ford's Paris years. Fashion design icons were always whisking in and out of the George V's lobby, like elegantly dressed ghosts appearing and then suddenly vanishing. That golden period from 2000 to 2012 *really* was the perfect time in fashion. Philip Treacy and Alexander McQueen's magnificent interpretation of flowers were fascinating to me. When looking back, their influence and tutelage have taught me so much about how my brand has grown today. Fashion was inspiring then; it was all about *art*. Having the honor to even be around these legendary designers during this period still strikes me as unbelievable. They really shaped me into the person I am now. How could they not? It goes without saying that, just like movies, fashion is another one of the most important influences in my designs.

As I travel around the world and experience different peoples, cultures, and places, I cannot help but be amazed at the impact one hotel can have. The influence of the George V is mind blowing, and I am proud to say I am a member of the team who continues to keep it that way. They have always given me artistic freedom that allowed me to create spectacular displays, which is something I will forever be grateful for. Each one of the hotel lobbies I've curated is like one of my children. They're significant and different in unique ways— just like the cities they're a part of. From the glitz and glamour of the Four Seasons Los Angeles at Beverly Hills to the sleek and modern Four Seasons Philadelphia, it's always hard to choose my favorite. However, even though I have offices in different parts of the world now, the Four Seasons George V will always and forever be my mothership.

Four Seasons George V Rooftop.
Hydrangeas and vanda orchids.

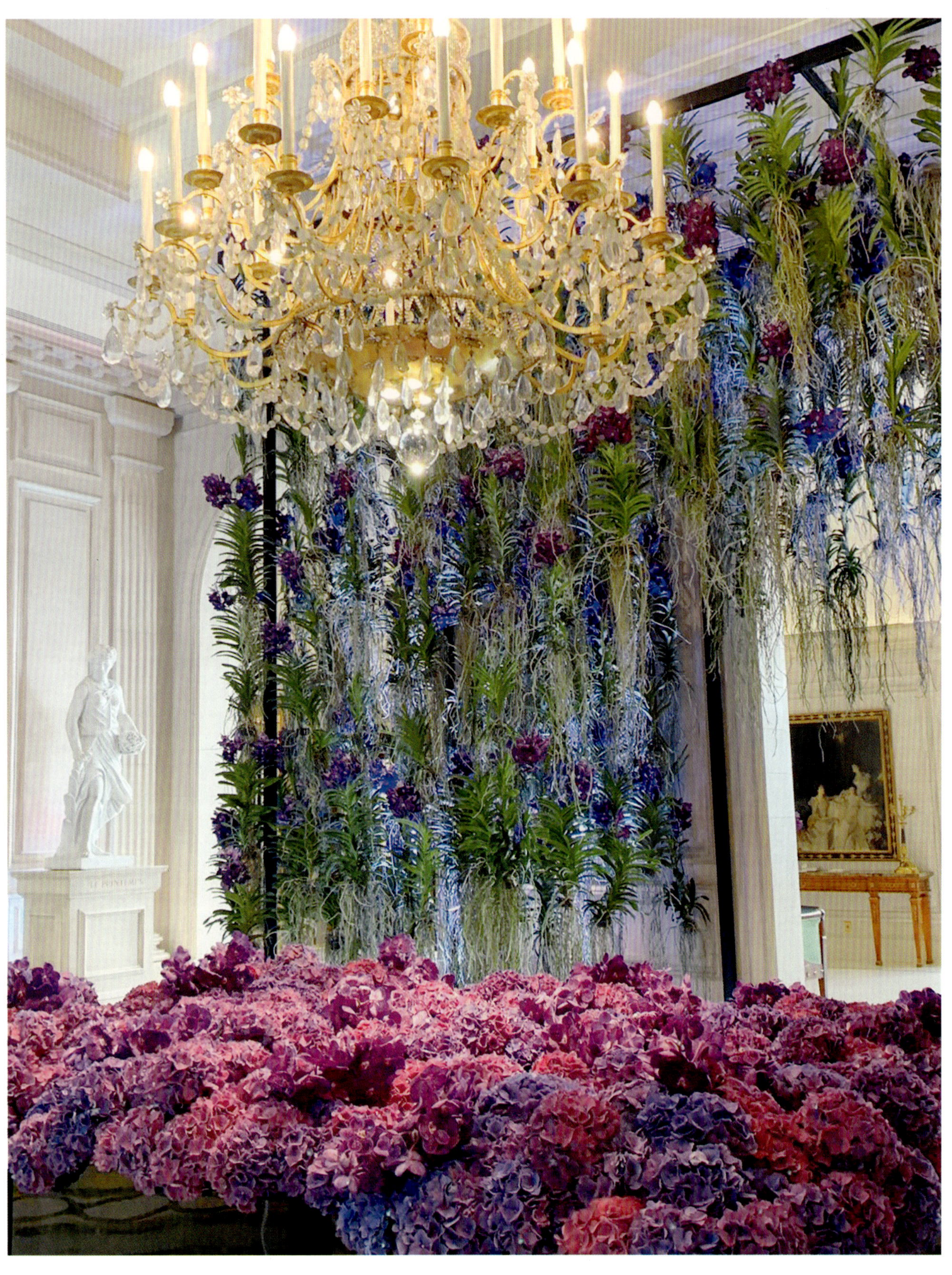

ABOVE: Four Seasons George V Lobby.
Hanging vanda orchids and hydrangeas.
OPPOSITE: Statice, hydrangeas, and roses.

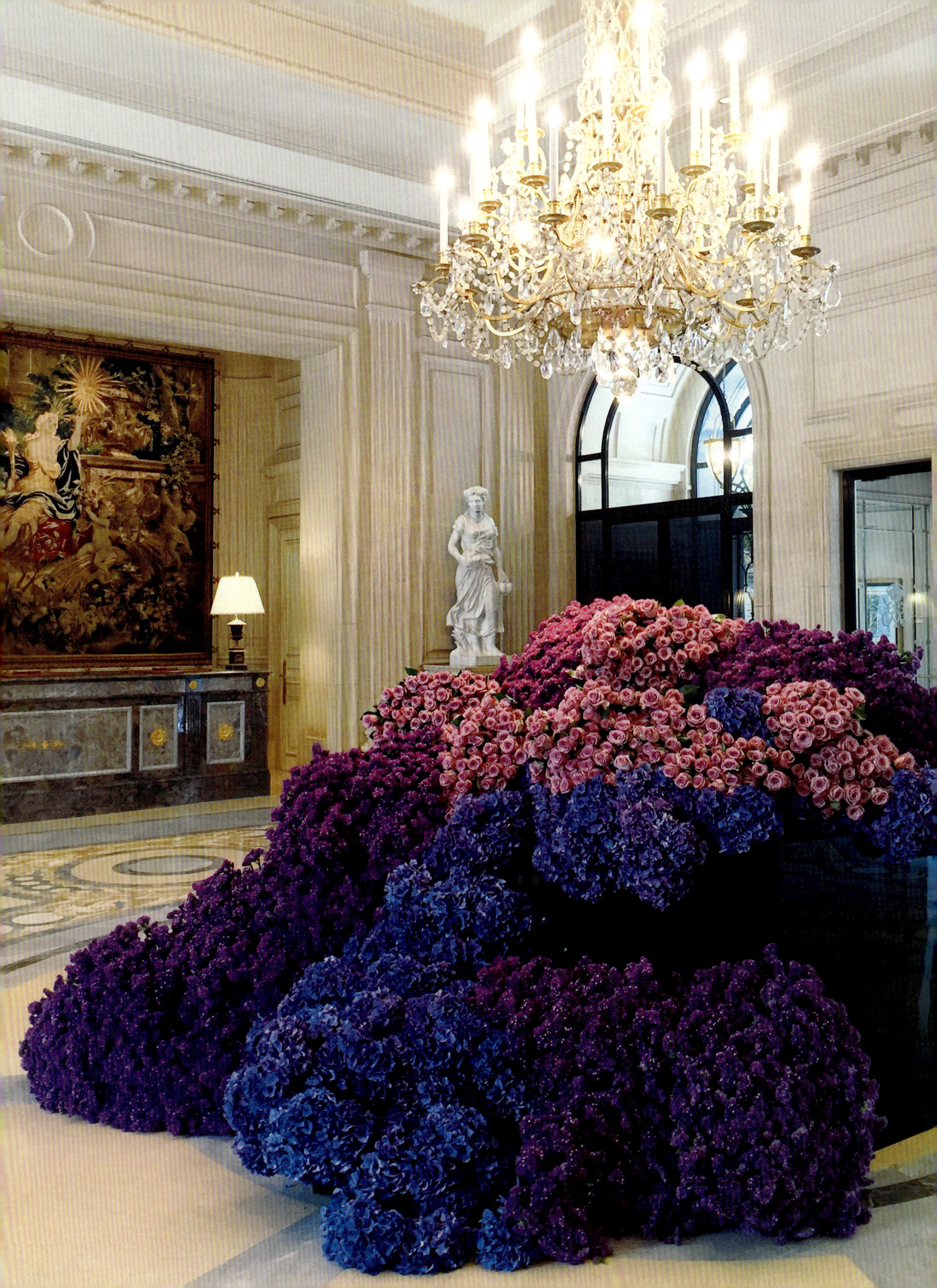

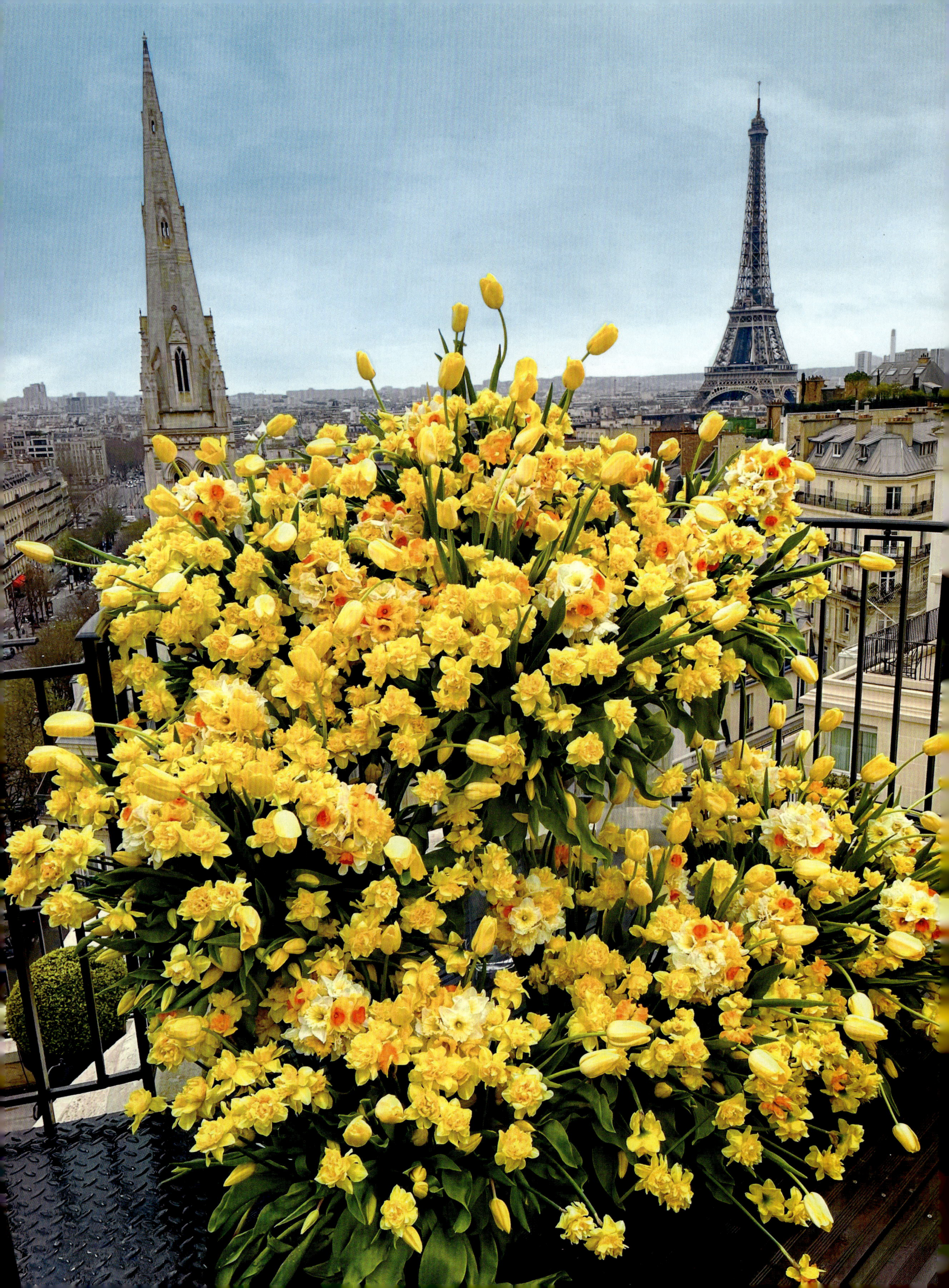

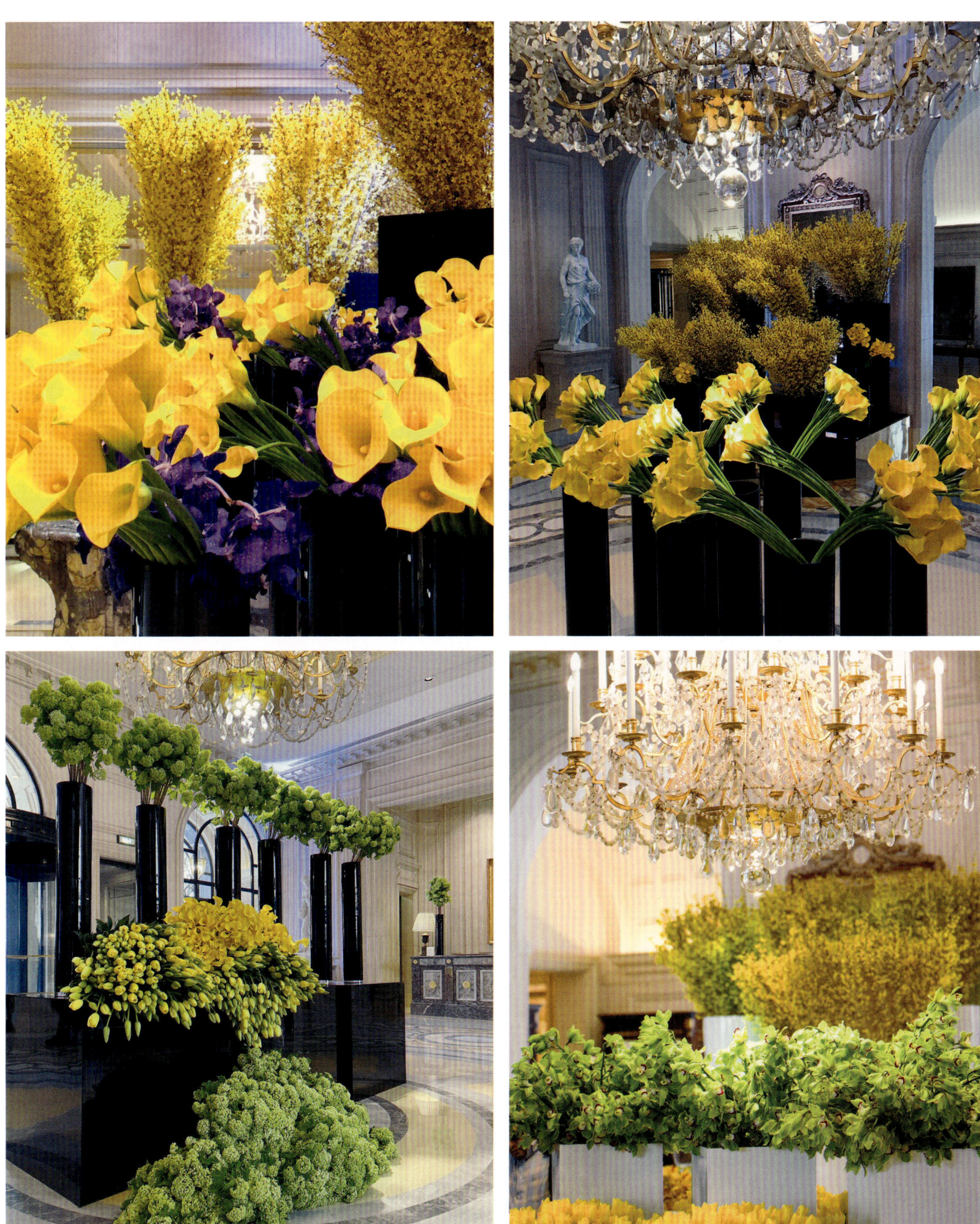

Four Seasons George V Lobby and Rooftop.
Tulips, cymbidiums, forsythia branches, calla lilies, daffodils, vanda orchids, and viburnum. FOLLOWING: Calla lilies, hydrangeas, phalaenopsis orchids, and hanging vanda orchids.

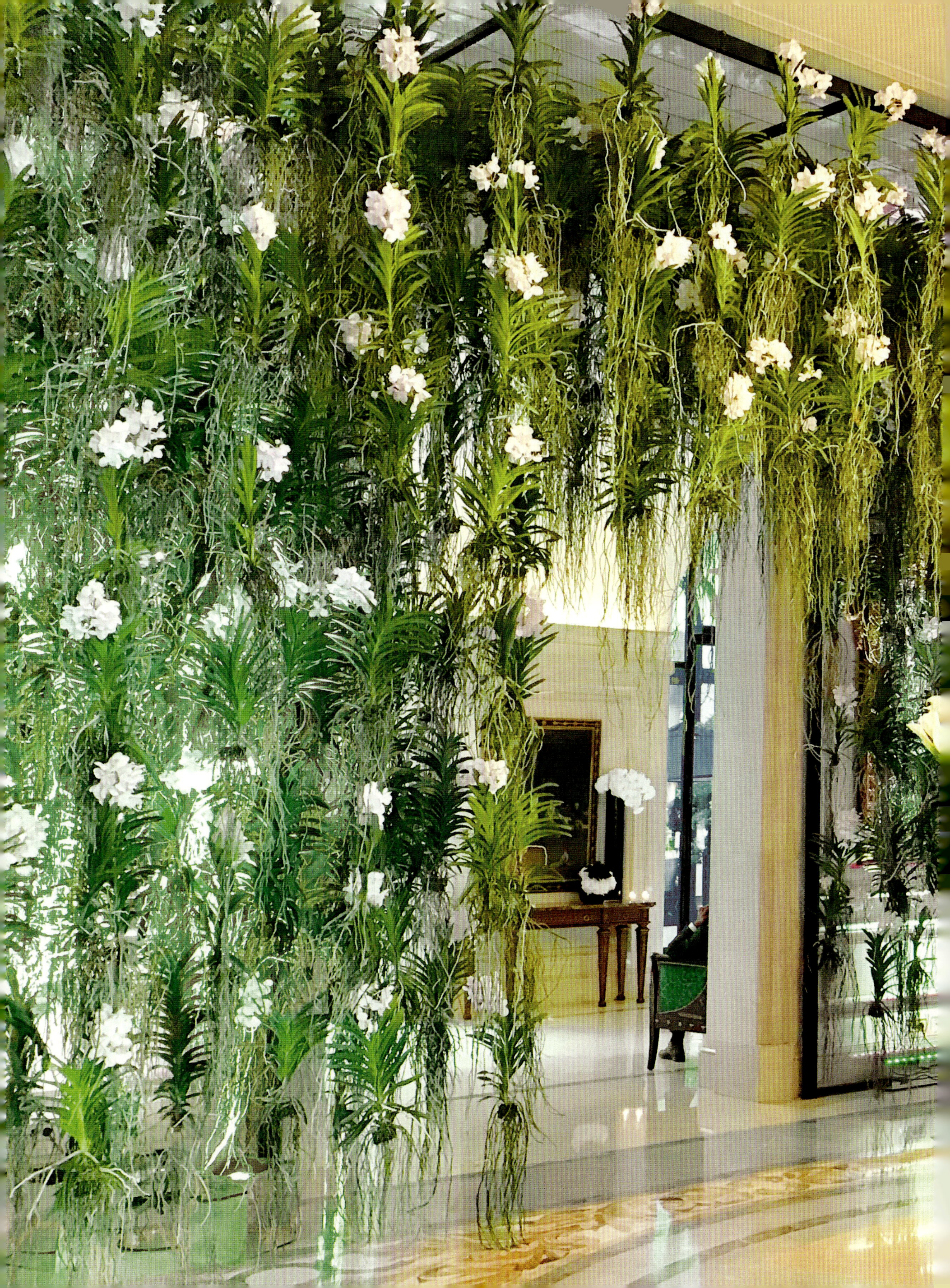

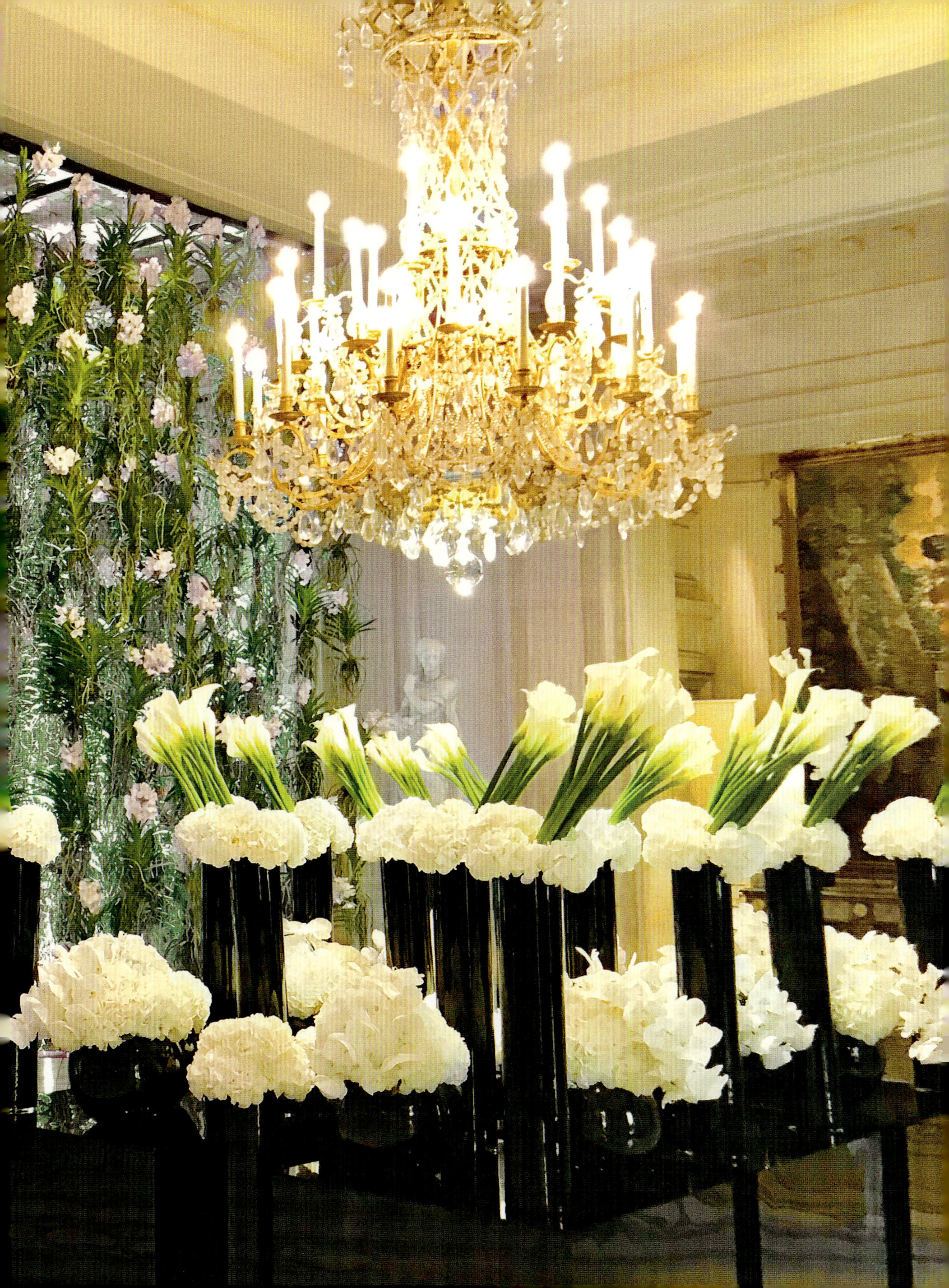

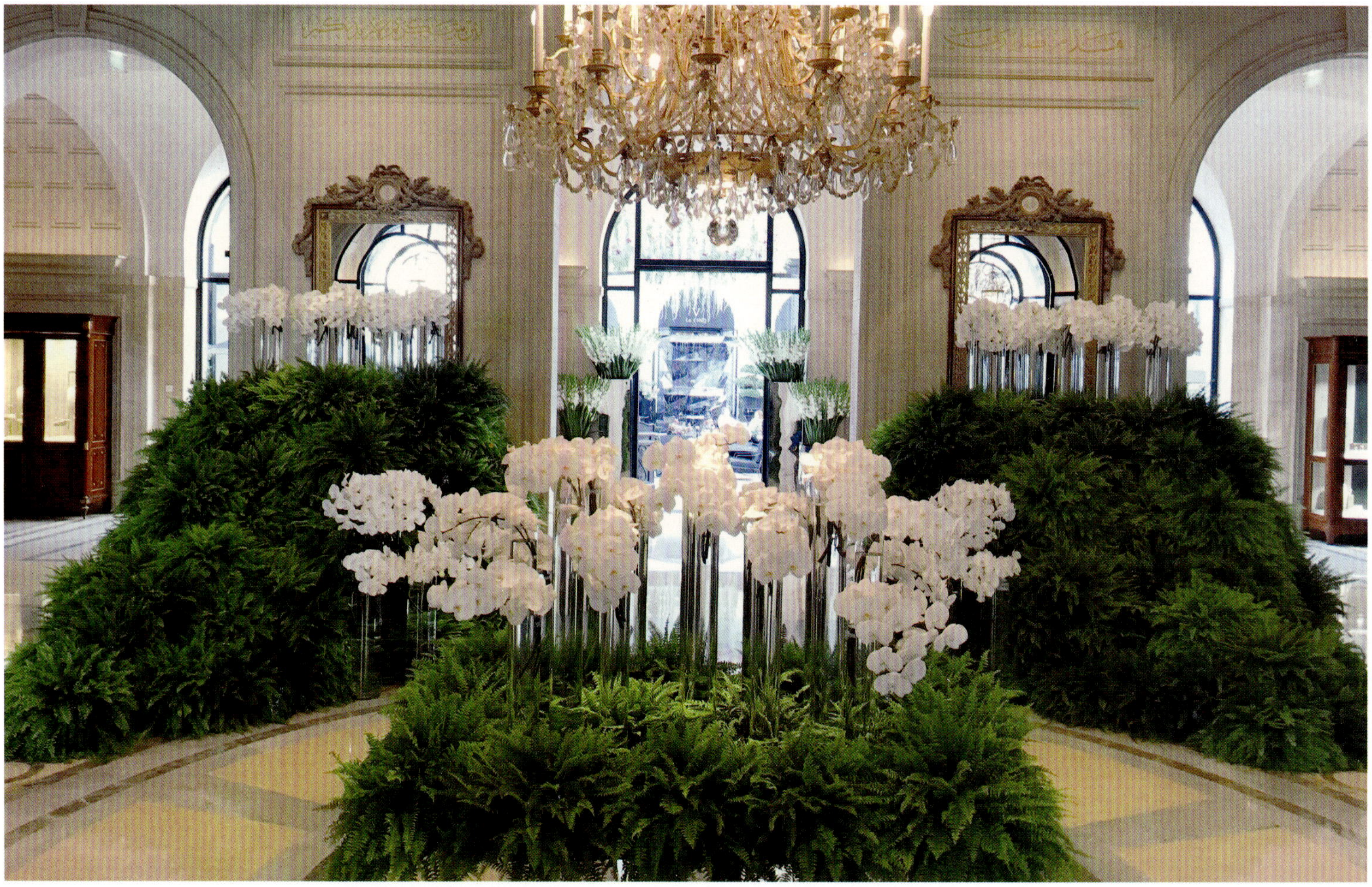

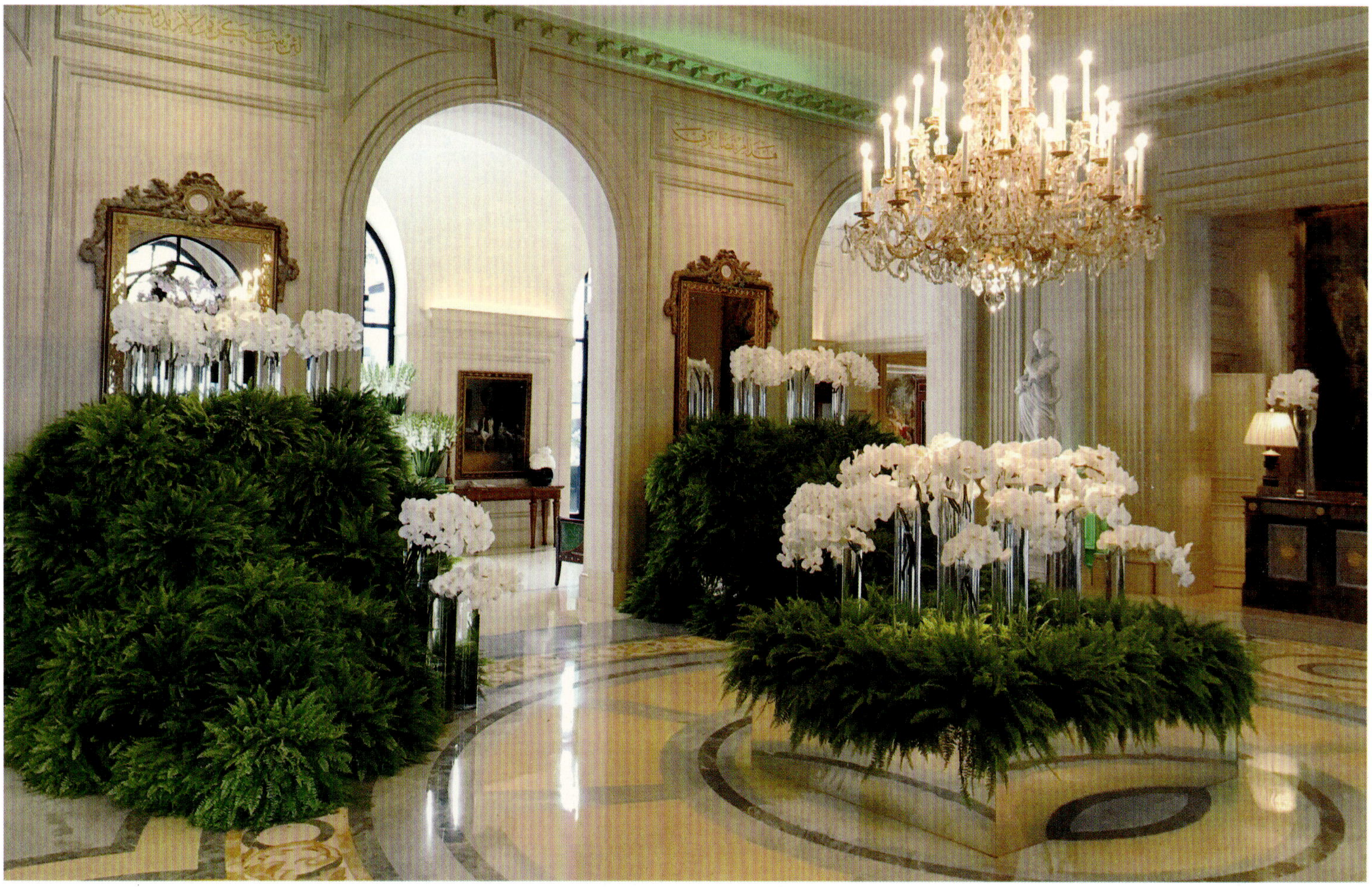

Four Seasons George V Lobby.
Fern plants and phalaenopsis orchids.

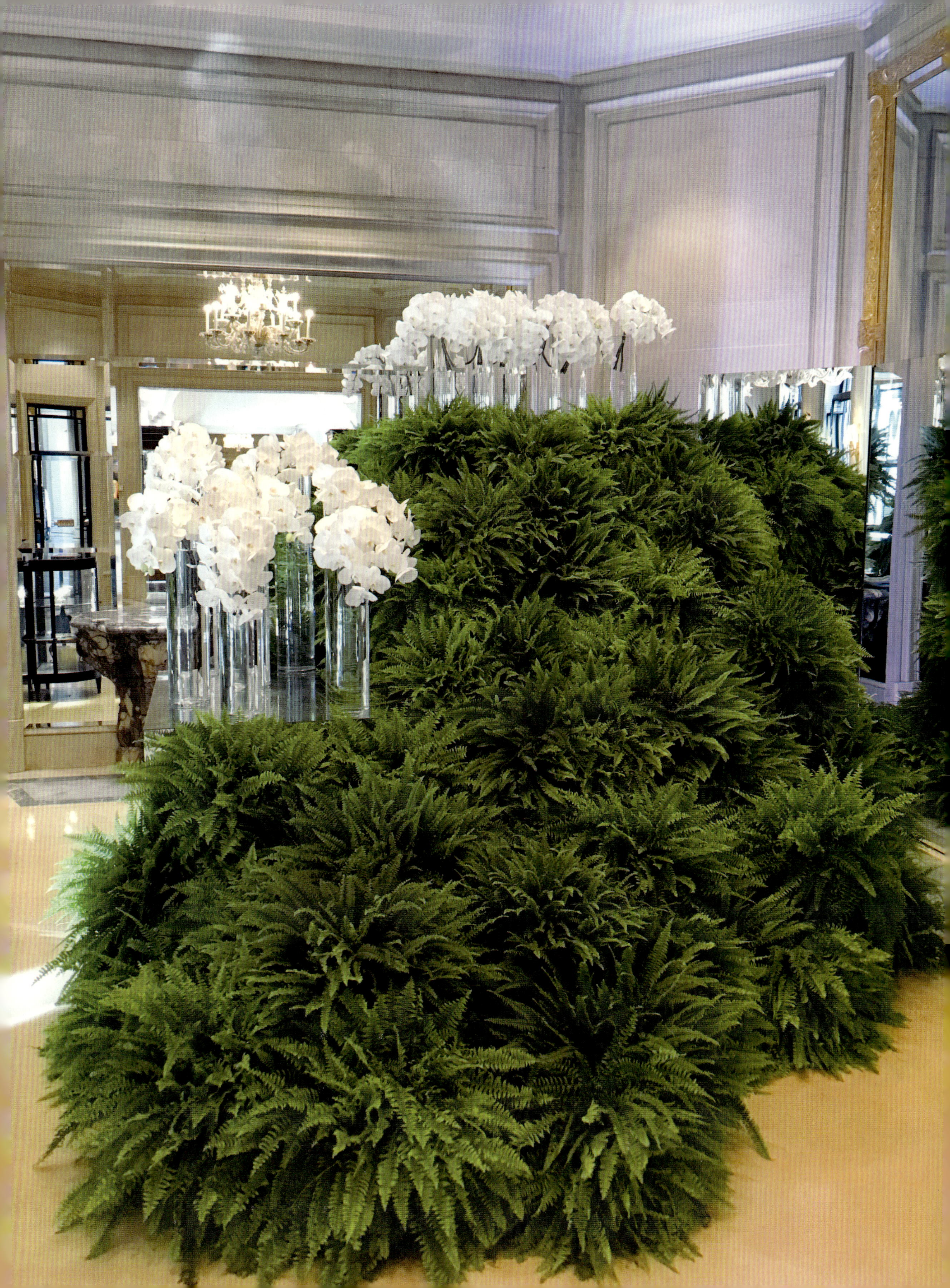

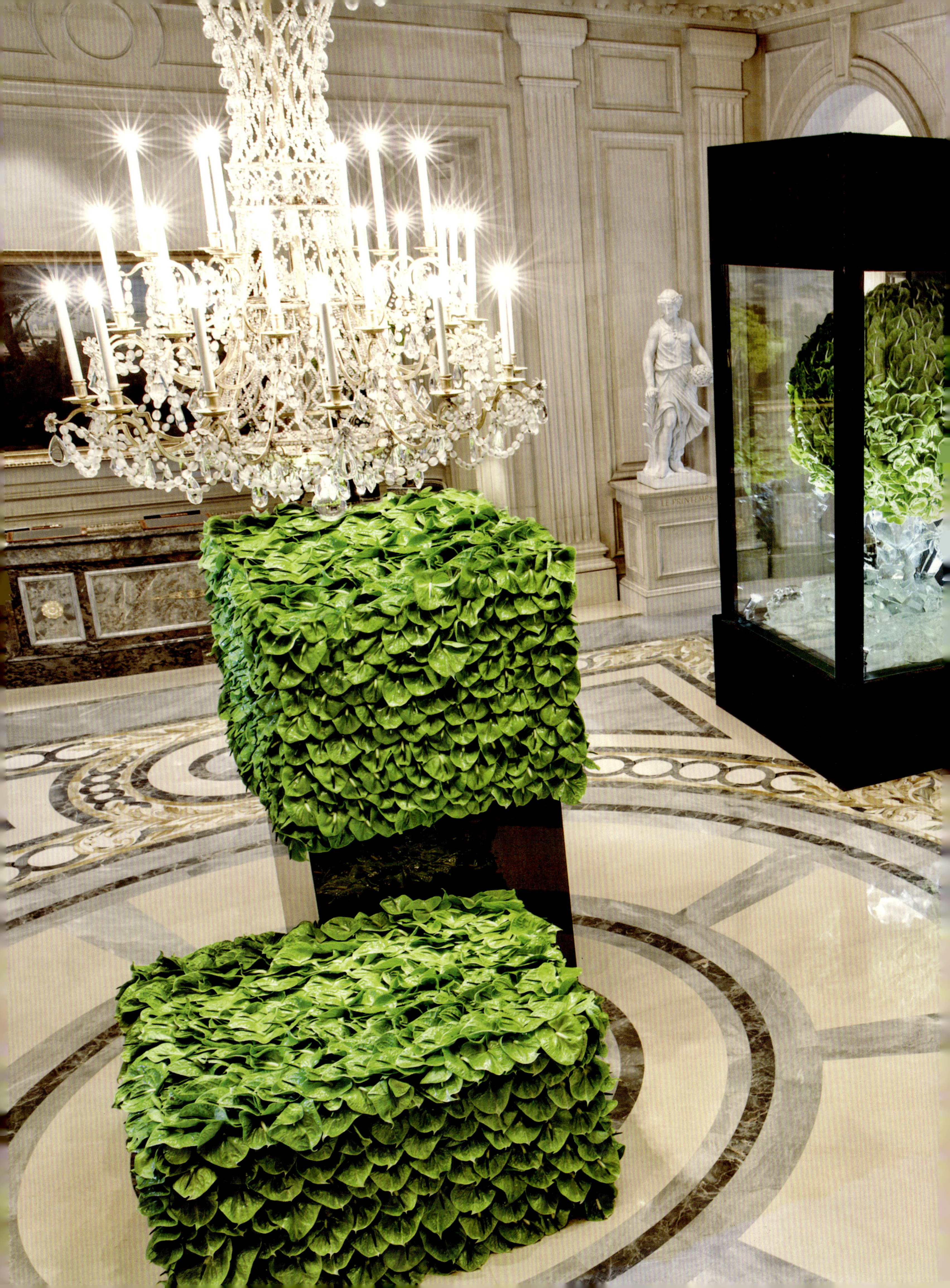

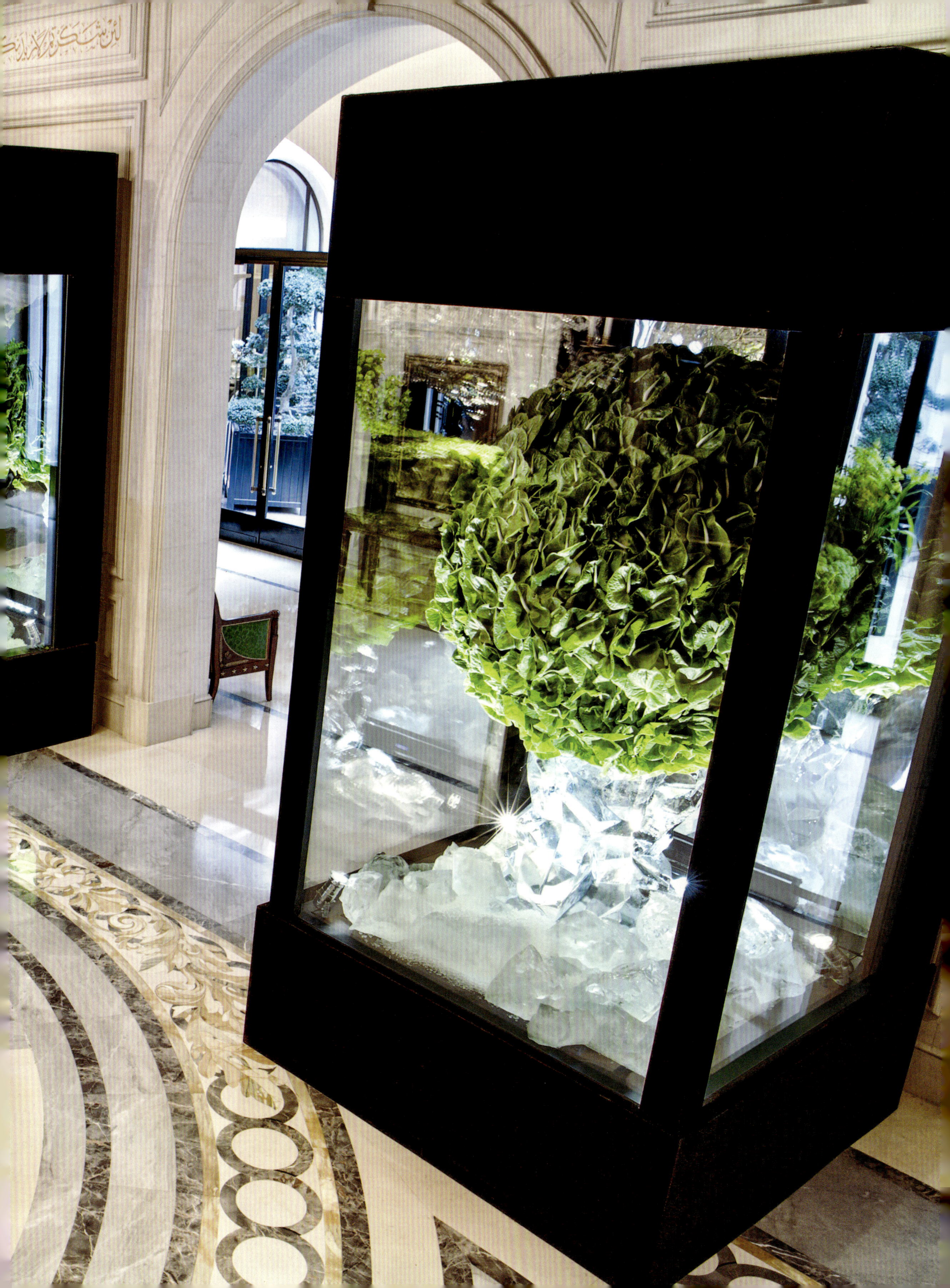

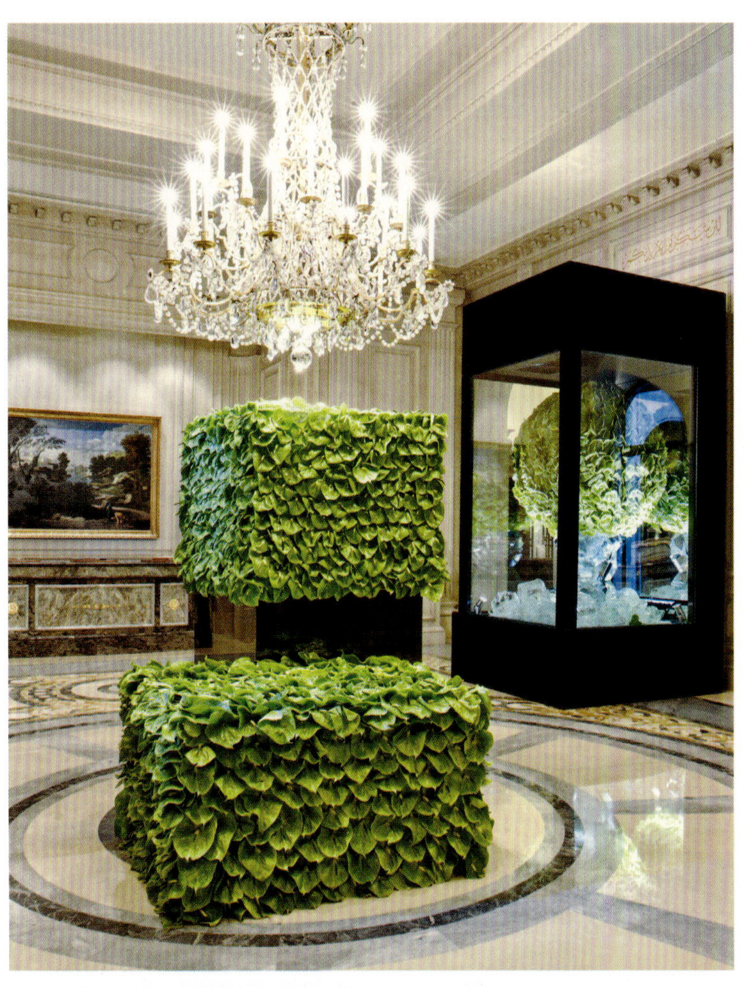
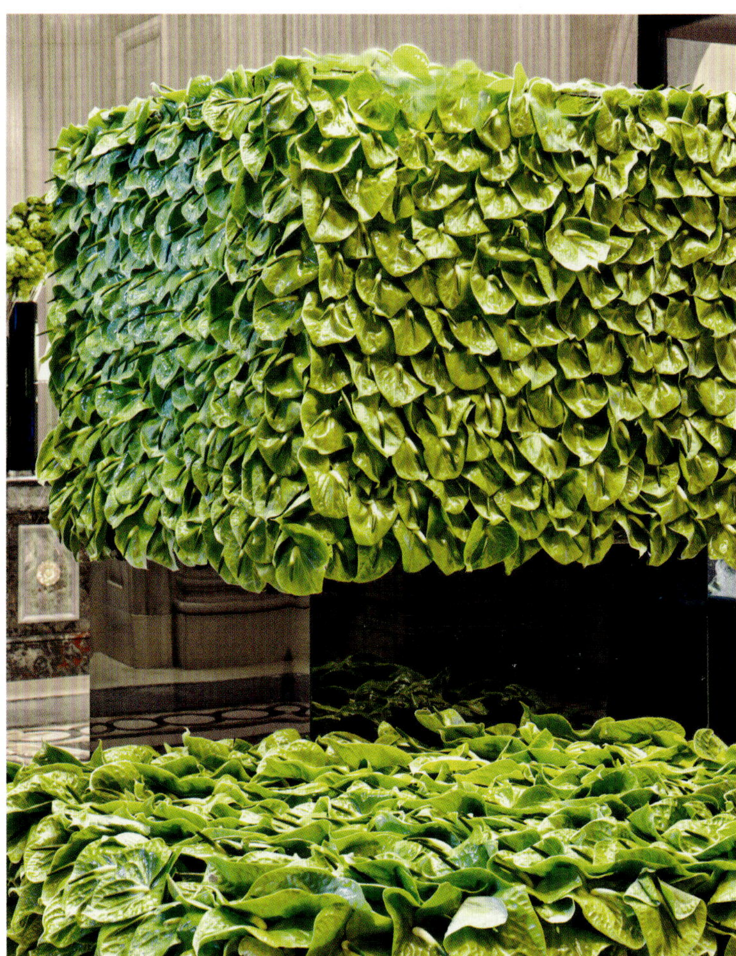
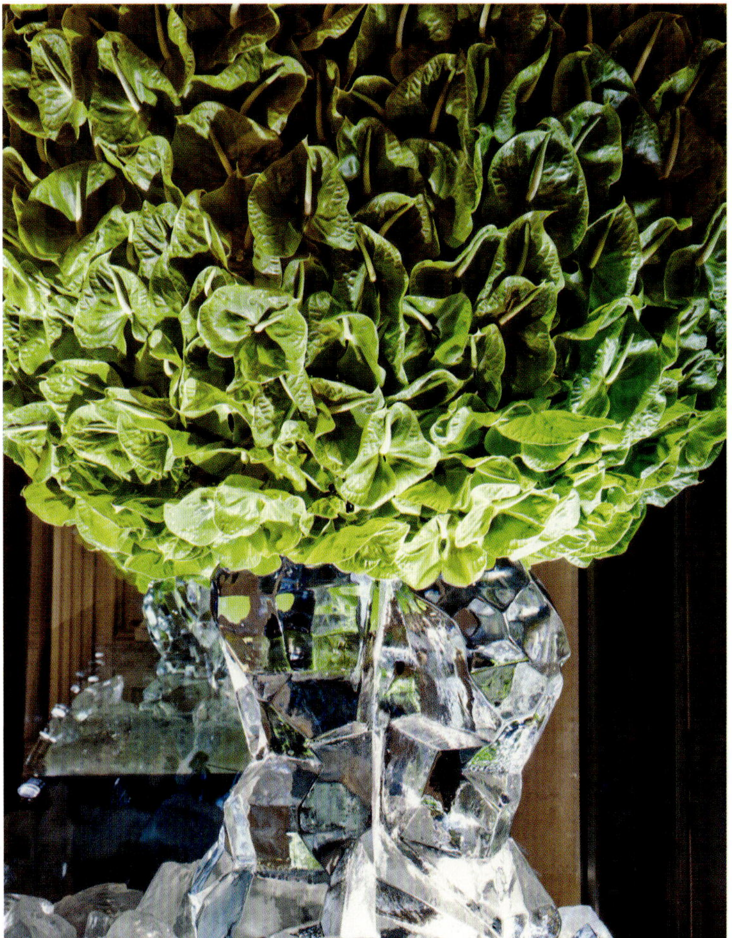
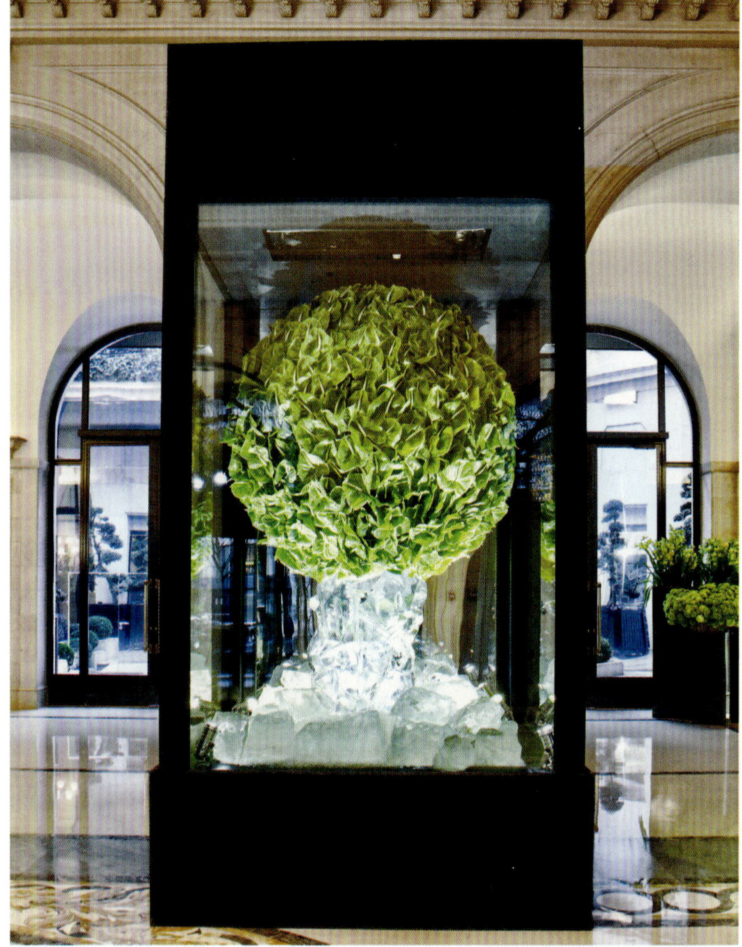

PREVIOUS AND ABOVE: Four Seasons George V Lobby. Anthurium.
OPPOSITE: Viburnum and phalaenopsis orchids.

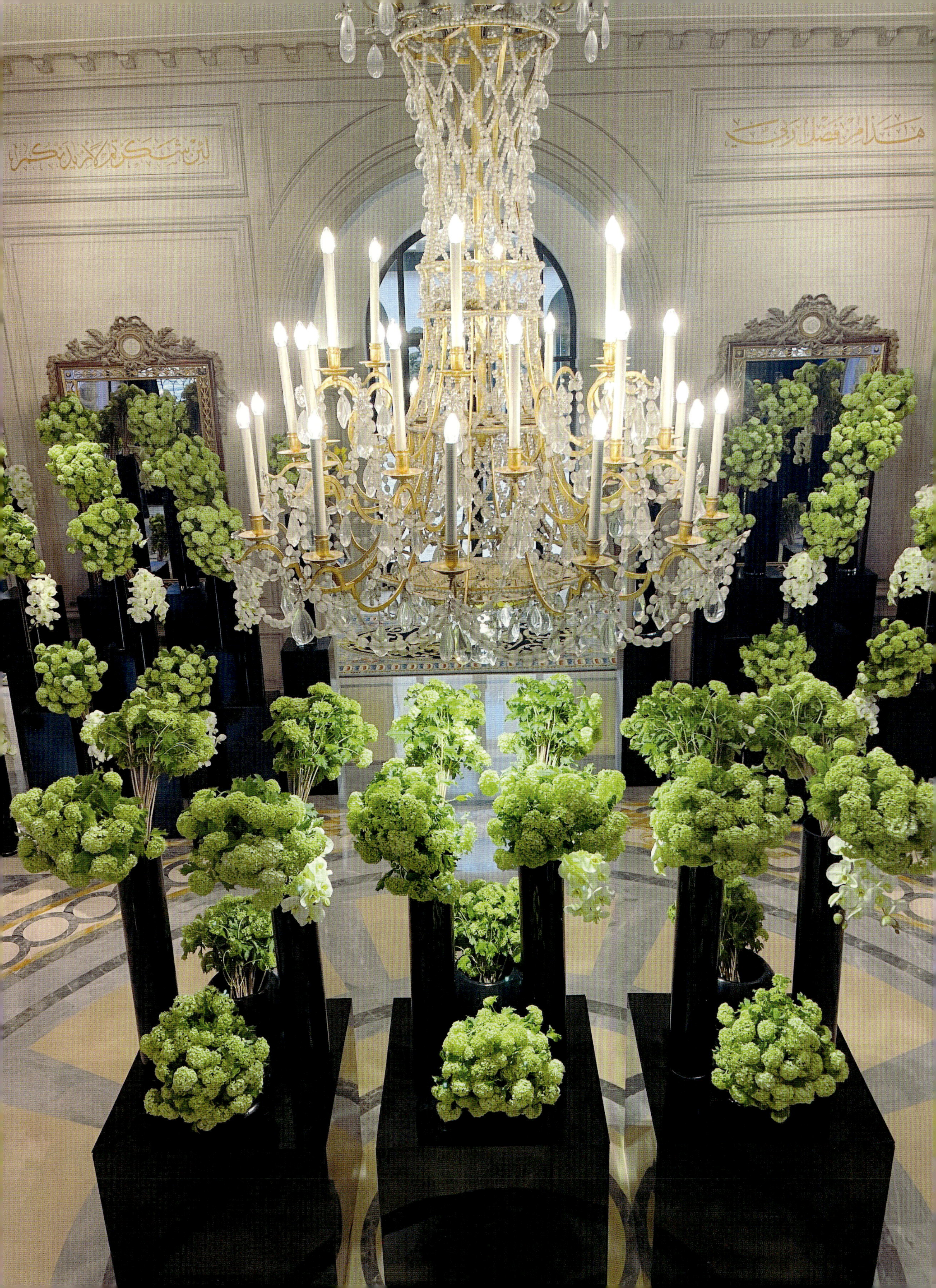
هذا من فضل ربي
لئن شكرتم لأزيدنكم

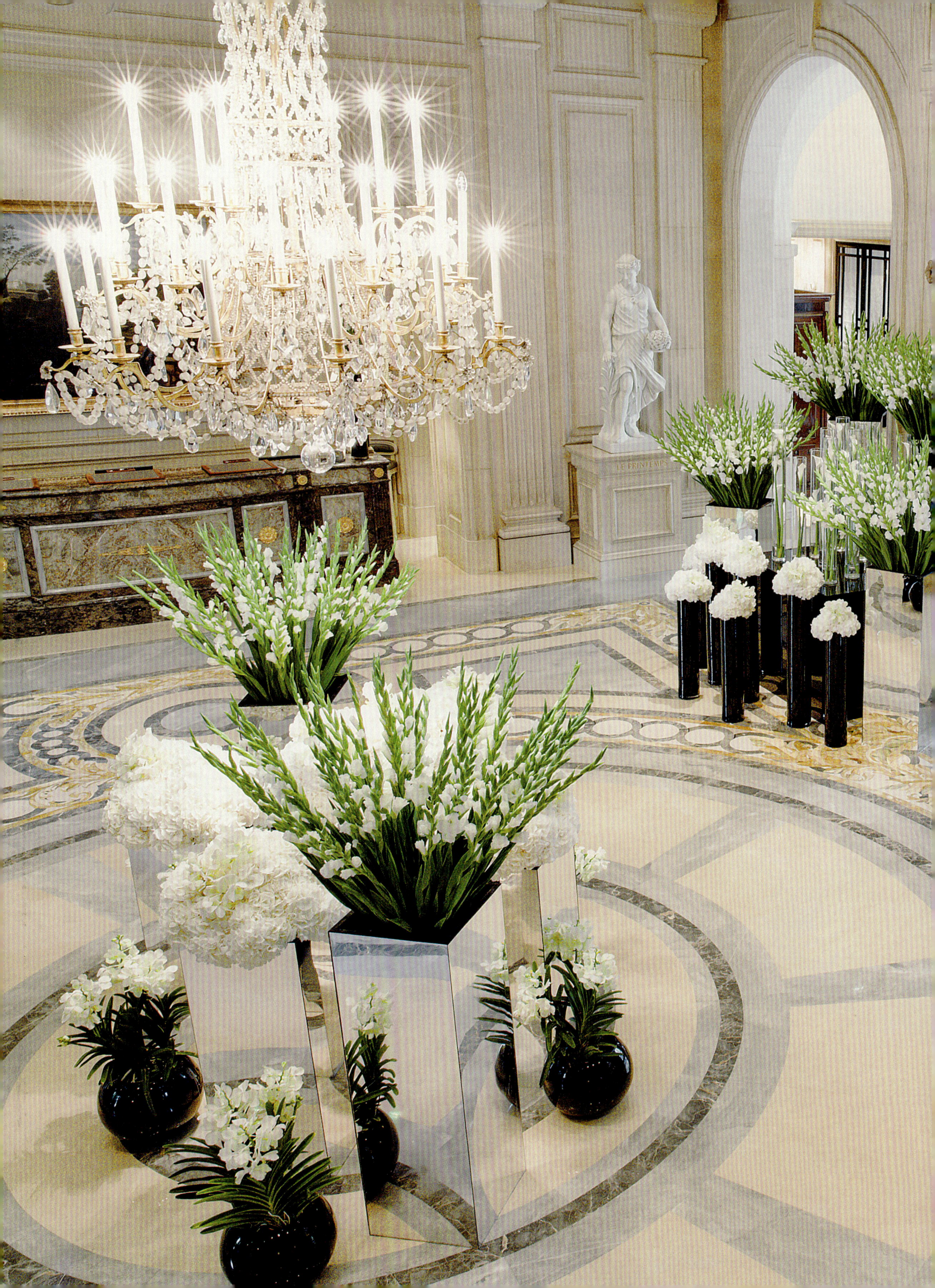

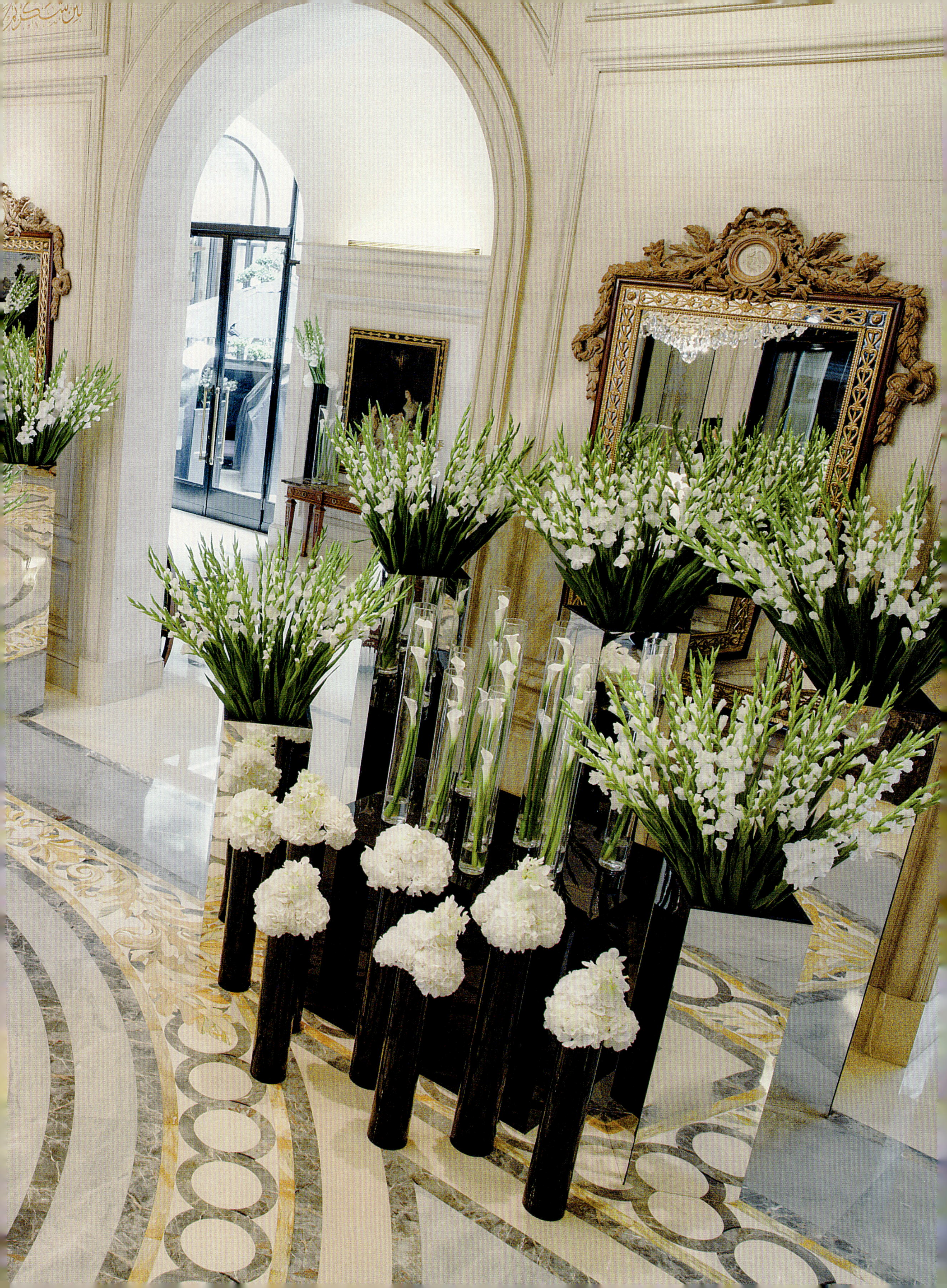

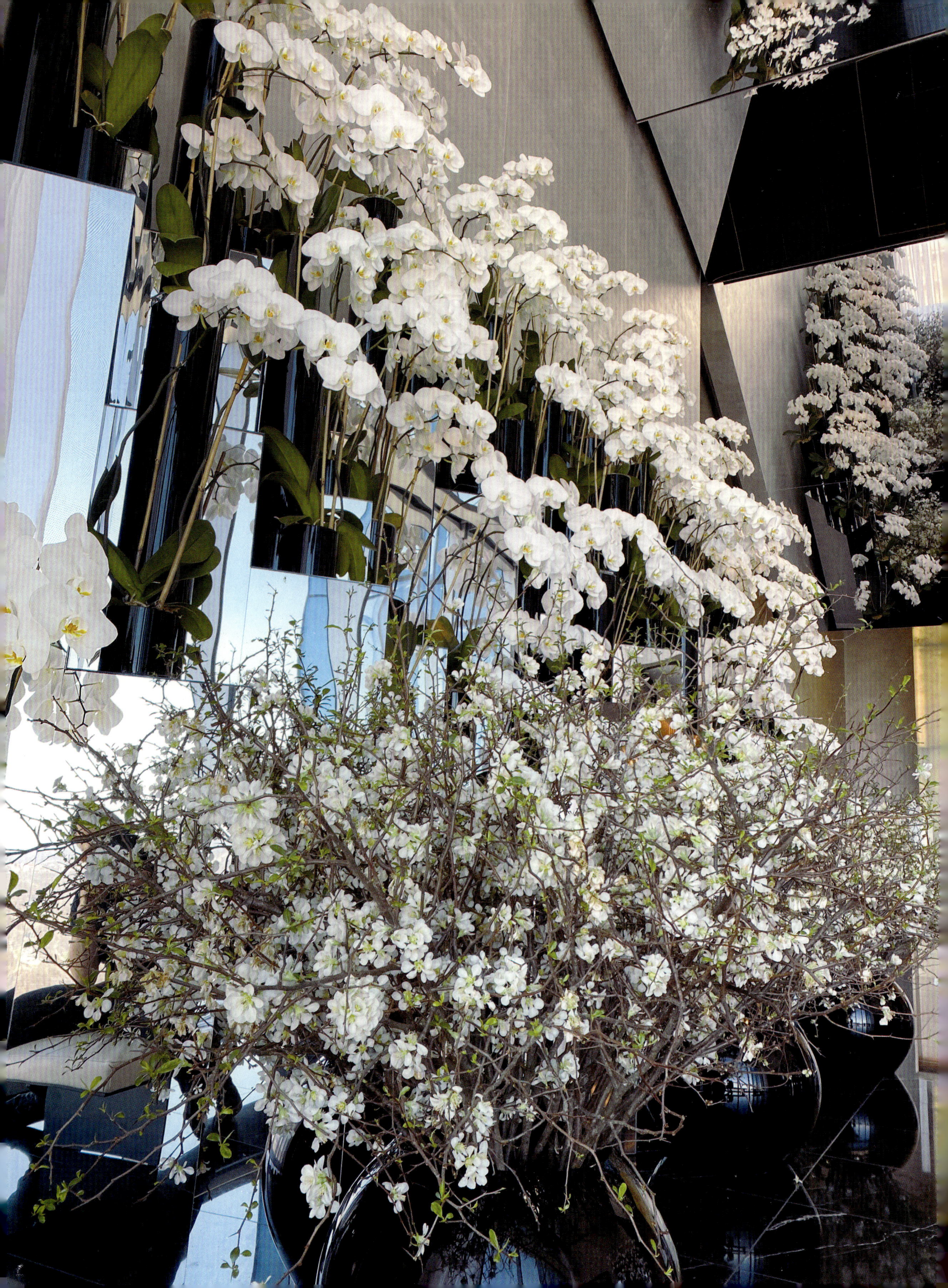

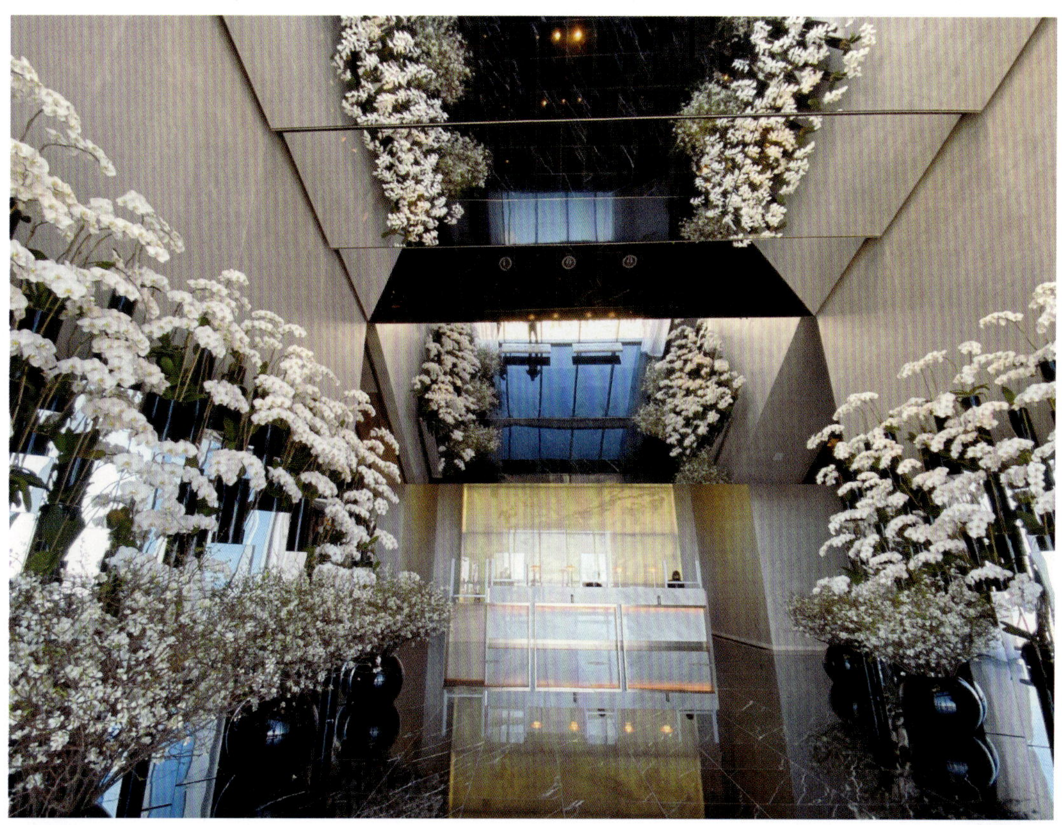

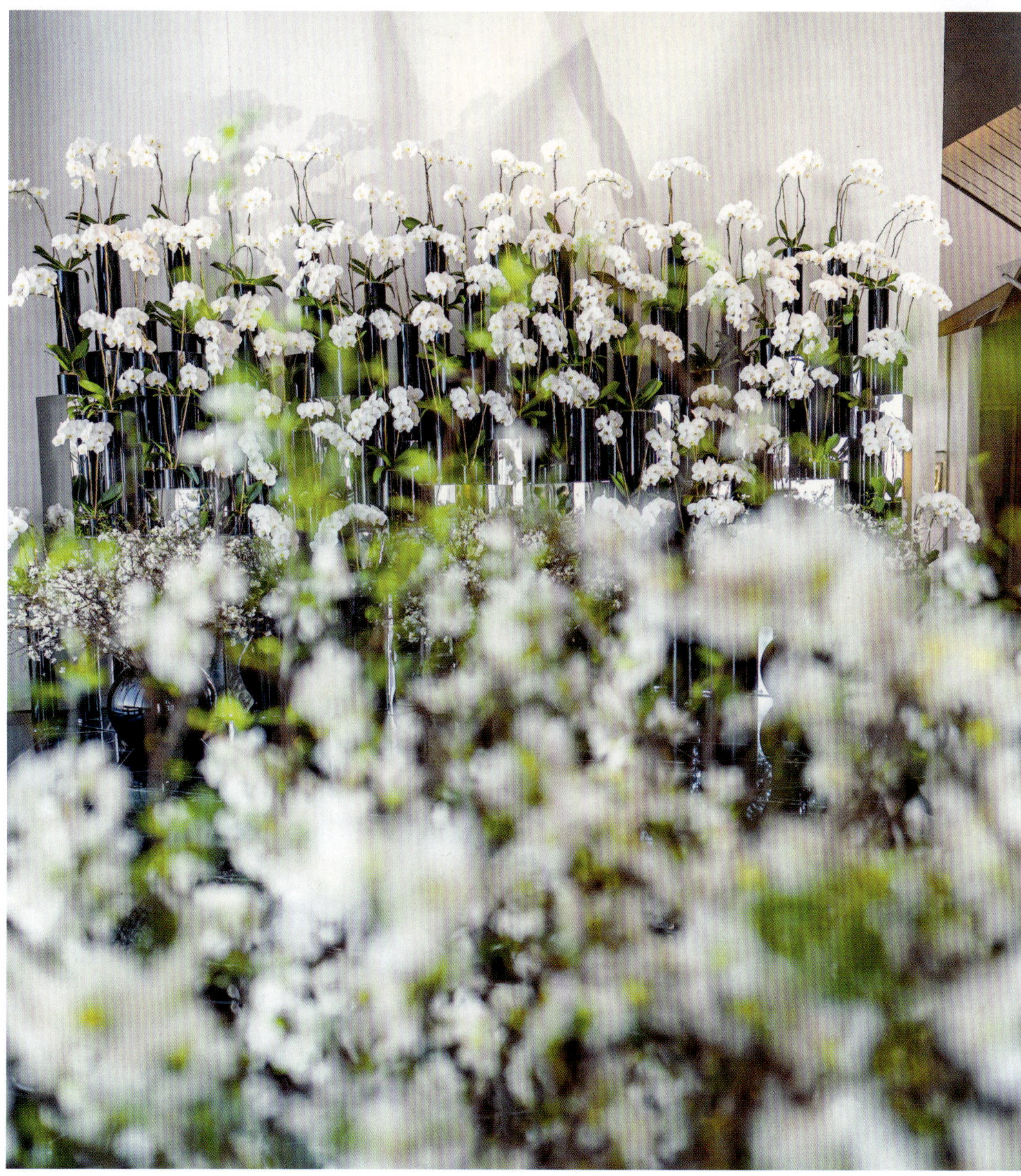

PREVIOUS: Four Seasons George V Lobby. Gladiolas, hydrangeas, and vanda orchids. OPPOSITE AND RIGHT: Four Seasons Philadelphia Lobby. Phalaenopsis orchids and quince. FOLLOWING: Four Seasons George V Lobby. Coral charm peonies and hydrangeas.

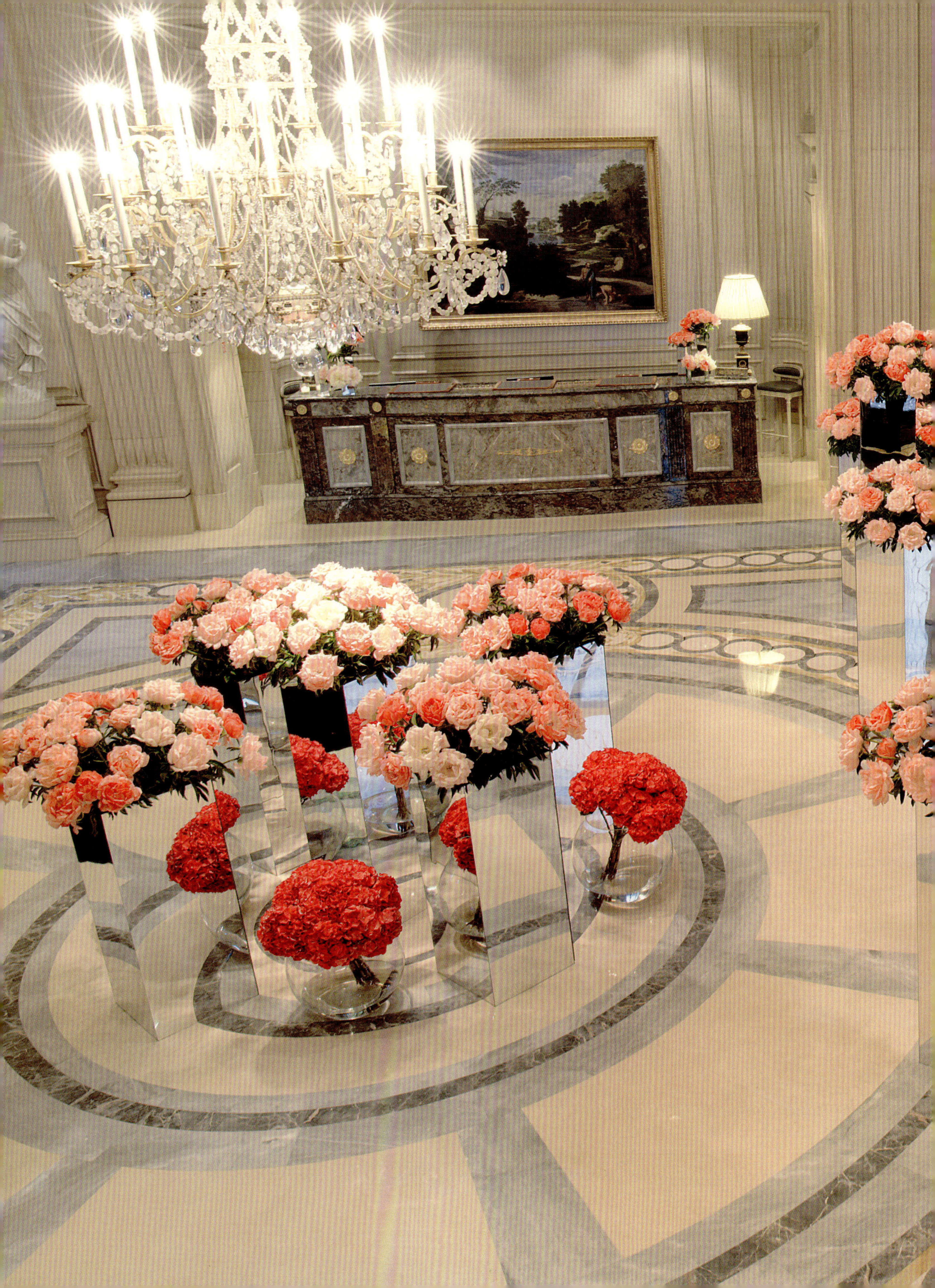

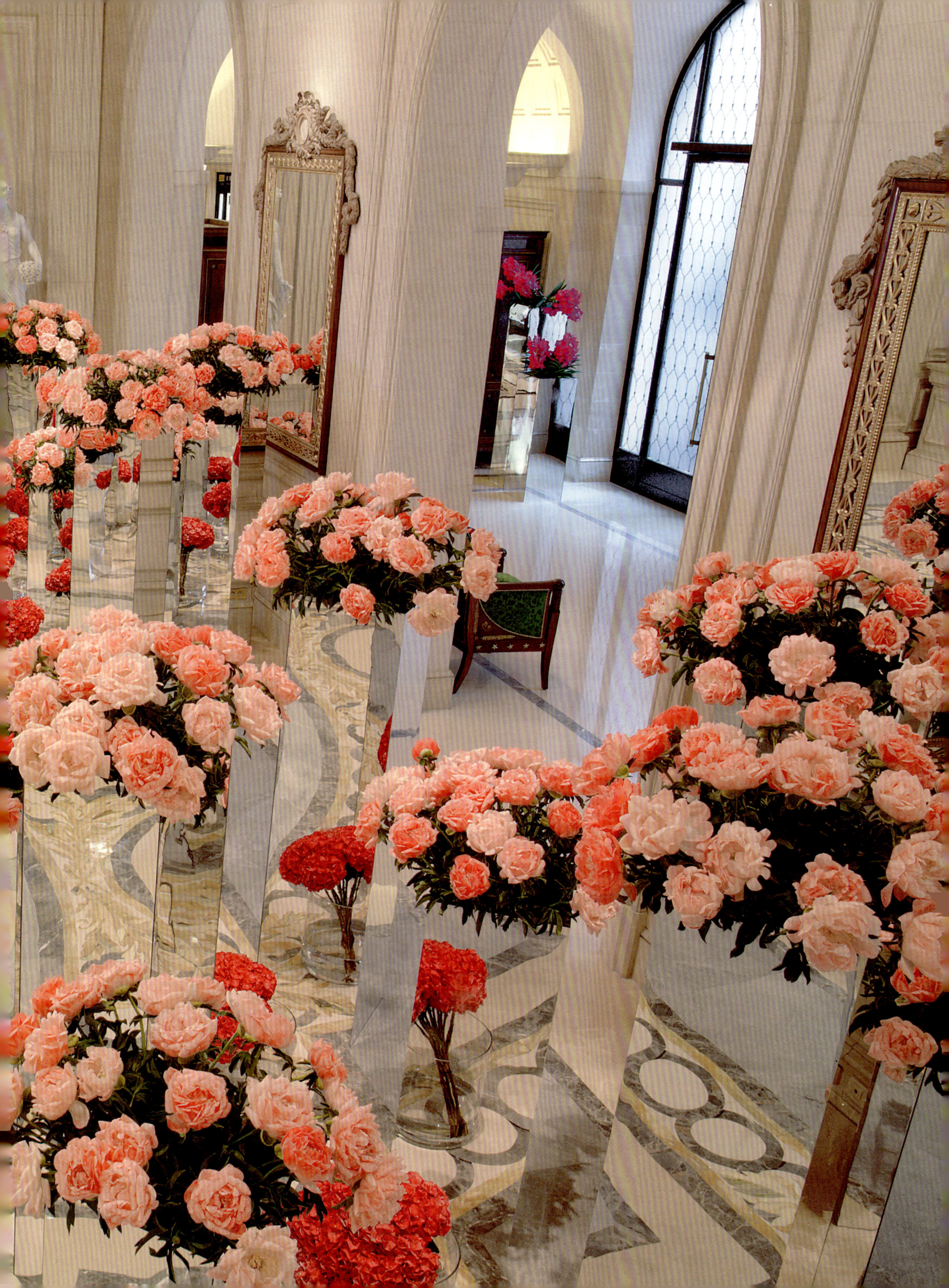

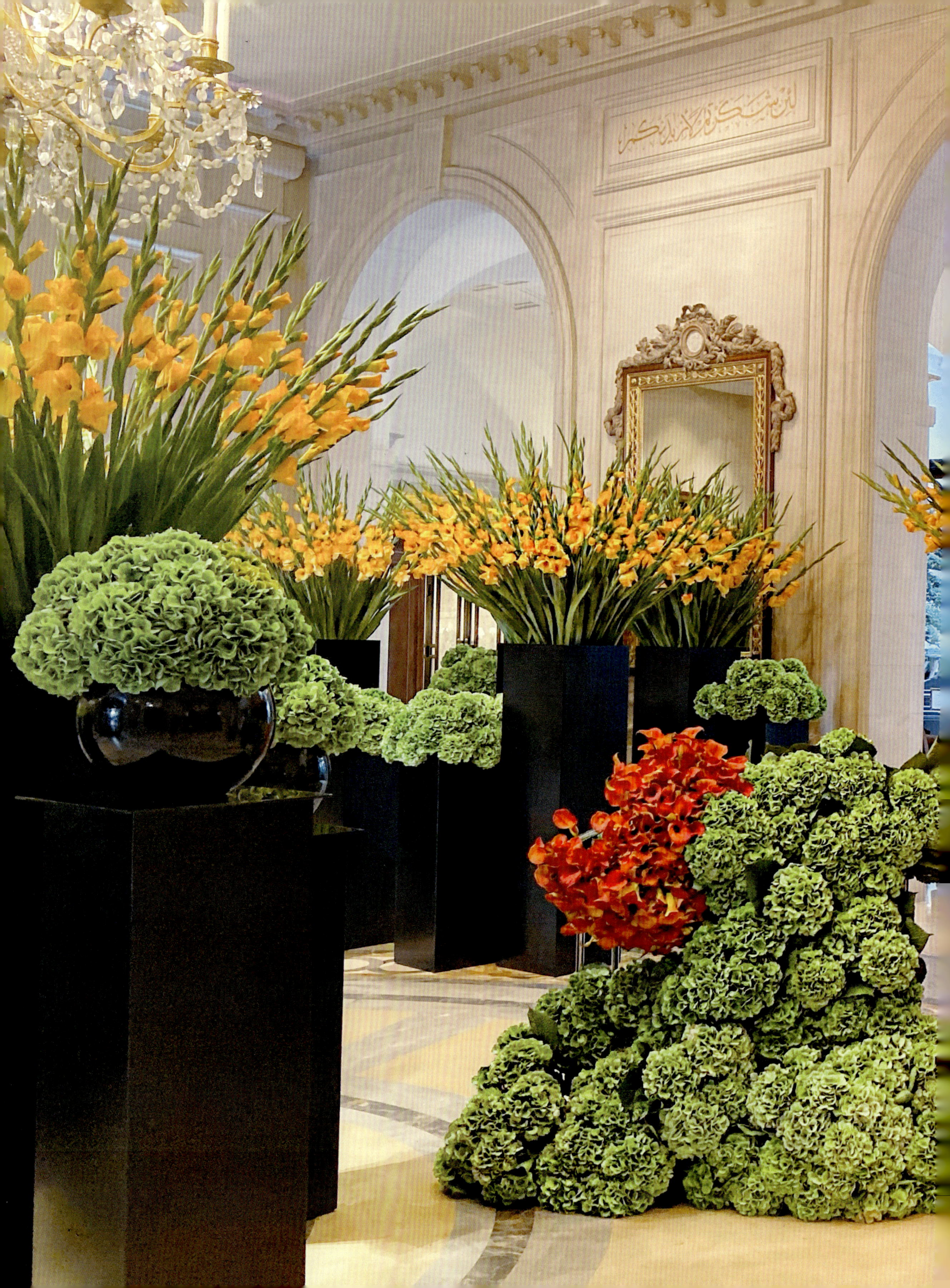

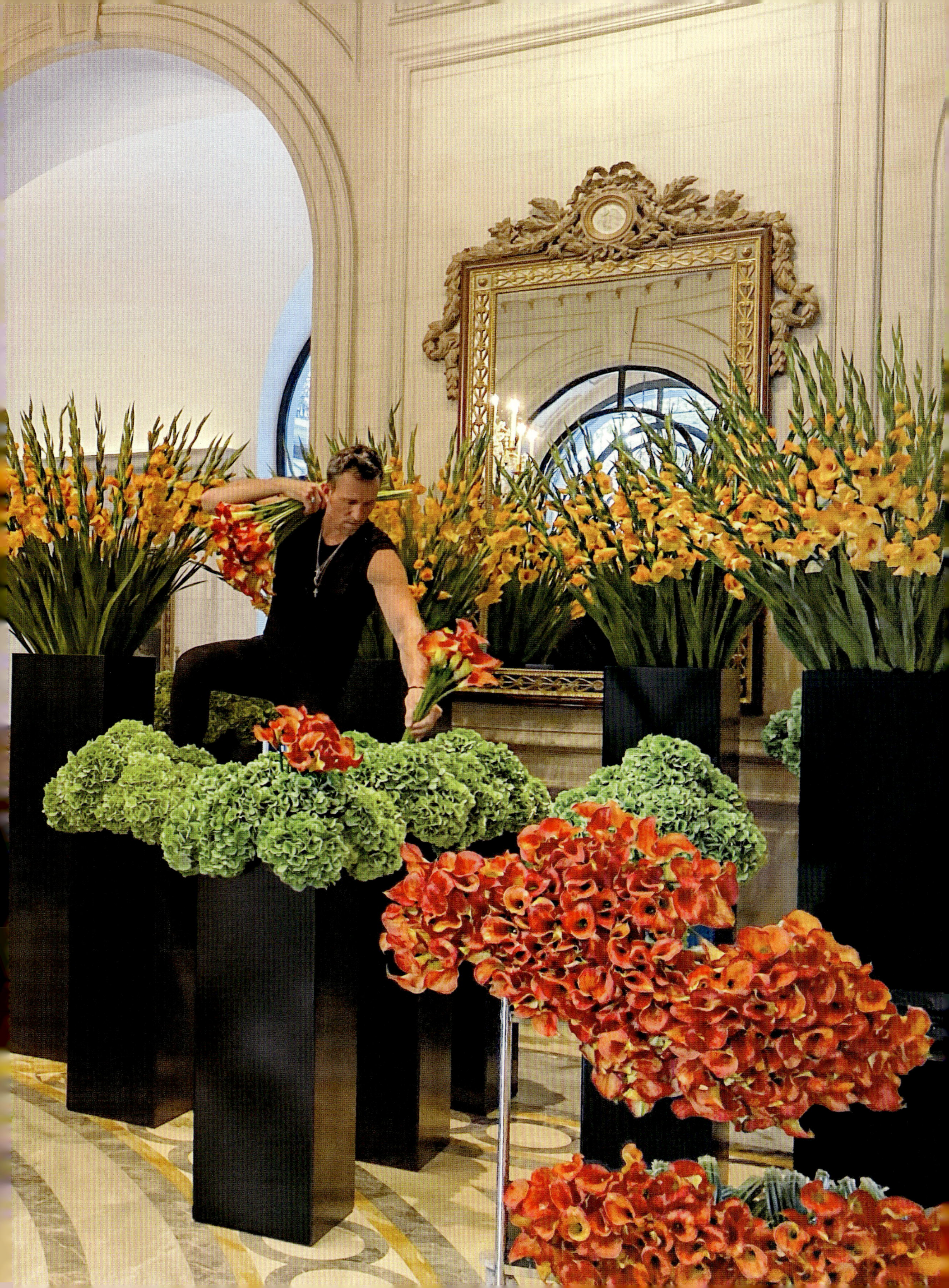

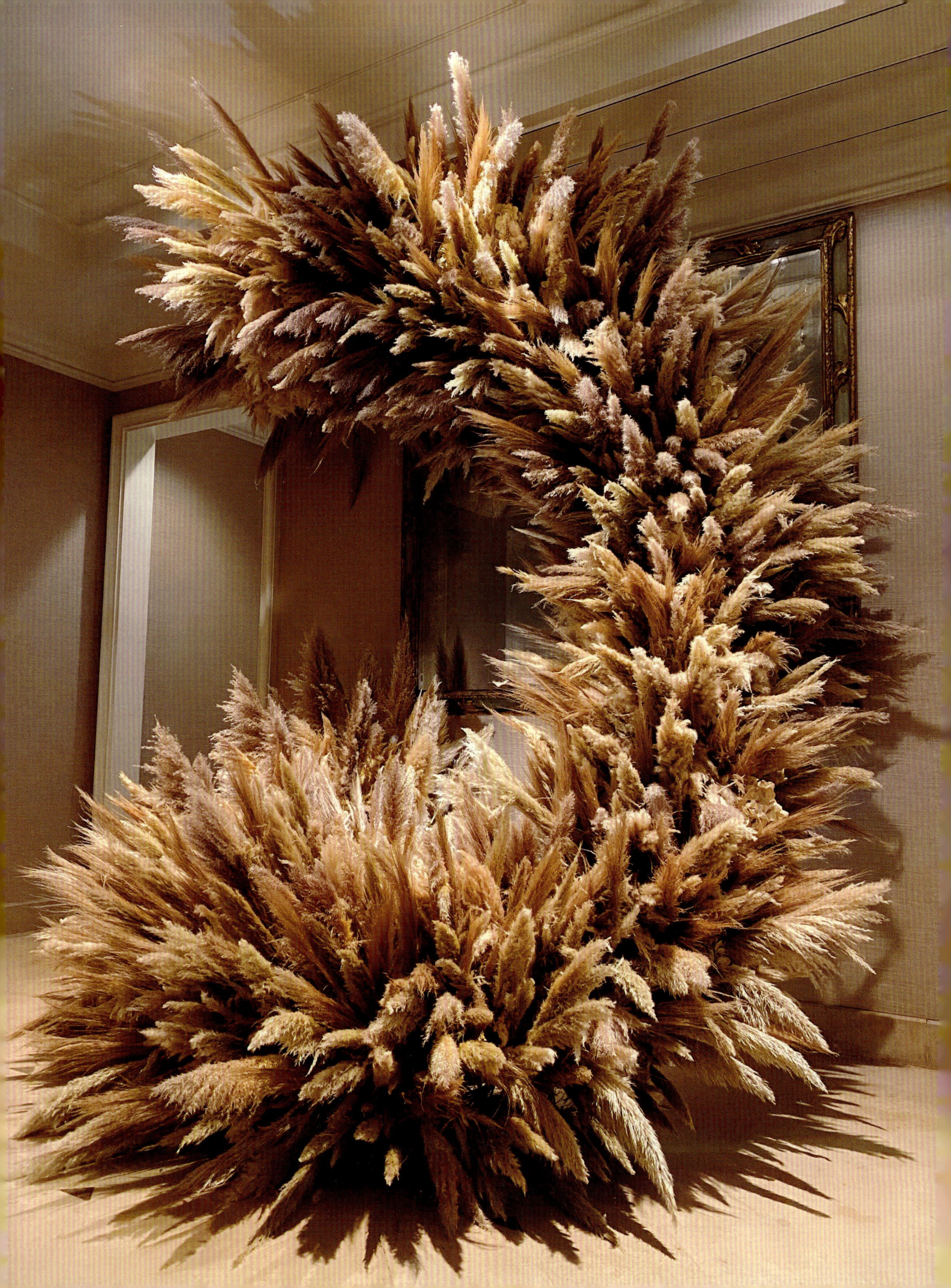

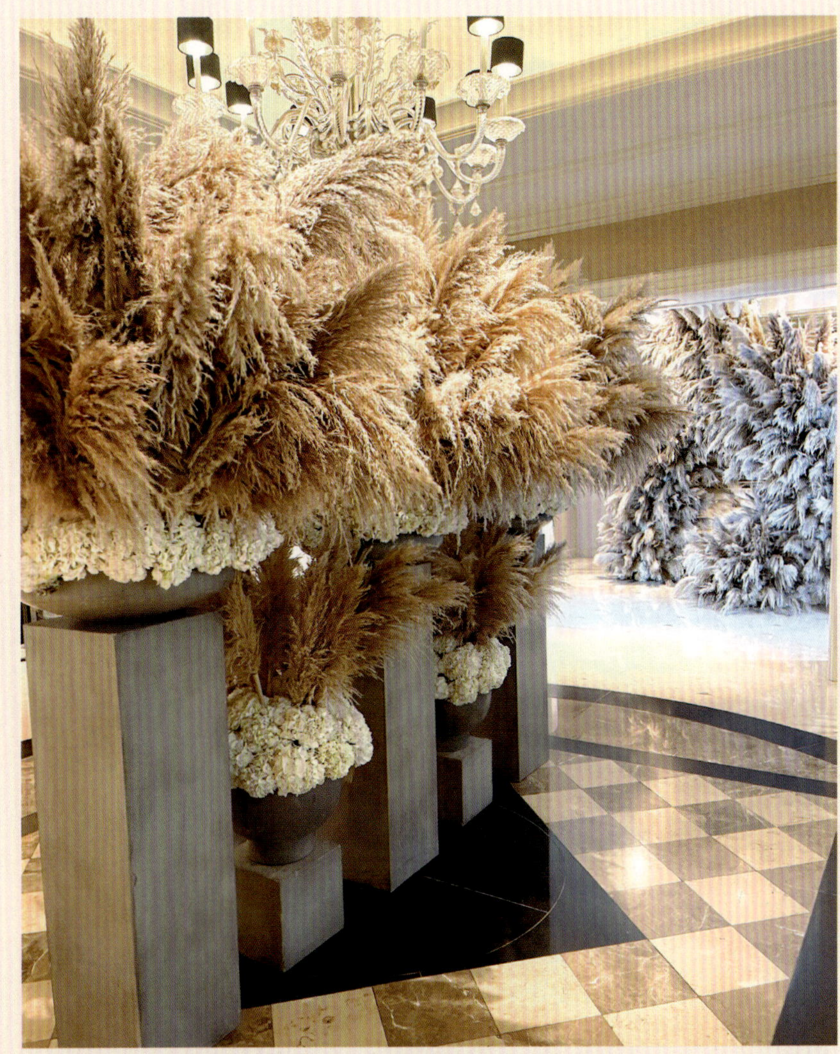

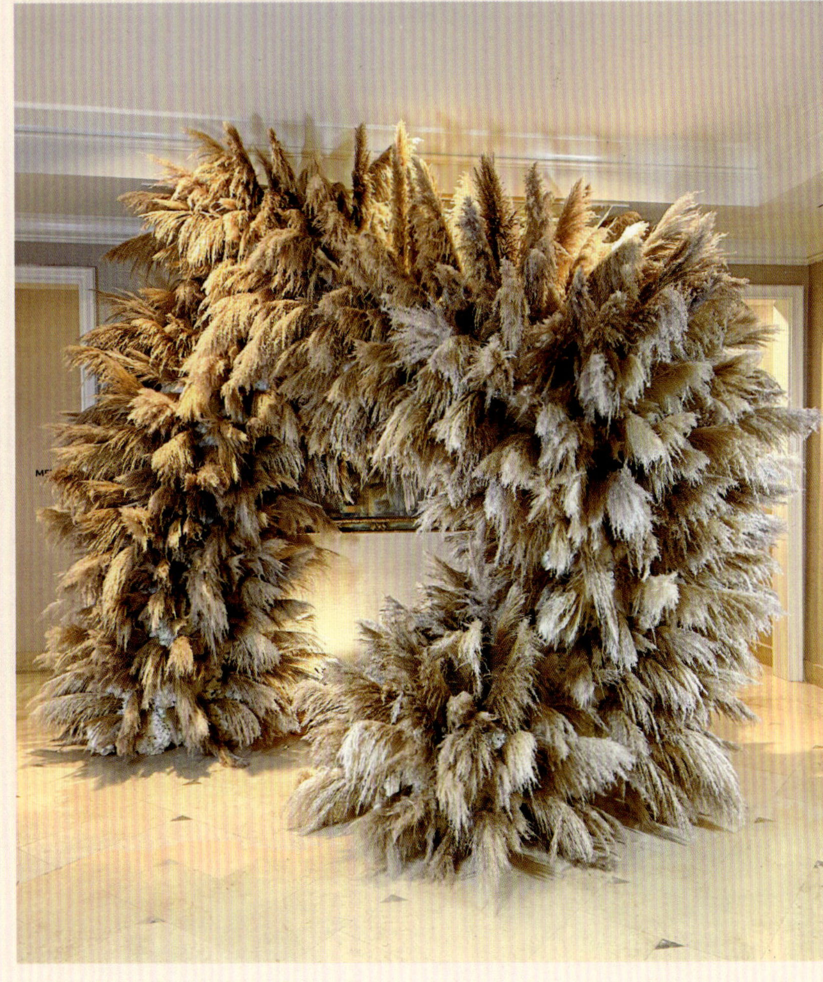

PREVIOUS: Four Seasons George V Lobby. Gladiolas, hydrangeas, and calla lilies. OPPOSITE AND RIGHT: Four Seasons Los Angeles at Beverly Hills Lobby. Pampas grass and hydrangeas (top).

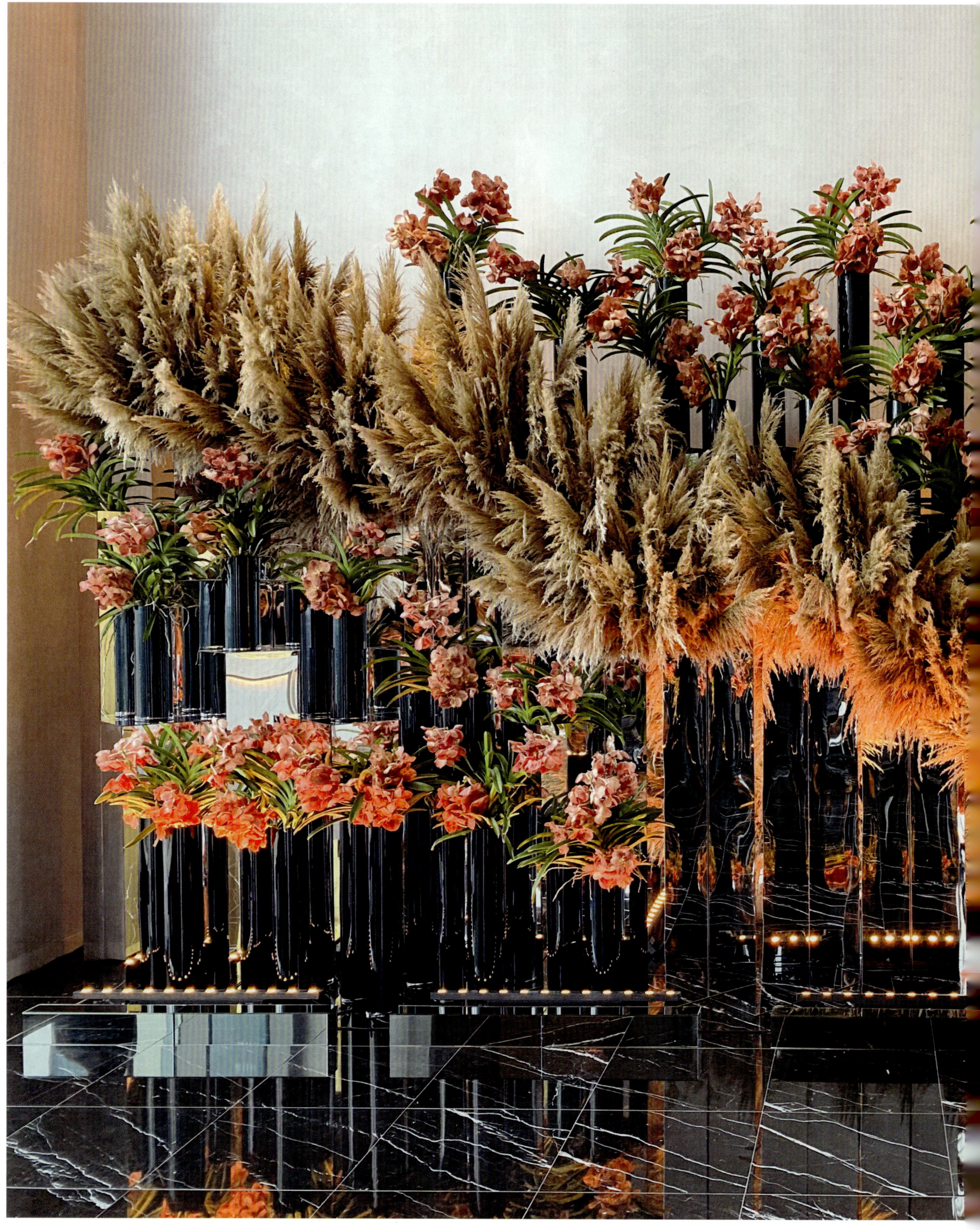

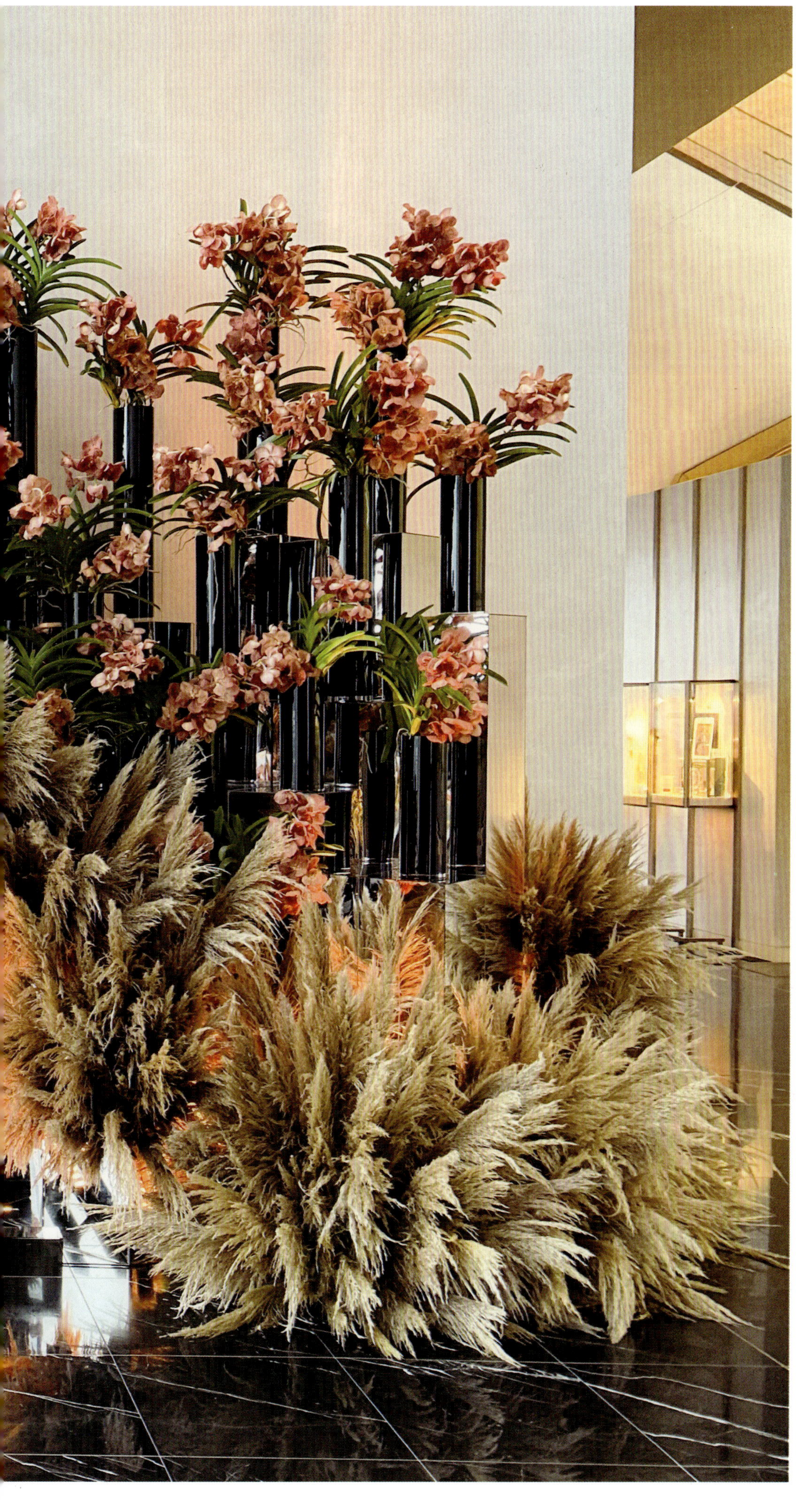

Four Seasons Philadelphia Lobby.
Pampas grass and vanda orchids.

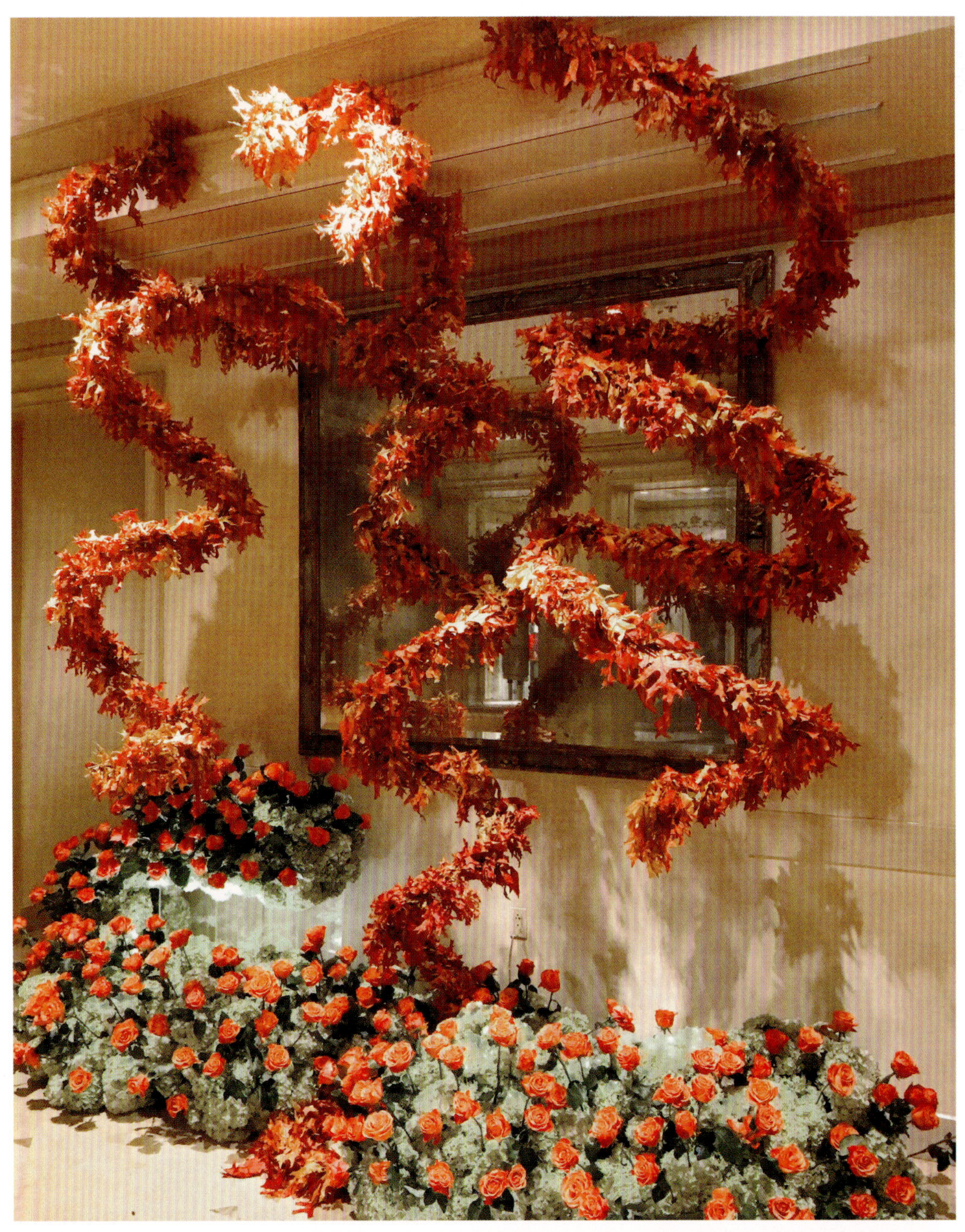

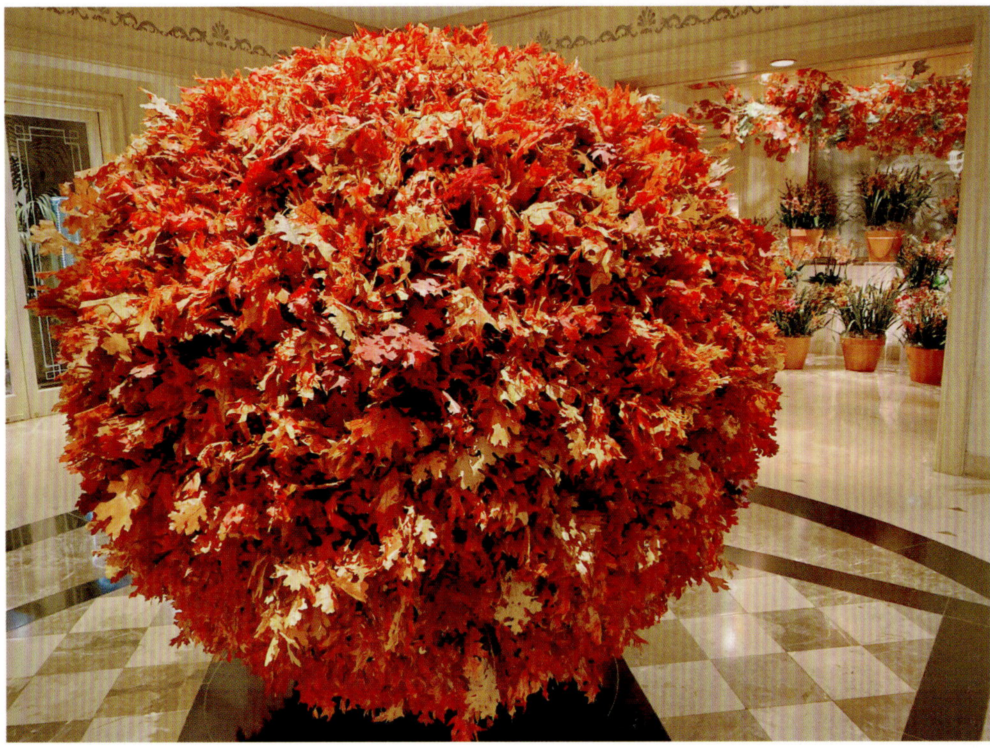

Four Seasons Los Angeles at Beverly Hills Lobby. Spiraling fall leaves over a garden of orange crush roses and hydrangeas.

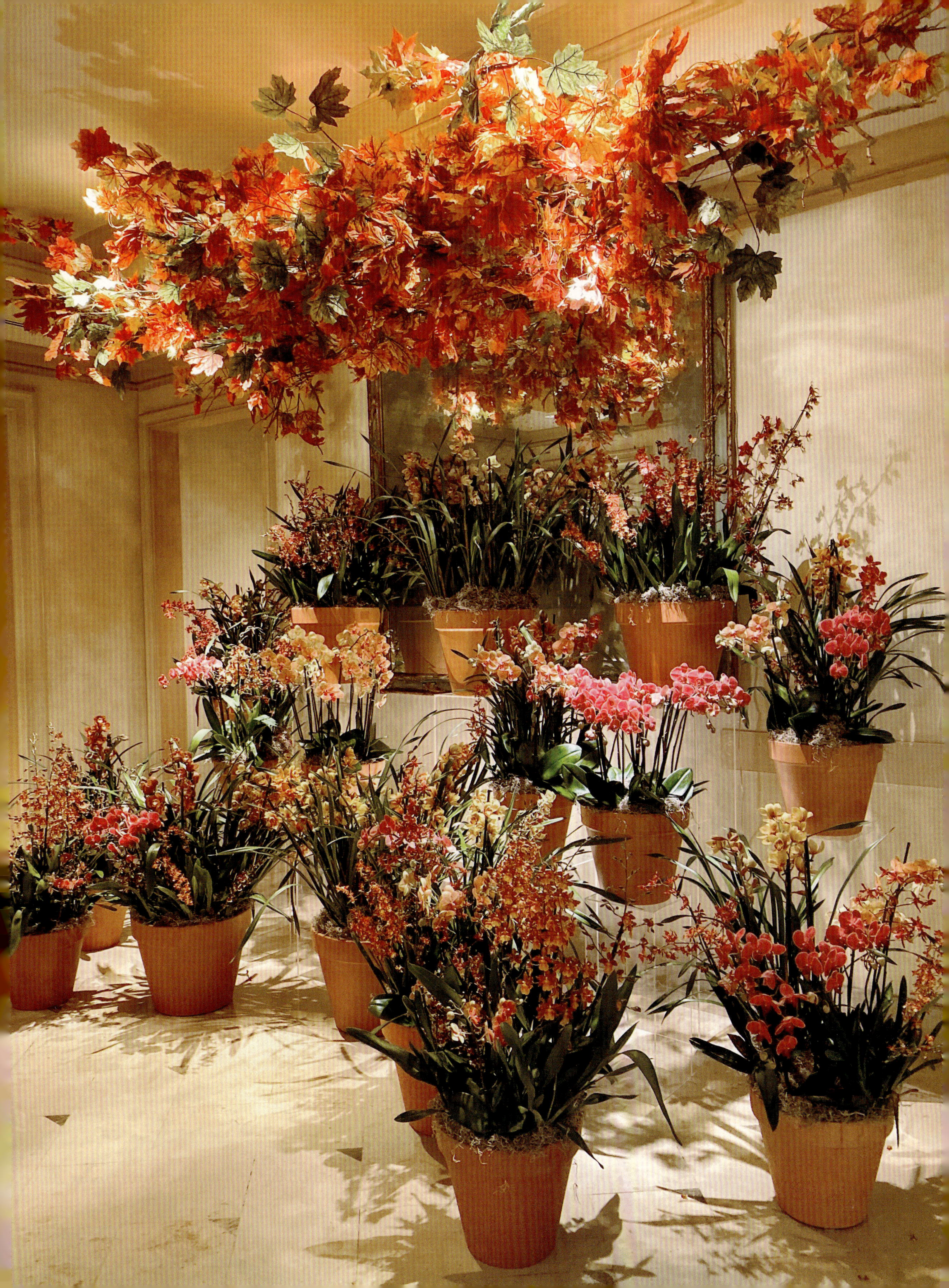

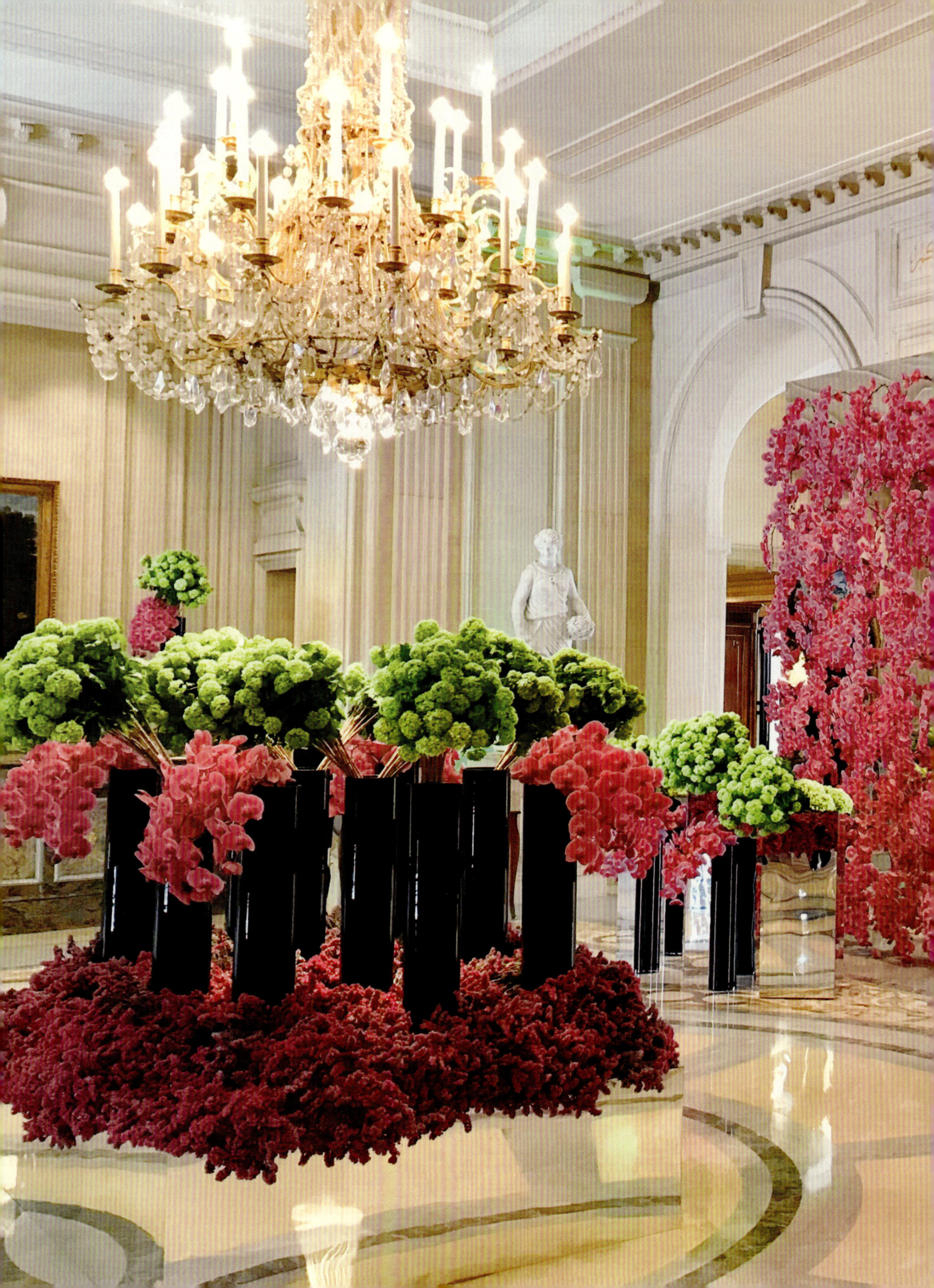

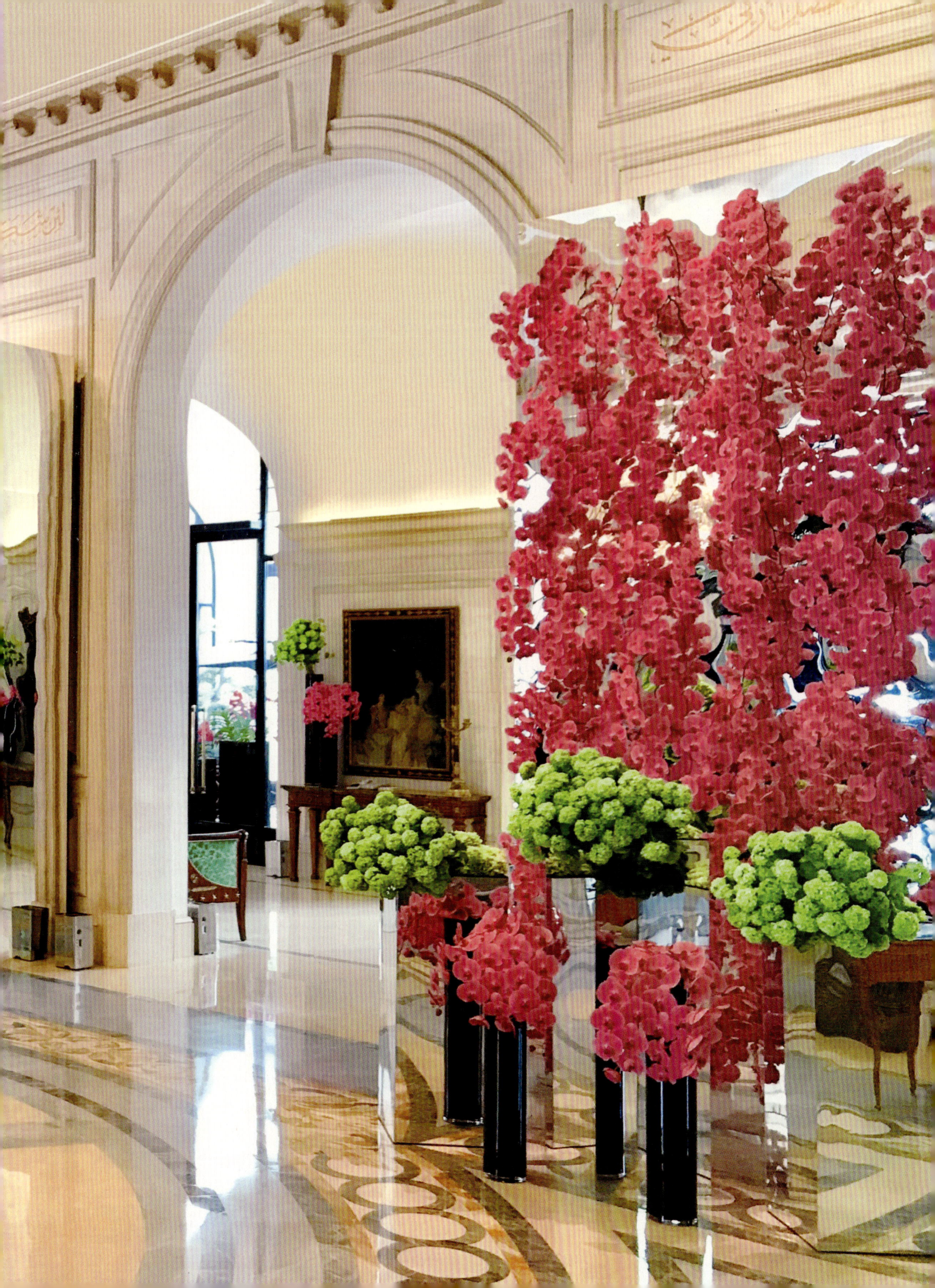

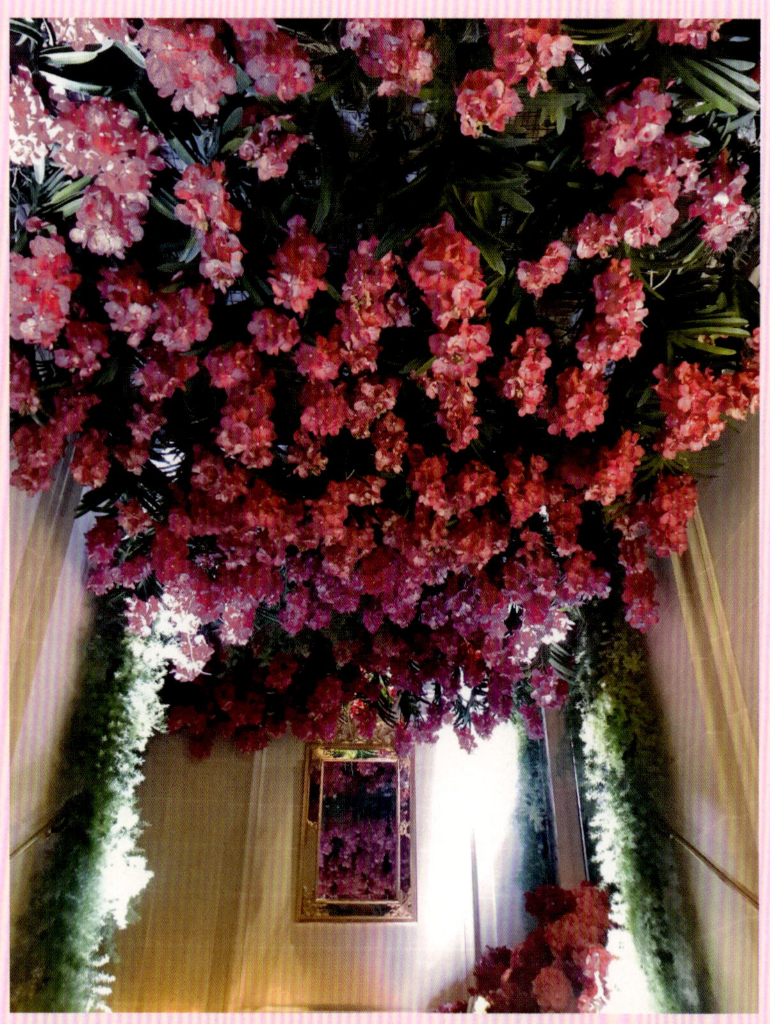

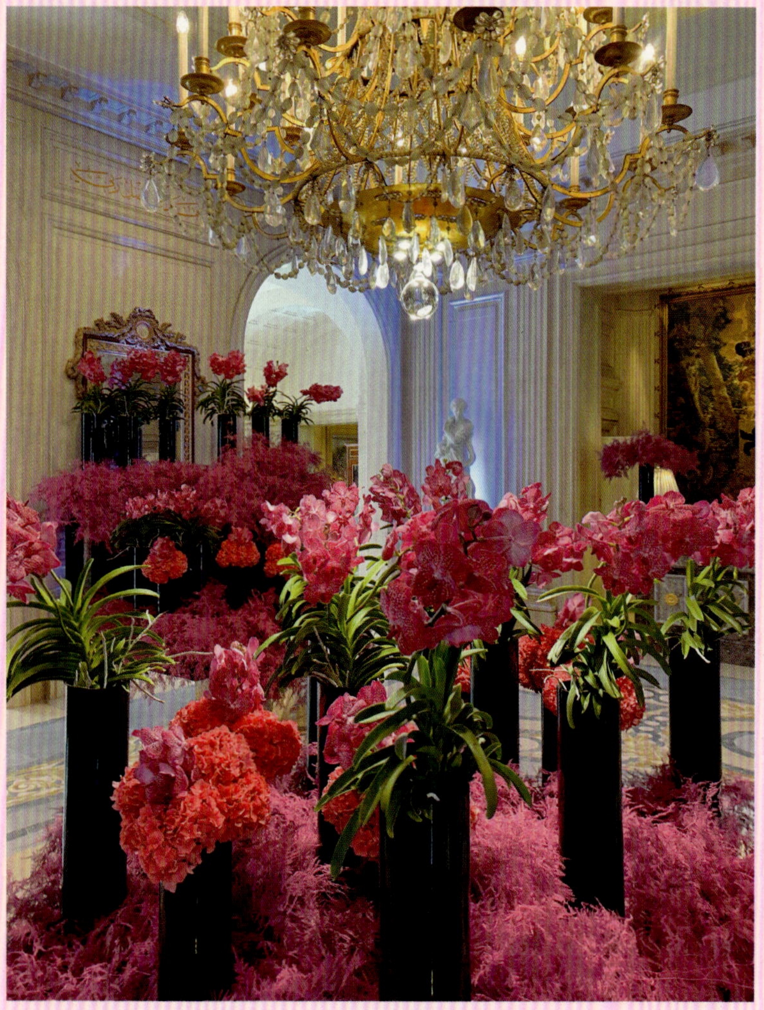

PREVIOUS: Four Seasons George V Lobby. Viburnum, phalaenopsis orchids, and statice. LEFT AND OPPOSITE: Phalaenopsis orchids, vanda orchids, hydrangeas, and plumosa.

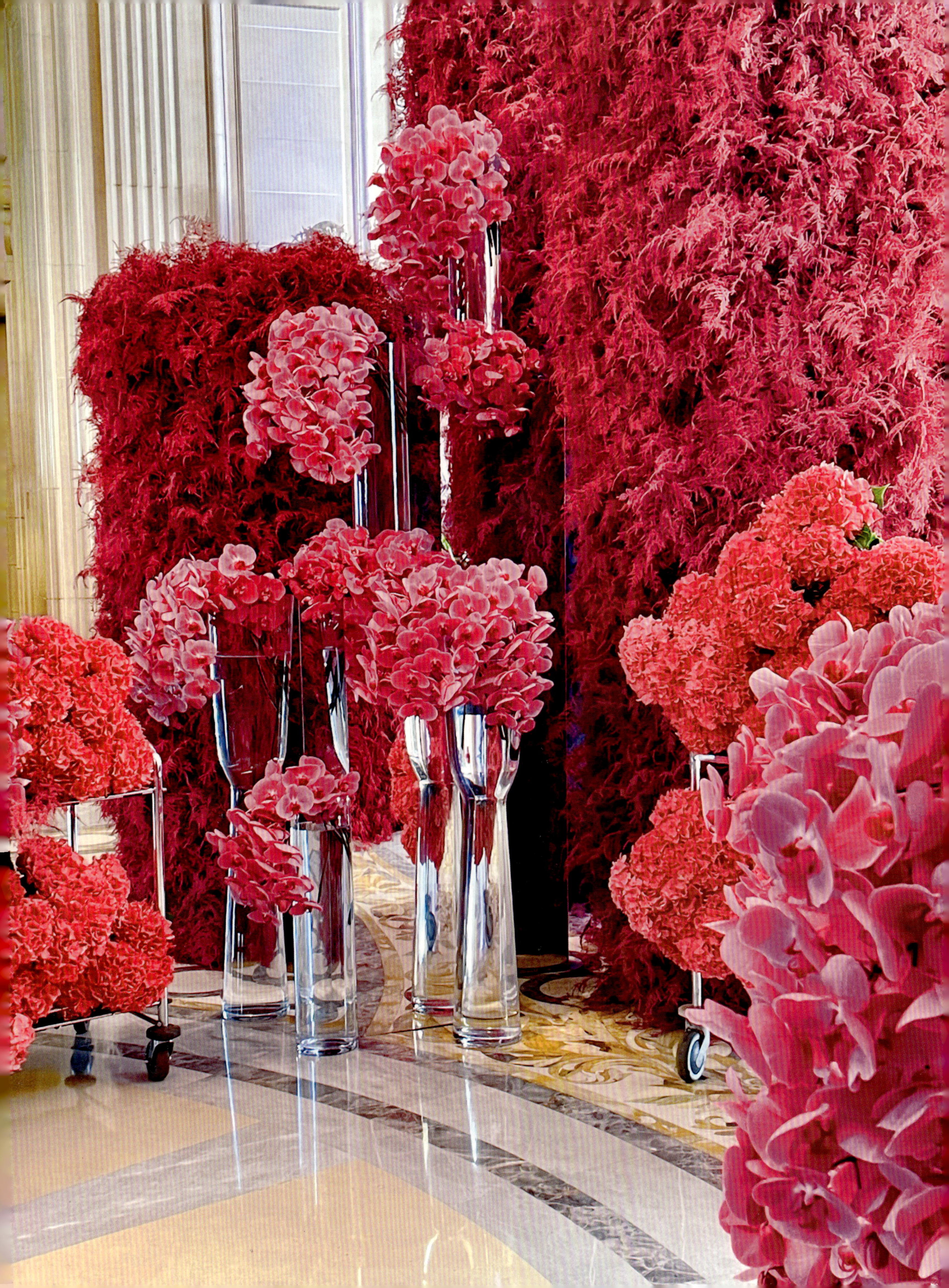

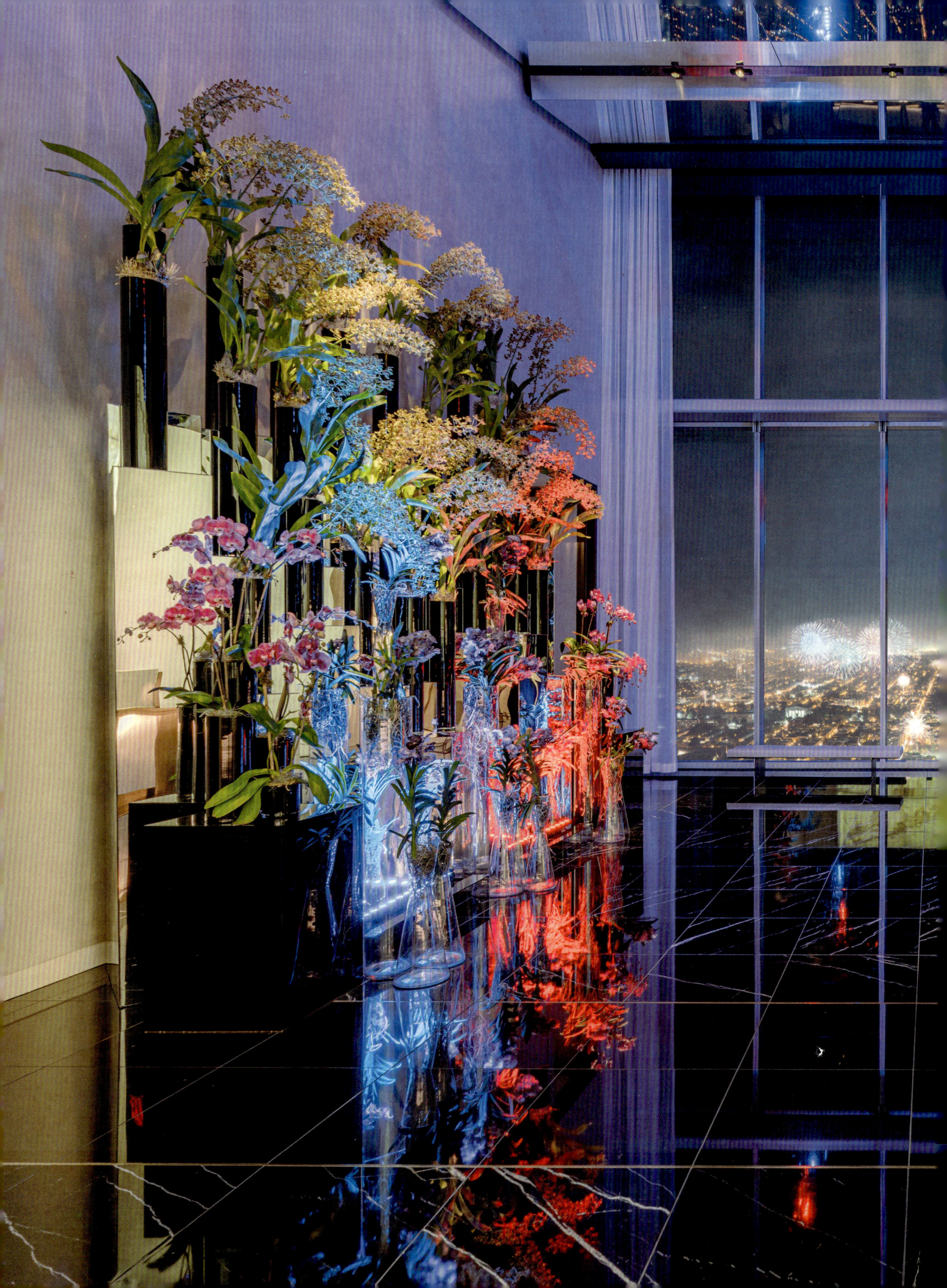

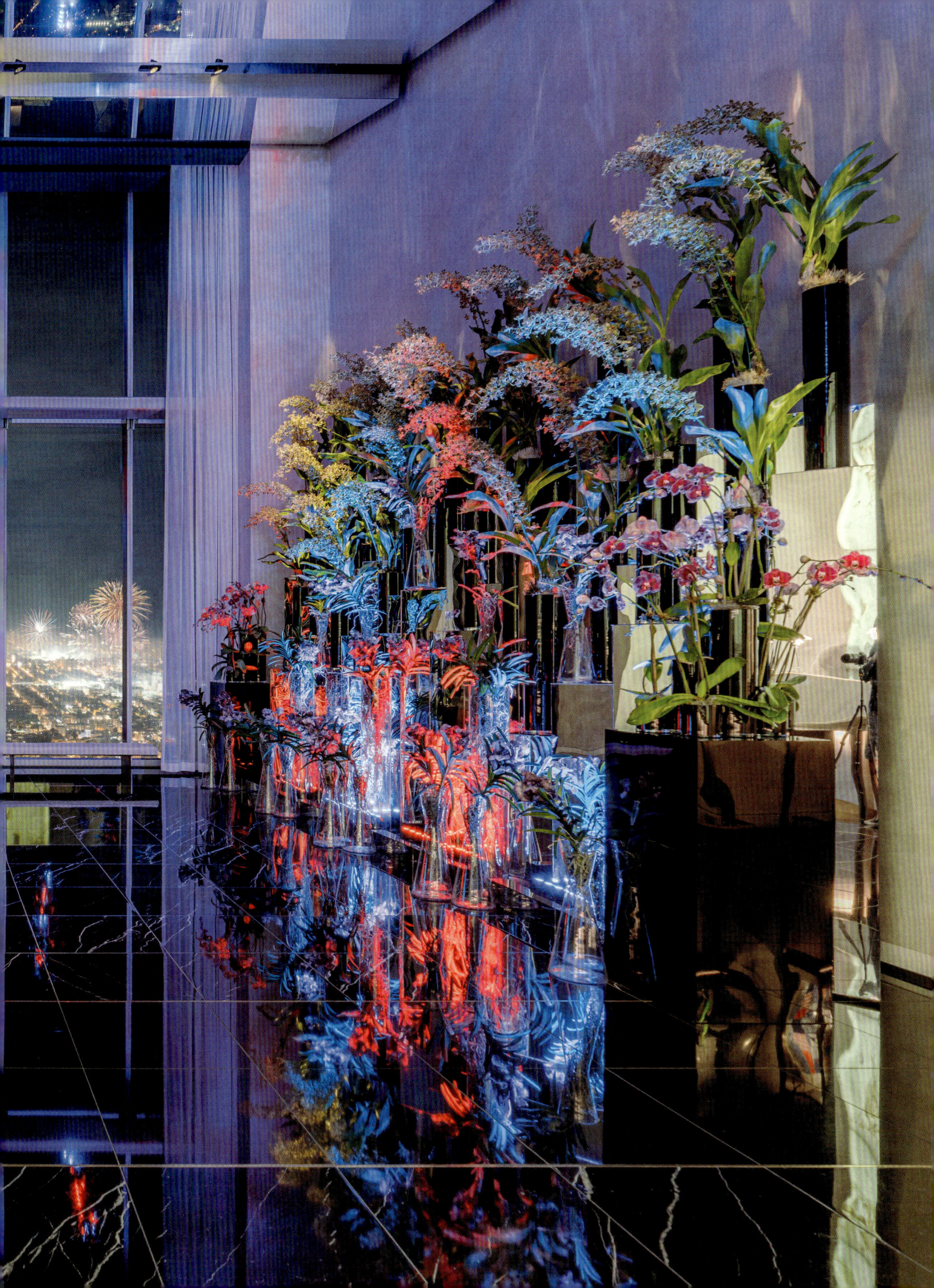

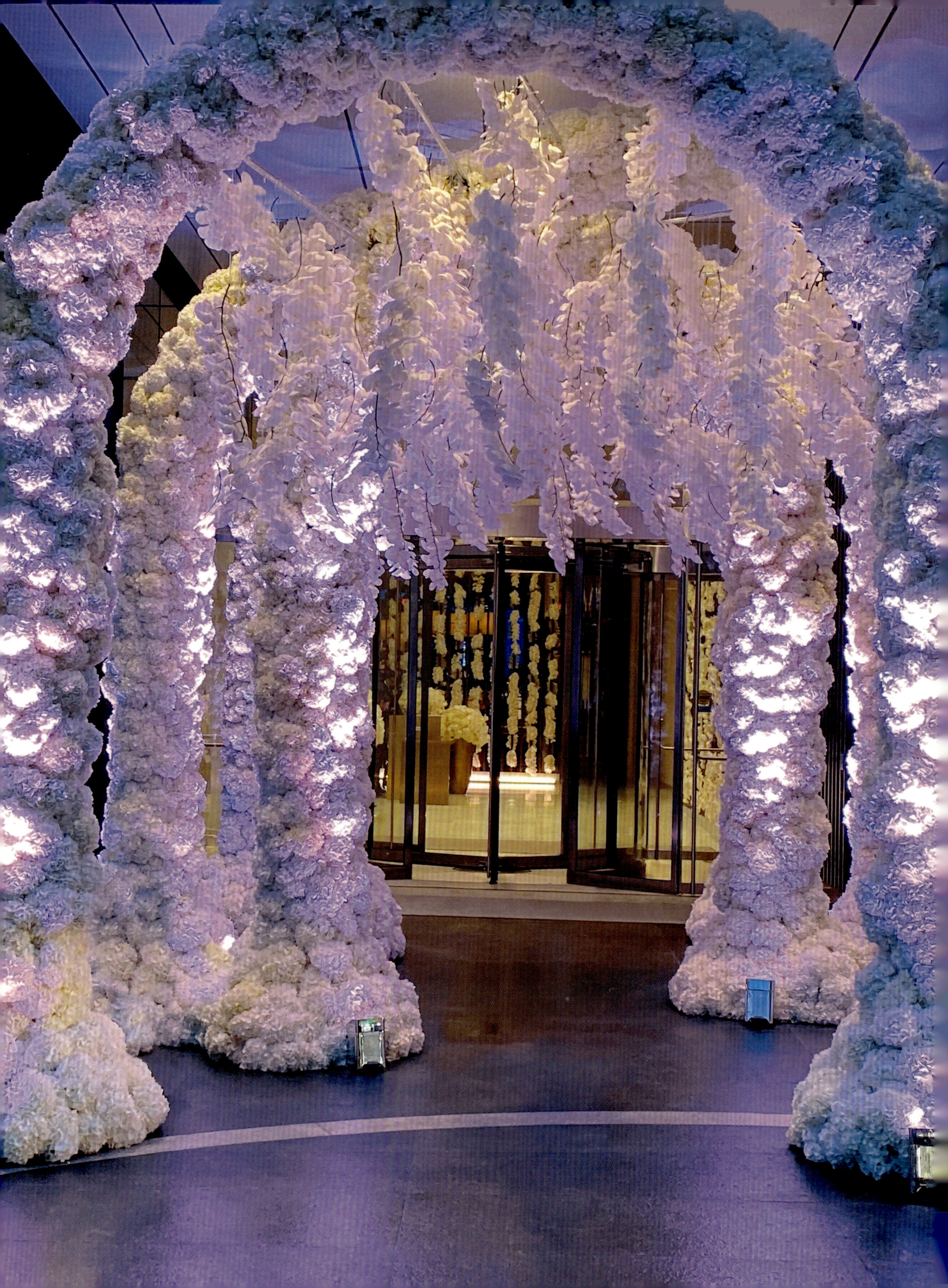

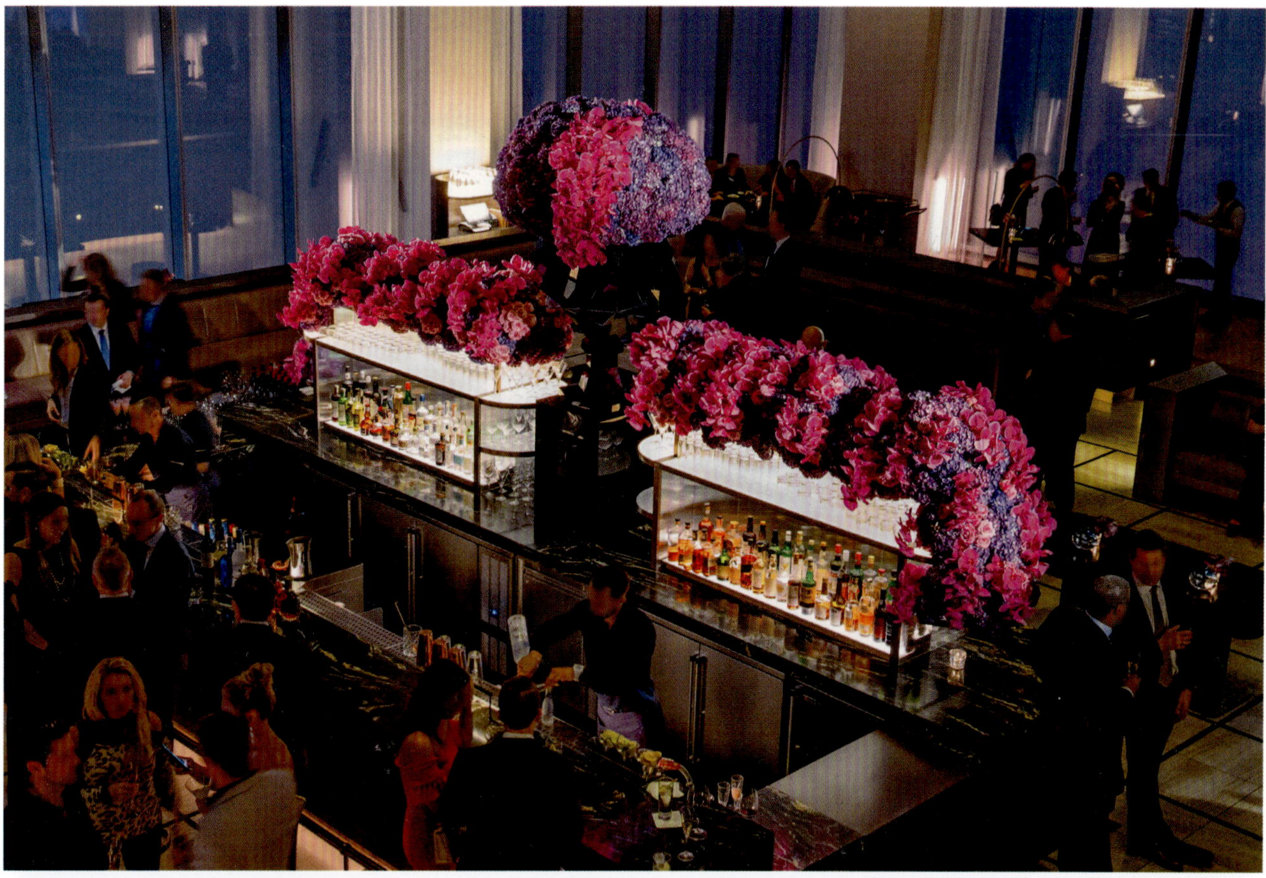

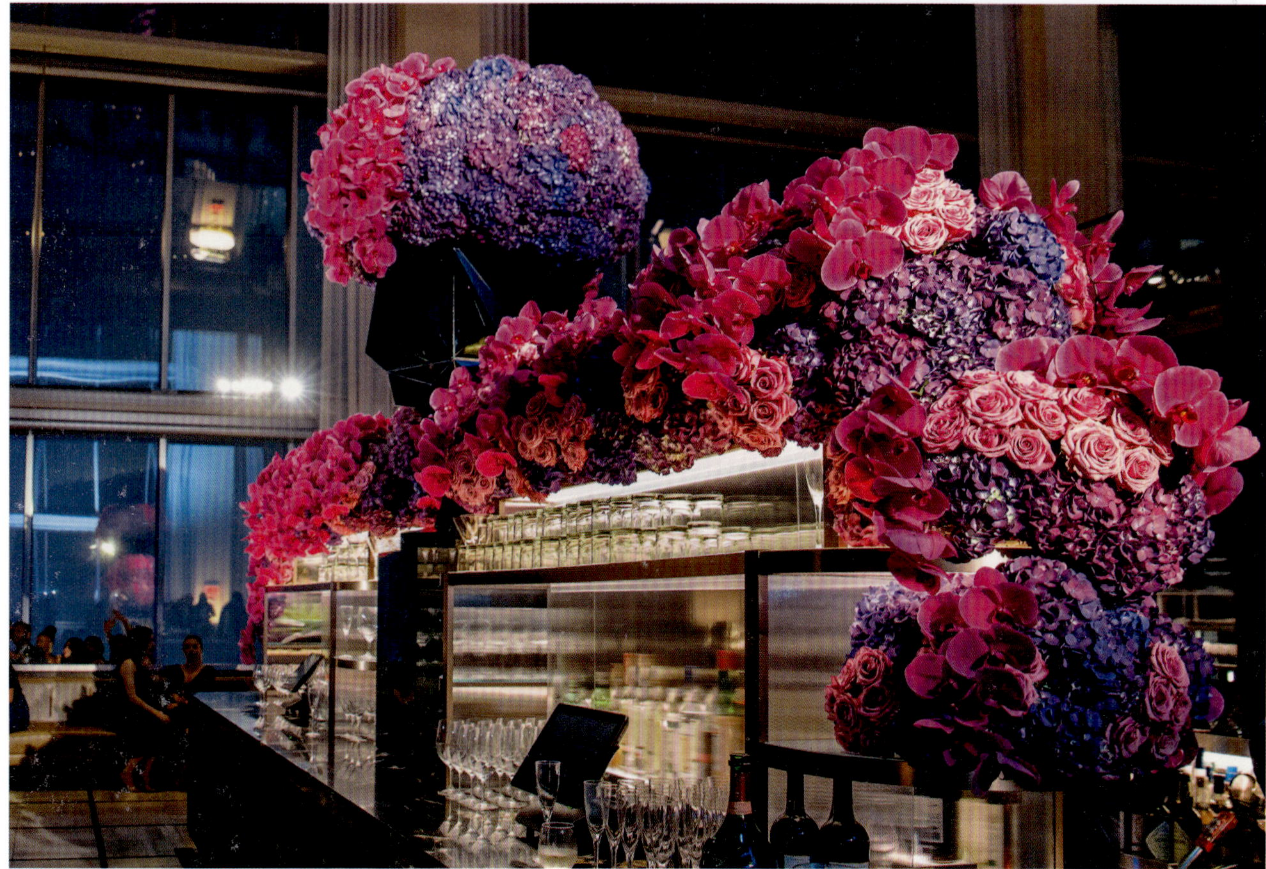

PREVIOUS: Four Seasons Philadelphia Lobby. Orchid varieties.

OPPOSITE: Four Seasons Philadelphia Lobby. Hydrangeas and phalaenopsis orchids.

ABOVE: Hydrangeas, phalaenopsis orchids, and roses.

FOLLOWING LEFT: Four Seasons George V Lobby. Hydrangeas and coral charm peonies.

FOLLOWING RIGHT: Four Seasons Philadelphia Lobby. Cherry blossoms, phalaenopsis orchids, and coral charm peonies.

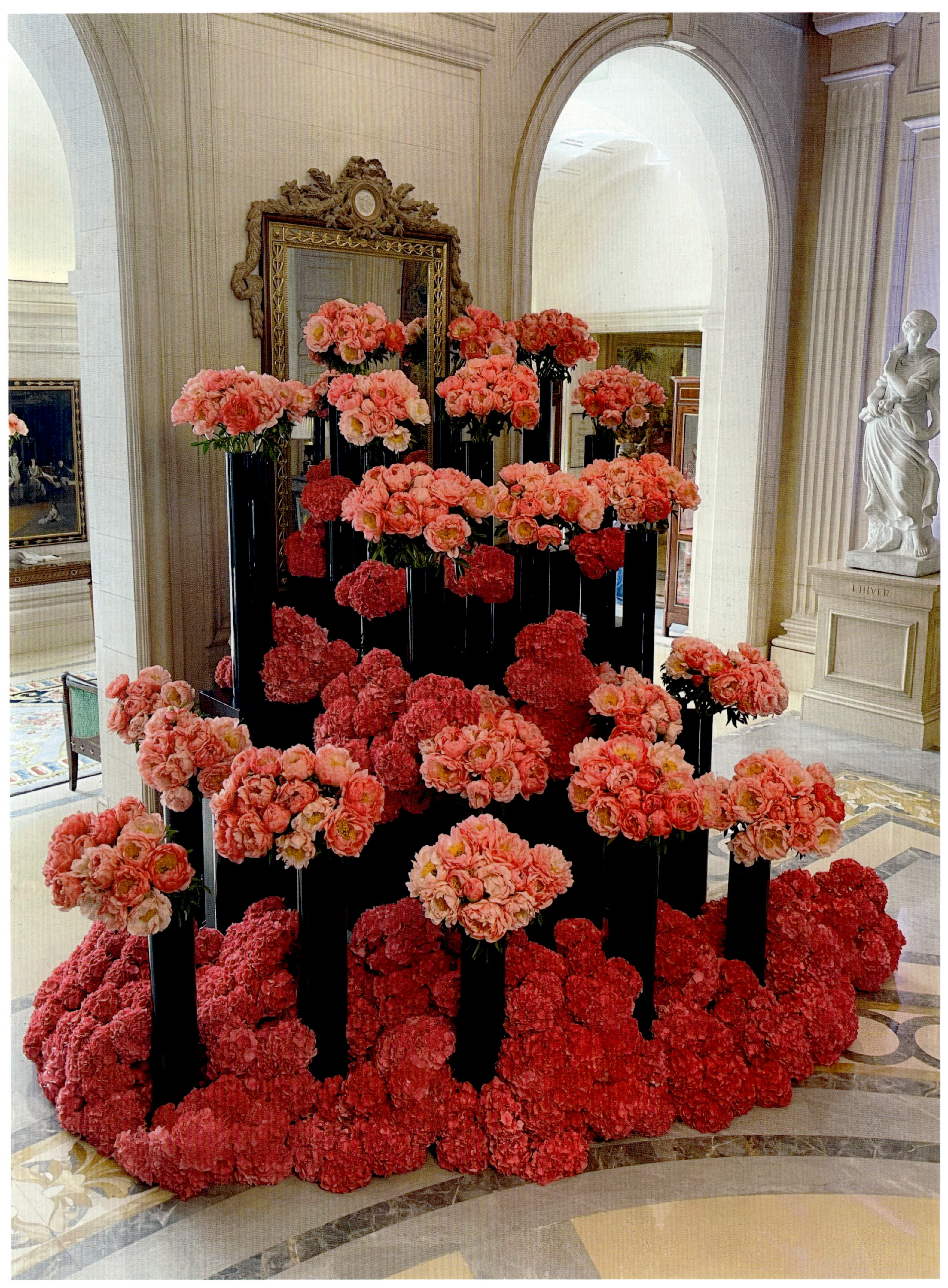

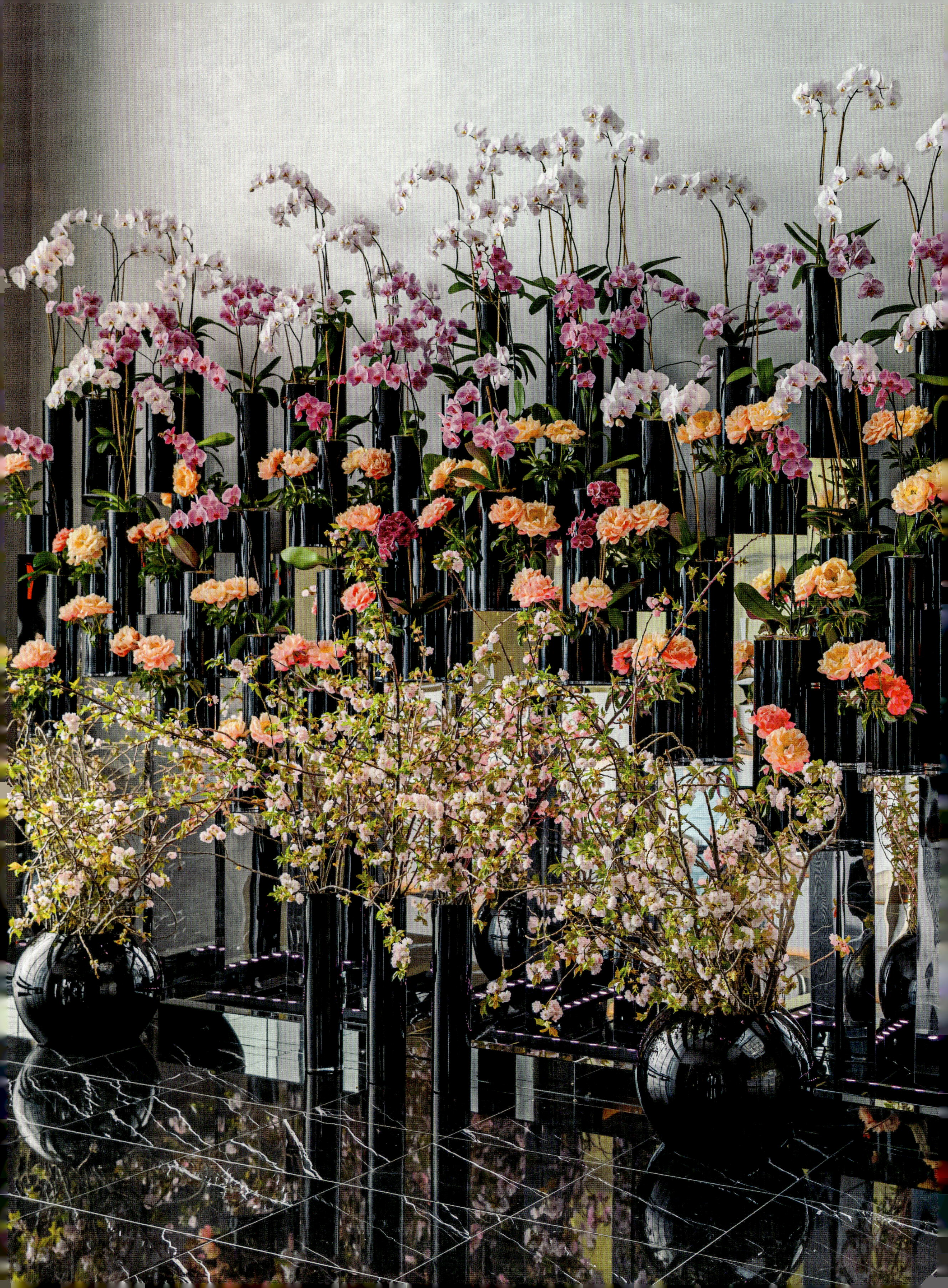

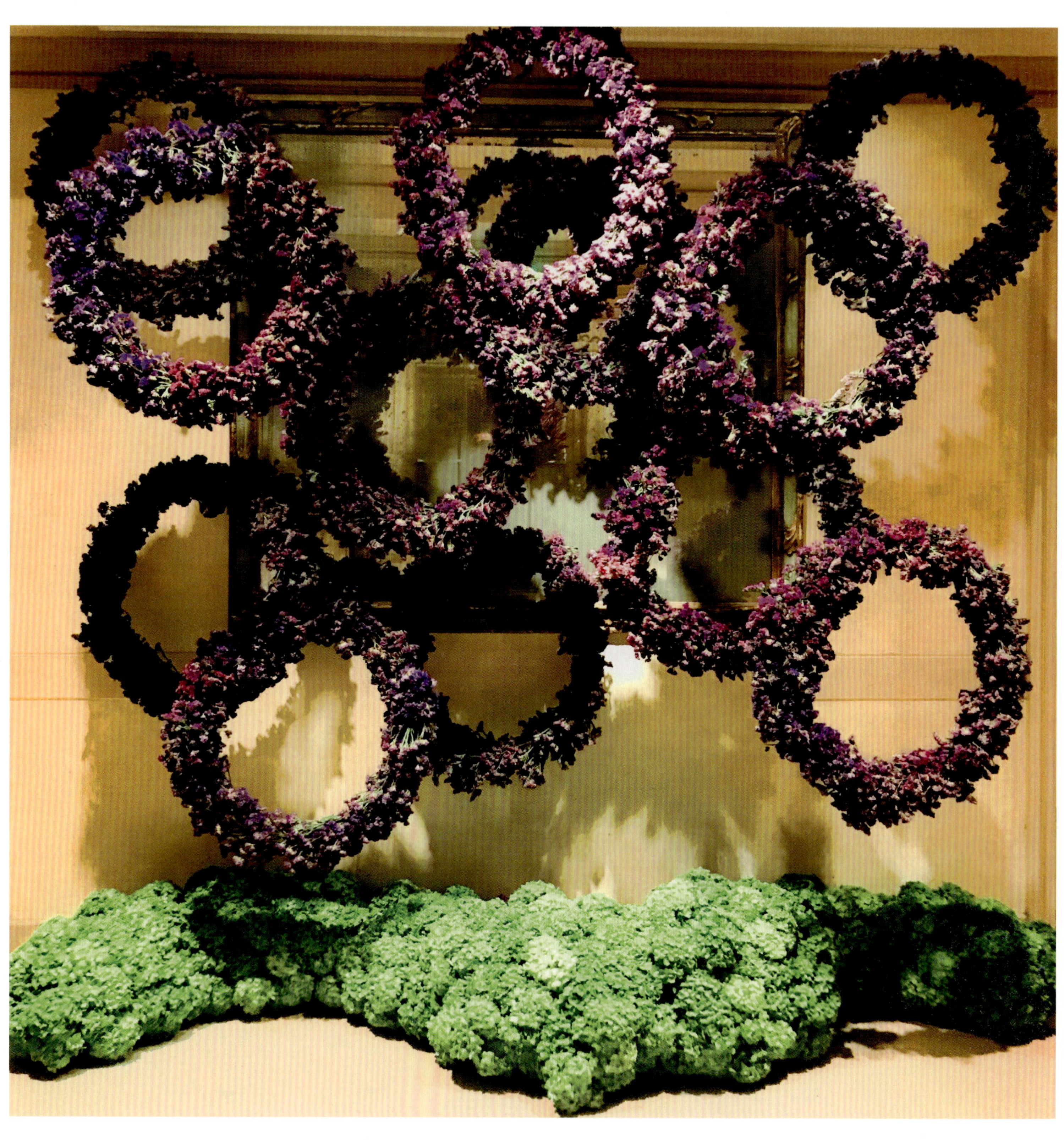

Four Seasons Los Angeles at Beverly Hills
Lobby. Liatris with hydrangeas (opposite).
FOLLOWING: Four Seasons George V Lobby.
Gladiolas and hydrangeas.

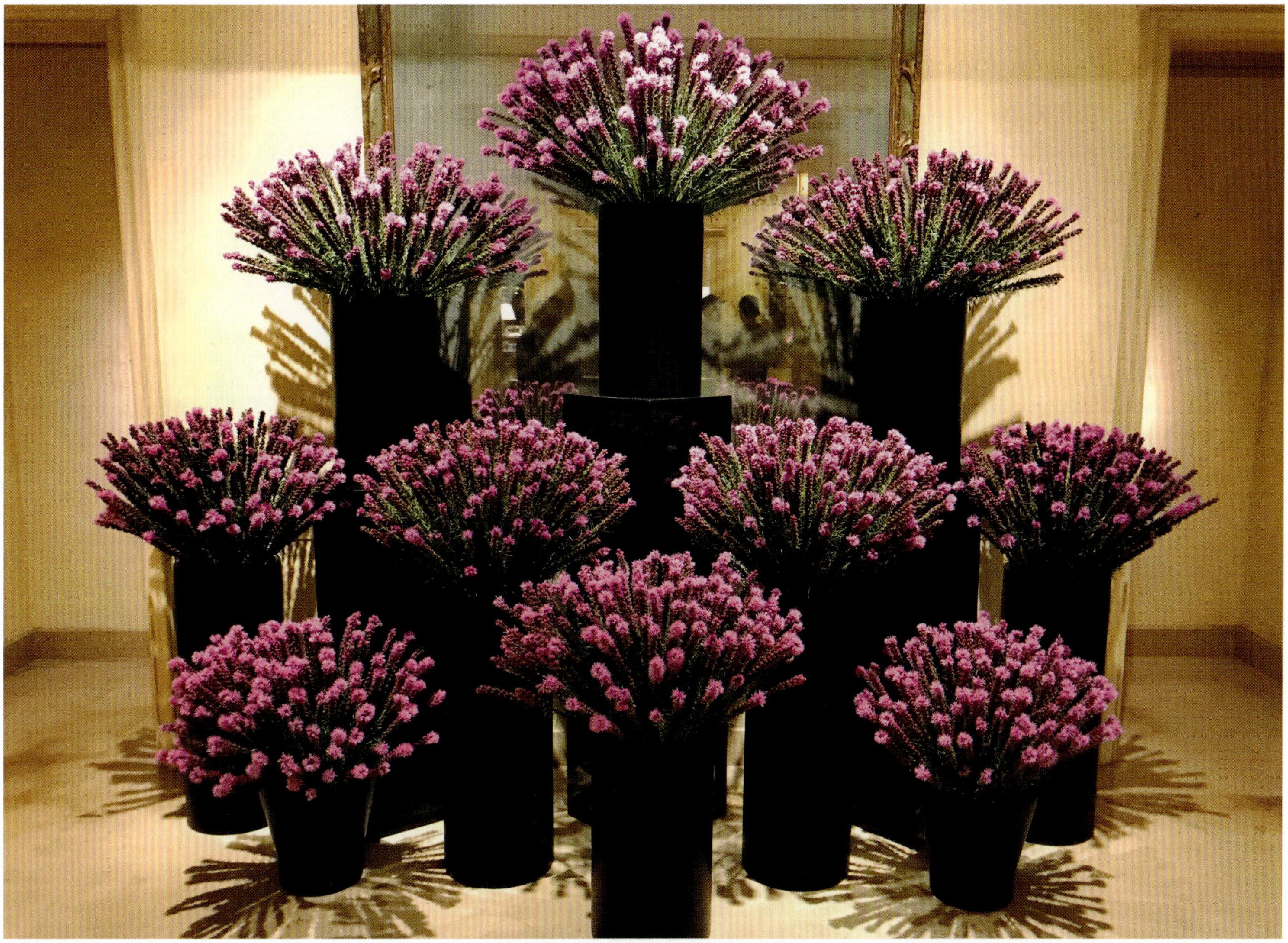

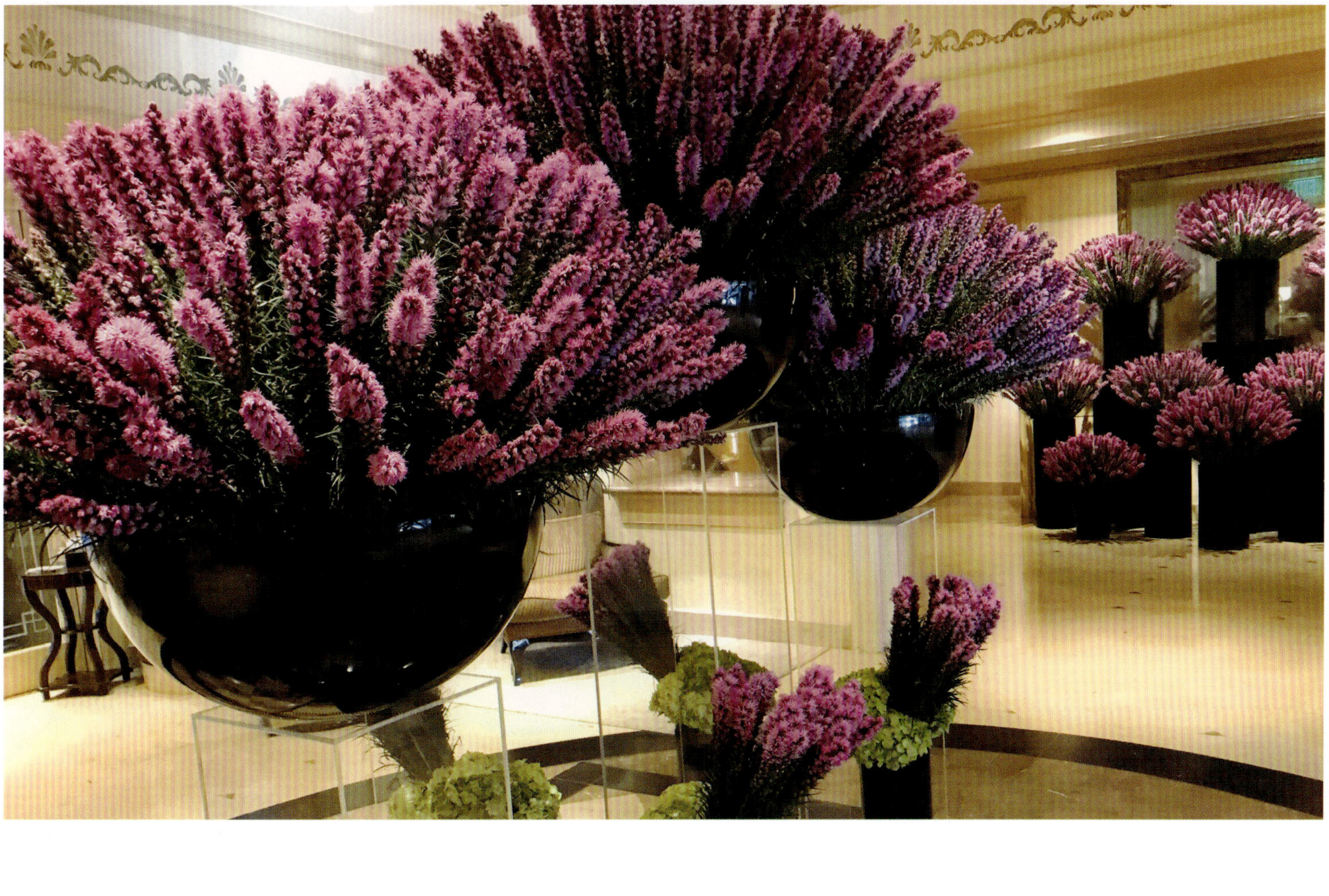

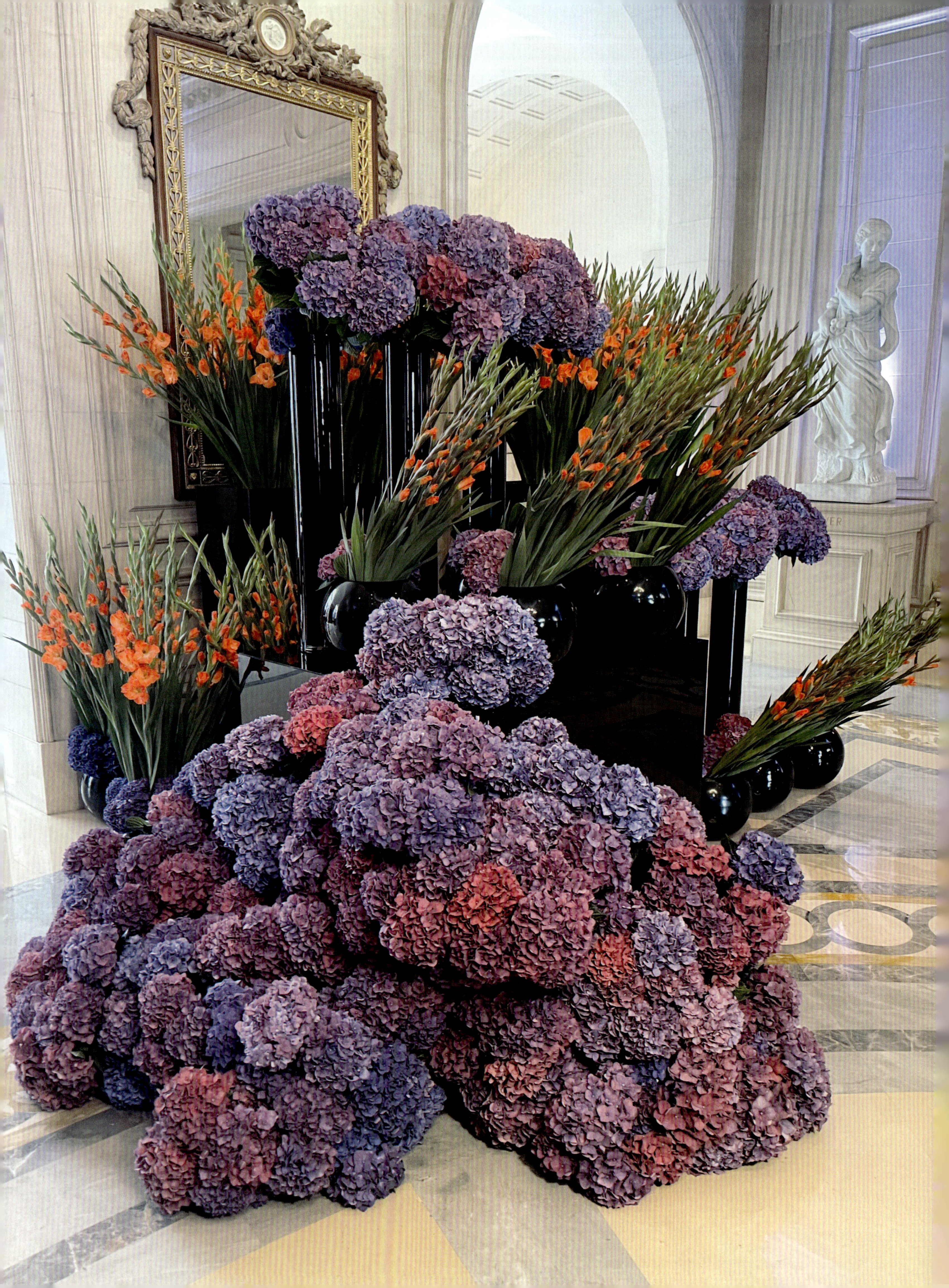

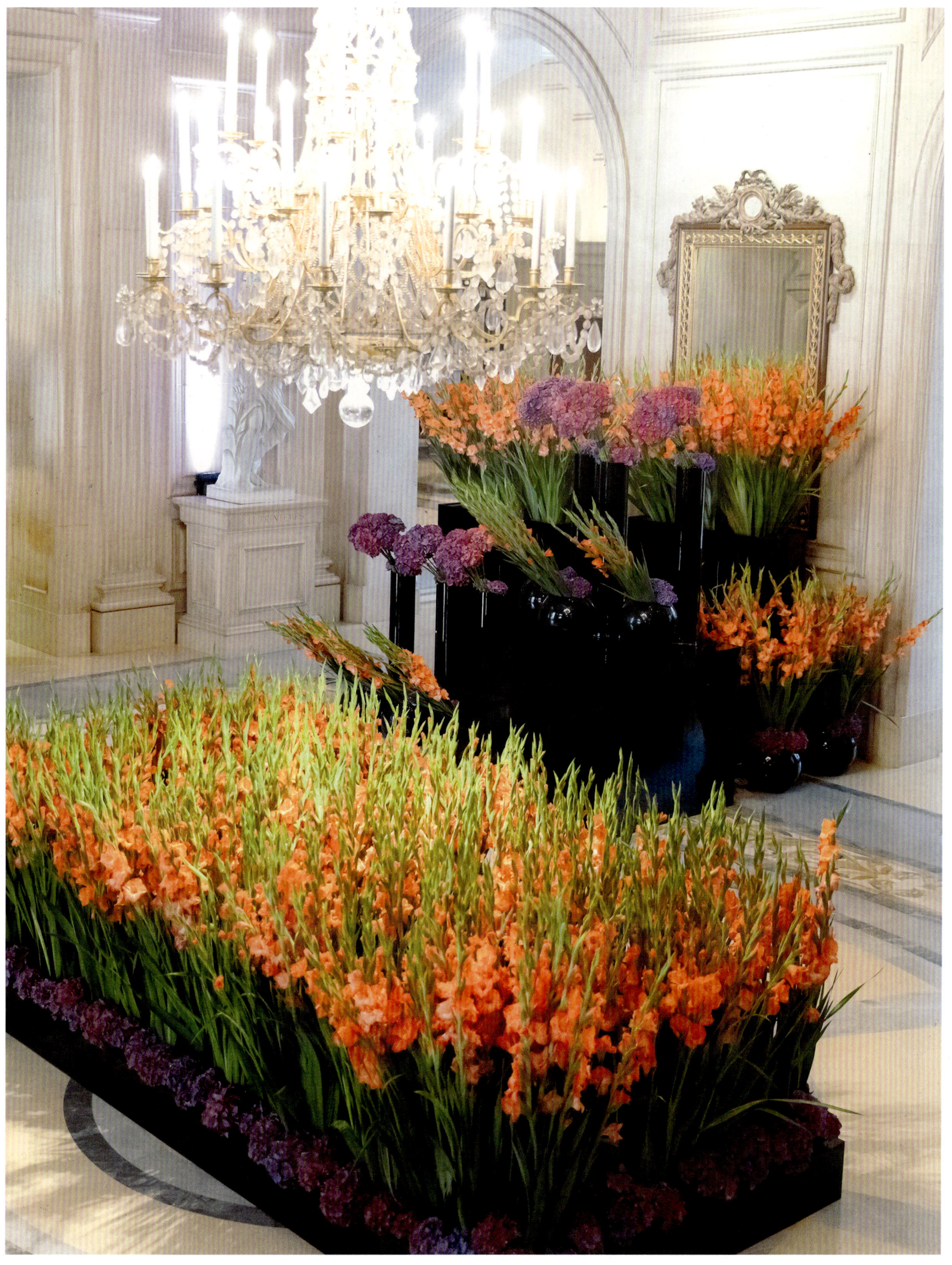

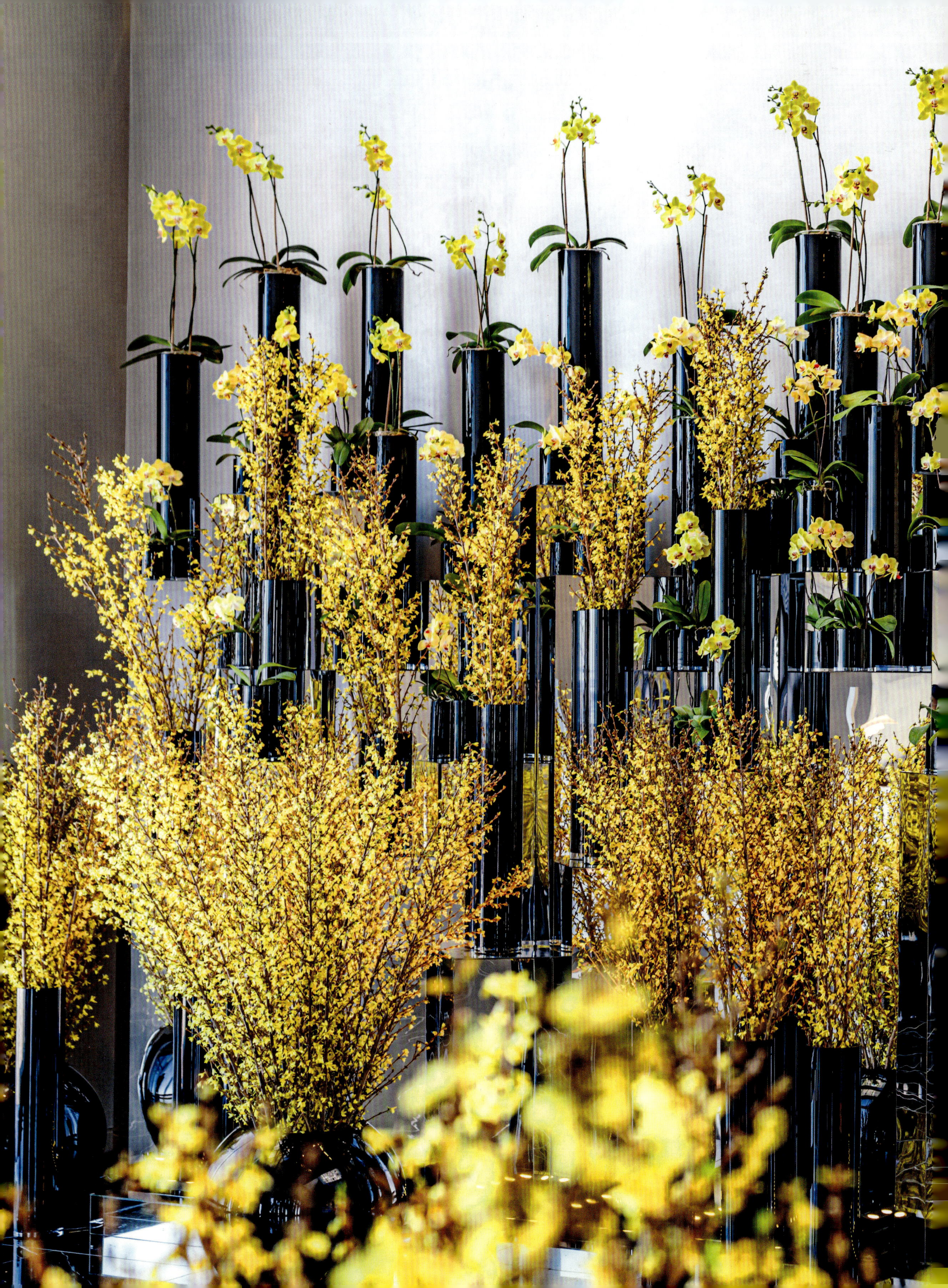

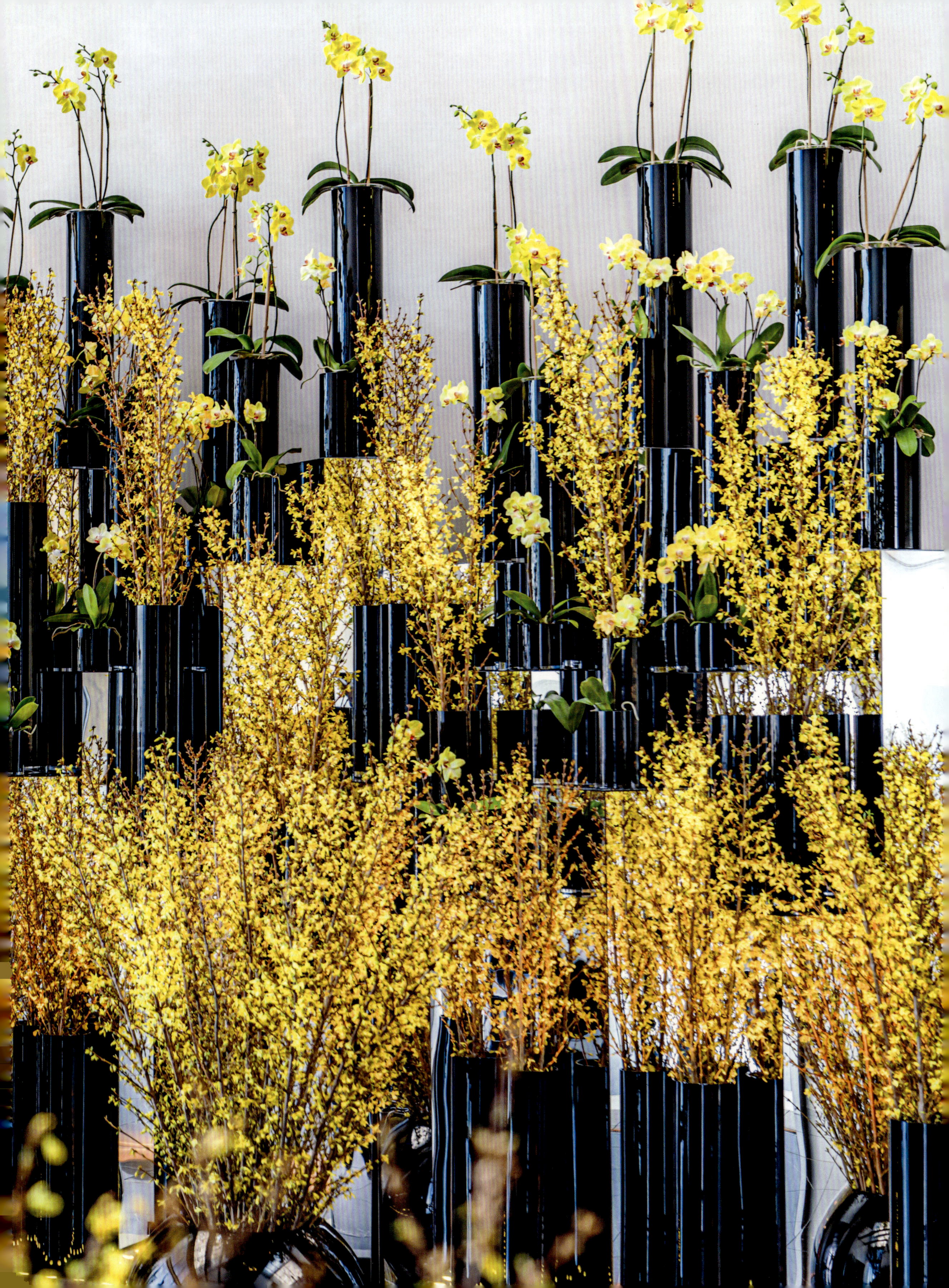

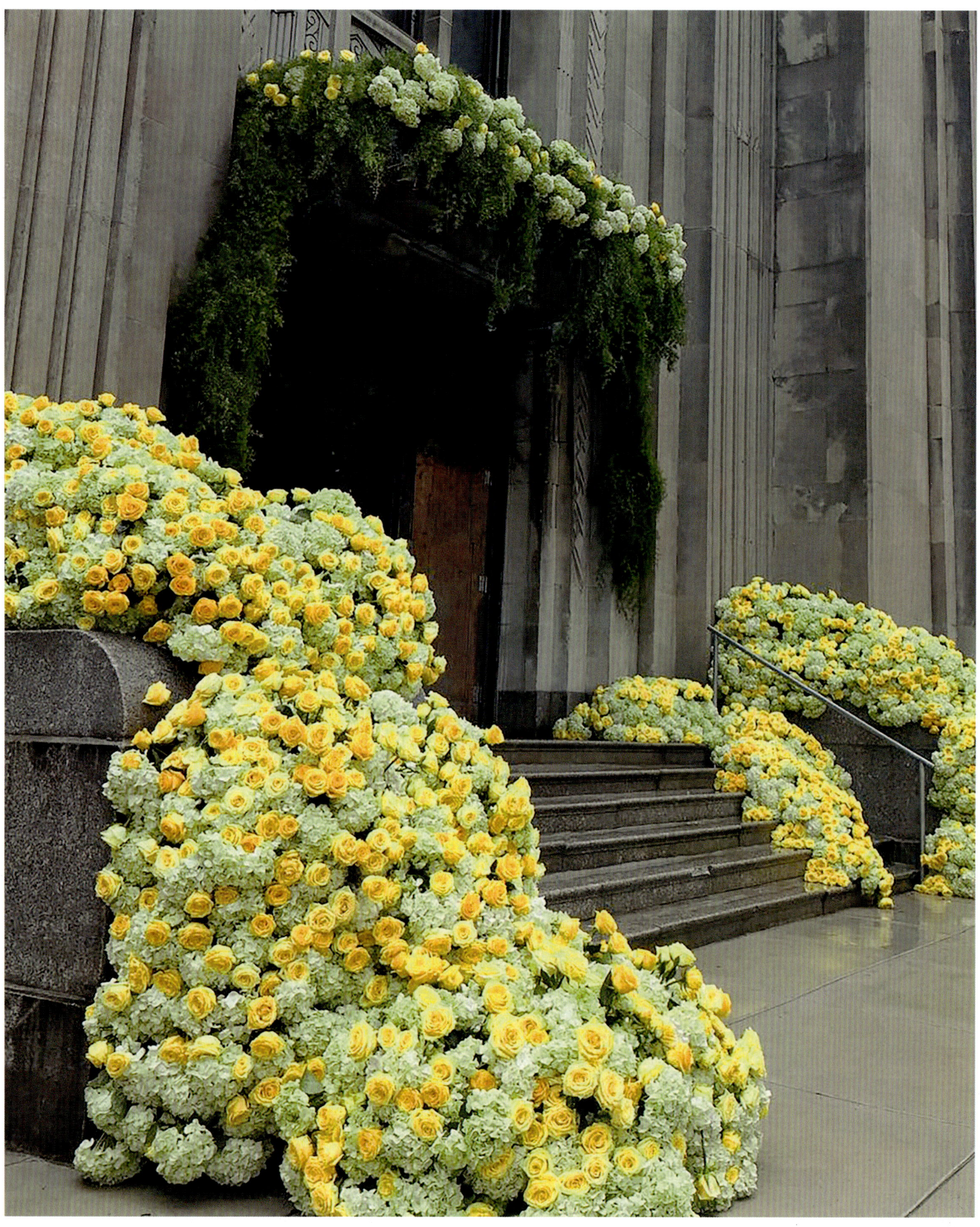

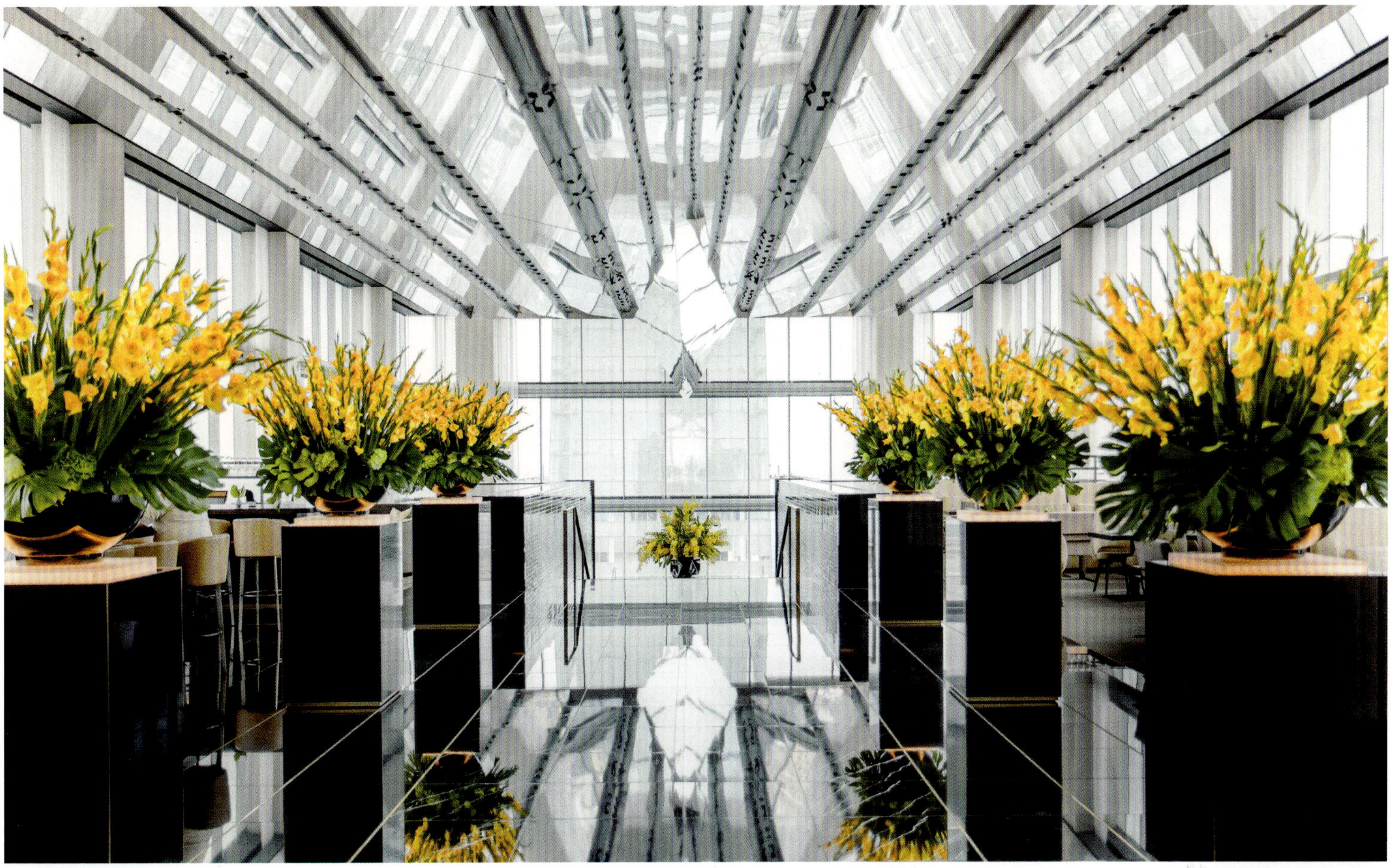

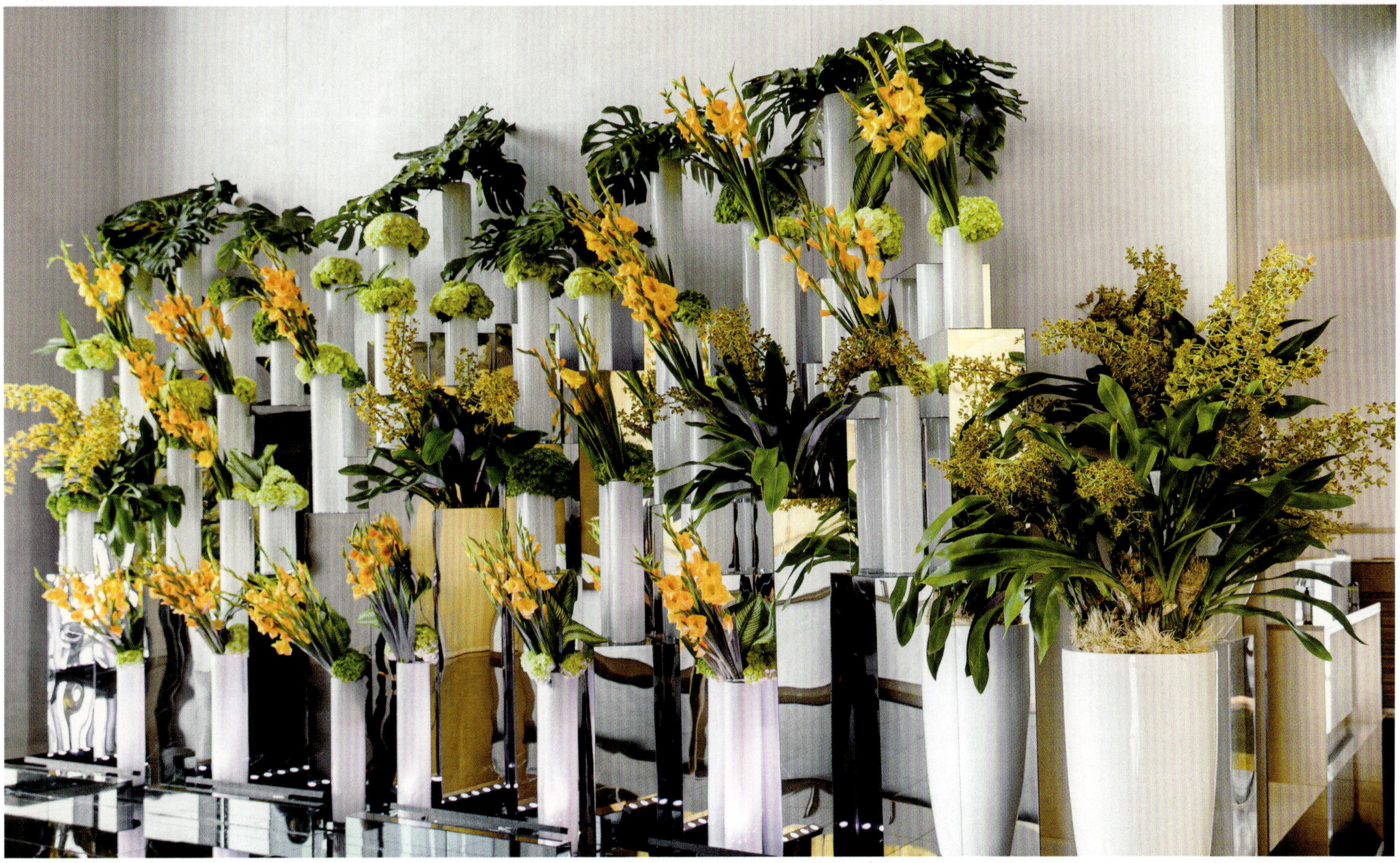

PREVIOUS: Four Seasons Philadelphia Lobby. Forsythia branches and phalaenopsis orchids. OPPOSITE: Four Seasons Philadelphia Entrance. Roses, hydrangeas, and pepper berry. ABOVE: Four Seasons Philadelphia Lobby. Tropical leaves, gladiolas, forsythia, and phalaenopsis orchids.

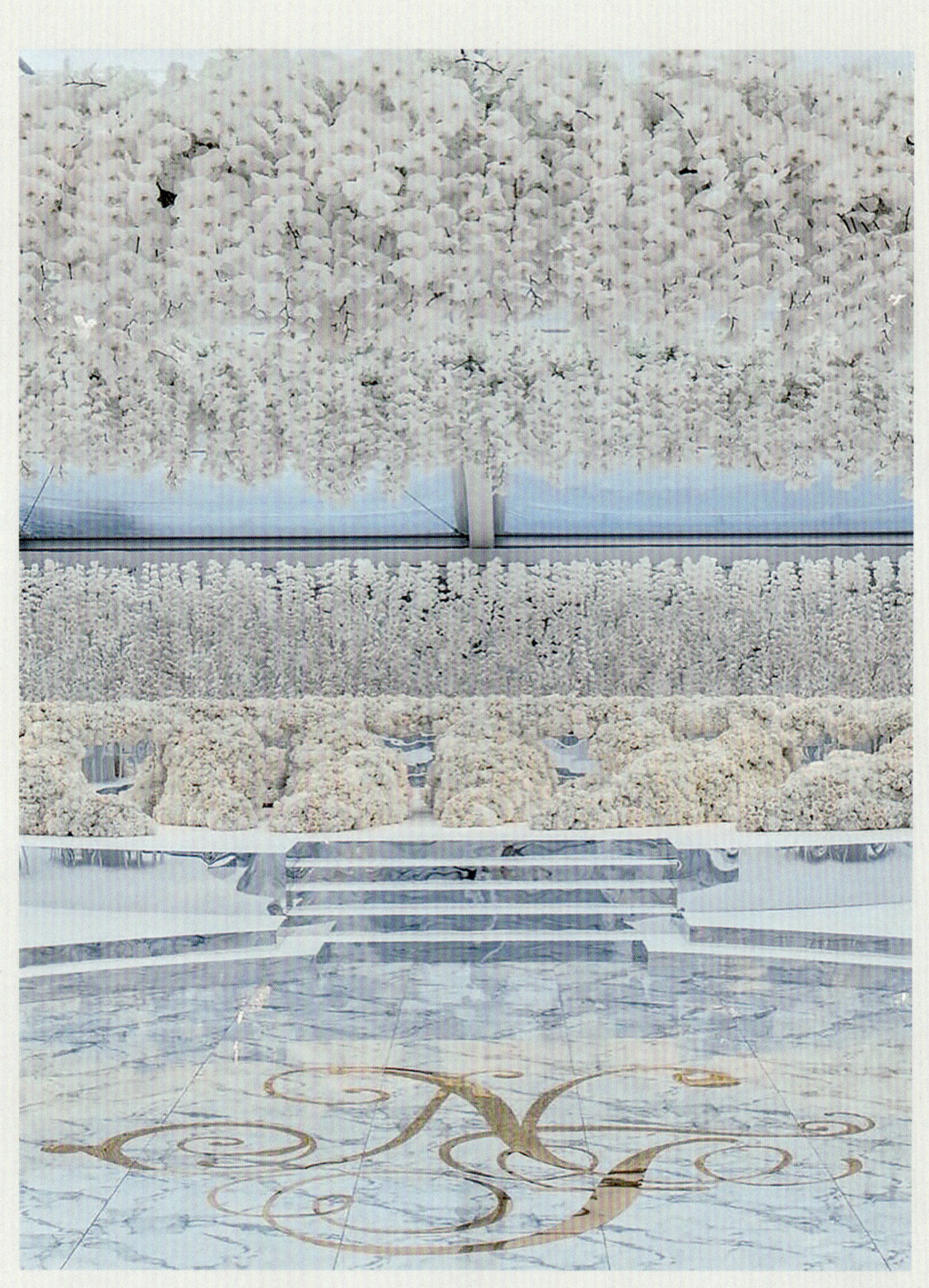

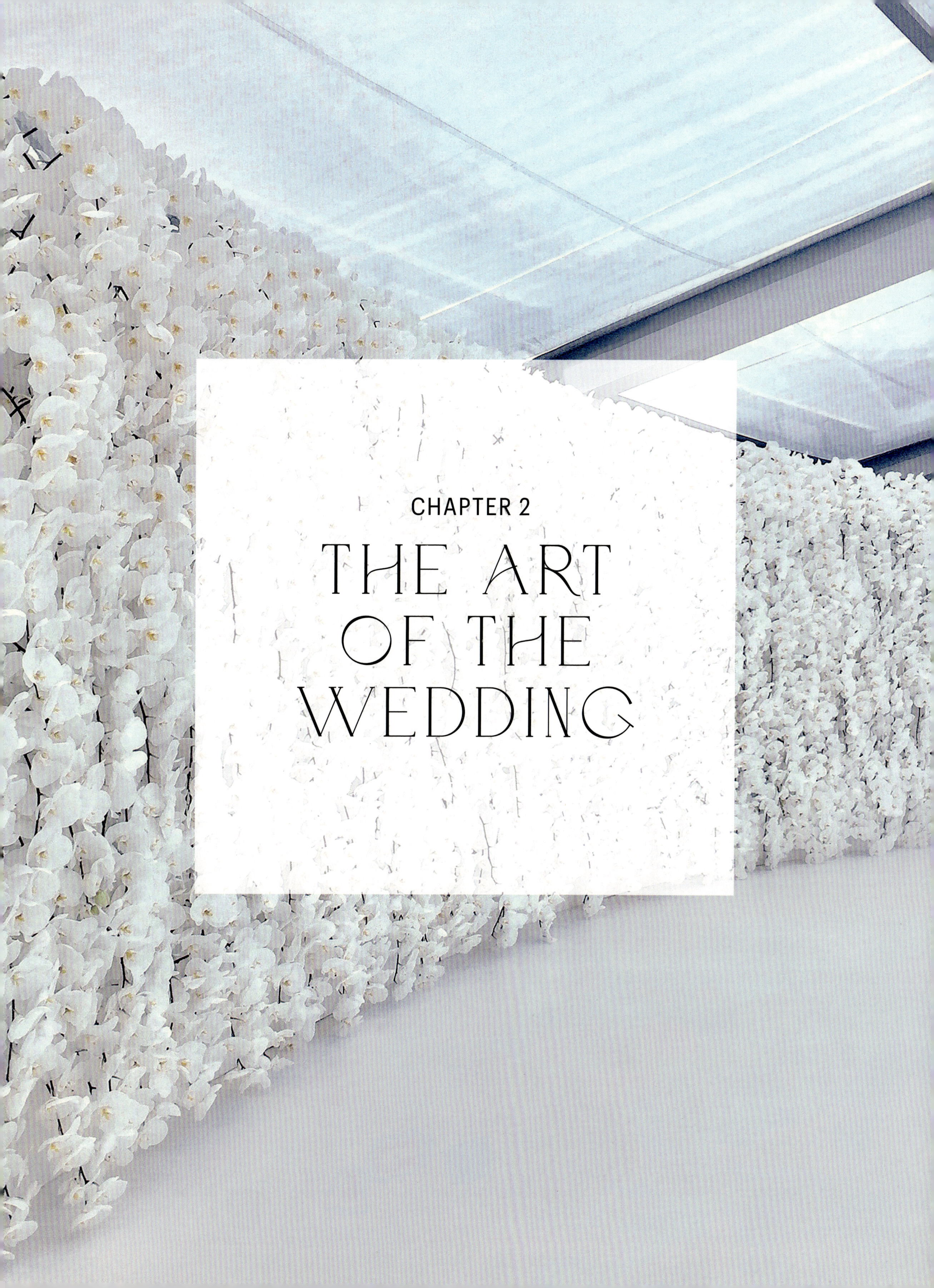
CHAPTER 2
THE ART
OF THE
WEDDING

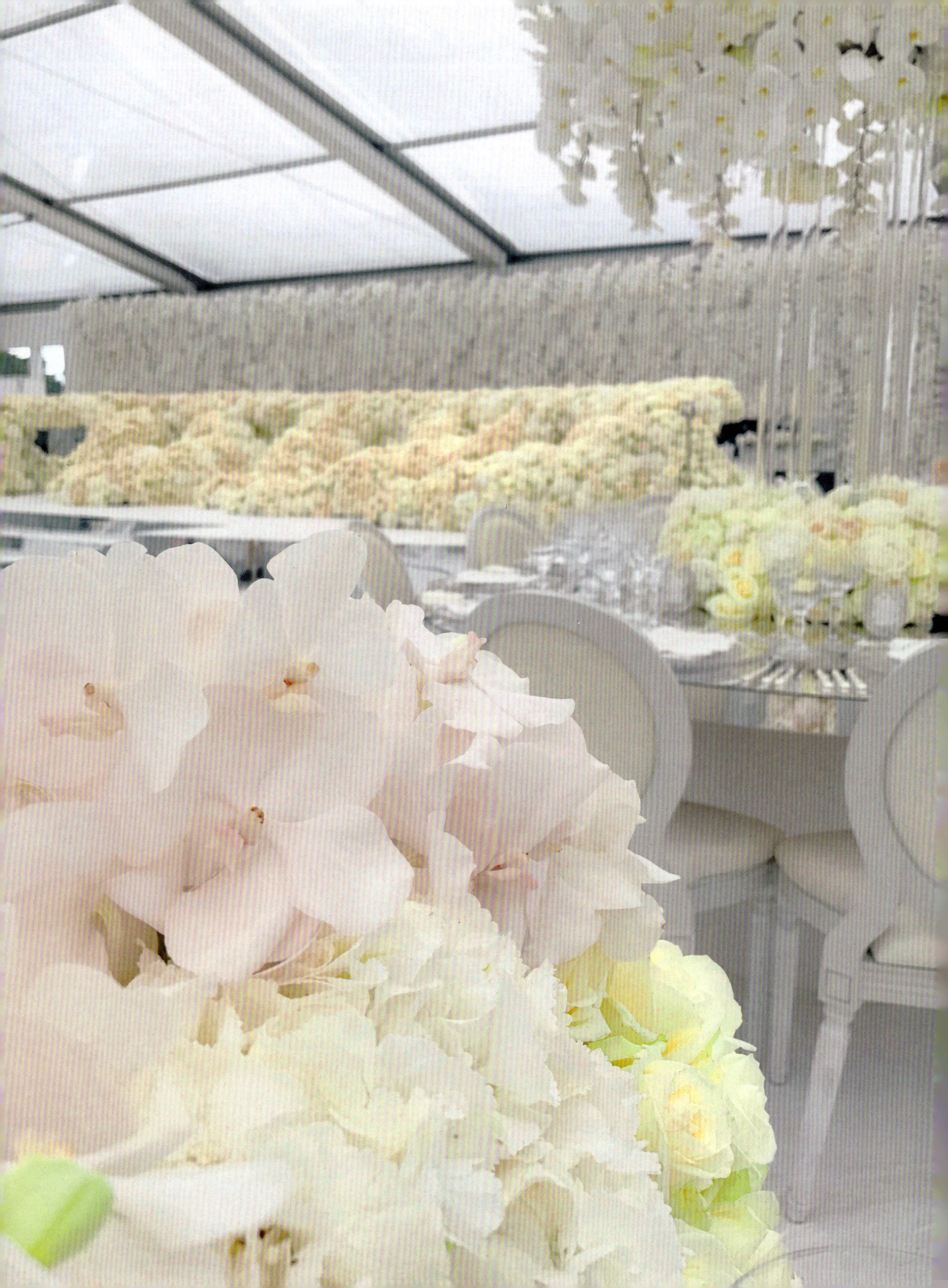

W hether it's extremely intimate or over the top, weddings have a certain personality. They are always an exciting celebration, and I take great care and pride in designing them. Weddings are my most intimate events, and where I aim to create a dream experience. I derive my inspiration when I first meet the couple and learn about their unique relationship. Weddings are also where my personal relationship with a bride—and the bride's family—factors into play. I always ask brides to close their eyes and tell me how *they* see their wedding and how they've dreamt about it their whole life, because I want their dreams to come true. Of course, I also like to surprise brides with little additions they did not even ask for—which never ceases to delight them.

Truthfully, though, as beautiful and joyful as they are, weddings can also be complicated with many opinions being offered from everyone involved. I also feel that, nowadays, weddings have become very competitive, which I don't like. They should be personal and focused on the couple getting married, not a contest to outdo another wedding. In the end, everyone needs to remember that a wedding is a celebration of a union and of love. I'm a romantic soul to the extreme—when a person works with flowers every day, how can they not be? Love is my inspiration in creating unforgettable weddings.

I enjoy small weddings just as much as big ones. I try to keep my designs simple and keep in mind that each part of the wedding can, and should, be a different experience for the guests. From cocktail hour to the ceremony, and from dinner to dancing, each wedding stage matters and is a place to create an eye-catching spectacle. Of course, the ceremony is certainly important, and you never want the flowers to overpower the bride or groom. The art of the perfect wedding is all about *people*. It's the most personal time in any couple's life and, as a designer, I always want the couple and their guests to feel special—however it is they wish to achieve that.

Trust me, it's the right way to do it. I also enjoy working with different planners and families and incorporating the visions they have for the most important day of the couple's life, and it is something that I take pride in. I also take into account any cultural heritages the couple and their families would like to celebrate.

The best weddings I have done have been in destinations all over the world, which makes location scouting extremely important. Wedding installations can take weeks to create, yet just a couple of hours to take down—which makes me laugh every time. The location acts as my design partner to determine how it will feature into my design by either completely transforming the space or turning it into an accessory. Whether converting a sparse ballroom into an enchanted garden, a grand Florentine palazzo into an intimate dinner, a sterile golf course into a romantic rose garden, or remodeling a simple swimming pool into an elaborate Monet-like painting, the important thing is that each wedding is based on making a romantic moment into a living romantic dream.

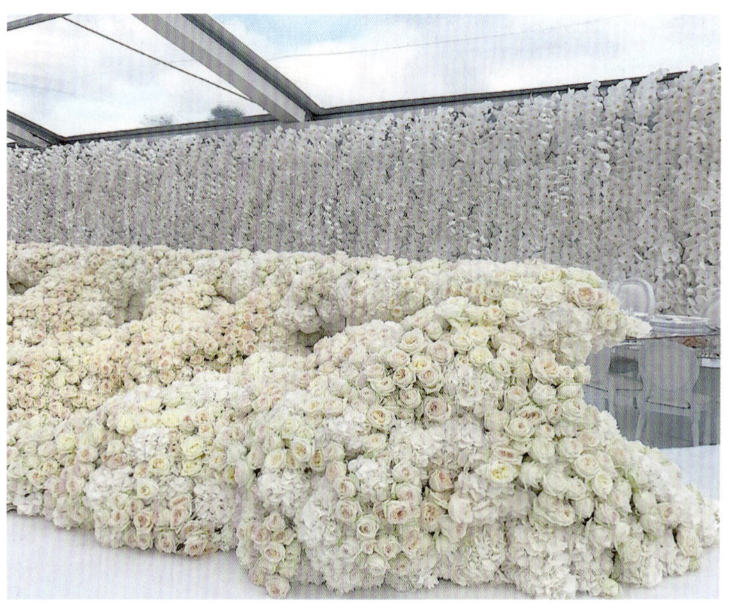

PAGES 64–71: Private Wedding, Woodstock, England. Hydrangeas, phalaenopsis orchids, and roses.

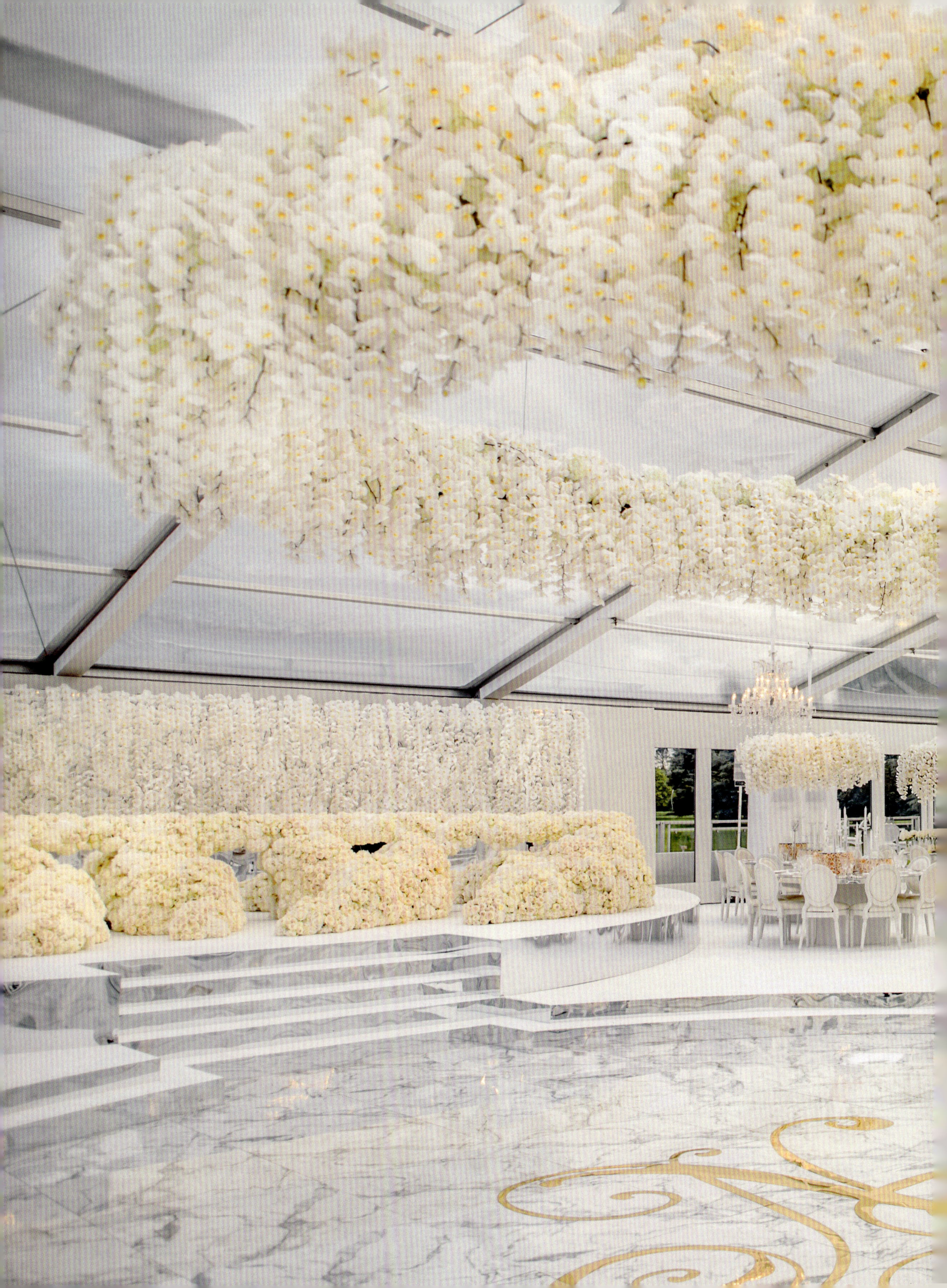

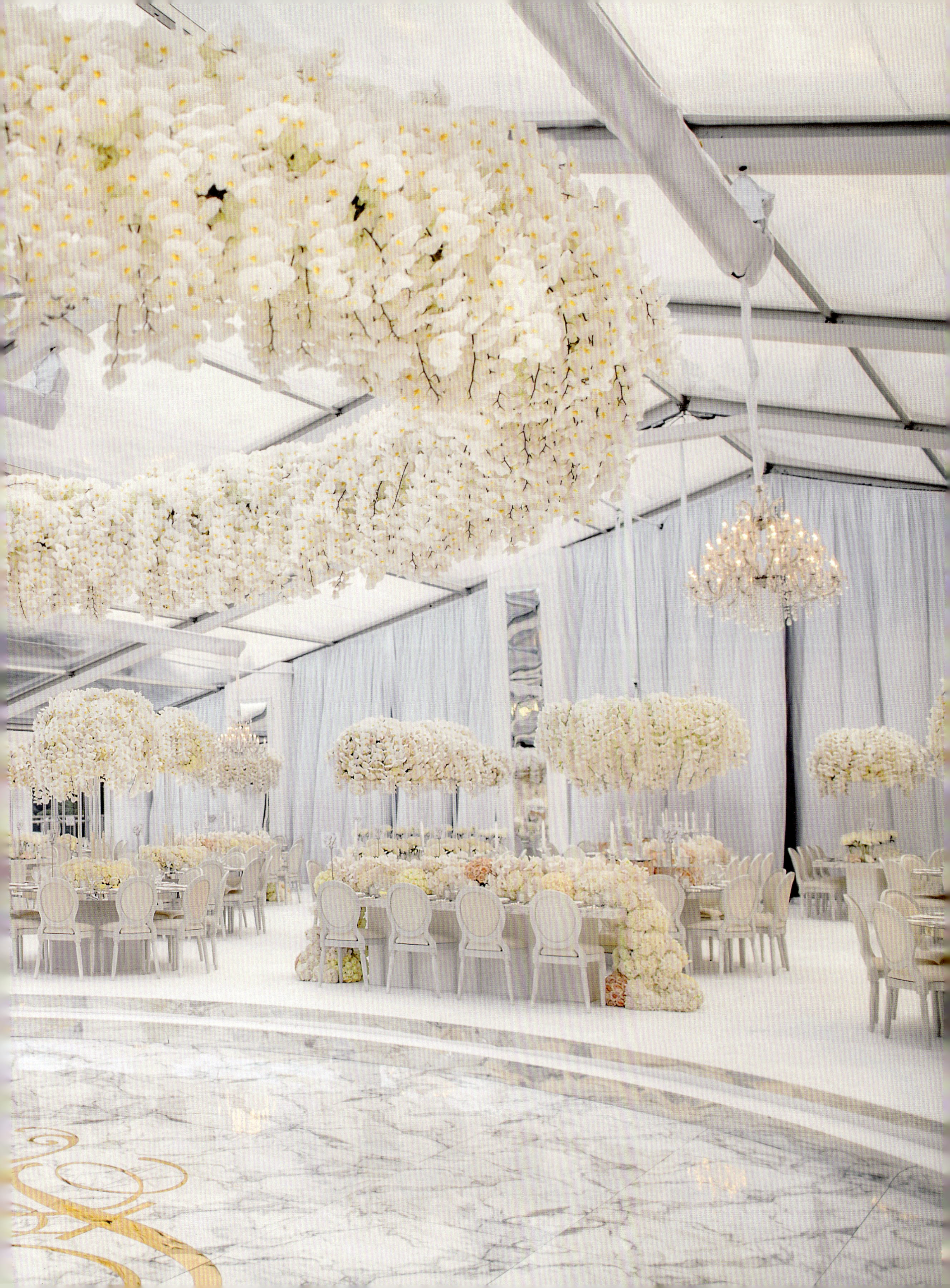

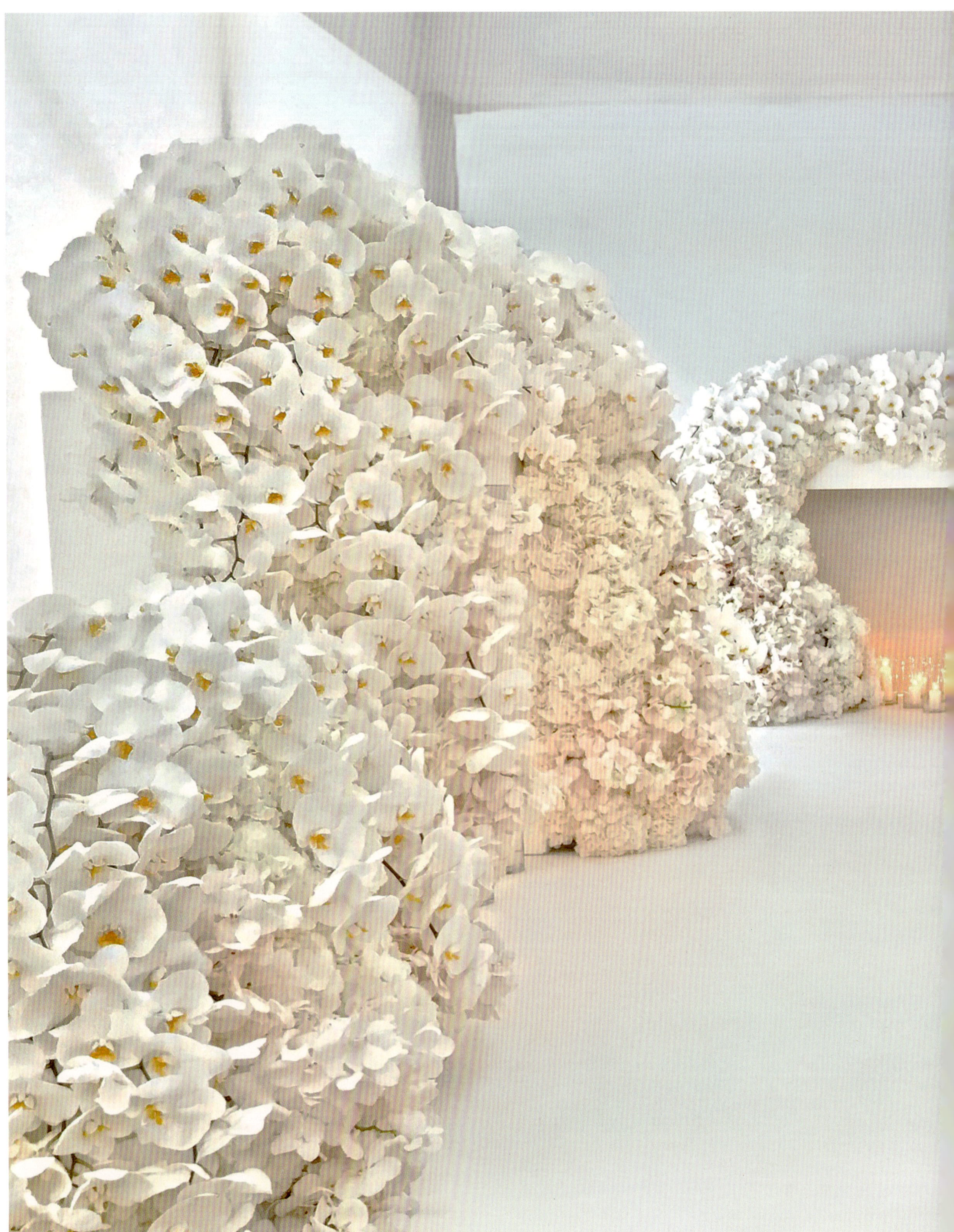

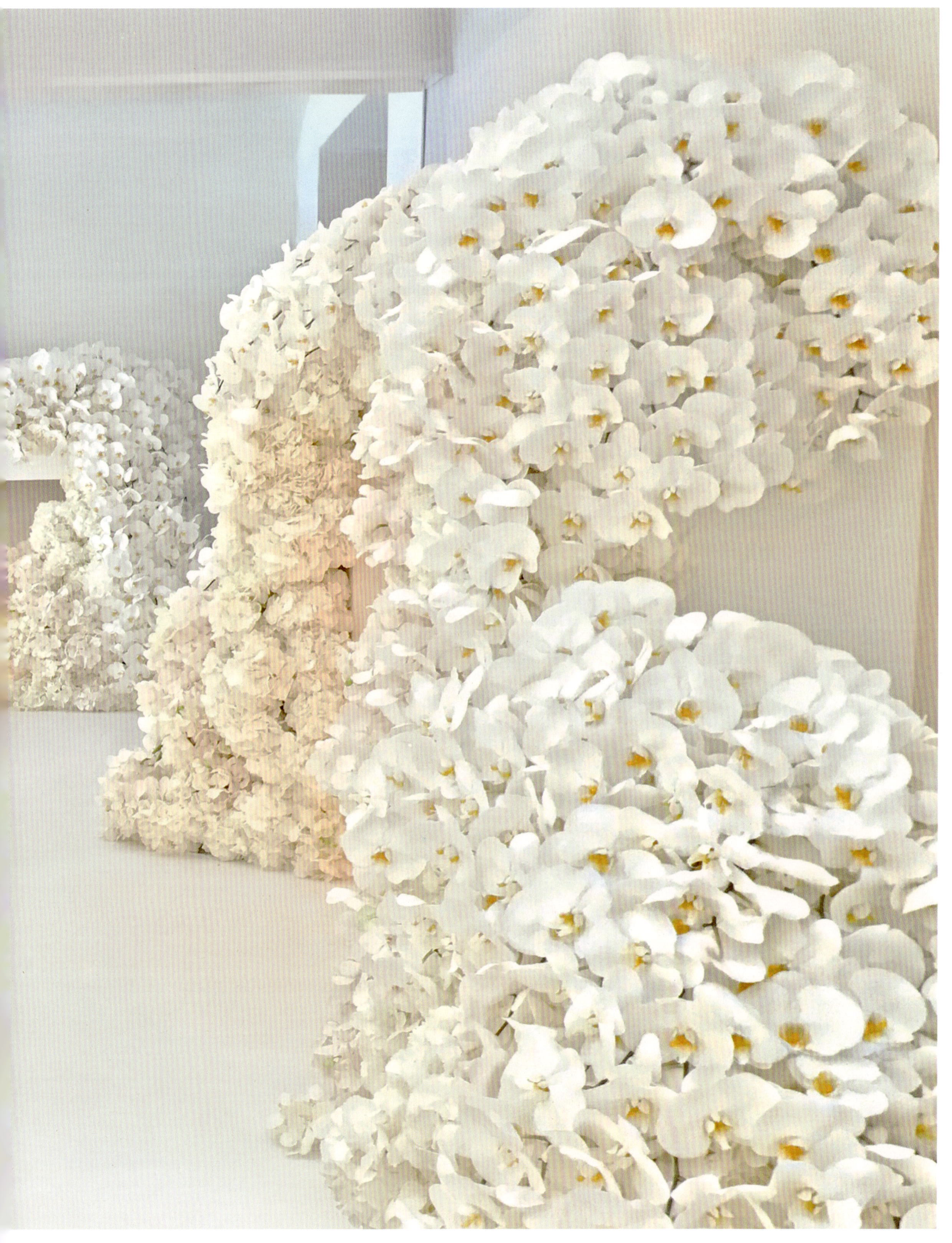

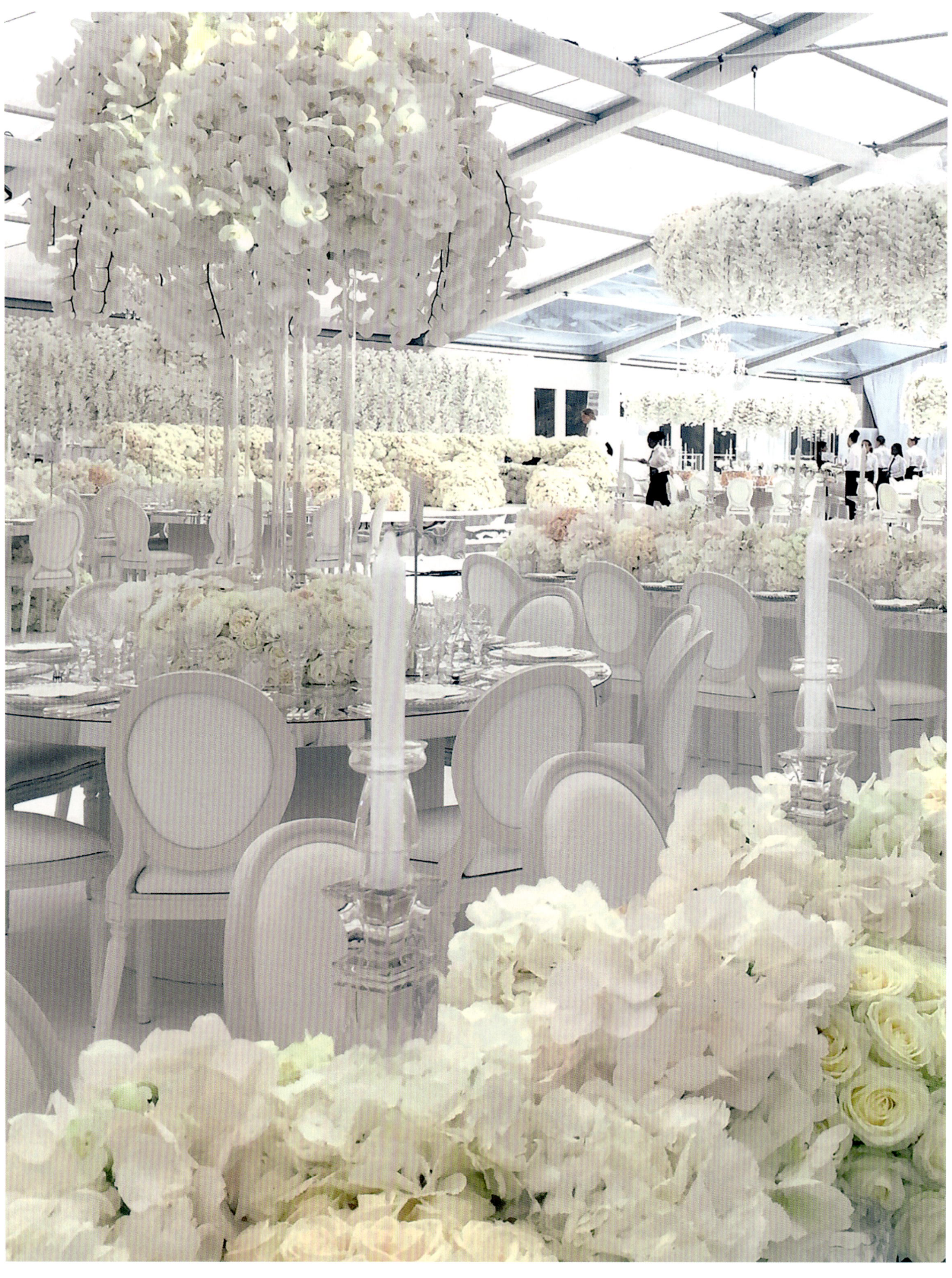

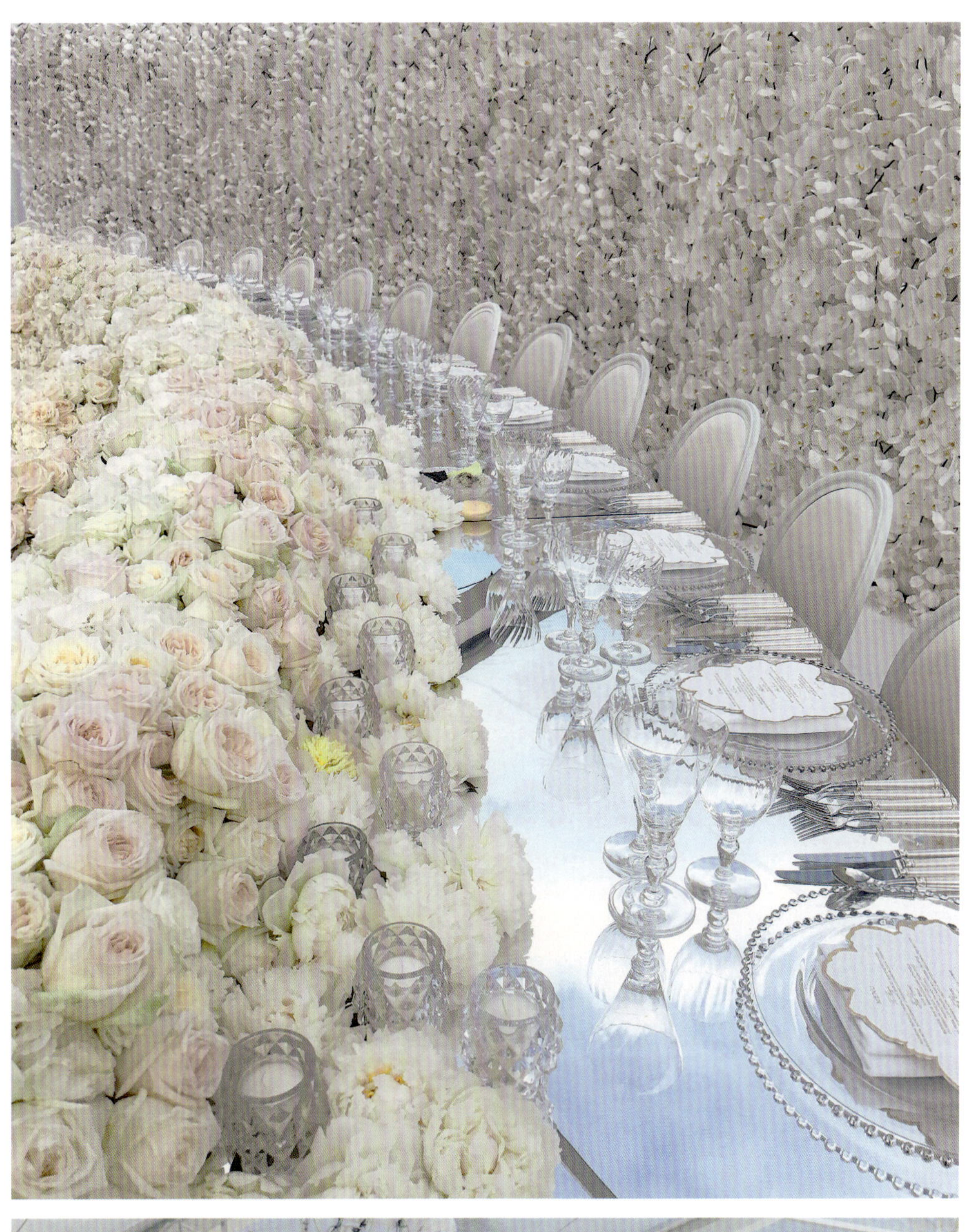

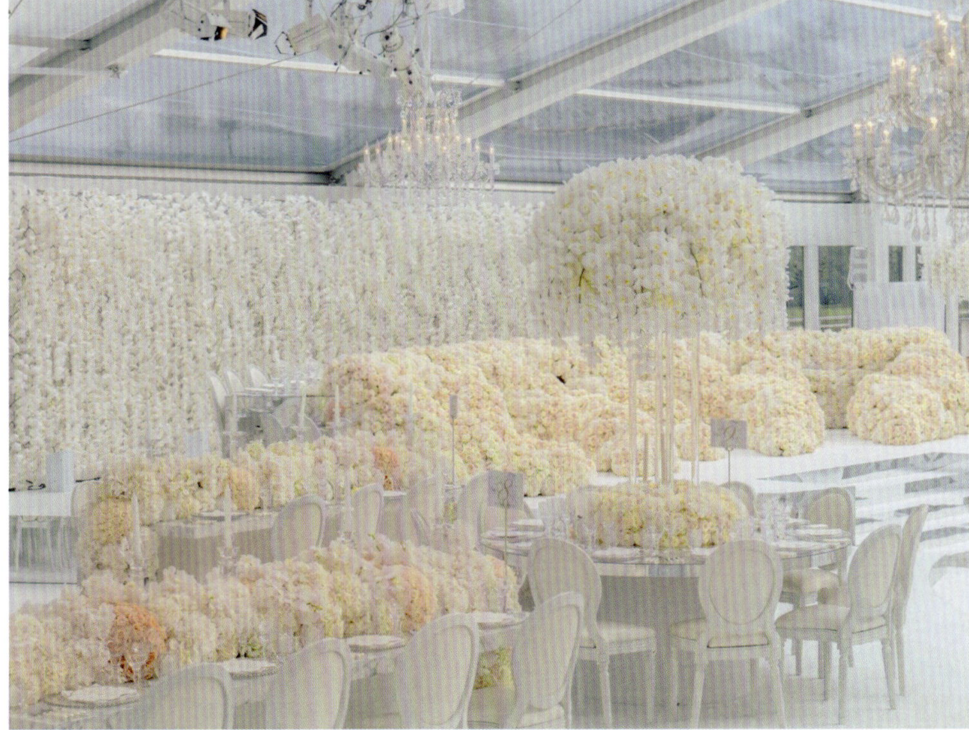

PAGES 72–75: Private Wedding, Beverly Hills. Roses, calla lilies, peonies, hydrangeas, and baby's breath.

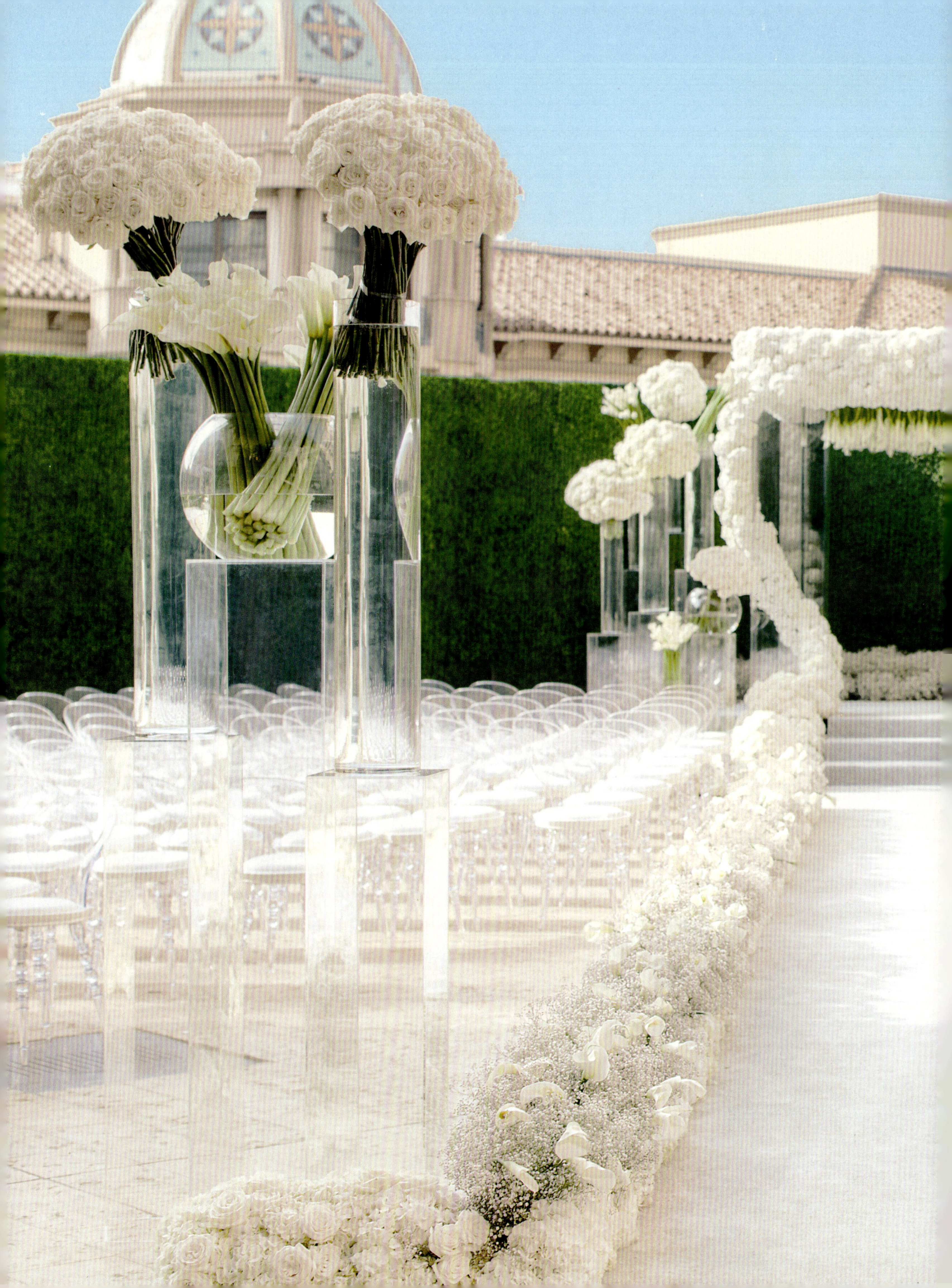

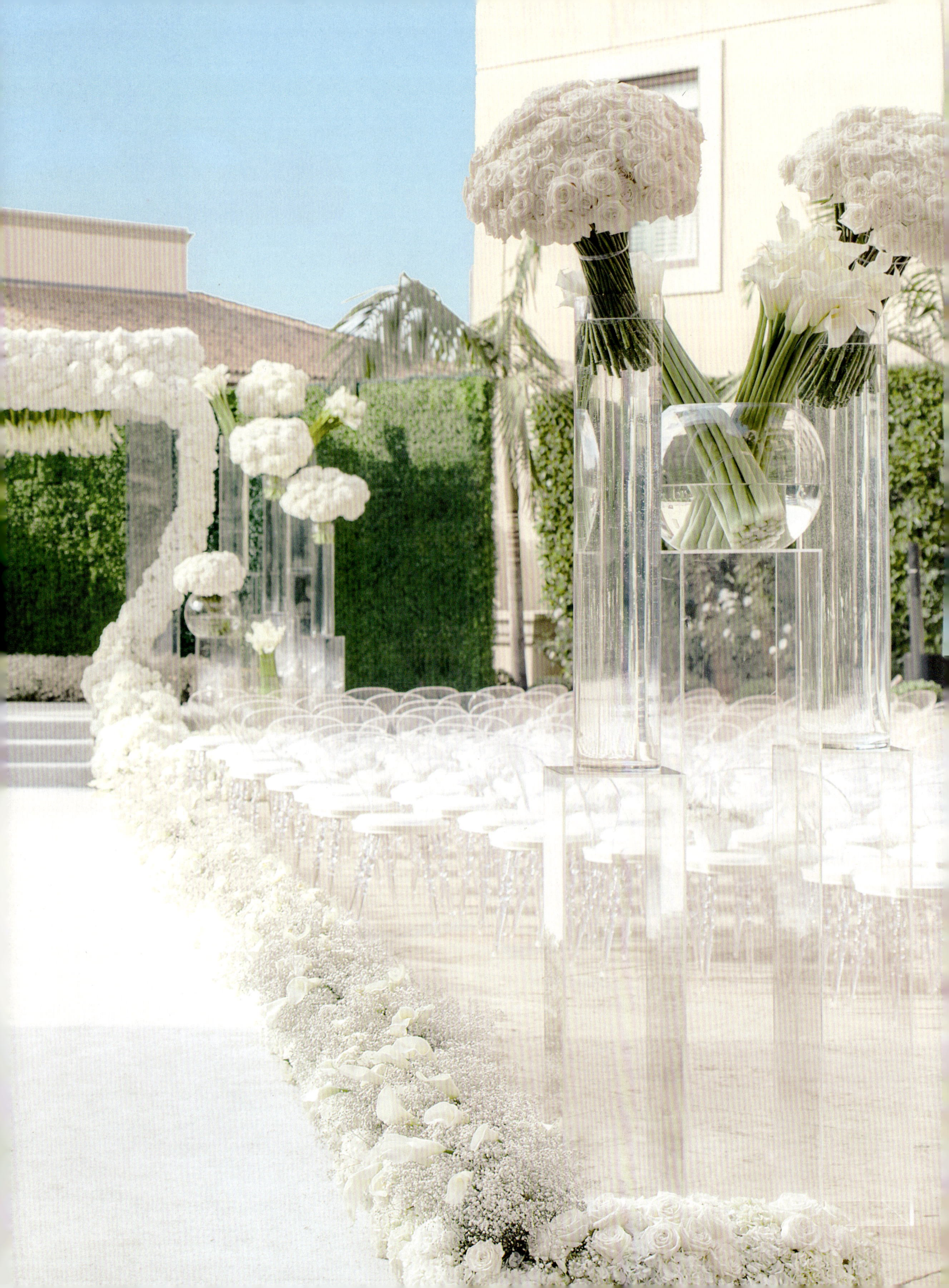

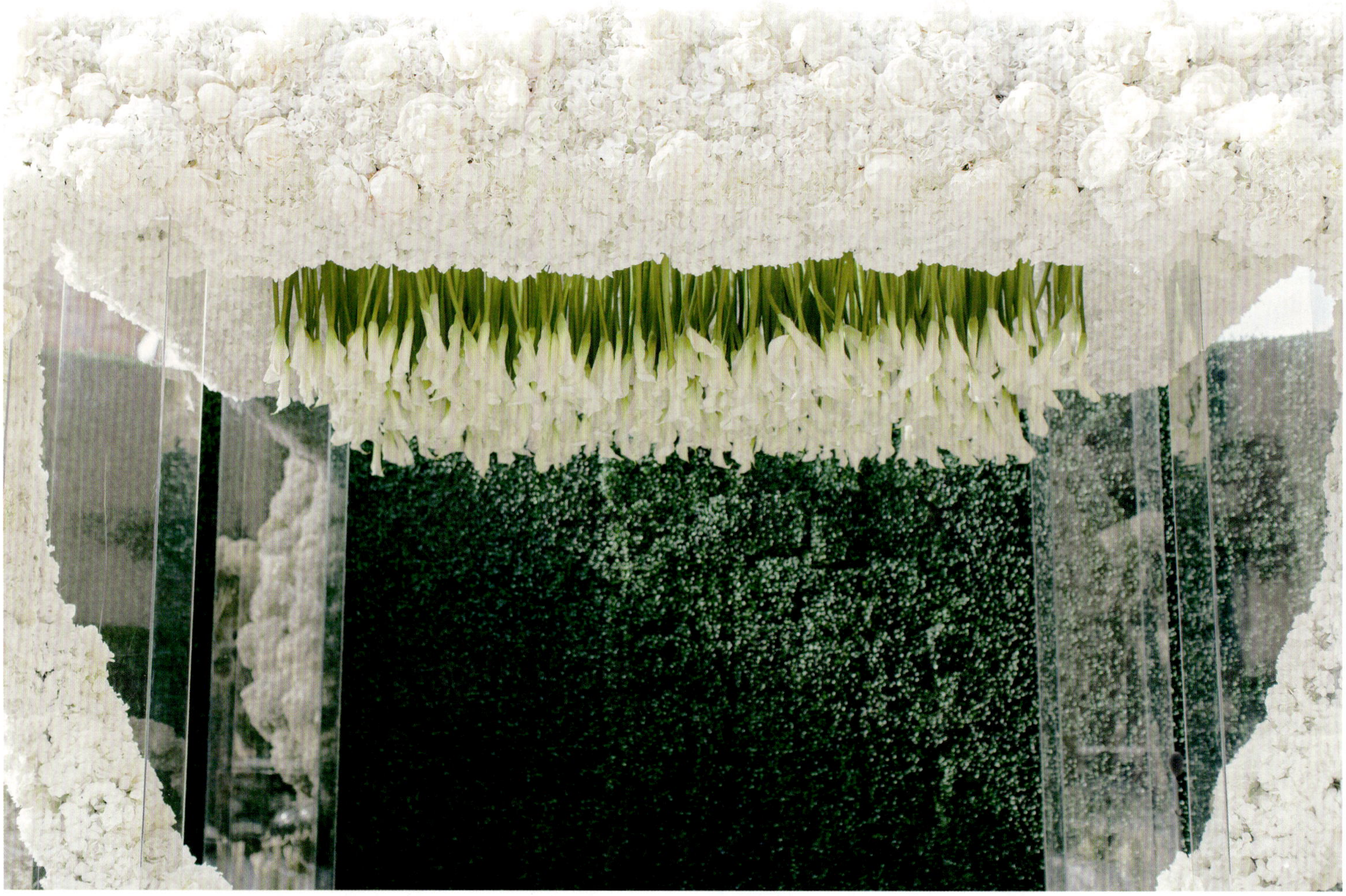

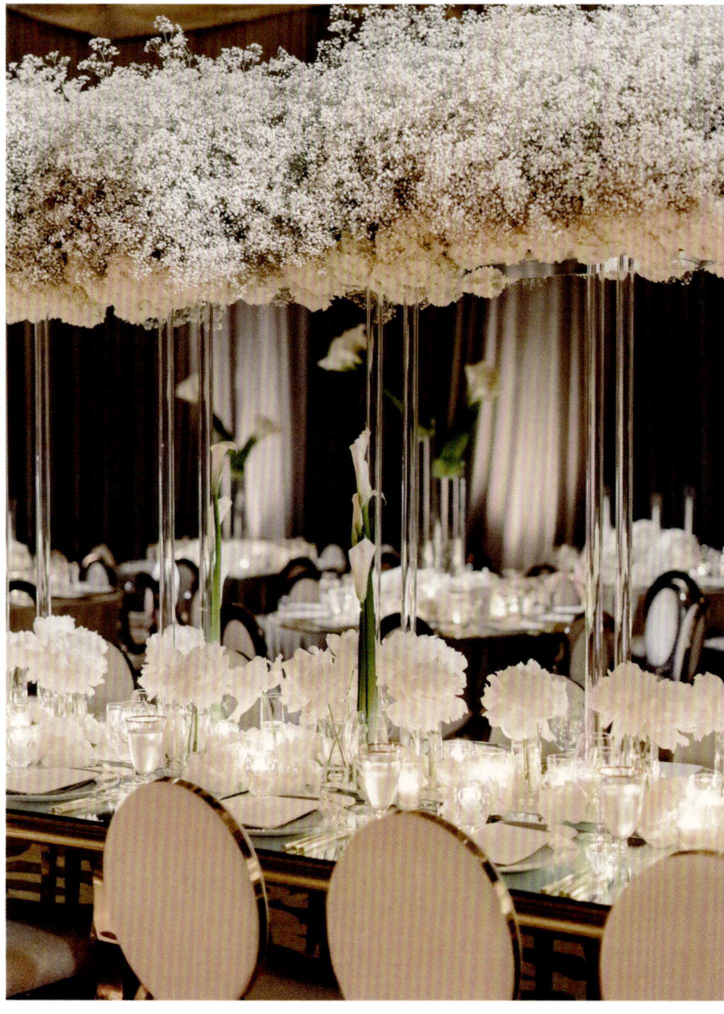
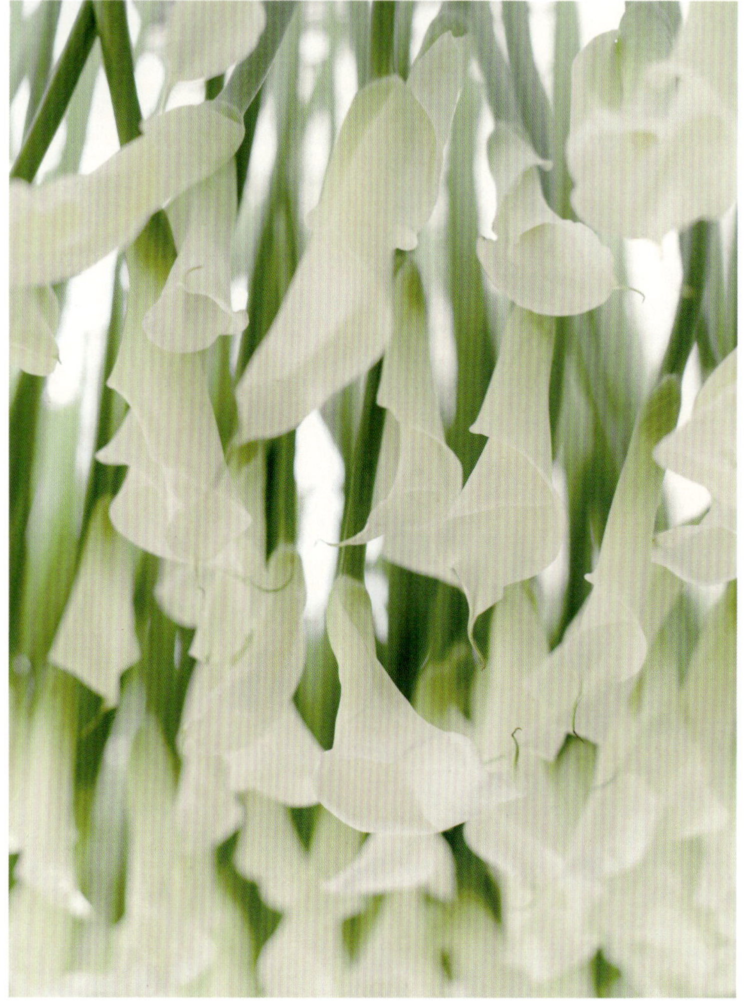

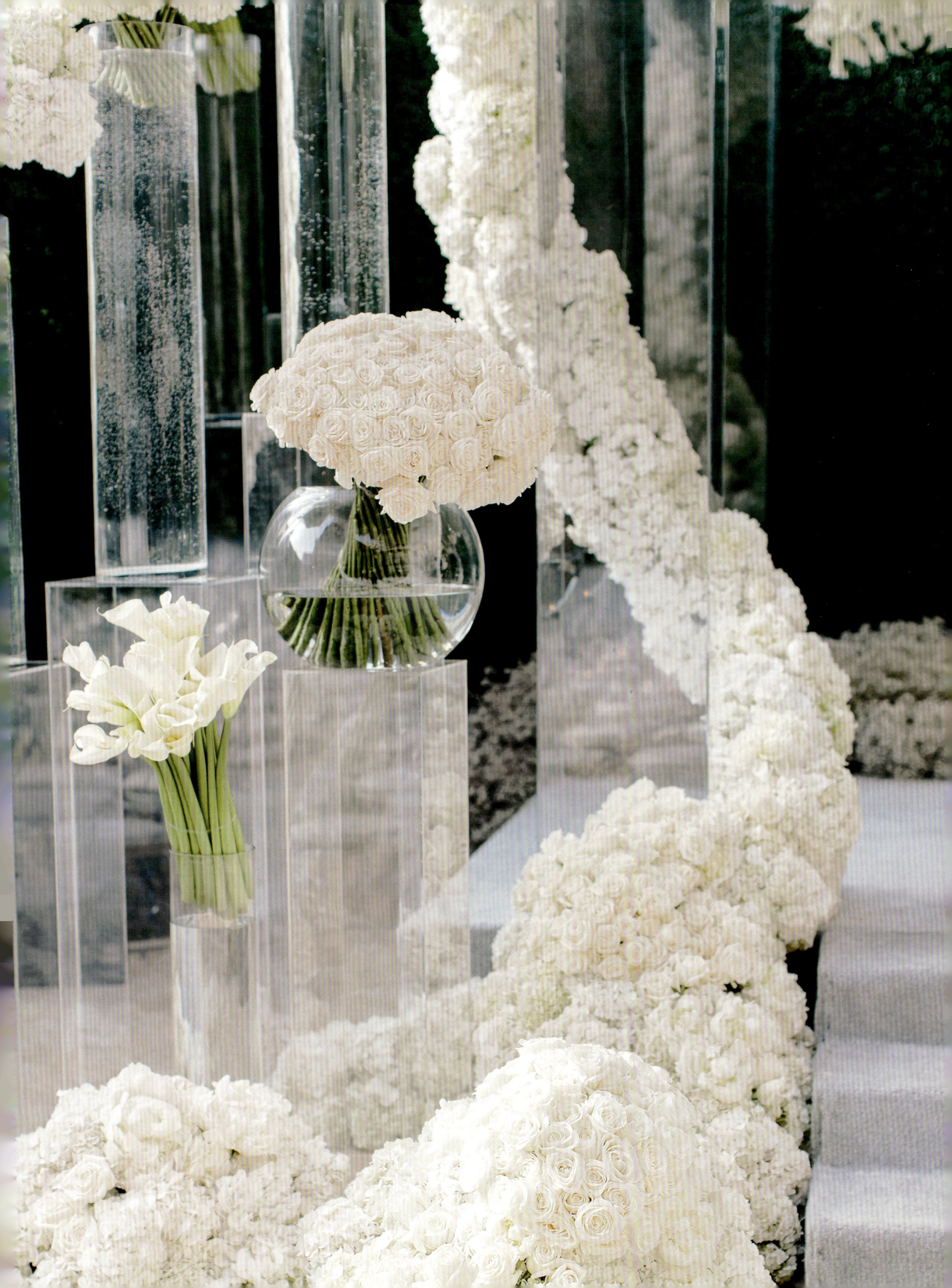

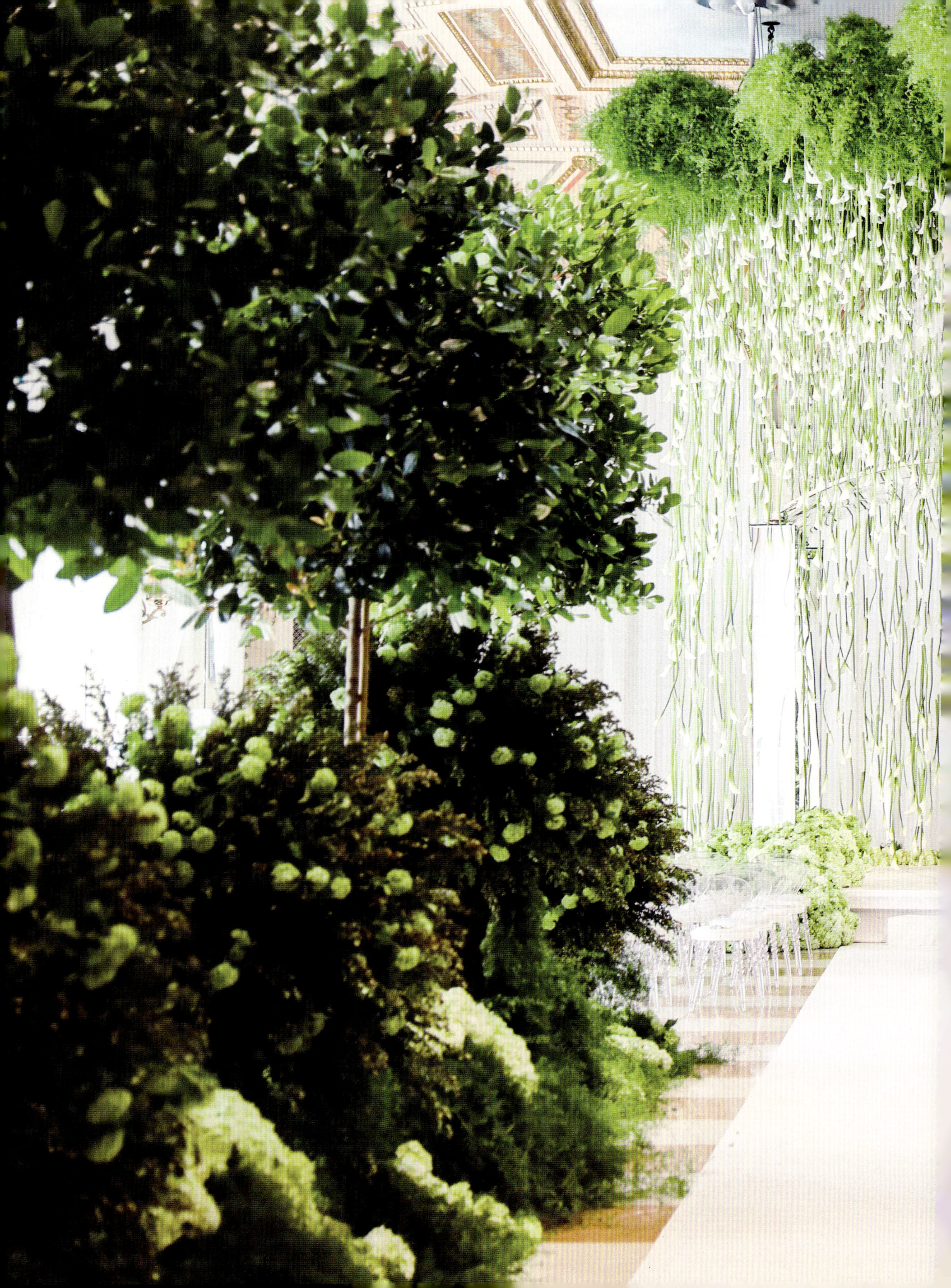

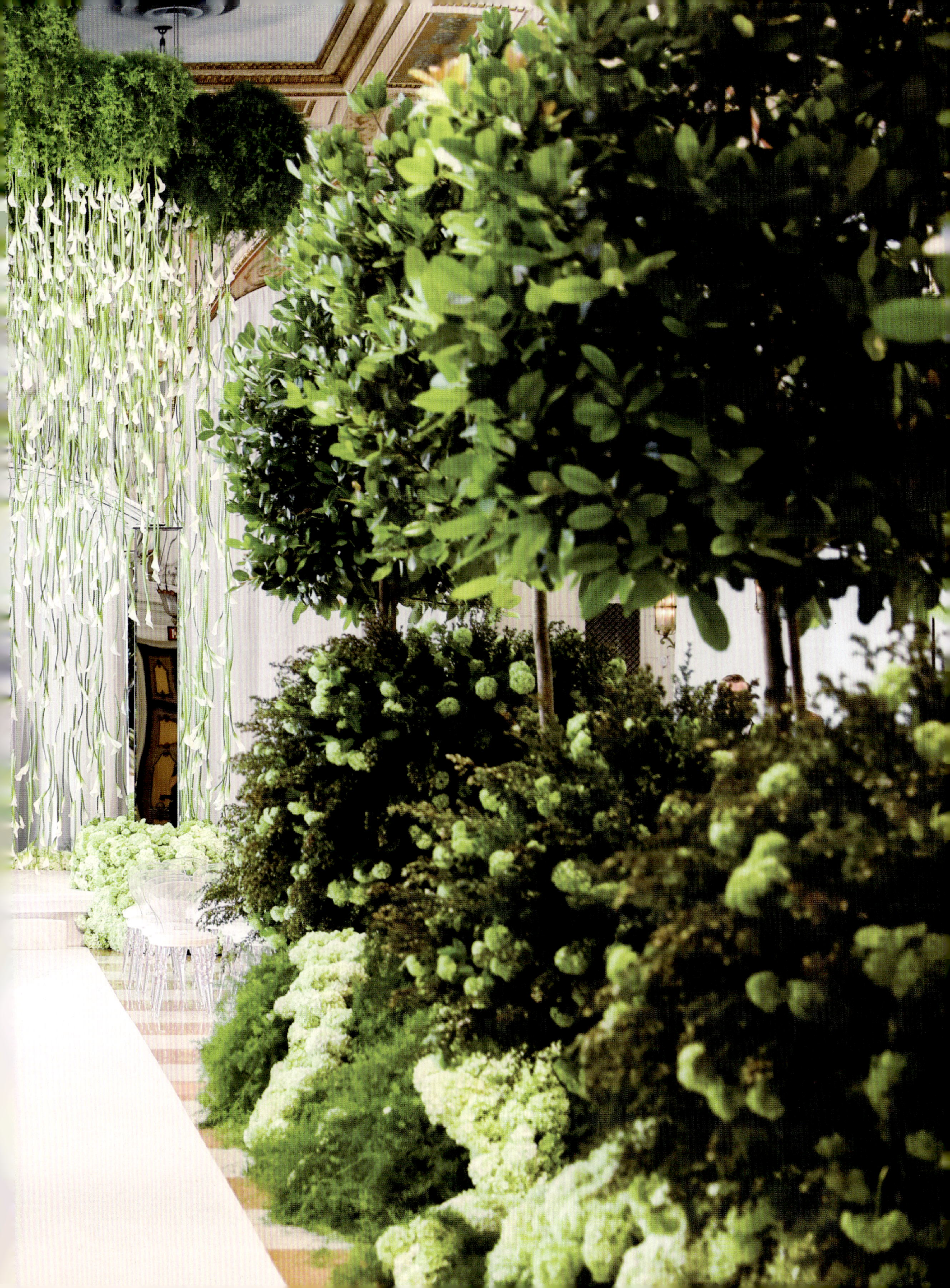

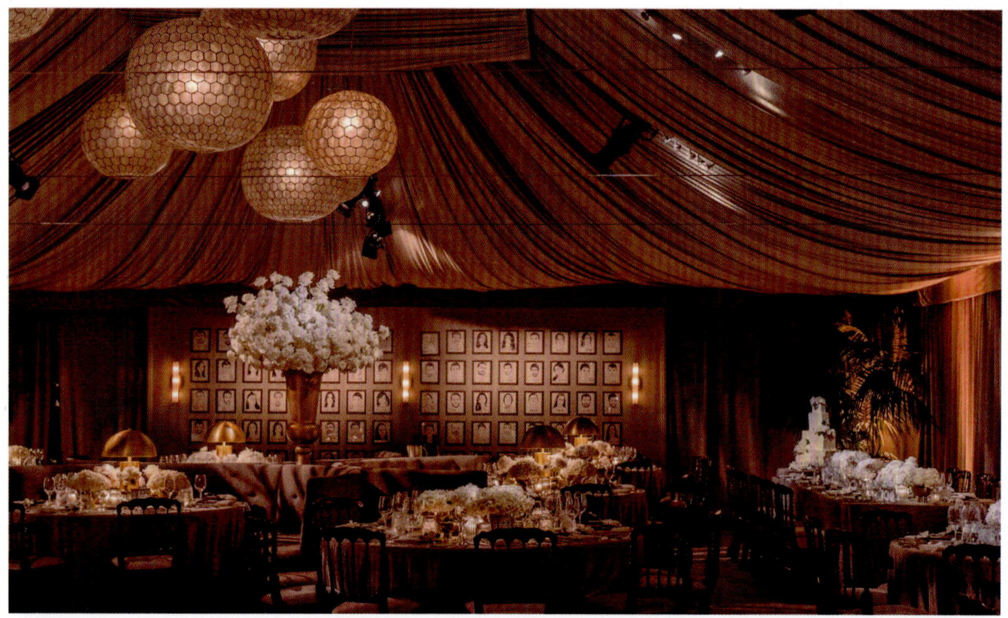

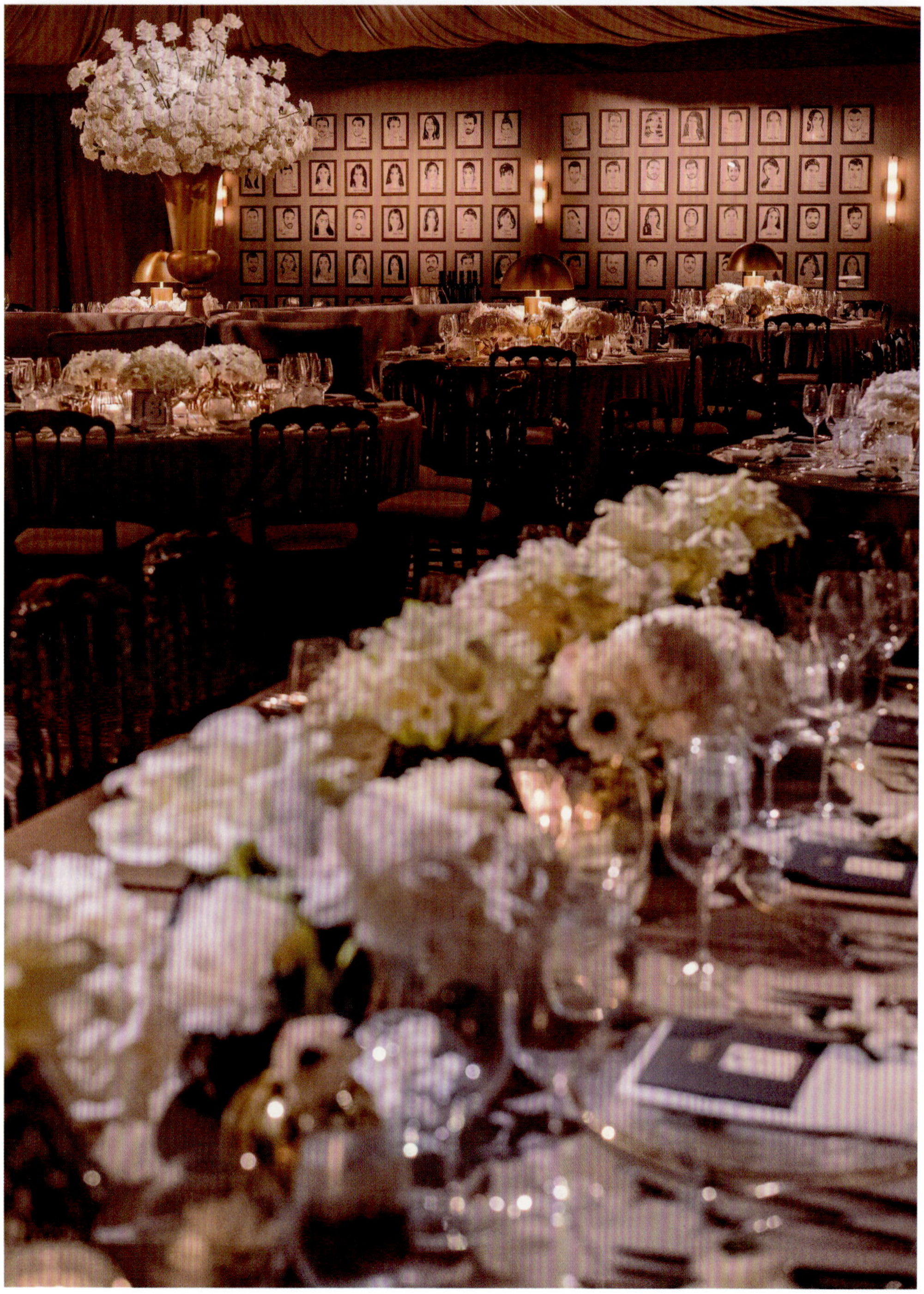

PREVIOUS: Private Wedding, Palm Beach, Florida. Hanging calla lilies, hydrangeas, and viburnum. LEFT AND OPPOSITE: Private Wedding, Bel-Air, Los Angeles. Roses, calla lilies, and anemones.

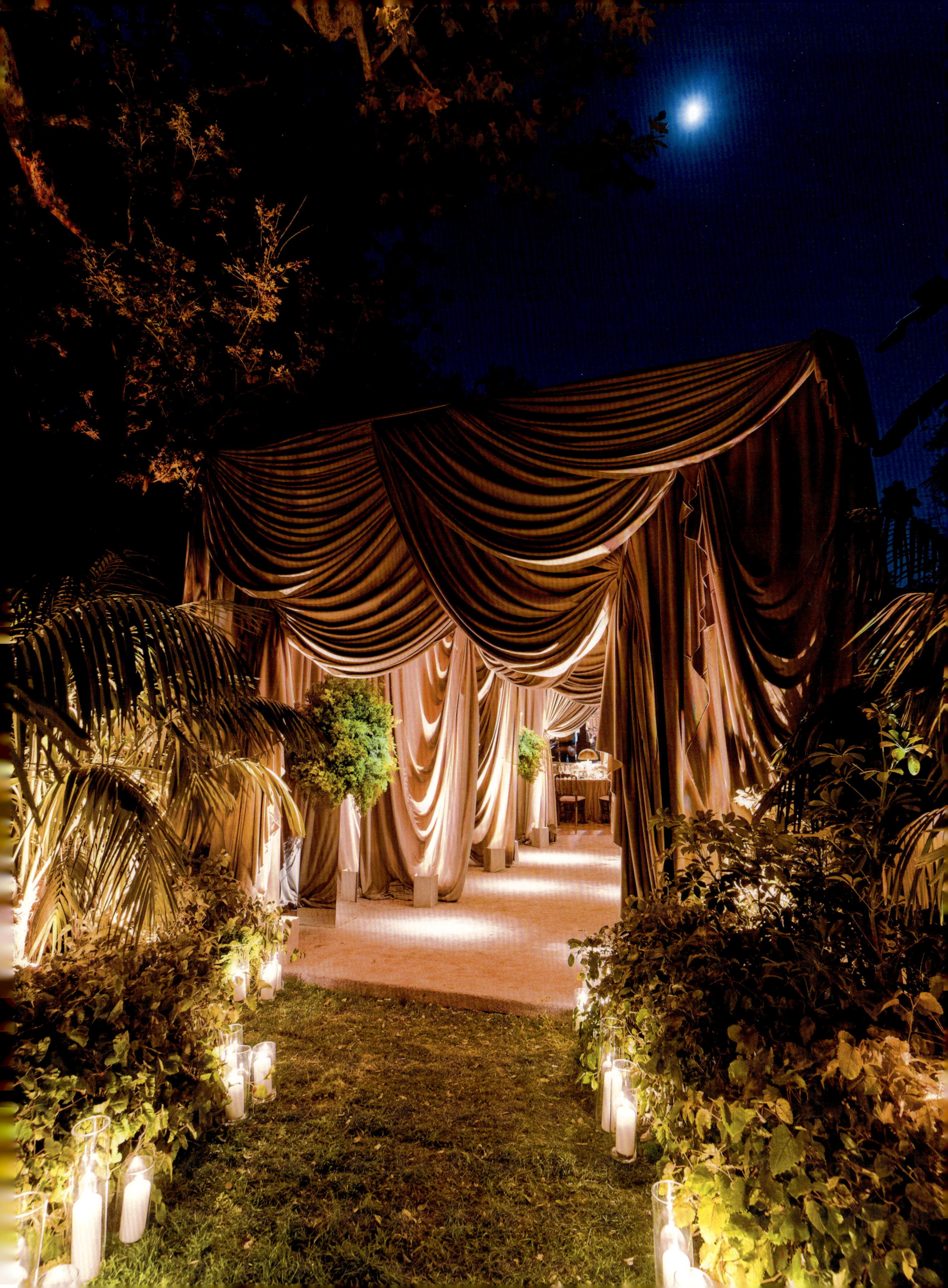

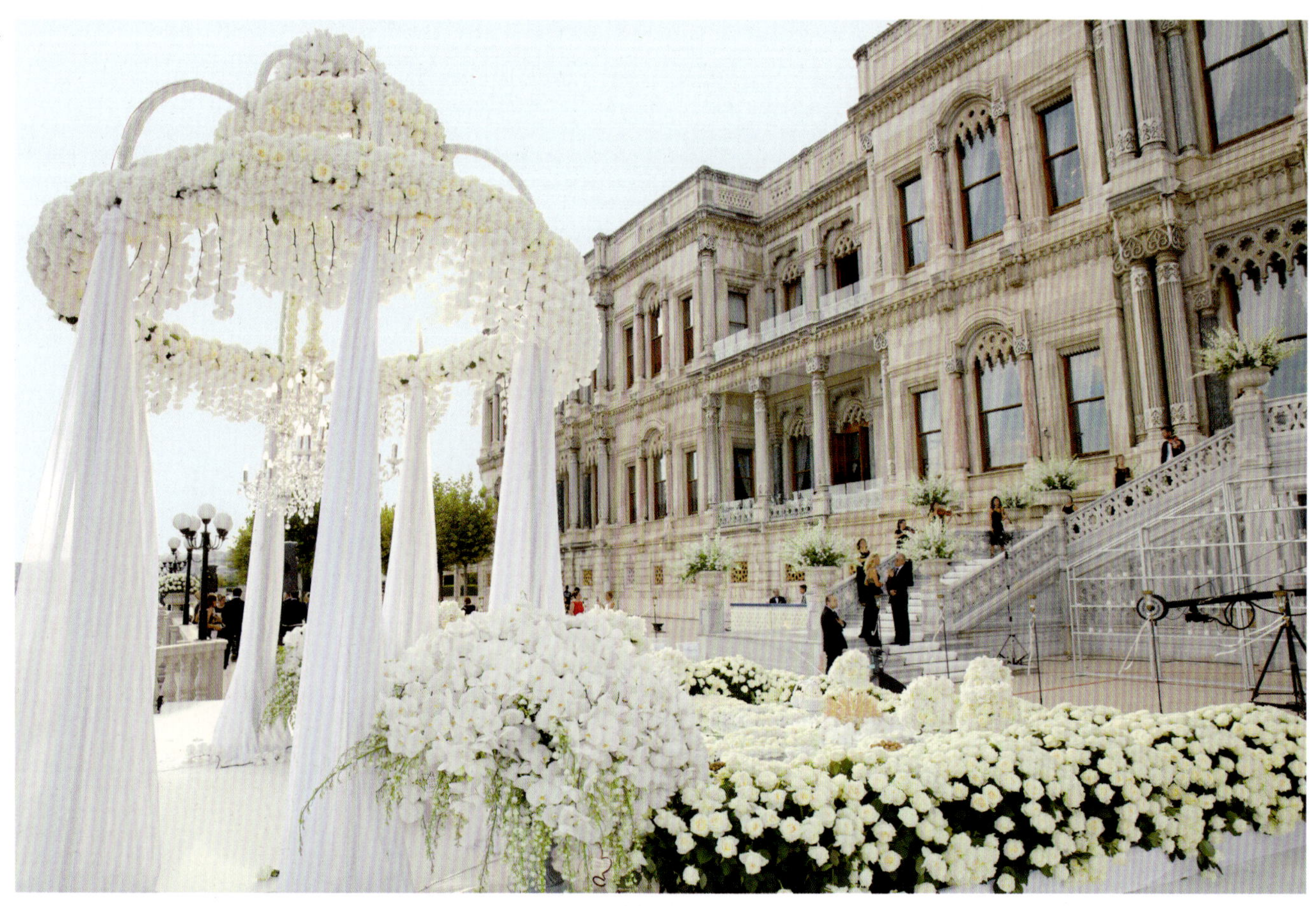

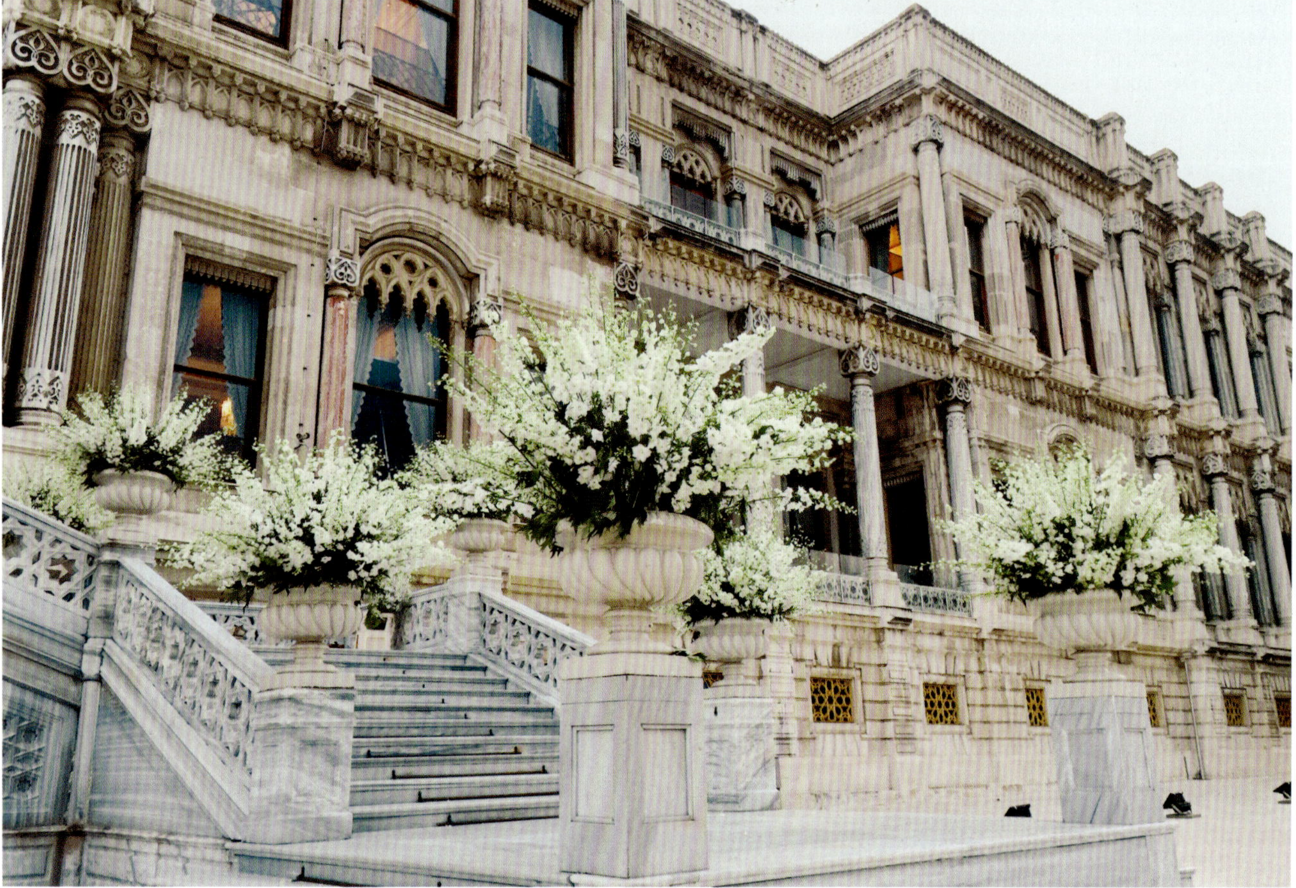

Private Wedding, Istanbul, Turkey.
Roses, delphinium, and orchids.

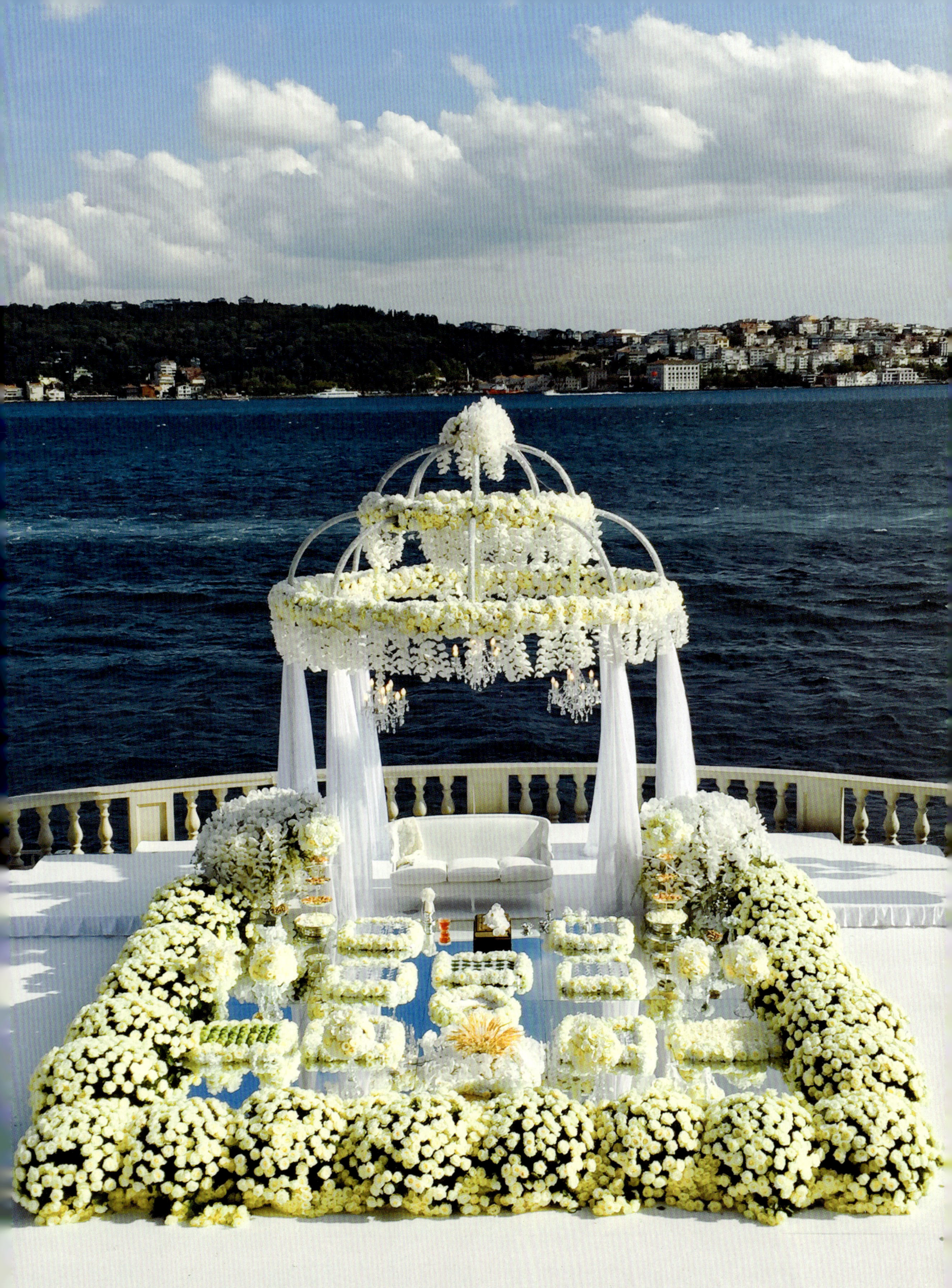

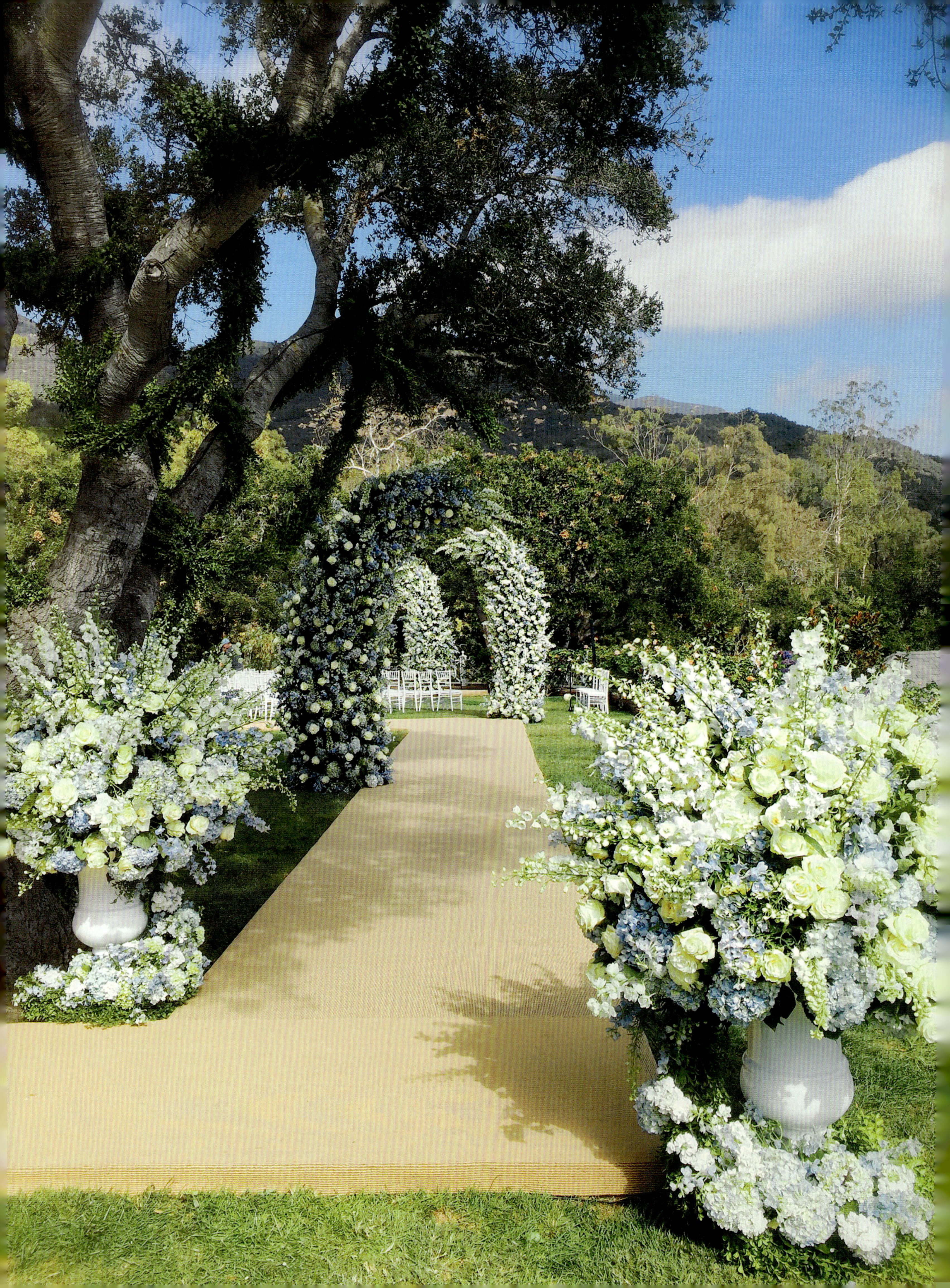

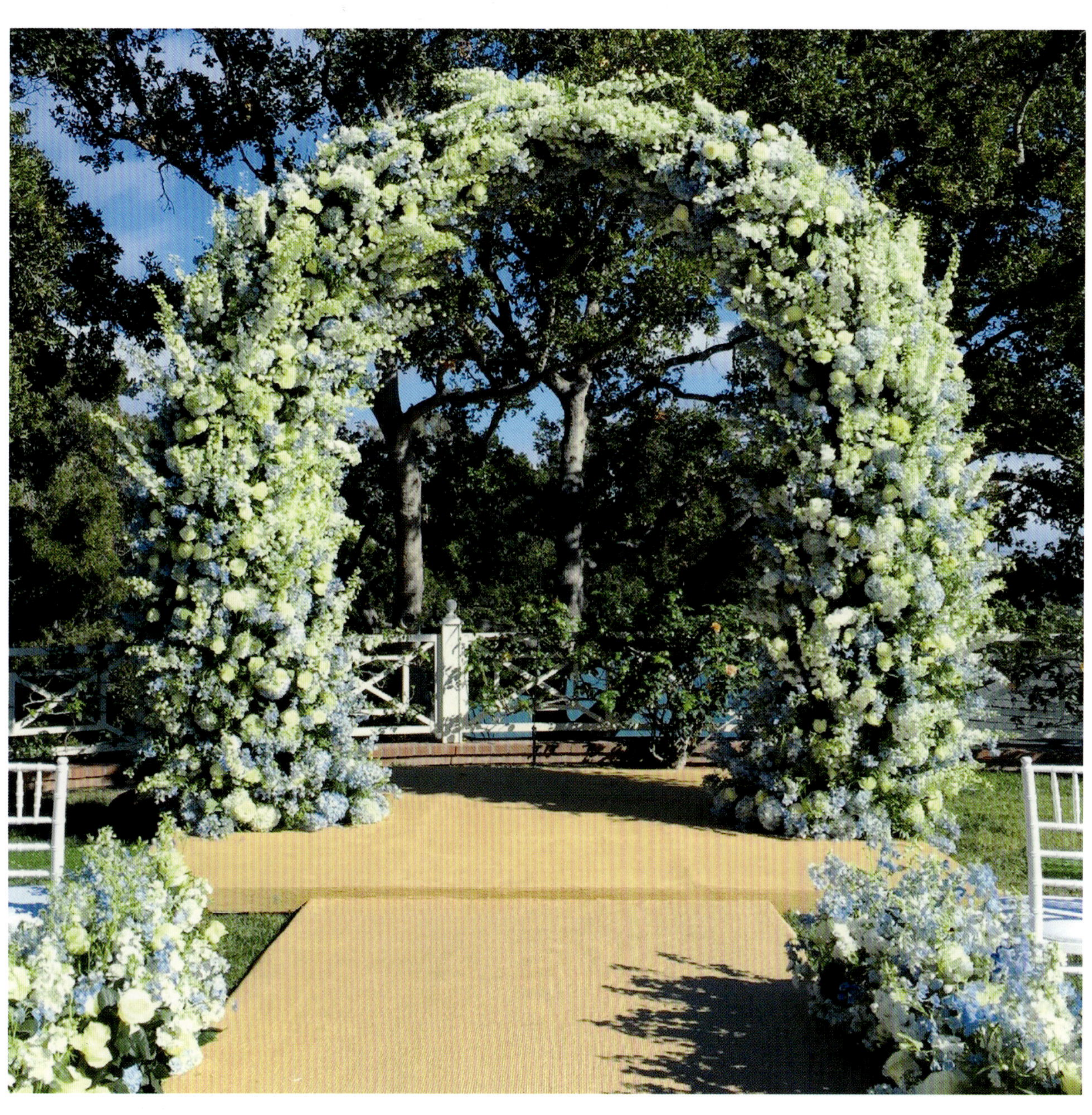

PAGES 82–85: Private Wedding, Montecito,
California. Delphinium, hydrangeas, and roses.

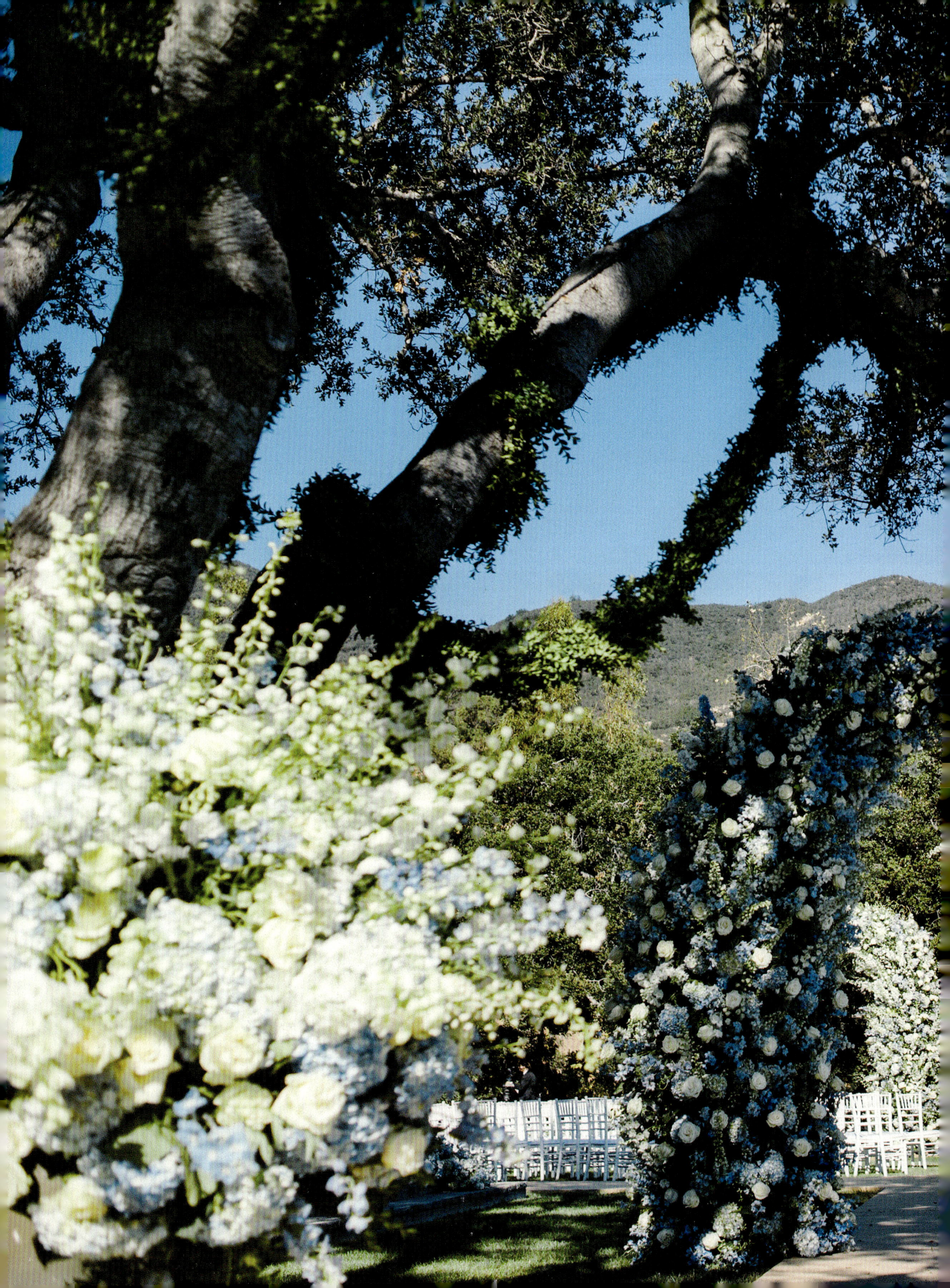

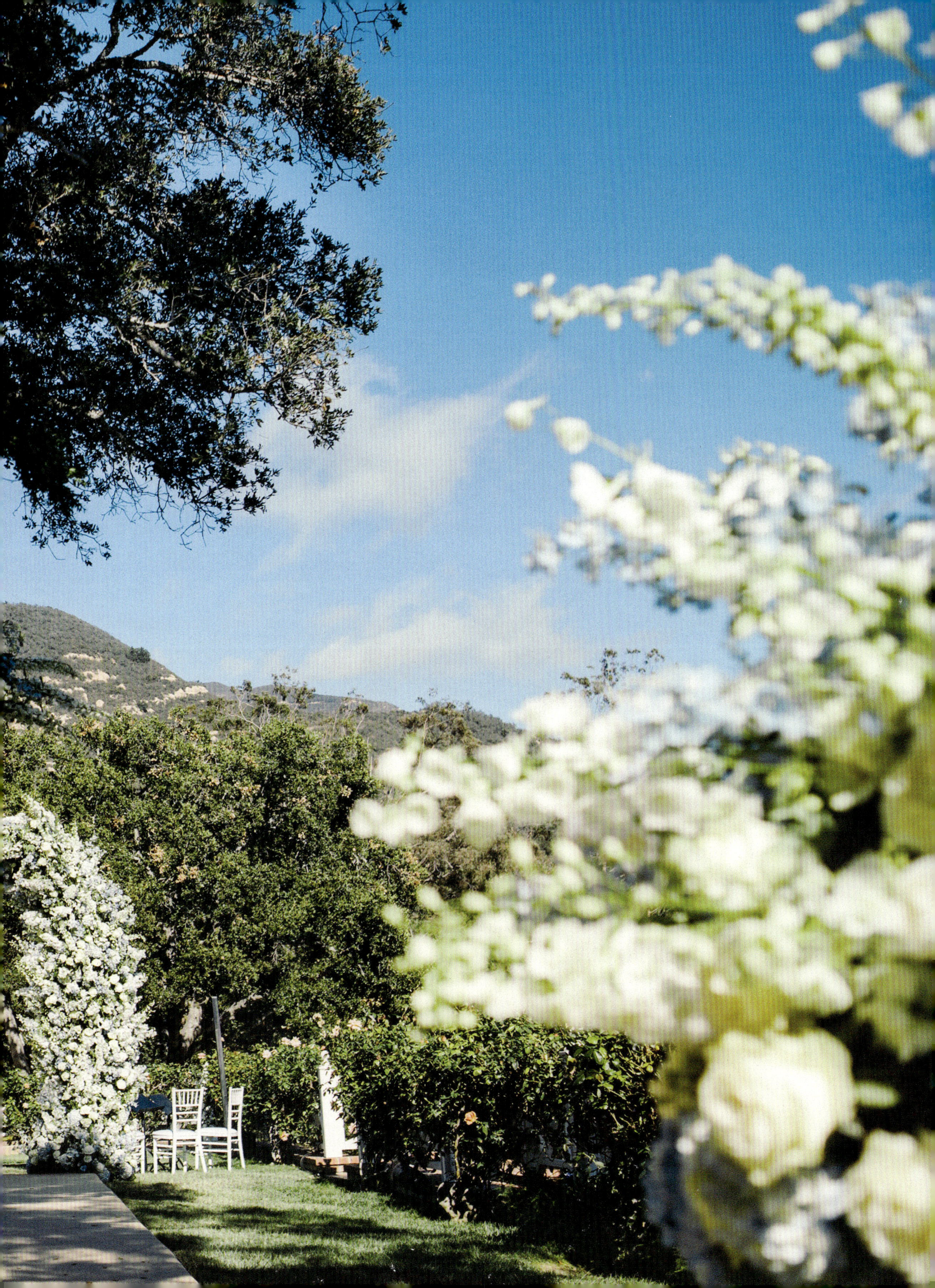

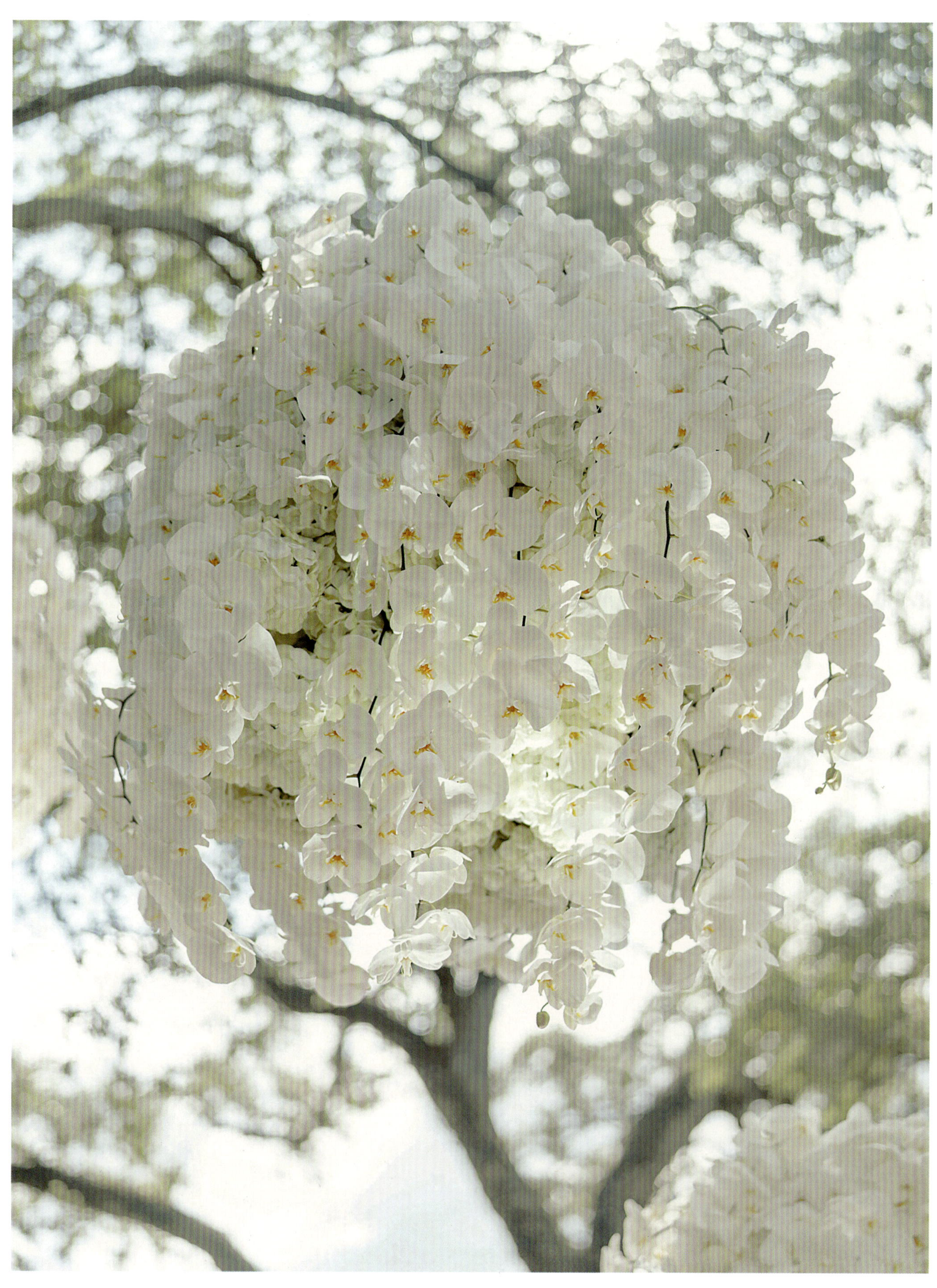

Private Wedding, Beverly Hills. Orchids (above).
Hydrangeas and orchids (opposite).

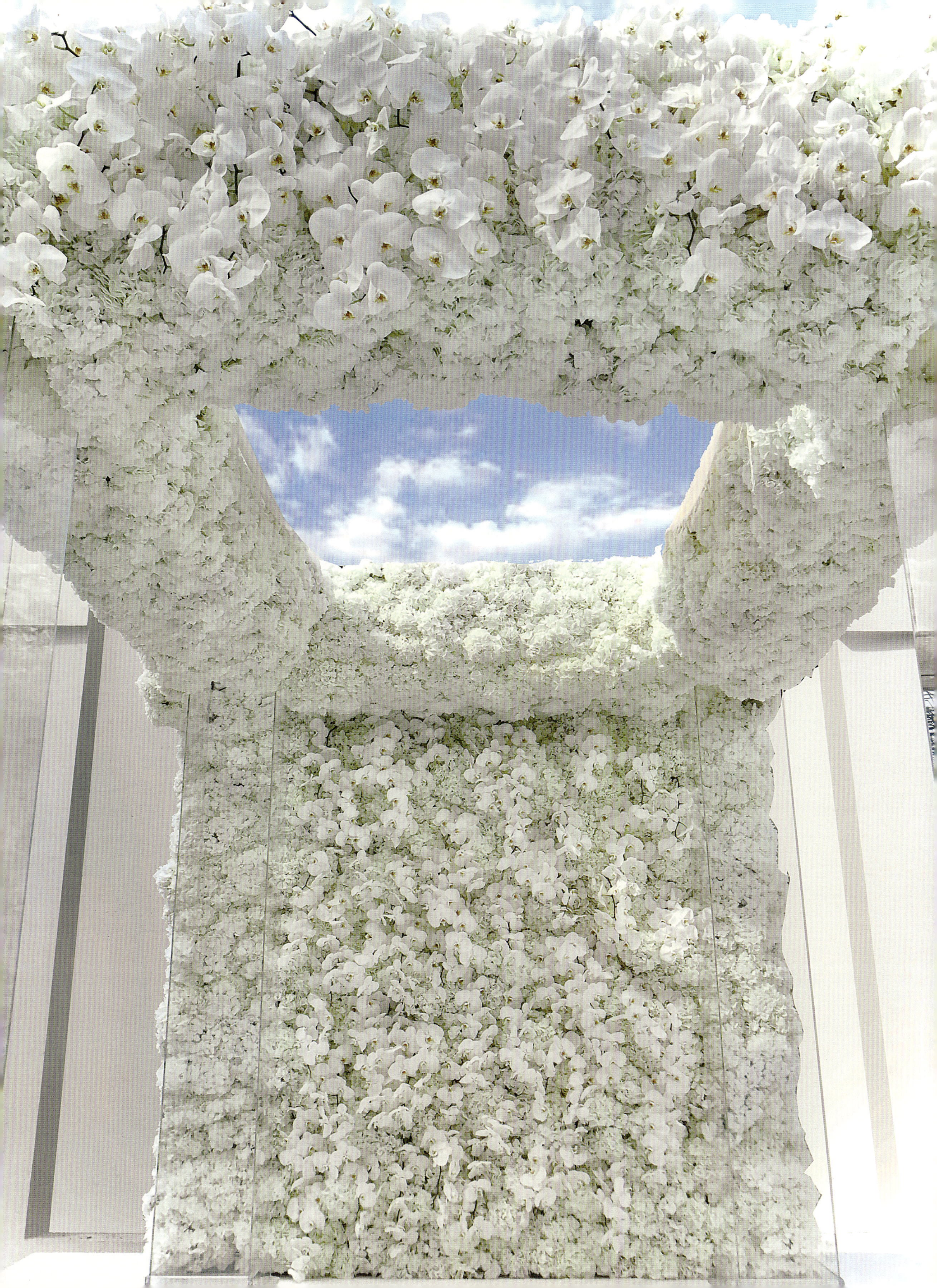

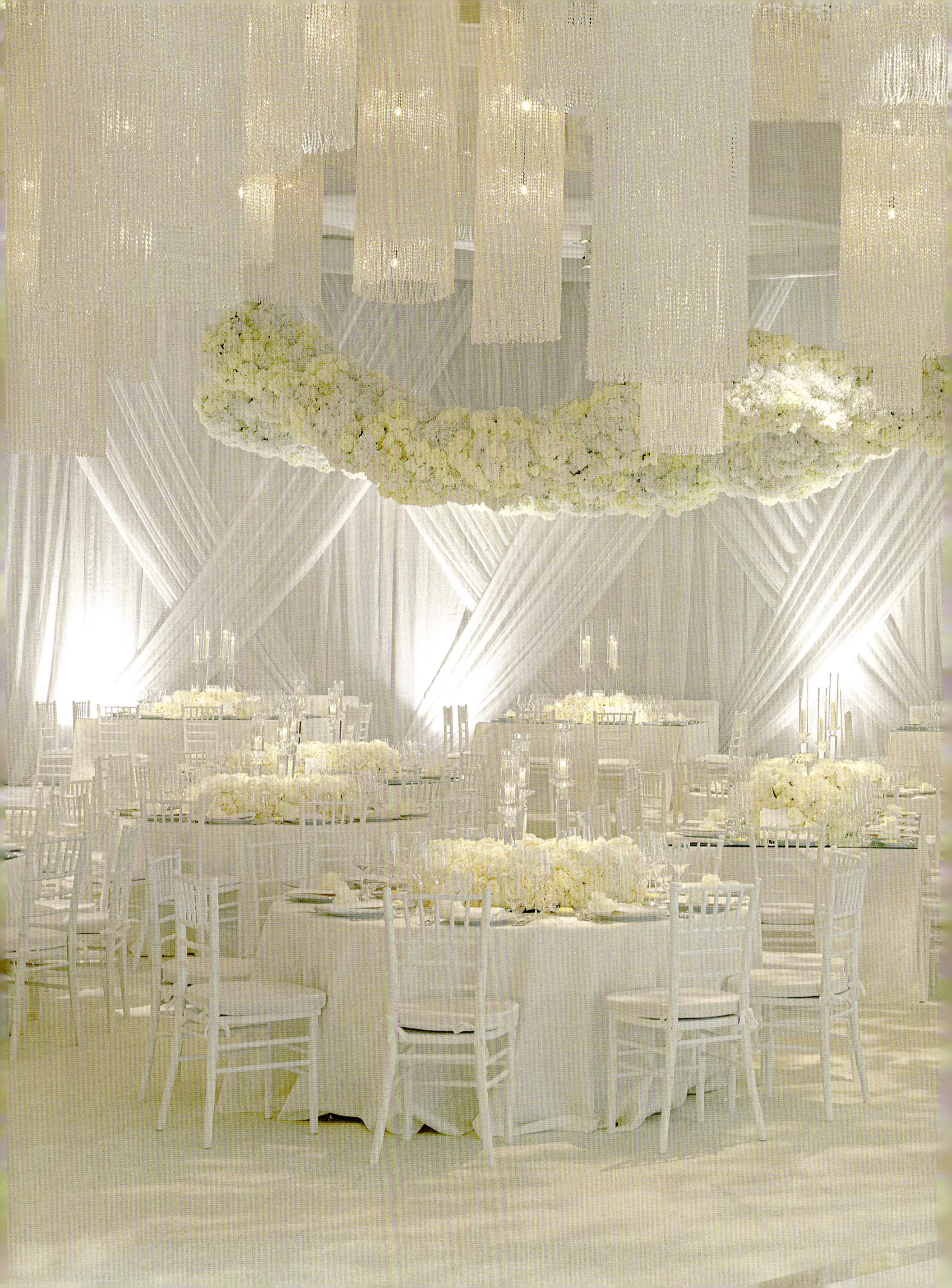

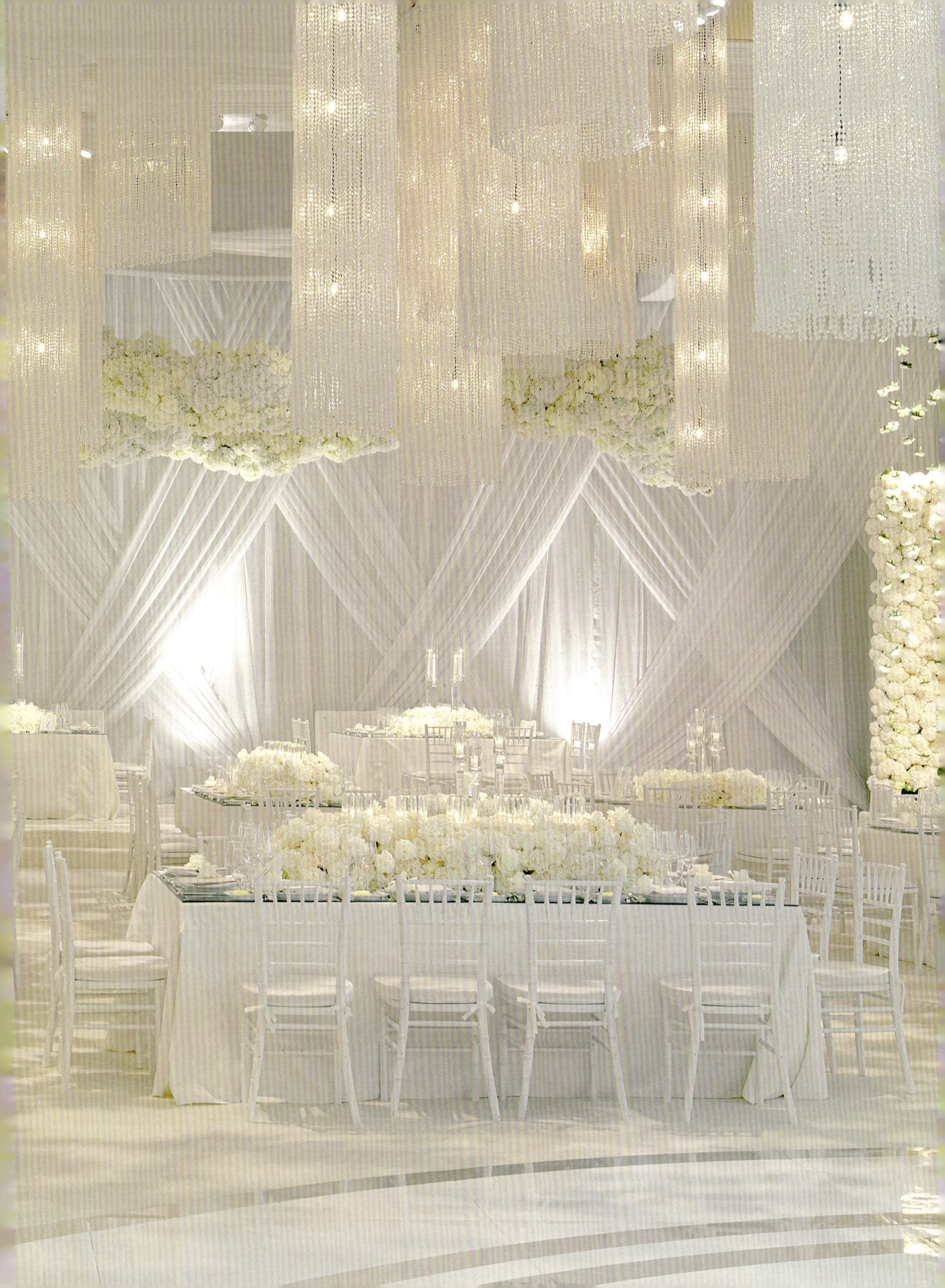

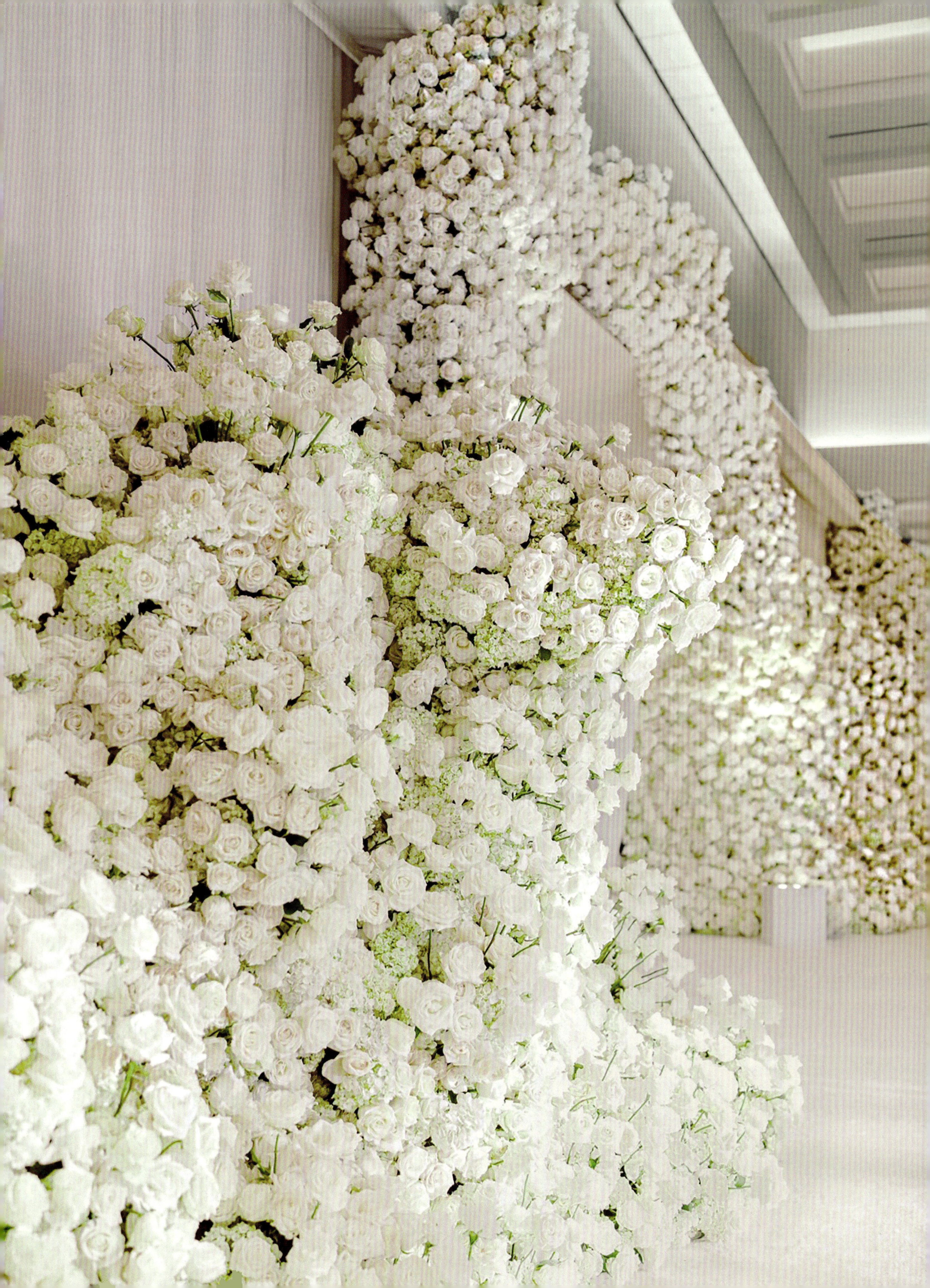

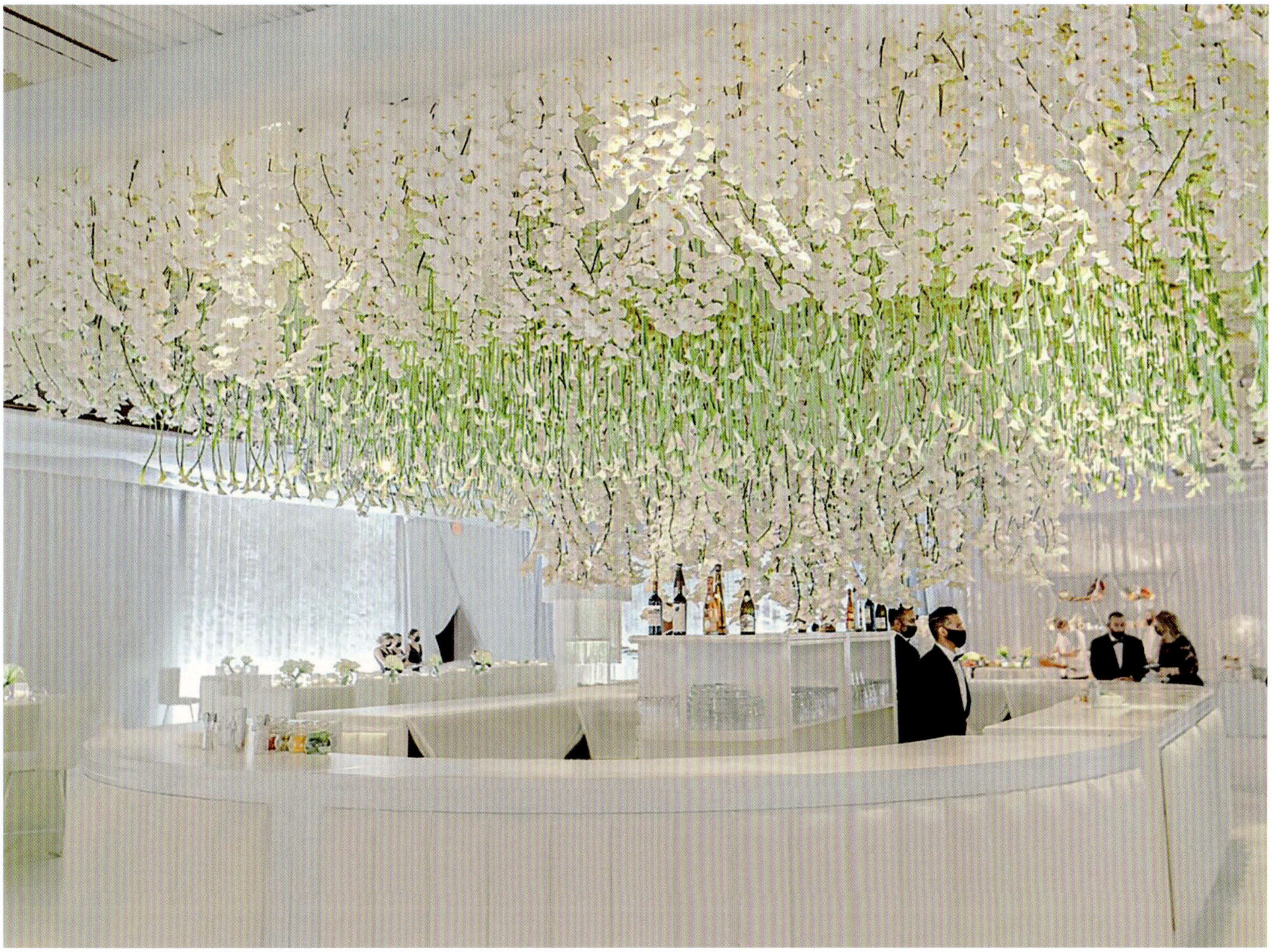

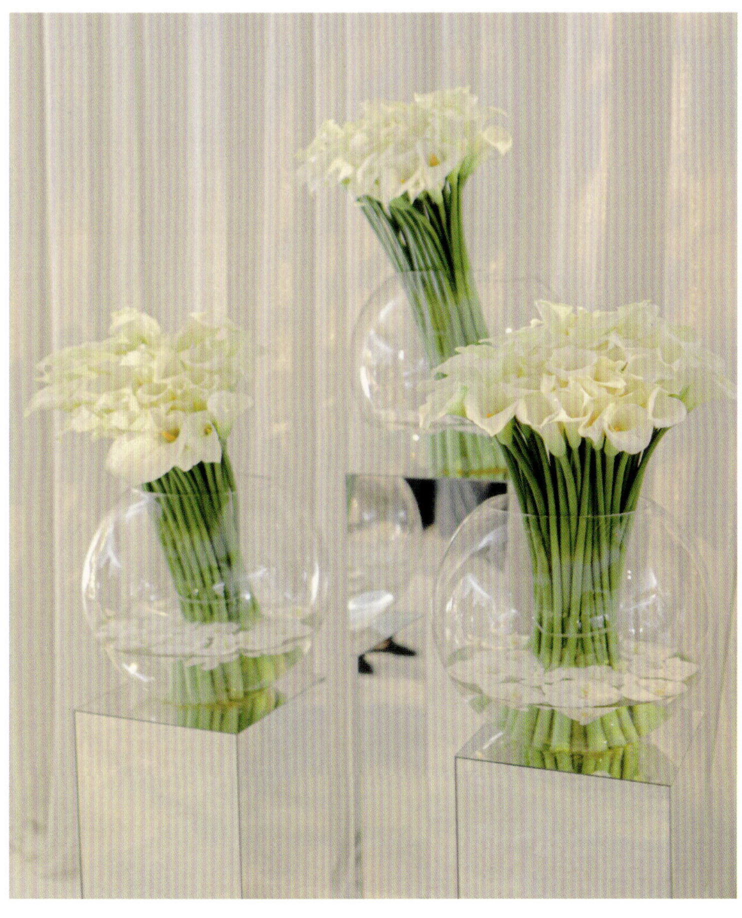
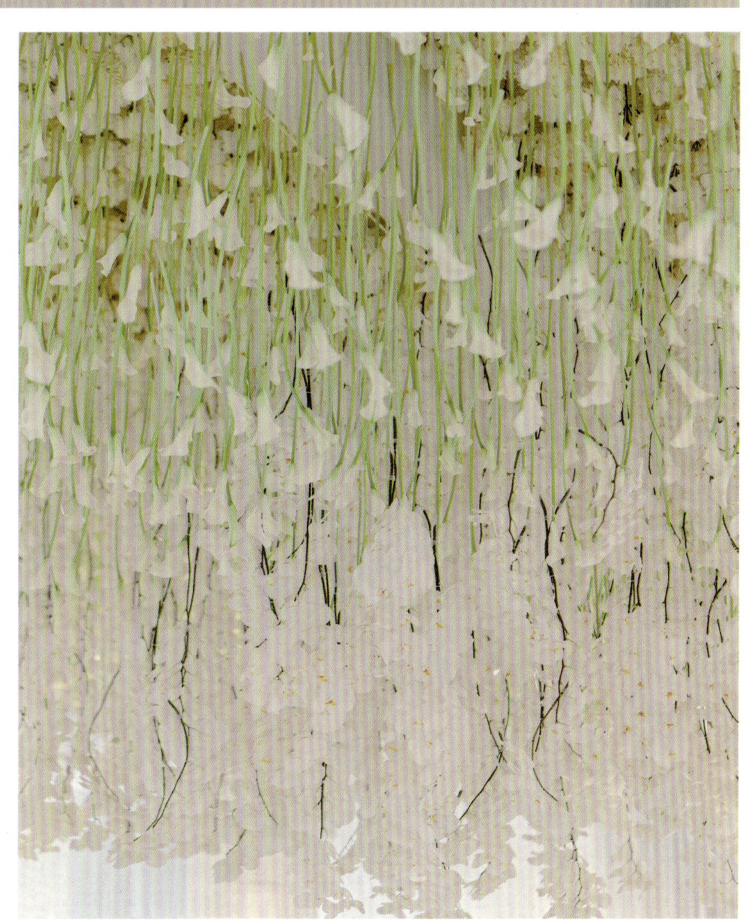

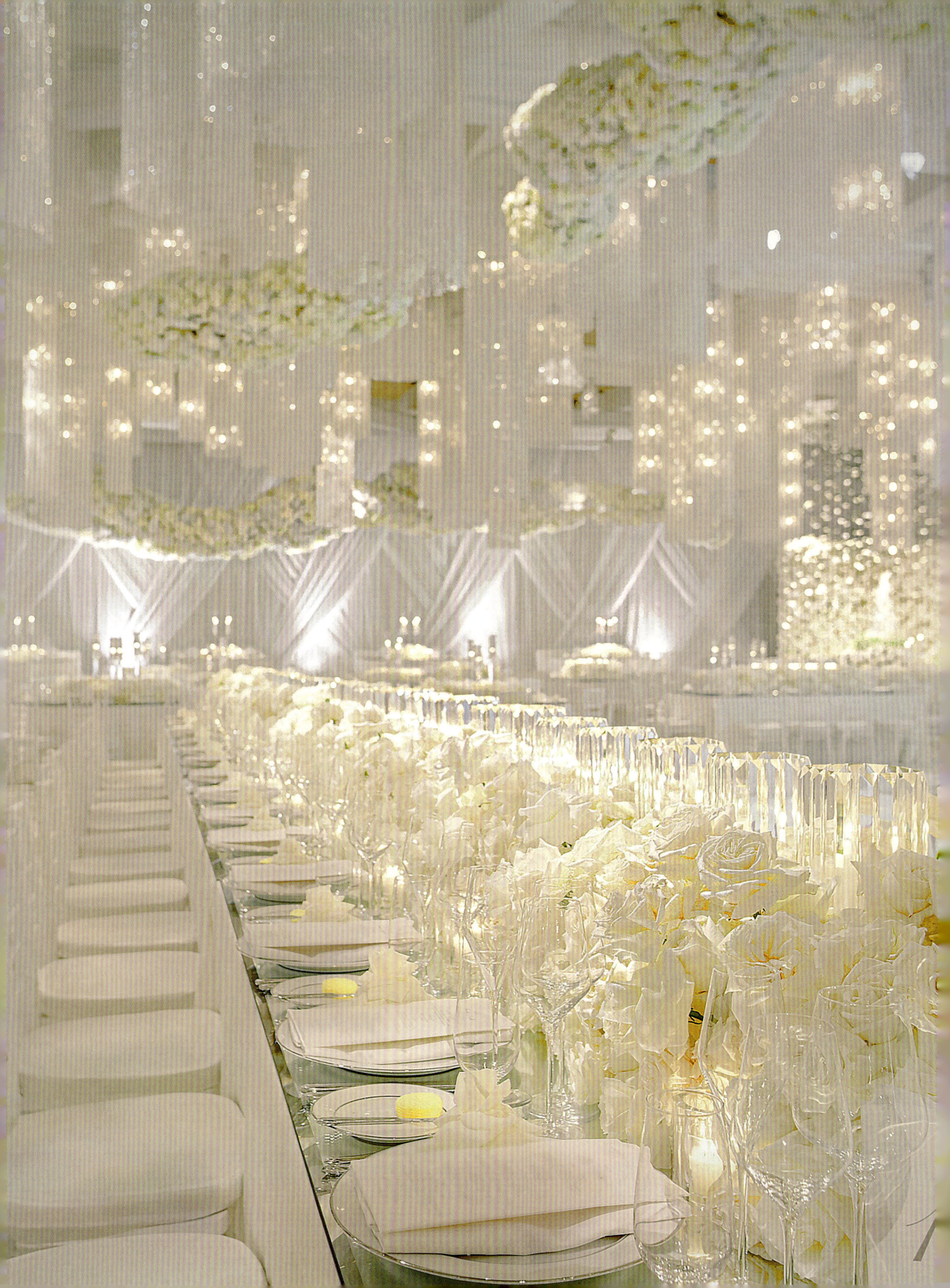

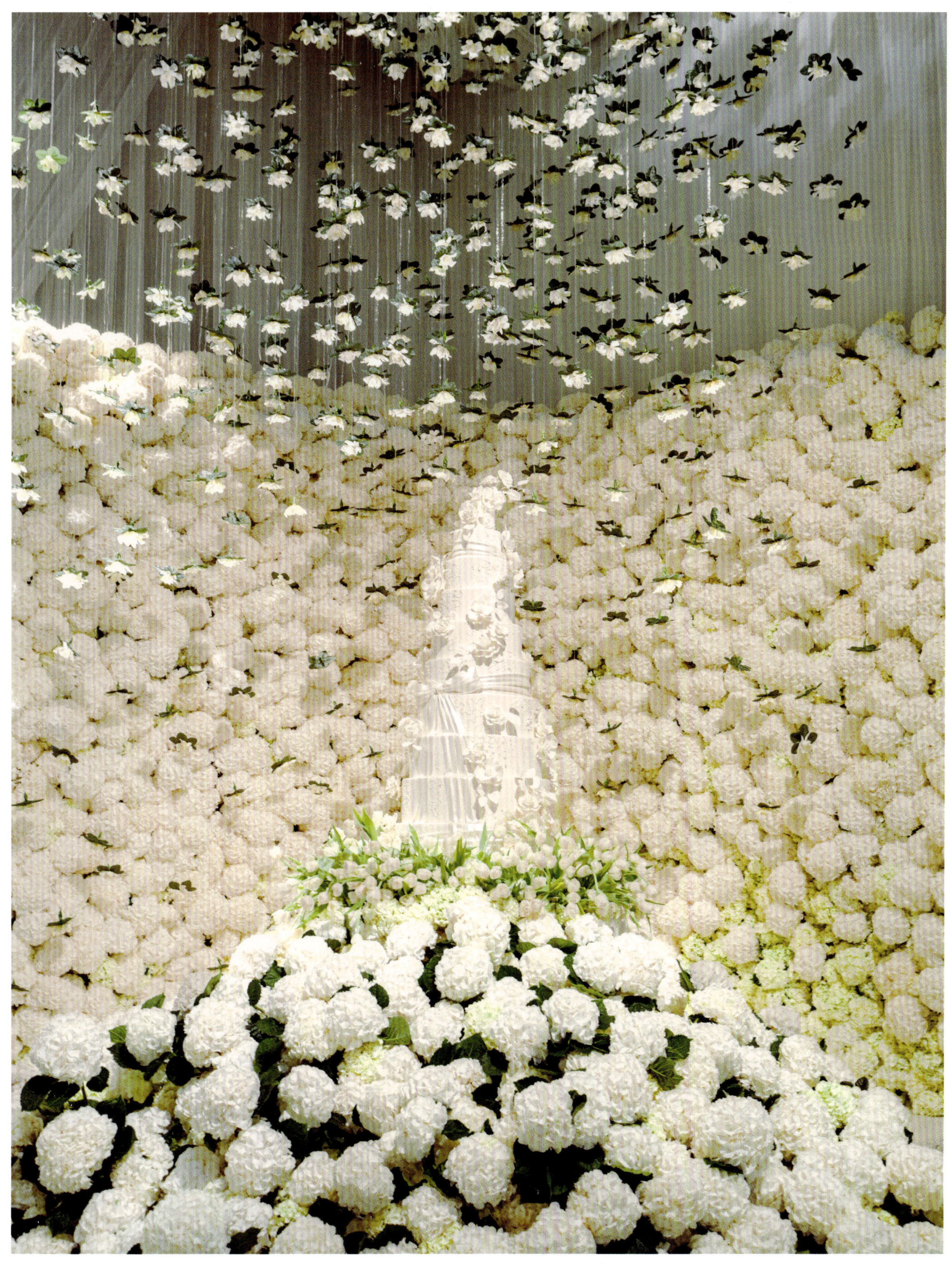

PAGES 88–93: Private Wedding, Las Vegas. Orchids, hydrangeas, and roses.
PAGES 94–97: Private Wedding, Texas. Roses, hydrangeas, and leather leaf.

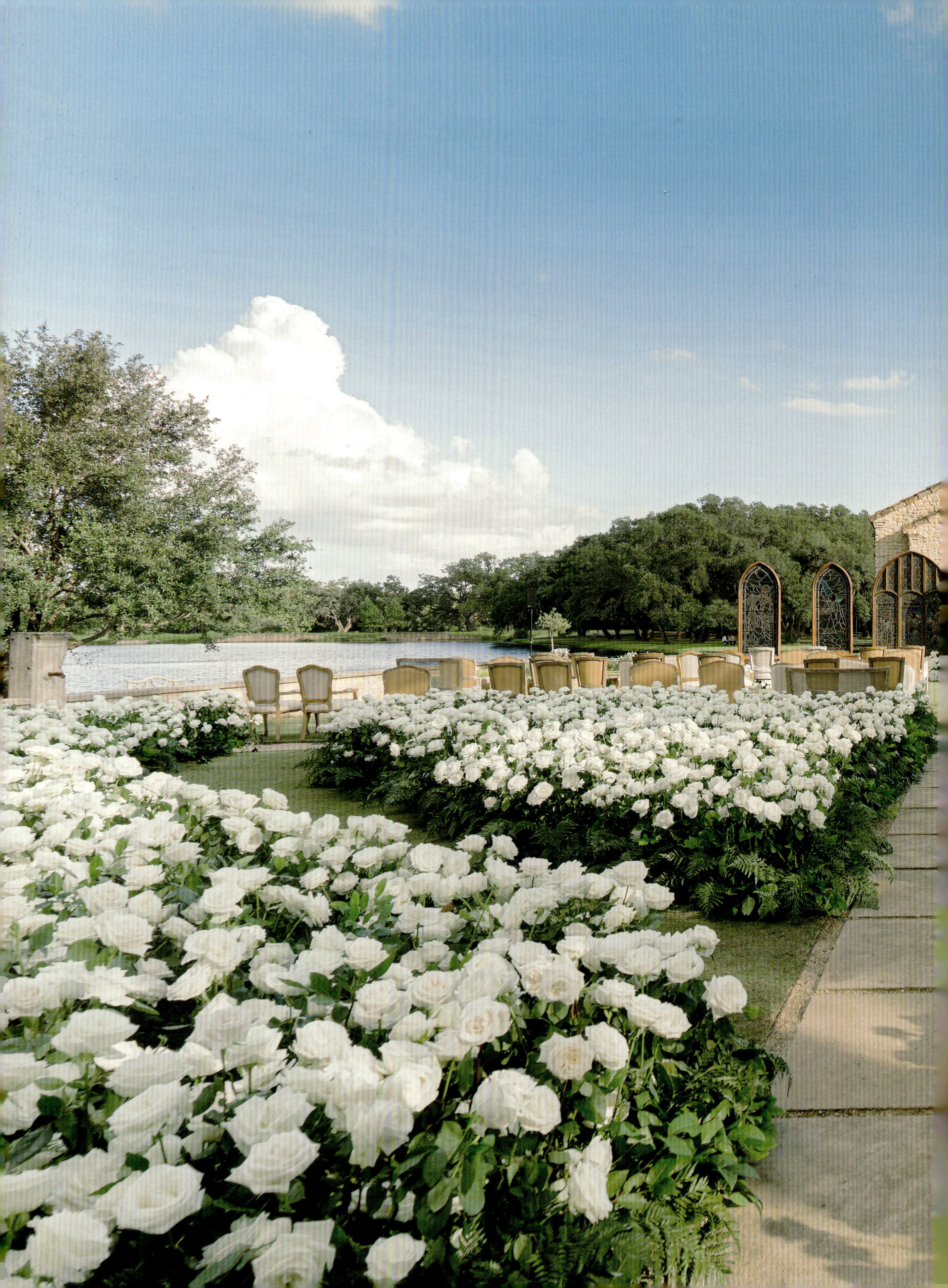

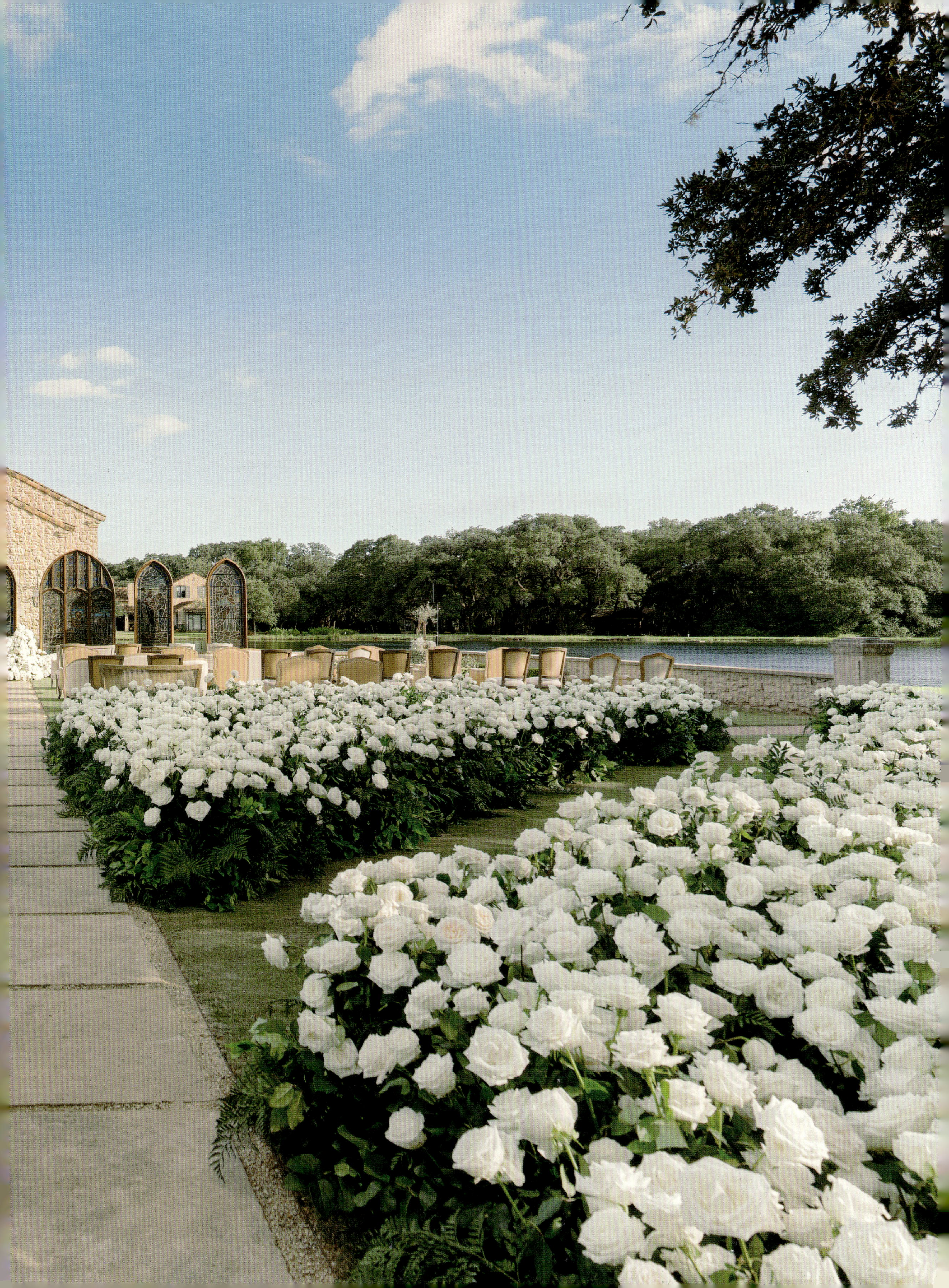

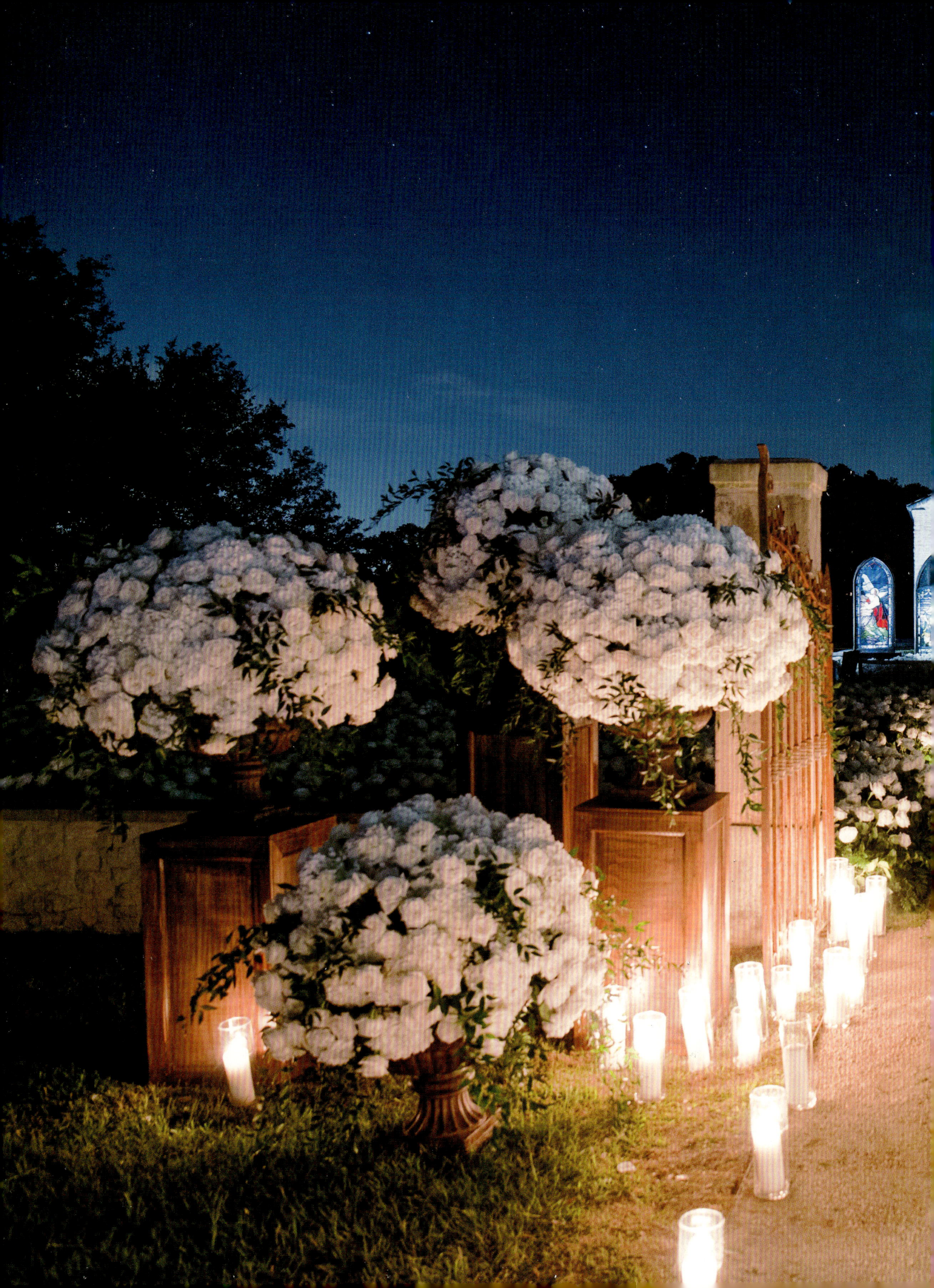

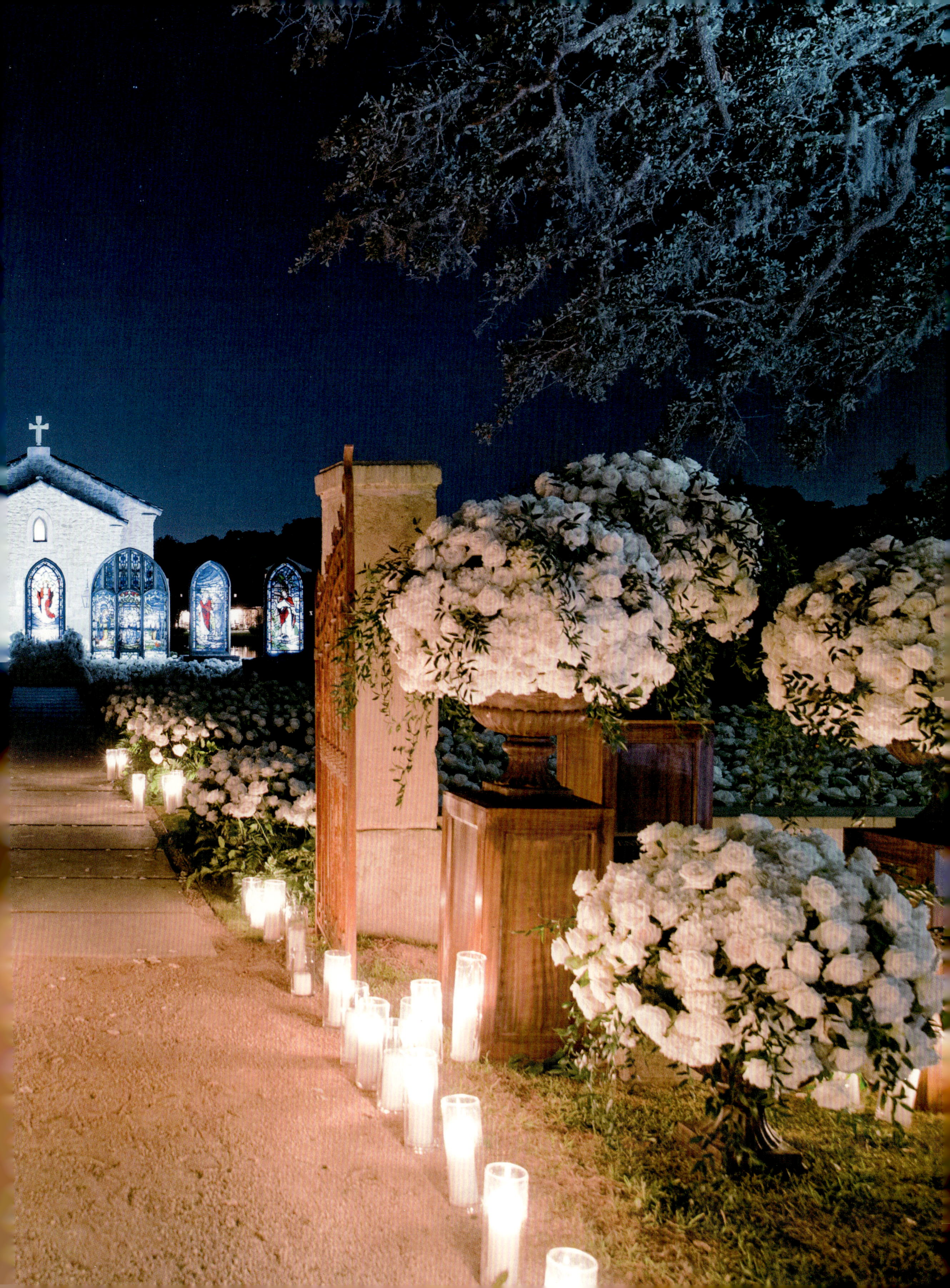

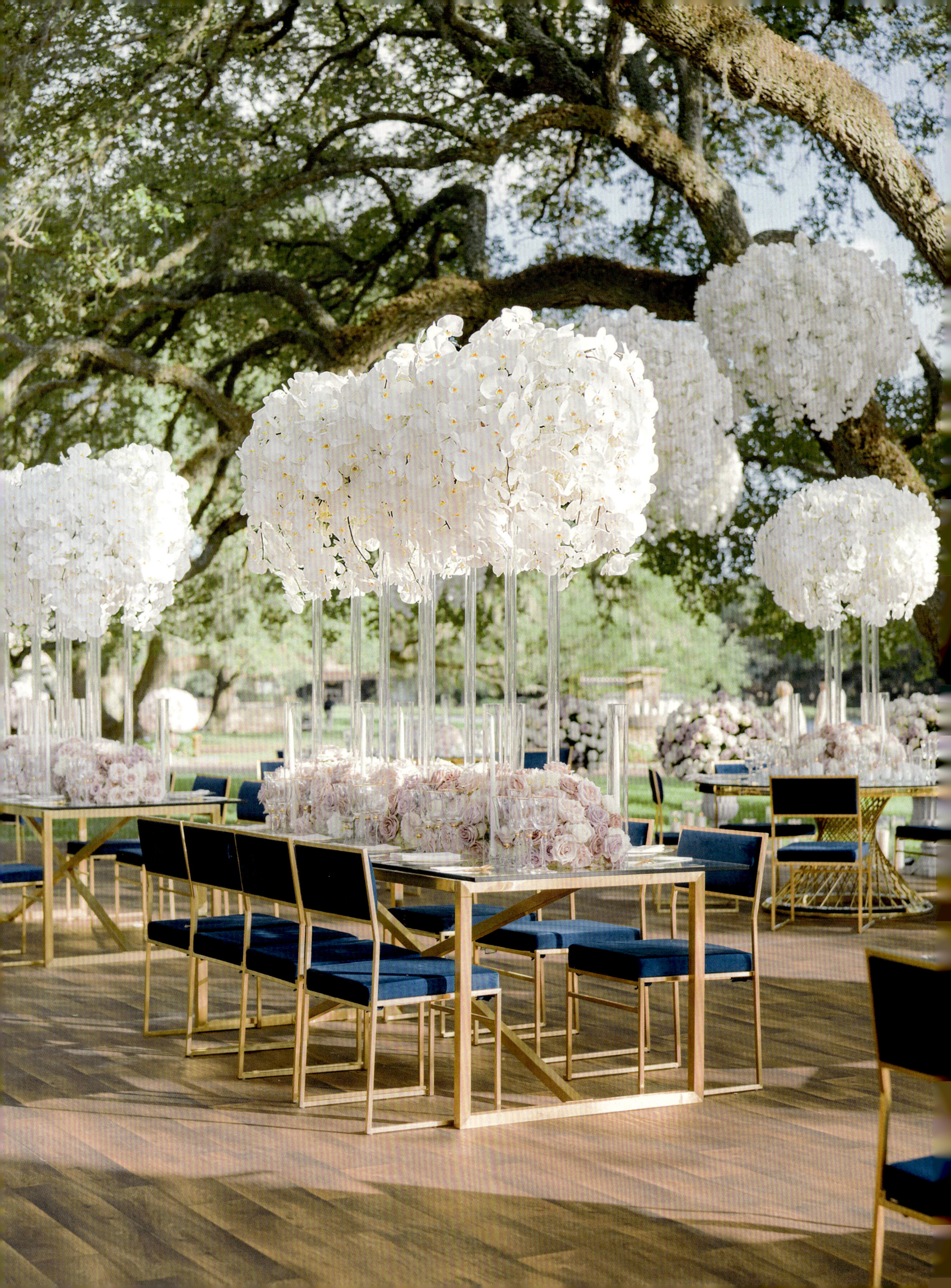

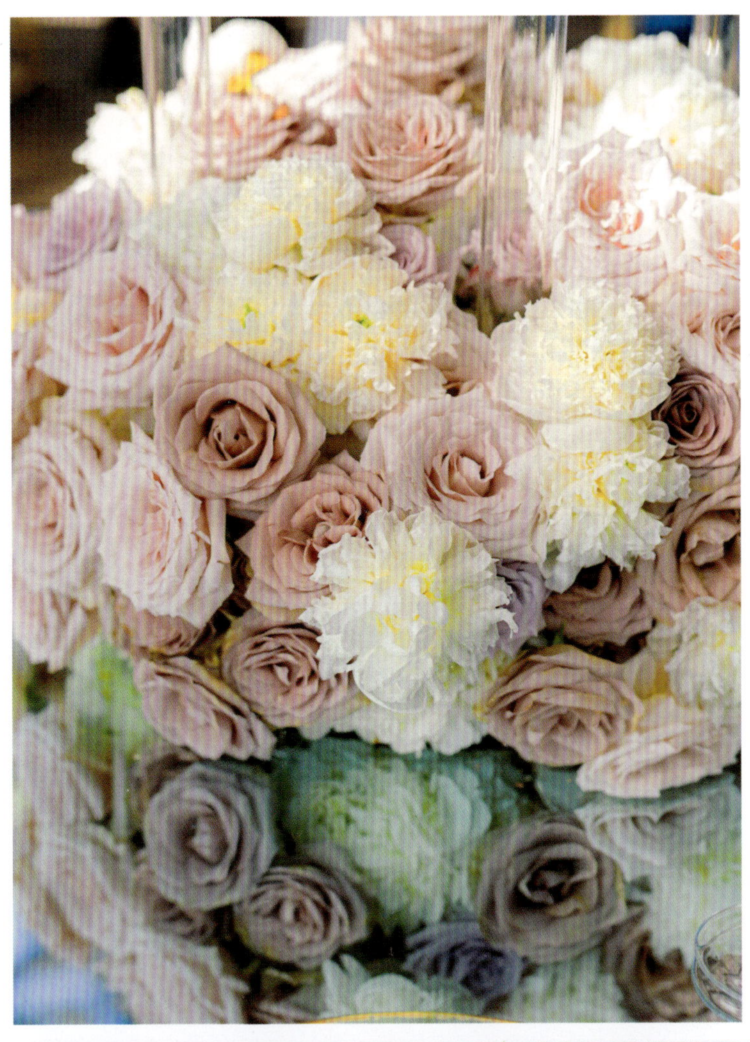
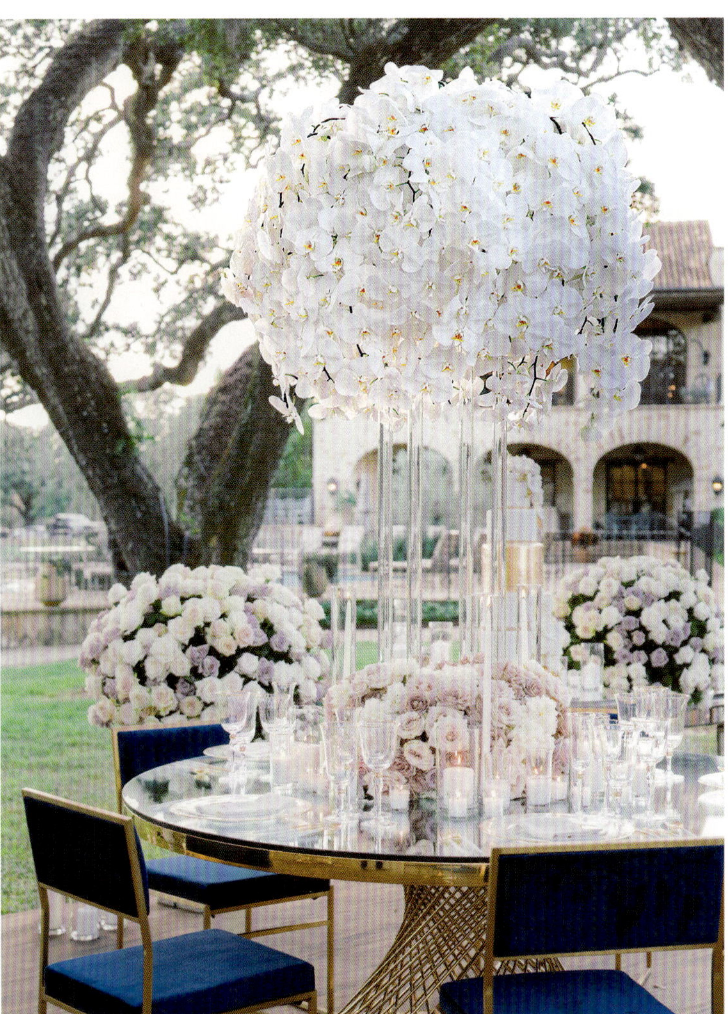

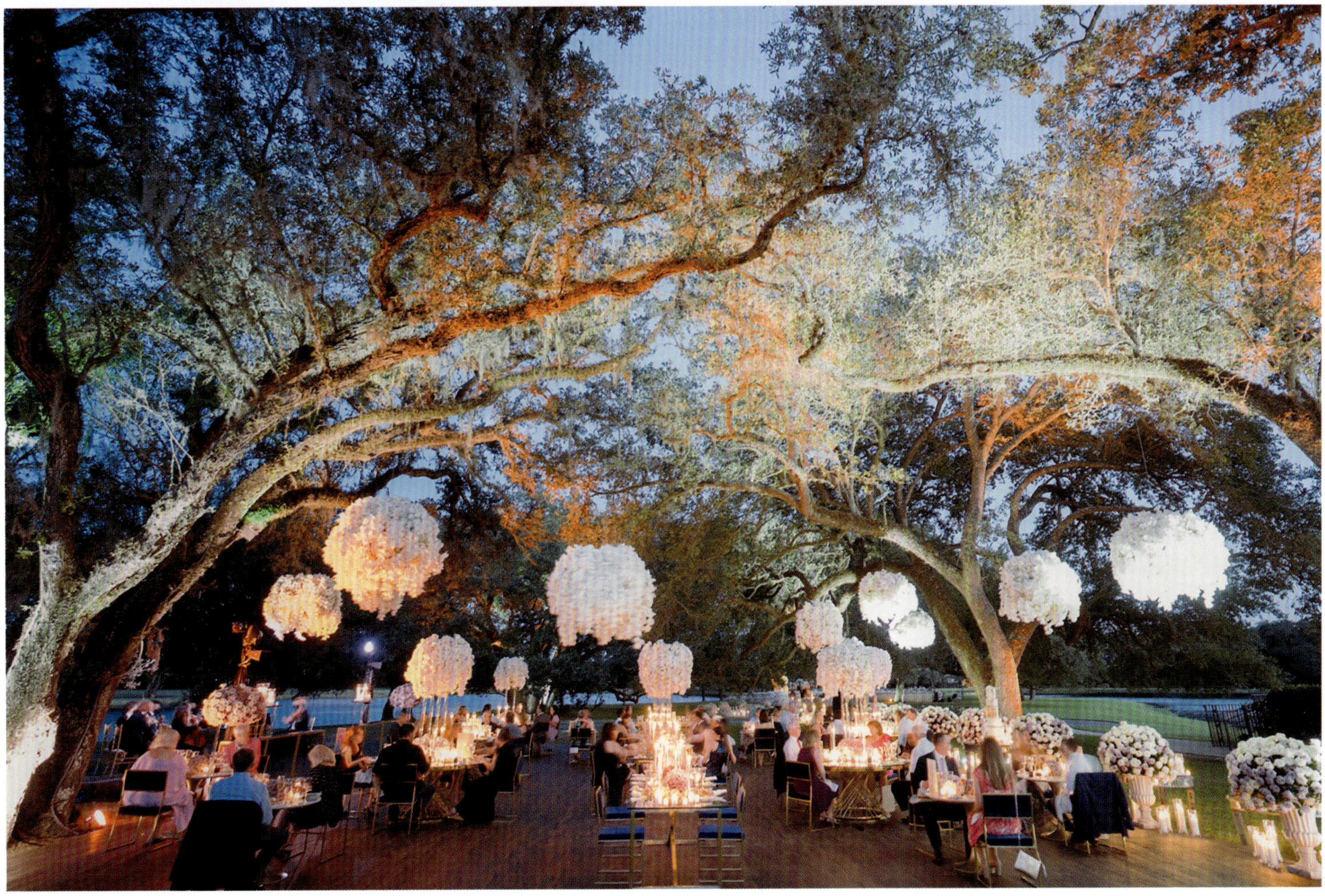

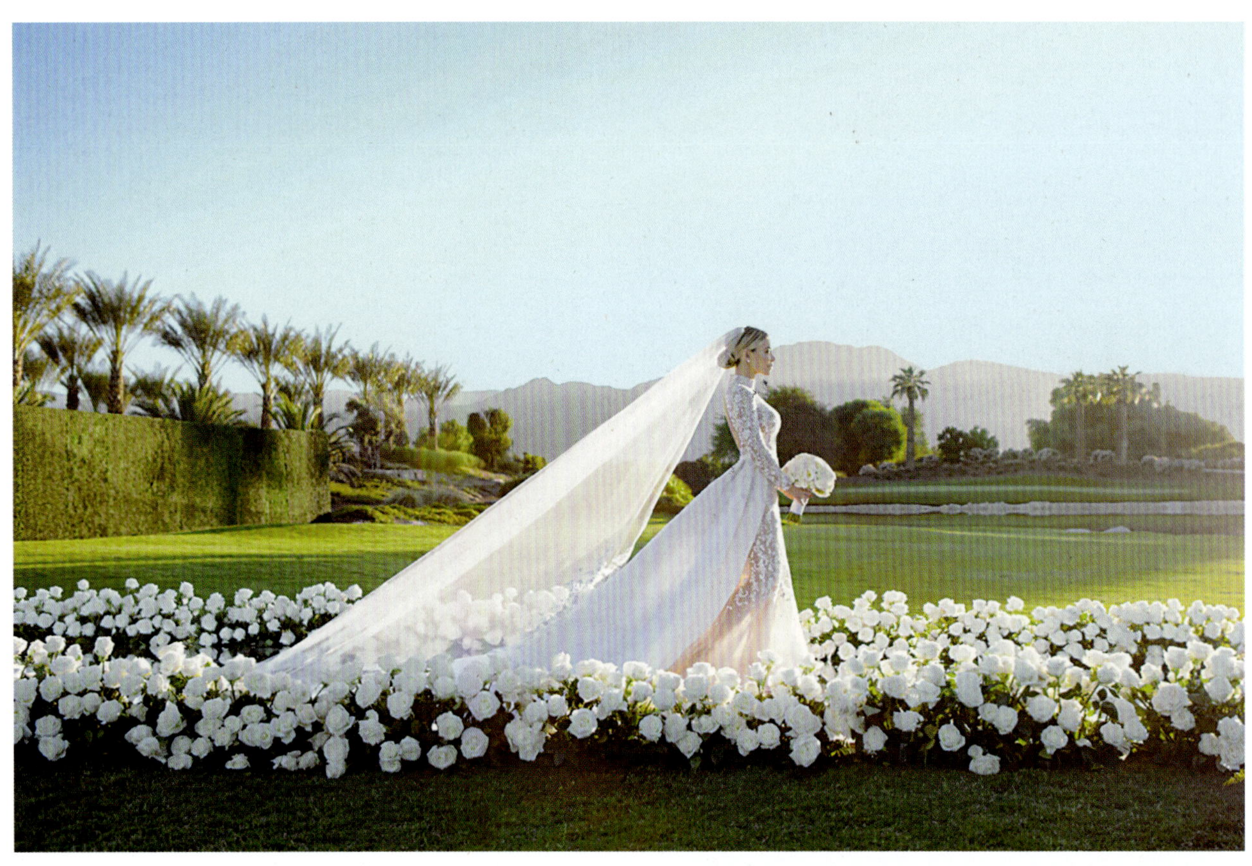

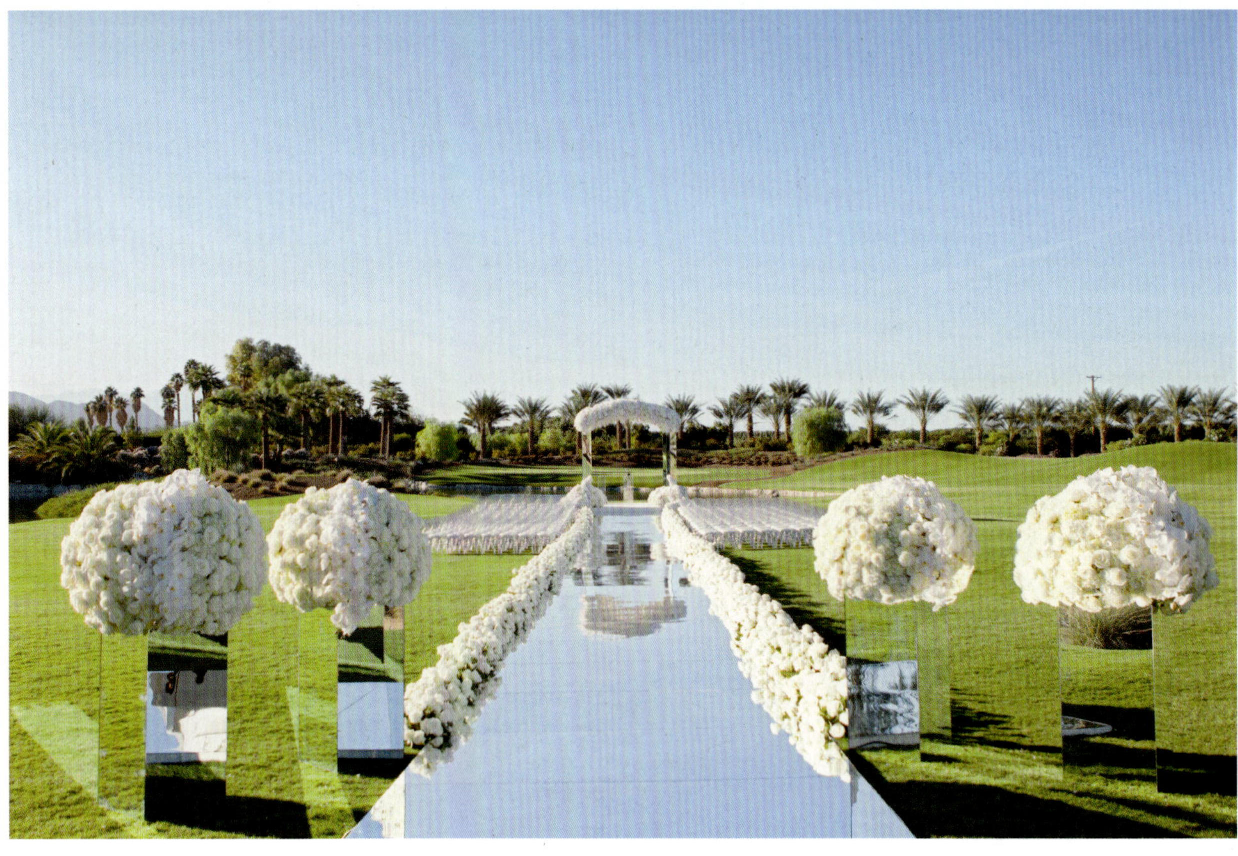

PAGES 98–99: Private Wedding, Texas. Quicksand and amnesia
roses, peonies, and phalaenopsis orchids. ABOVE AND OPPOSITE:
Private Wedding of Tara Dollinger (top). Palm Springs. Roses.

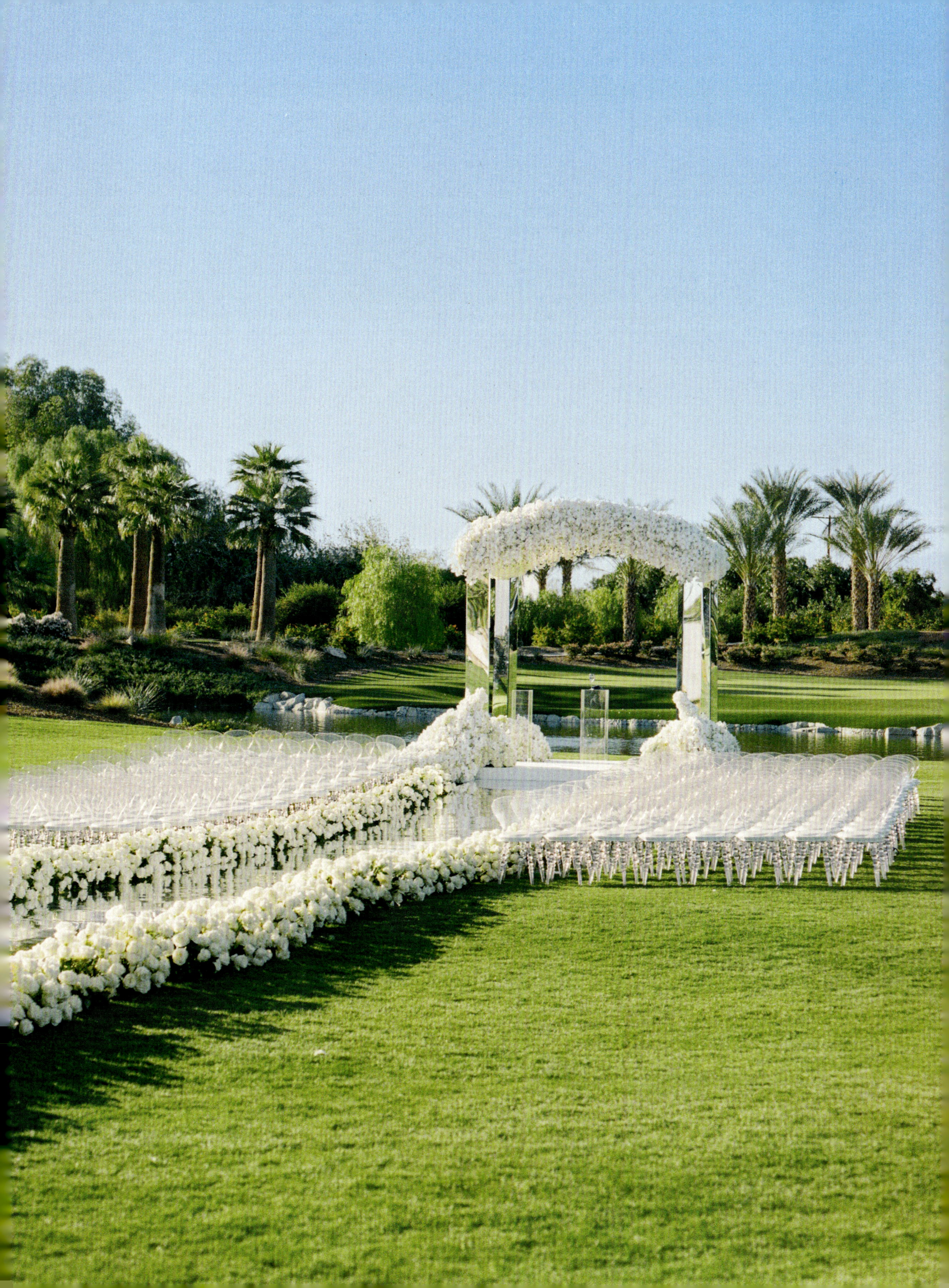

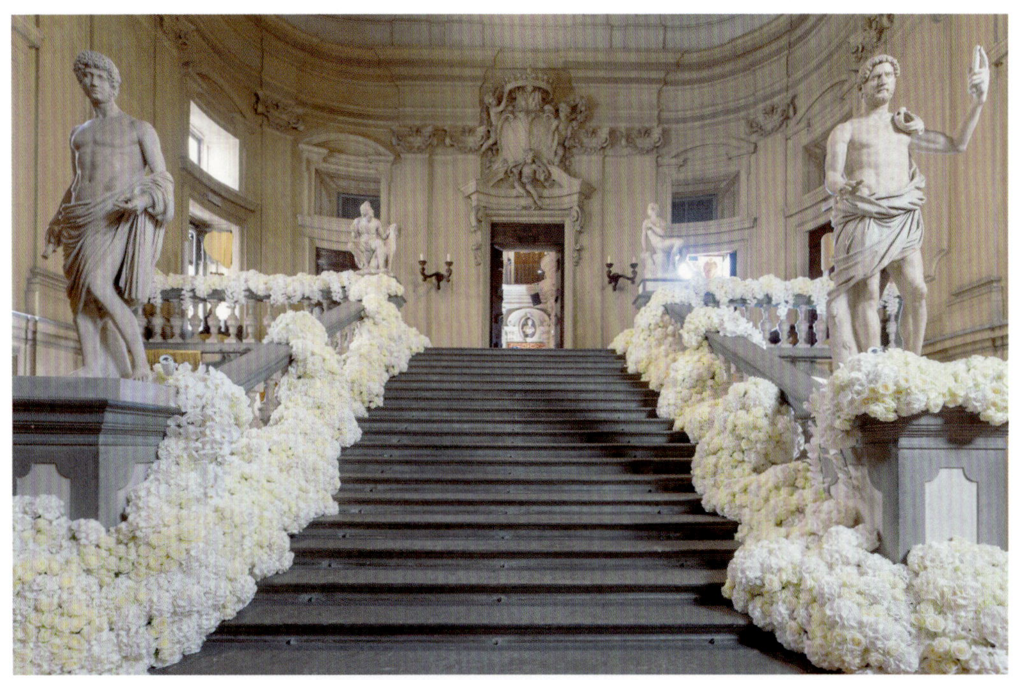

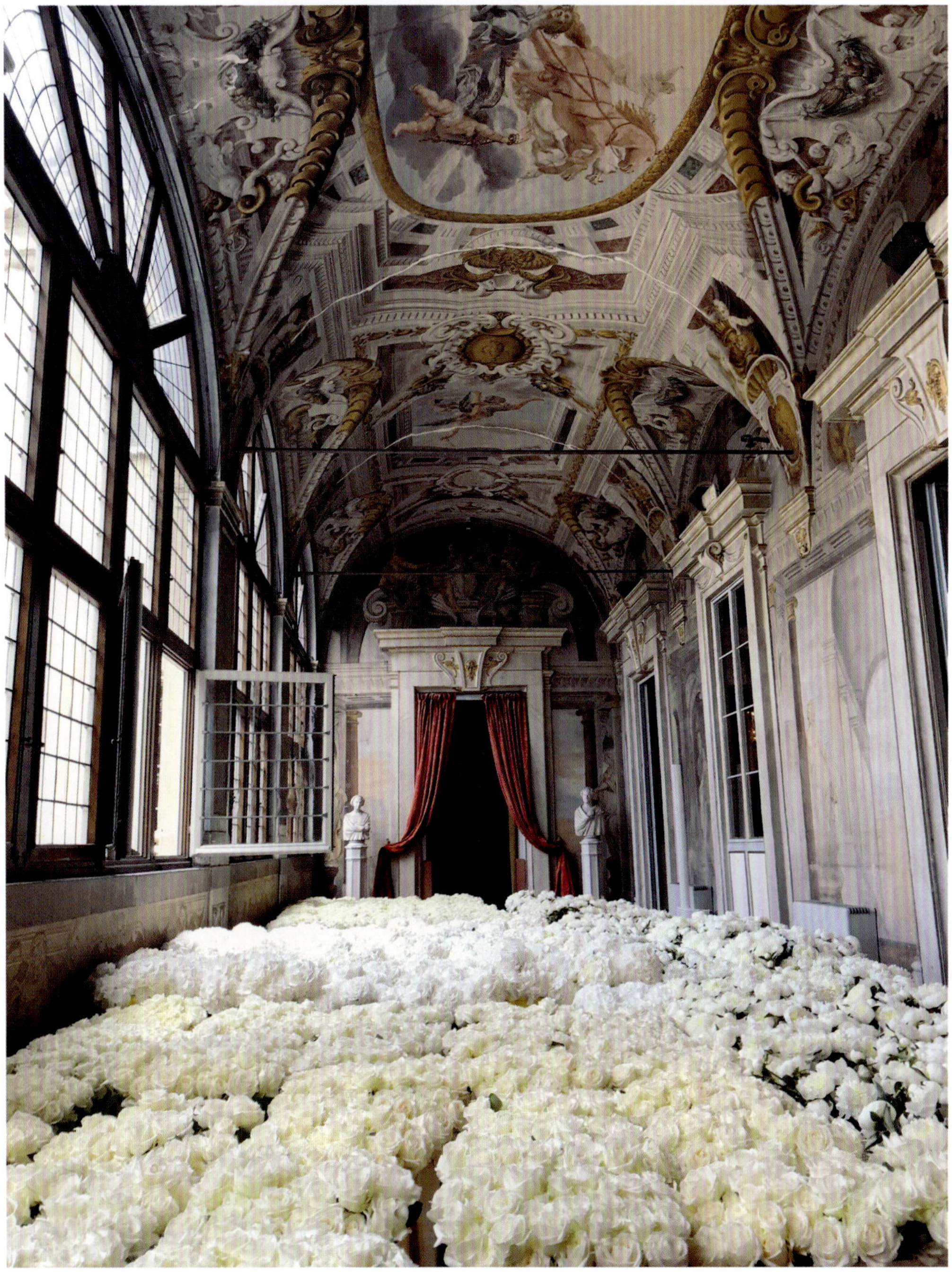

PAGES 102–109: Private Wedding, Florence, Italy. Roses, hydrangeas, and phalaenopsis orchids.

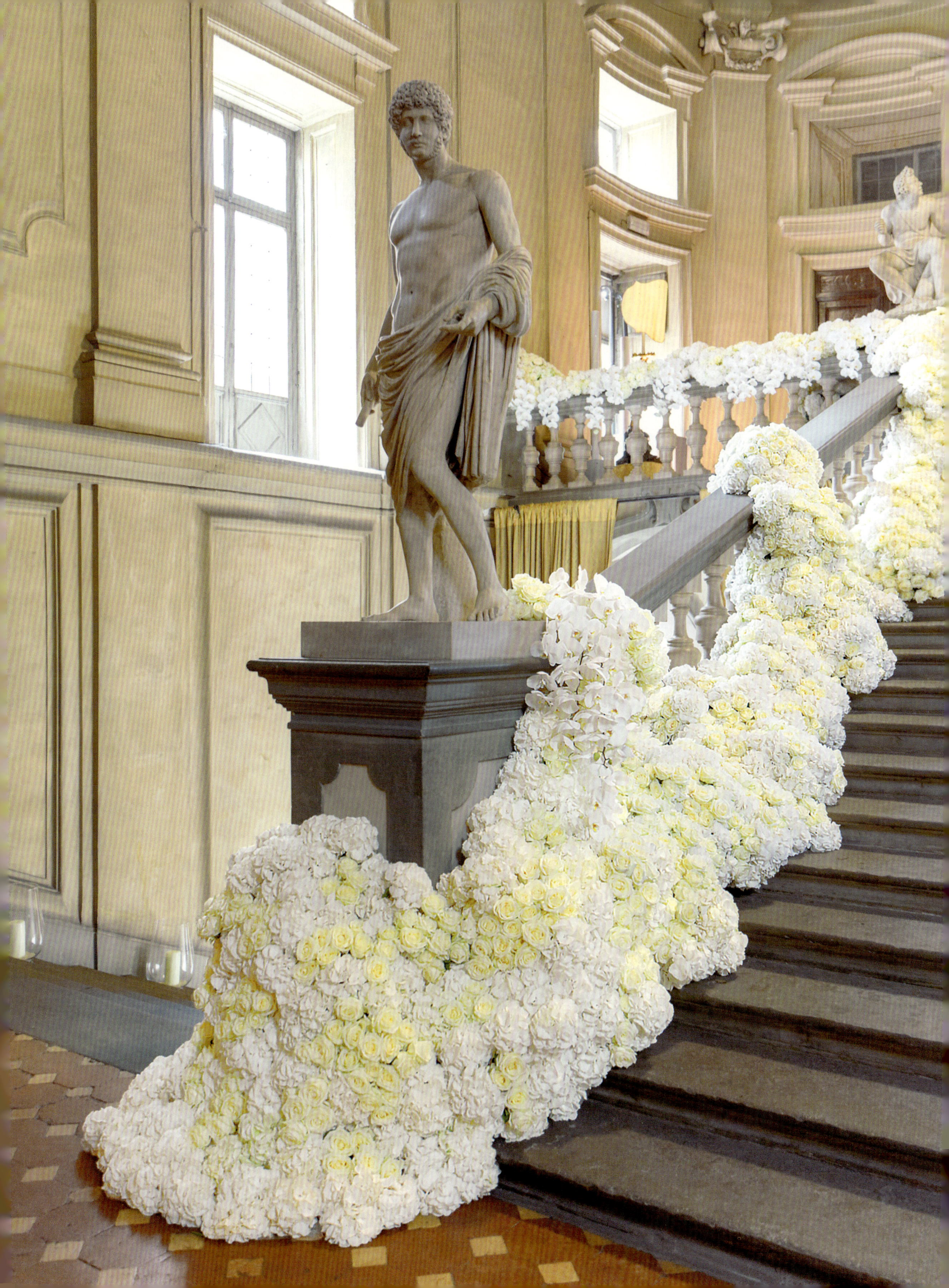

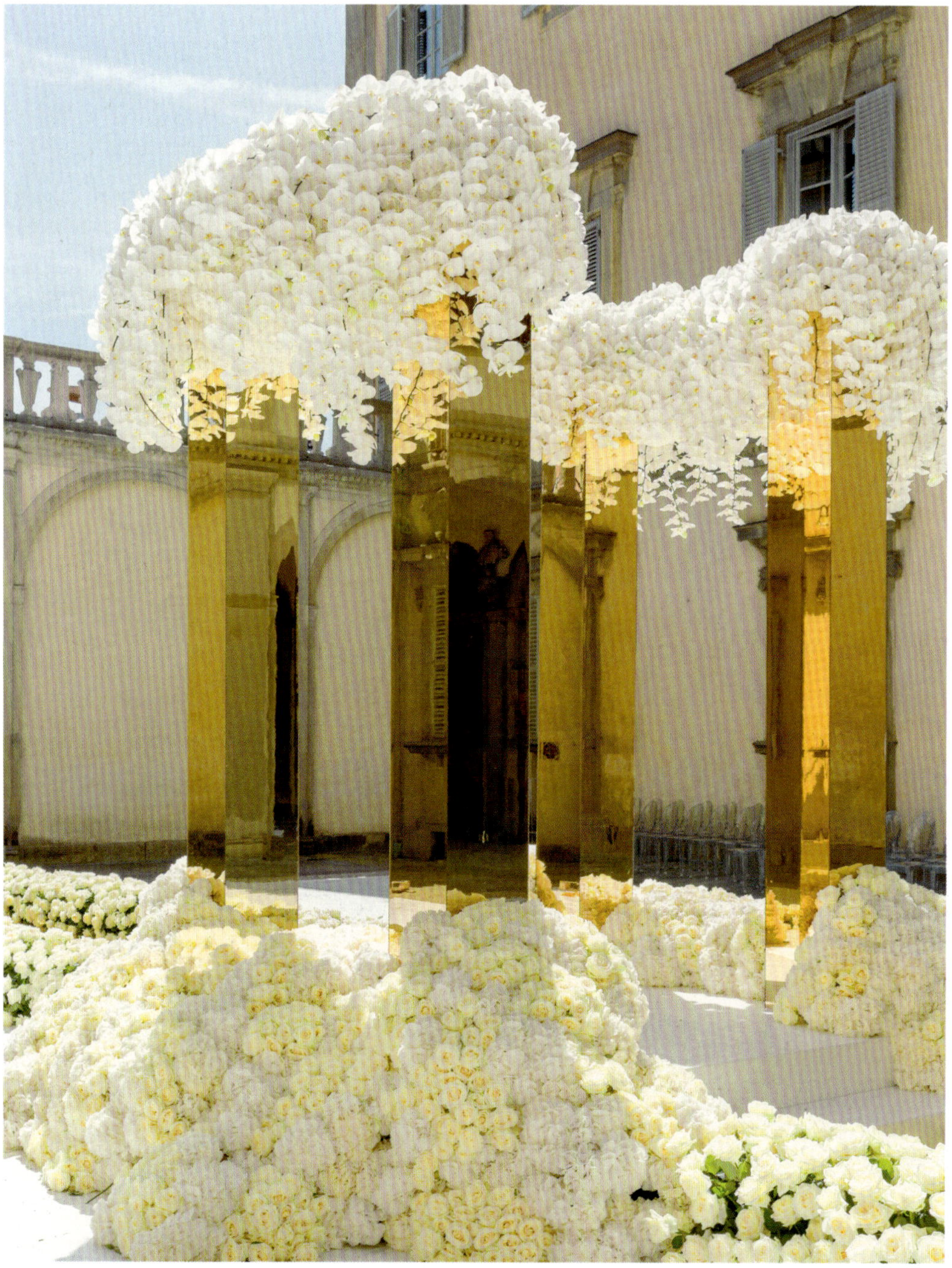

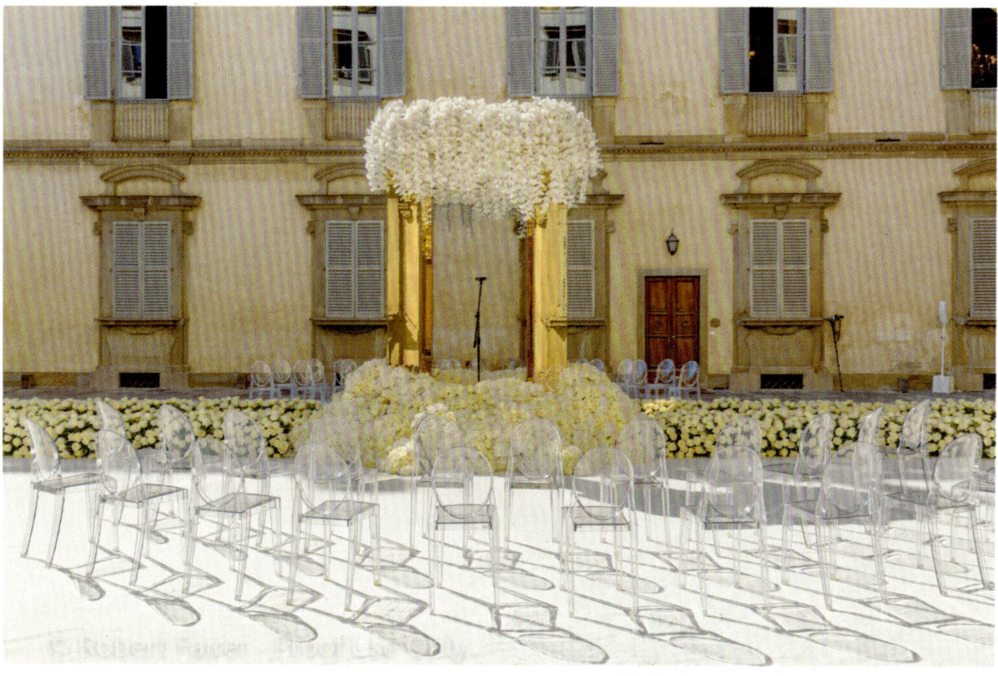
© Robert Fairer

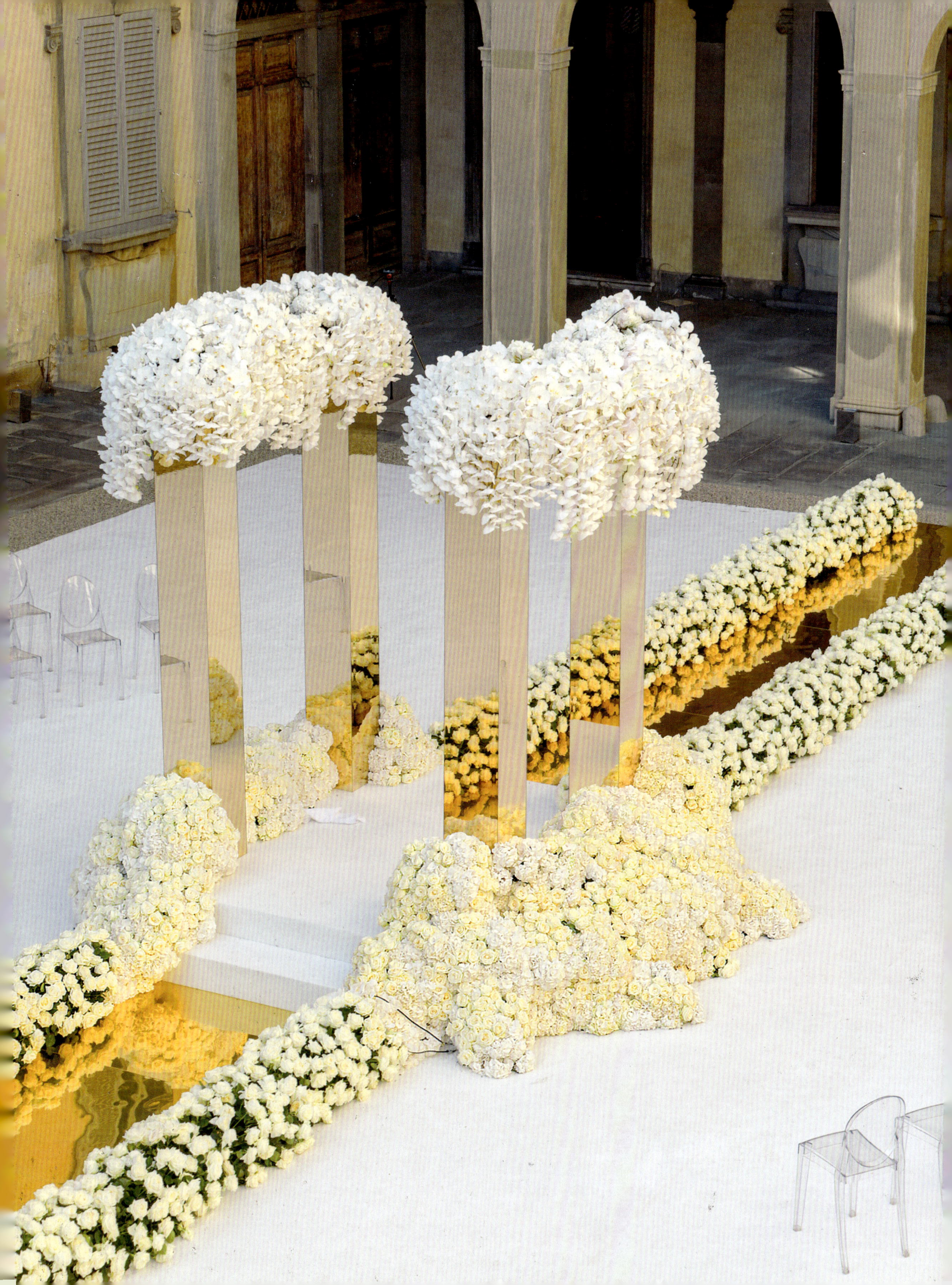

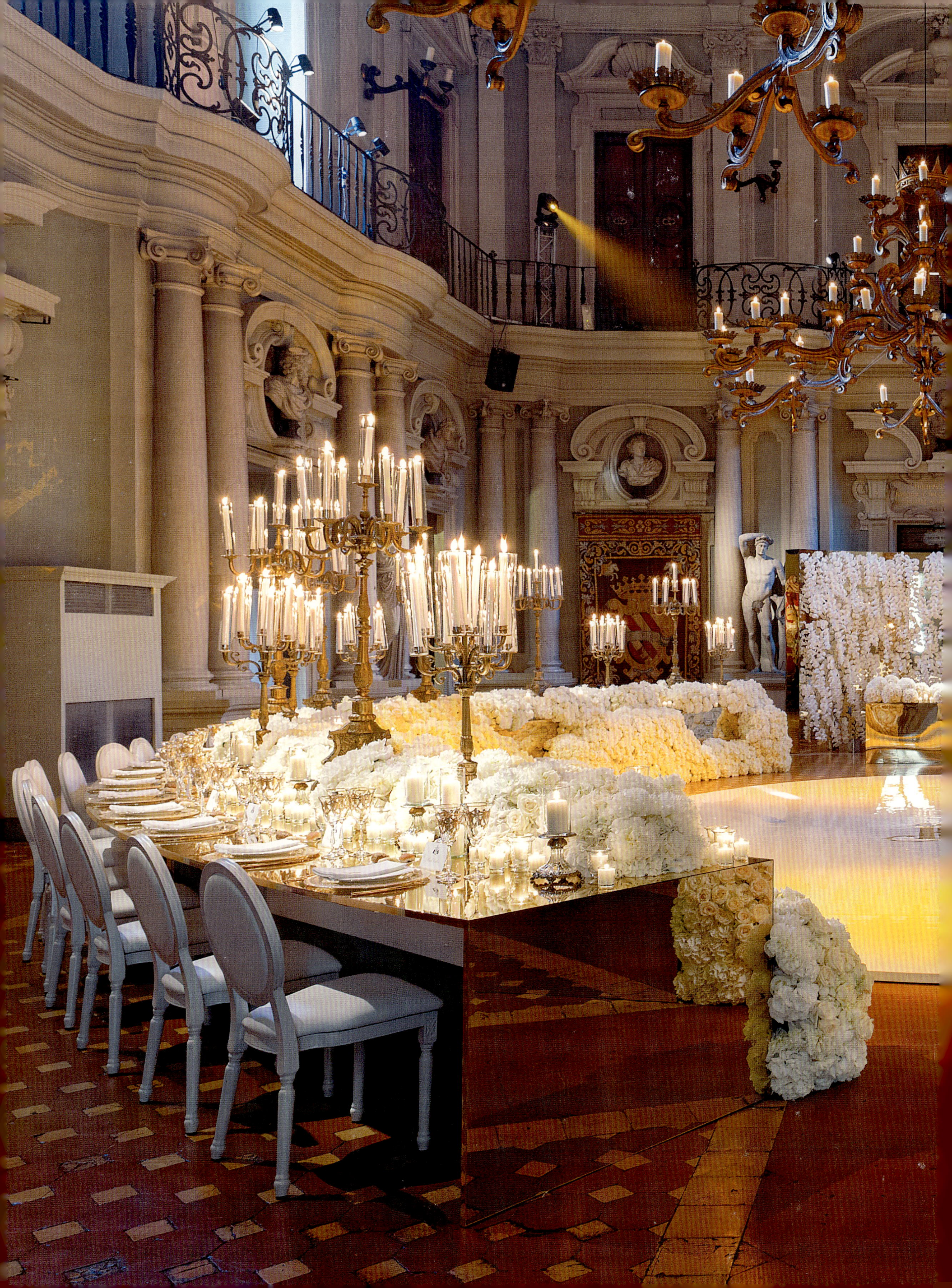

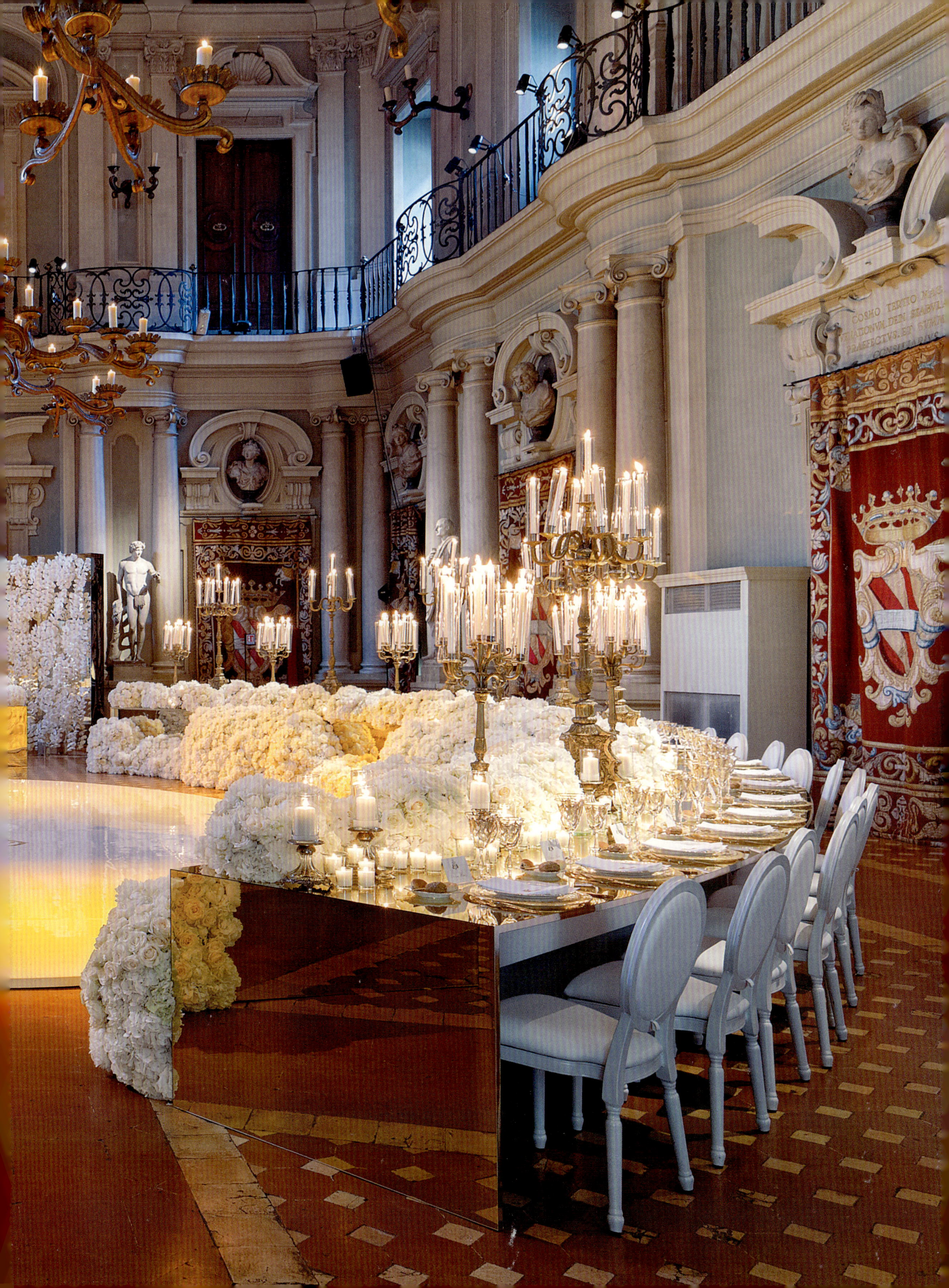

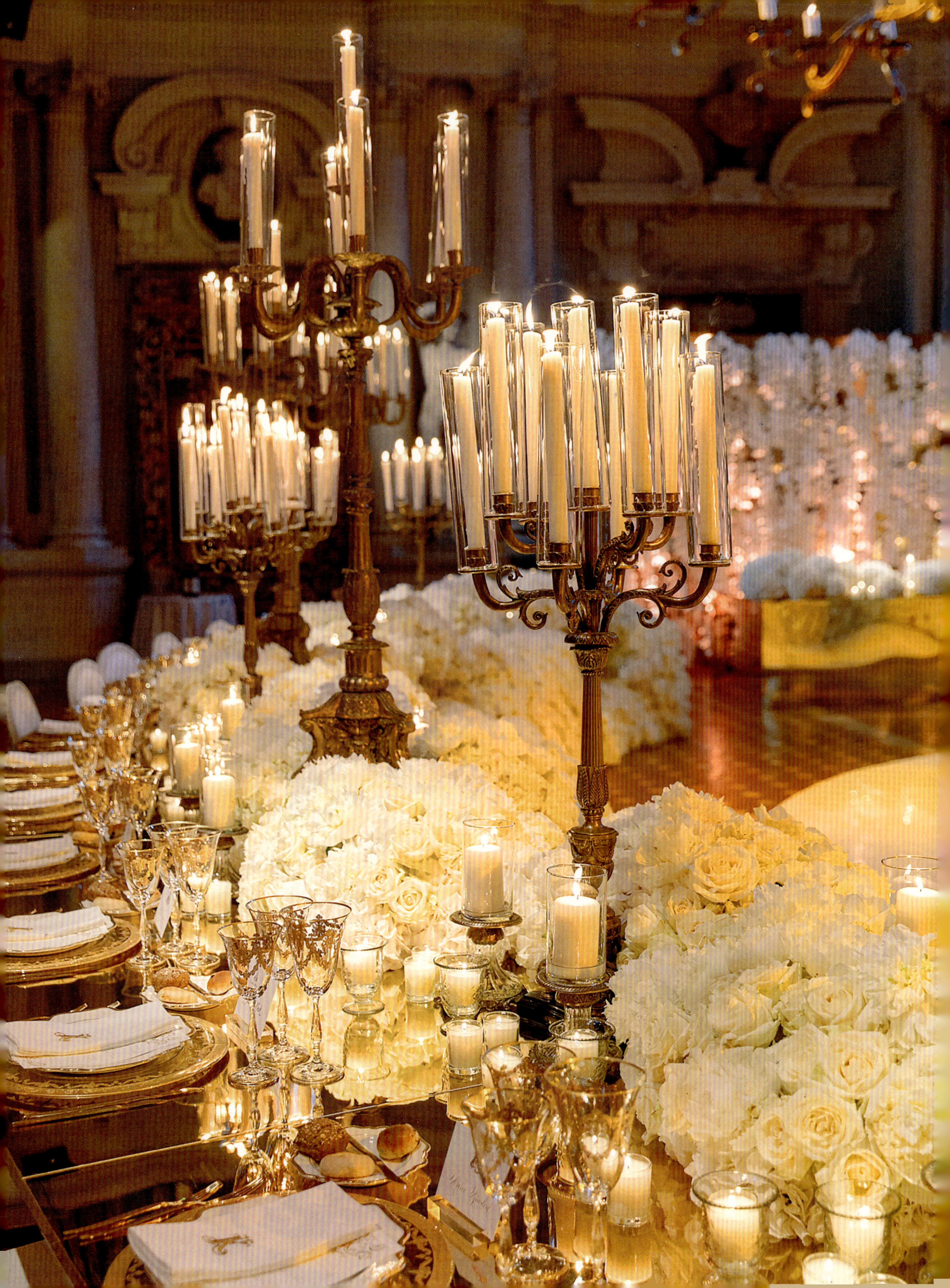

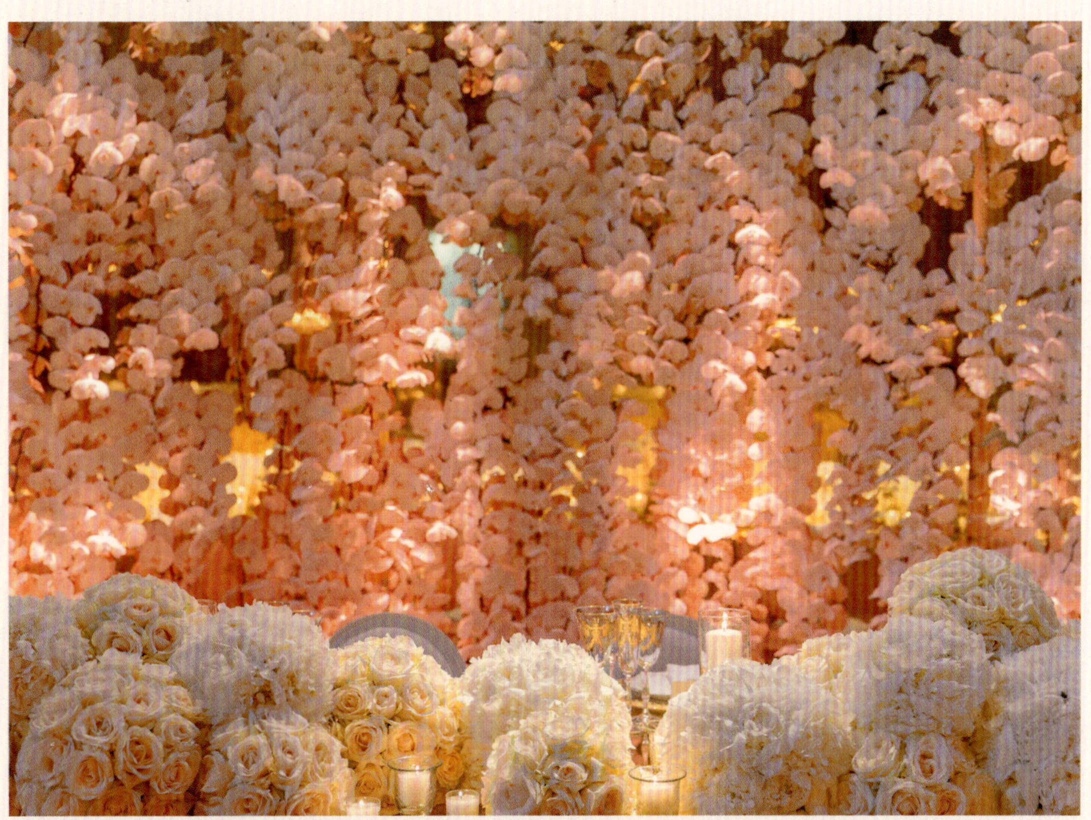

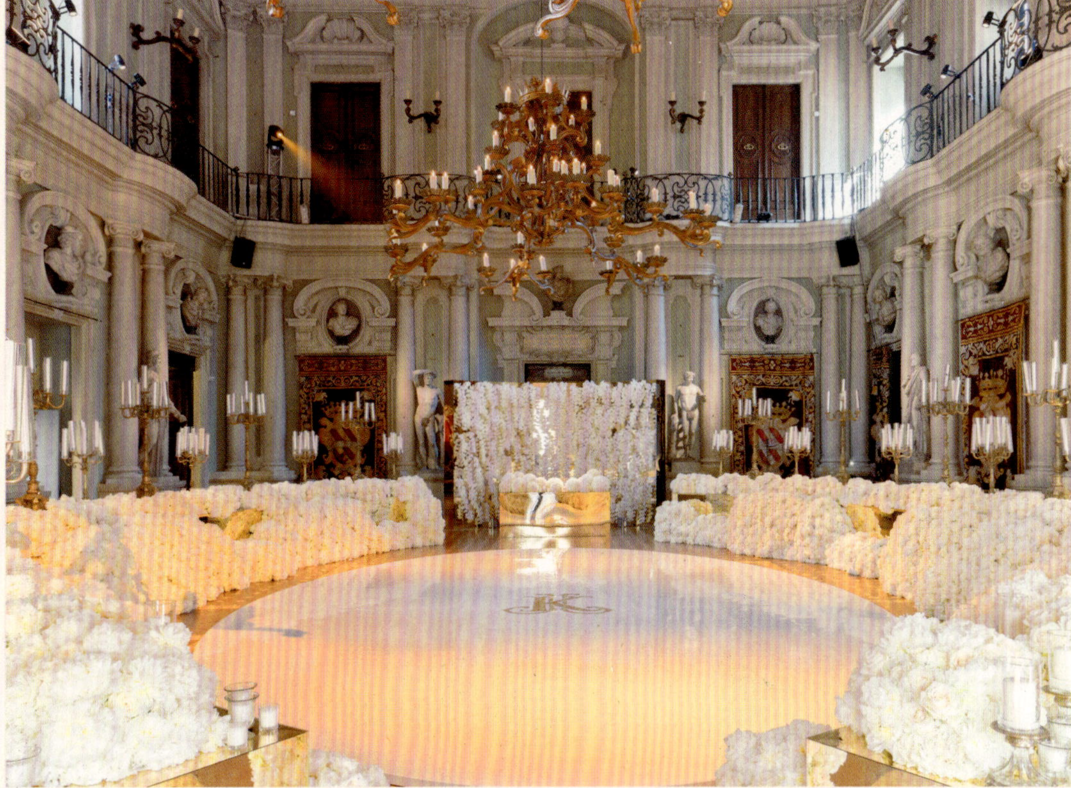

FOLLOWING: Private Wedding, Palm Beach,
Florida. Train of roses, hanging phalaenopsis
orchids, and leis of dendrobium orchids.

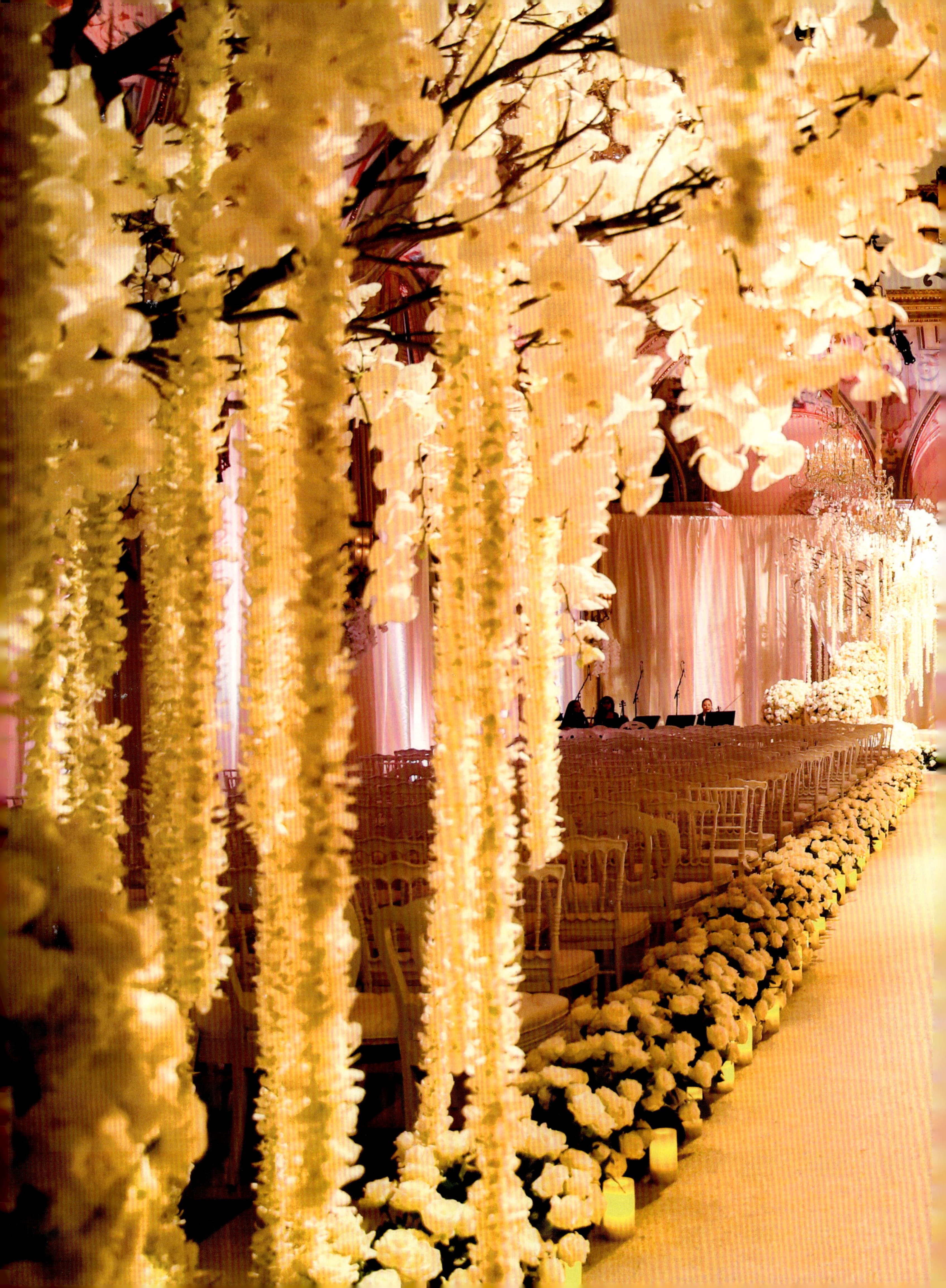

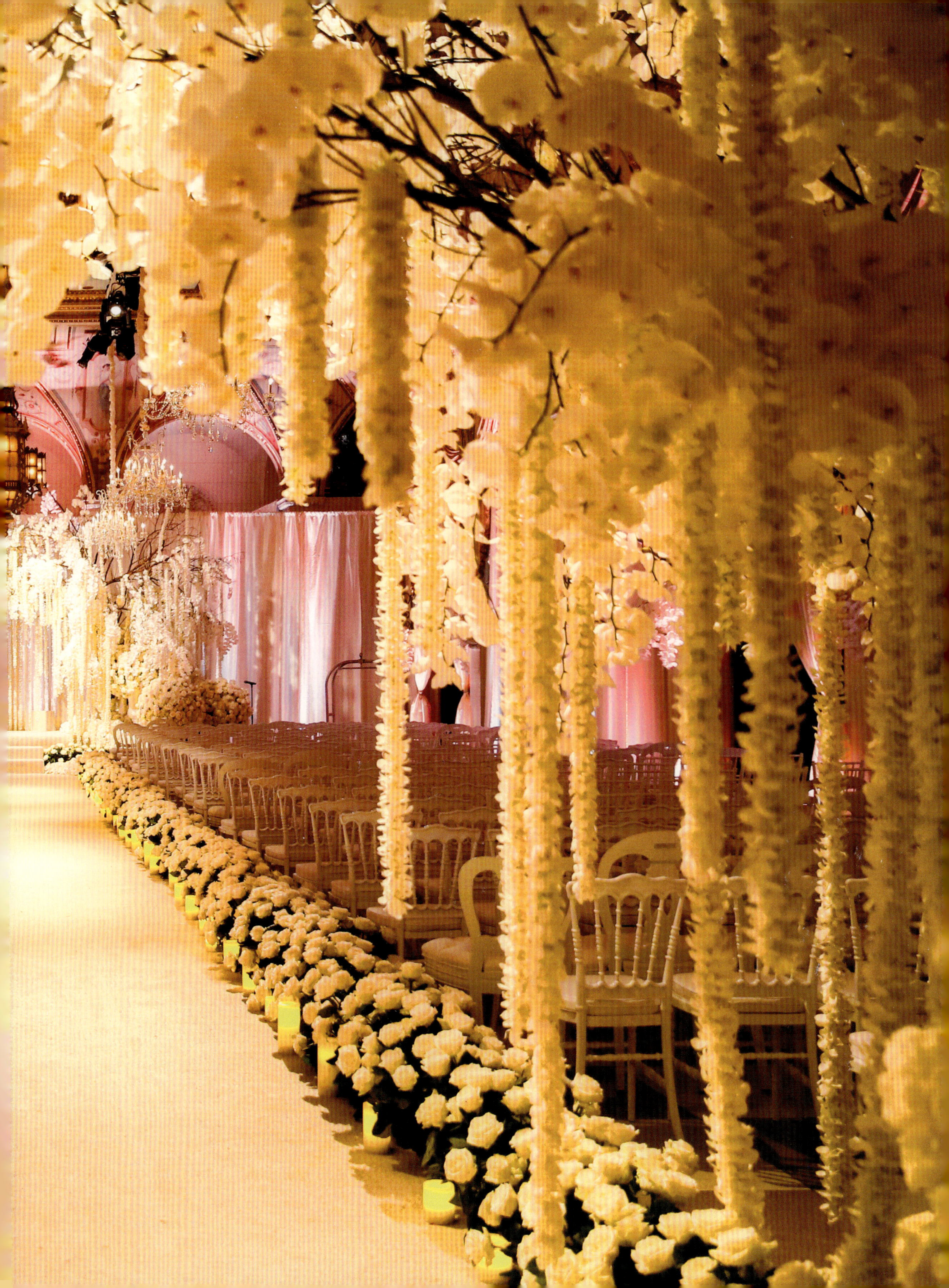

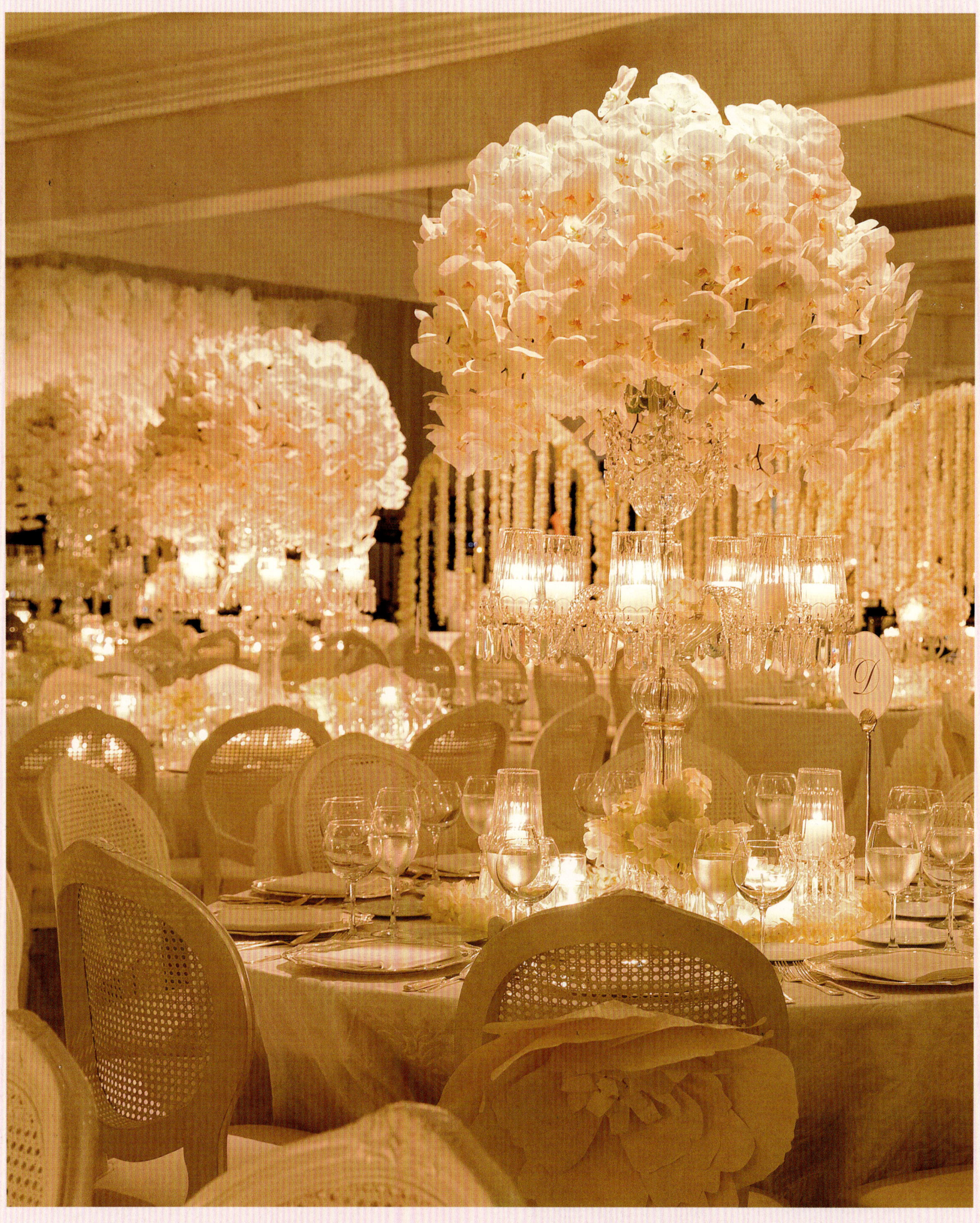

ABOVE: Private Wedding, Turkey. Orchids and leis of dendrobium orchids. OPPOSITE: Private Wedding, Palm Beach, California. Phalaenopsis orchids and and leis of dendrobium orchids.

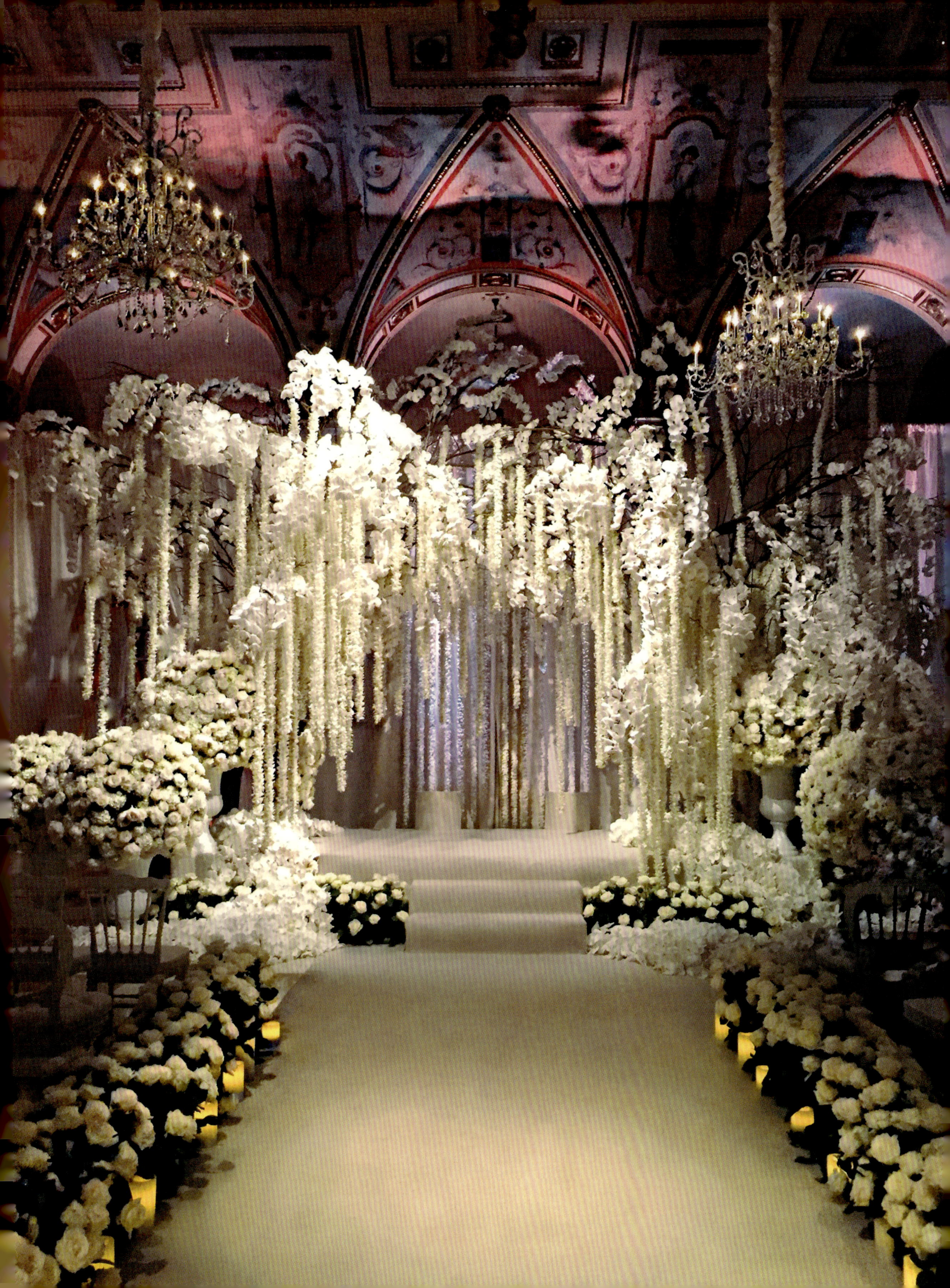

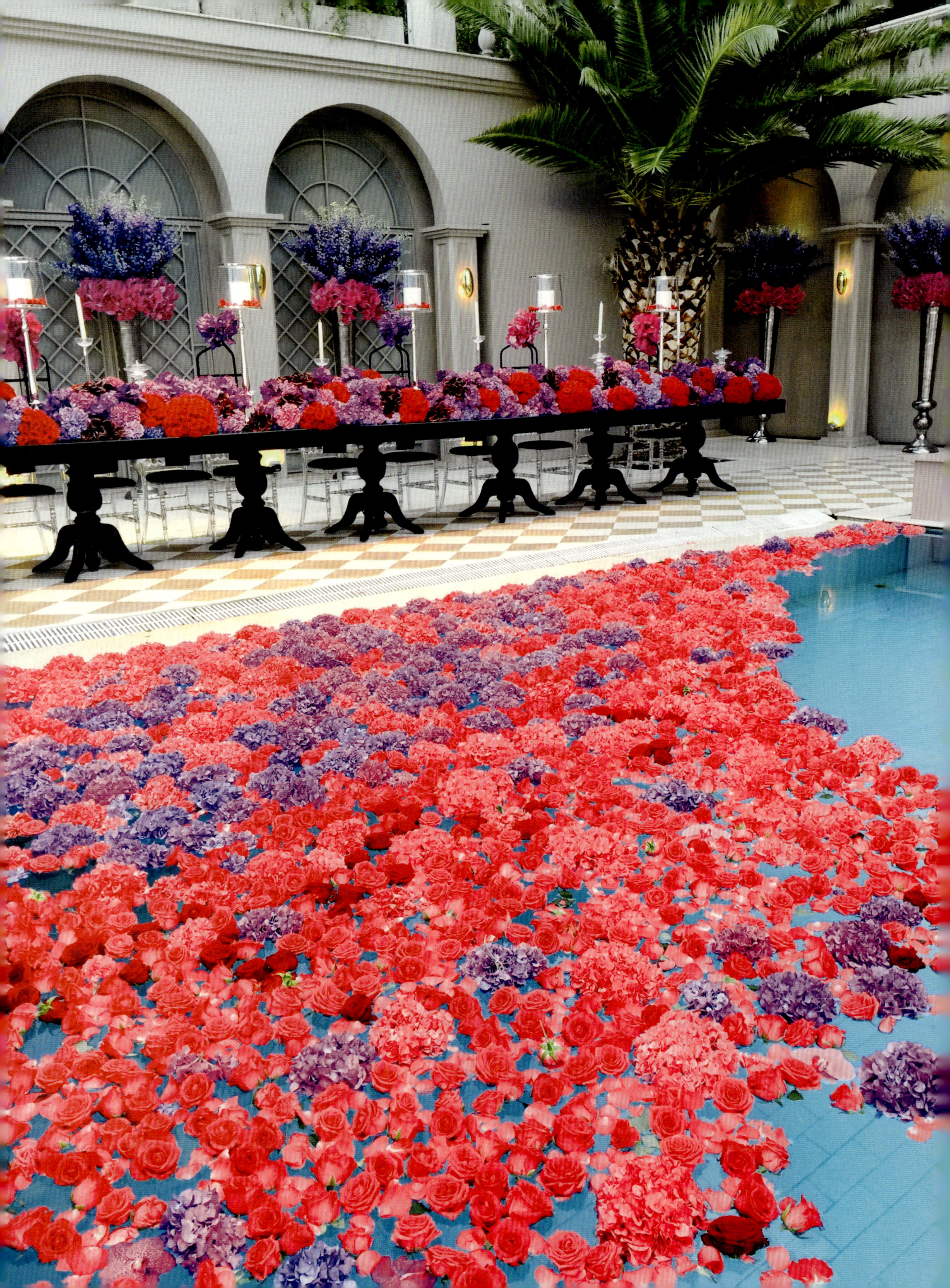

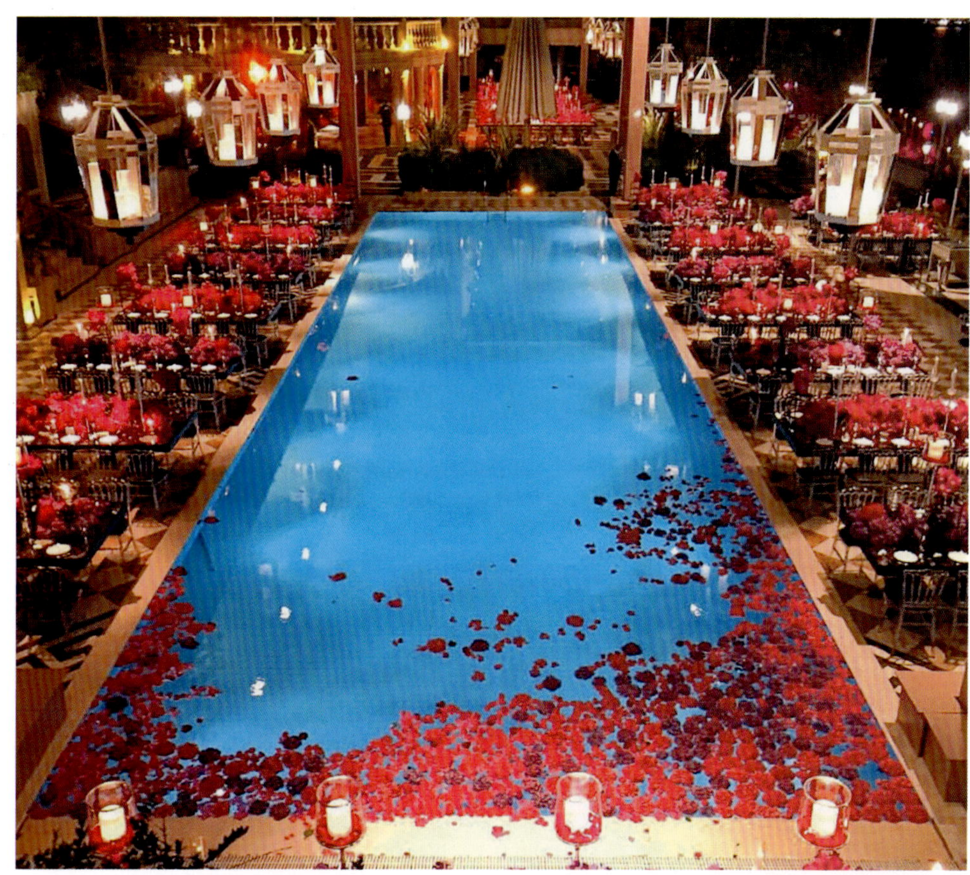

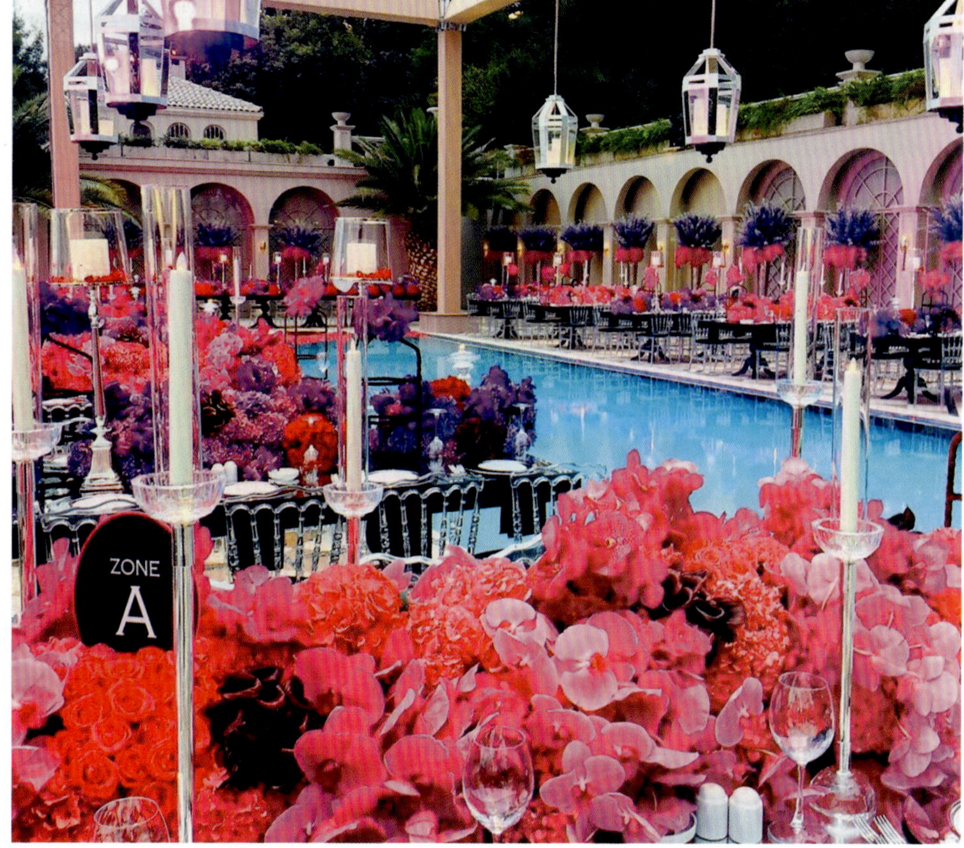

Private Wedding, Turkey. Floating Pink Floyd
rose heads, hydrangea heads, and roses.
Delphinium in vases, phalaenopsis orchids,
and hydrangeas. FOLLOWING: Private
Wedding, Los Angeles. Leis of dendrobium
orchids and hydrangeas.

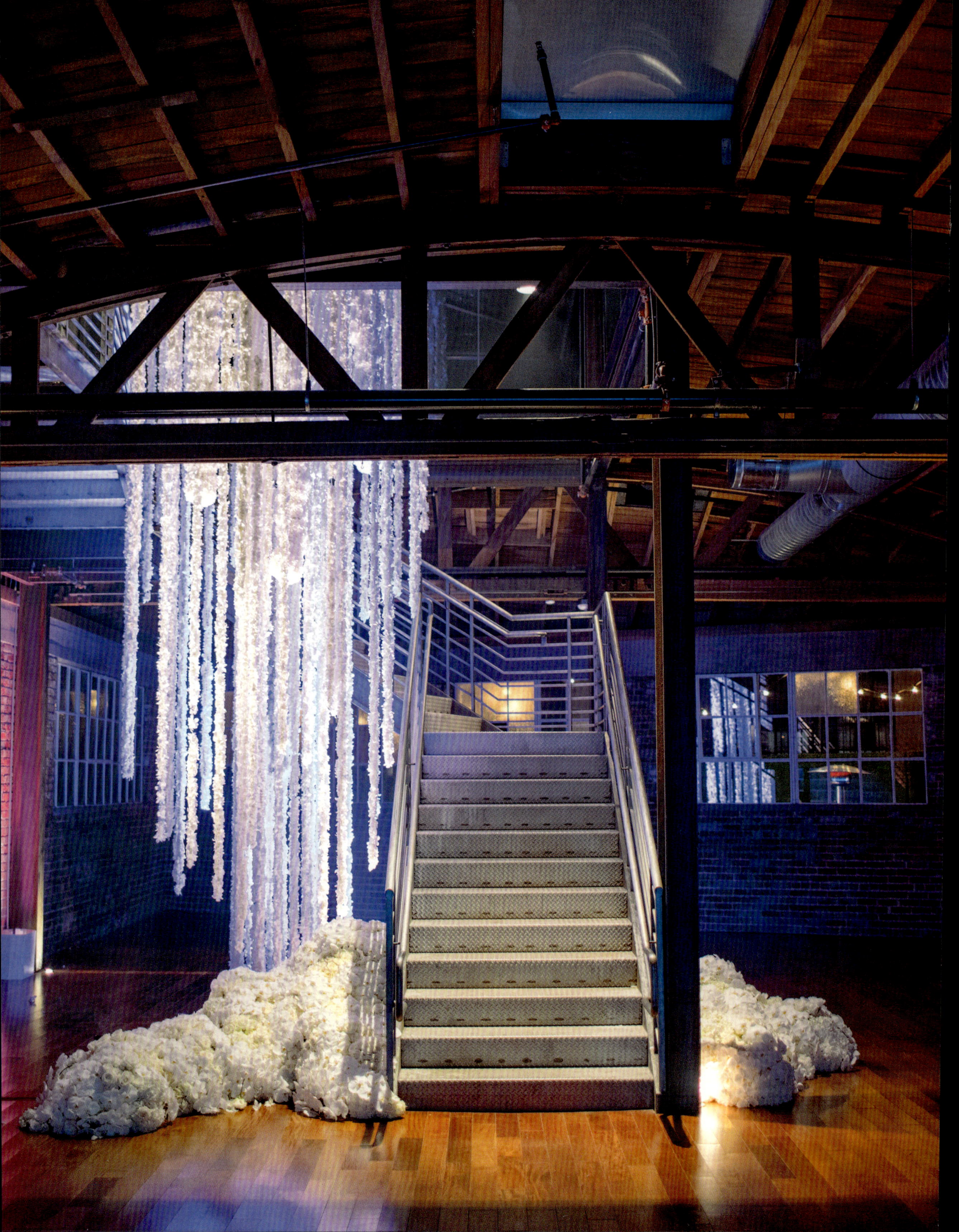

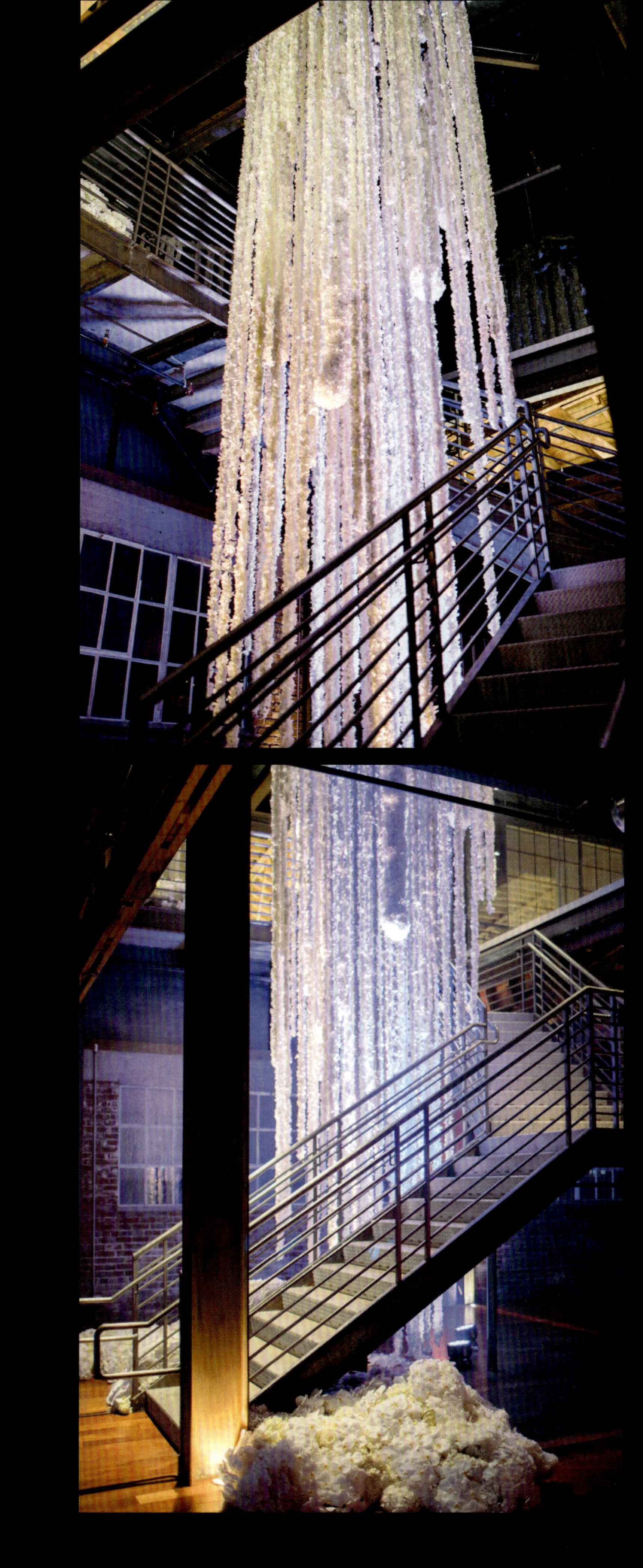

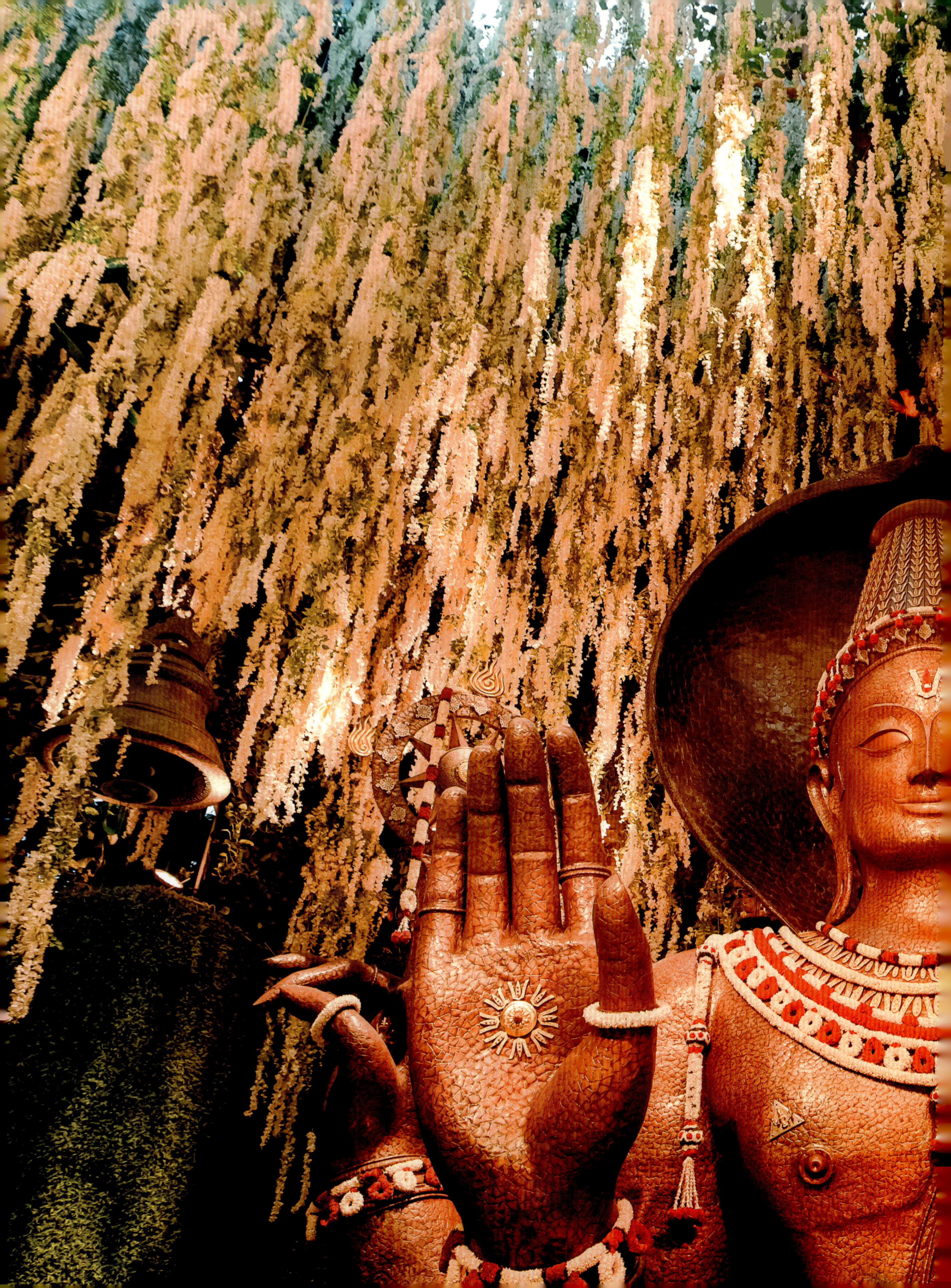

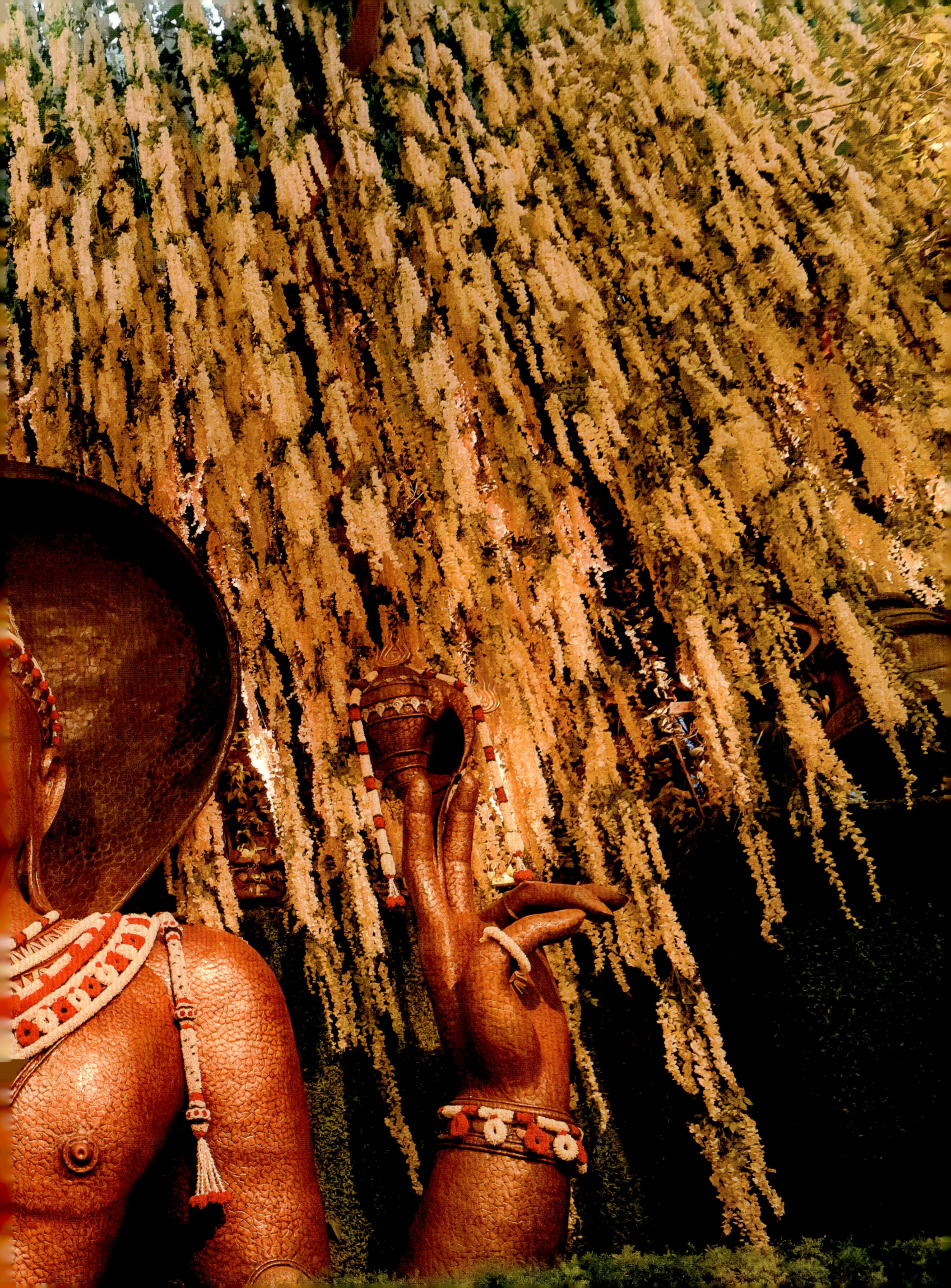

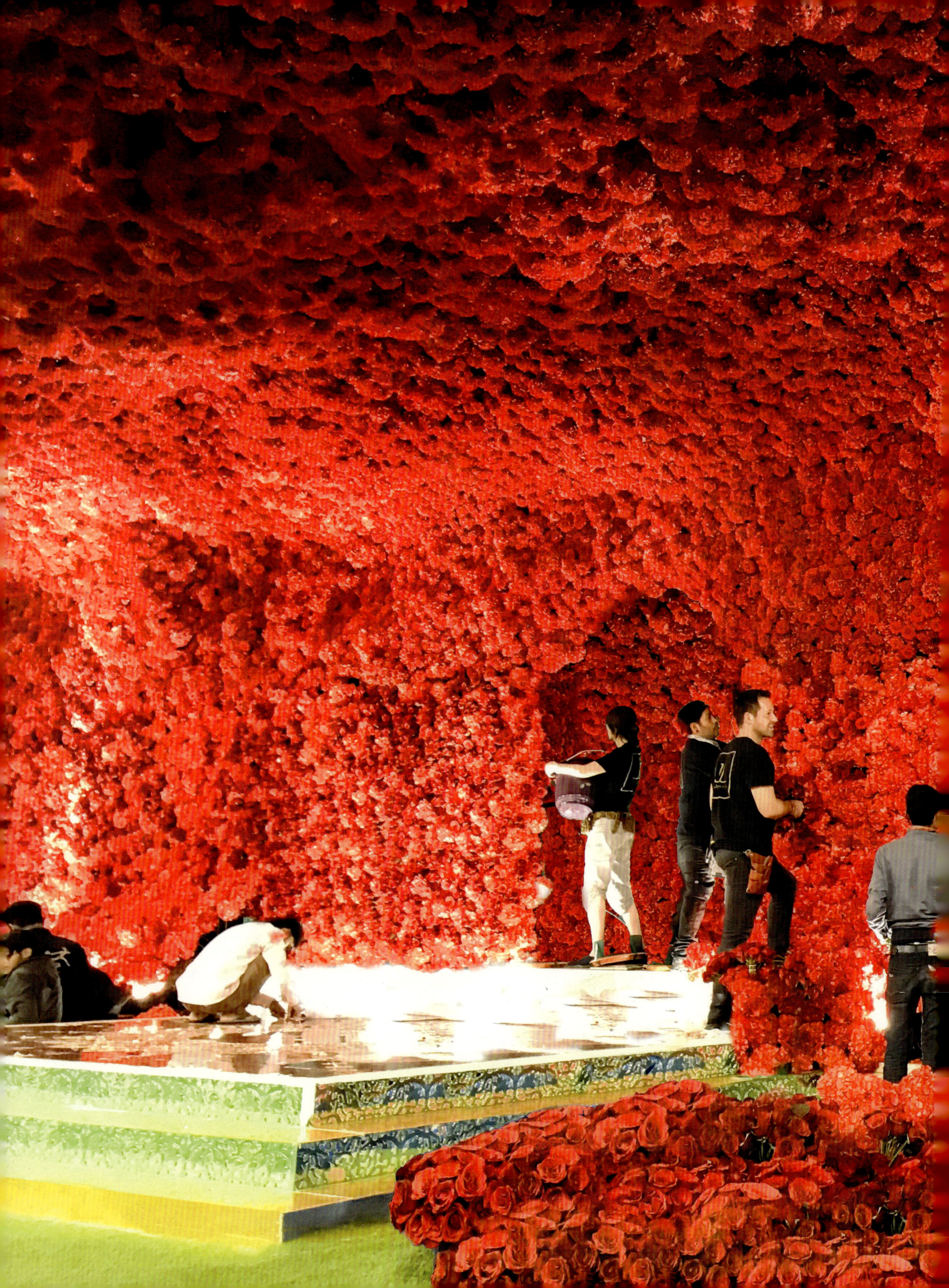

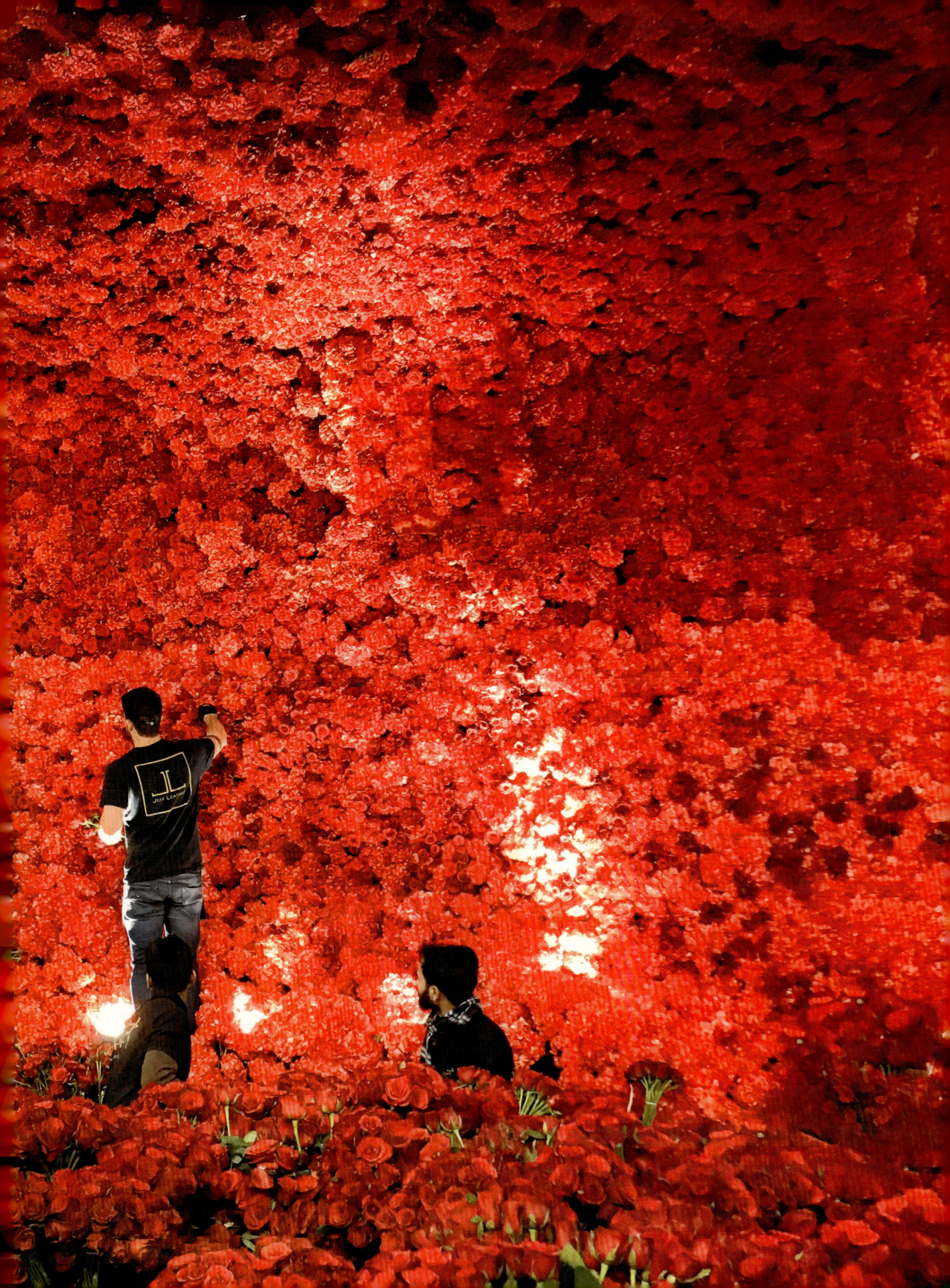

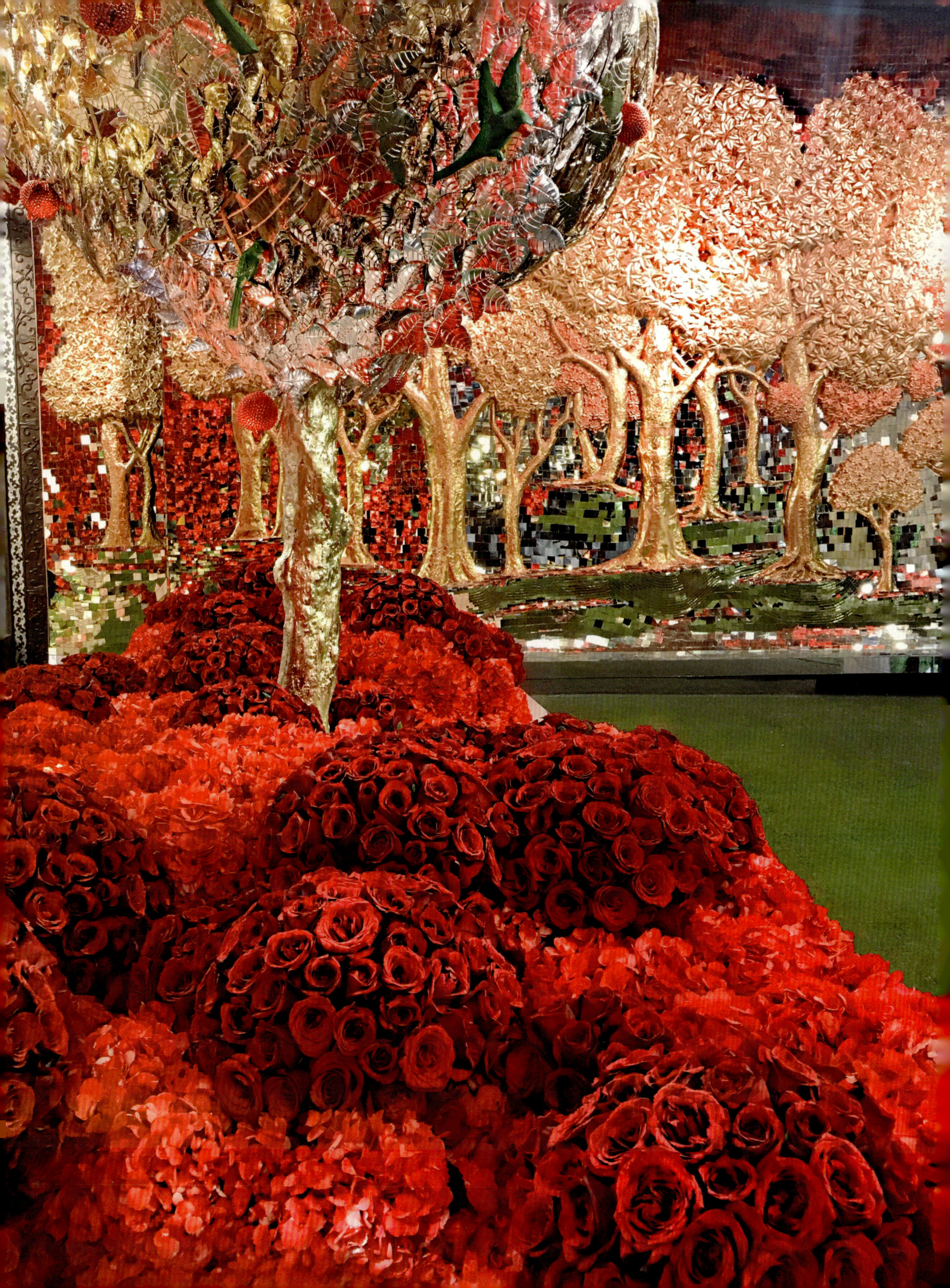

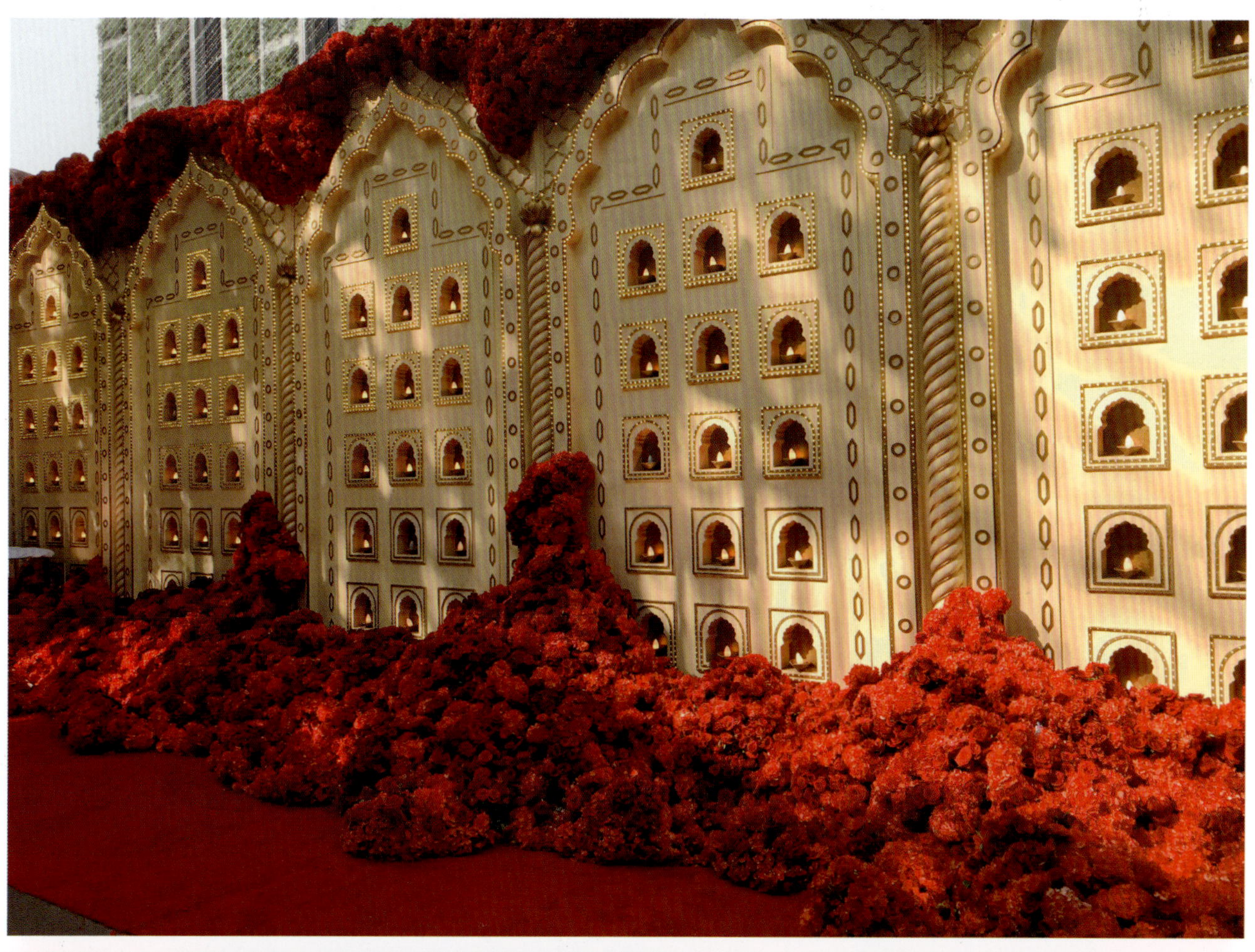

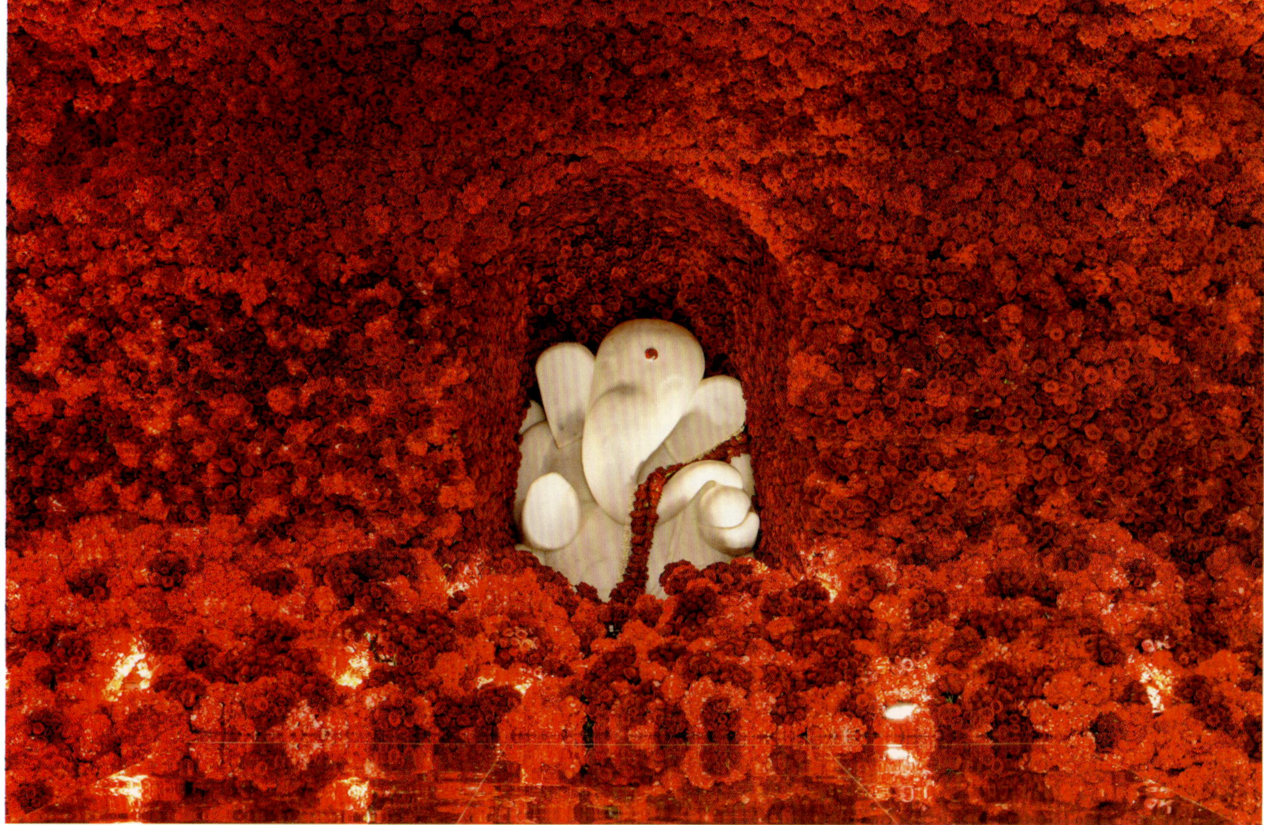

PAGES 118–125: Private Wedding, Mumbai, India. Wisteria, roses, and hydrangeas. PAGES 126–127: Private Wedding, Palm Springs, California. Roses.

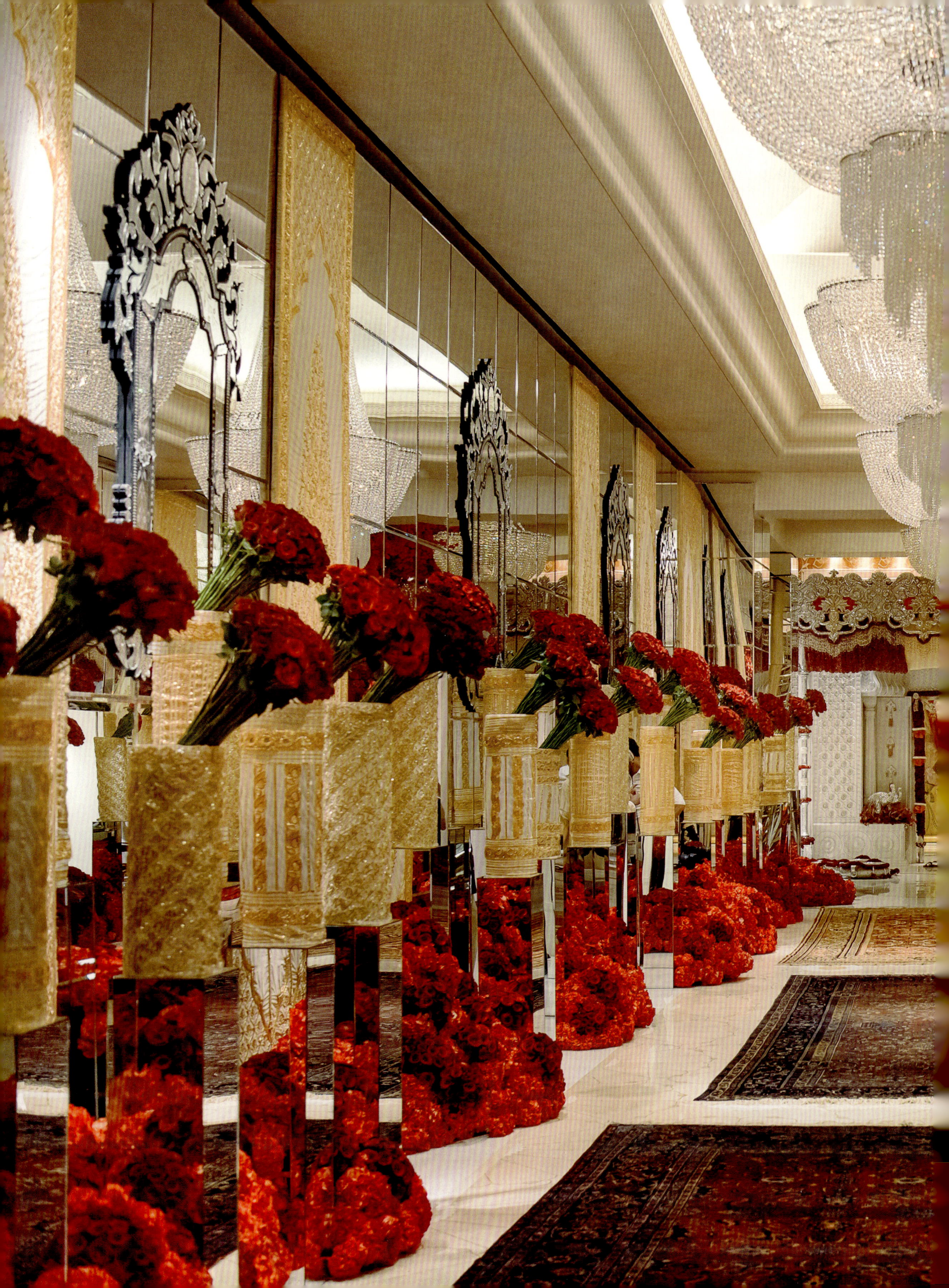

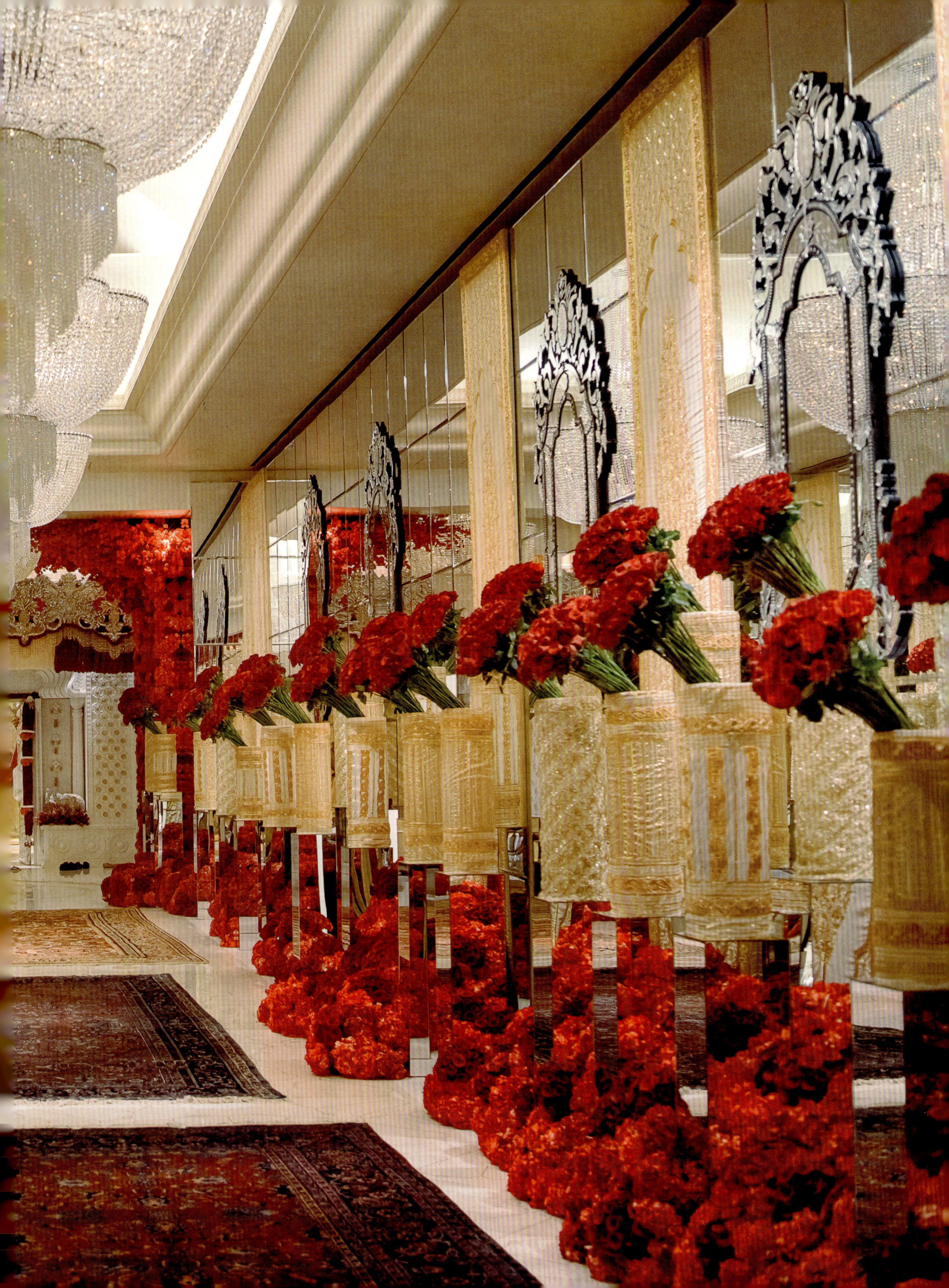

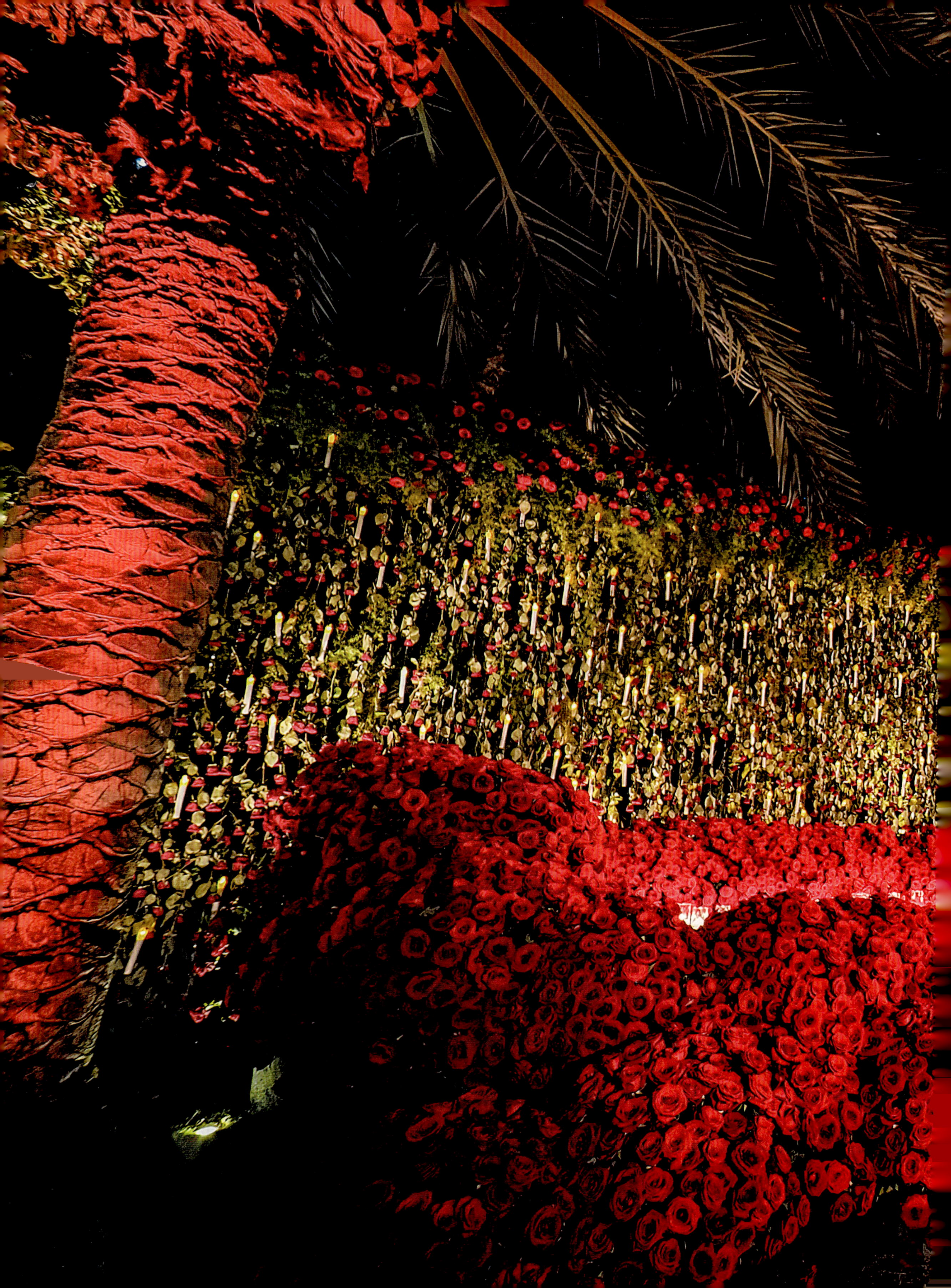

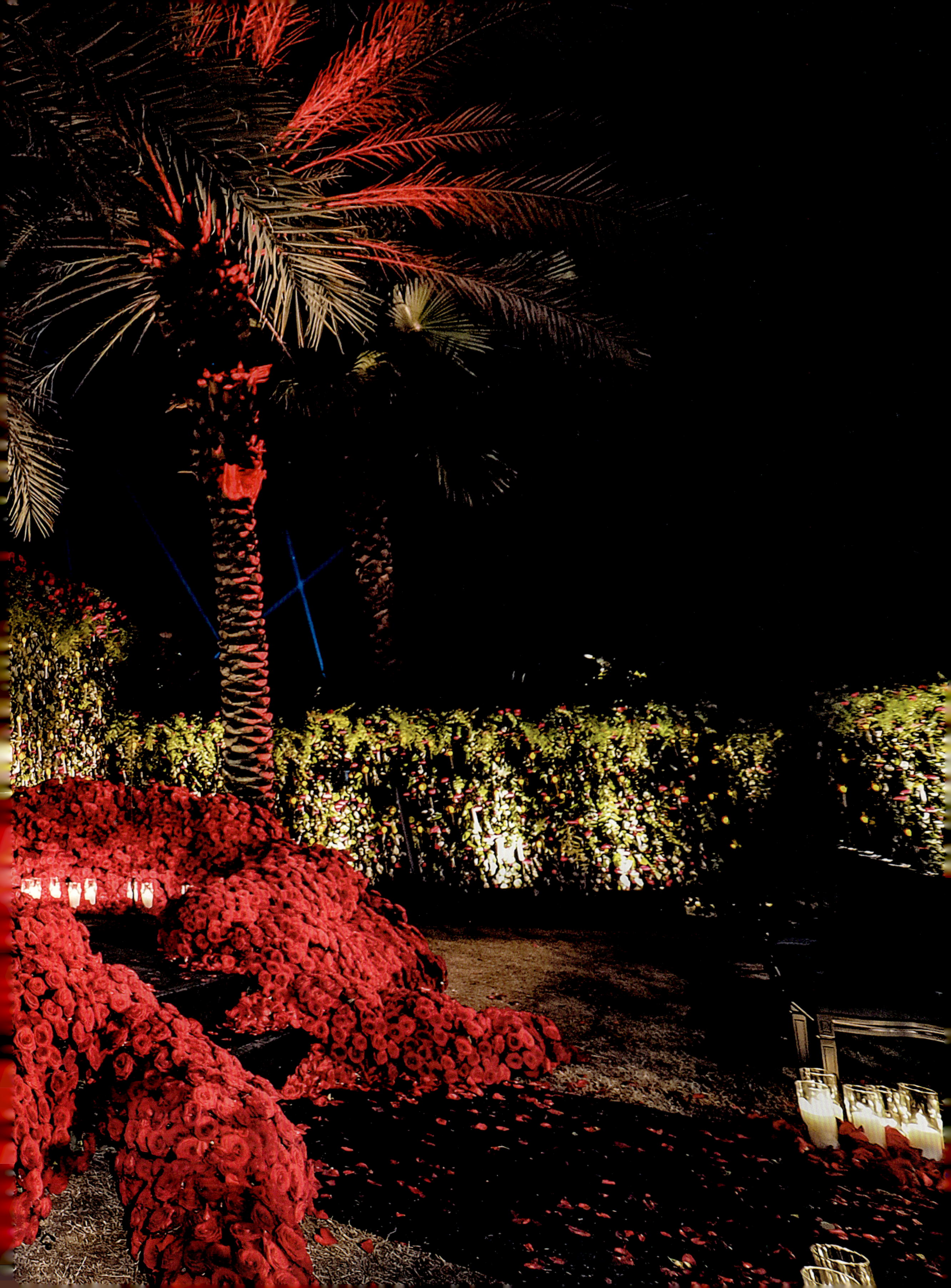

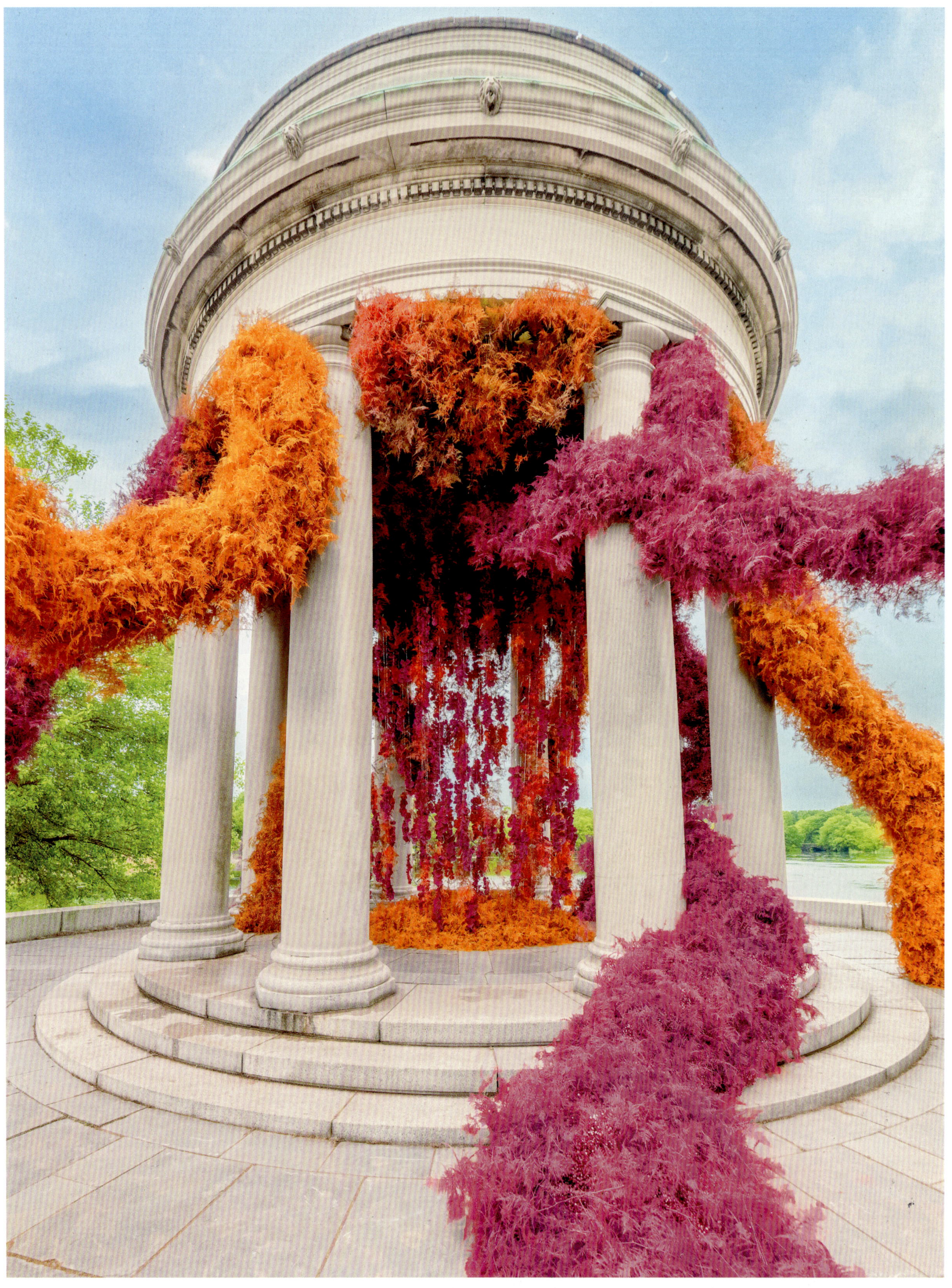

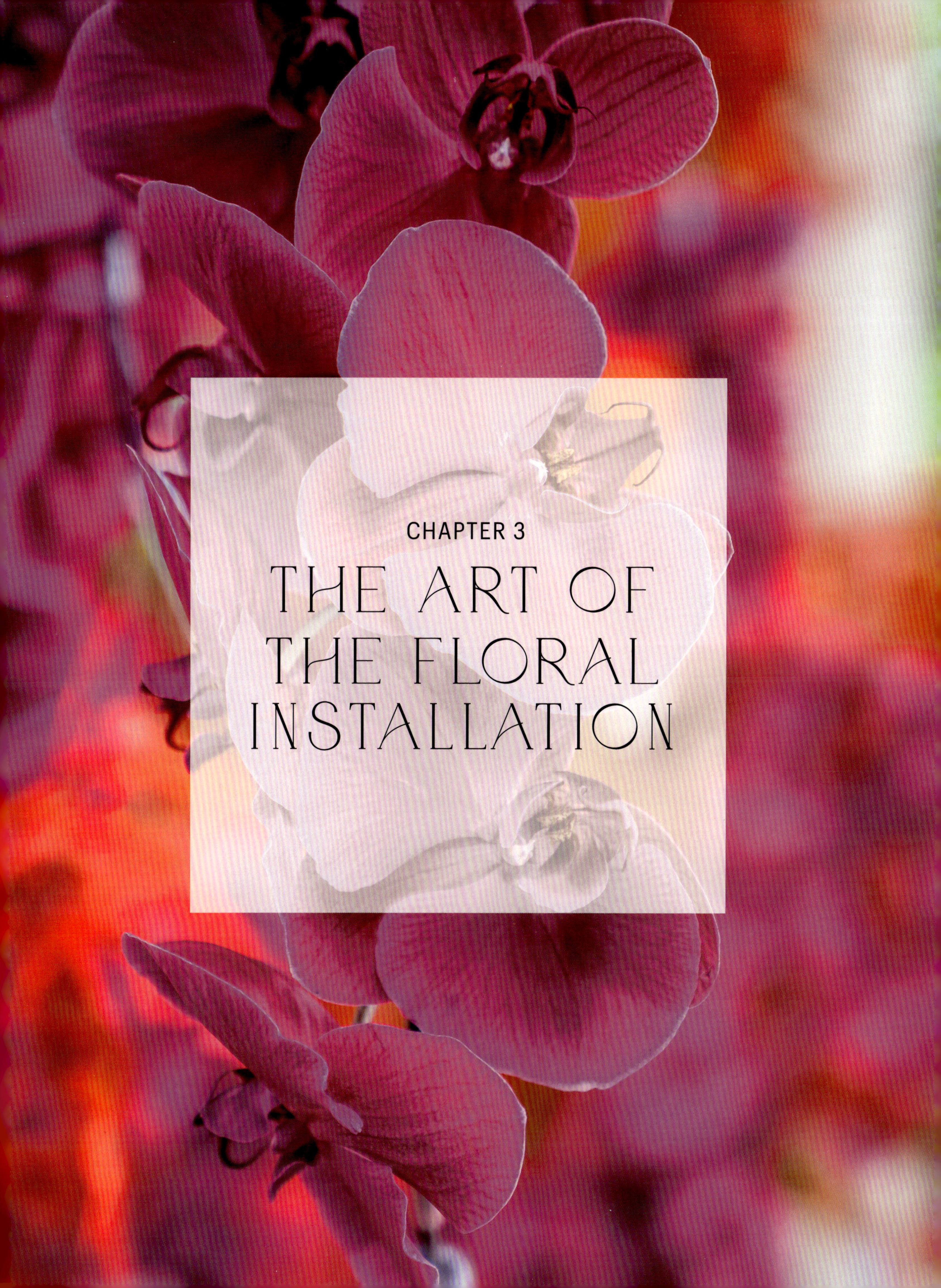
CHAPTER 3

THE ART OF
THE FLORAL
INSTALLATION

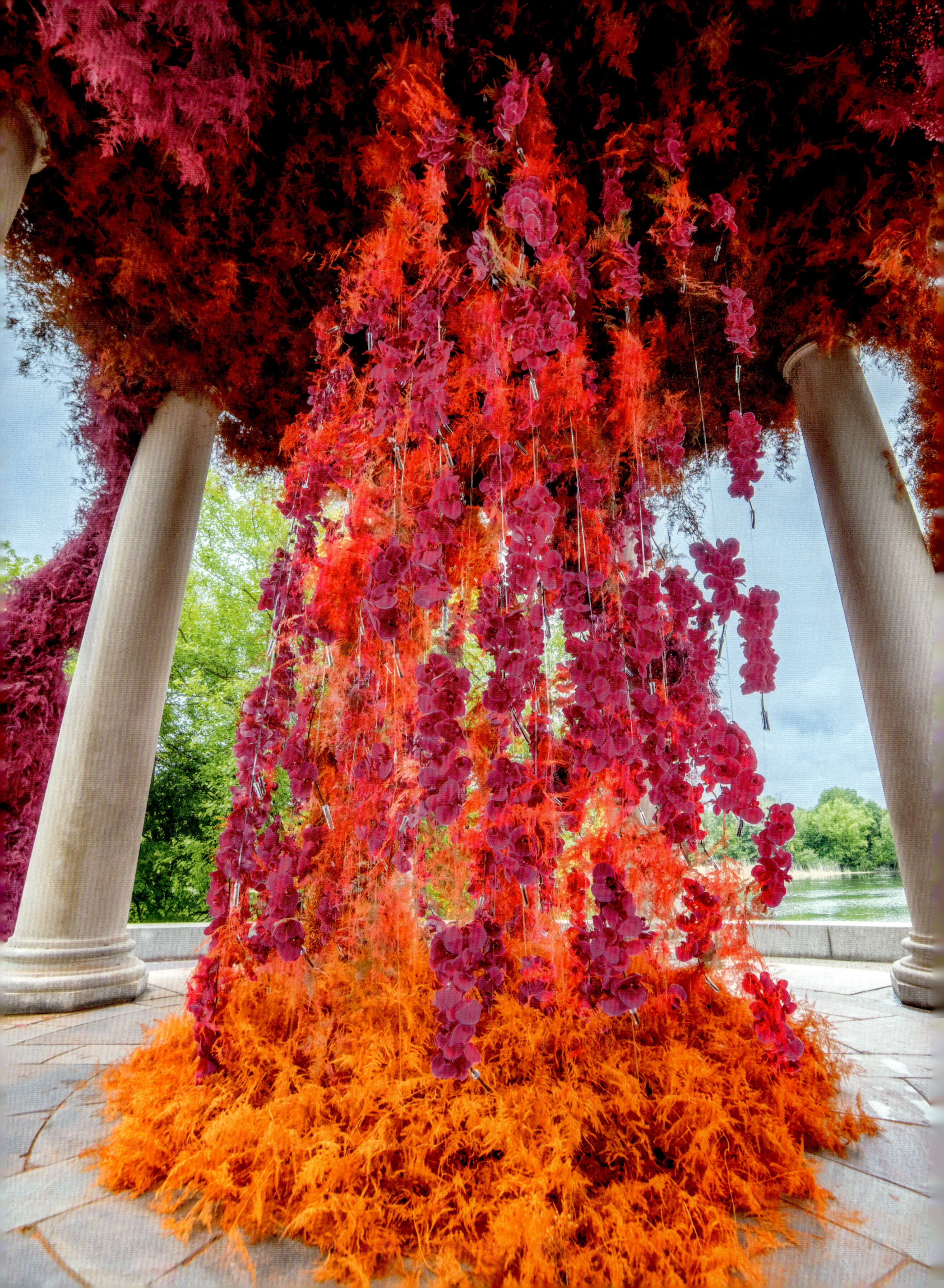

When it comes to installations, my goal is for the attendees to become a part of the immersive experience and participate in the transformation of the installation's space. Therefore, I concentrate on creating pure art, while keeping in mind how viewers will interact with the space. Whether they are built for one month, one week, or one day, installations need to be impactful and unforgettable. They need to *wow*. Through the lens of my artistic expression and via flowers as my medium, my installation art aims to capture a fleeting moment.

As an artist and an art collector myself, I approach each installation as if I were taking part in the immersive process, too. I use magnolias, which are my favorite flower, as a metaphor when thinking about an installation's design. You only have a short amount of time to appreciate a magnolia's beauty once it has been picked, as it fades soon after. I always begin with the installation's theme and then design around it using flowers, mirrors, lighting—or all three—to transform the space and my vision into another realm. For example, I used reflective mirrors in the "Reflective Nature" installation at Intersect by Lexus and utilized roses to transform a simple bus into a rich, textured, purple fantasy. I like the term "pop art" when it comes to my floral installation designs, because I purposely create them to *pop* with *art*.

Collaboration and inclusion are what bring in new ideas and allow for evolution. I am fortunate to have many different people from all around the world be a part of my teams, and I value each one of their creative suggestions. In the same way that flowers have a personal effect on the people who admire them, I think it is as just as important to have an appreciation of the artistic vision of those who work with them.

I also want each viewer to feel as if they are having a curated experience with my flower designs. Each person, and each pair of eyes, is as individual as each flower in the installations. Observing people seeing my designs for the first time and taking photos is one of the most rewarding parts of the process. Whether or not they keep the picture for themselves, post it for the world to see, or send it to a loved one, their response is very special to me. Being able to evoke such a positive response in others through my art gives me joy and is a blessing, even if they can't quite describe it. I want people to always say, "Did you see that *thing* that Jeff Leatham made?"

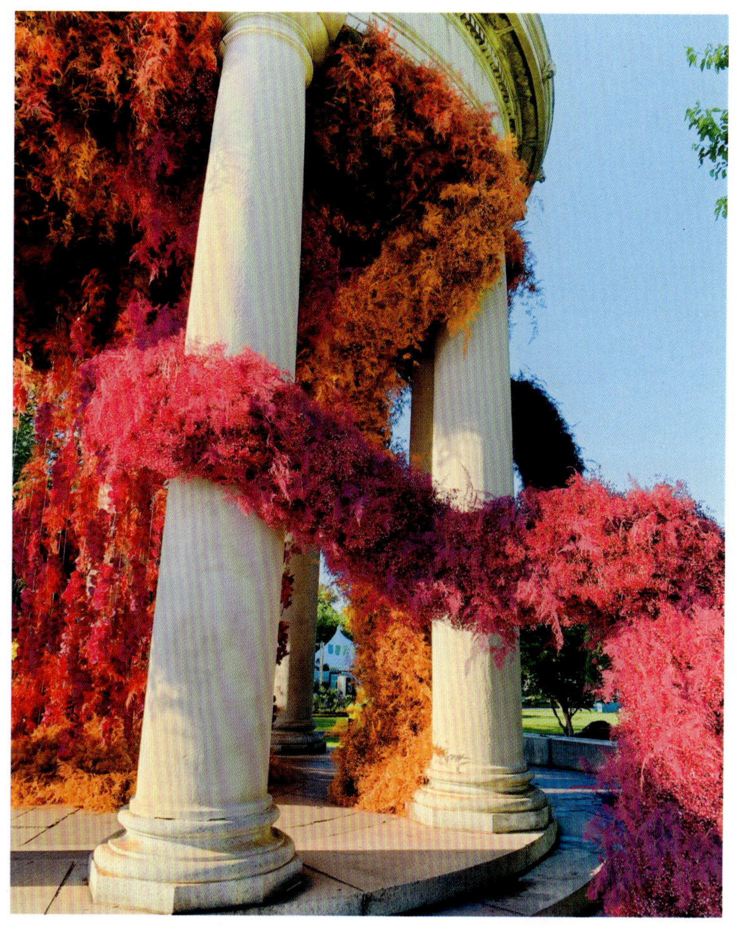

PAGES 130–133: The Main Pavilion of the Franklin Delano Roosevelt Park for the Philadelphia Flower Show. Dyed plumosa and orchids.

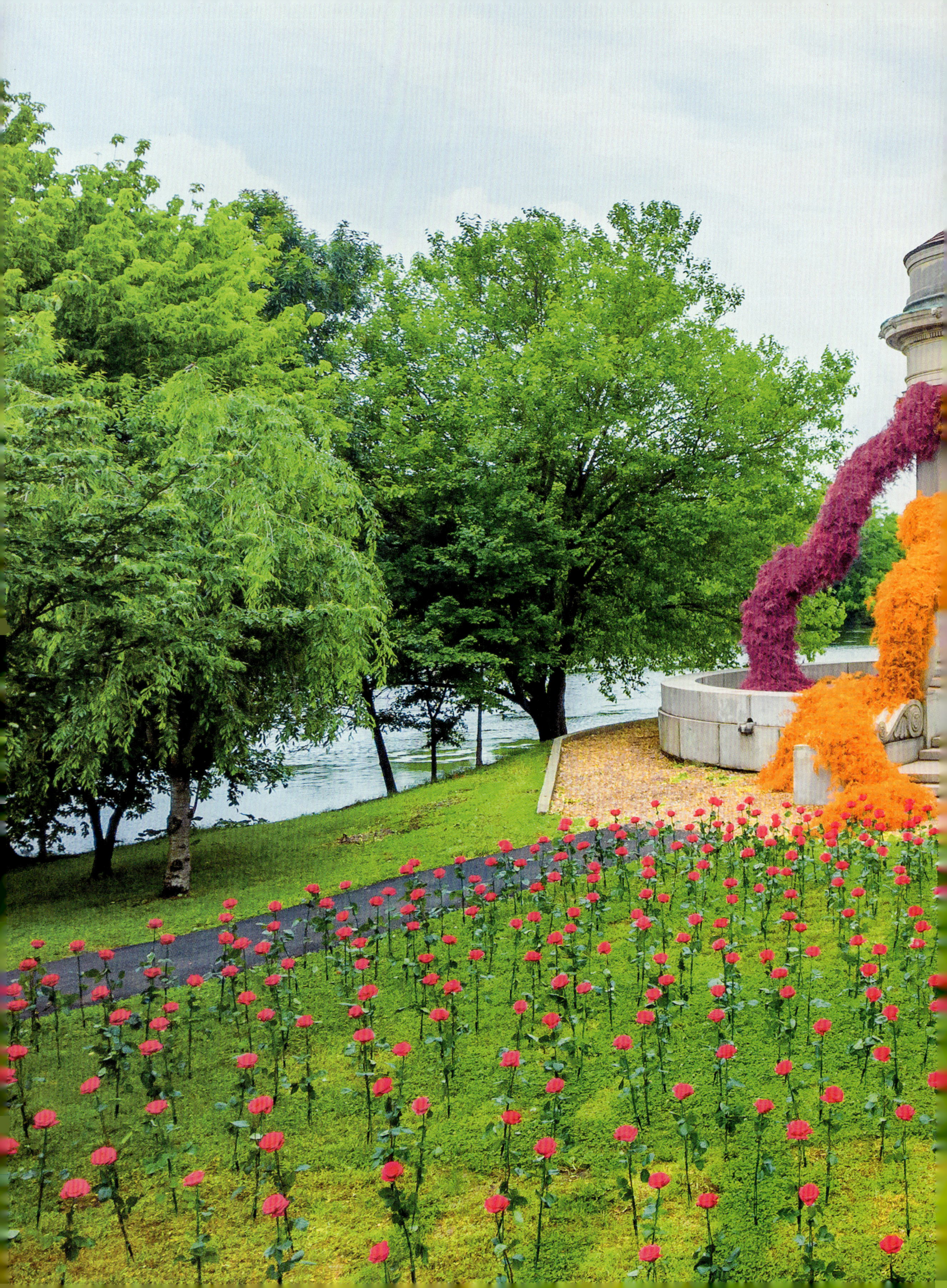

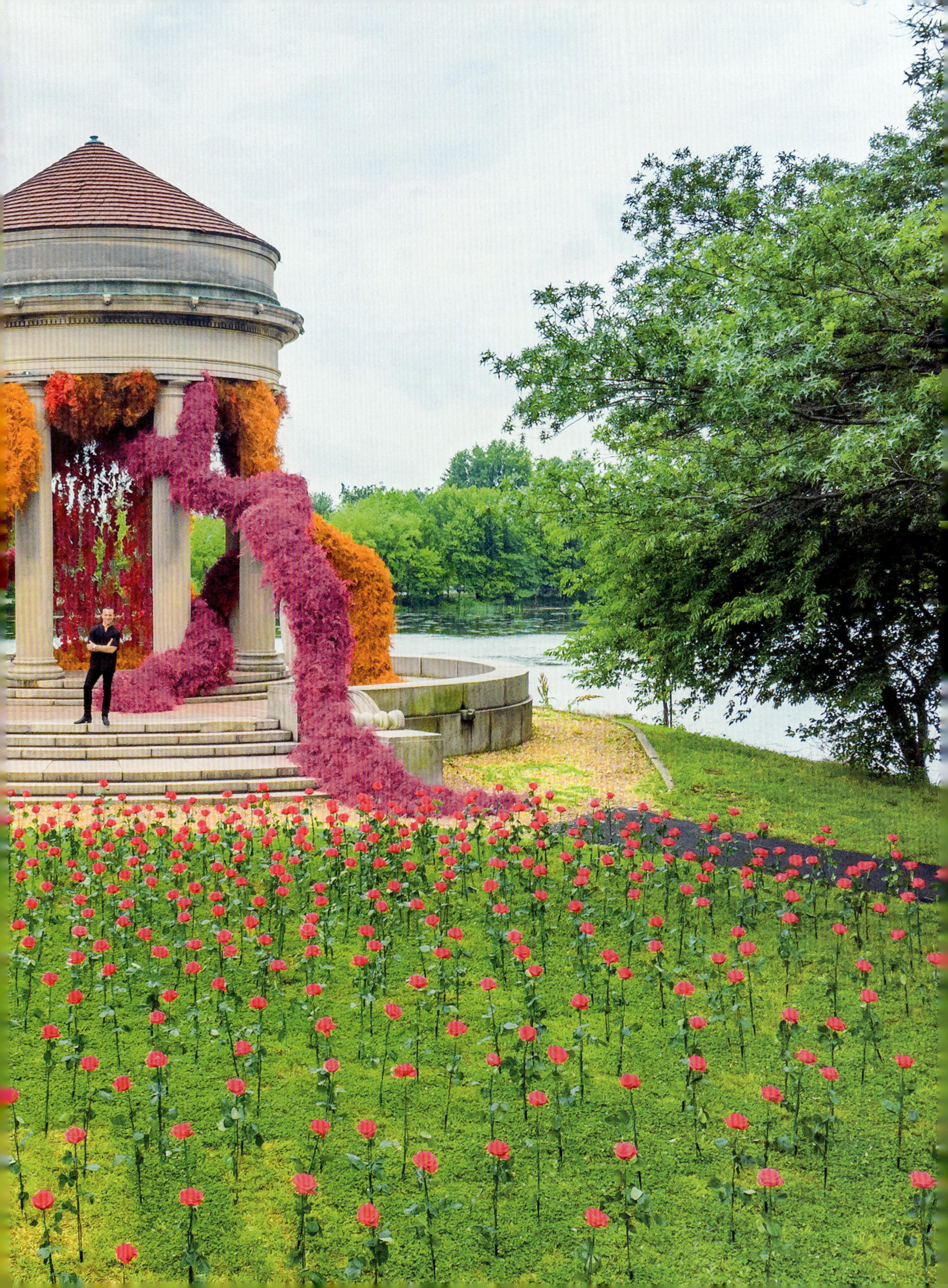

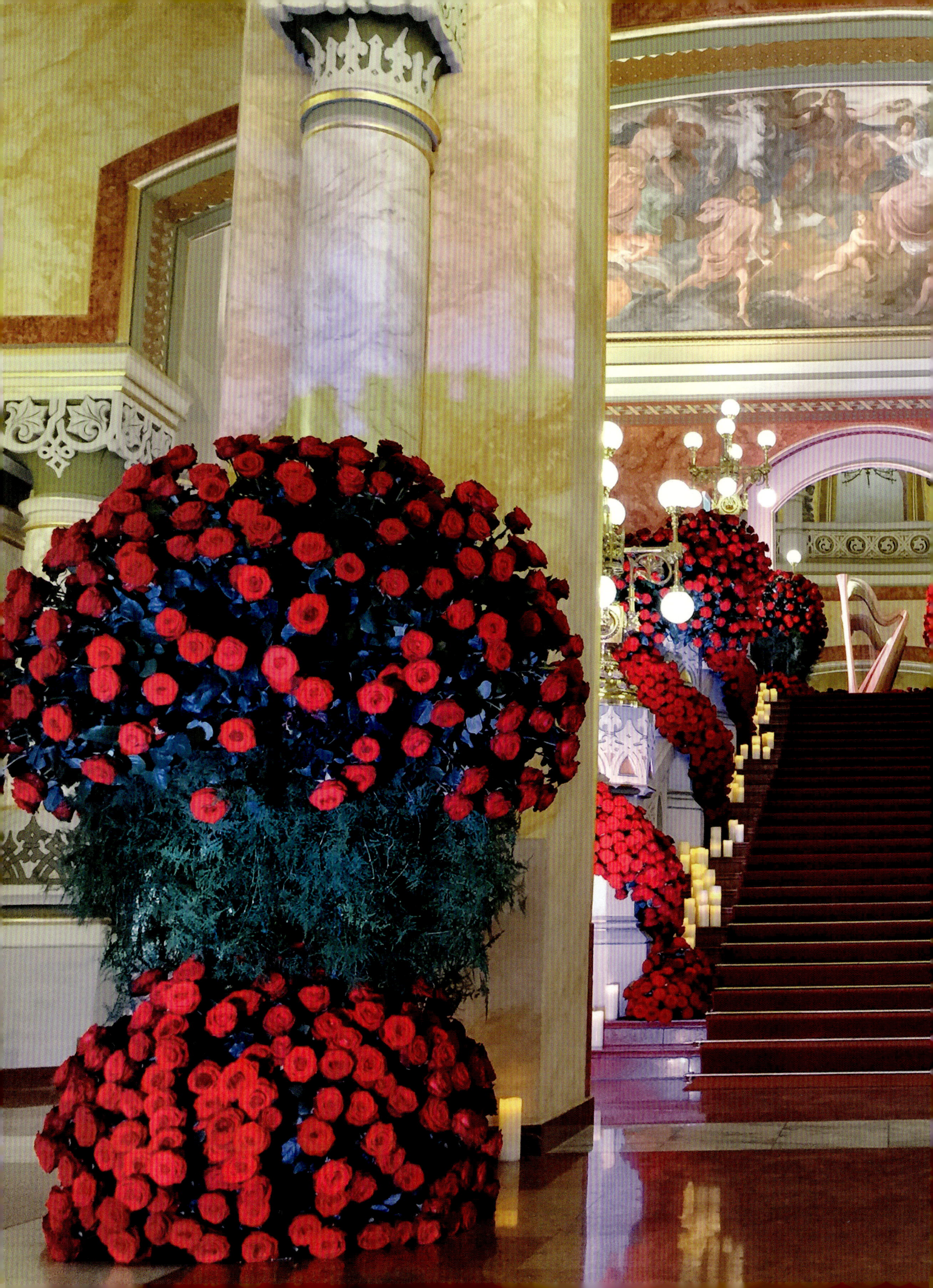

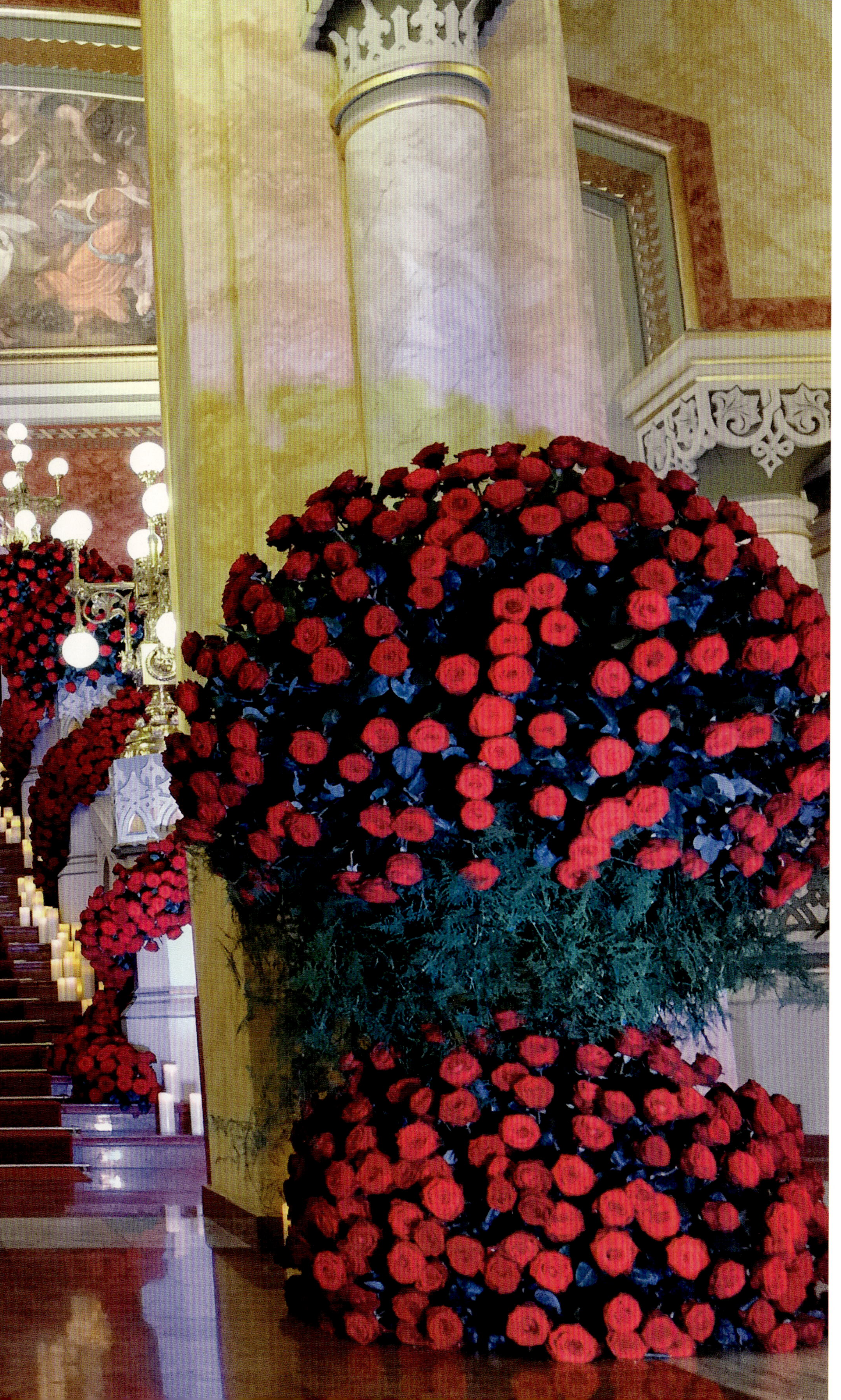

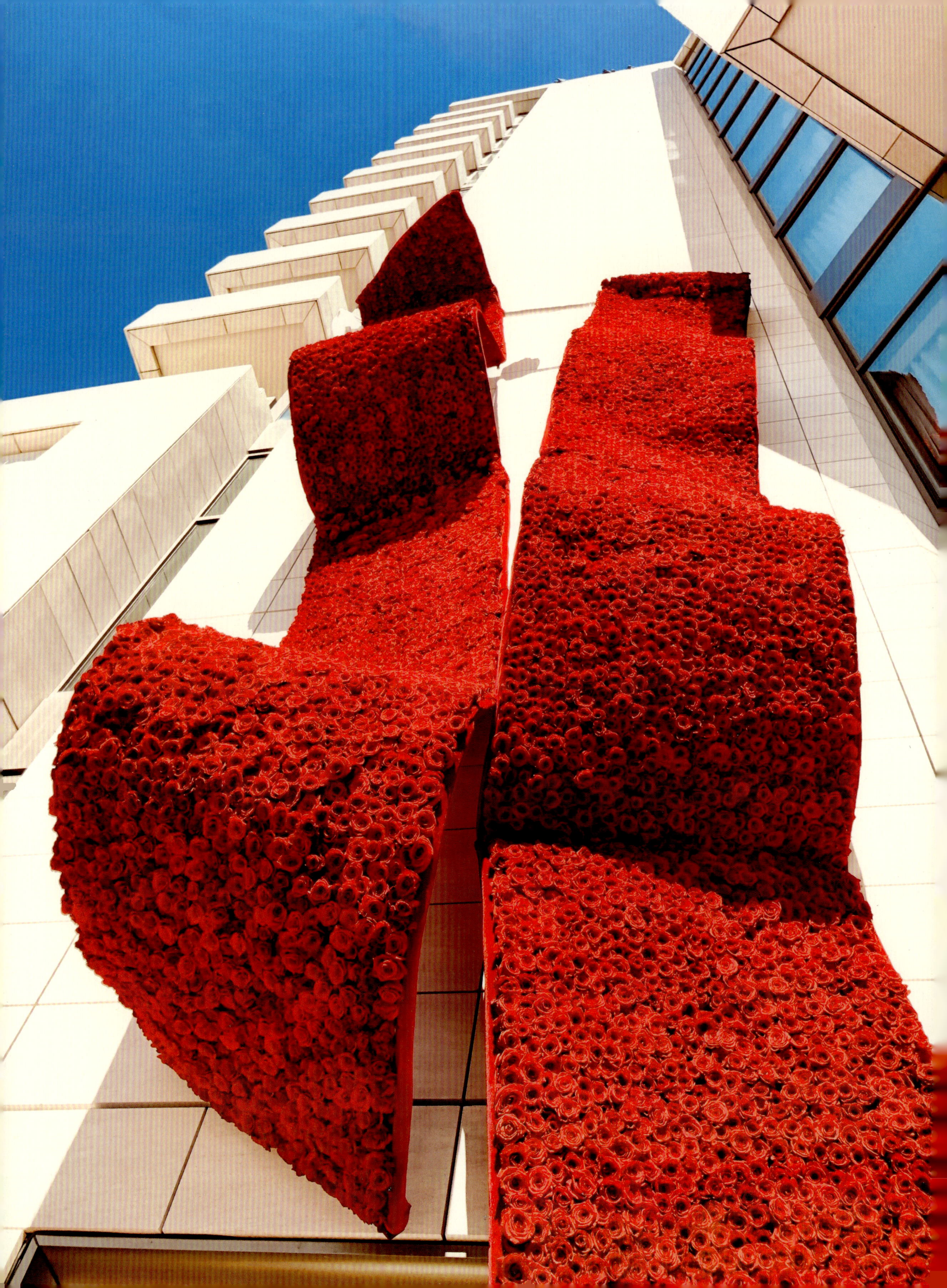

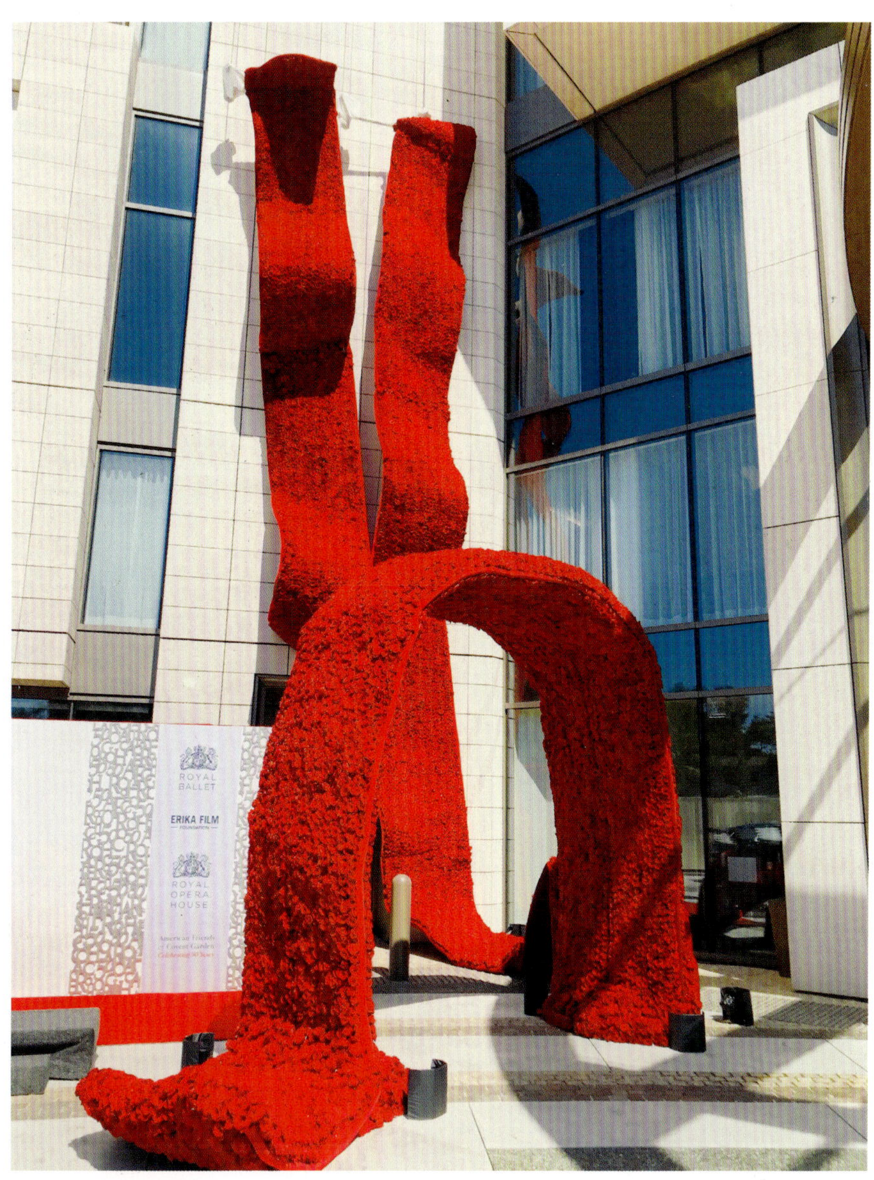

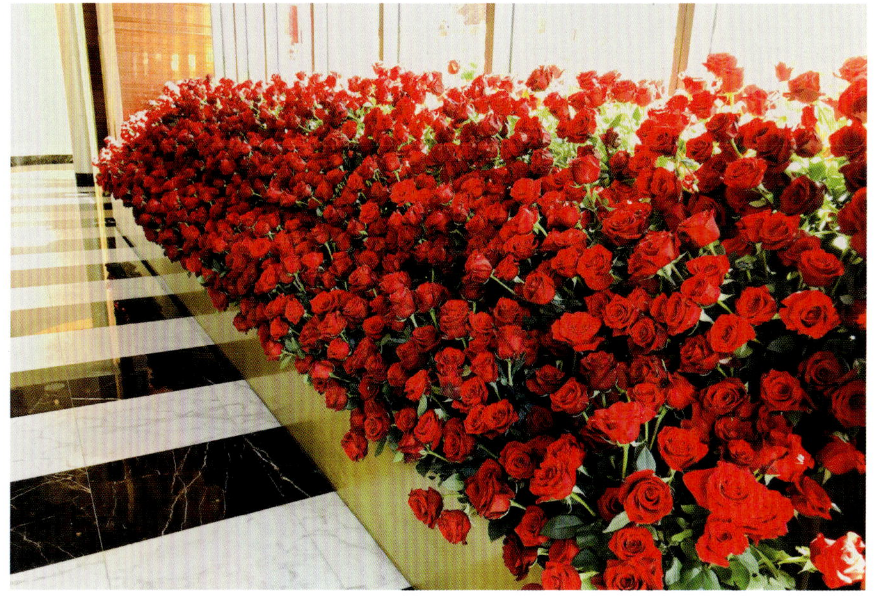

PREVIOUS: Hungarian State Opera House Lobby, Budapest, Hungary. Roses. OPPOSITE AND RIGHT: Waldorf Astoria Beverly Hills, Private Event for The Royal Ballet. Roses.

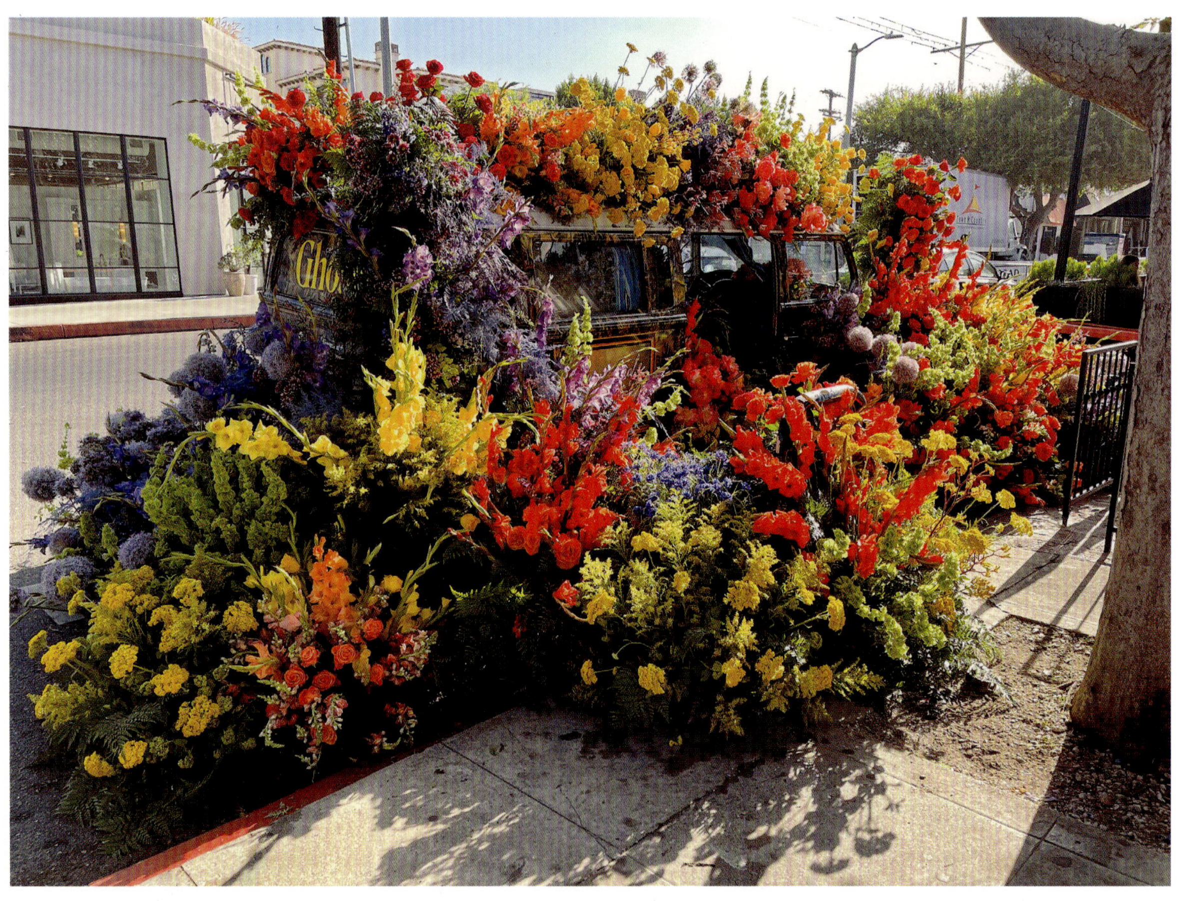

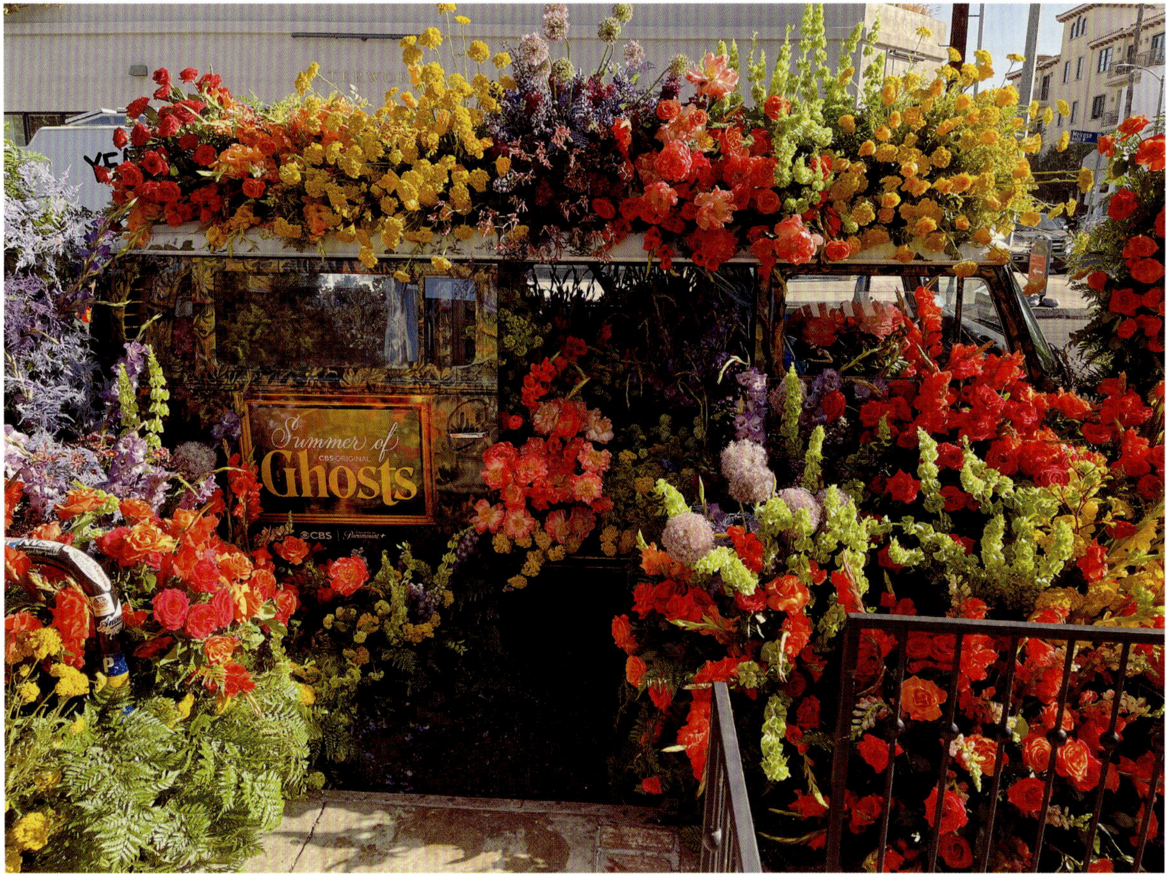

Private Event, Los Angeles. A mix of gladiolas, roses, peonies, yarrow, delphinium, snapdragons, mums, bells of Ireland, solidaster, alliums, blue cornflowers, and plumosa. FOLLOWING: Private Event, Los Angeles. Sunflowers, delphinium, variety of roses, magnolia branches, and kangaroo paws.

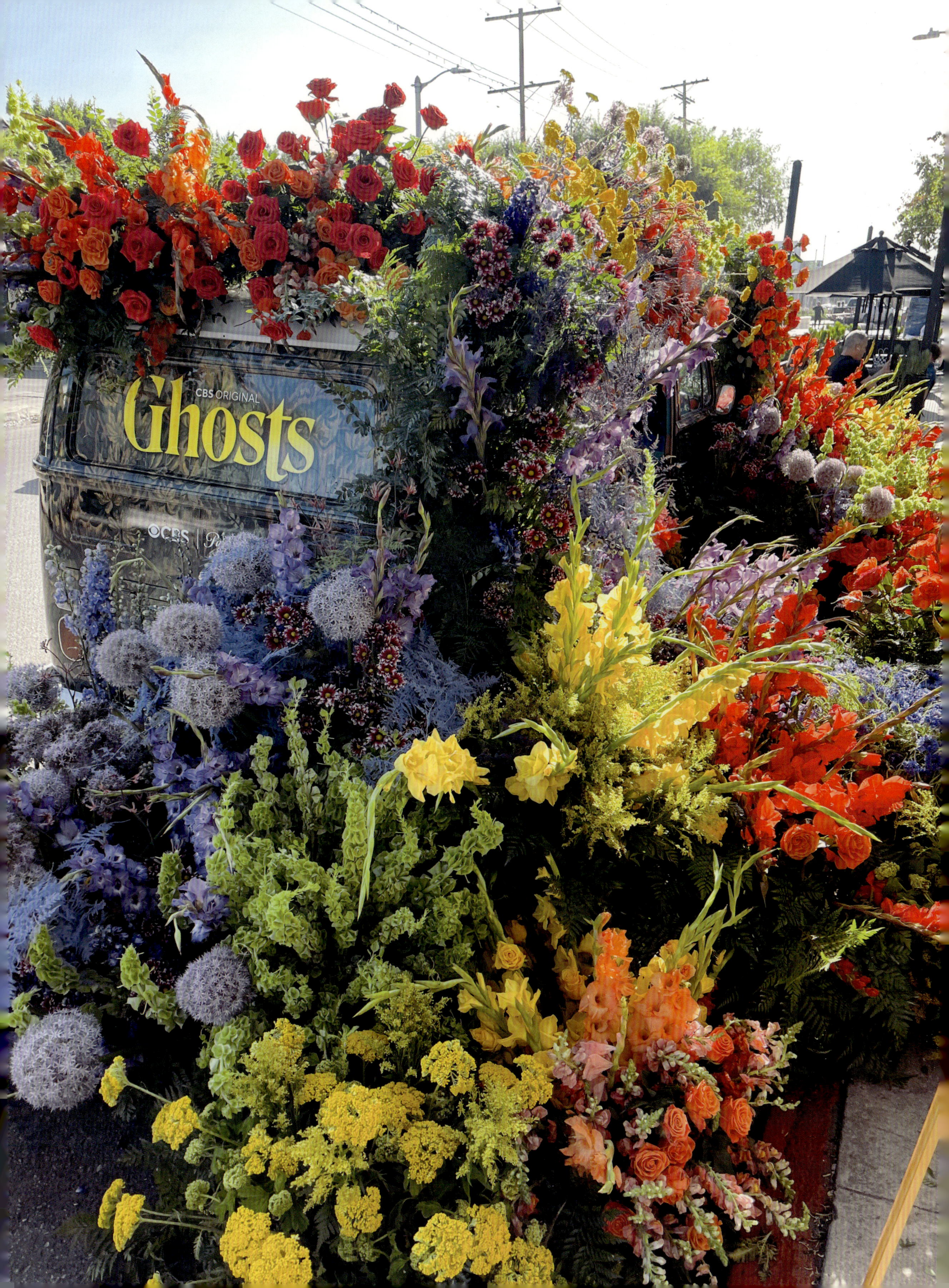
CBS ORIGINAL
Ghosts

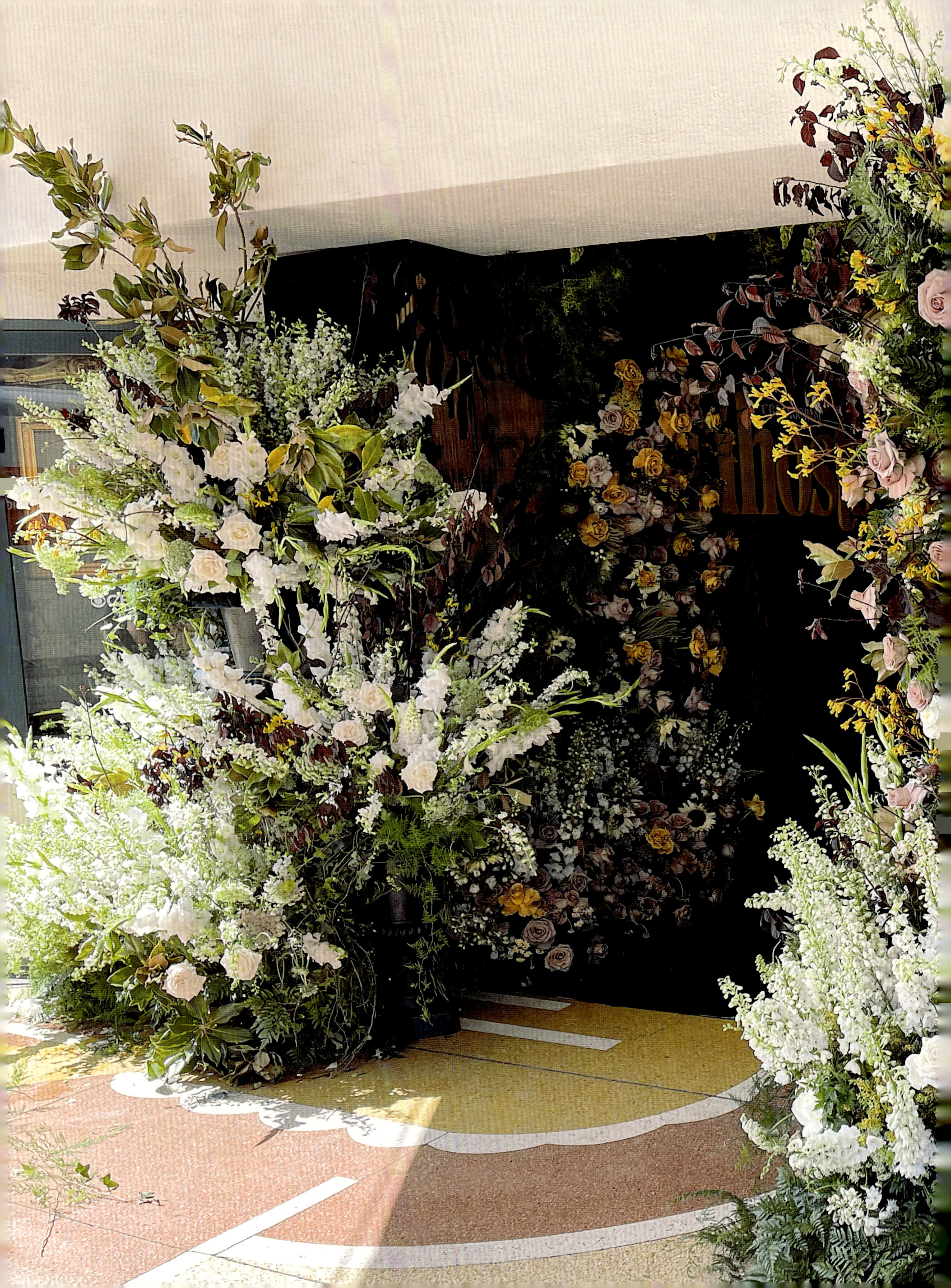

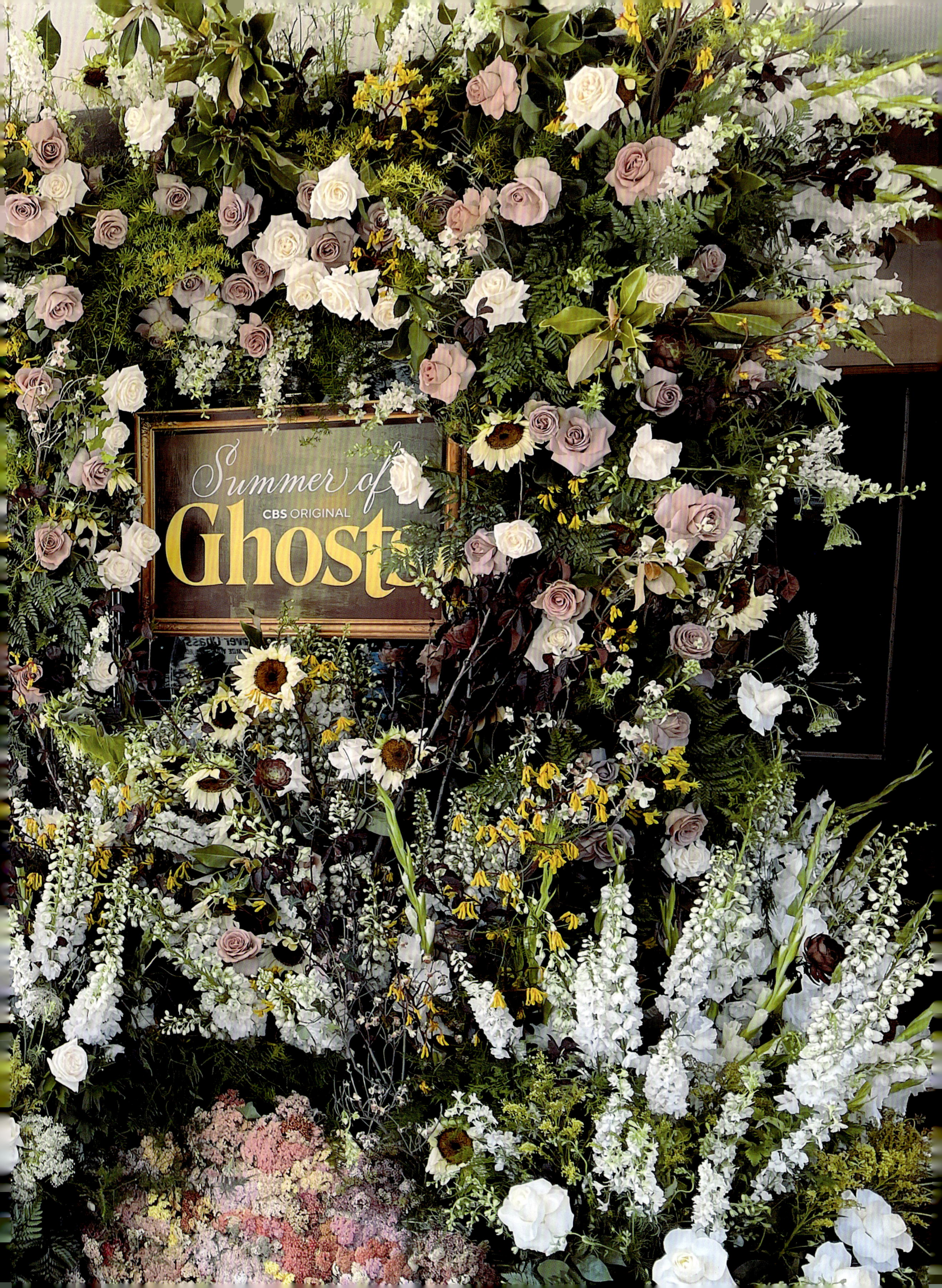

Summer of
CBS ORIGINAL
Ghosts

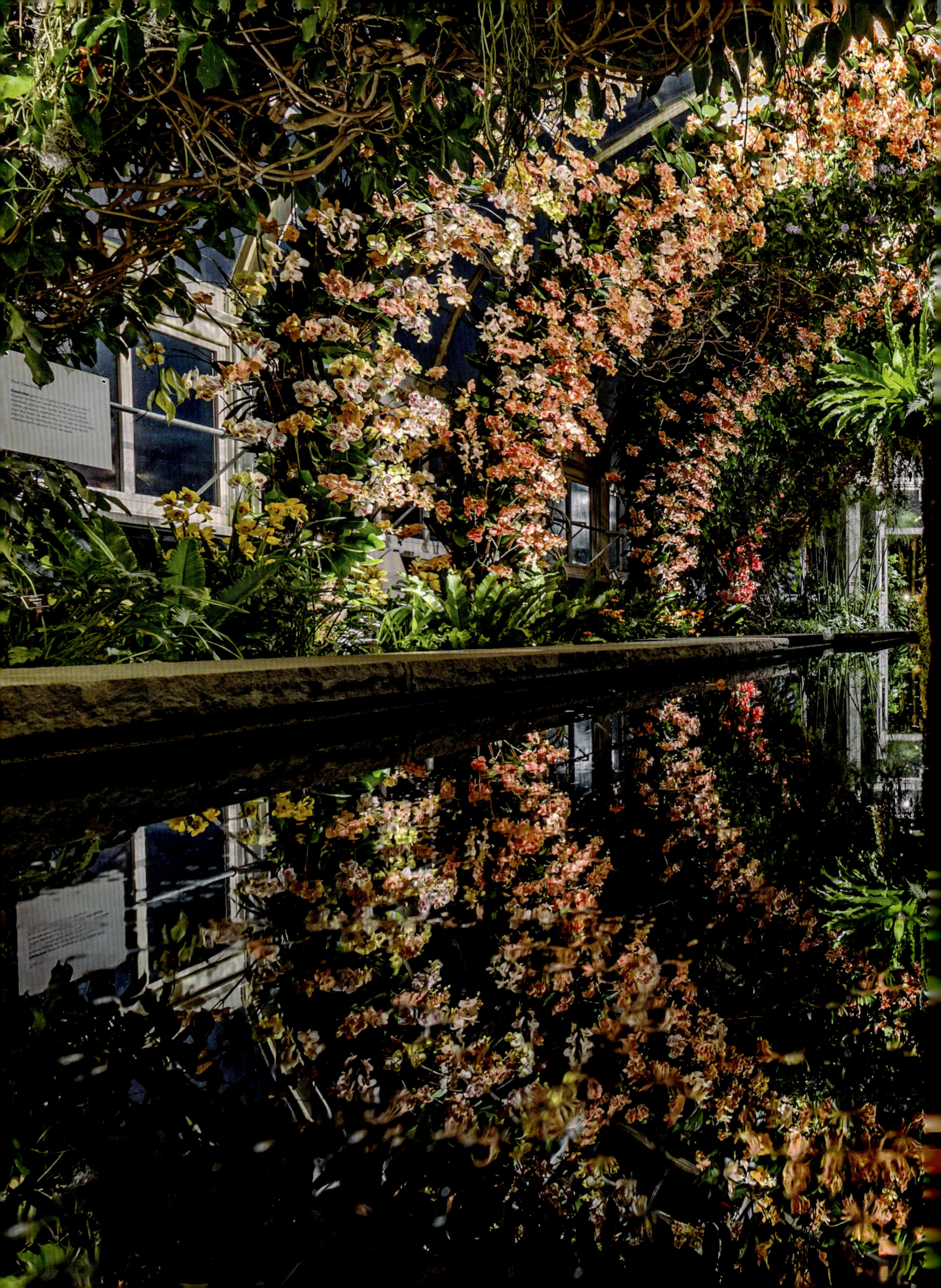

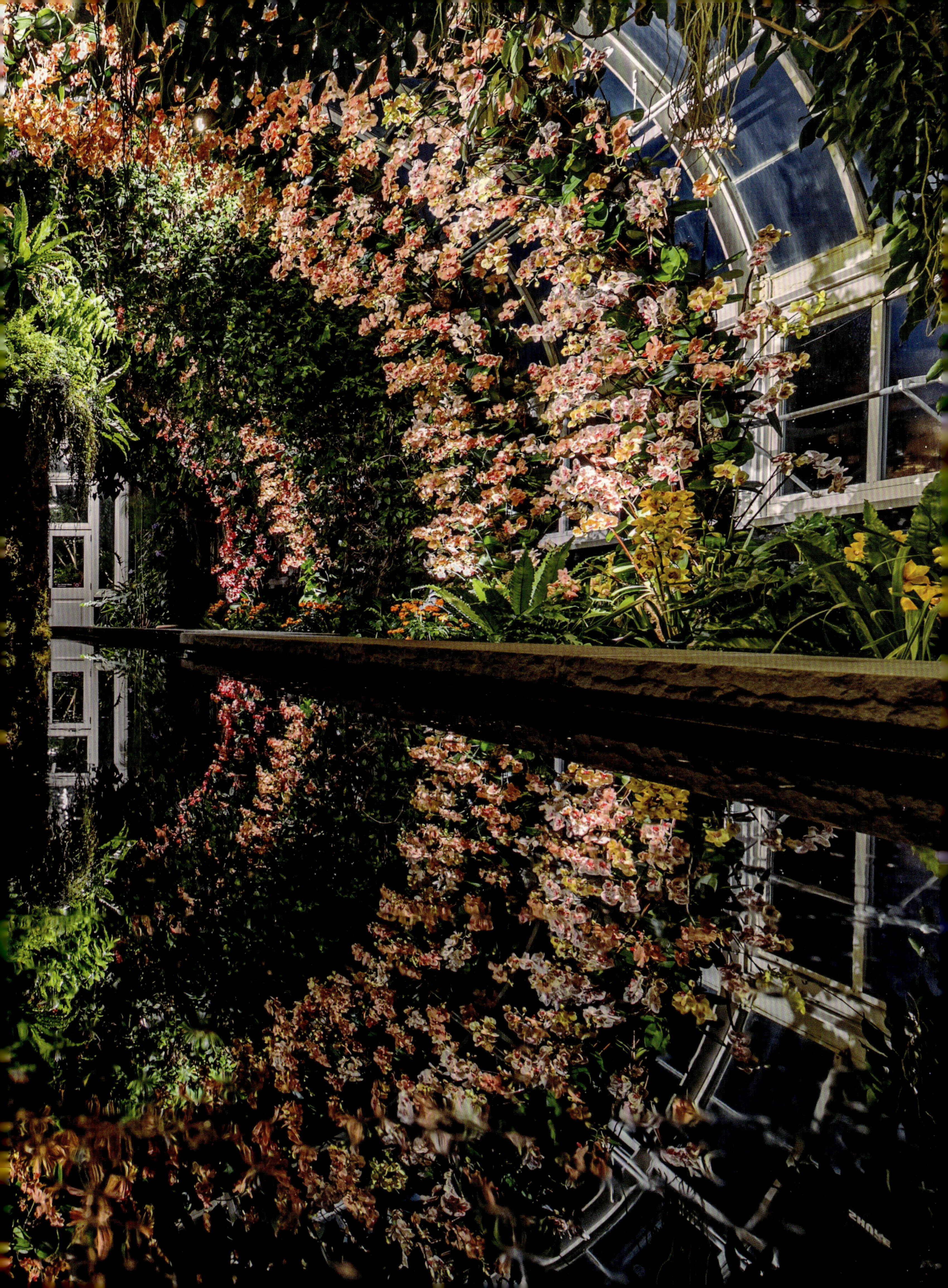

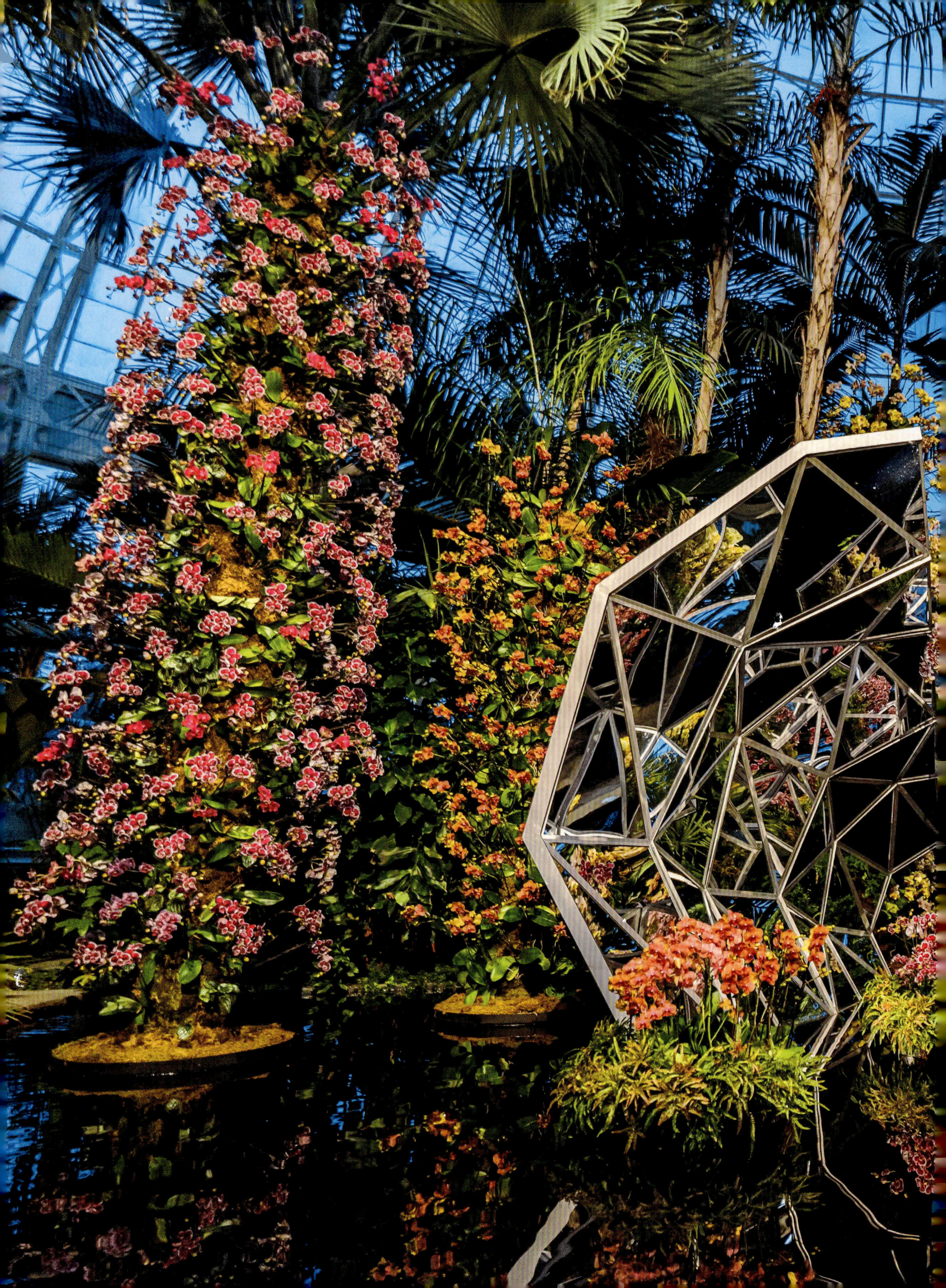

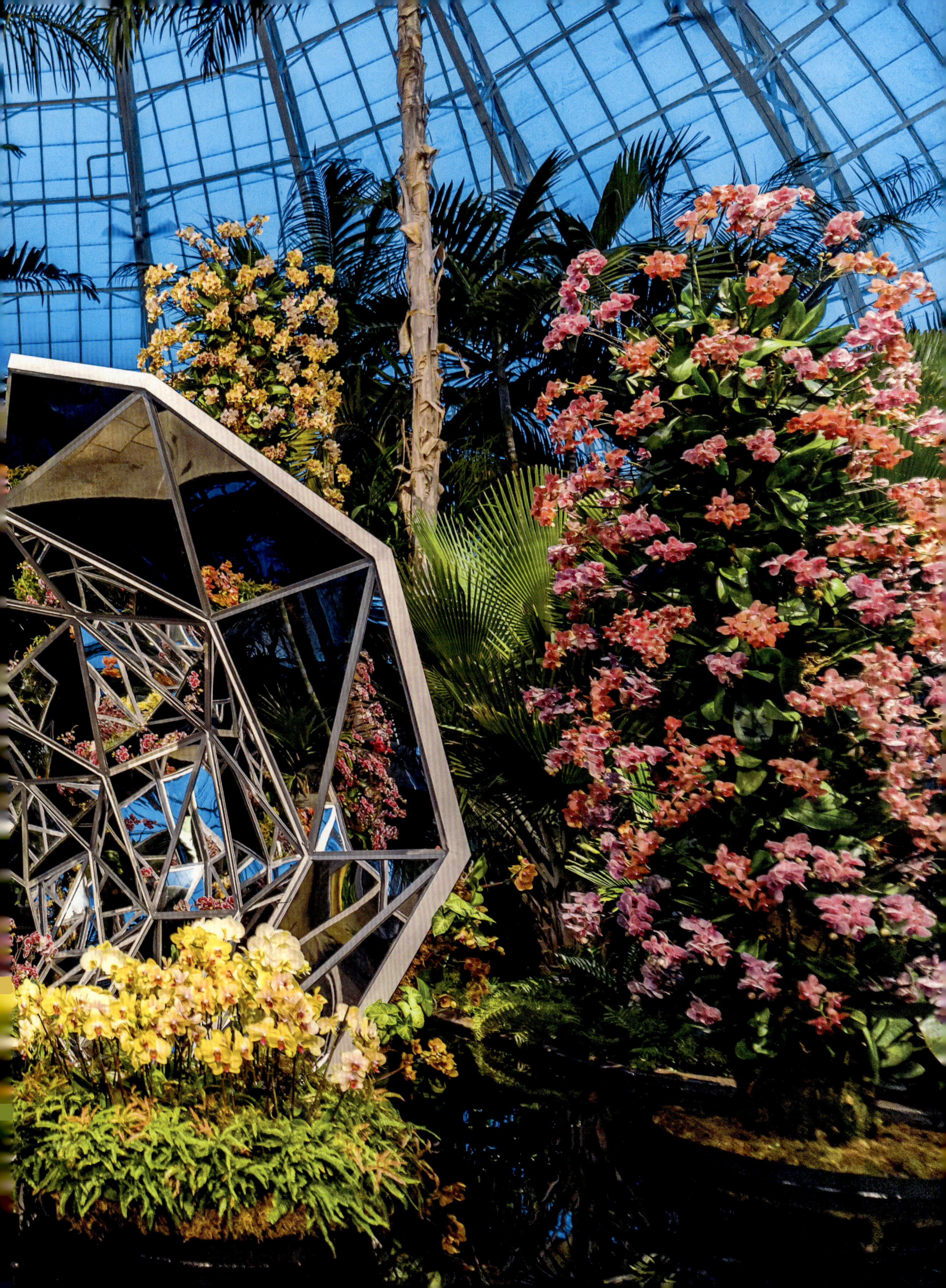

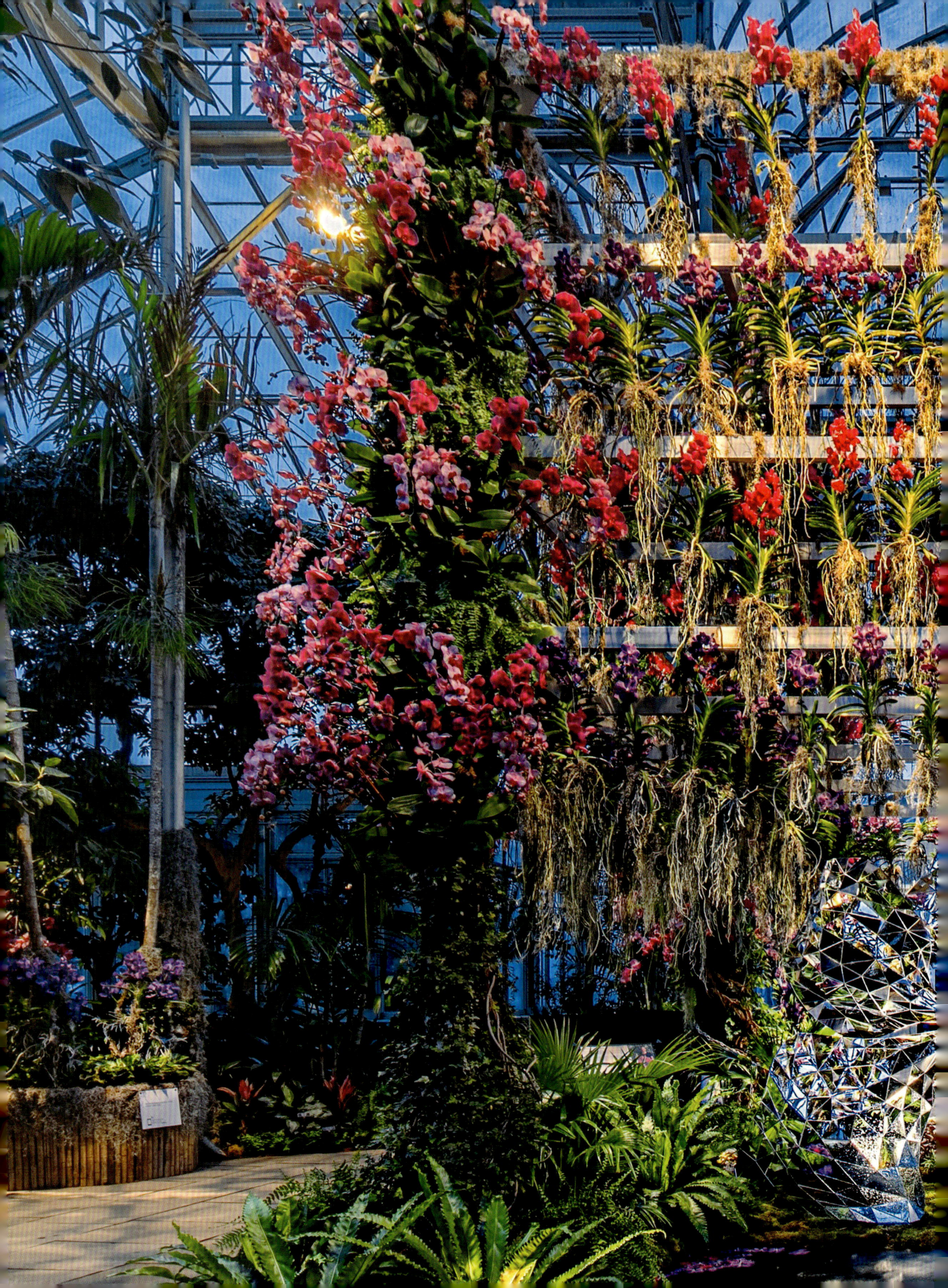

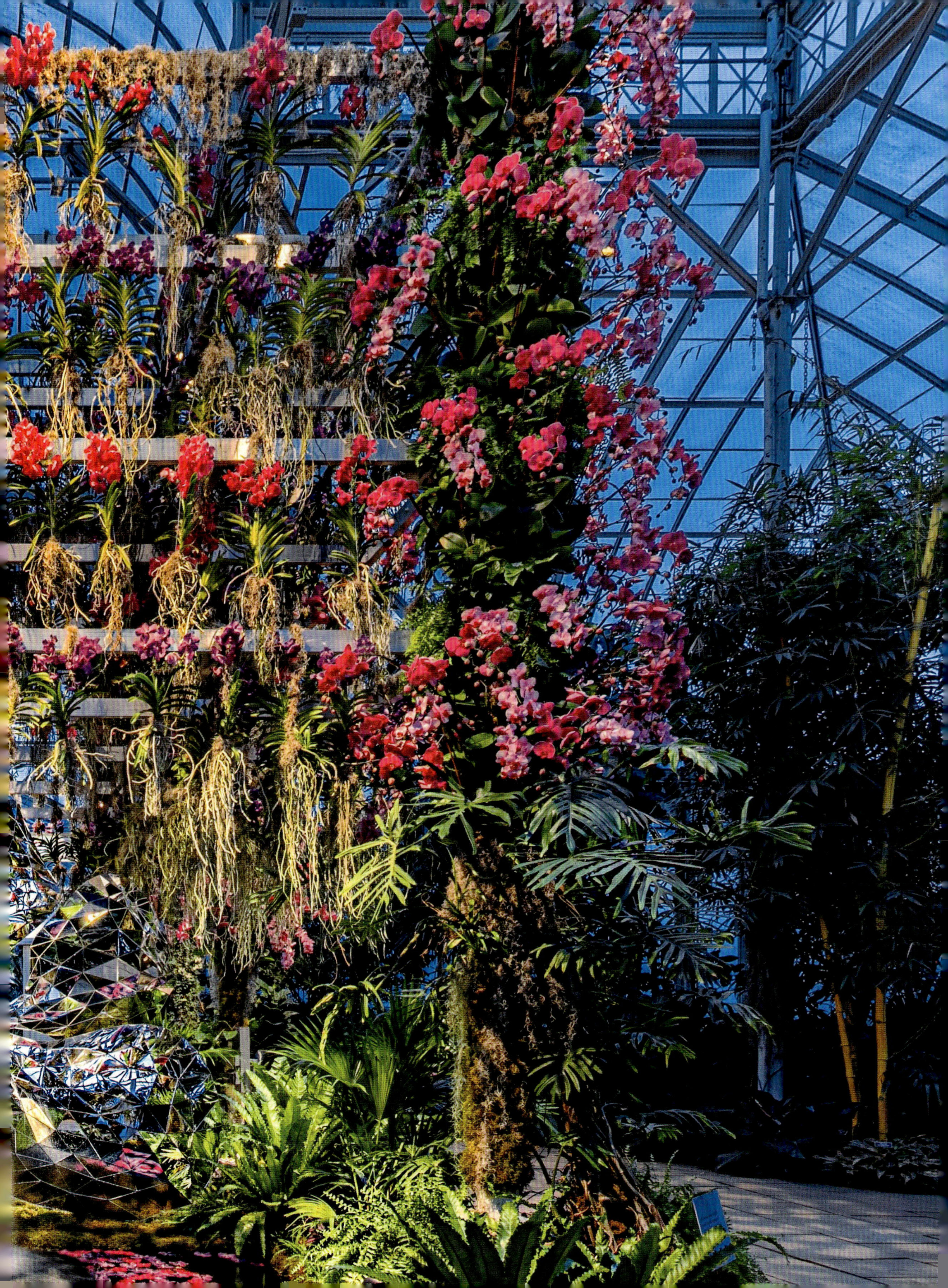

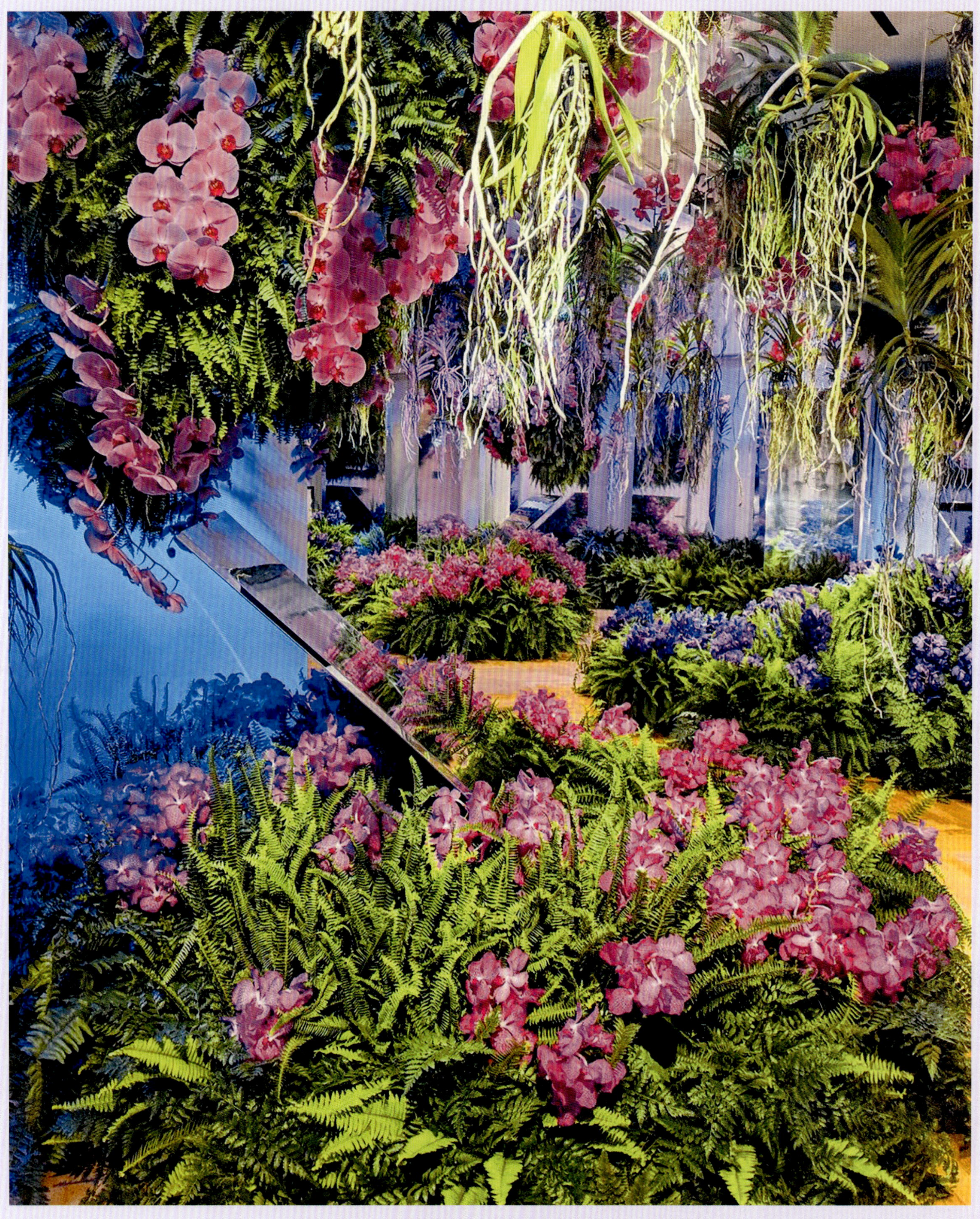

PAGES 142–147: *The Orchid Show* at The New York Botanical Garden, New York City. A variety of vanda orchids. ABOVE AND OPPOSITE: "Reflective Nature" Installation at Intersect by Lexus, New York City. A celebration of orchids. FOLLOWING: Private St-Germain Event at The Houdini Estate, Los Angeles. Eremurus, delphinium, roses, and liatris.

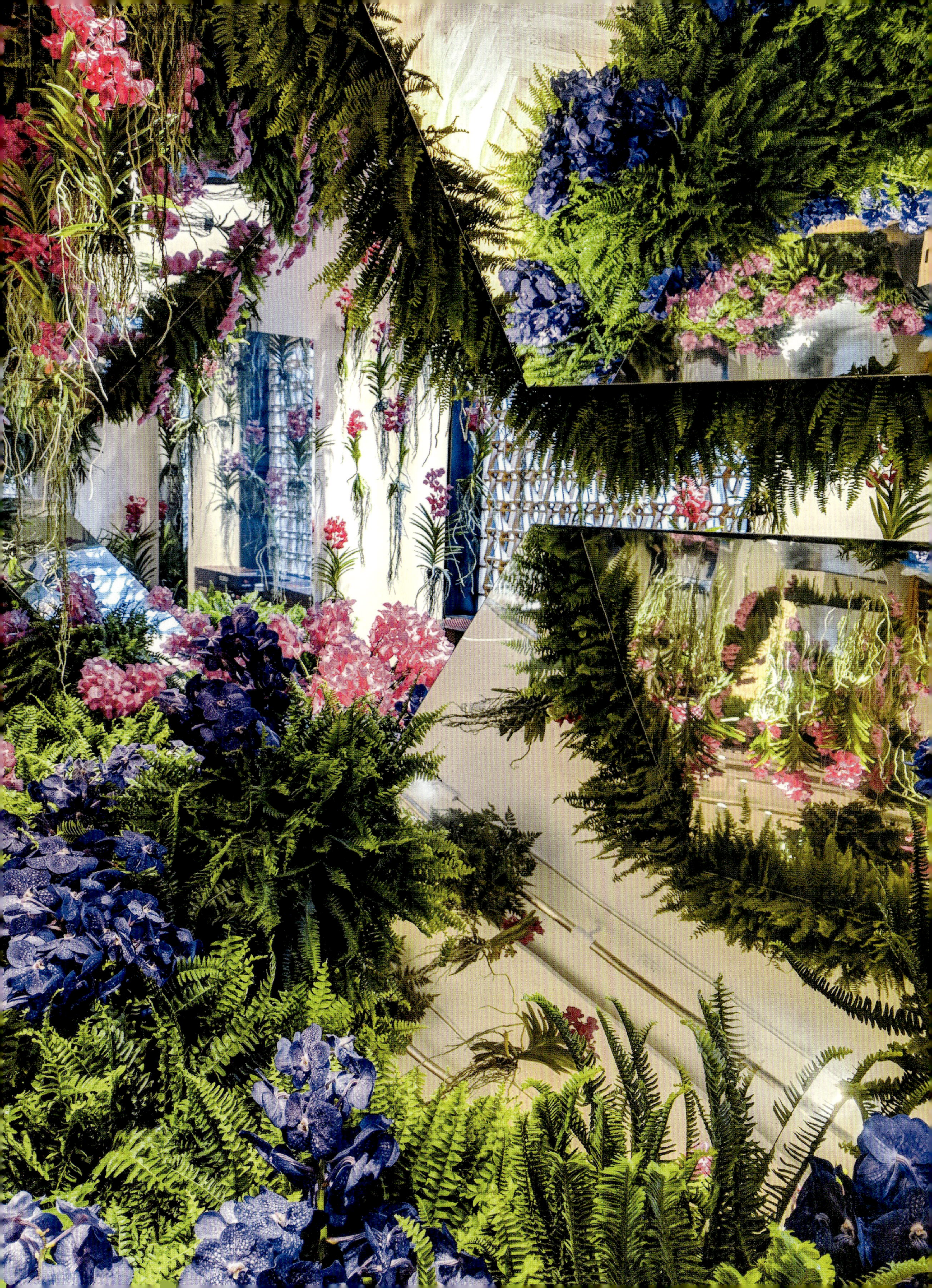

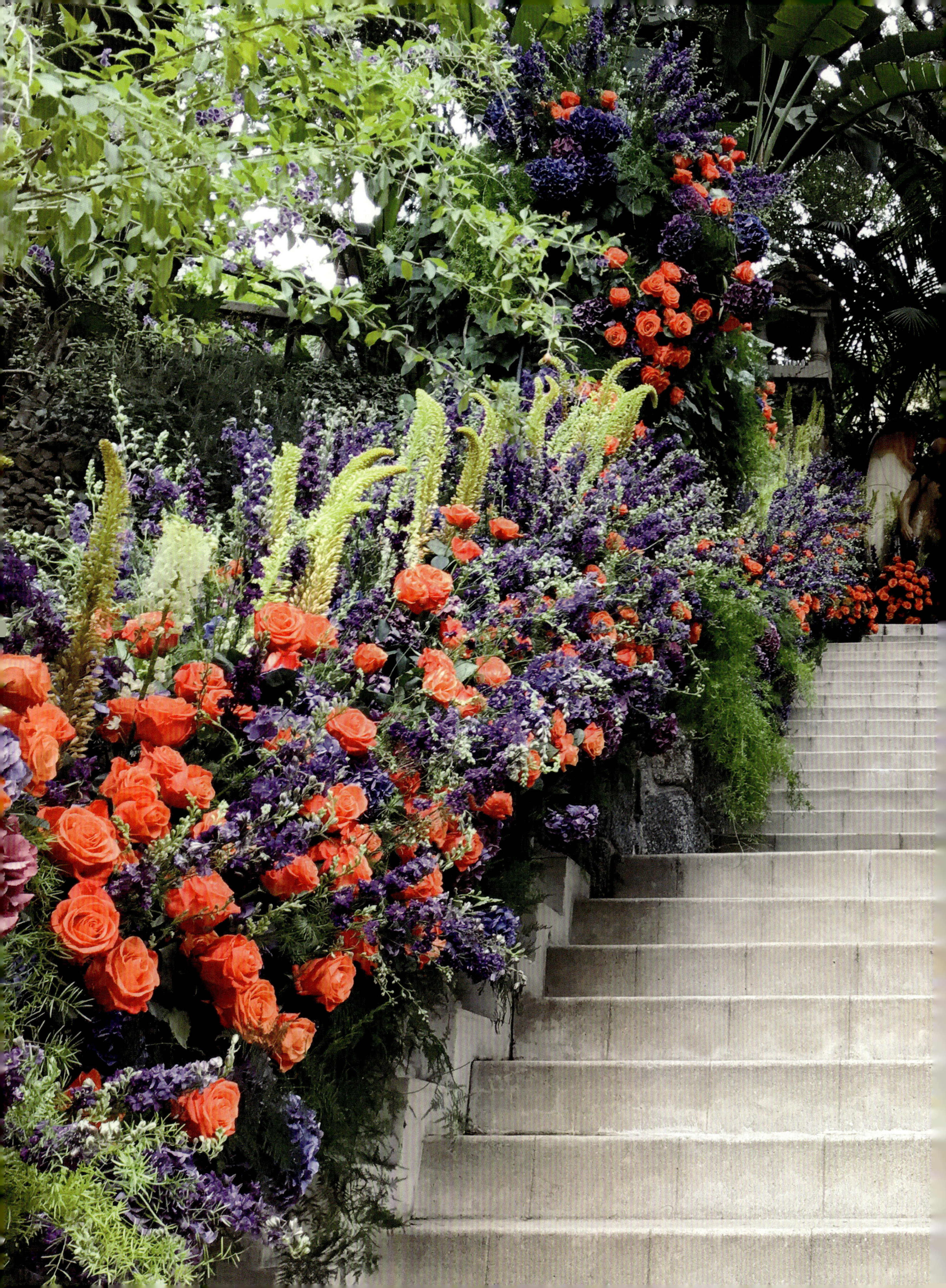

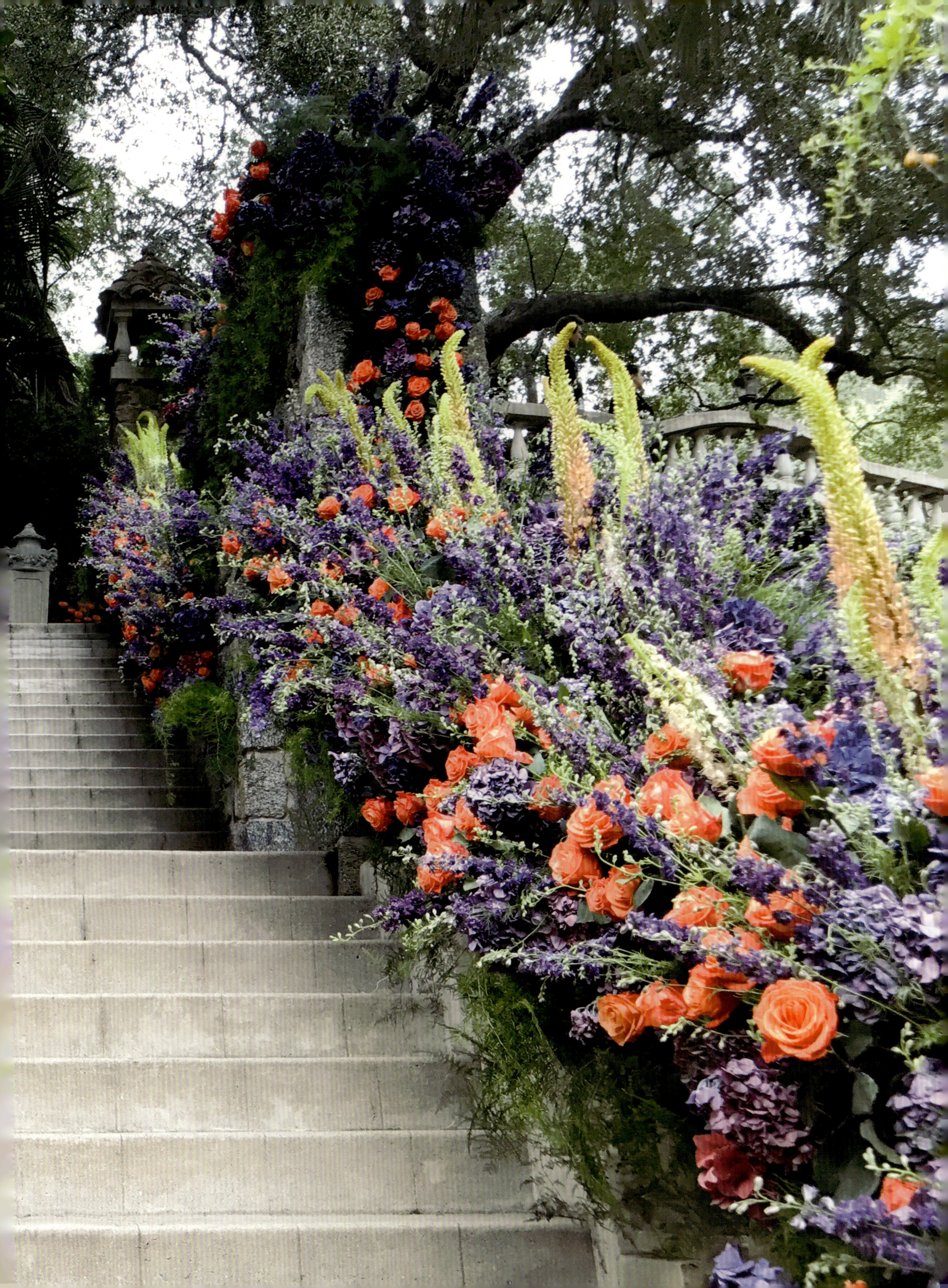

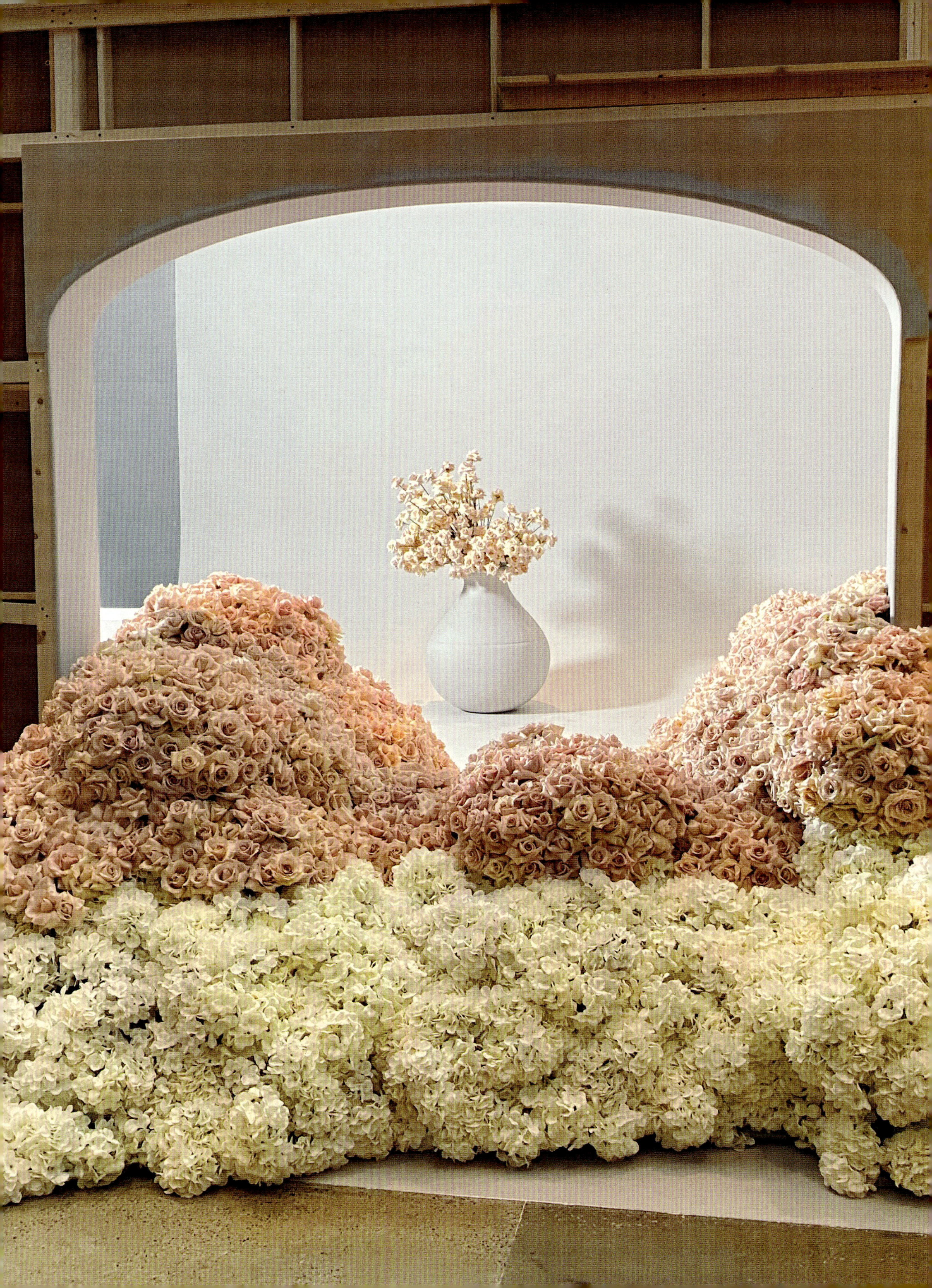

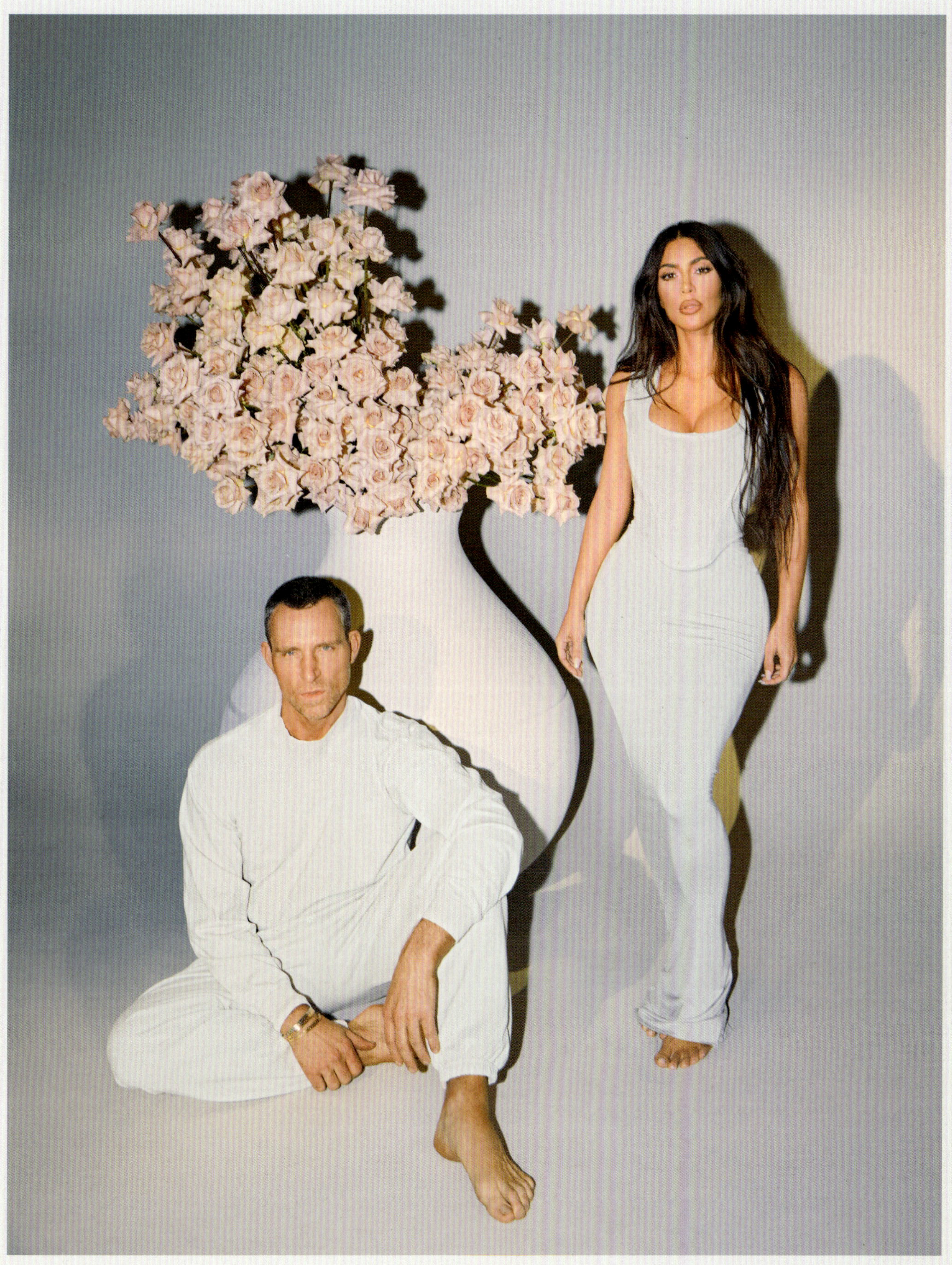

PAGES 152–155: Jeff Leatham and Kim Kardashian Fragrance
Photo Shoot, Los Angeles. Quicksand roses, hydrangeas, and
pampas grass.

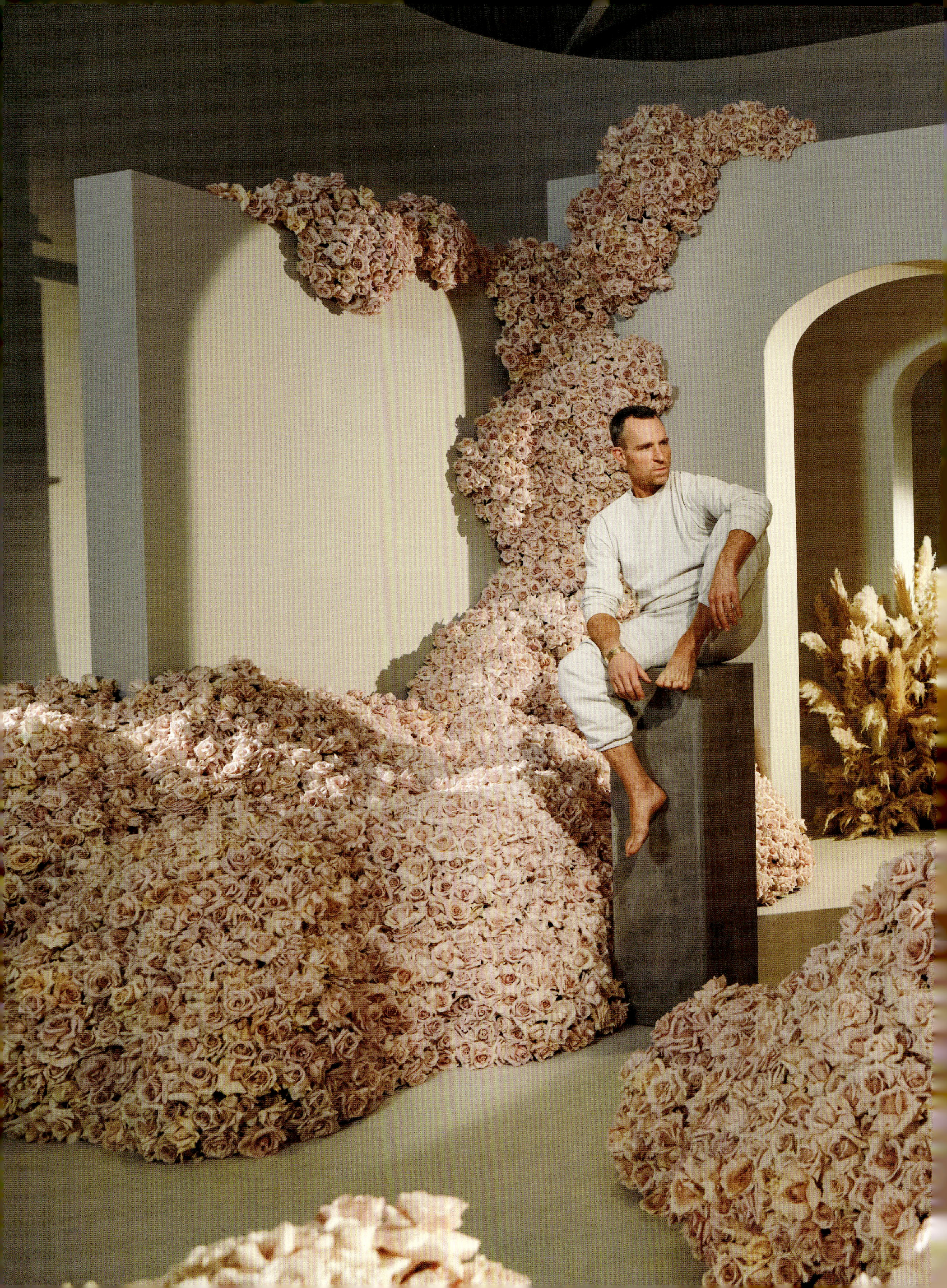

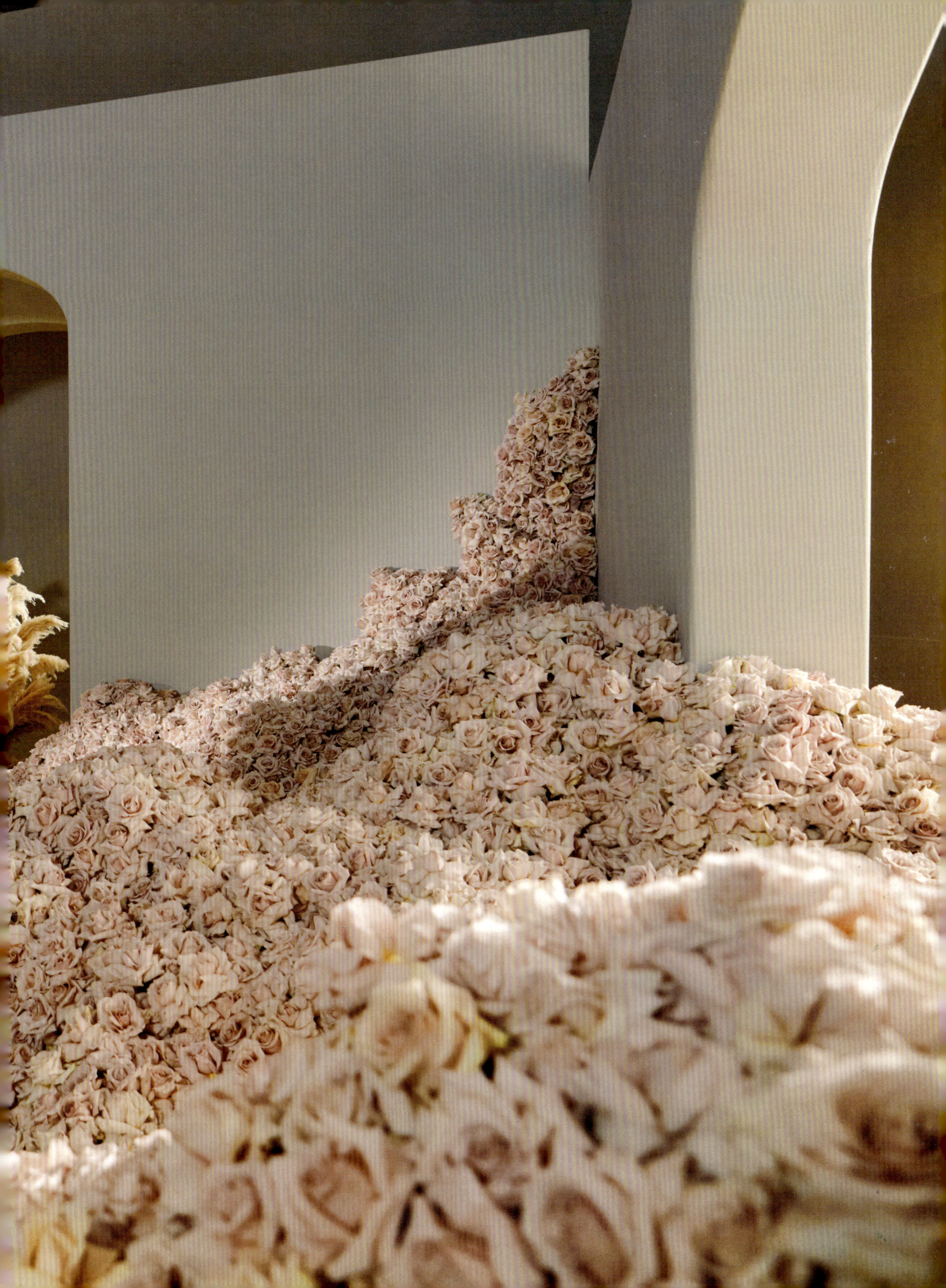

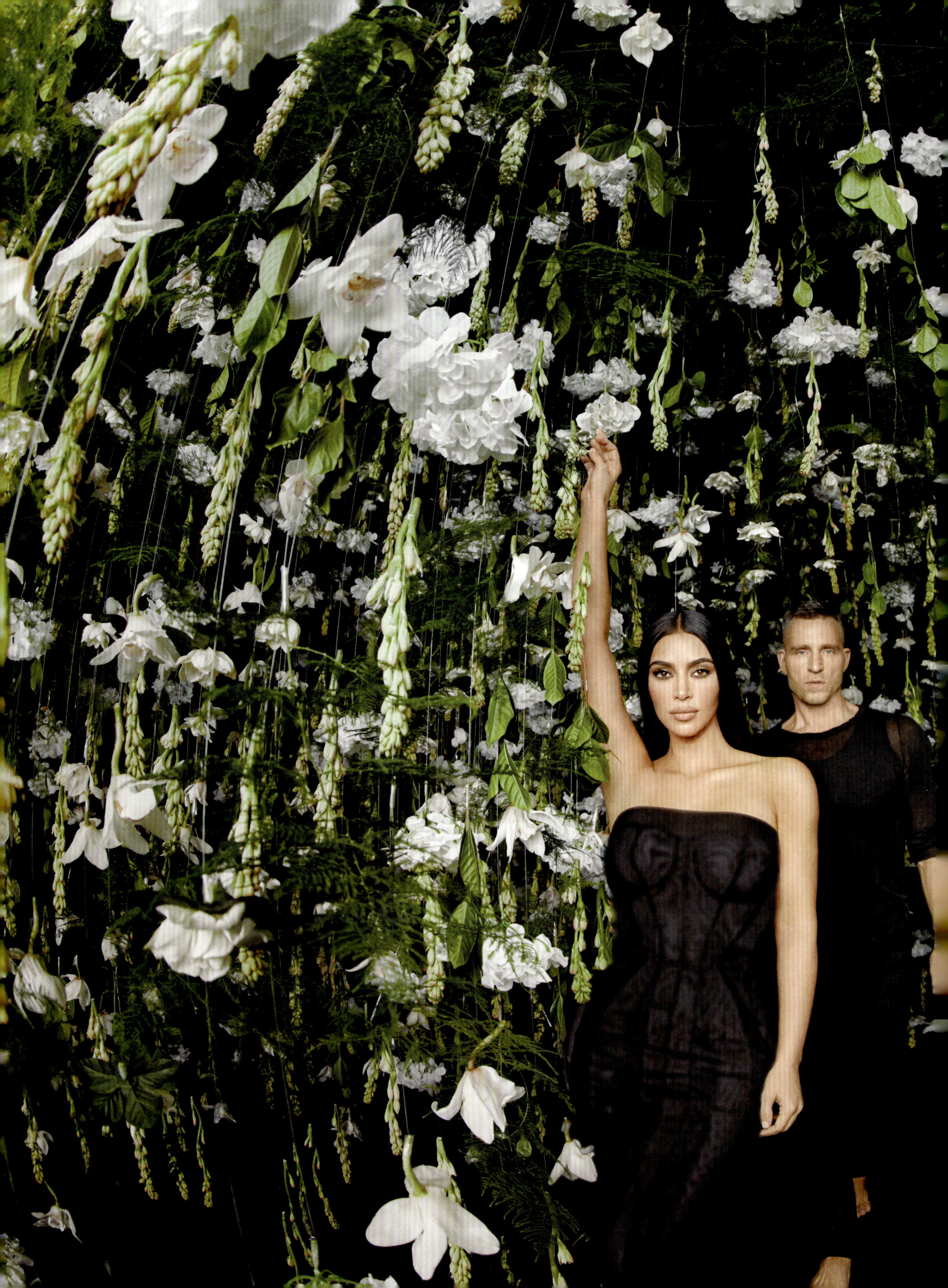

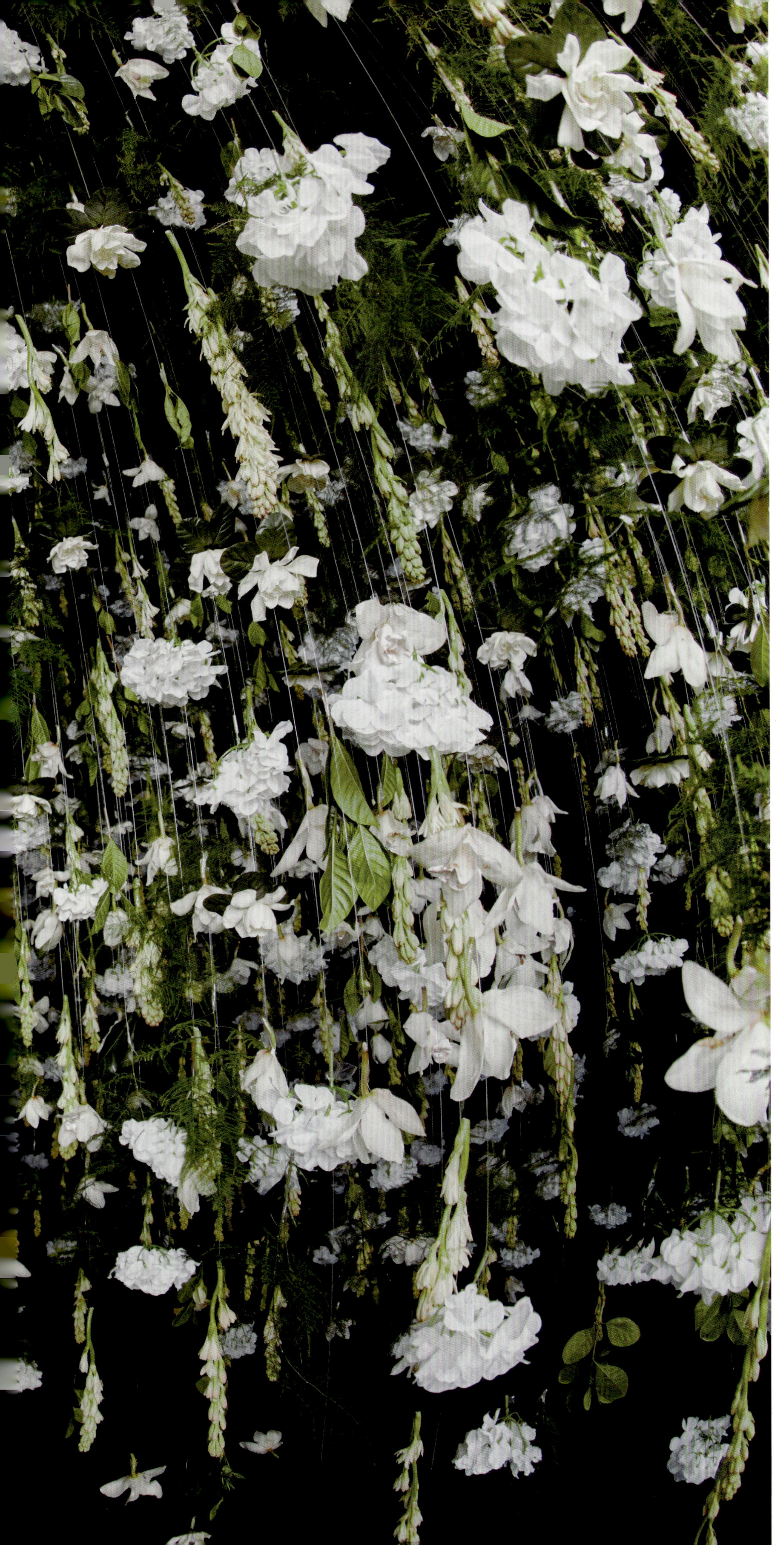

Jeff Leatham and Kim Kardashian
Photo Shoot, Los Angeles. Hydrangeas,
tuberose, white cymbidiums, gardenias,
and plumosa.

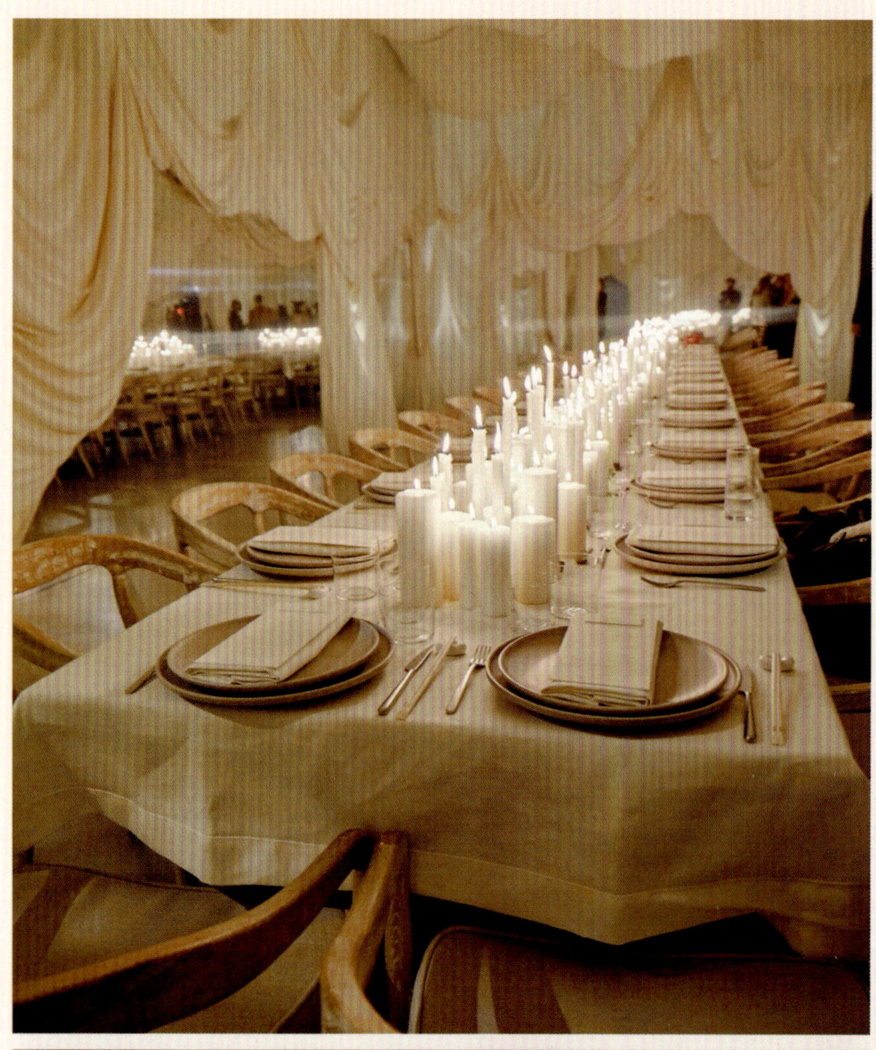

Private Event, Calabasas, California.
Table setting and giant bouquet of
quicksand roses.

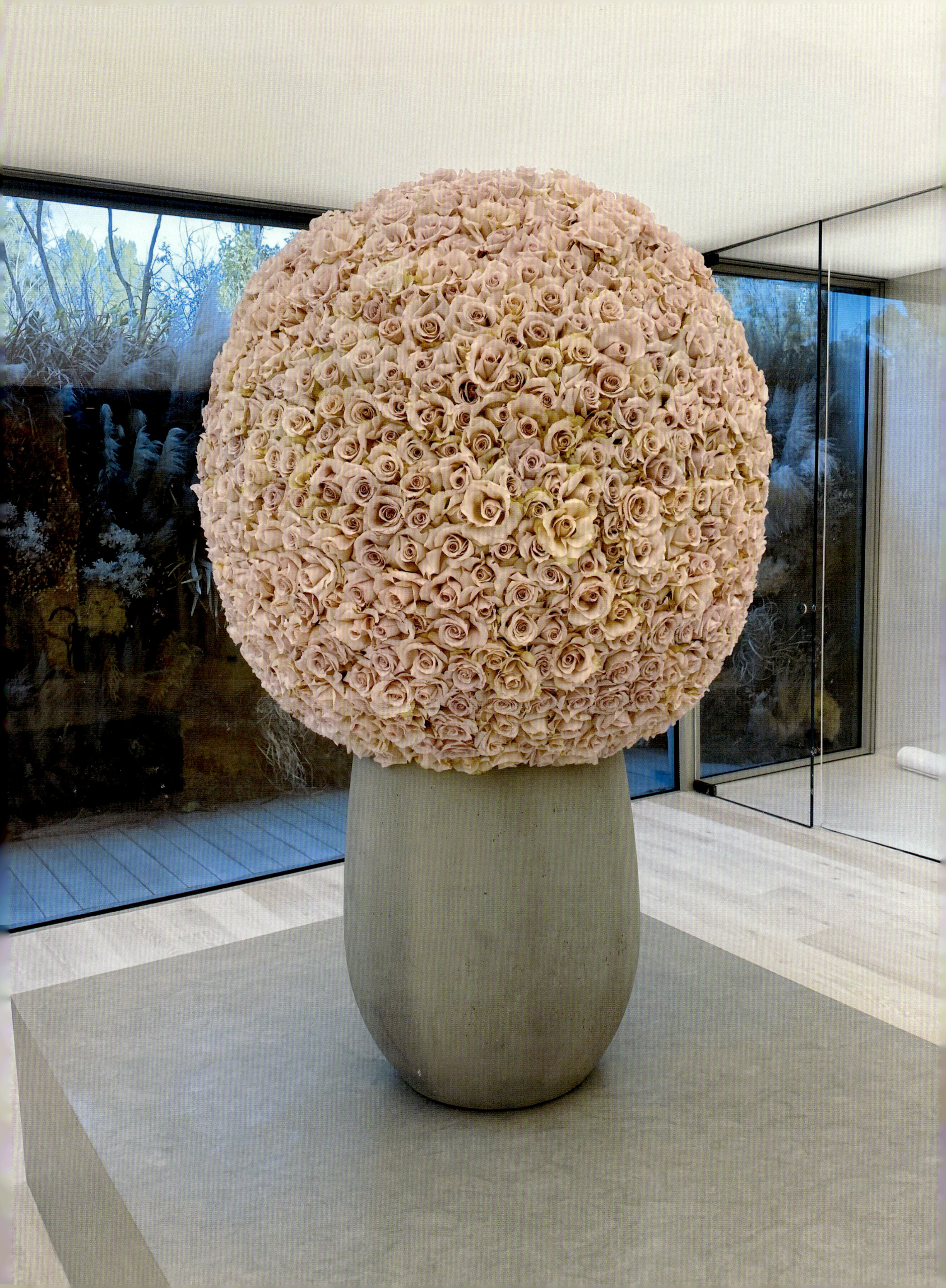

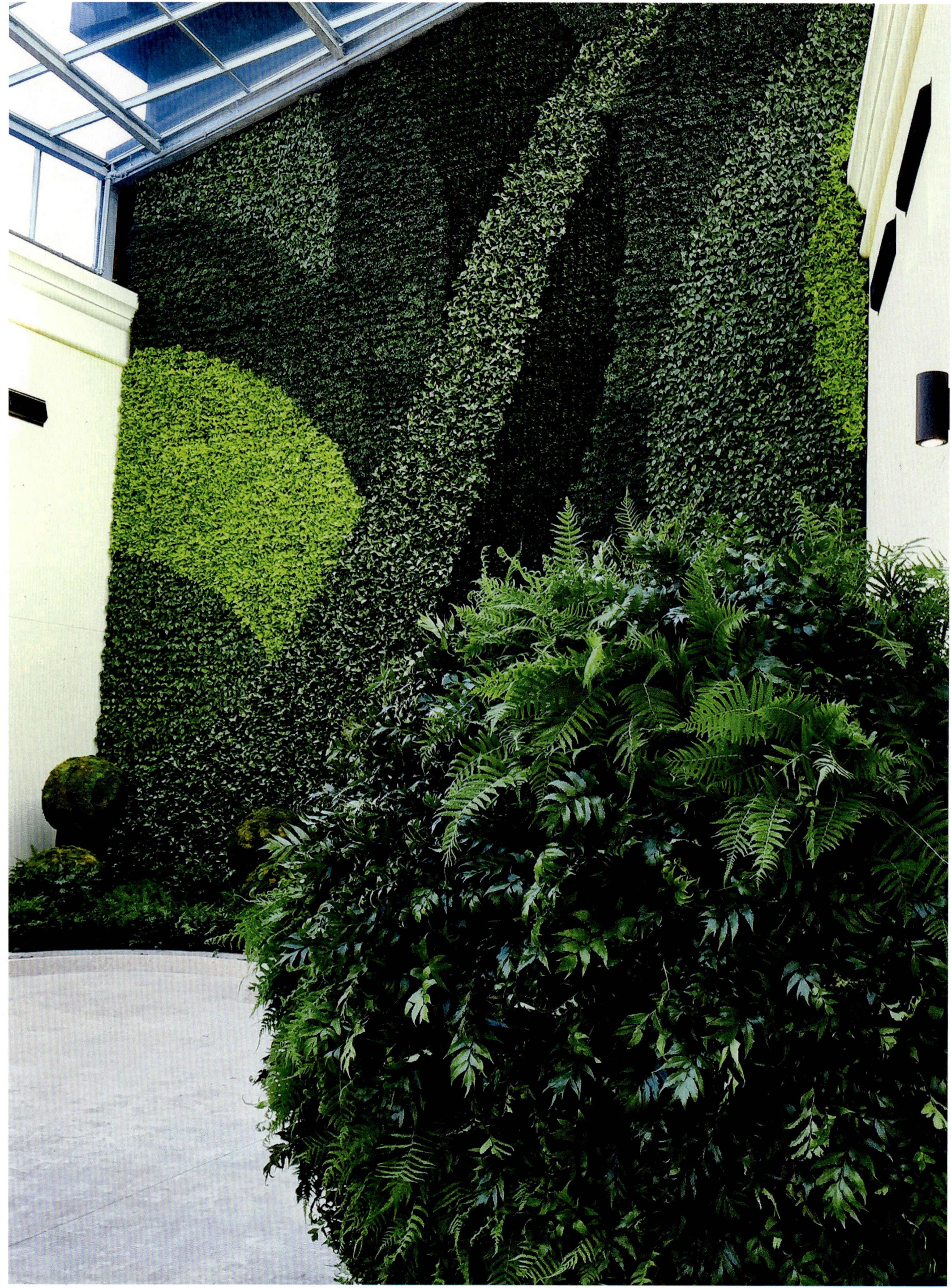

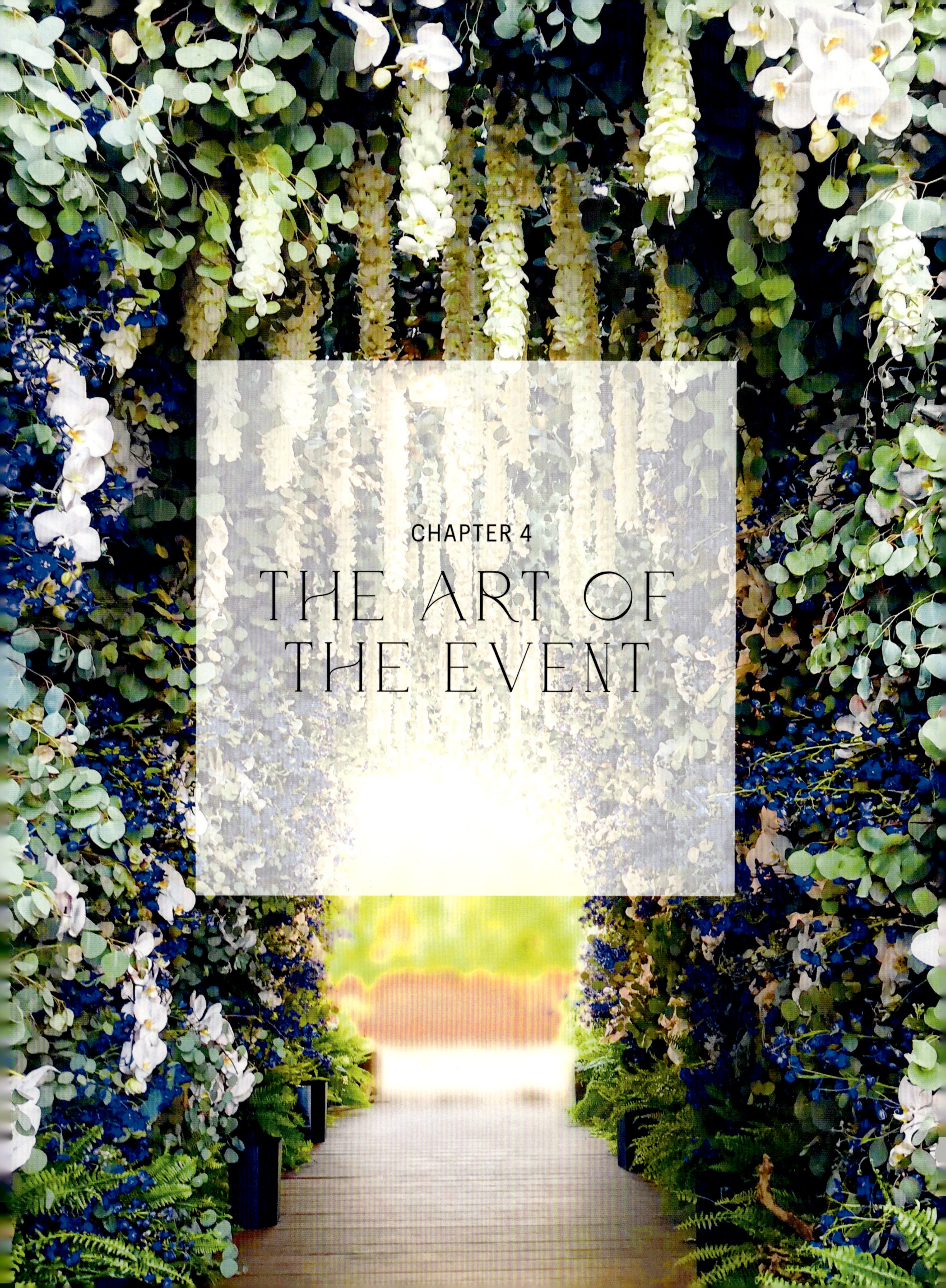

CHAPTER 4
THE ART OF
THE EVENT

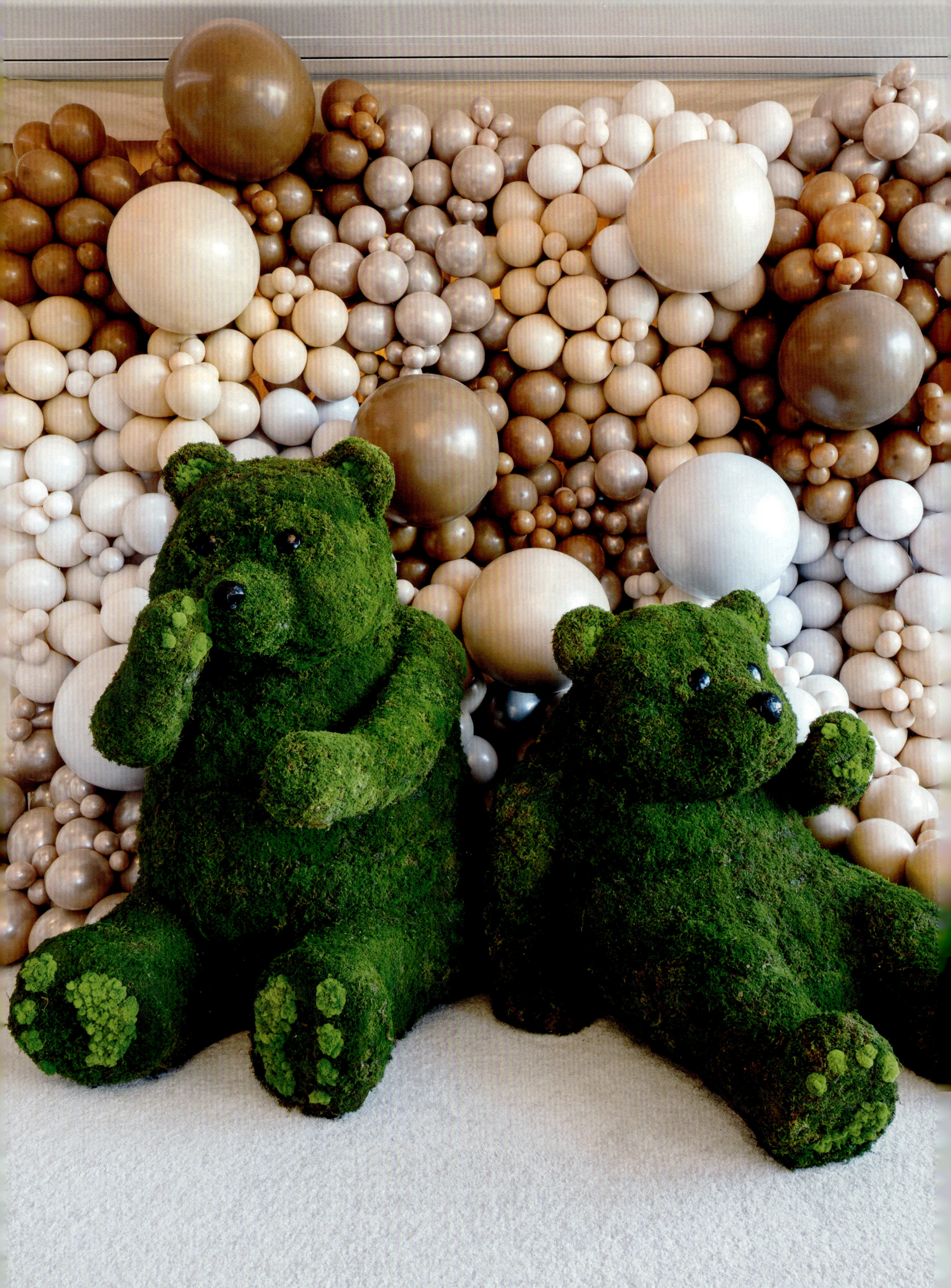

I have always loved F-words: flowers, food, fun, friends, family, and, of course, fashion. And to create truly memorable events, all my favorite F-words need to be in play. Whether it's a birthday, a baby shower, an engagement, a grand opening, or a product launch—which are increasingly popular now—each event needs to feel special and unique. I absolutely love a themed party, and if you really want to get me excited as a designer, allow me to design for a surprise party! I have found throughout my career that it's always easier to design around a theme. I've also learned that it's not just about the event, but also the art of the celebration, because, honestly, who doesn't love to celebrate?

Any theme that turns my mind on and is engaging is fair game. I like to design parties as if I were one of the guests, which means I always want to be wowed and see something different. When hiring me and my team, you'll always get an experience you've never seen before . . . and one you won't ever forget. Unique and inspirational moments are everywhere, and there is always something you can find to use as a starting point to make events special—you just need to search for it. The key is to think about what type of experience you want to give your guests that they will remember—and not just in the moment but in the future as well.

Every detail, whether big, small, or somewhere in between, matters. The first step to creating memorable moments lies in finding what will excite and inspire the attendees, and then adding details to emphasize it. Every single detail makes a huge difference and possesses the power to transform a simple event into an unforgettable experience. They say the devil is in the details, but I think it's more appropriate to say, "the design is in the details," which is what we're all searching for. The second step to the art of creating special events is focusing on many groups of people, not just one, and emphasizing the joy of celebrating together.

Events should also be treated as the iconic moments they are, which is something that the designers I worked with, and admired, in Paris always ensured. Every single Karl Lagerfeld show for Chanel was a spectacle and guests felt lucky just to be there. Every single Alexander McQueen show was distinct. They were not easy to create nor easy to forget; they were once-in-a-lifetime gatherings that would never happen again.

Making events special in a new way is something that matters to me and that I take seriously. How many birthdays have you been to? More than you can remember, I bet, but the good ones, the ones you do remember, featured elements that were different and special. This is where flowers enter. They create a déjà vu moment where you see something you've seen a thousand times before and, yet, it's different. It's beautiful and it makes you feel special because you're there for just that moment in time. That's what I try to remember and incorporate into each of my events.

PAGES 162–167: Private Event, Calabasas, California. Green moss sculptures, scabiosa, sweet peas, and a variety of roses.

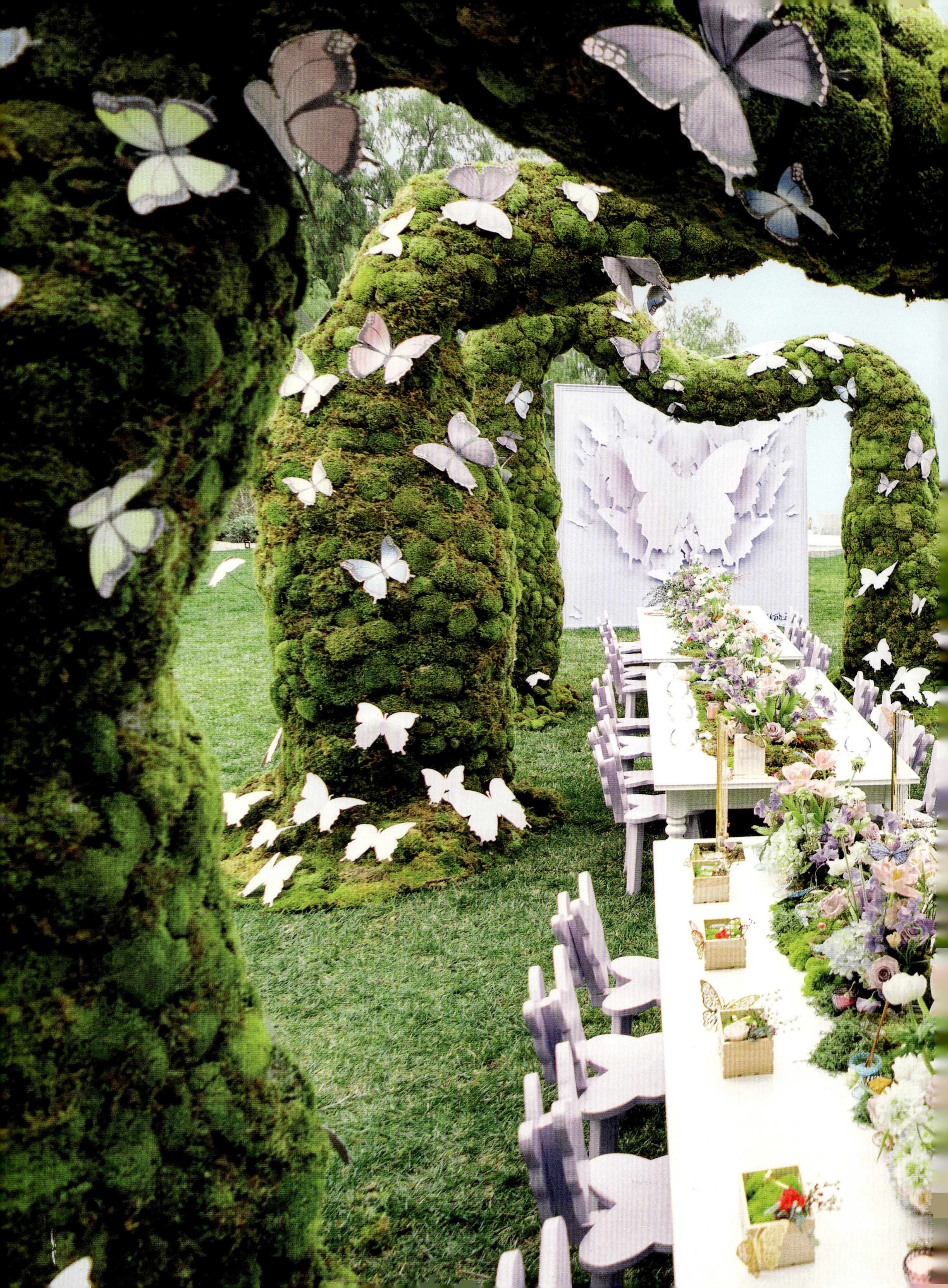

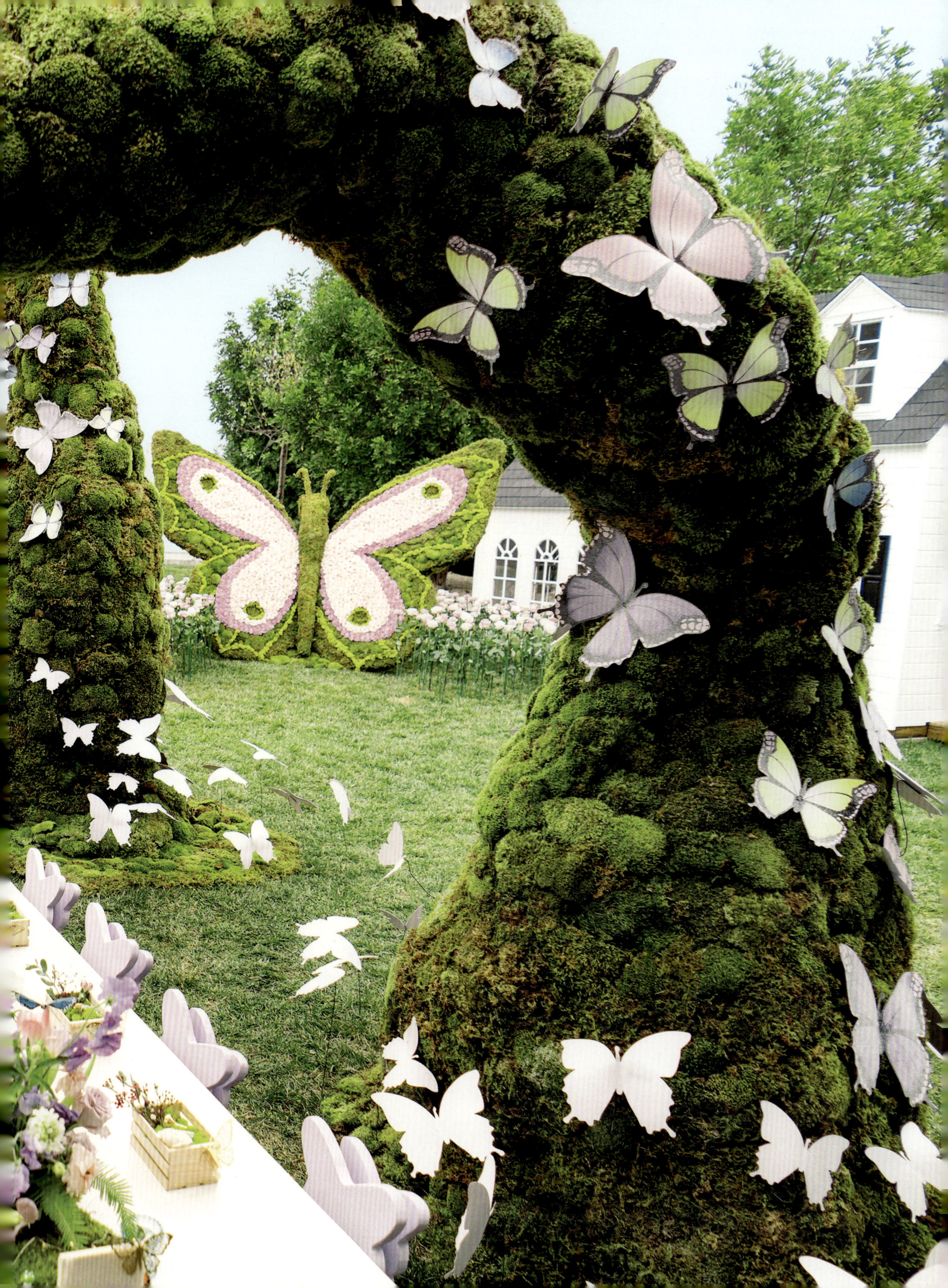

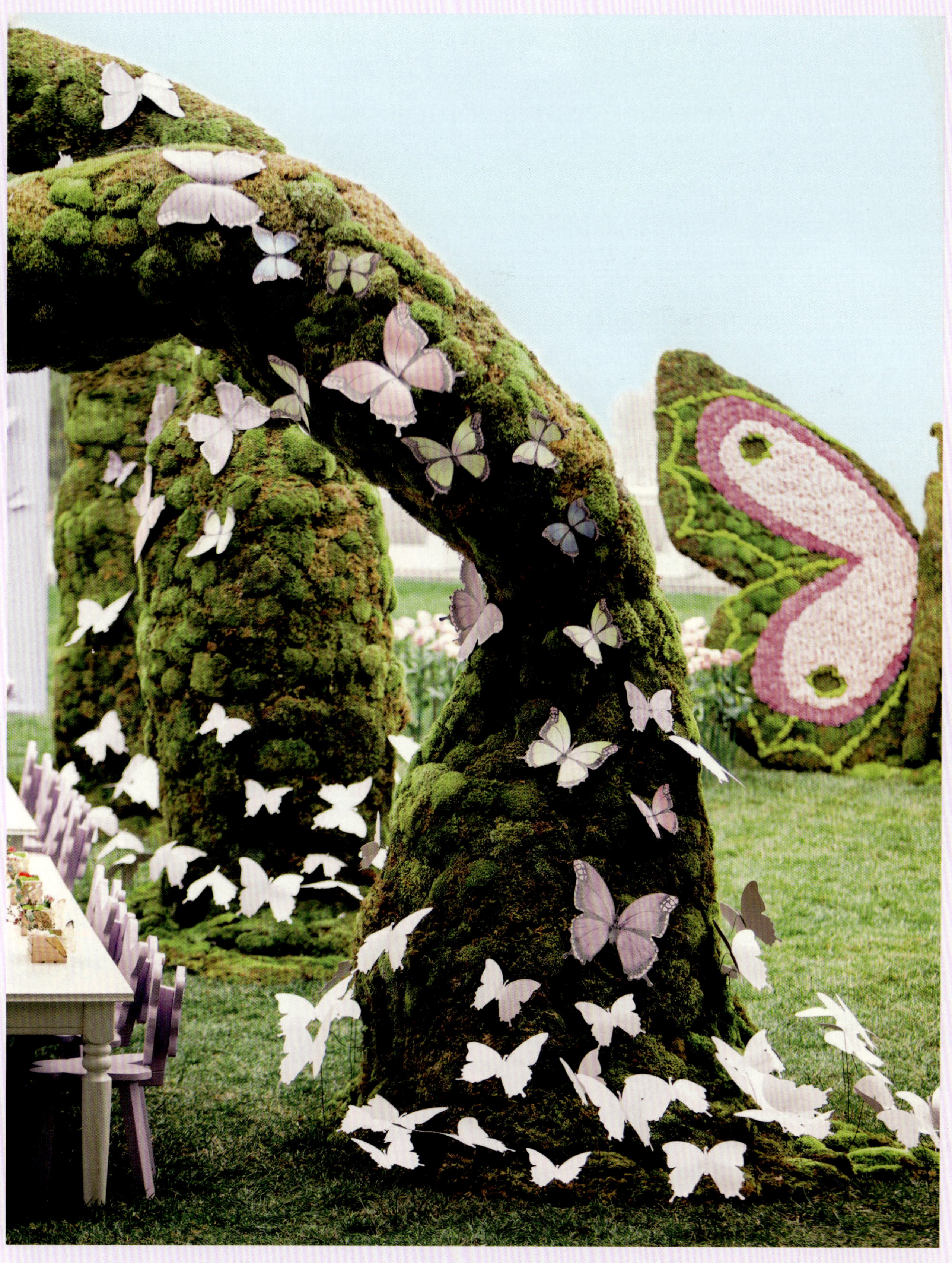

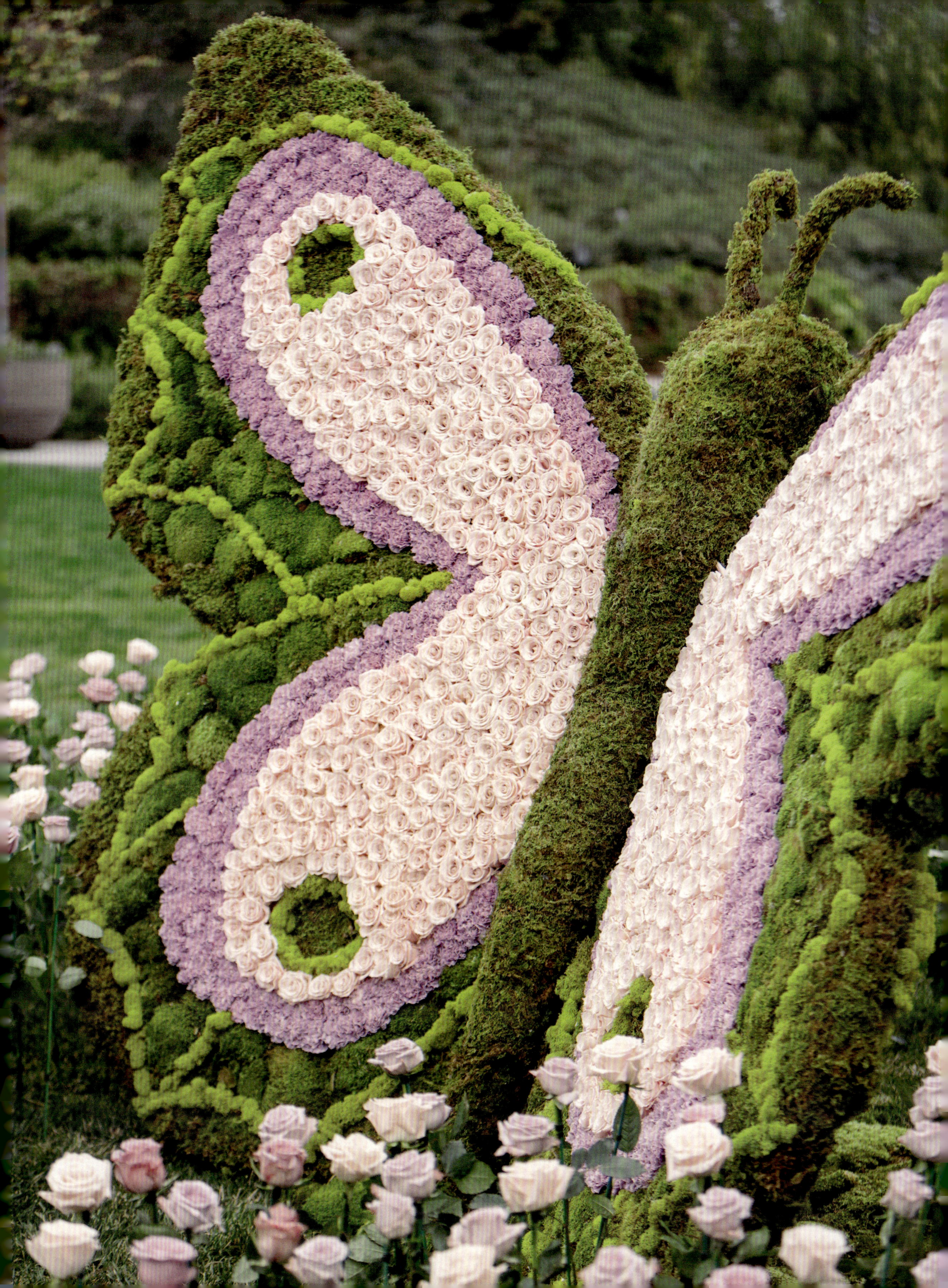

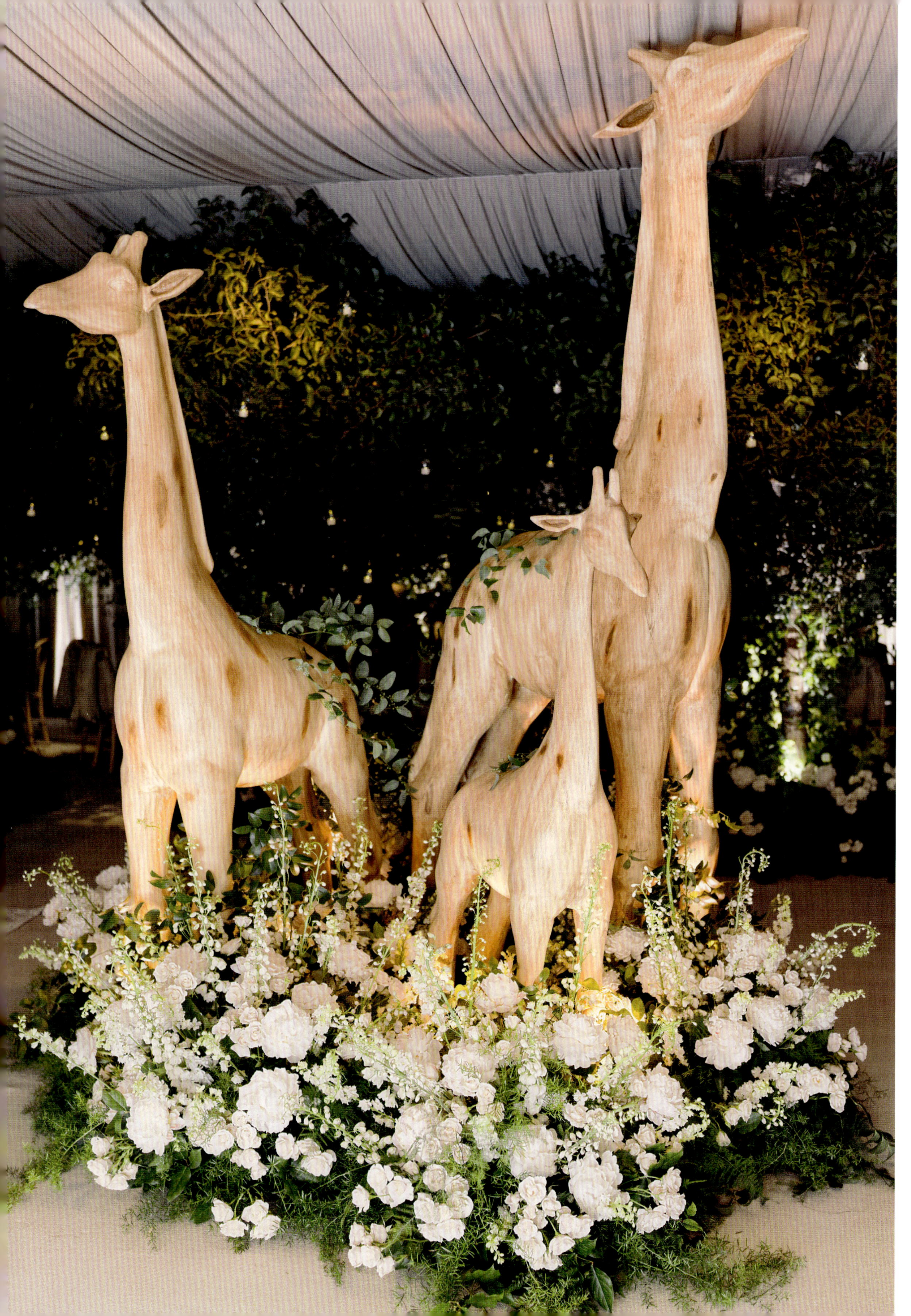

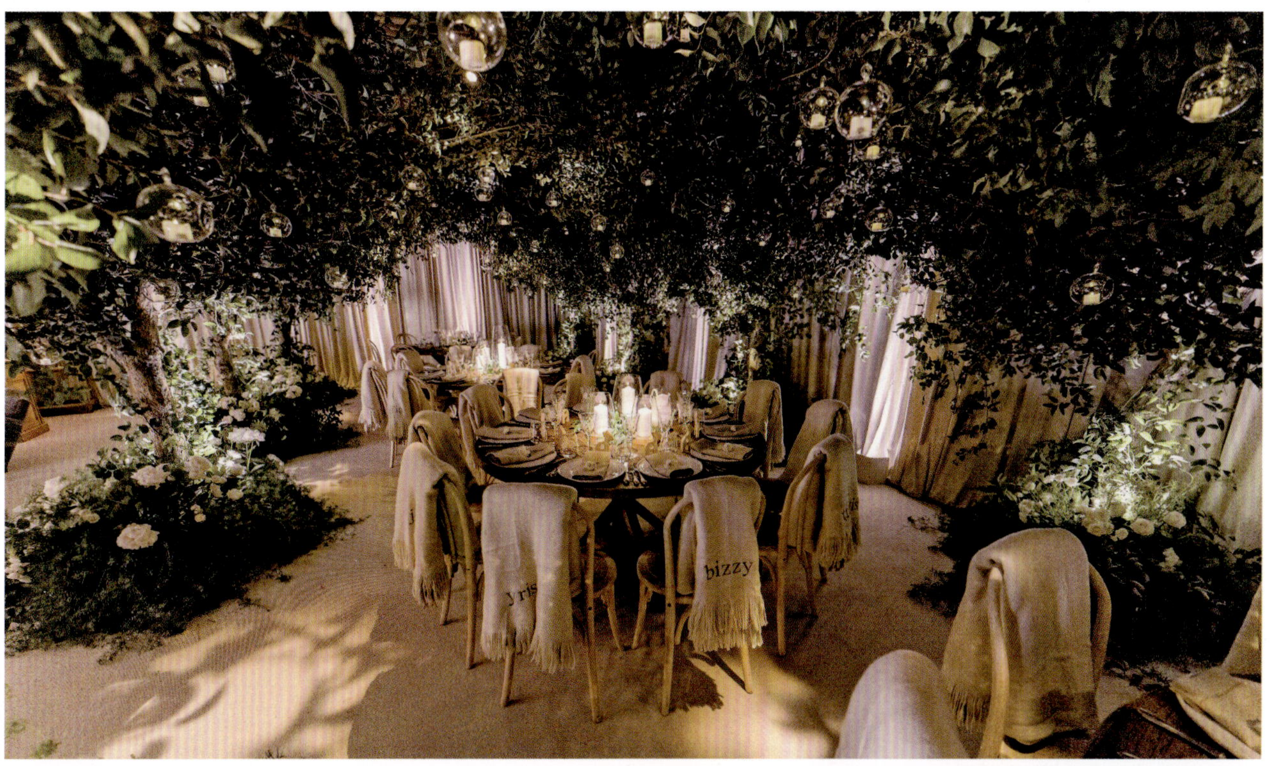

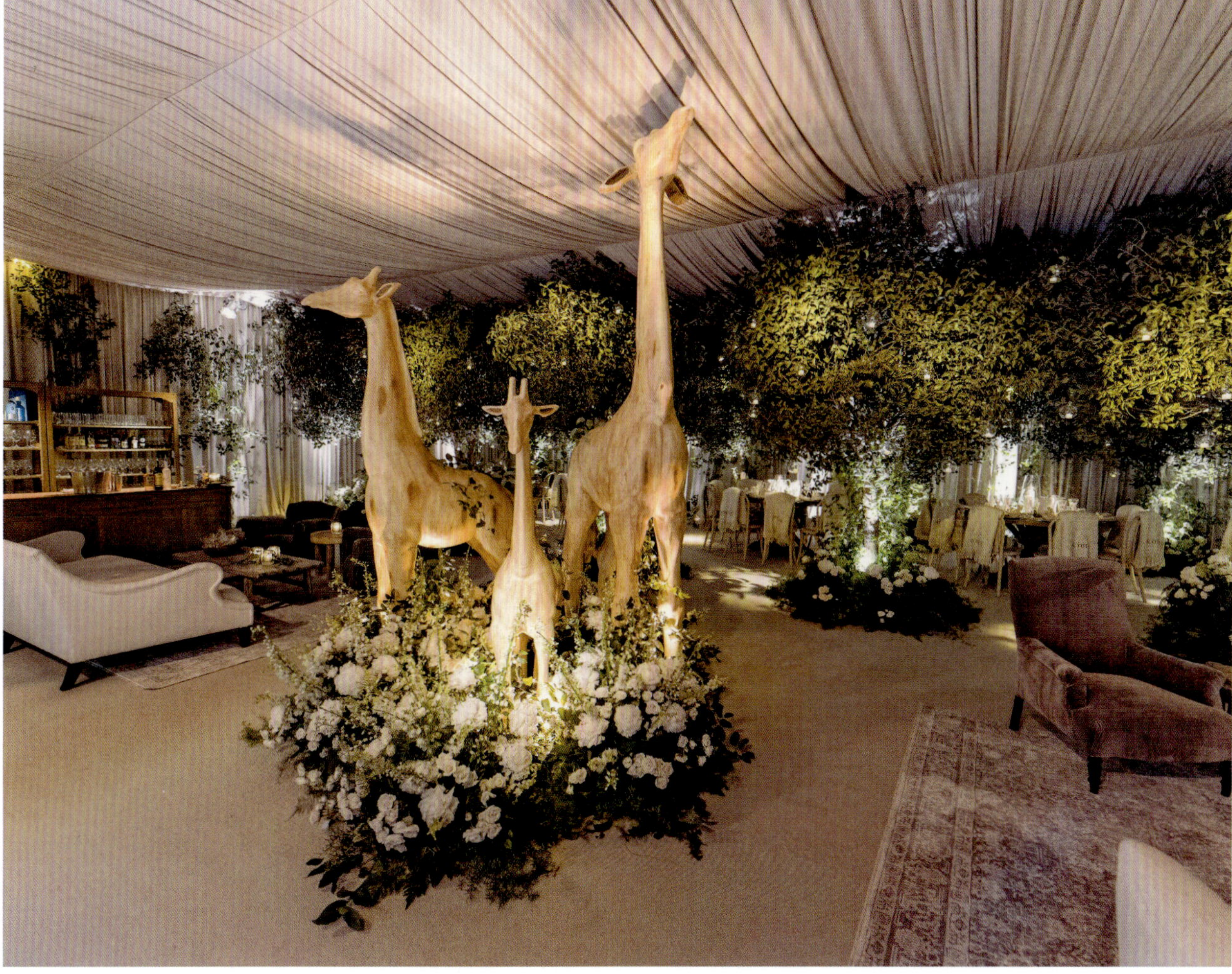

Private Event, Calabasas, California.
Roses and delphinium. PAGES 170–173:
Private Event, Calabasas, California.
Roses, hydrangeas, and carnations.

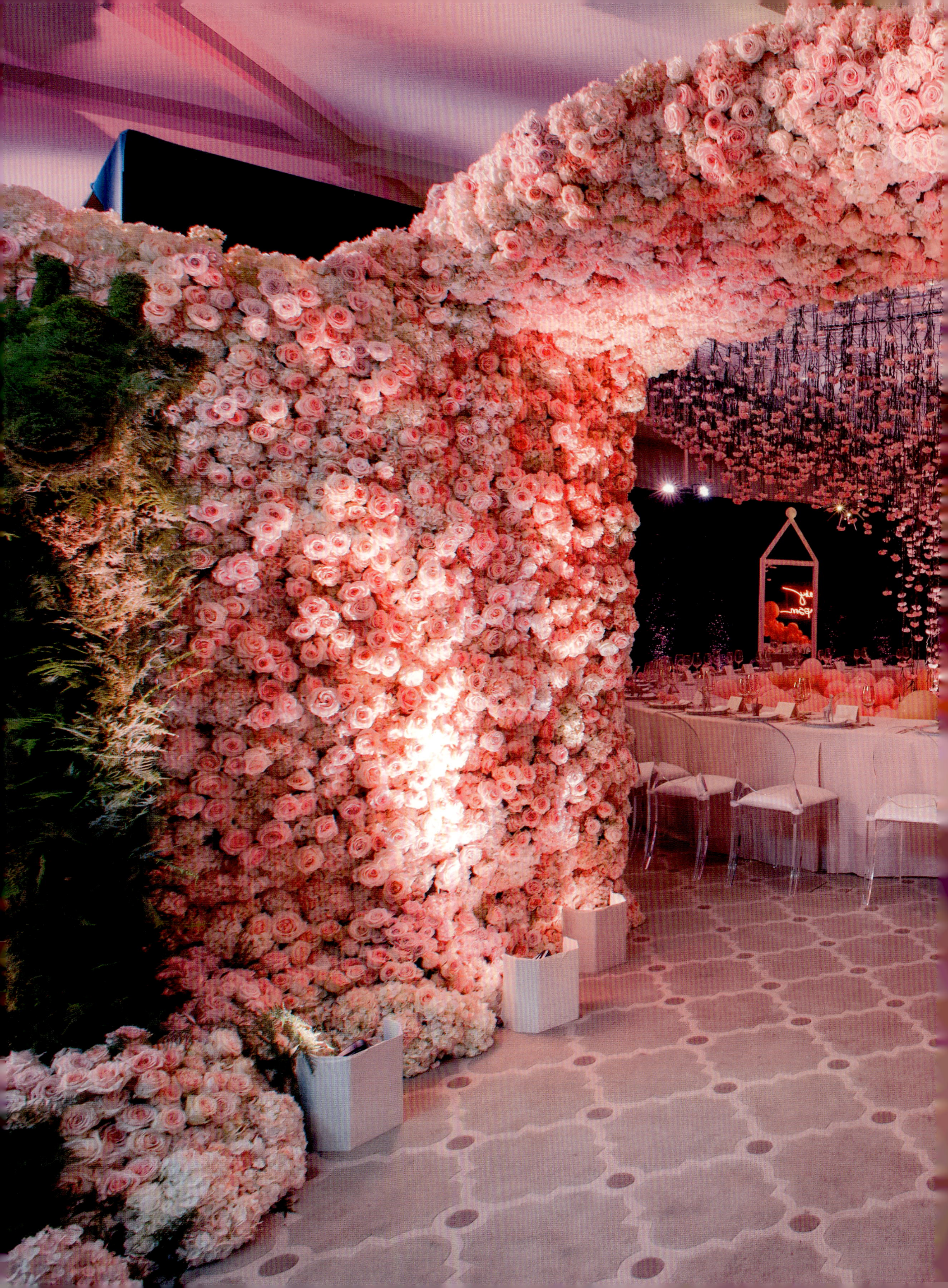

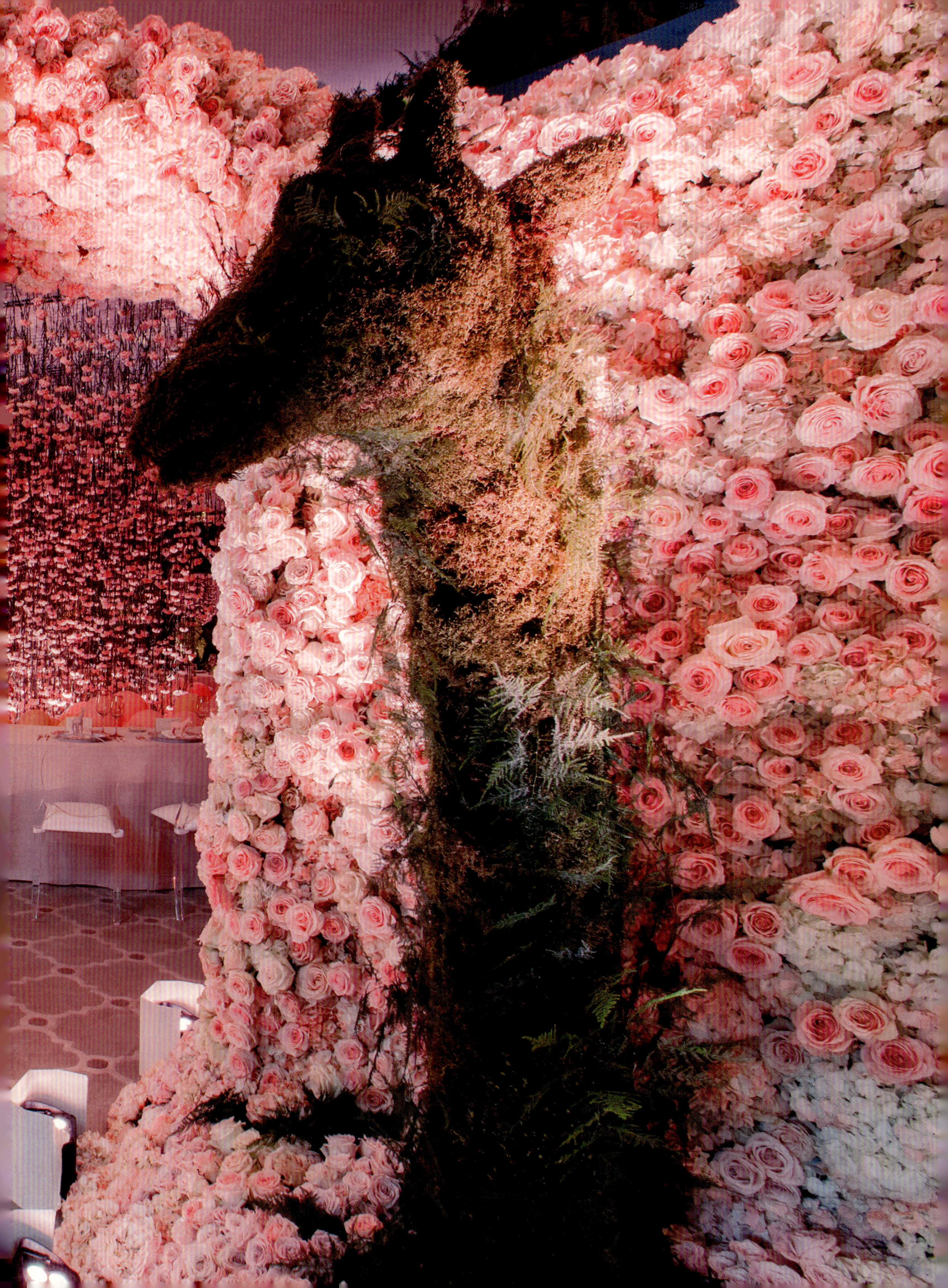

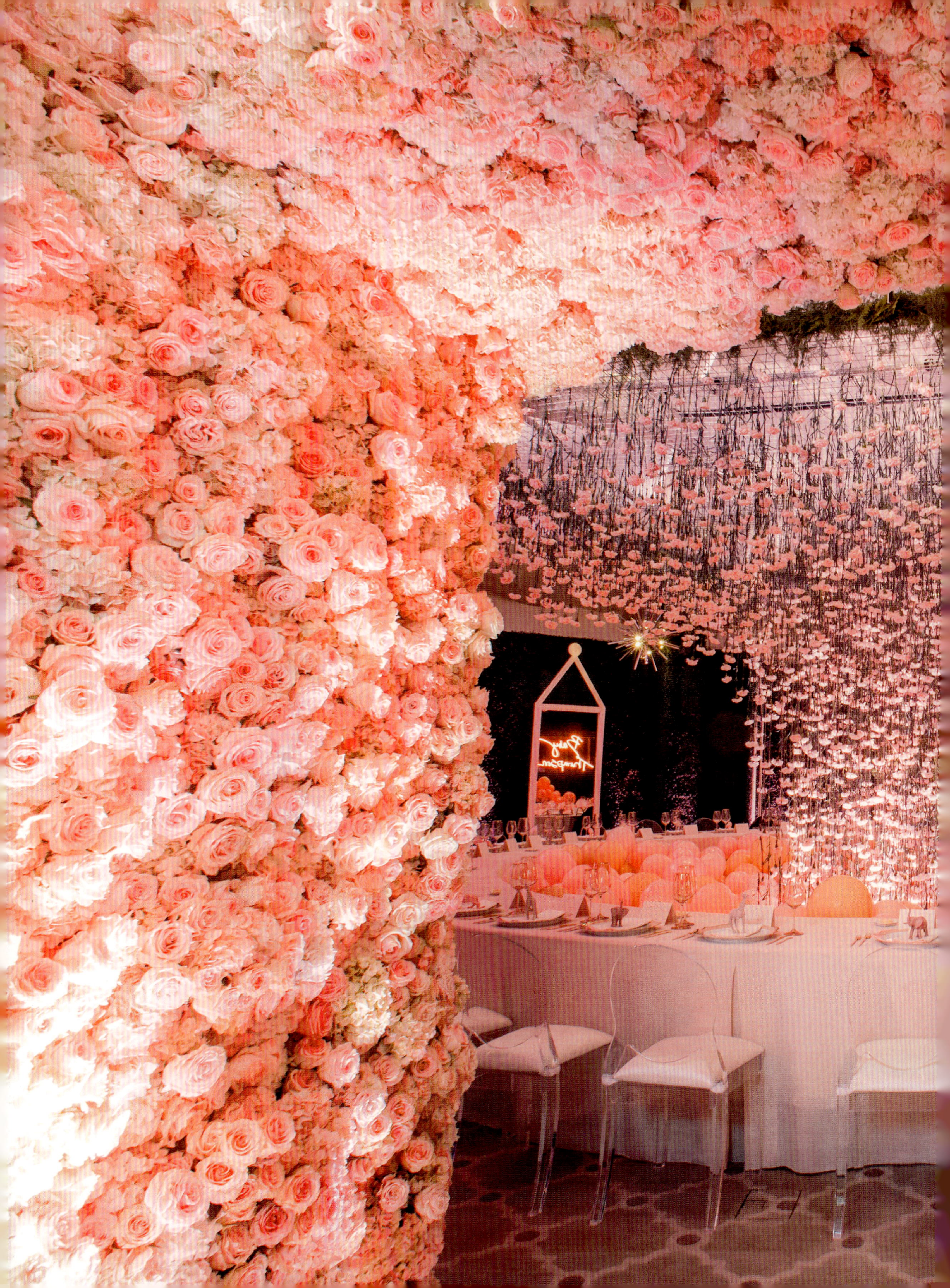

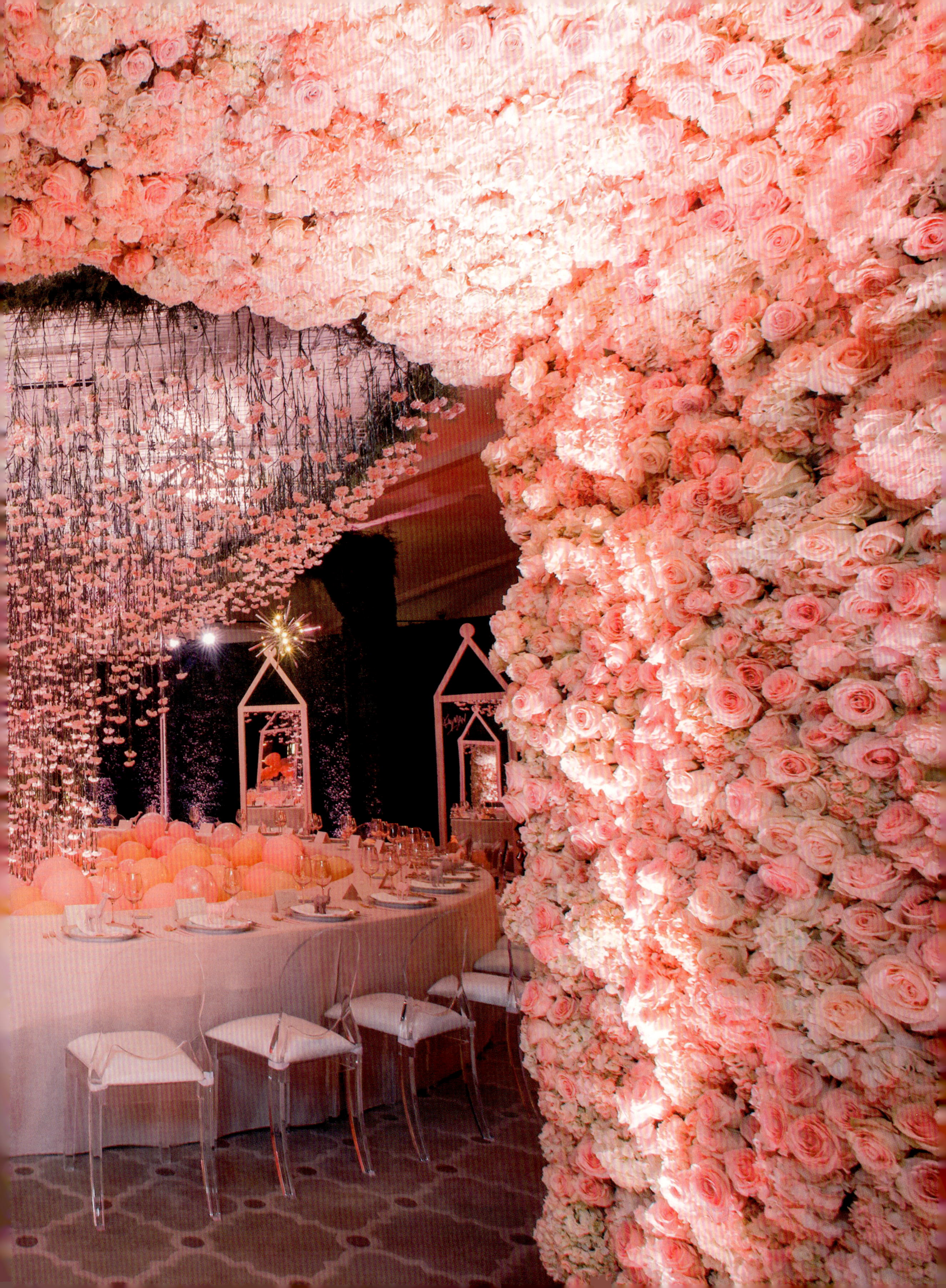

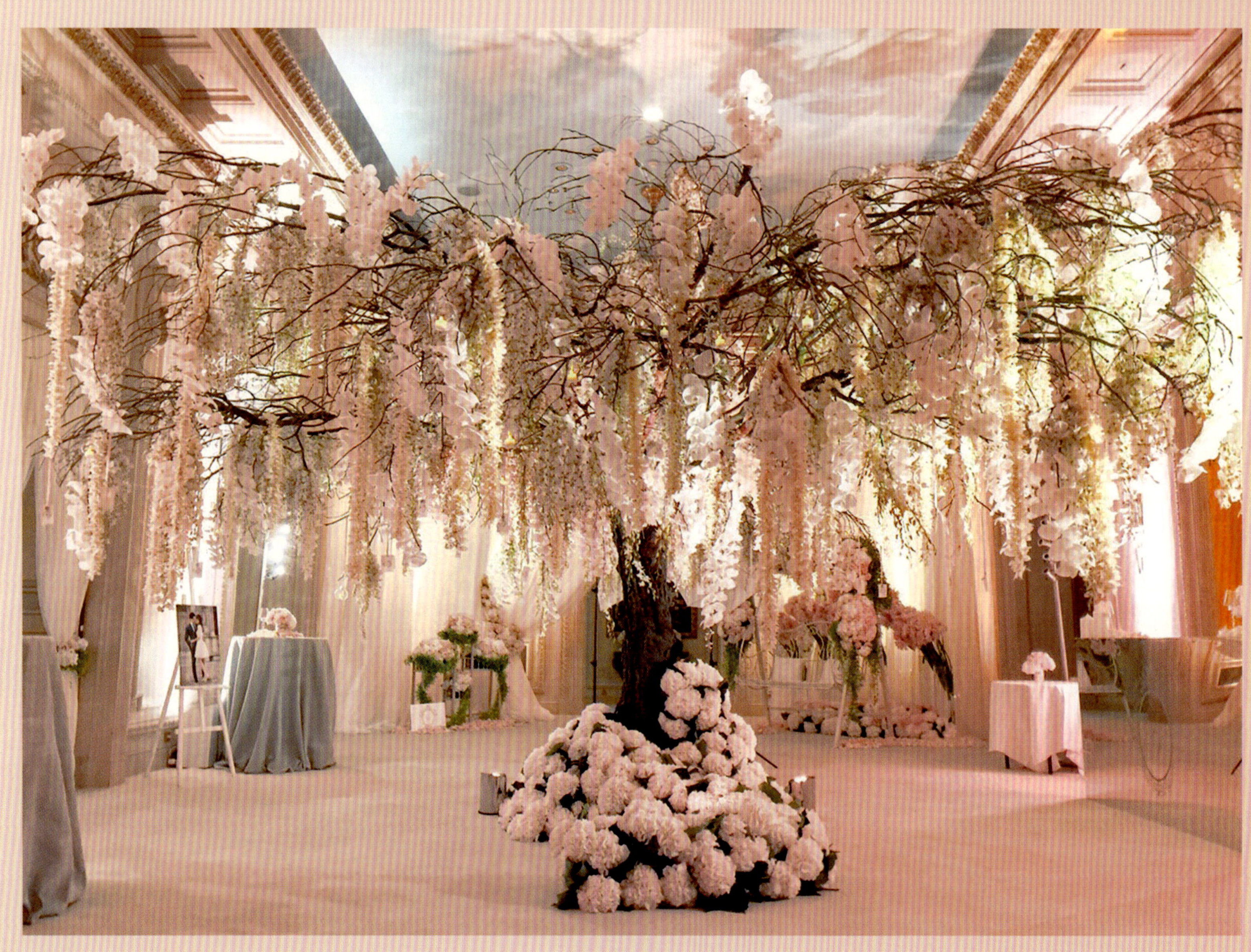

Private Event at Four Seasons George V. Hydrangeas. FOLLOWING: Private Event, Bel-Air, Los Angeles. Cherry blossoms and hydrangeas.

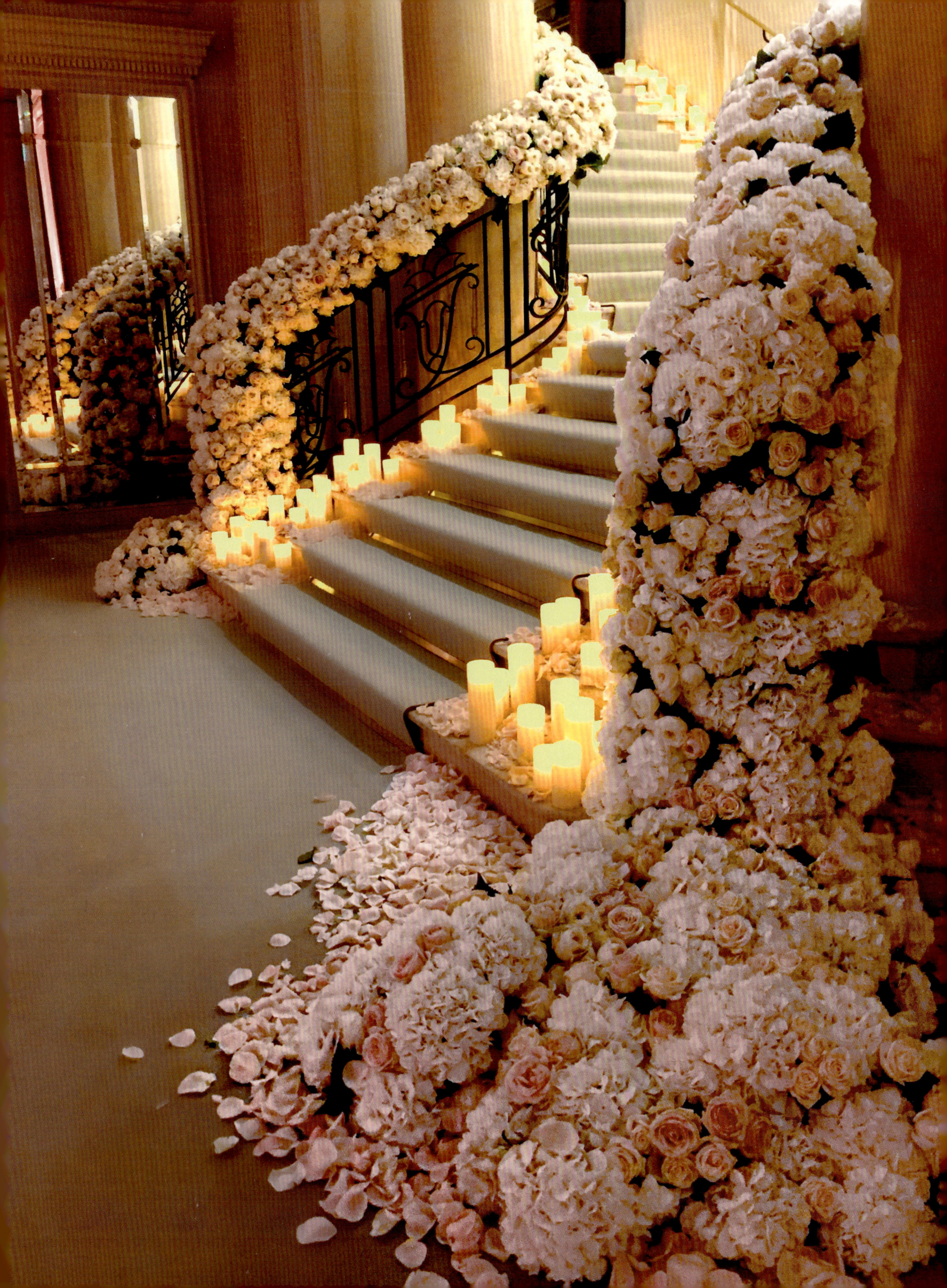

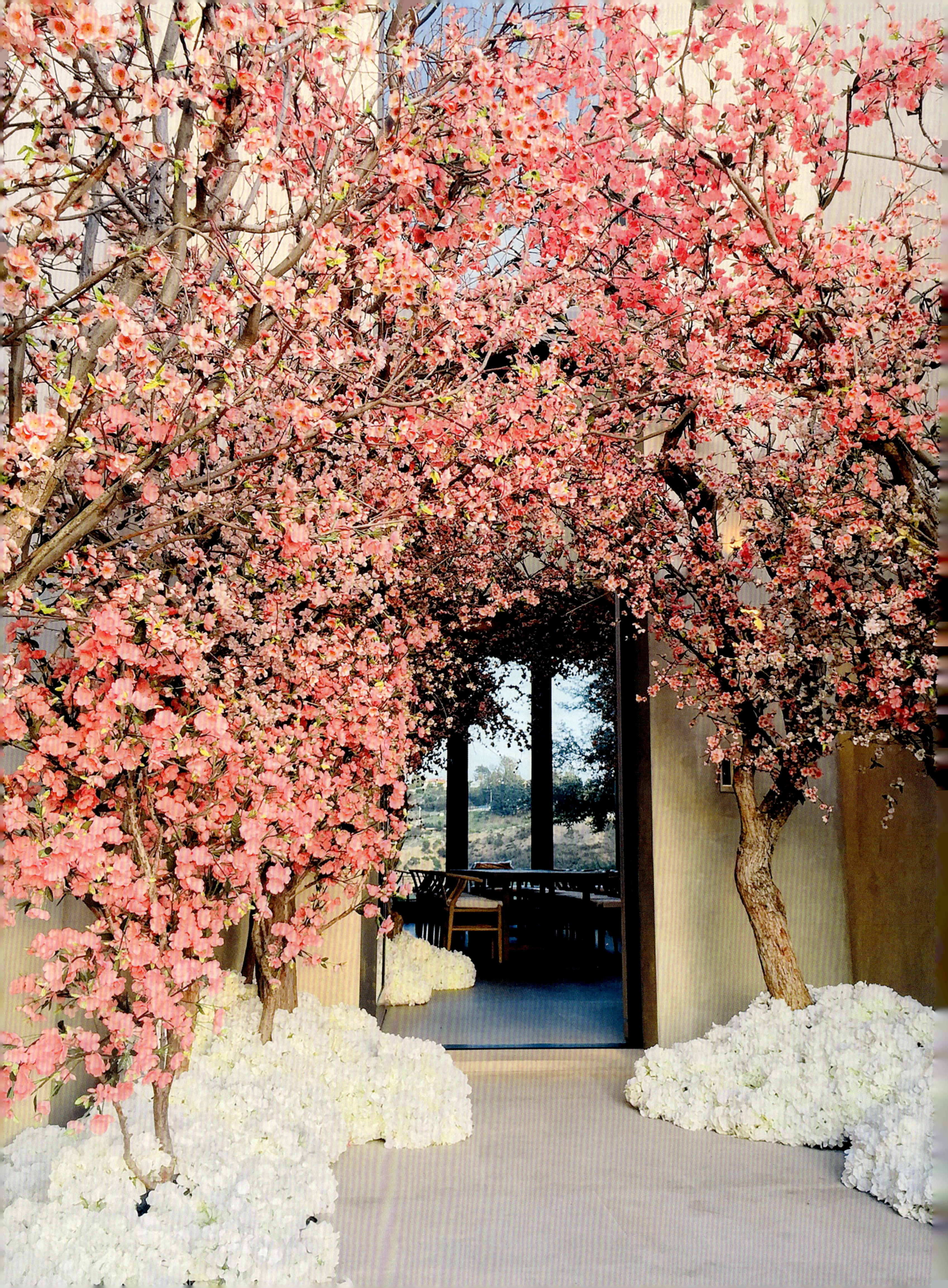

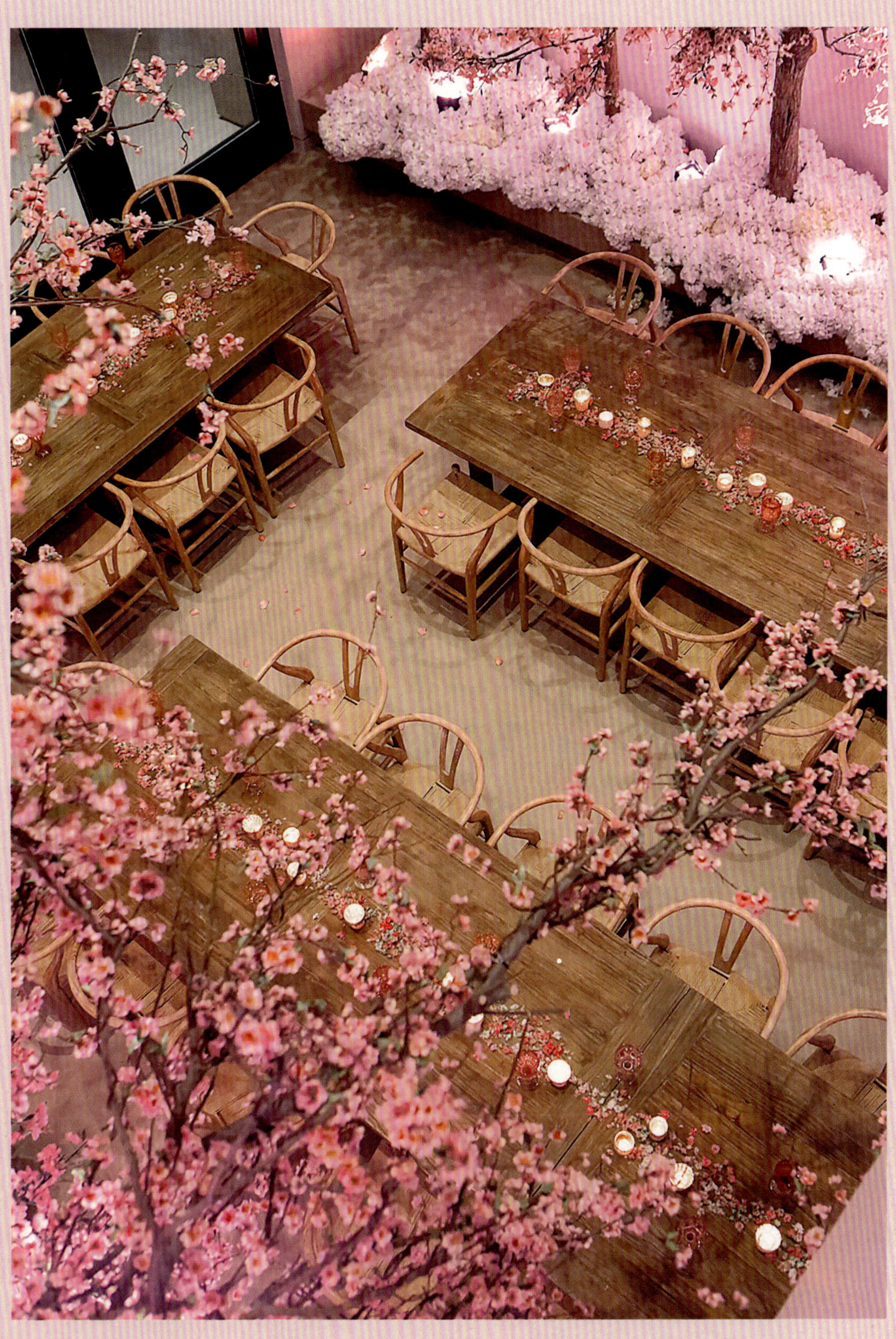

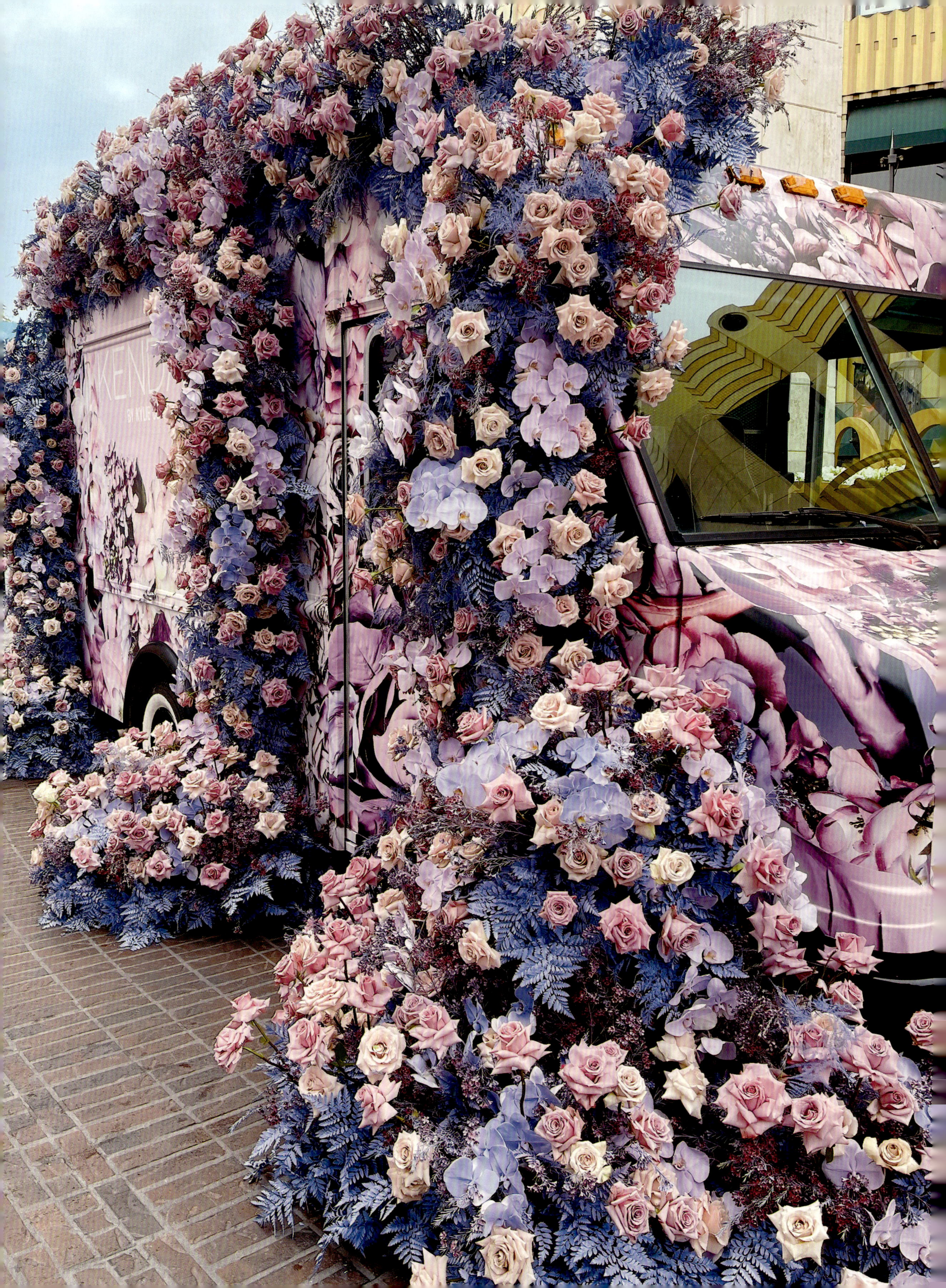
KEN
BY KYLIE

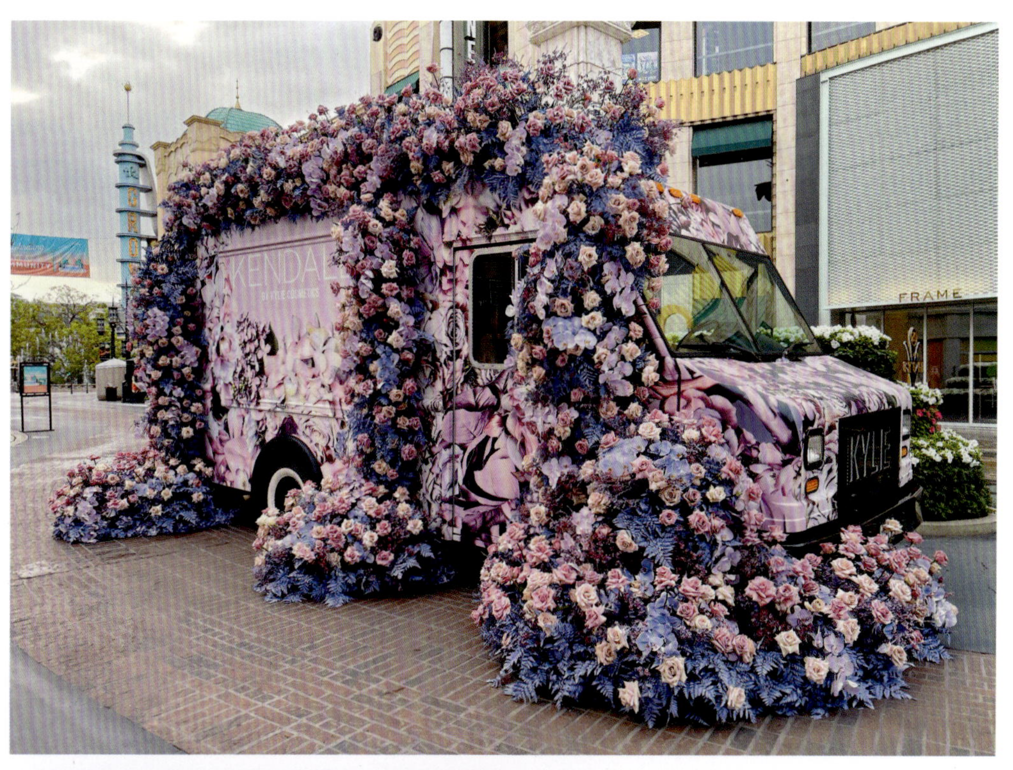

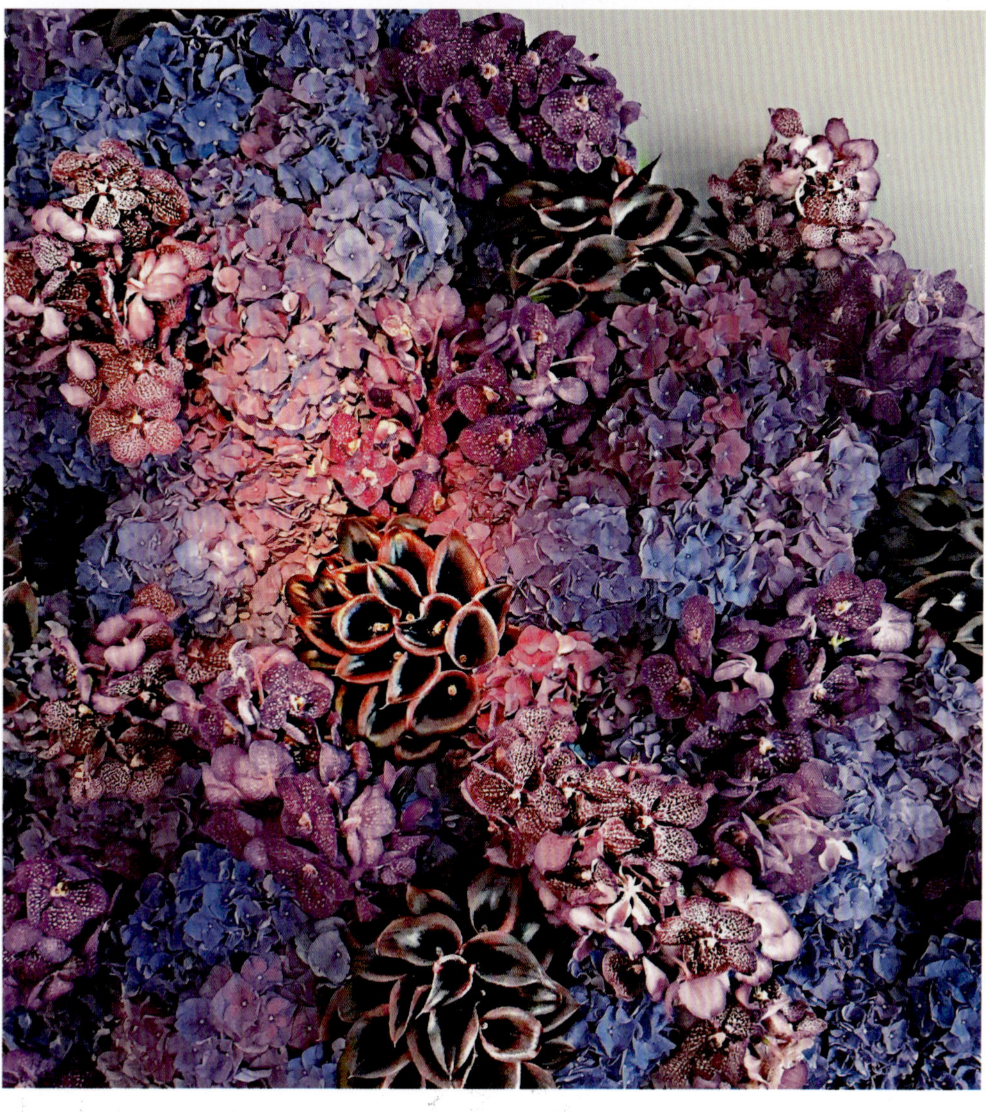

Shopping Center, Los Angeles. Leather leaf plumosa, orchids, calla lilies, and roses.

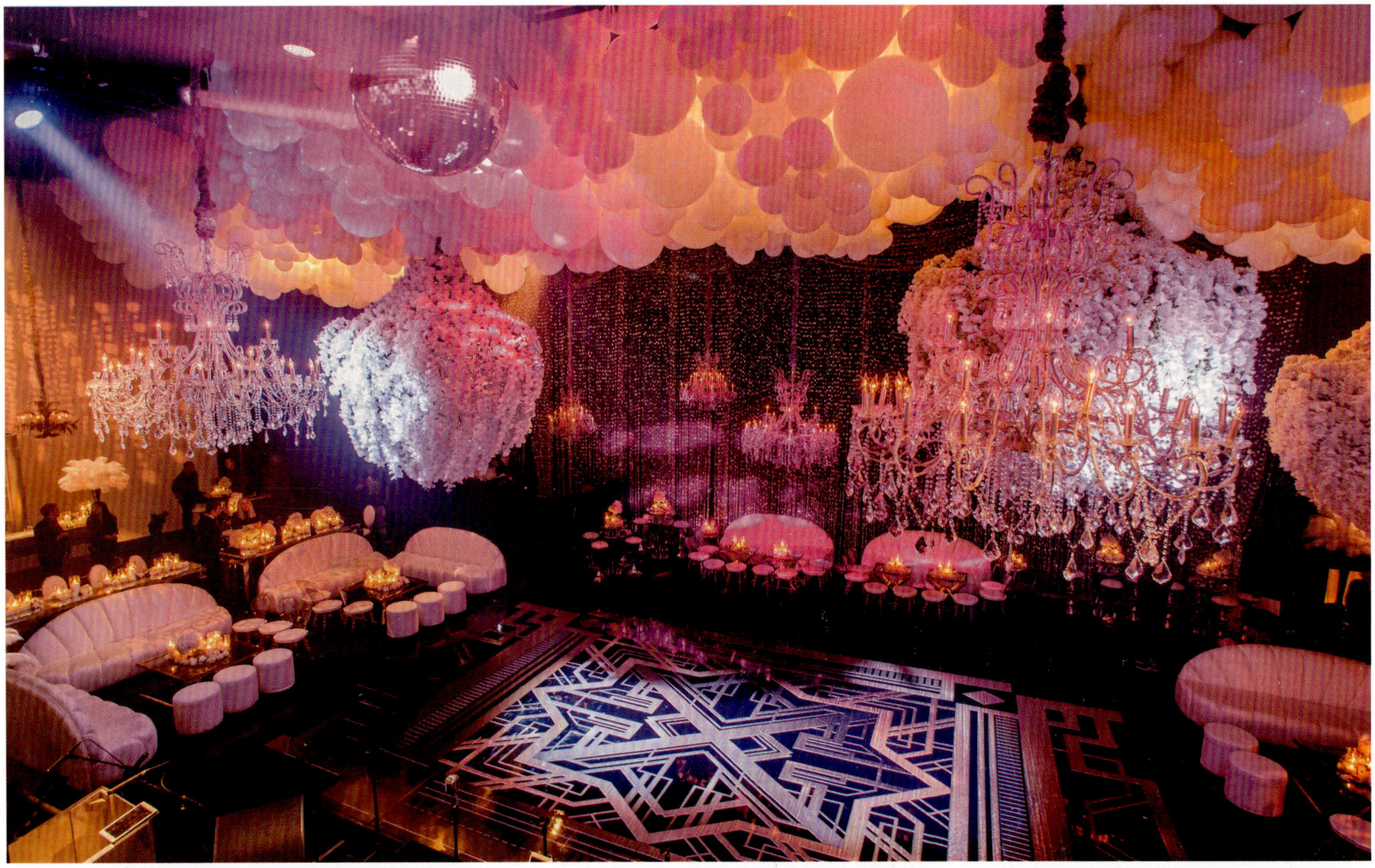

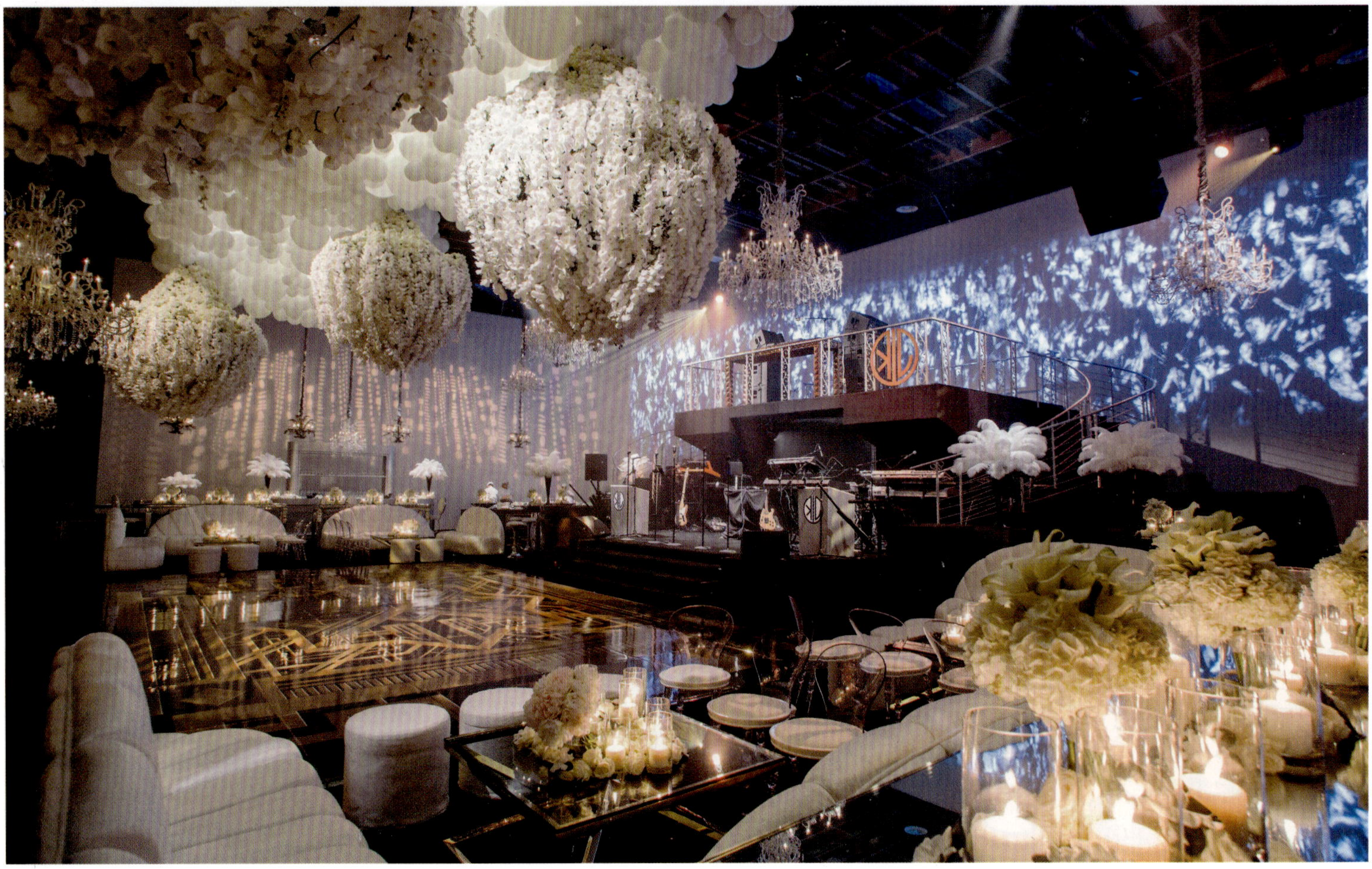

Private Event, Los Angeles. Orchids, calla lilies, and roses.
FOLLOWING: Private Event, Santa Barbara. Roses.

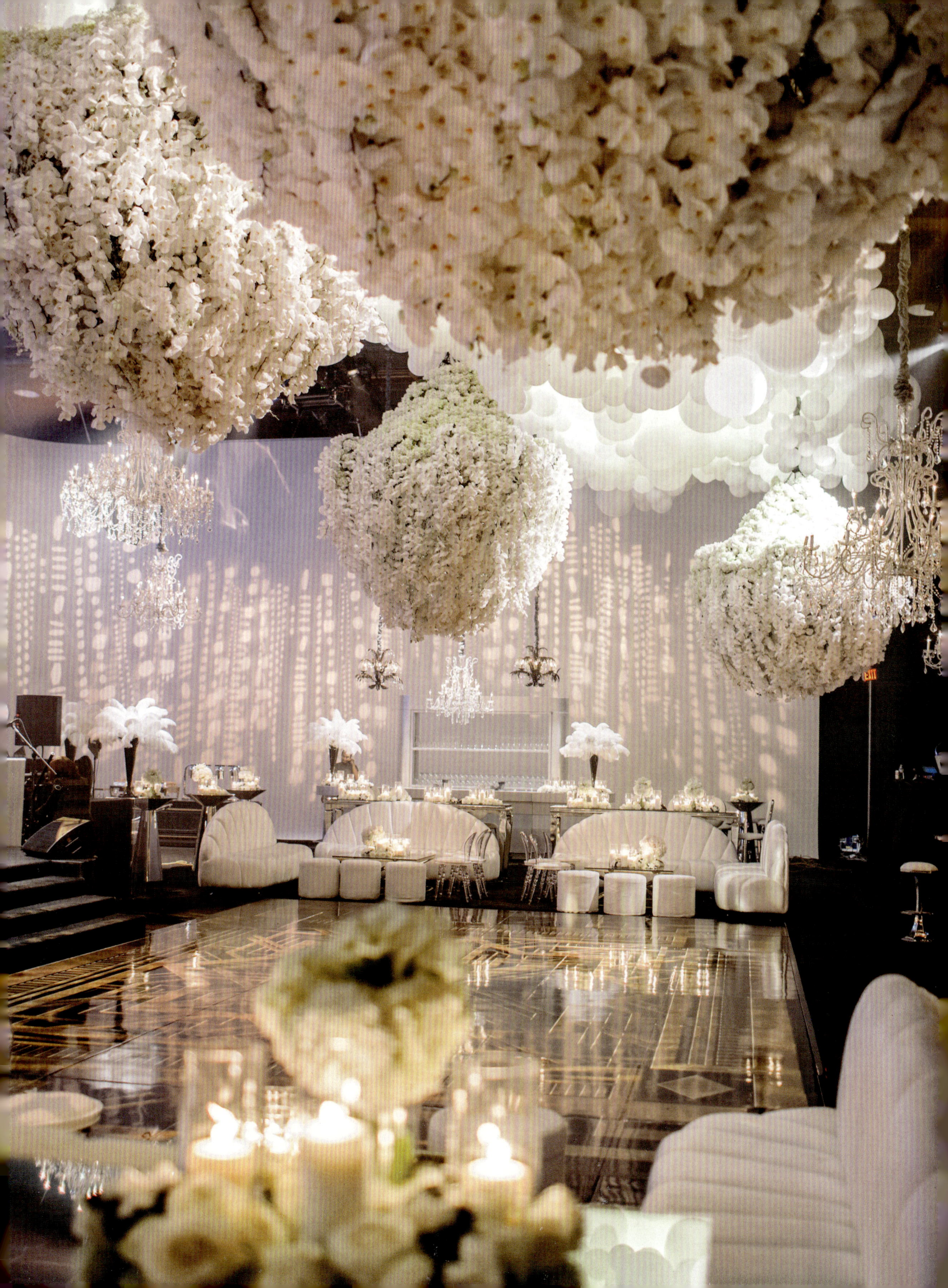

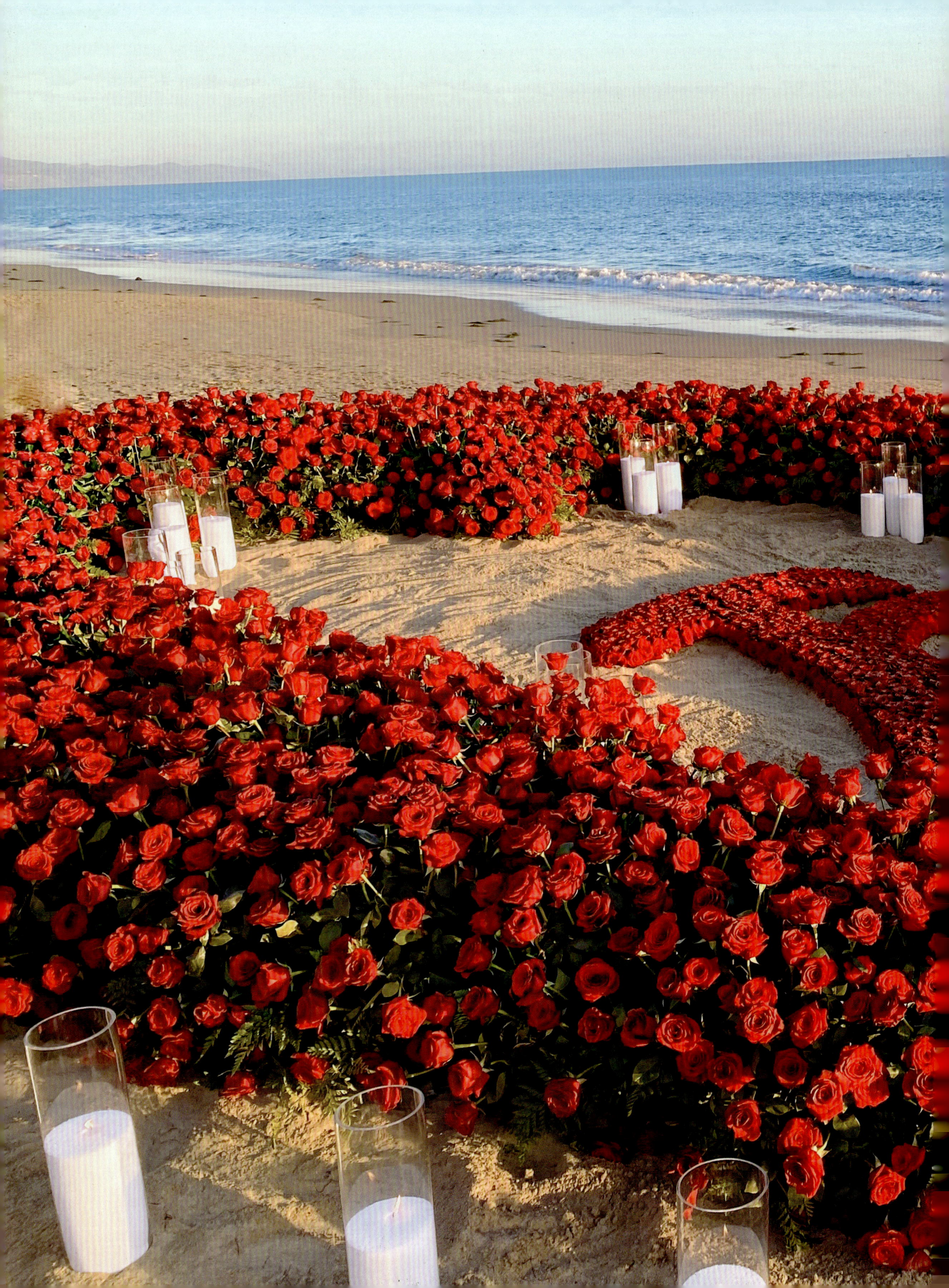

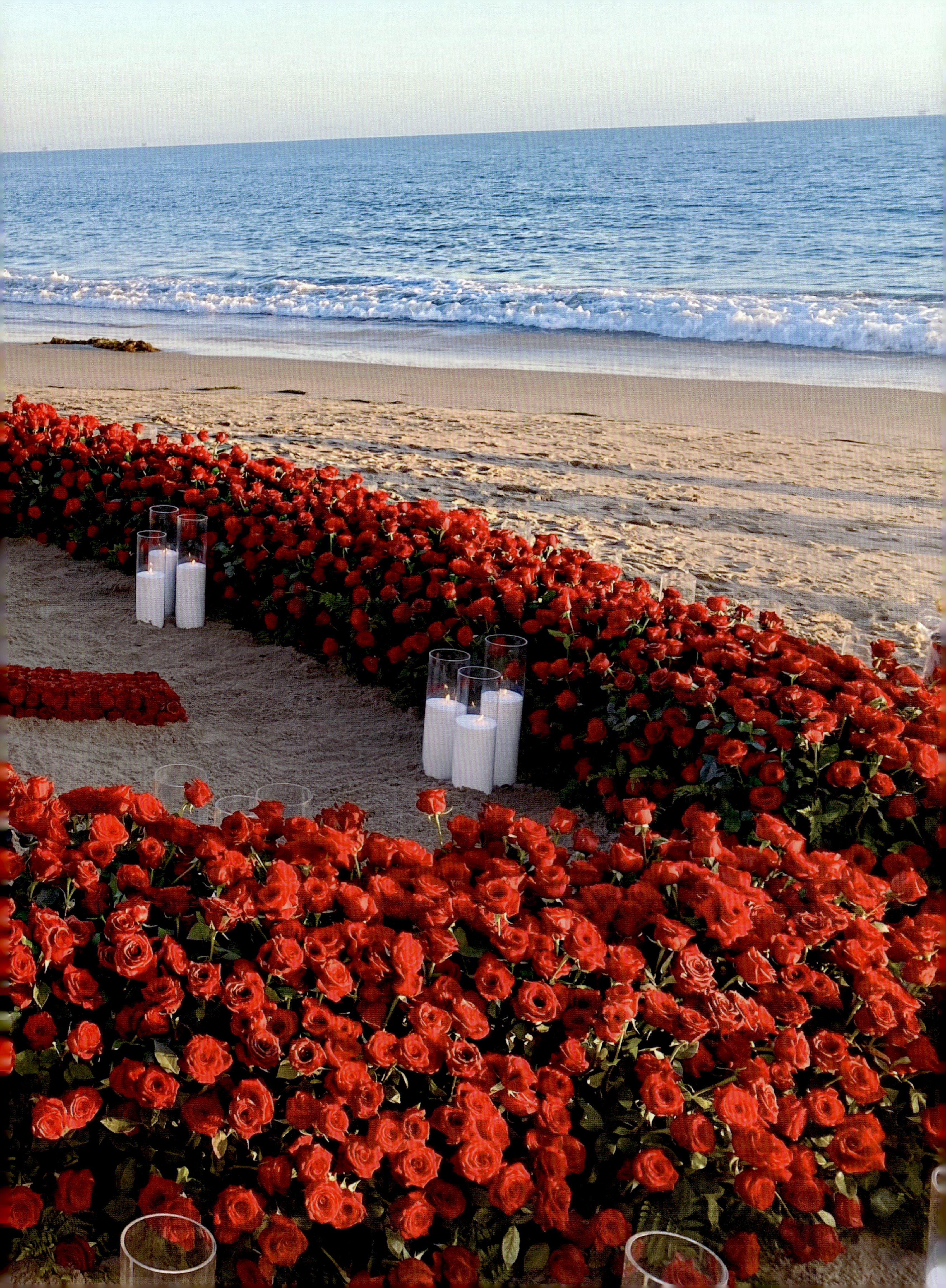

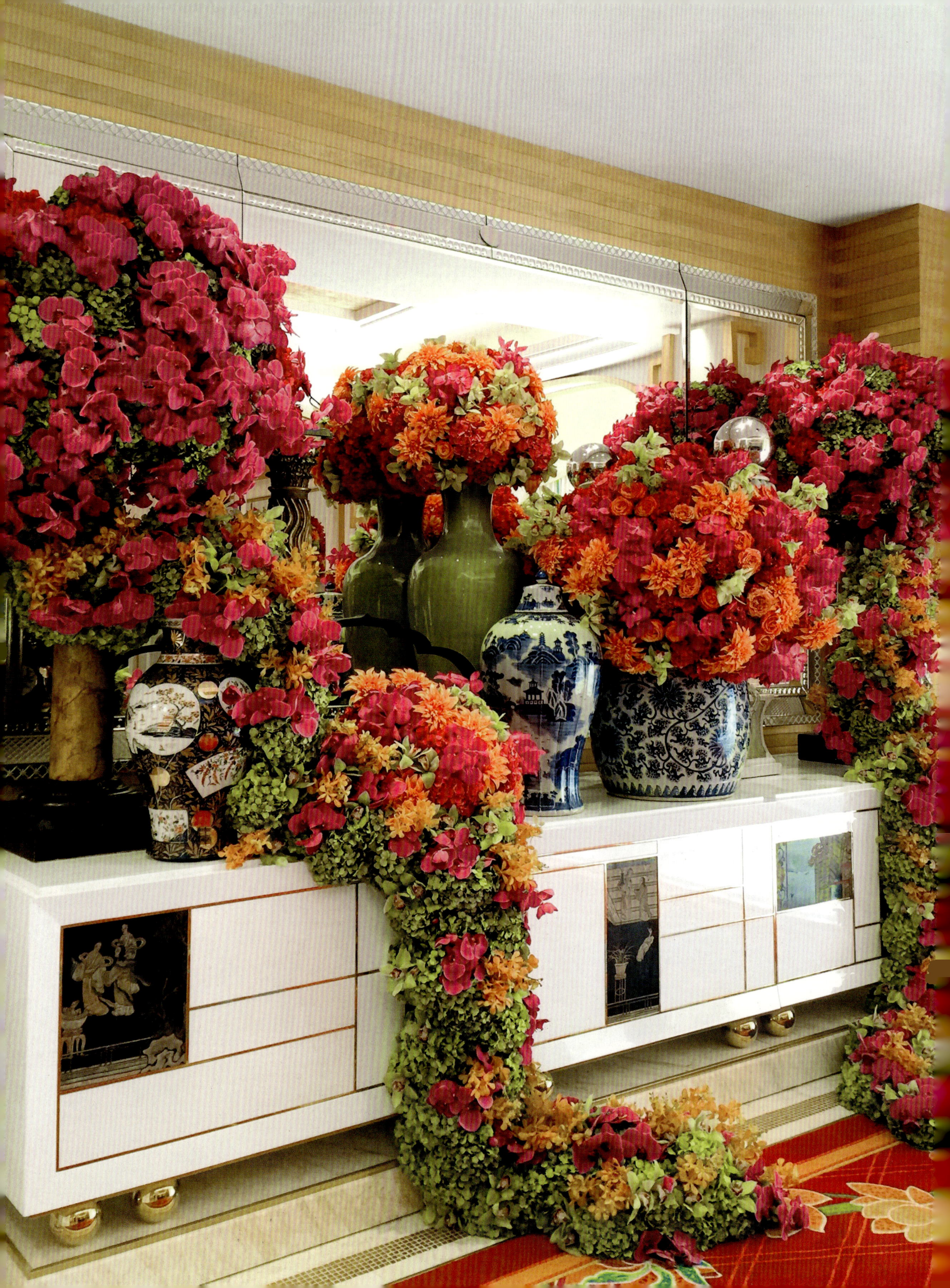

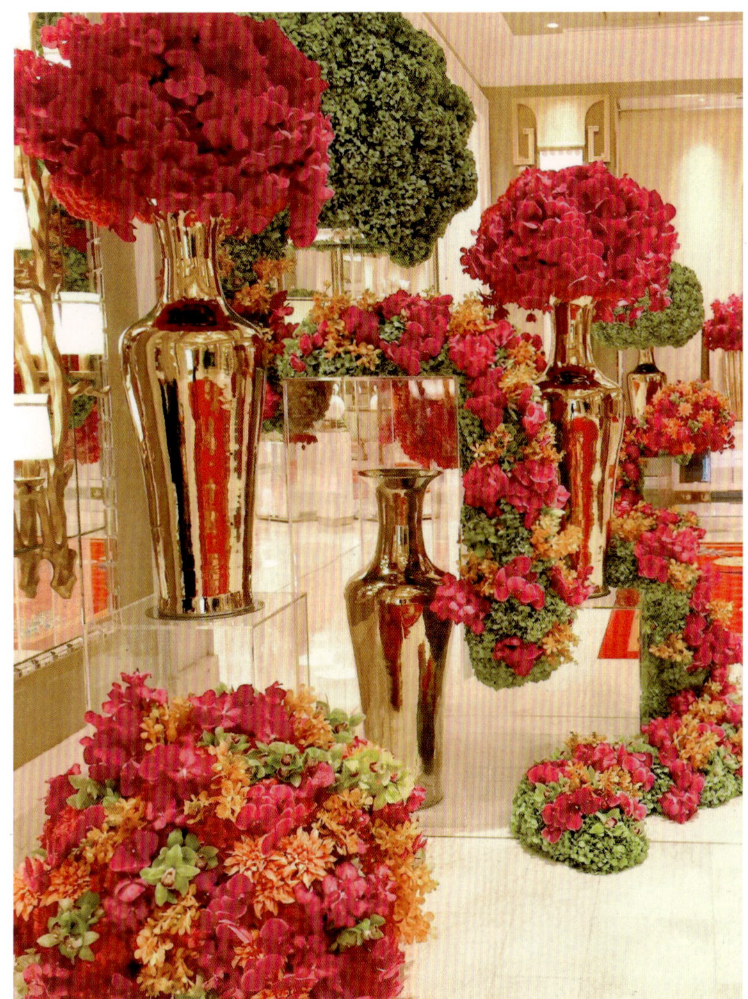

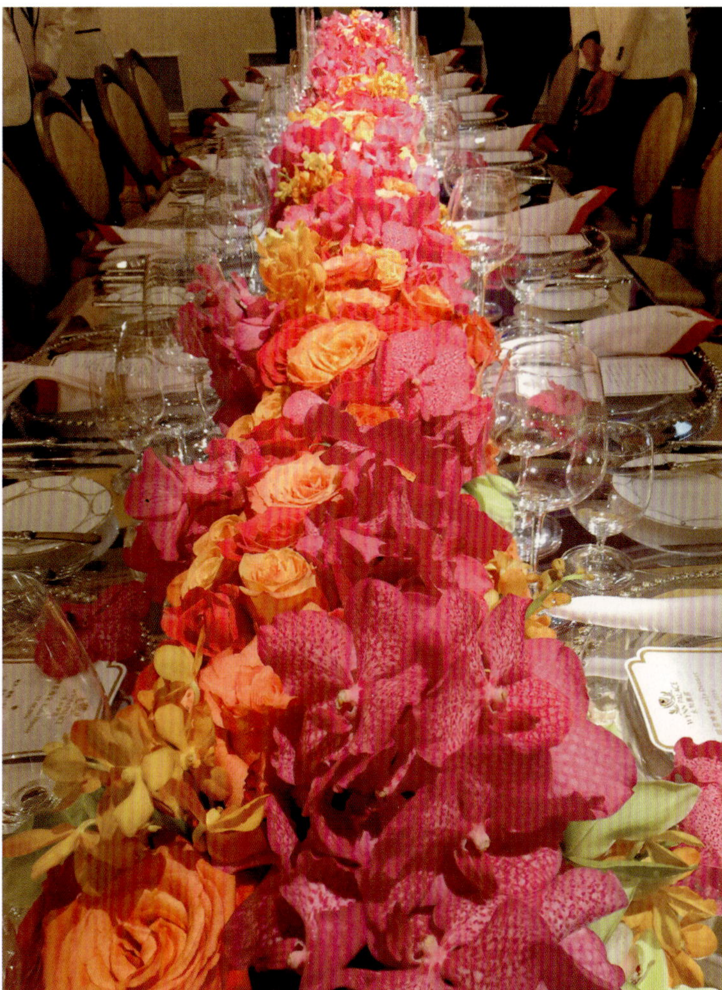

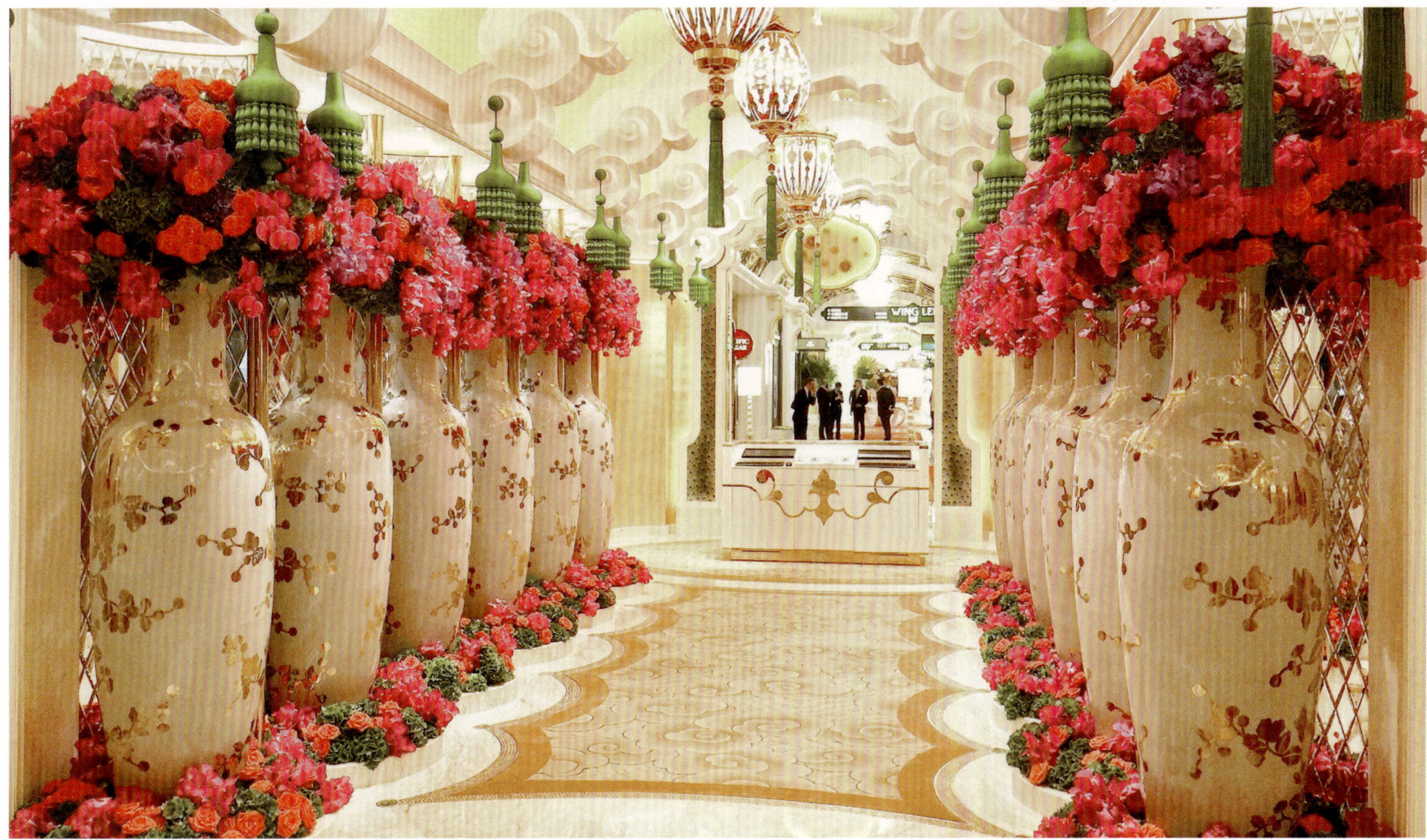

Wynn Palace Cotai Lobby. Hydrangeas, phalaenopsis and vanda orchids, and roses. FOLLOWING: Private Event, Arizona. Roses, calla lilies, and orchids.

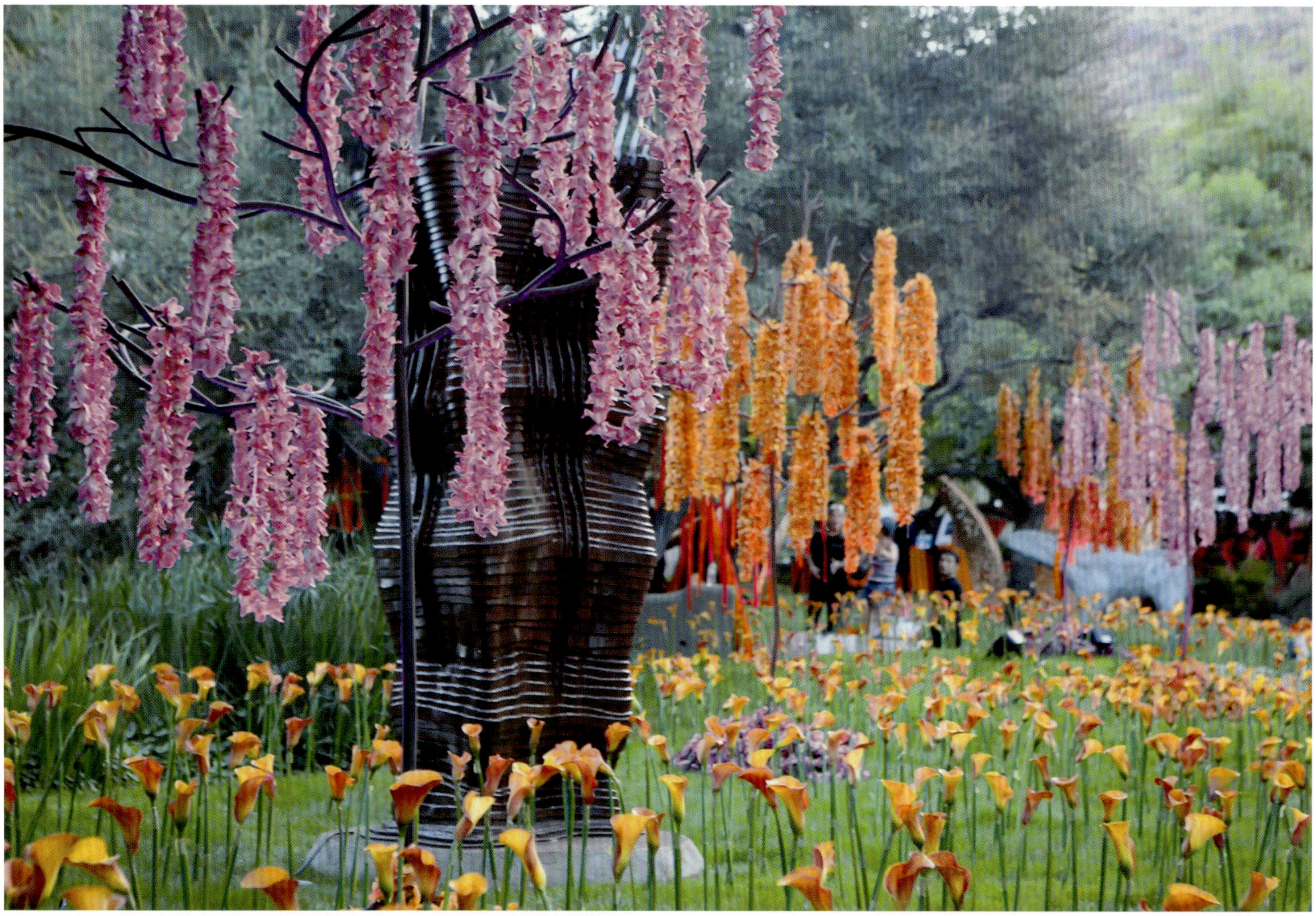

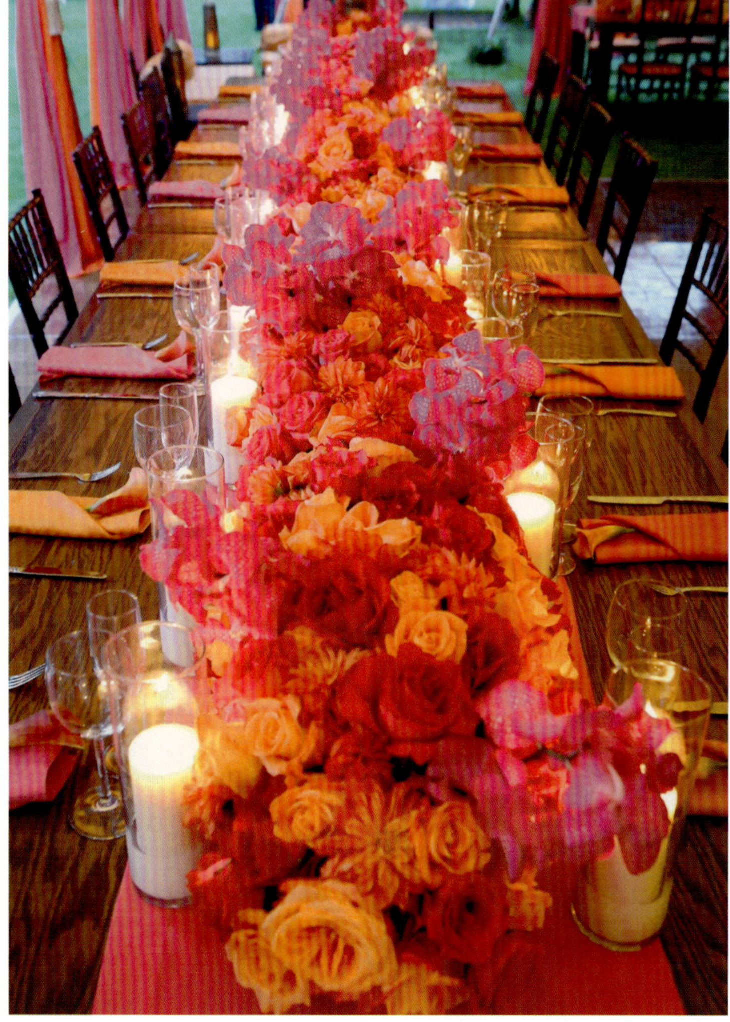

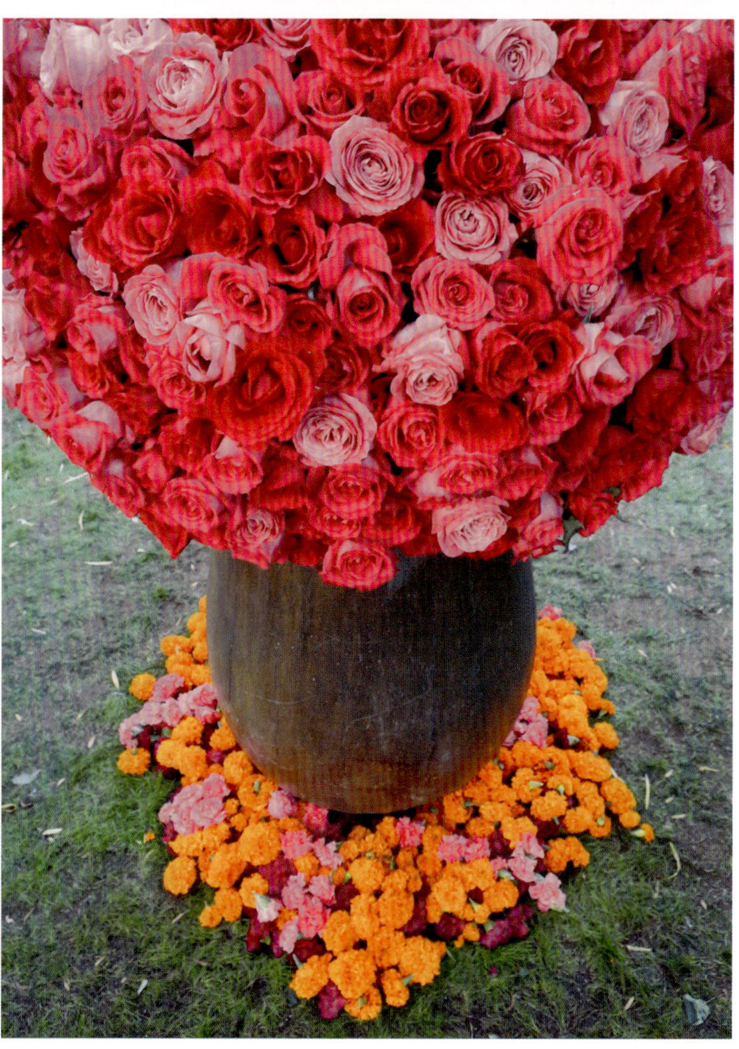

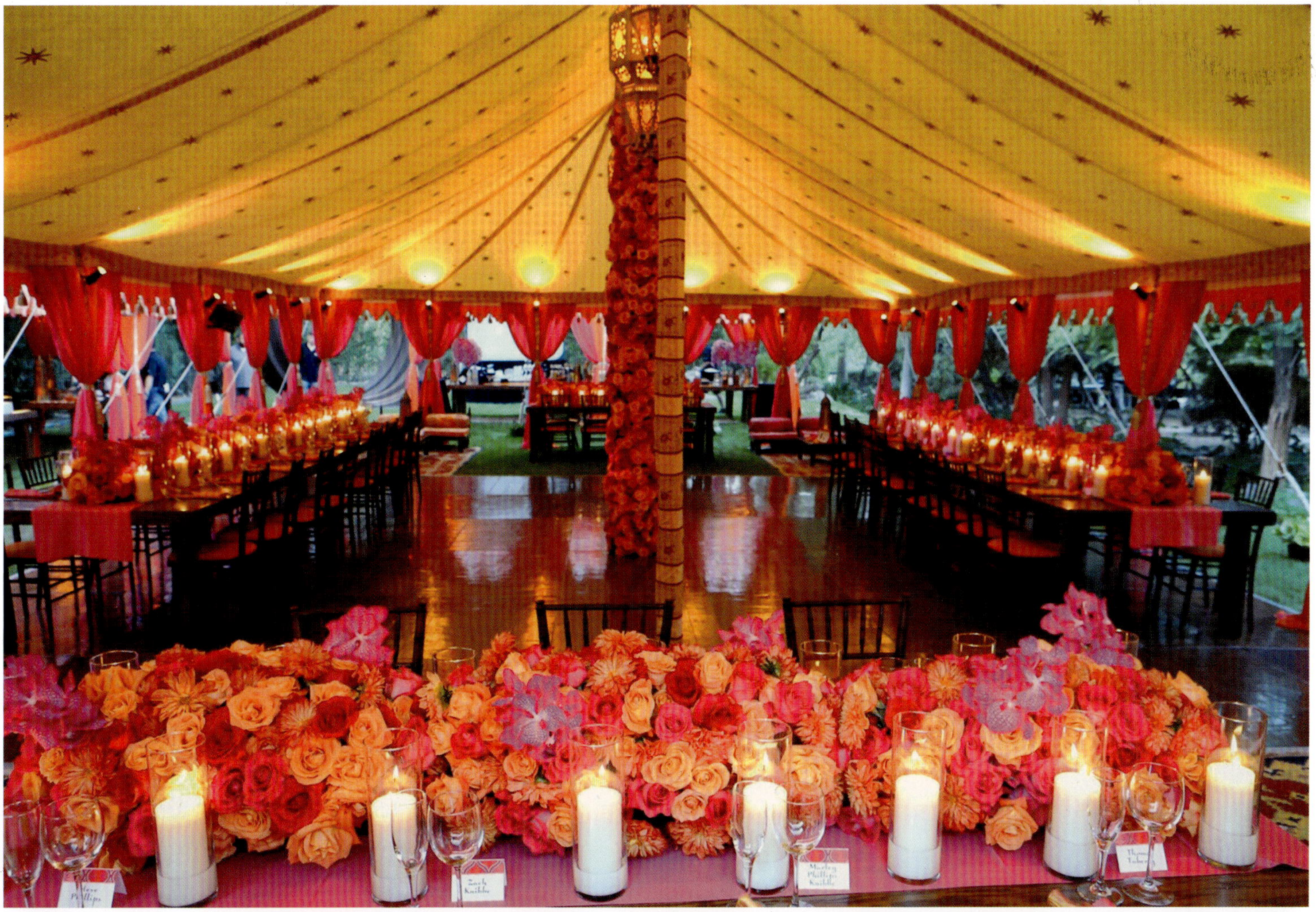

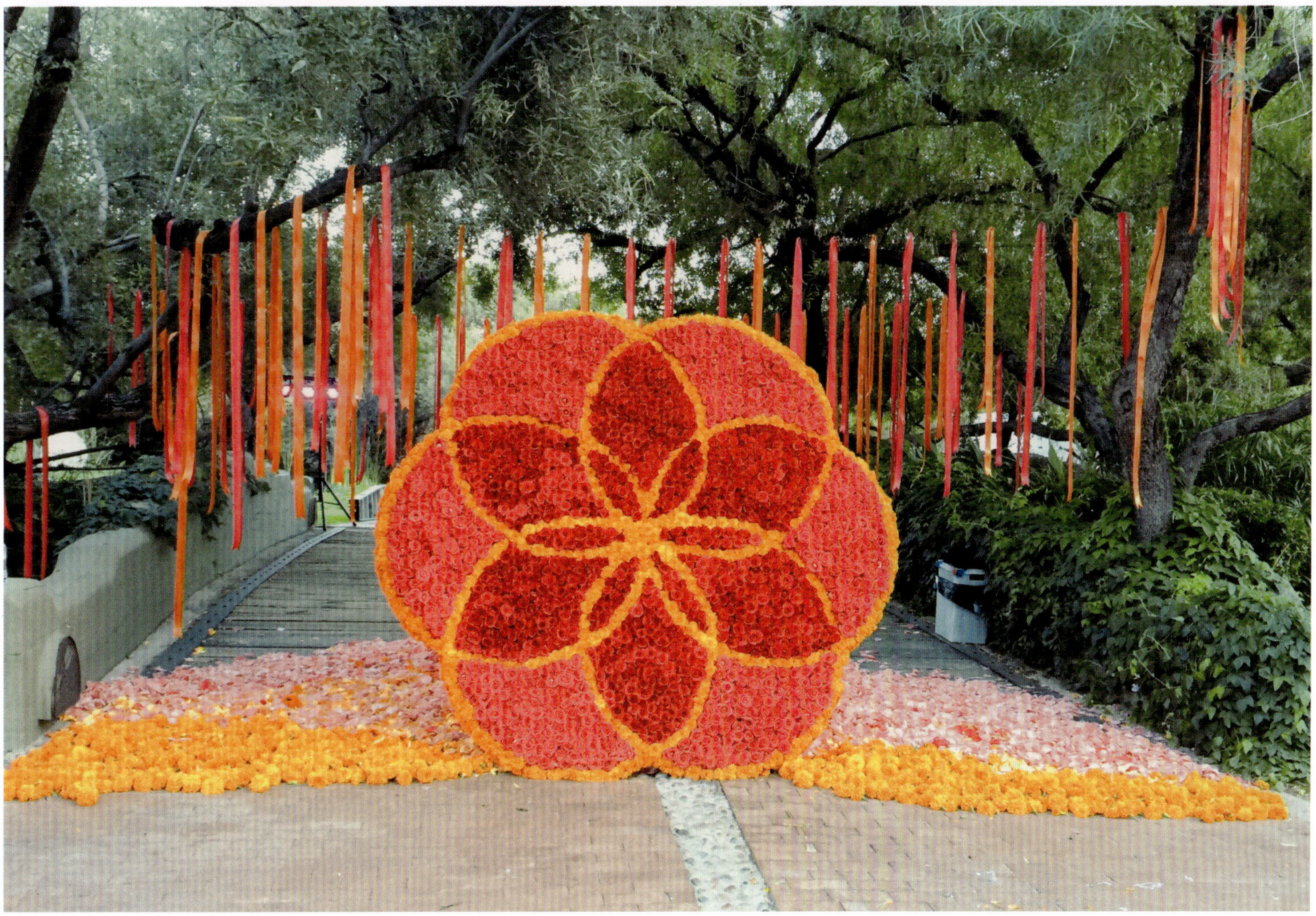

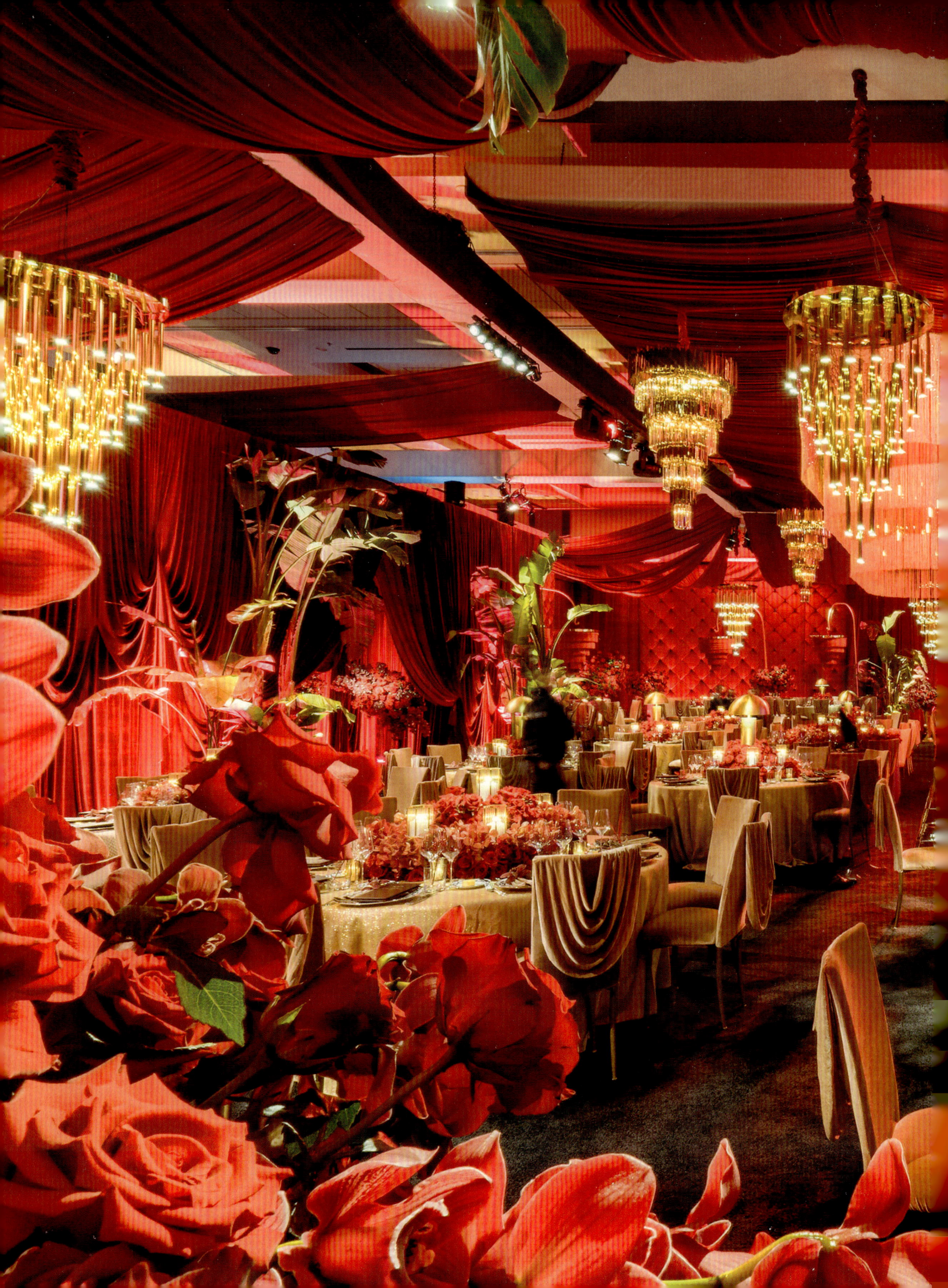

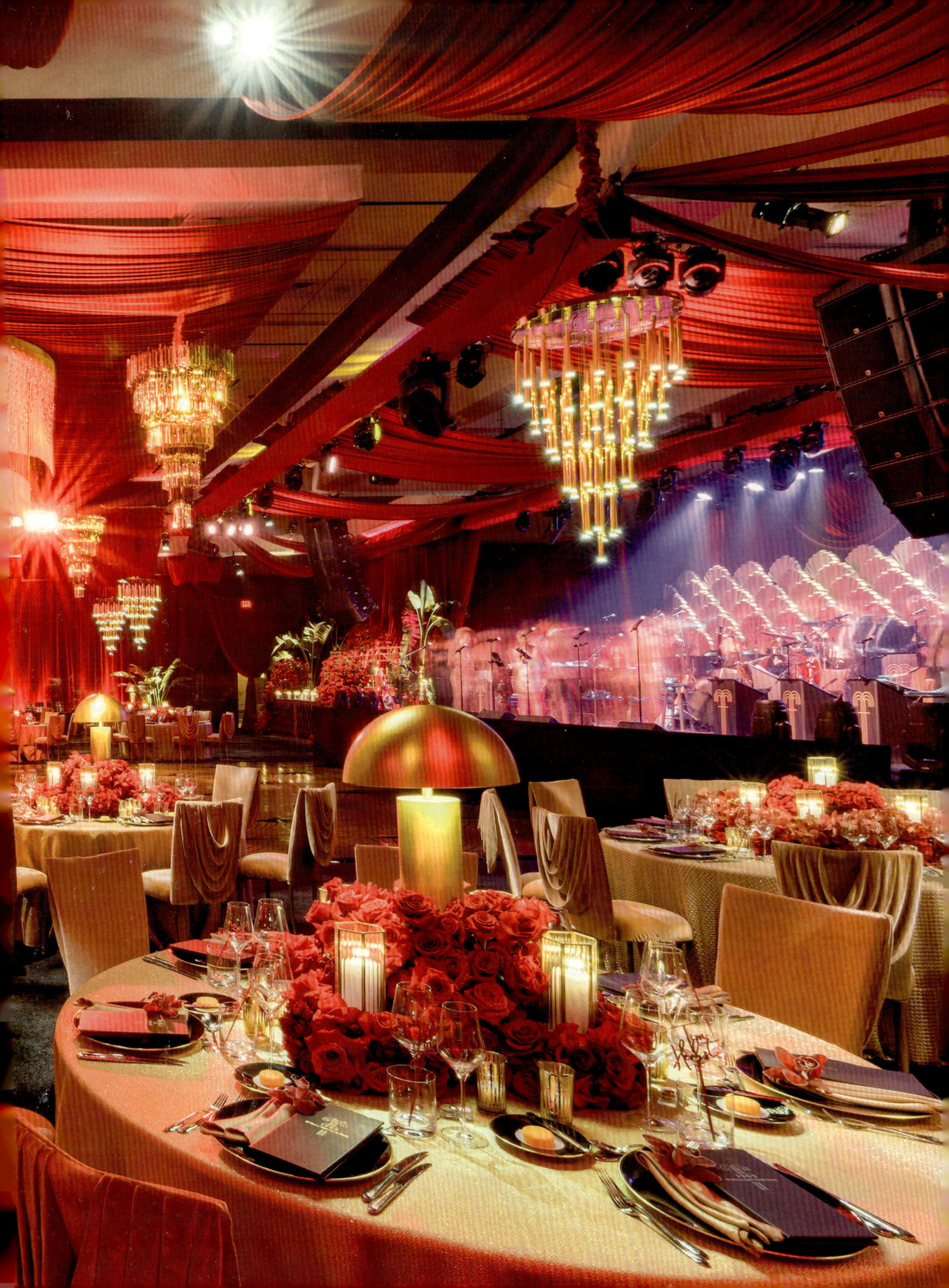

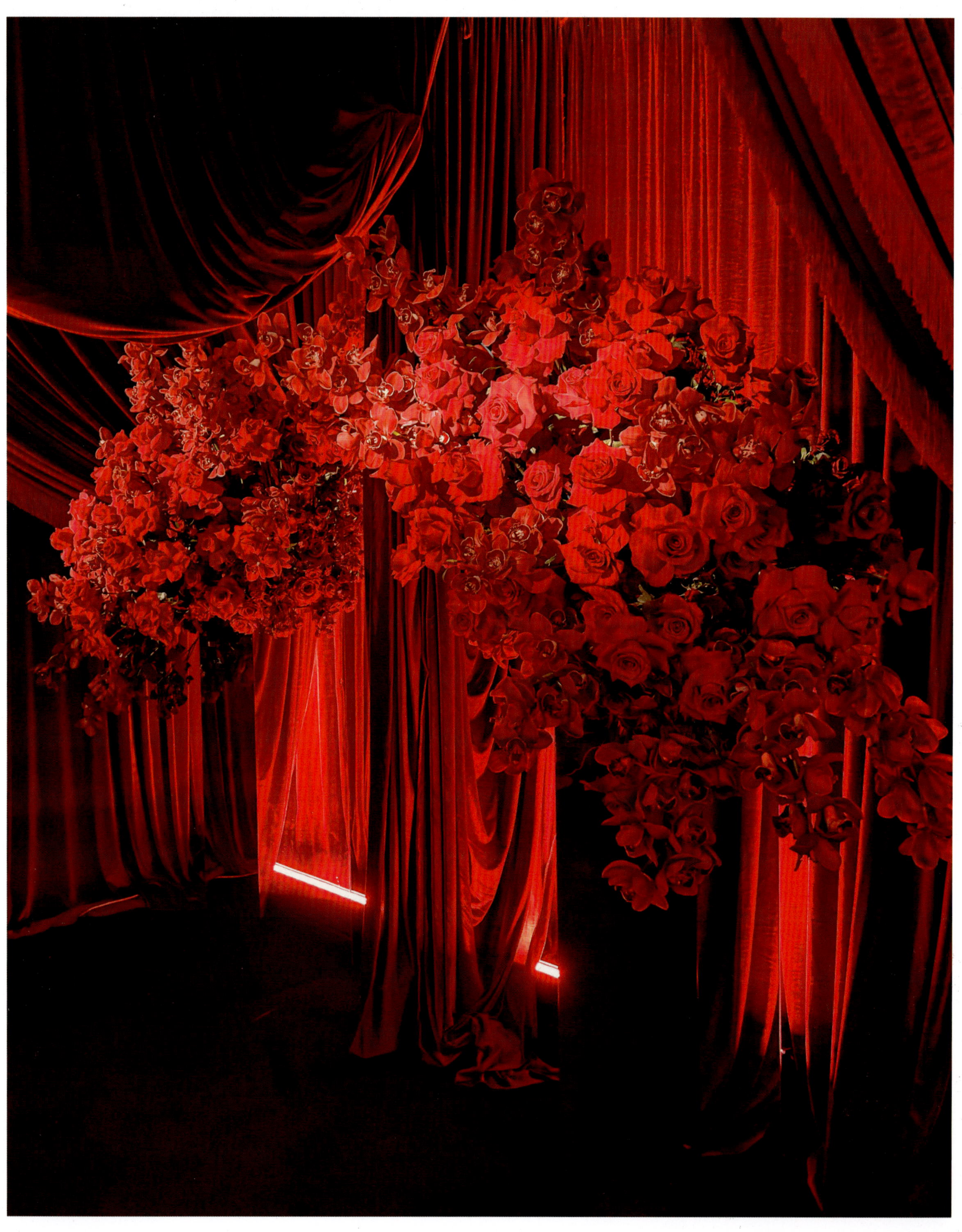

PAGES 188–191: Private Event, Las Vegas. Roses and cymbidium orchids. FOLLOWING: Private Event, Las Vegas. Roses, hydrangeas, and leis of dendrobium orchids.

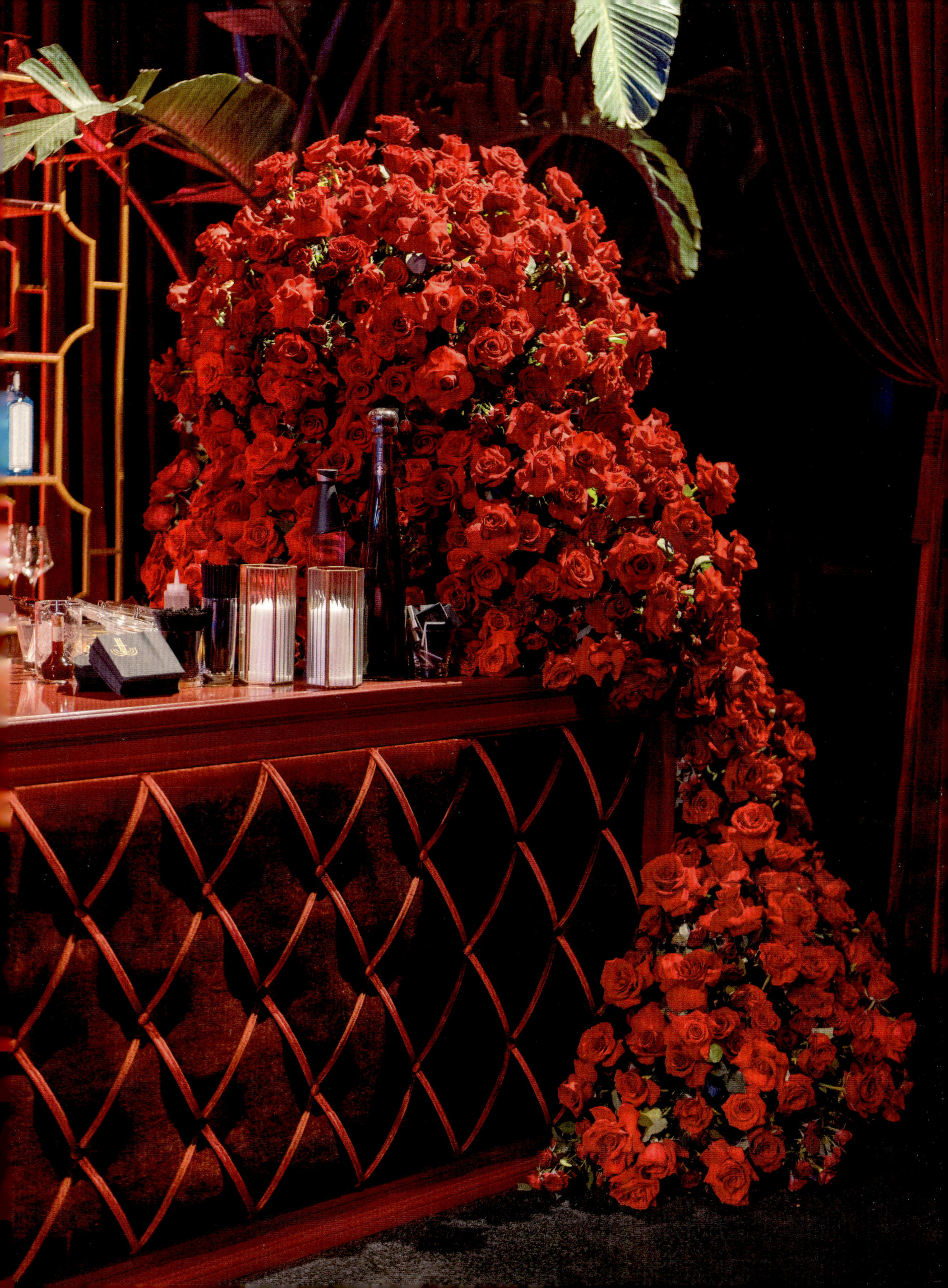

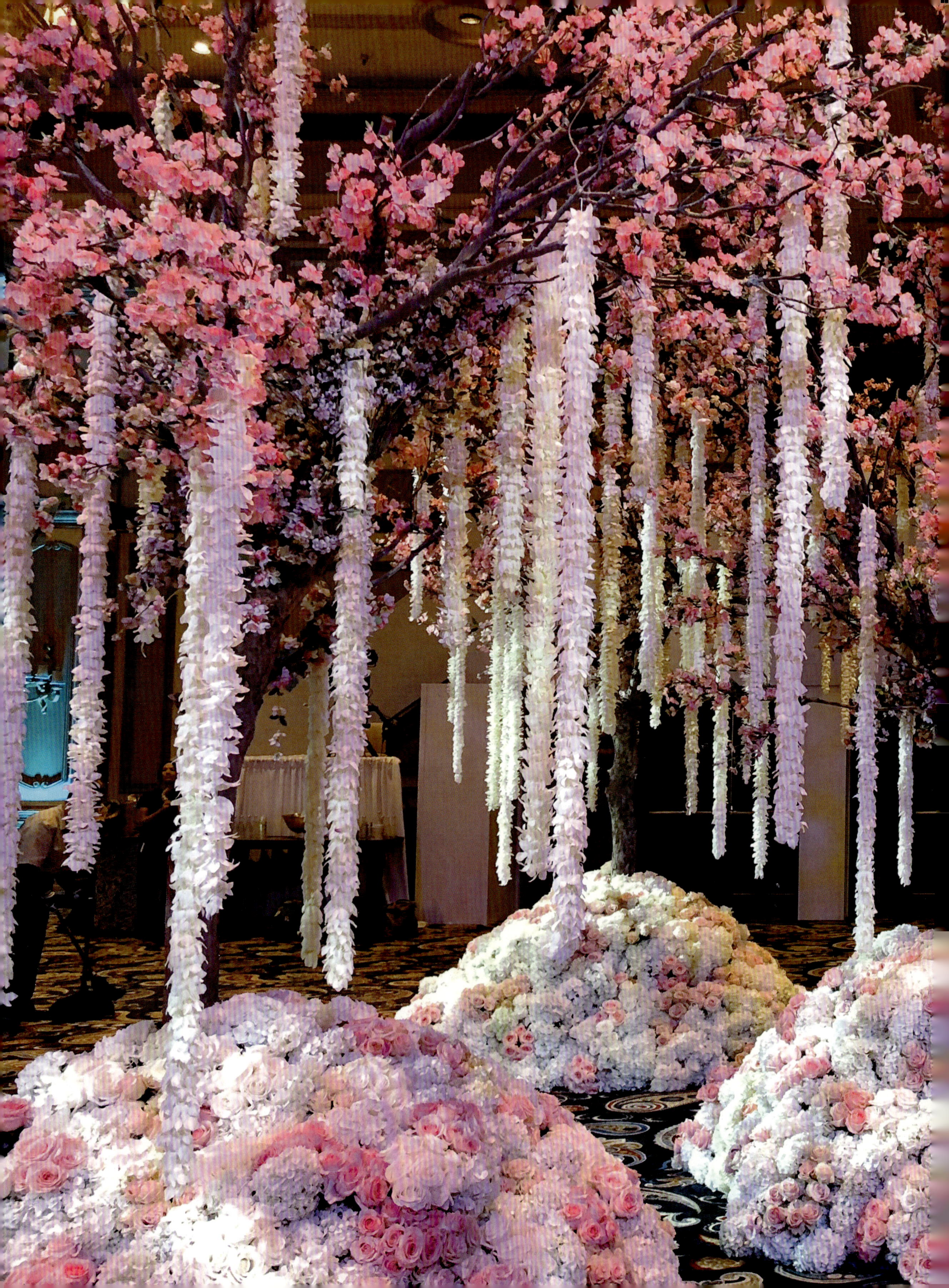

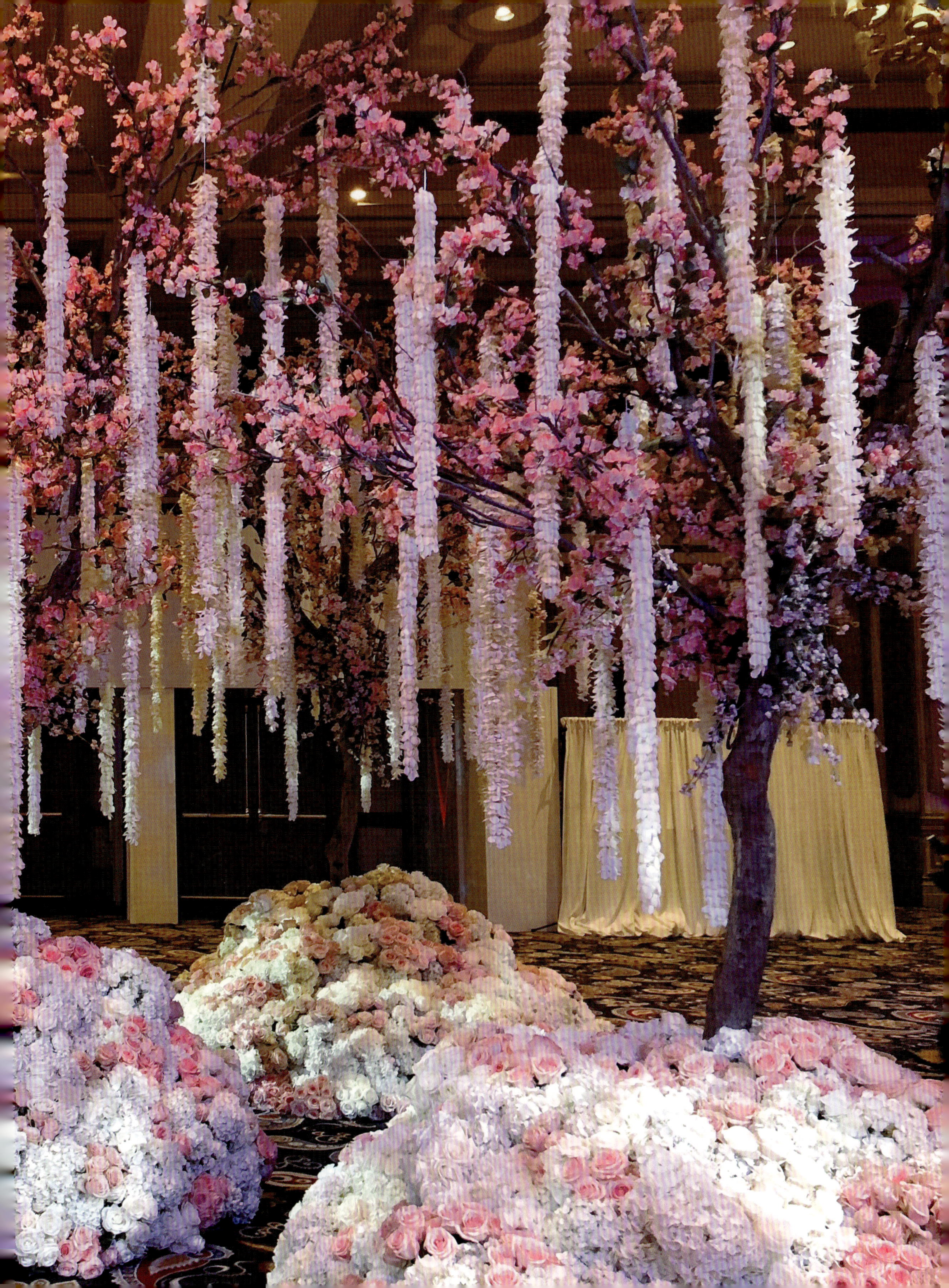

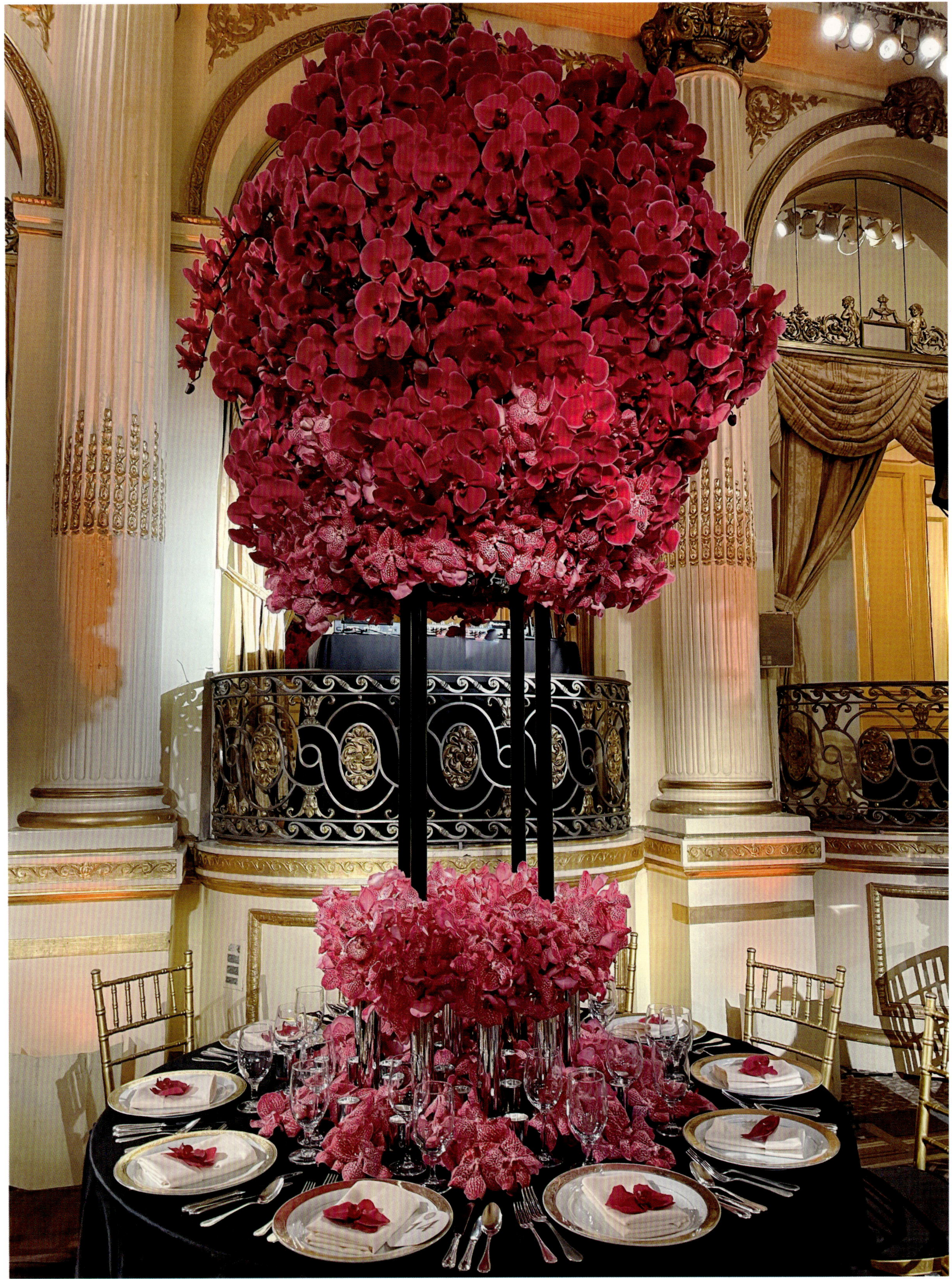

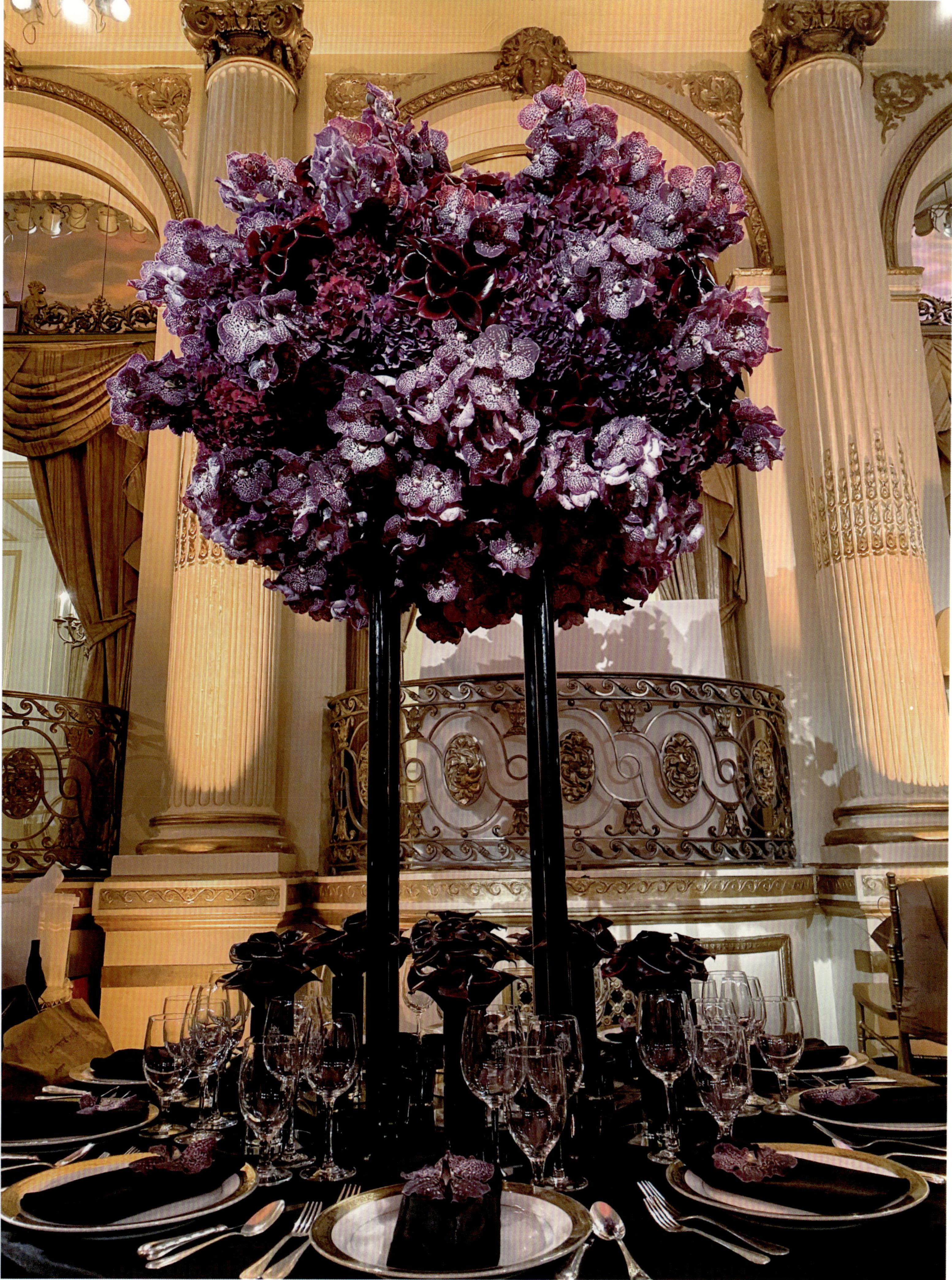

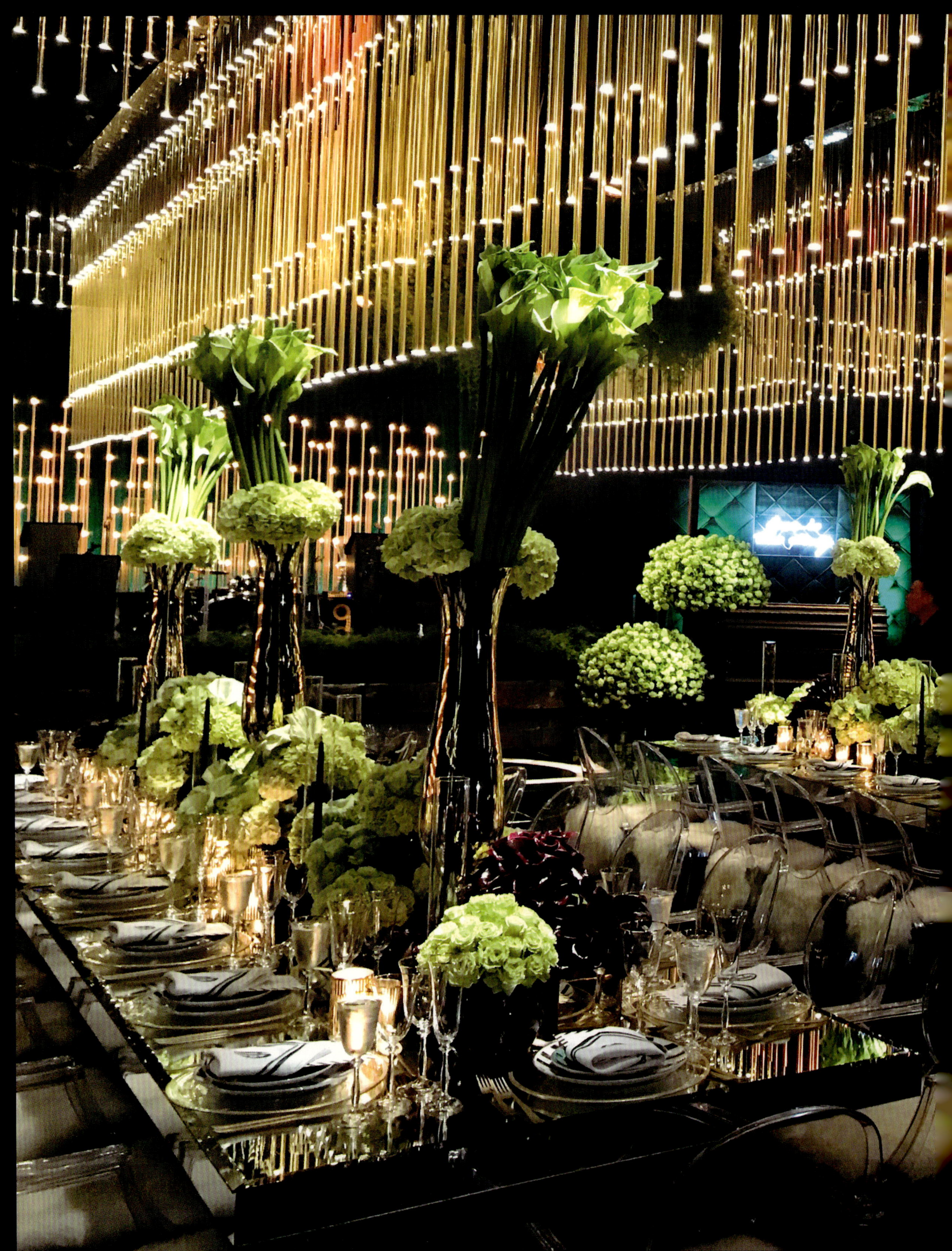

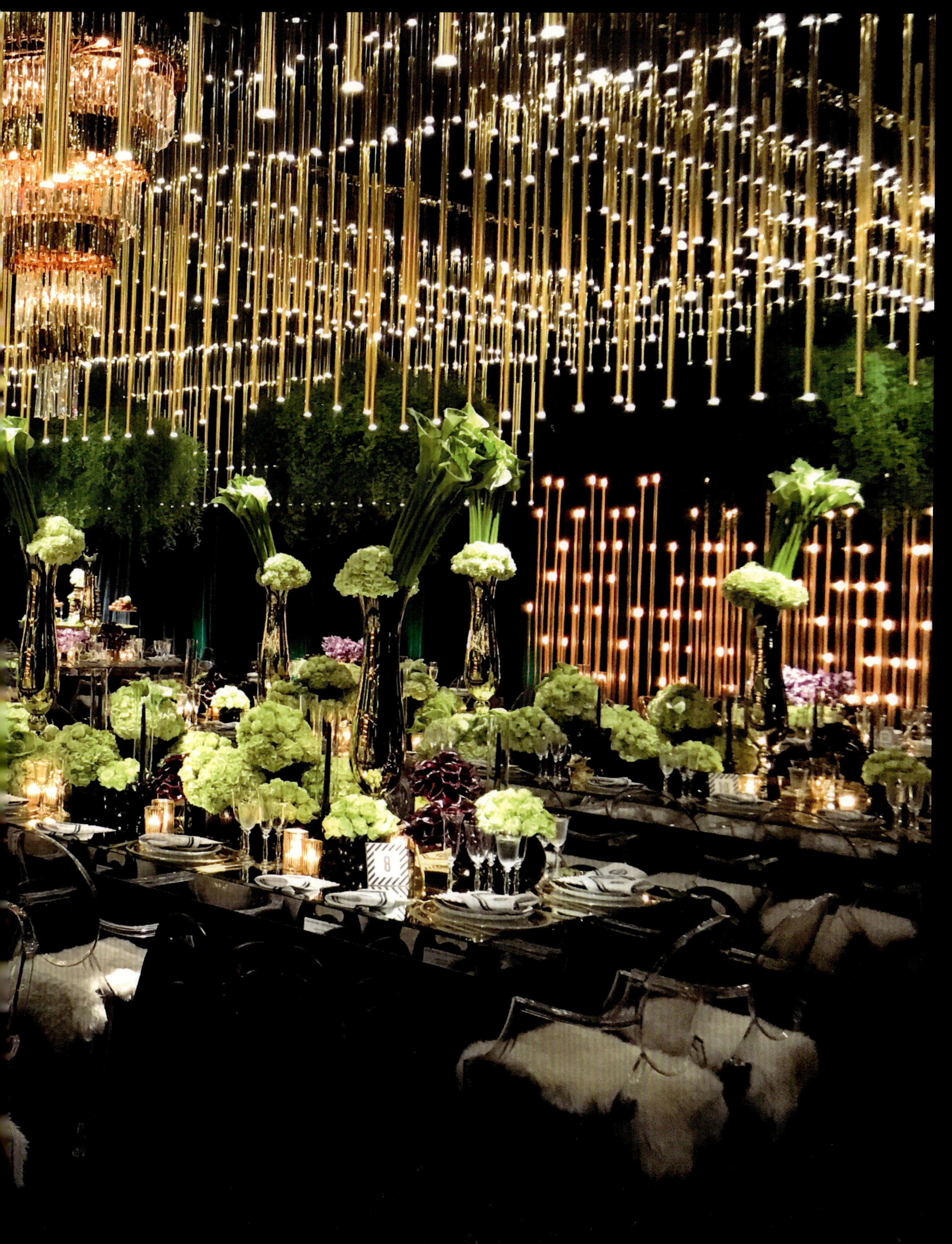

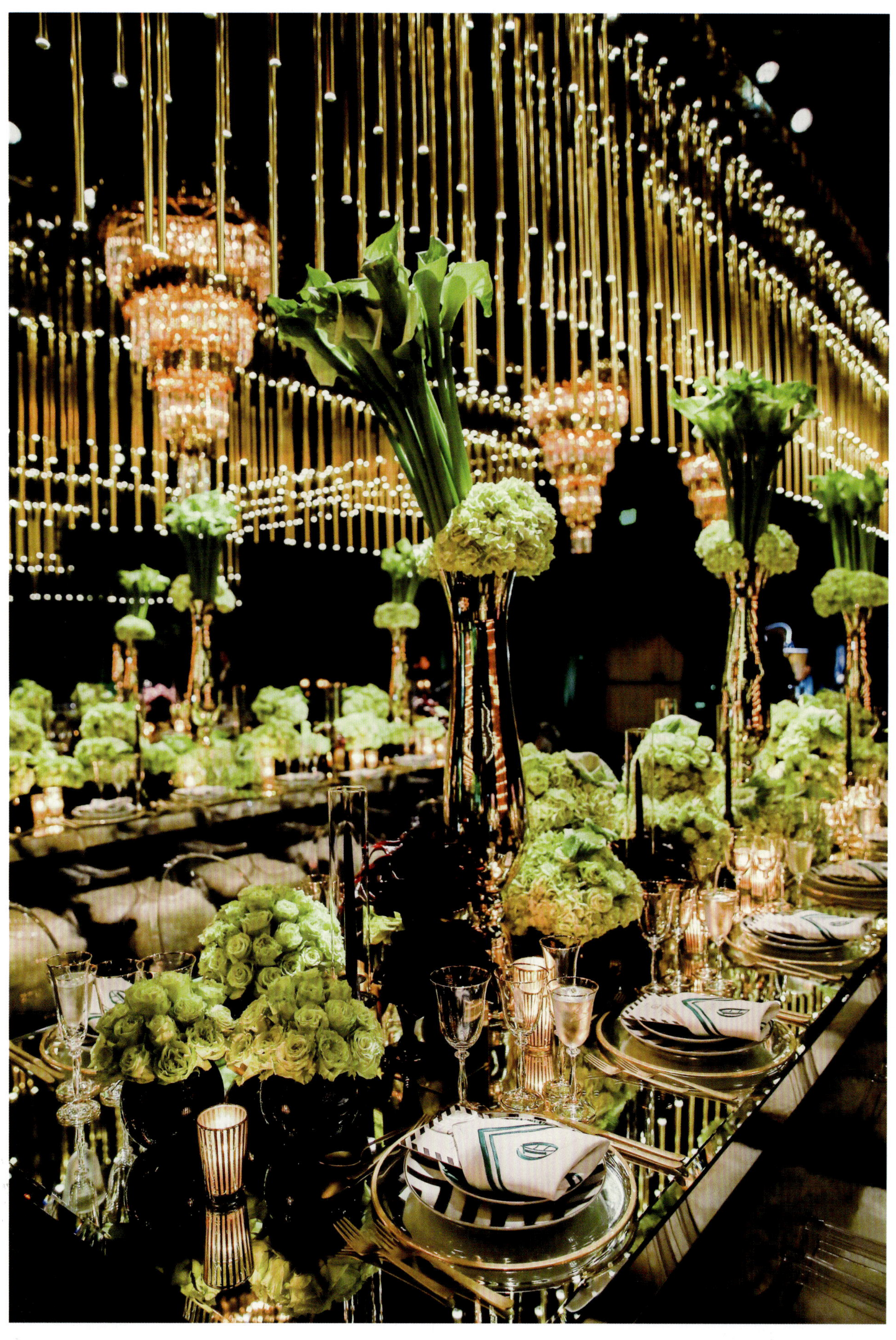

PAGE 194: Private Event, The Plaza New York. Variety of orchids.
PAGE 195: Variety of Vanda Sunanda Jeff Leatham orchids, calla lilies, and hydrangeas. PAGES 196–199: Private Event, Palm Beach, Florida. Calla lilies, vanda orchids, succulents, and roses.

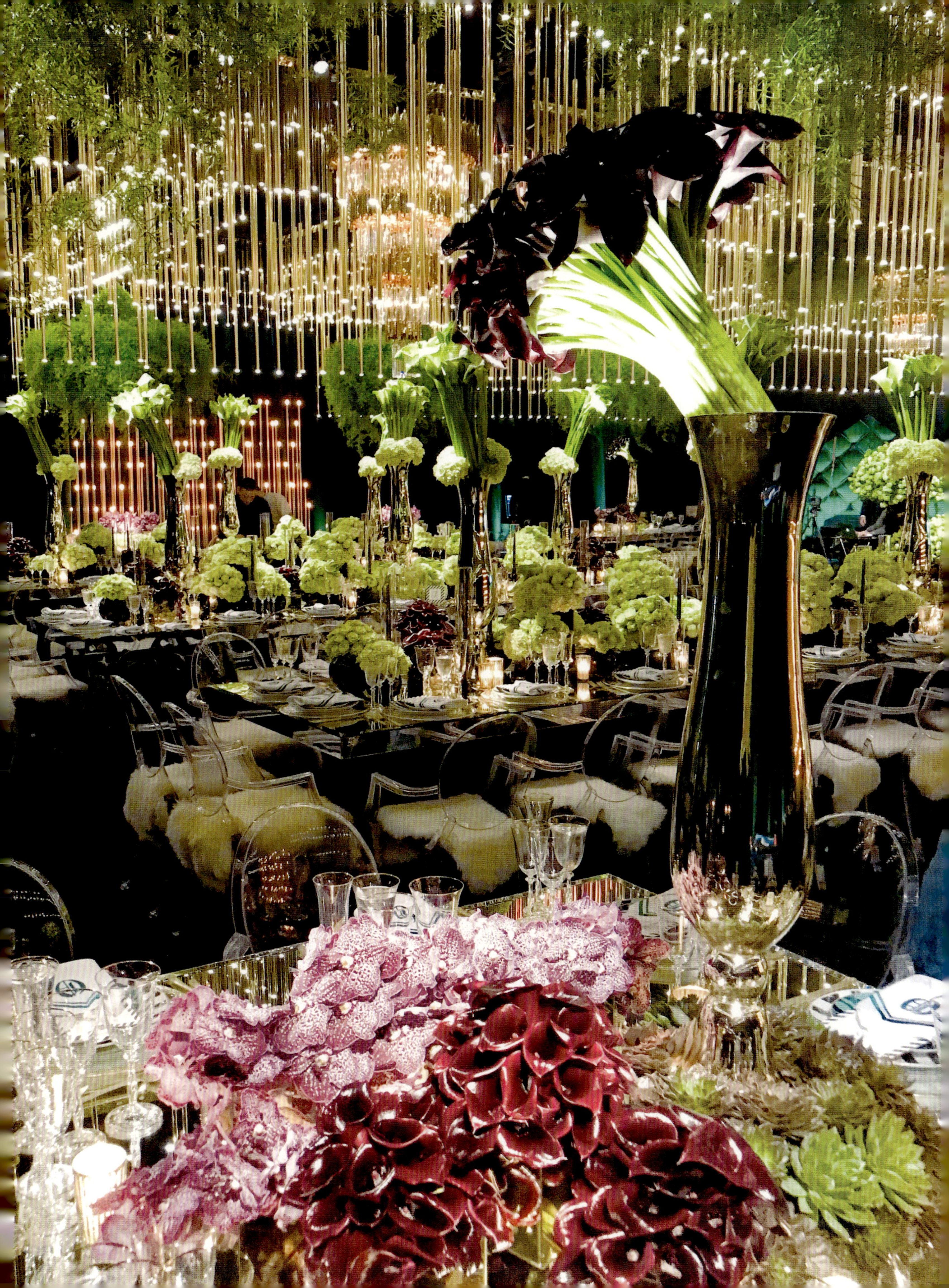

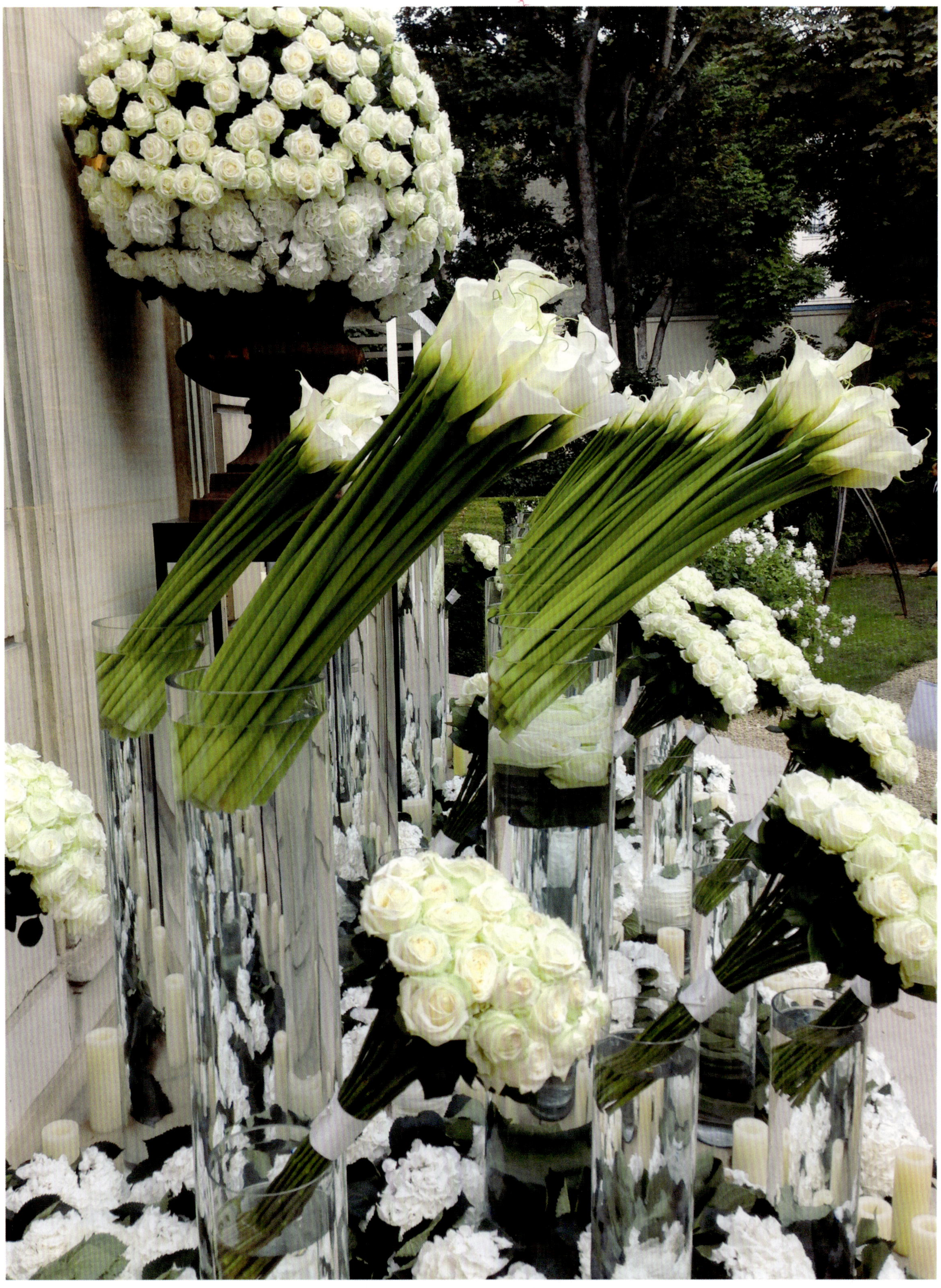

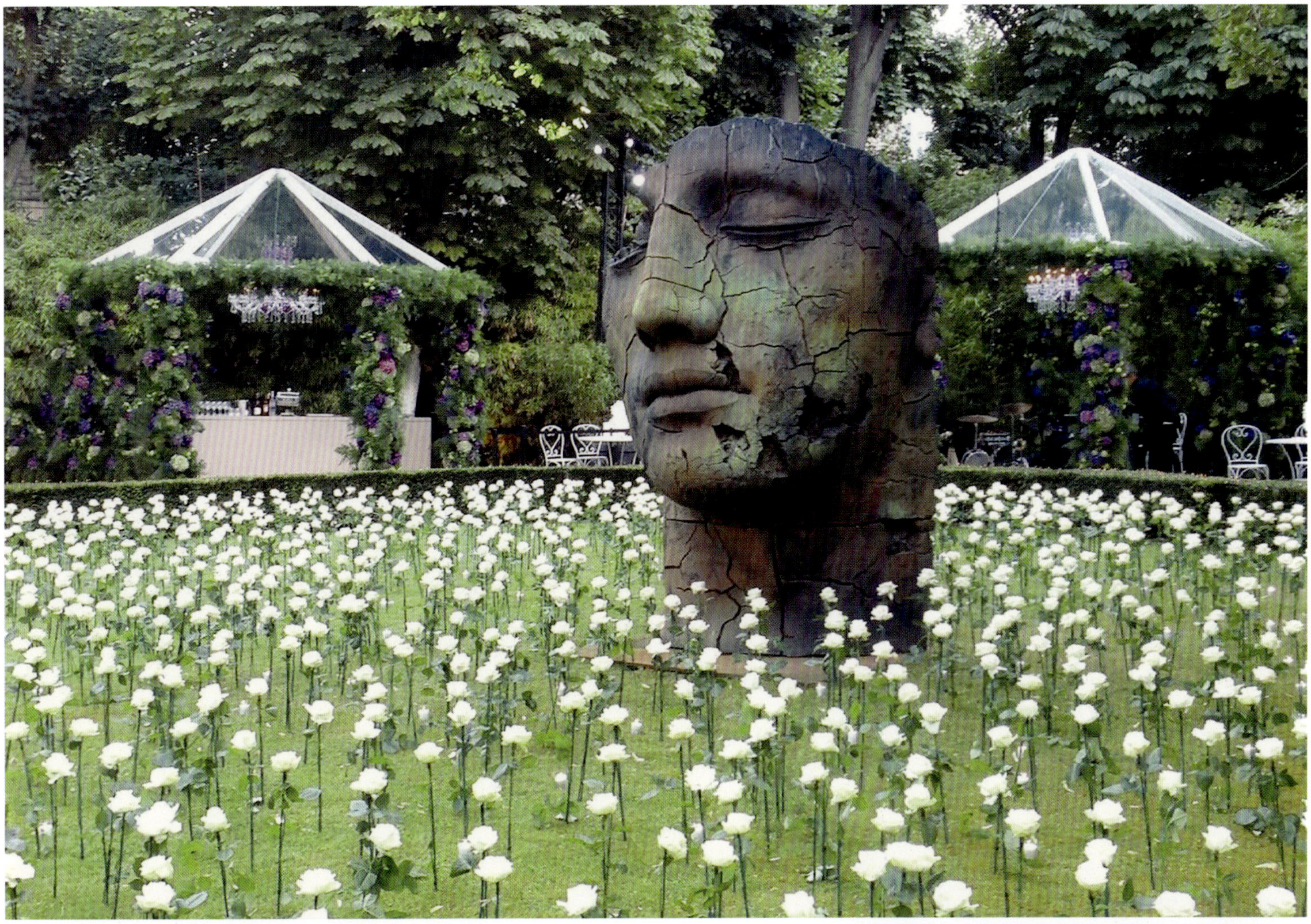

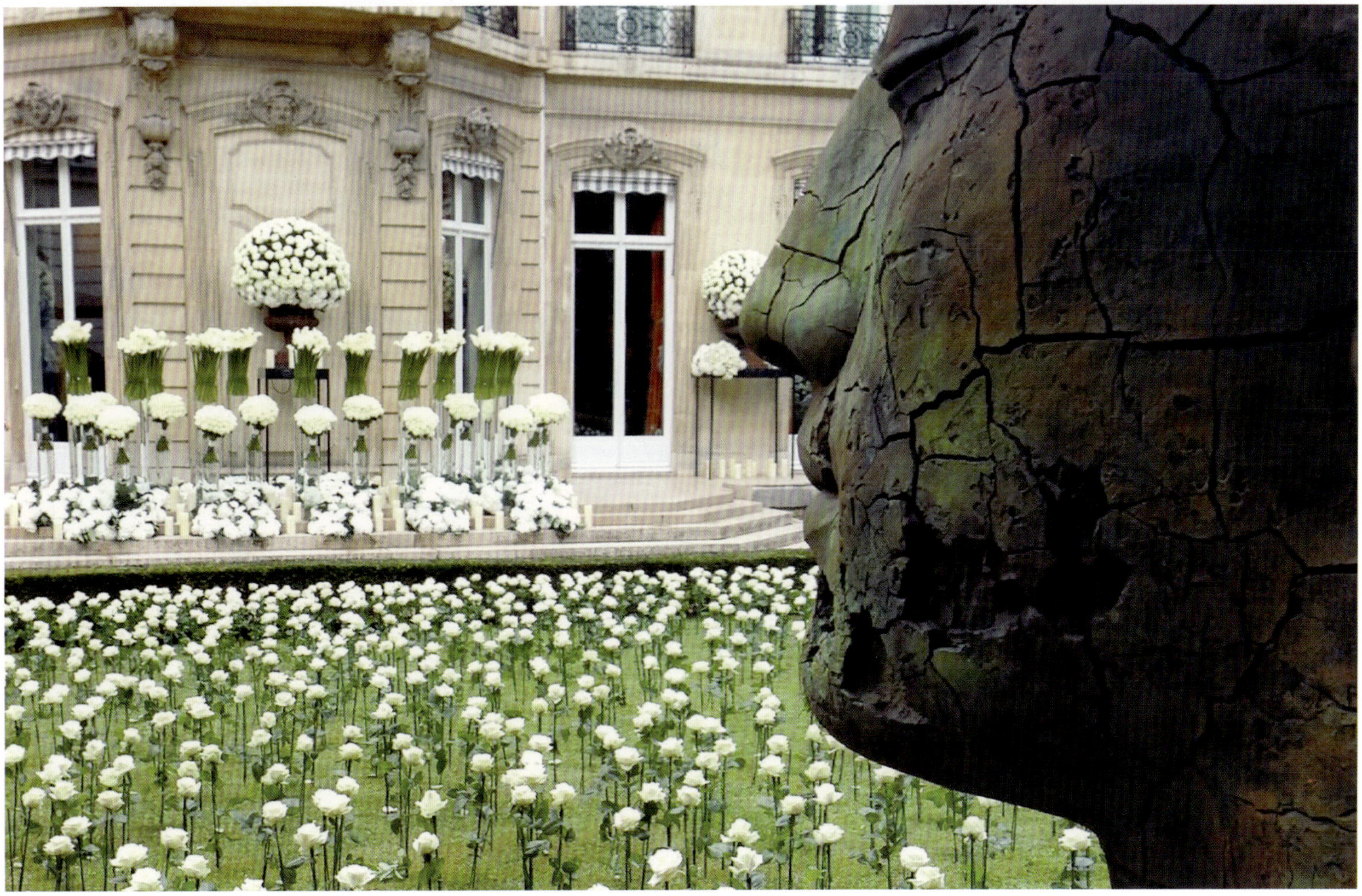

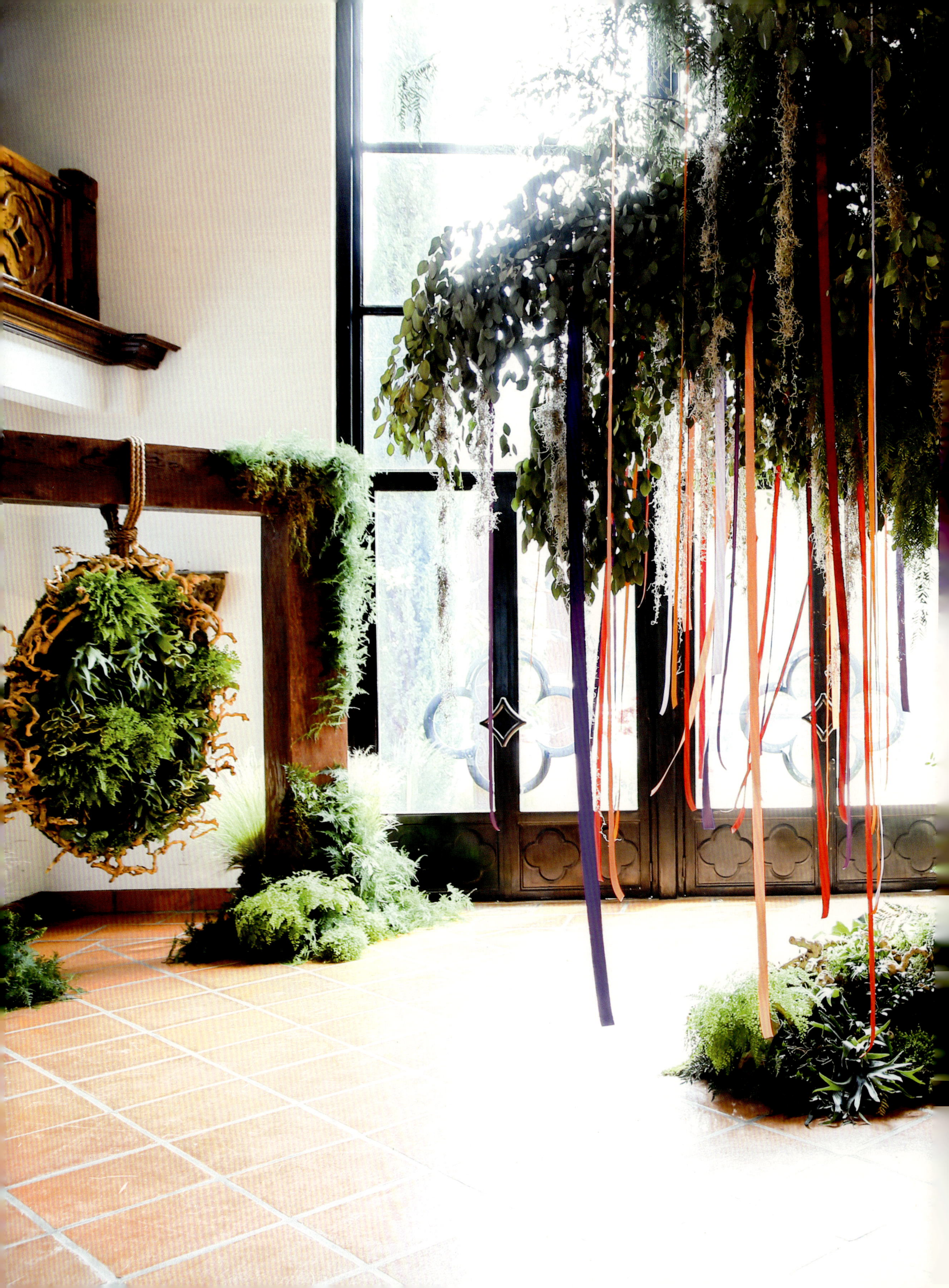

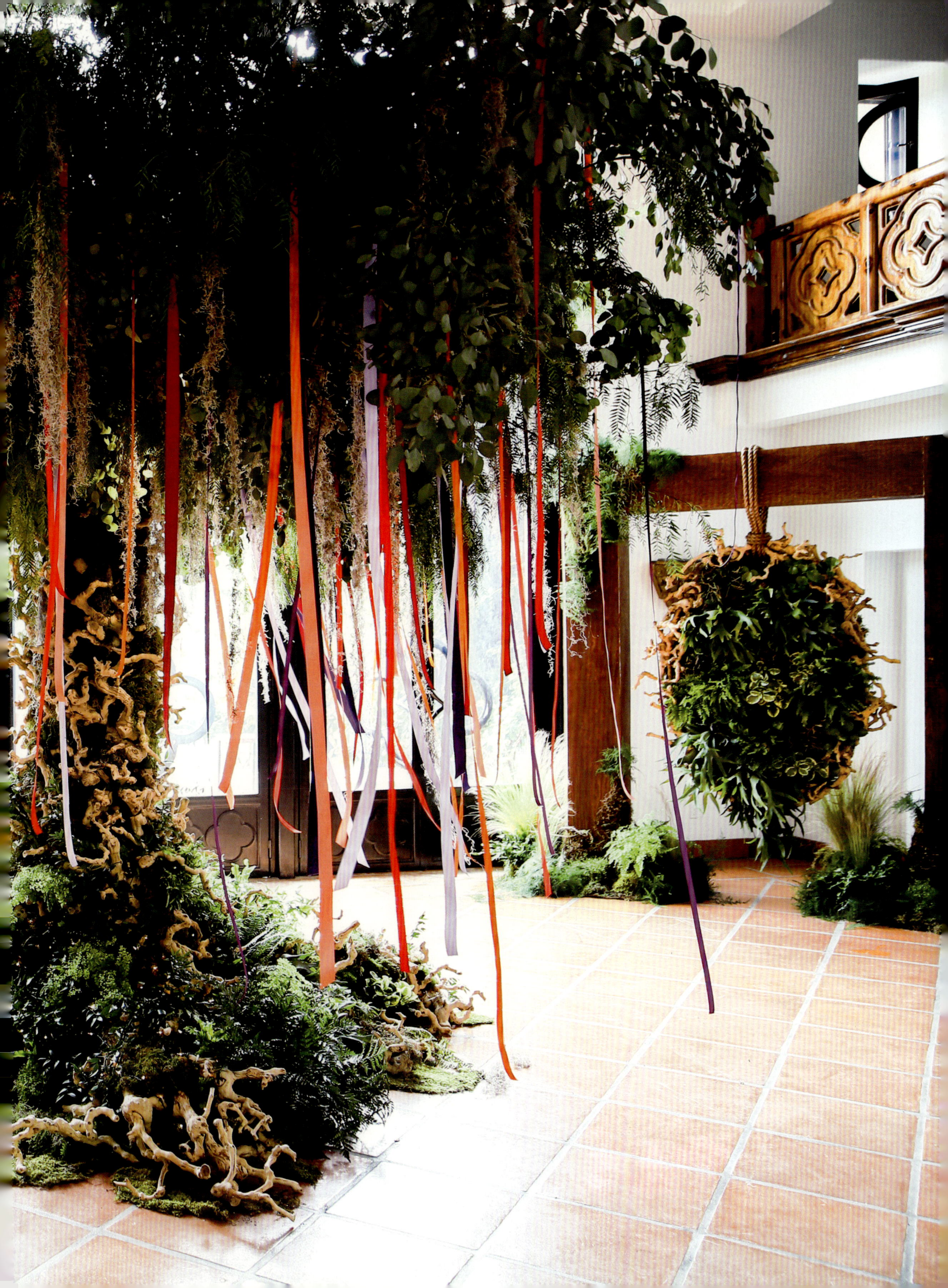

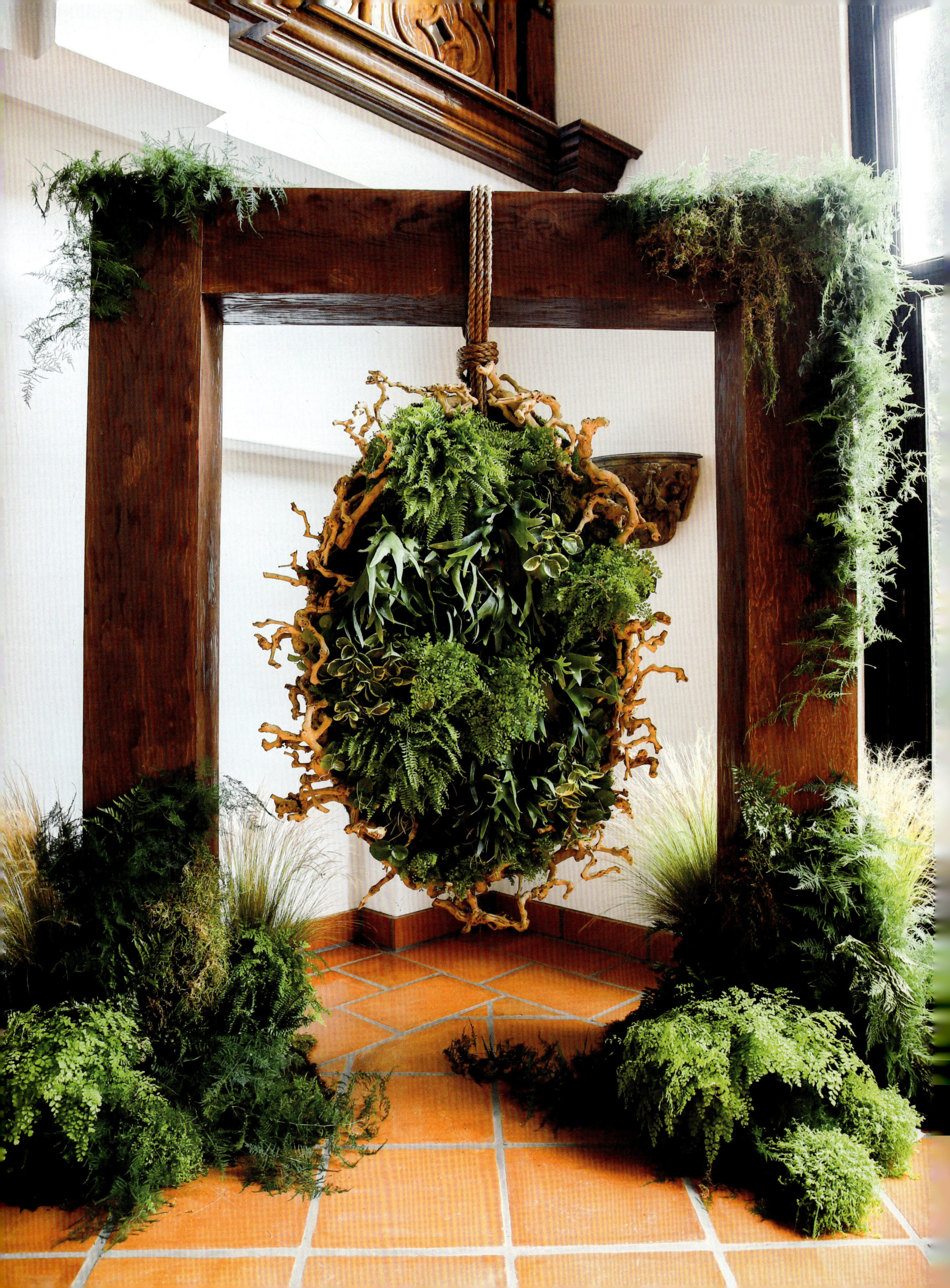

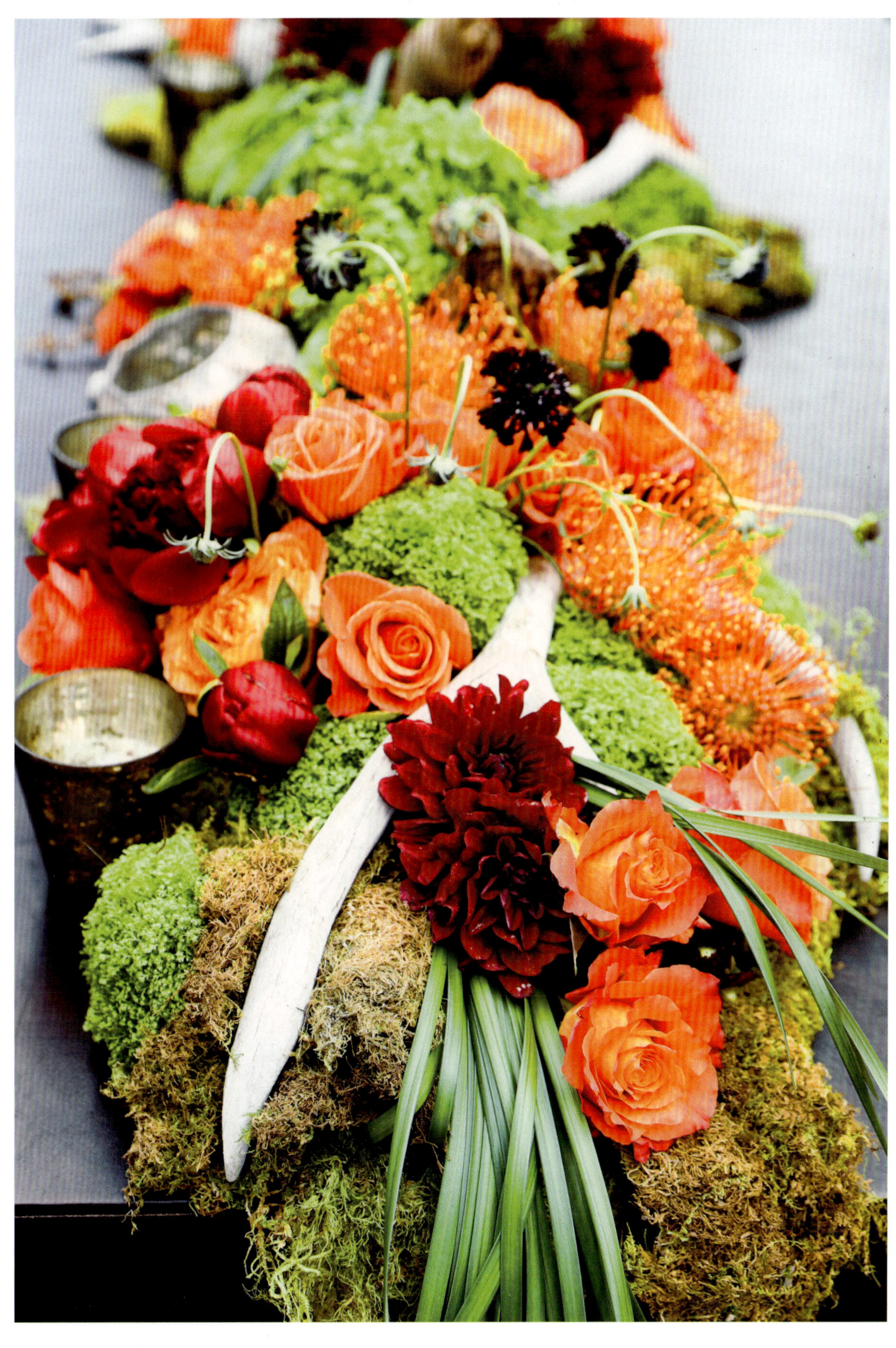

PAGES 200–201: Private Residence, Paris. Roses and calla lilies.
PAGES 202–205: Private Residence, Beverly Hills. A variety of greens, driftwood, and plants. FOLLOWING: Private Residence, Calabasas, California. Peonies, hydrangeas, toffee roses, and carnations.

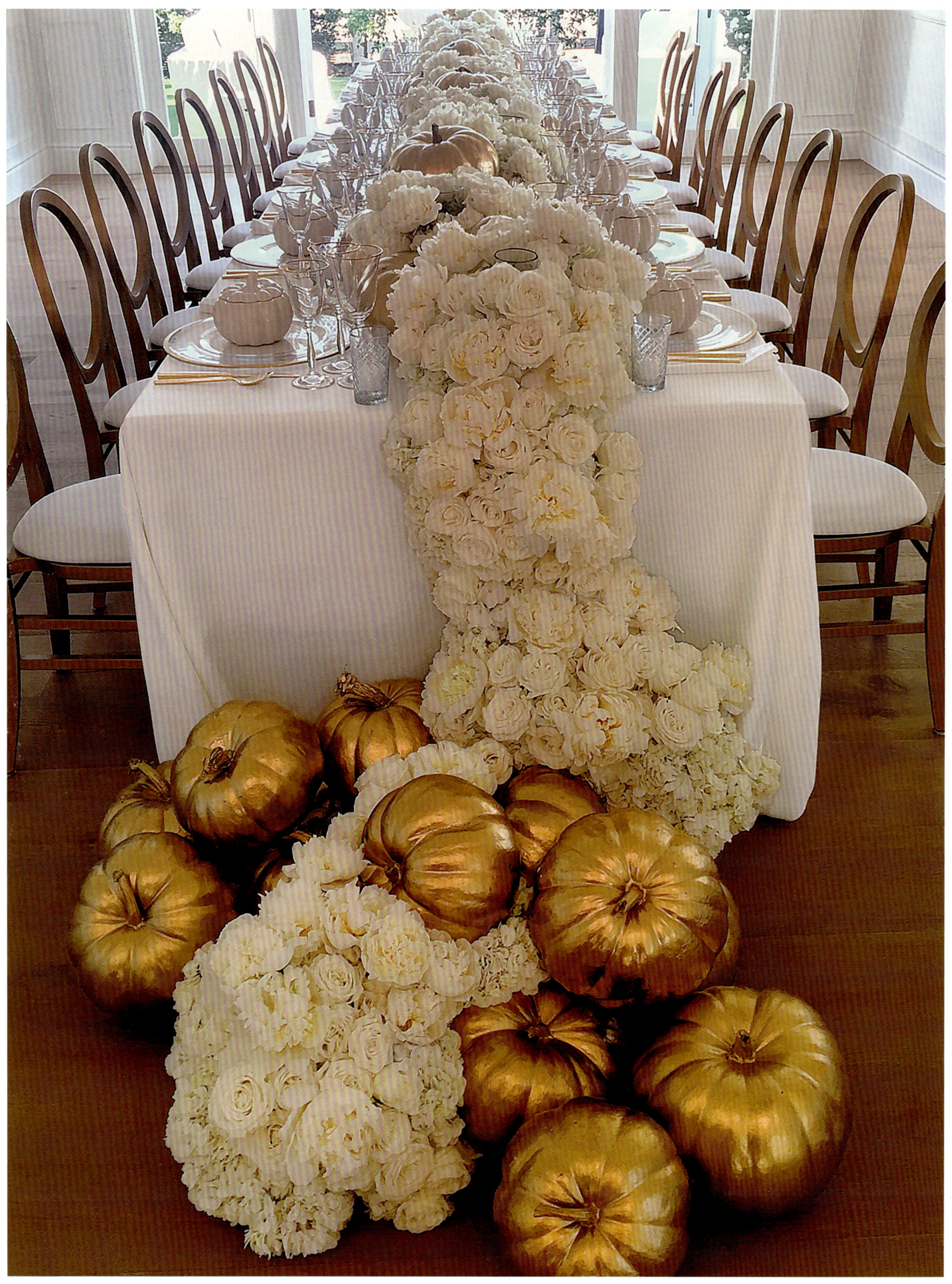

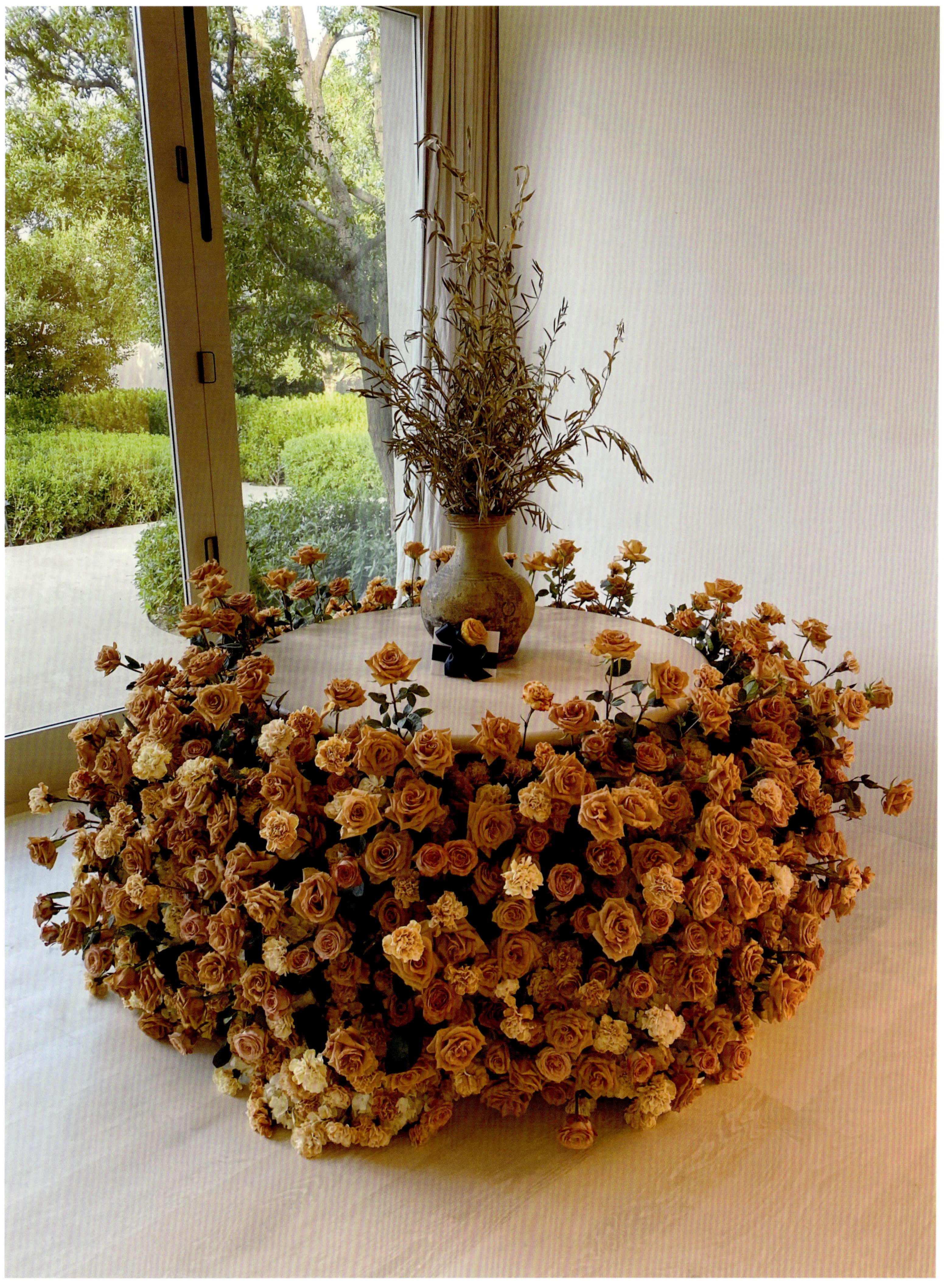

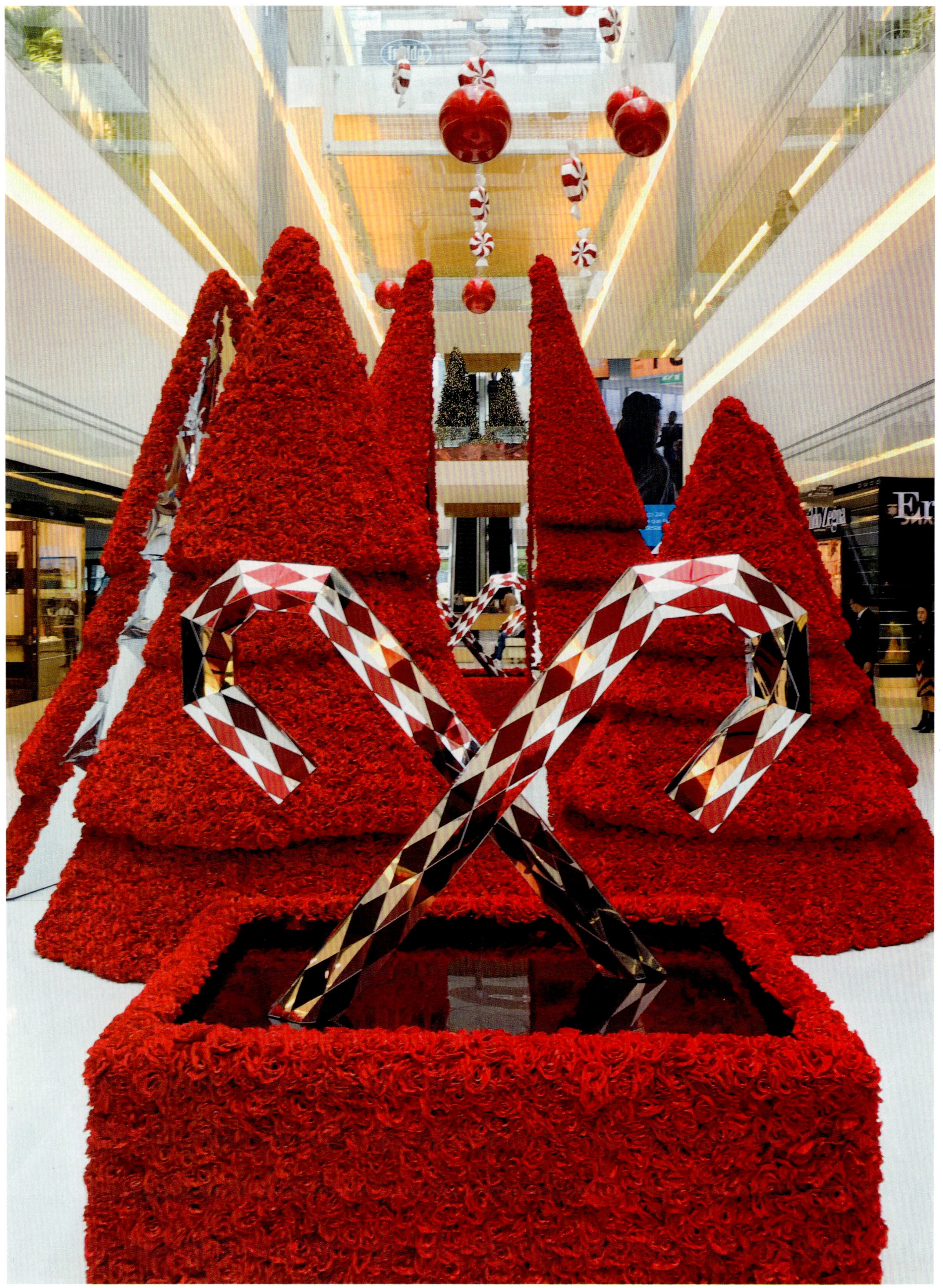

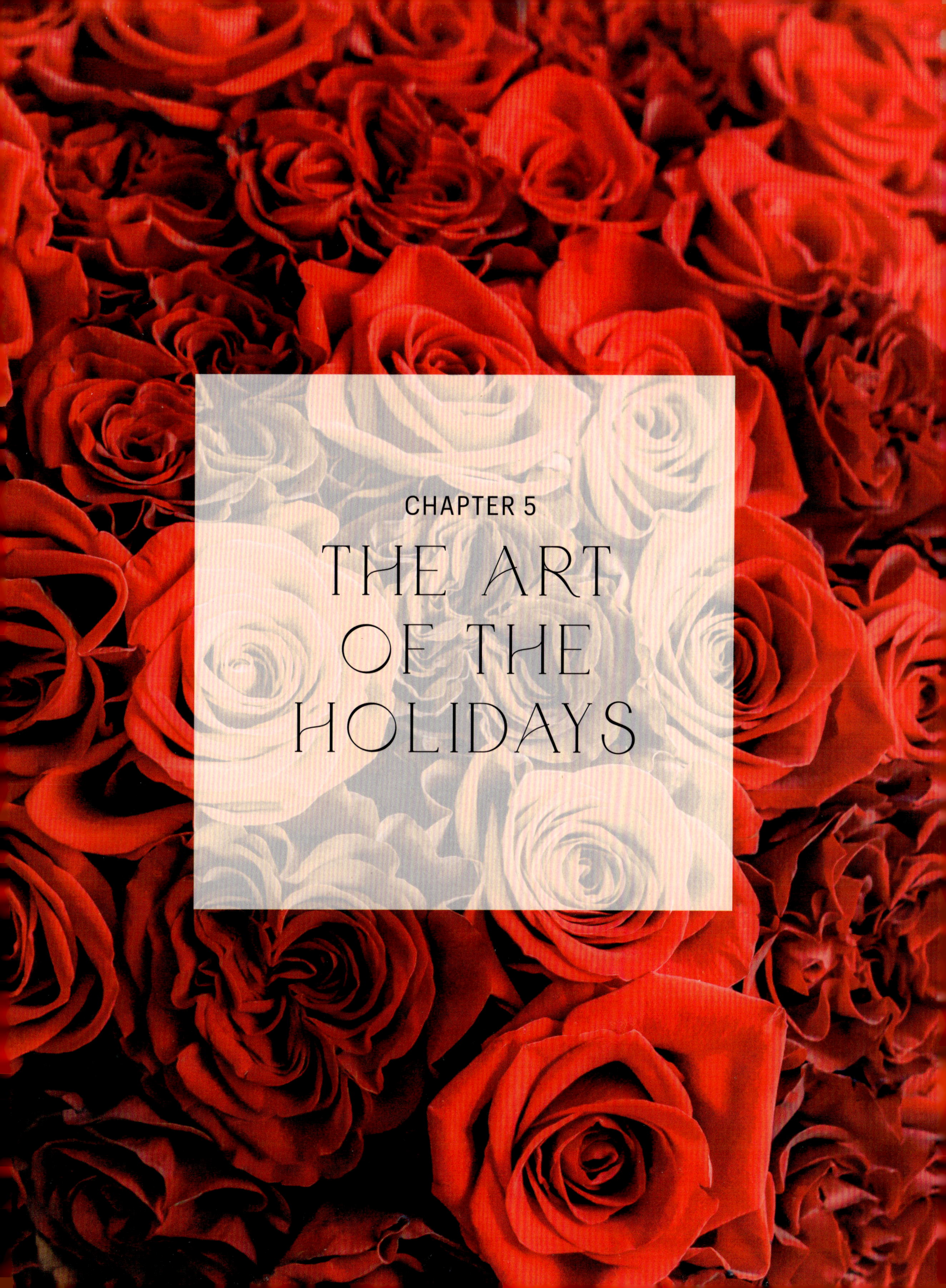

CHAPTER 5

THE ART
OF THE
HOLIDAYS

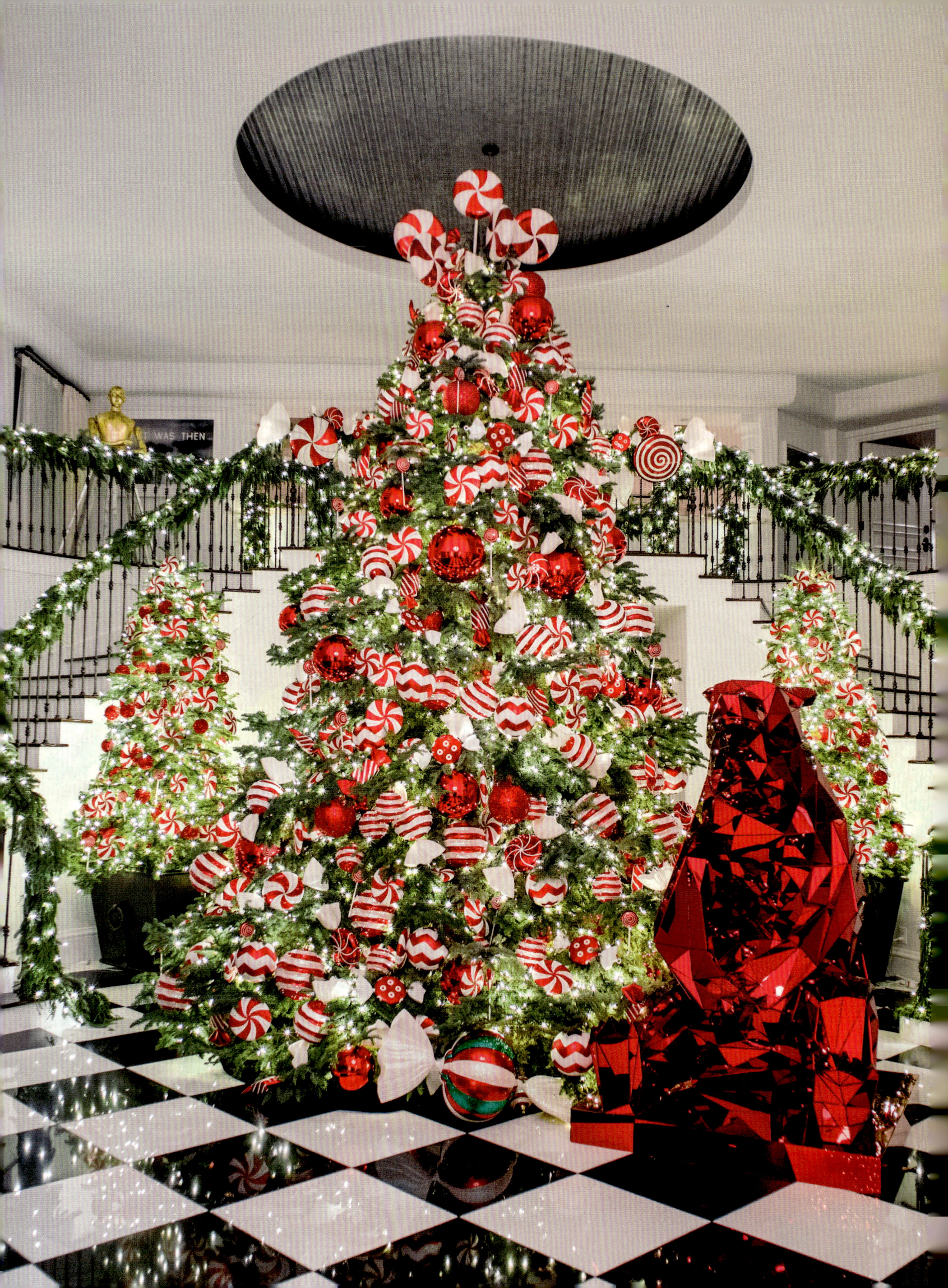
WAS THEN

Holidays are exciting for me because they're the one time where I get to truly show off my artistic abilities outside of flowers. I've had a love of the holidays since my childhood. I absolutely love them all . . . especially Christmas. As the self-proclaimed King of Christmas and the leading member of my team, Santa's Mafia, I *have* to—for the sake of my reputation. I do not care how old or how Scroogey you may be, but I find that this special five-week period is when everybody is their better selves: more joyful, less selfish, and happier. I also love that holidays have the power to bring you back to your childhood and reinforce the underlying importance of tradition.

For as long as I can remember, Christmas was always a big deal in my house growing up. From cutting down Christmas trees to working with my father to decorate them, the festive season brings an overload of nostalgia that I hold dear. From the first whiff of a fresh pine garland to the pure beauty of paperwhites, every moment is as magical as the time of the year itself. My parents loved Christmas, and the importance of a beautiful Christmas tree was instilled in me from an early age—and it continues to be important to me today. In fact, my first "real" job was putting lights on Christmas trees at Nordstrom when I was a teenager—never would I have imagined that one day I would design the iconic holiday windows at Bloomingdale's!

There's a true art to holiday decoration, and that's where tradition comes into play and which I strive to maintain when designing holiday events. There's nothing I love more than working in a client's home when they pull out heirloom family ornaments and decorations. It's important that there be a bit of family tradition within my holiday decorations. Christmas should be whimsical, unforgettable, magical, and *always* just a little over the top.

The holidays also allow for my inner artist to really shine. I've been so blessed to be able to go around the world to design my art for Christmas that I sometimes wonder whether Santa or I have more airline miles during the holidays. In my creative partnership with Michel Amann, we started the trend of creating large, faceted, mirrored animals. At first, they were just a cute idea. Something fun to make people smile during the holidays. They were immediately a hit, and people loved them and wanted more, so we expanded the collection and included almost every kind of animal imaginable, creating a zoo of elephants, bears, reindeer, penguins, bunnies, and flamingos. It never really occurred to us that people would borrow our concept, because we just simply loved making them, but now I see them everywhere—and I know in the back of my mind it's something we started at the Four Seasons Hotel George V. Nowadays, whenever I travel and I see them, I feel like I have my own traveling three-ring circus. When decorating for the holidays at the George V, I try to bring back our festive animals and add a twist by changing the colors. Guests look forward to seeing their favorites each year.

Like I said, the holidays are really about traditions and finding a way to keep them alive and treasured, as if the holiday were being celebrated for the first time. In the next pages are some of my favorite holiday installations featuring hundreds of poinsettias, bears made with roses, intricate infinity installations with lights, and over-the-top family celebrations that are synonymous with the holidays.

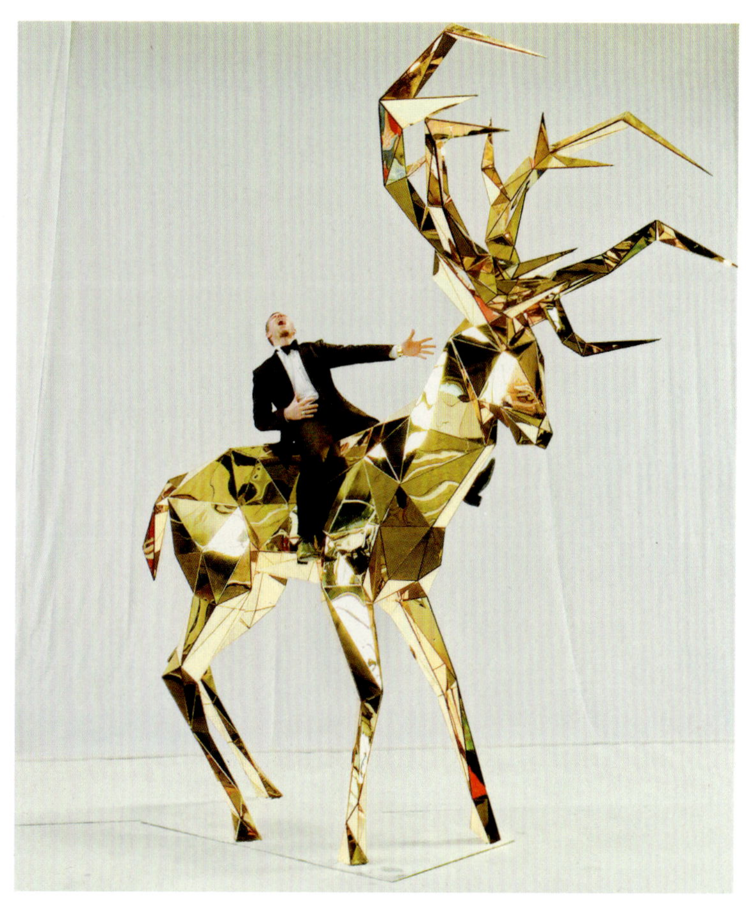

OPPOSITE: Private Residence, Calabasas, California. ABOVE: Faceted reindeer sculpture photo shoot. FOLLOWING: Iguatemi Shopping Center, São Paulo, Brazil. Playful bears made with roses and decorated pine trees.

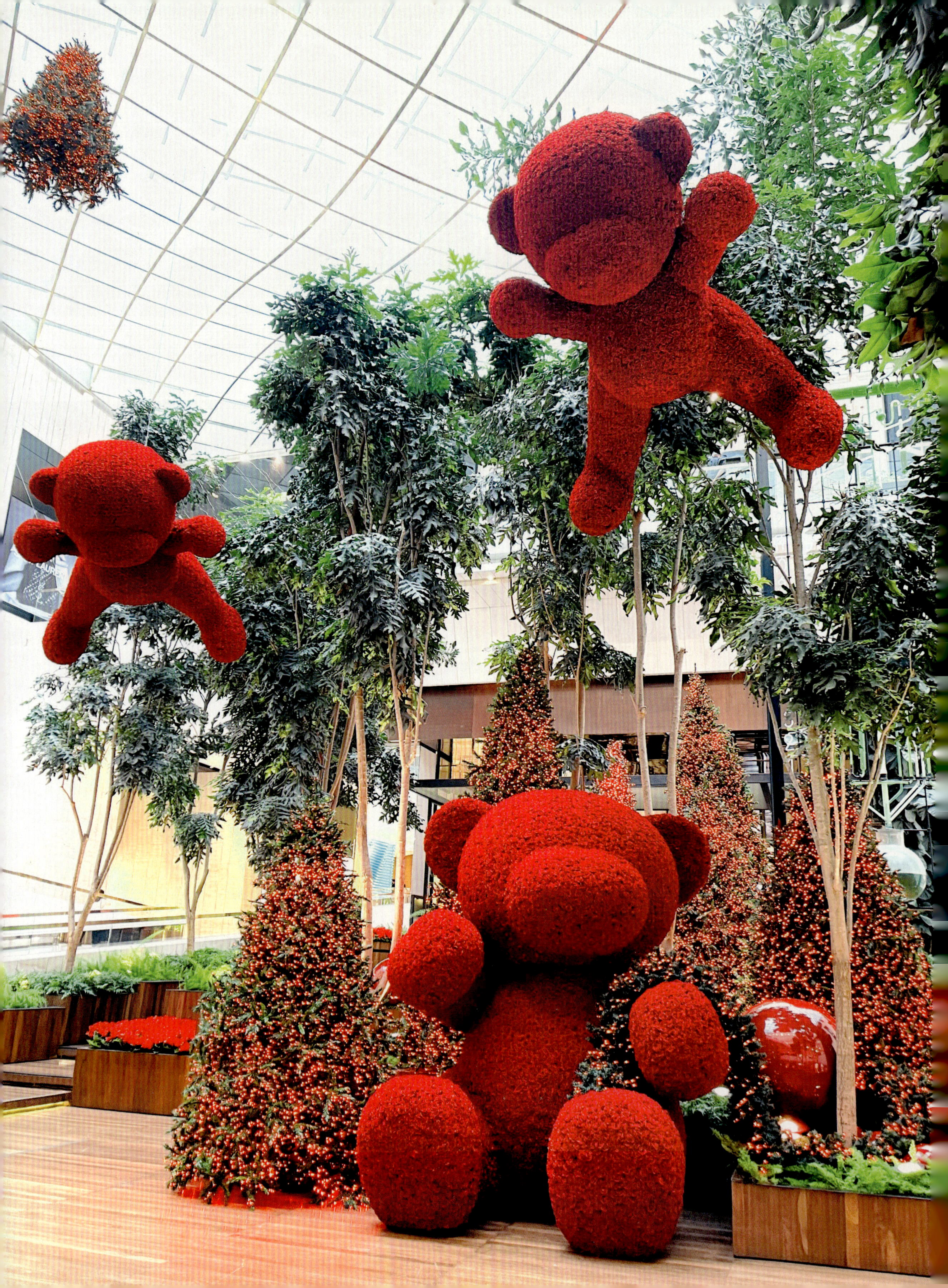

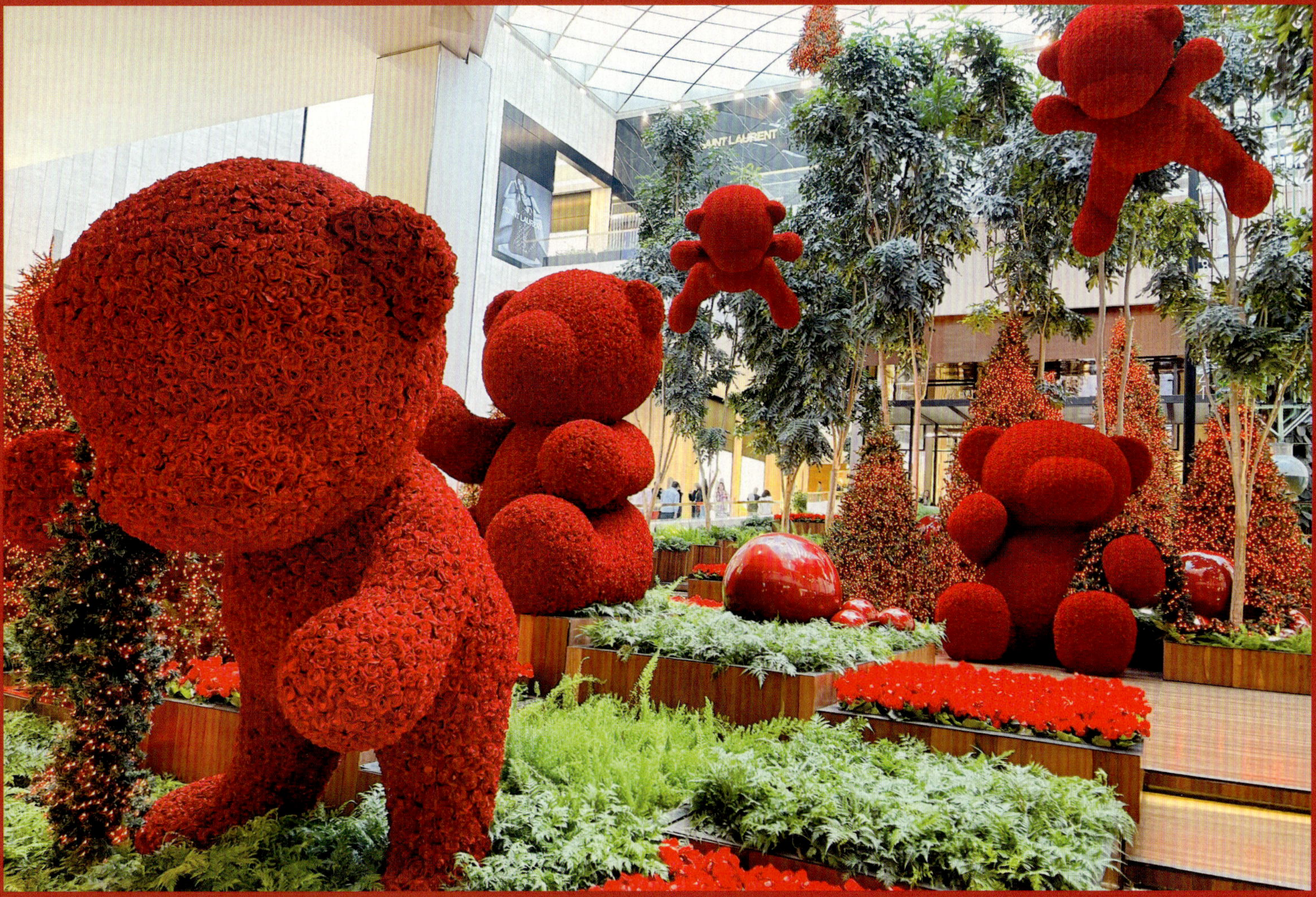

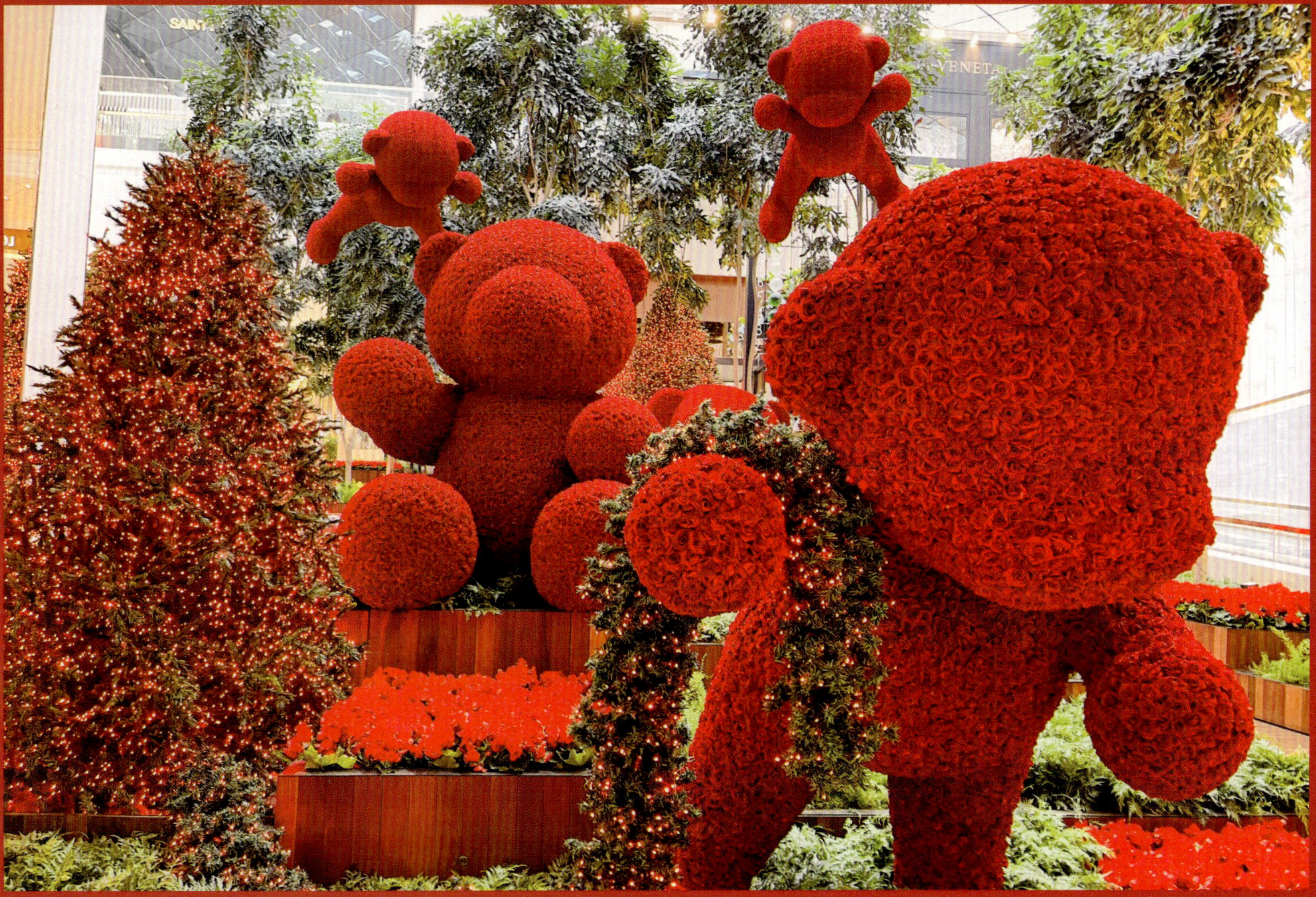

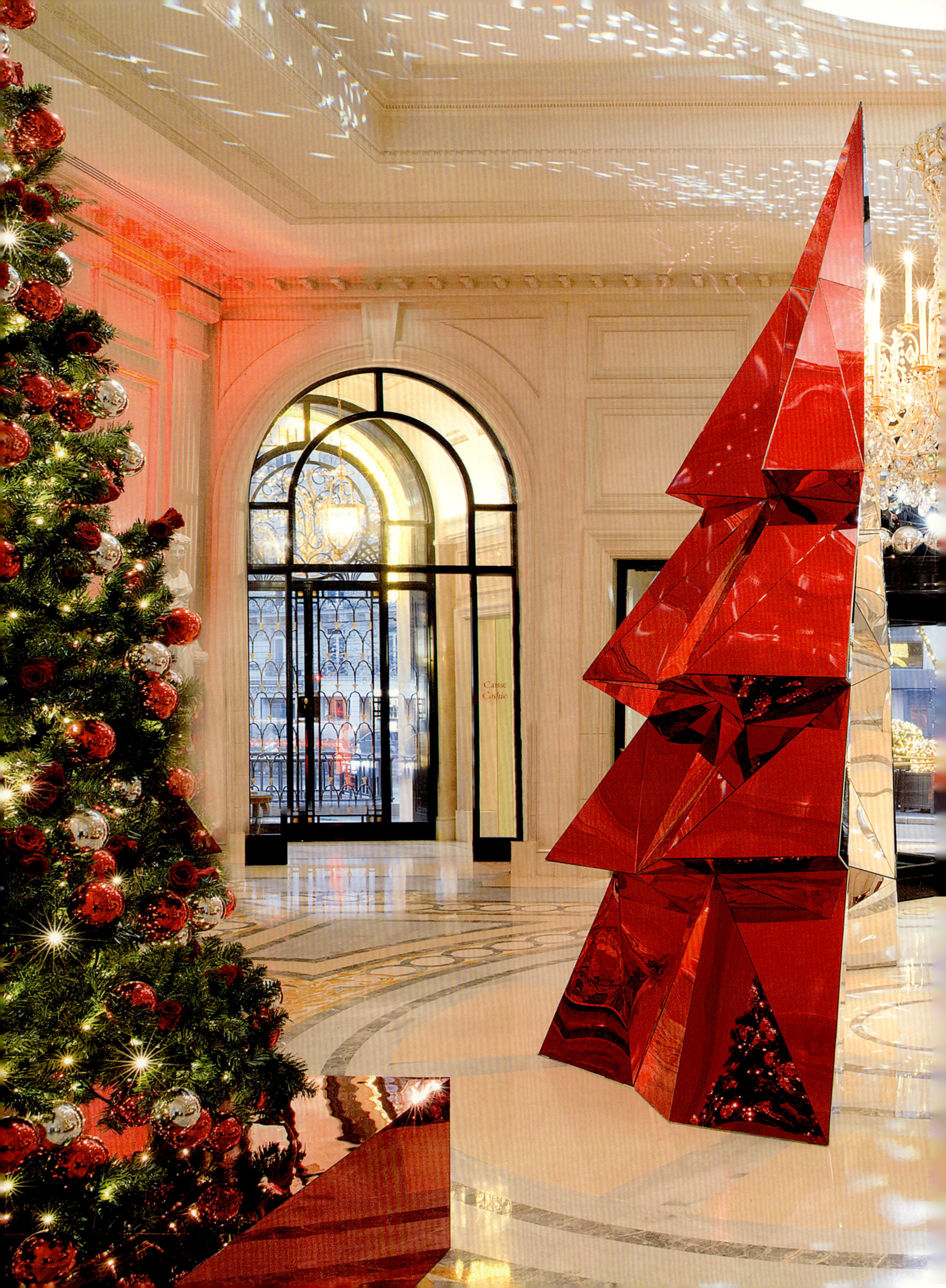
Caisse
Cashier

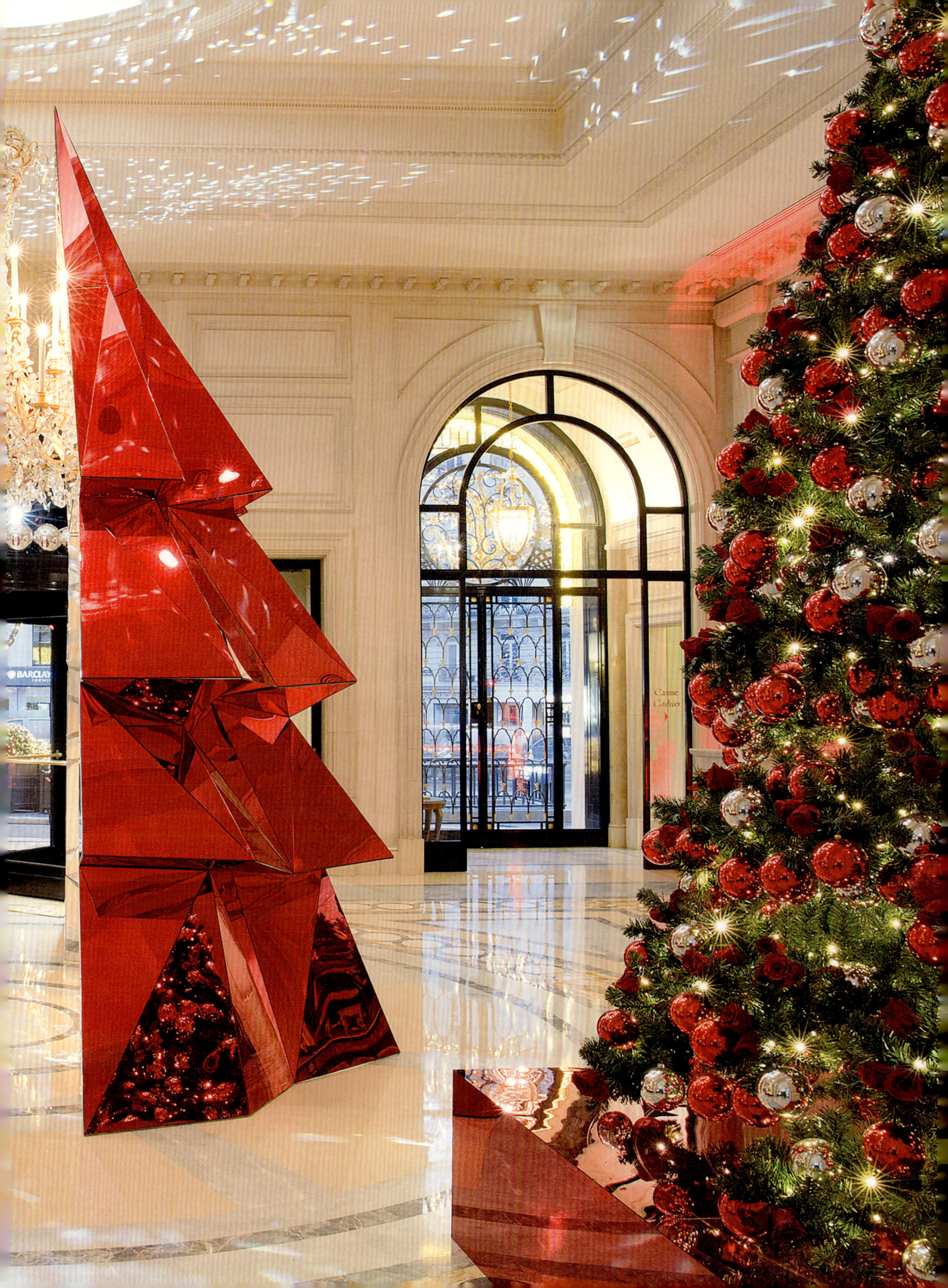

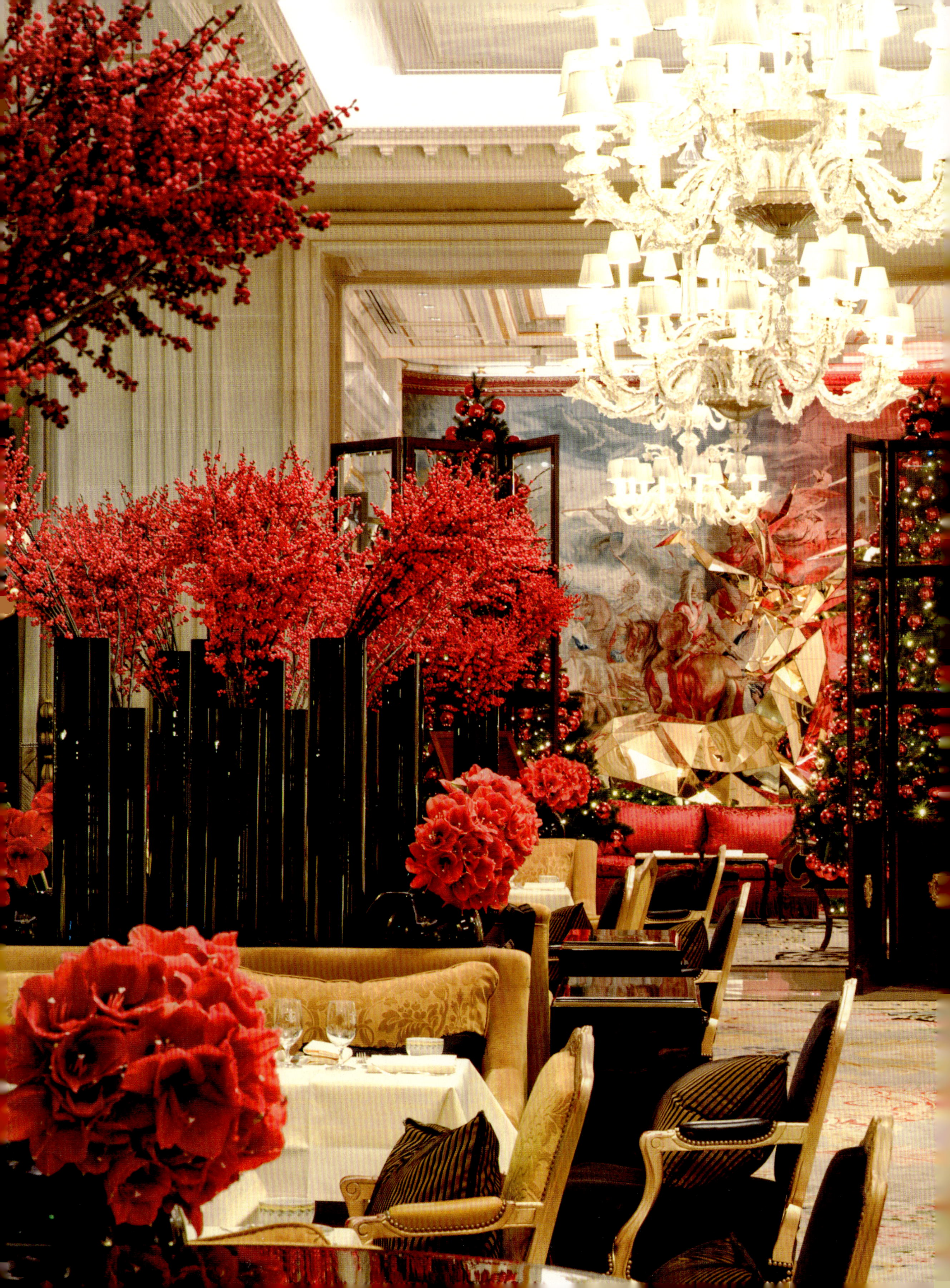

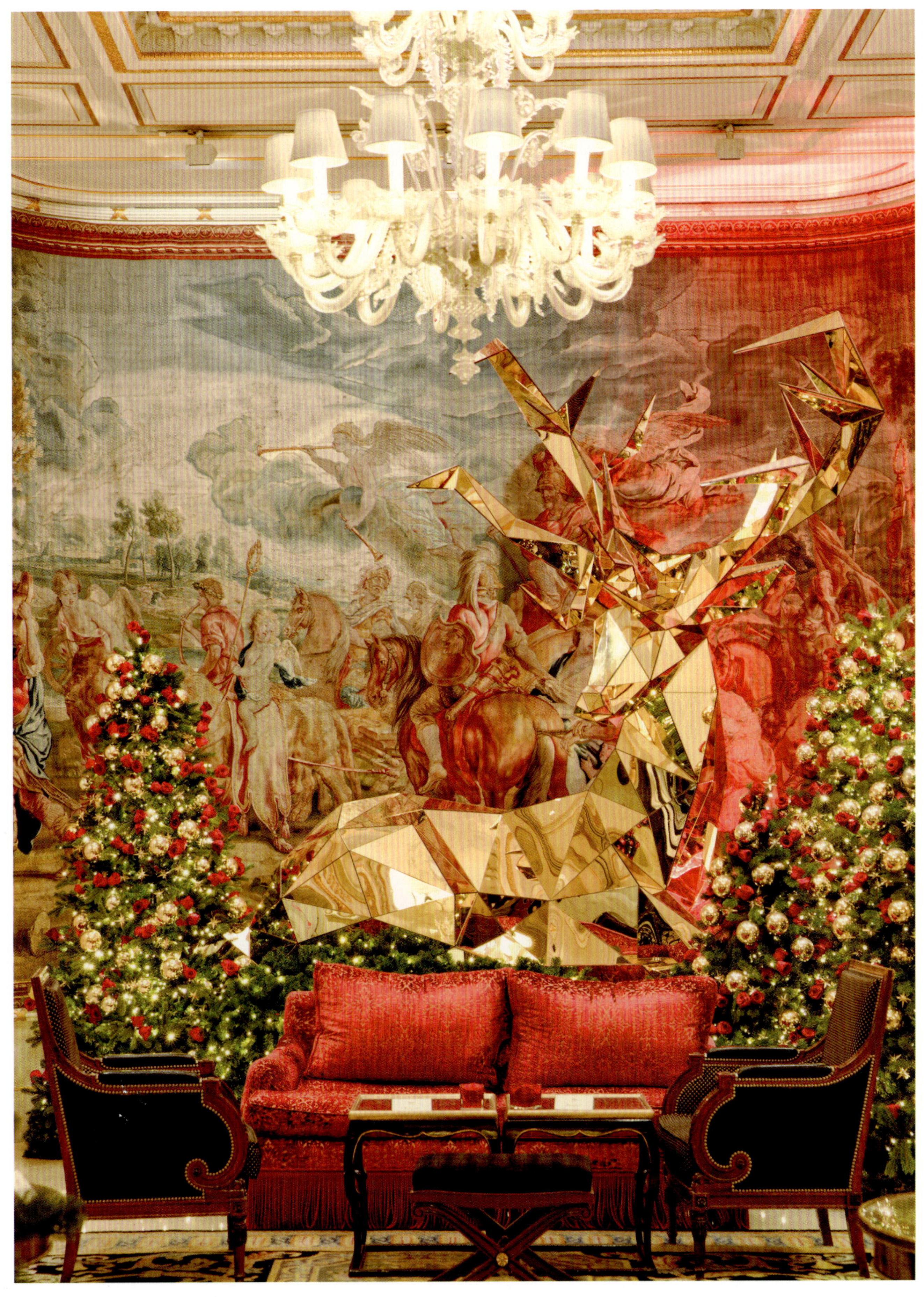

PREVIOUS: Four Seasons George V Lobby. Red acrylic tree sculptures alongside decorated pine trees. OPPOSITE AND ABOVE: Four Seasons George V Lobby. Ilex berries and amaryllis.

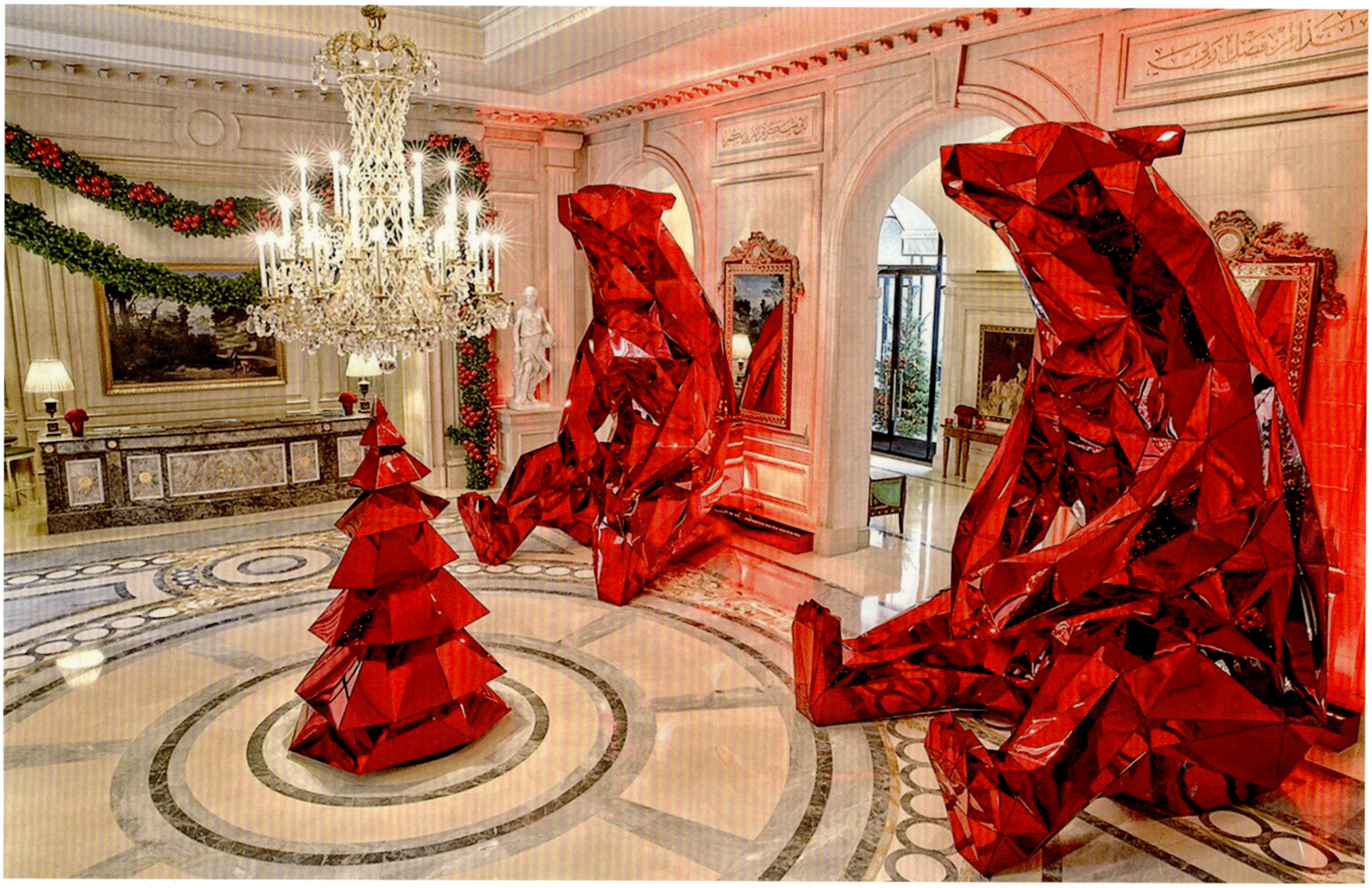

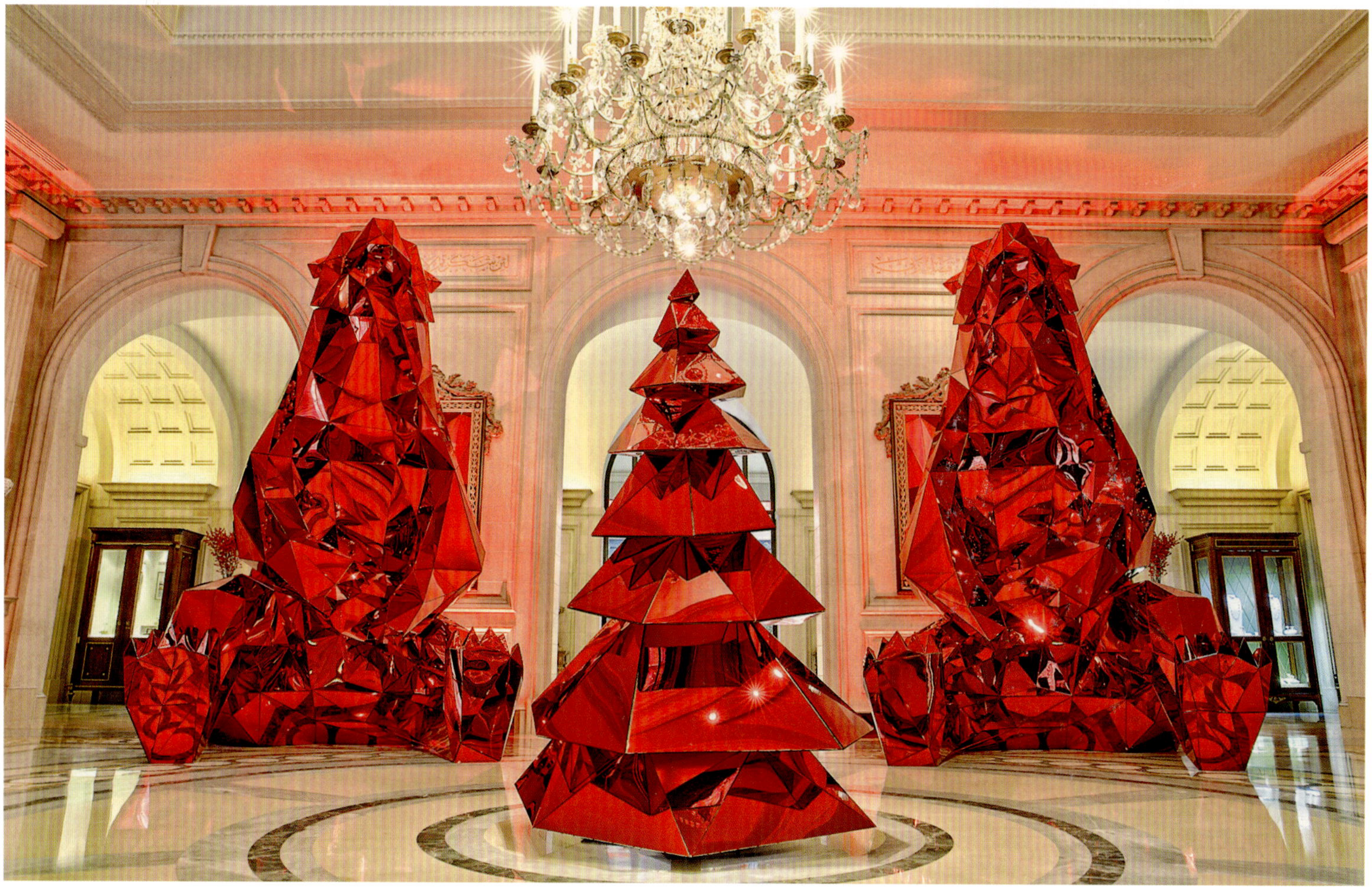

PAGES 218–221: Acrylic red bears and acrylic blue penguins continue the Four Seasons George V's seasonal tradition of animals, alongside decorated pine trees and lighted garlands.

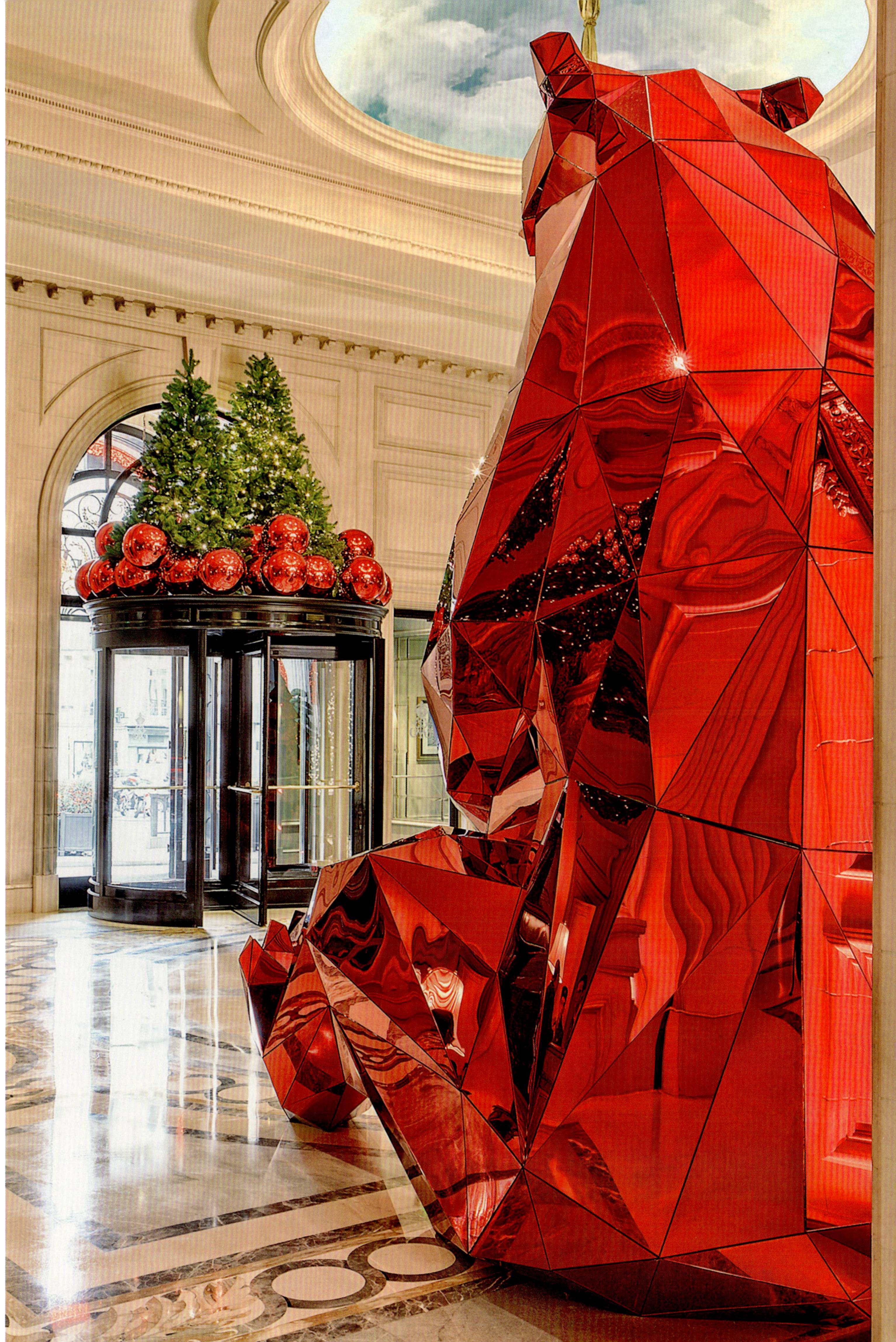

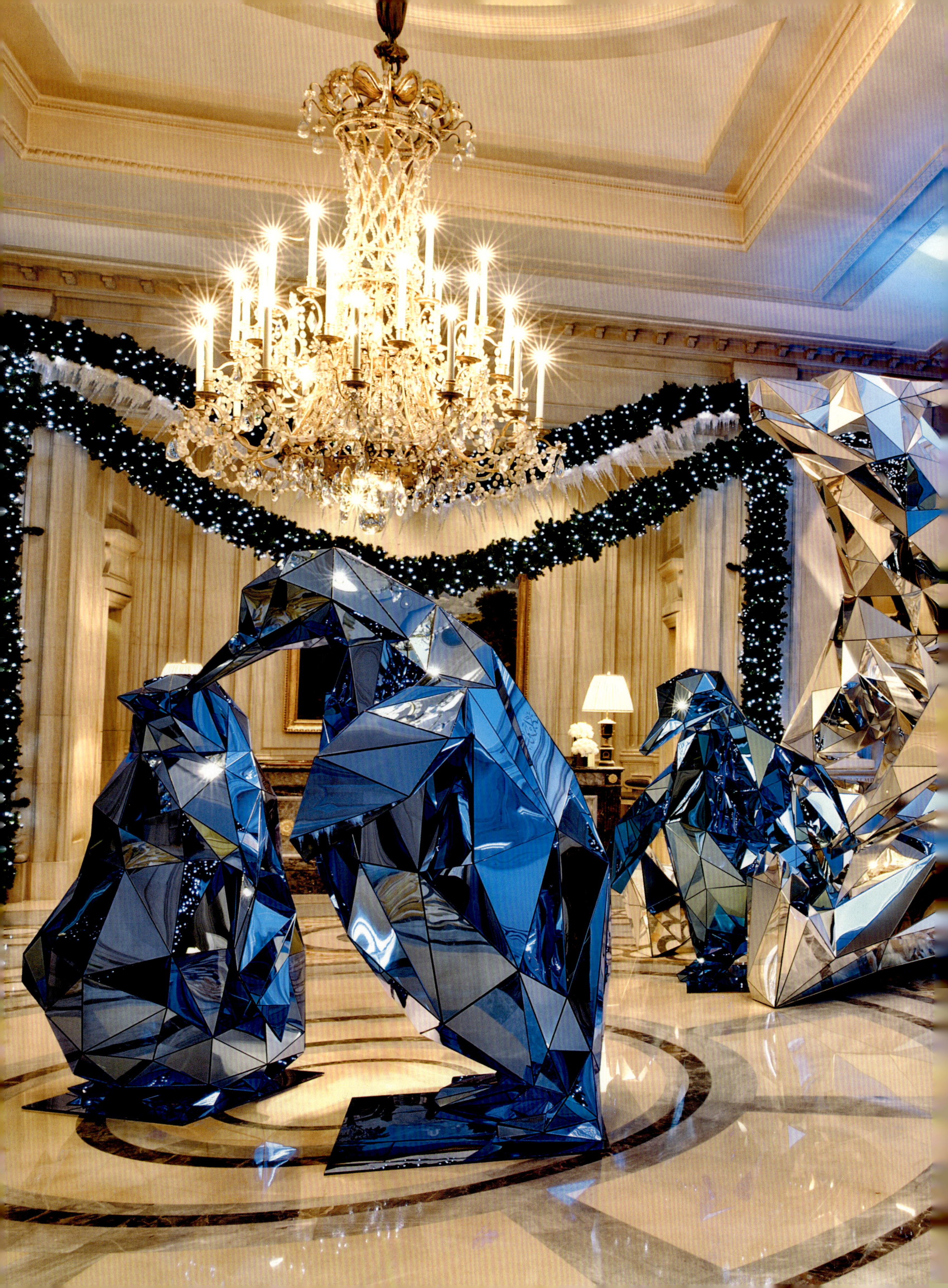

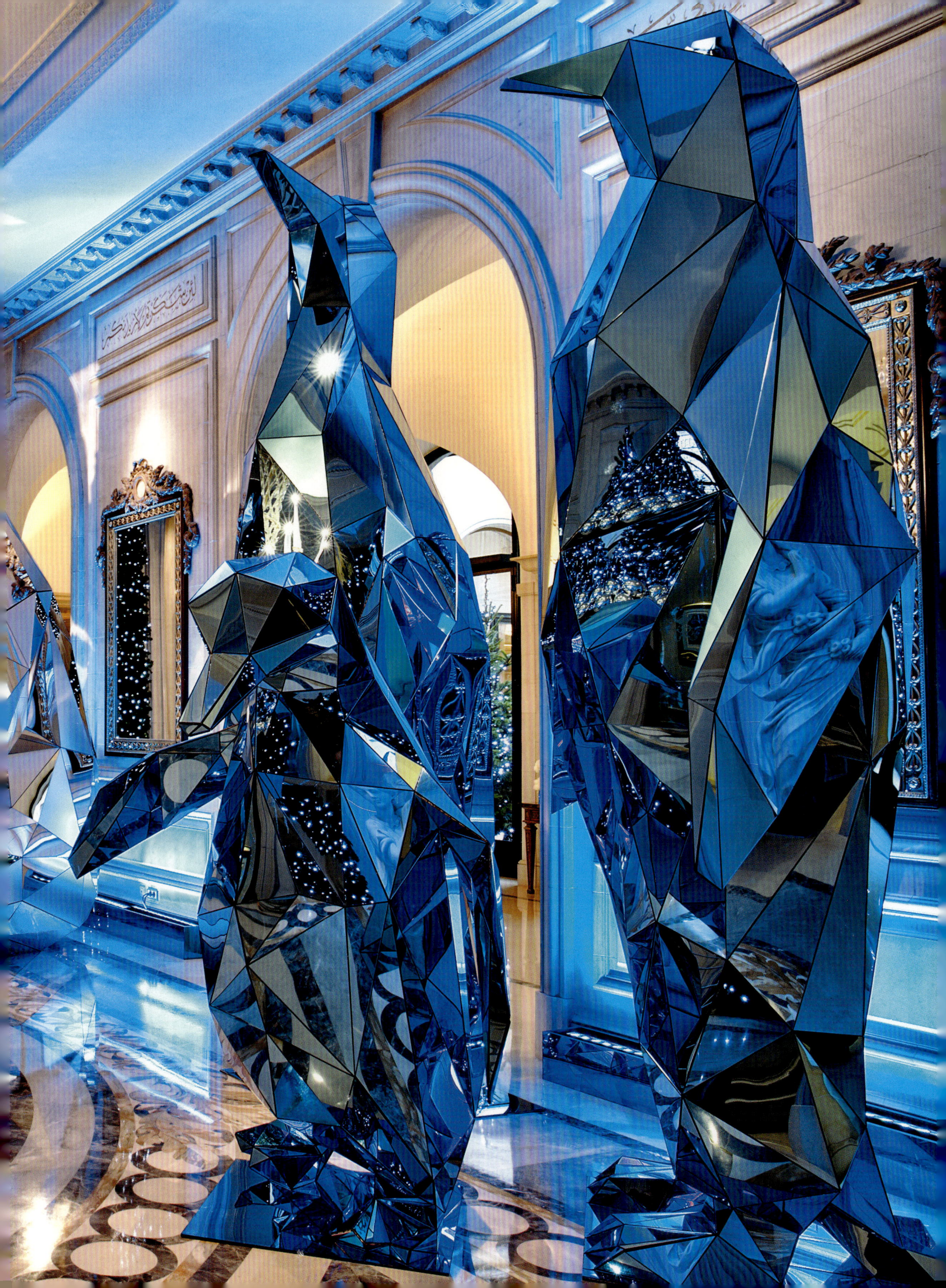

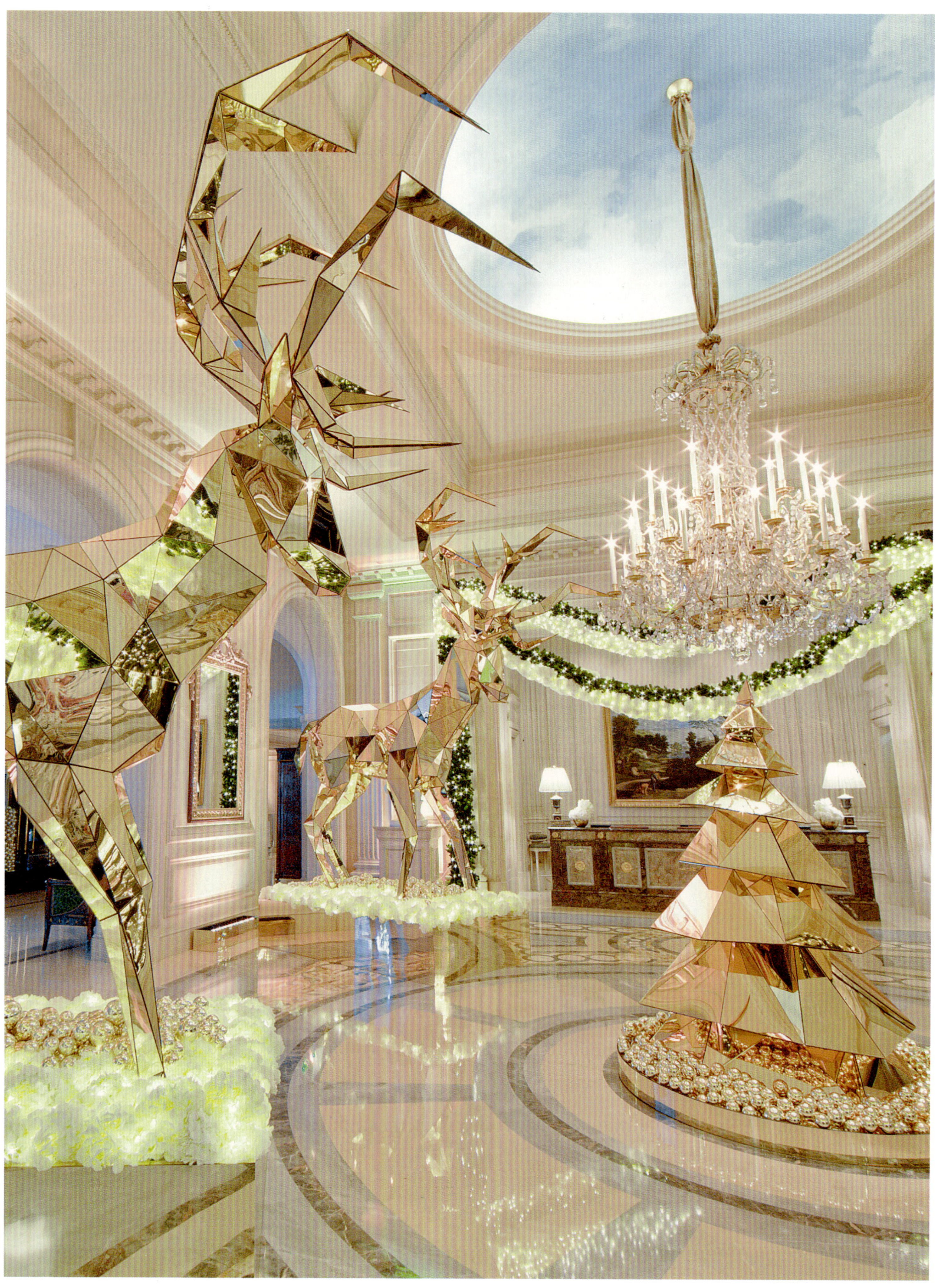

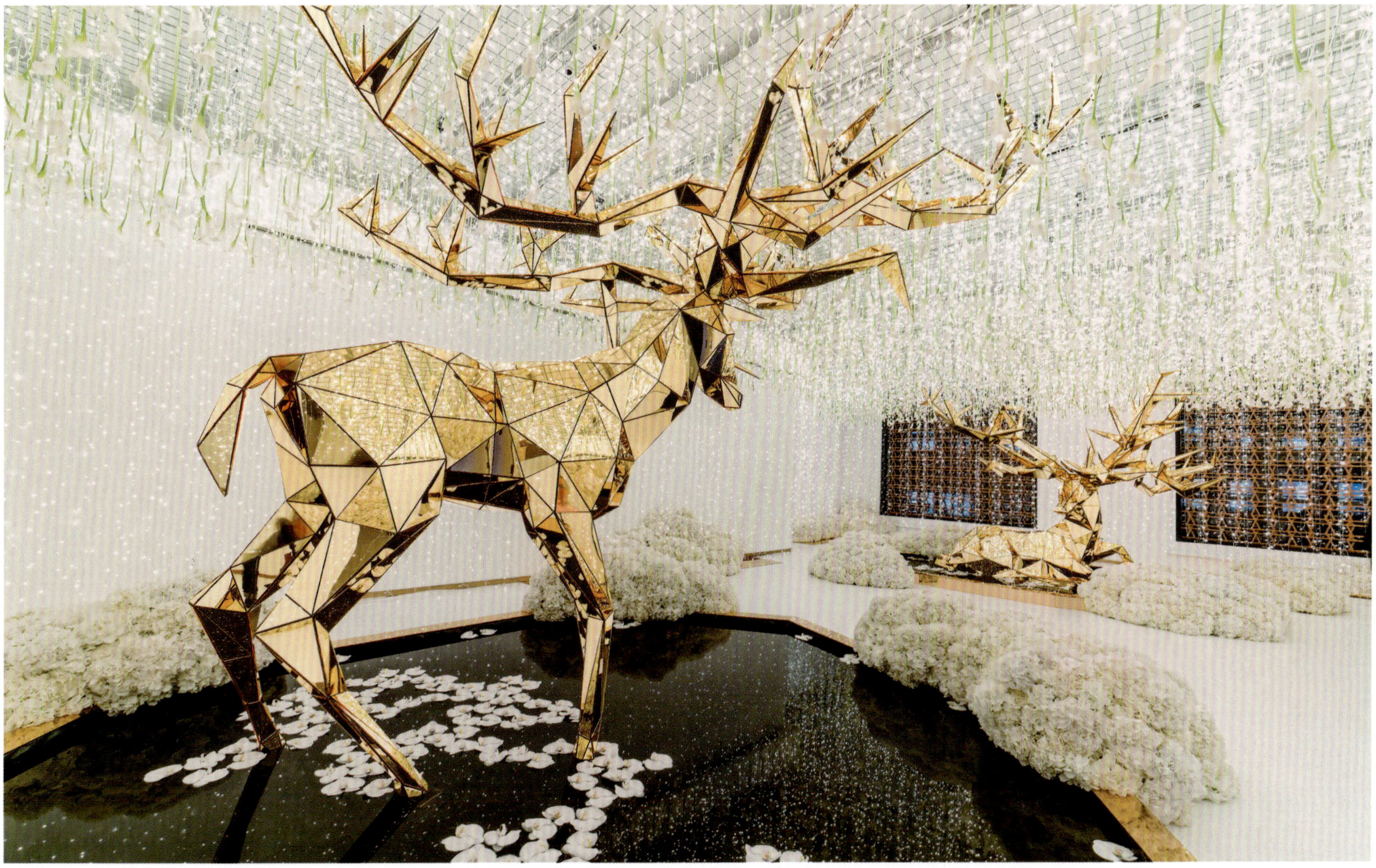

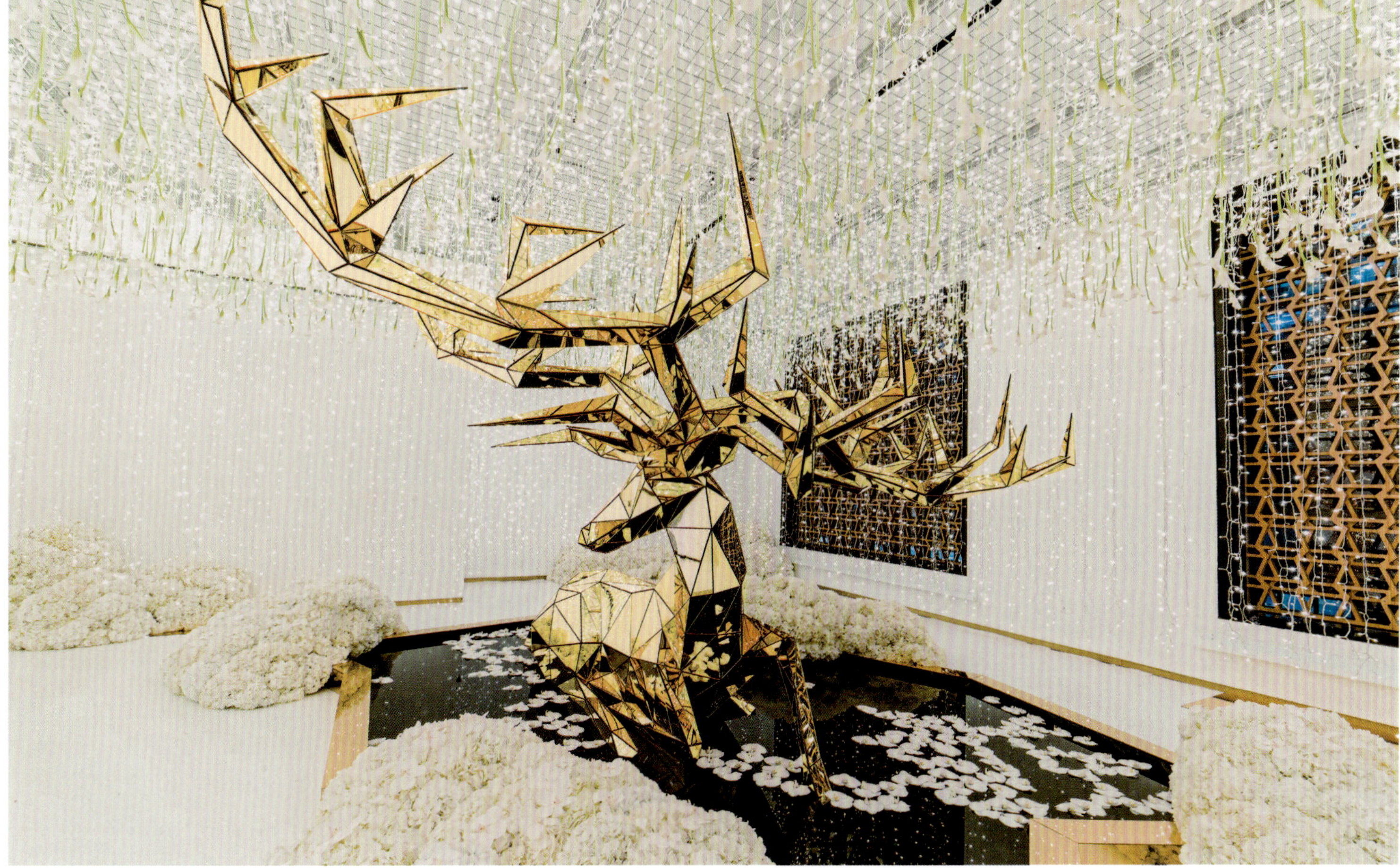

OPPOSITE: Four Seasons George V Lobby. Faceted glass reindeer.
ABOVE: "Winter Glow" Installation at Intersect by Lexus, New York City.
Hydrangeas, calla lilies, and phalaenopsis orchids.

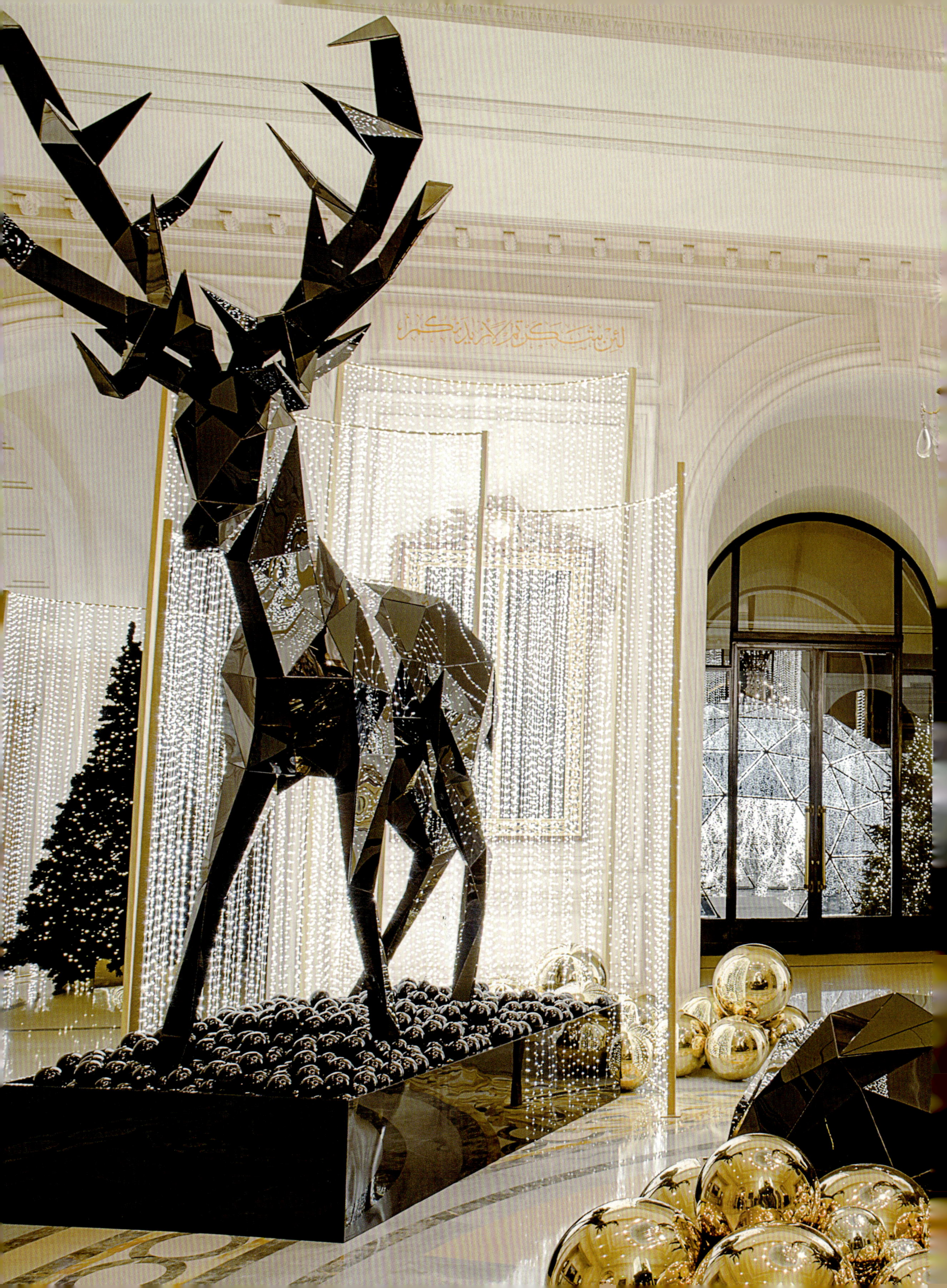

لئن شكرتم لأزيدنكم

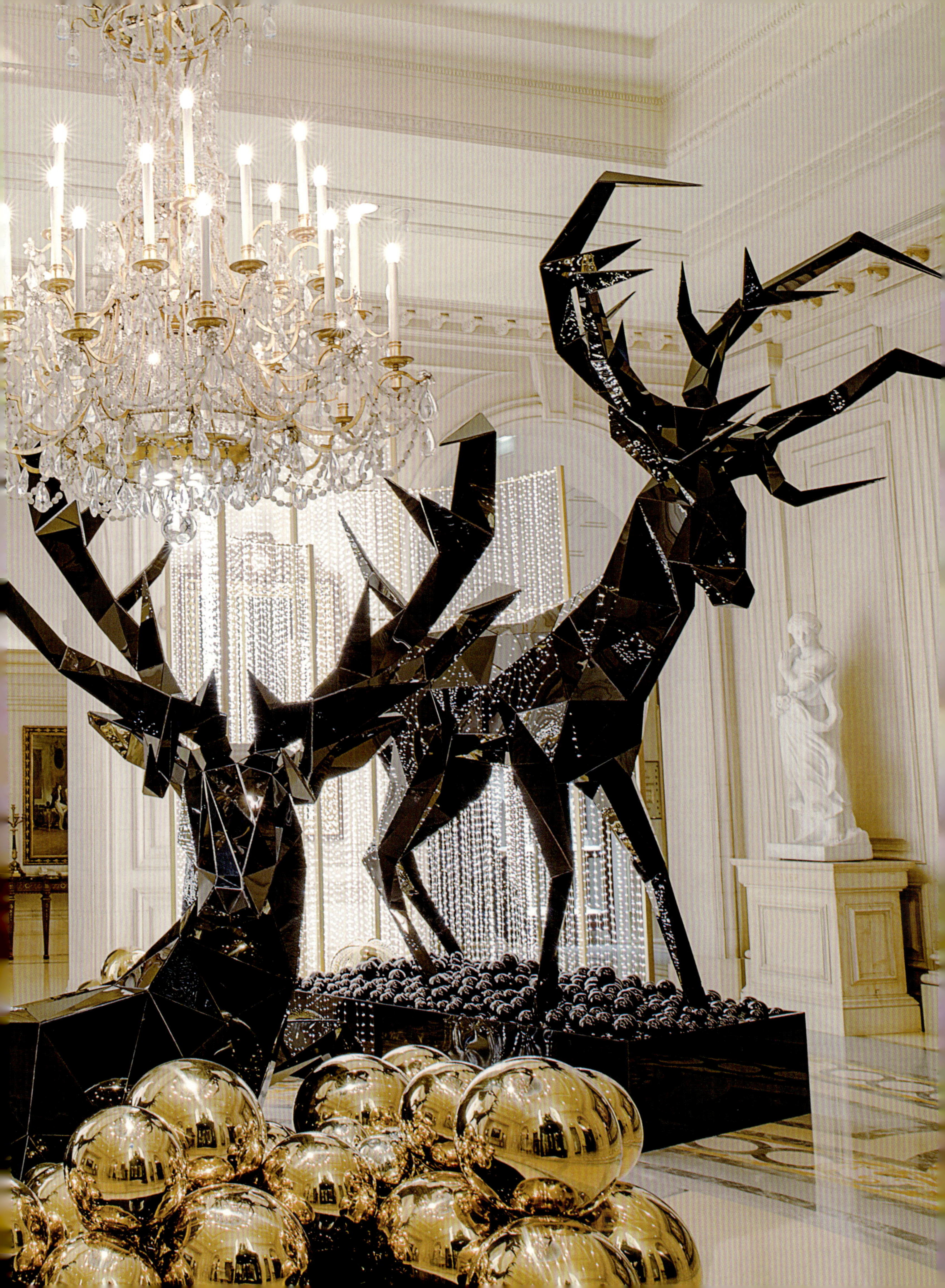

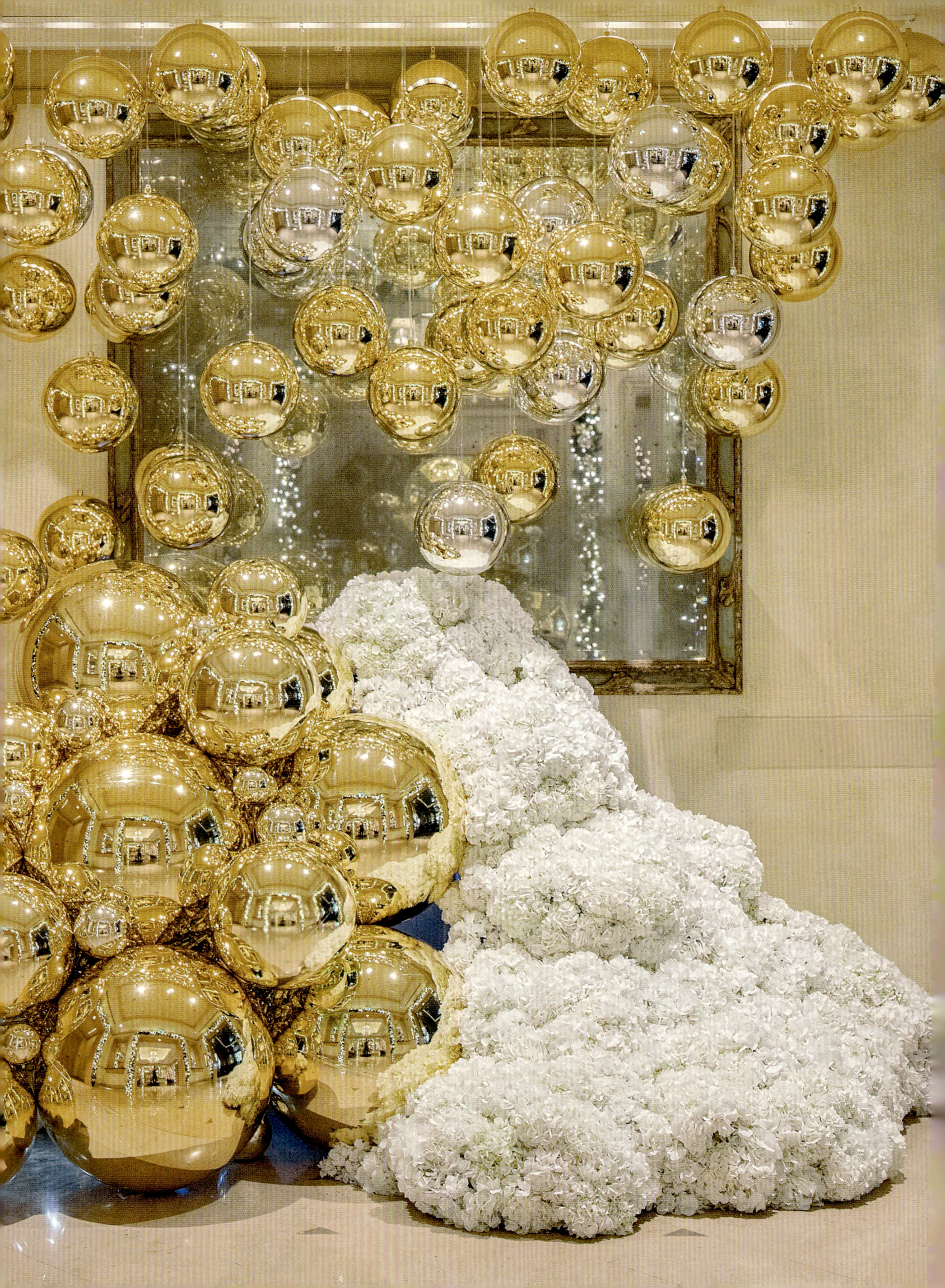

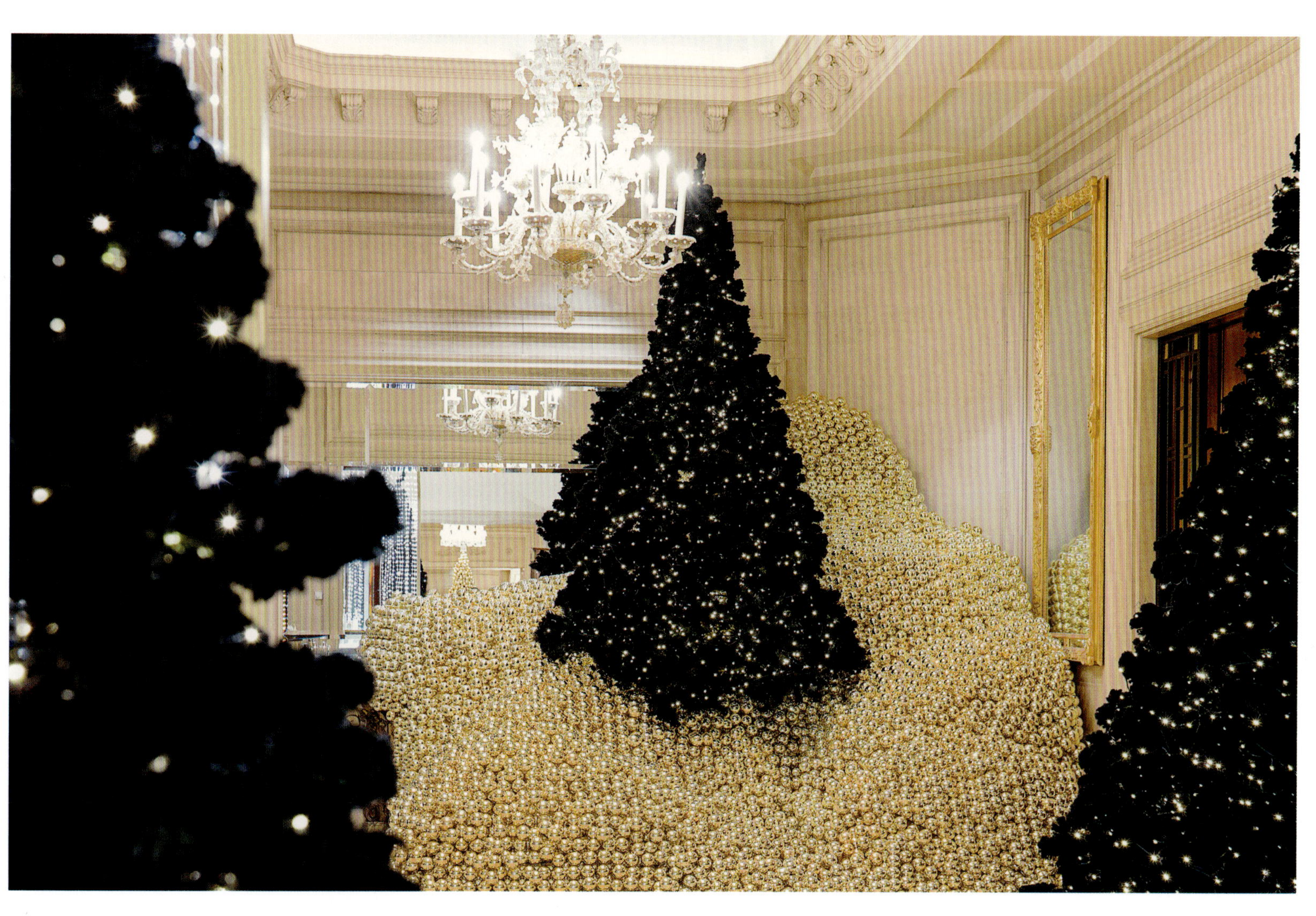

PAGES 224–227: Four Seasons George V Lobby.
Gold-and-black acrylic reindeer with black-and-gold
ornaments and hydrangea garland (opposite).

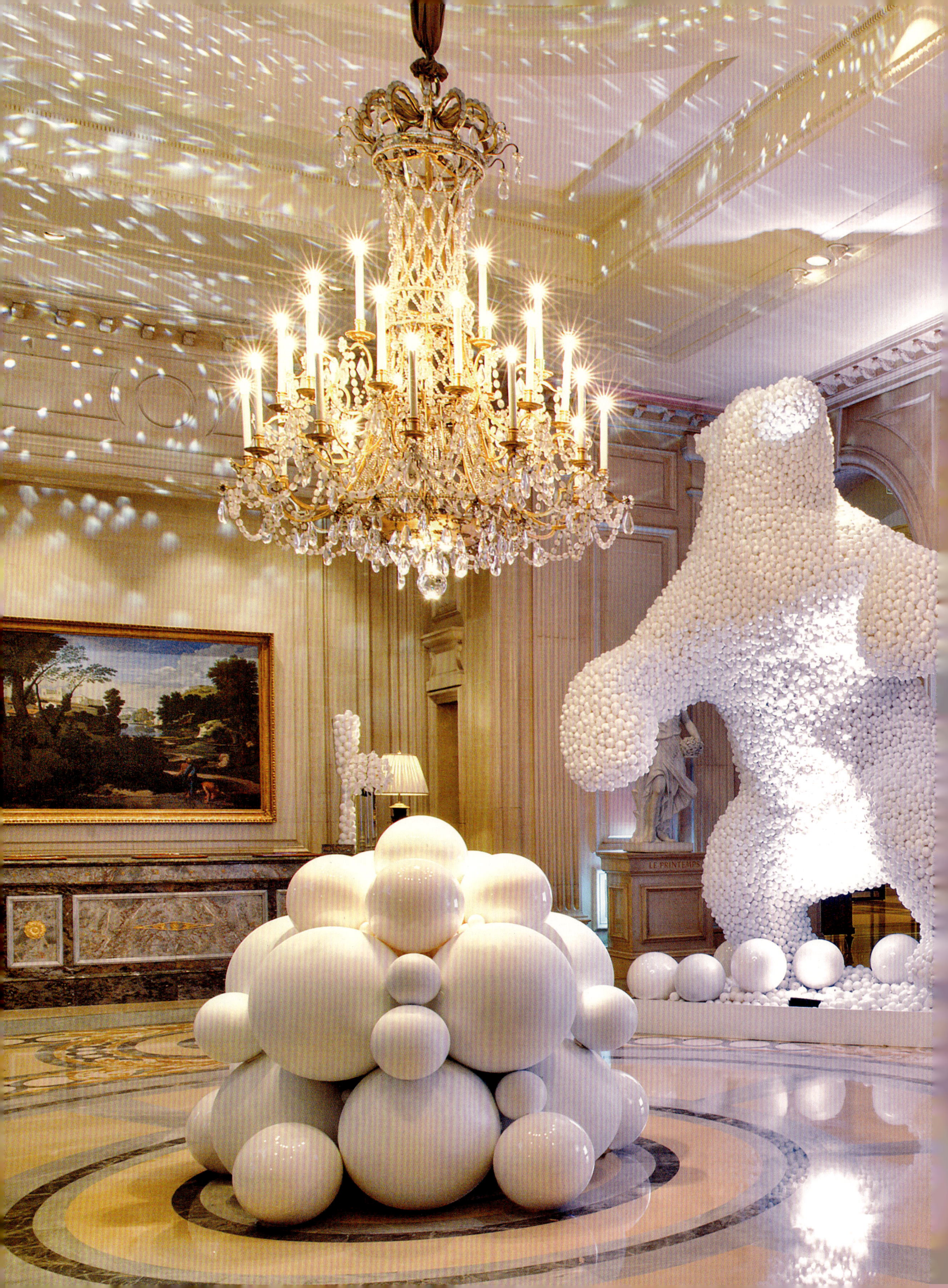

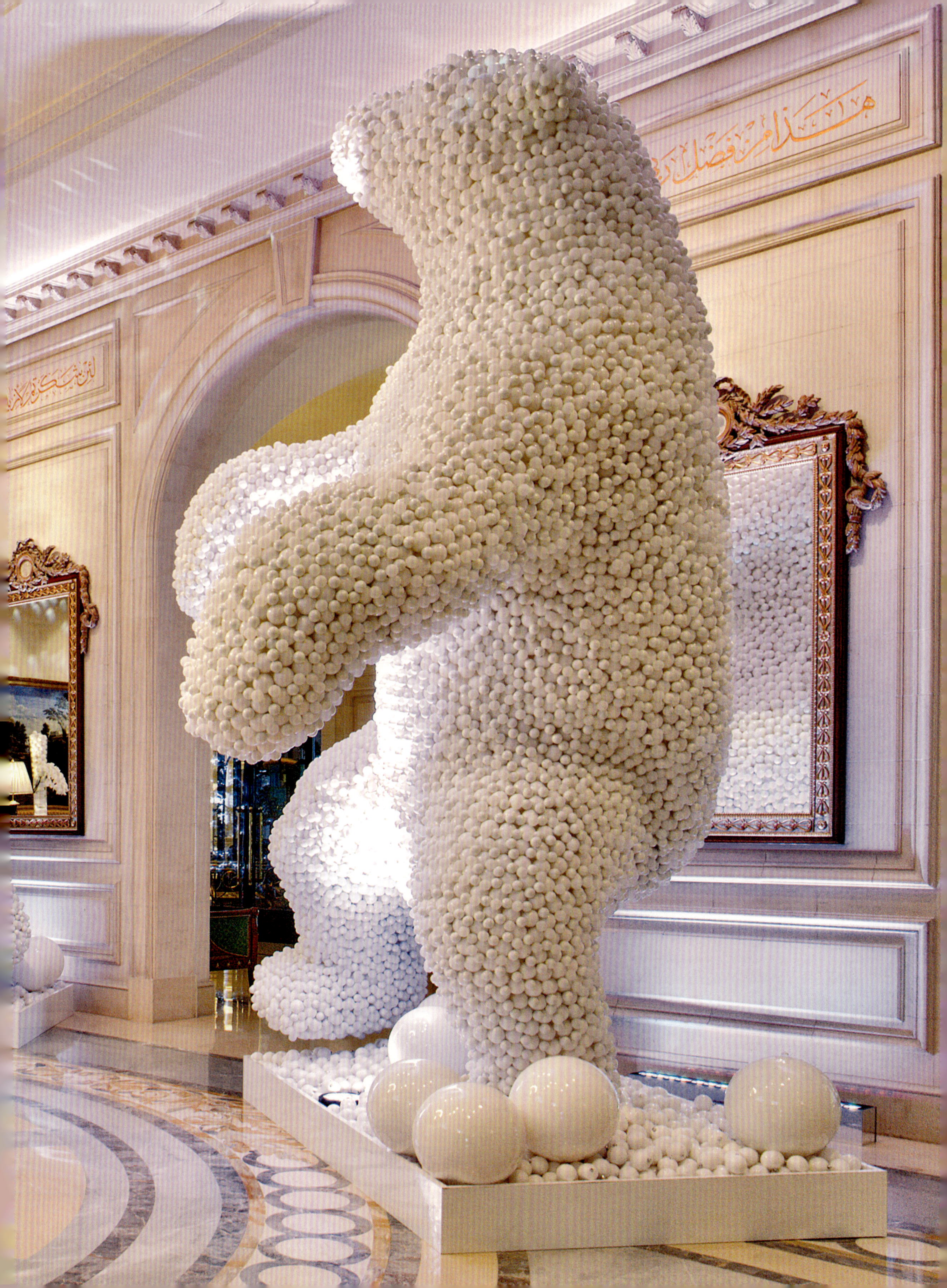

هذا من فضل ربي
لئن شكرتم لأزيدنكم

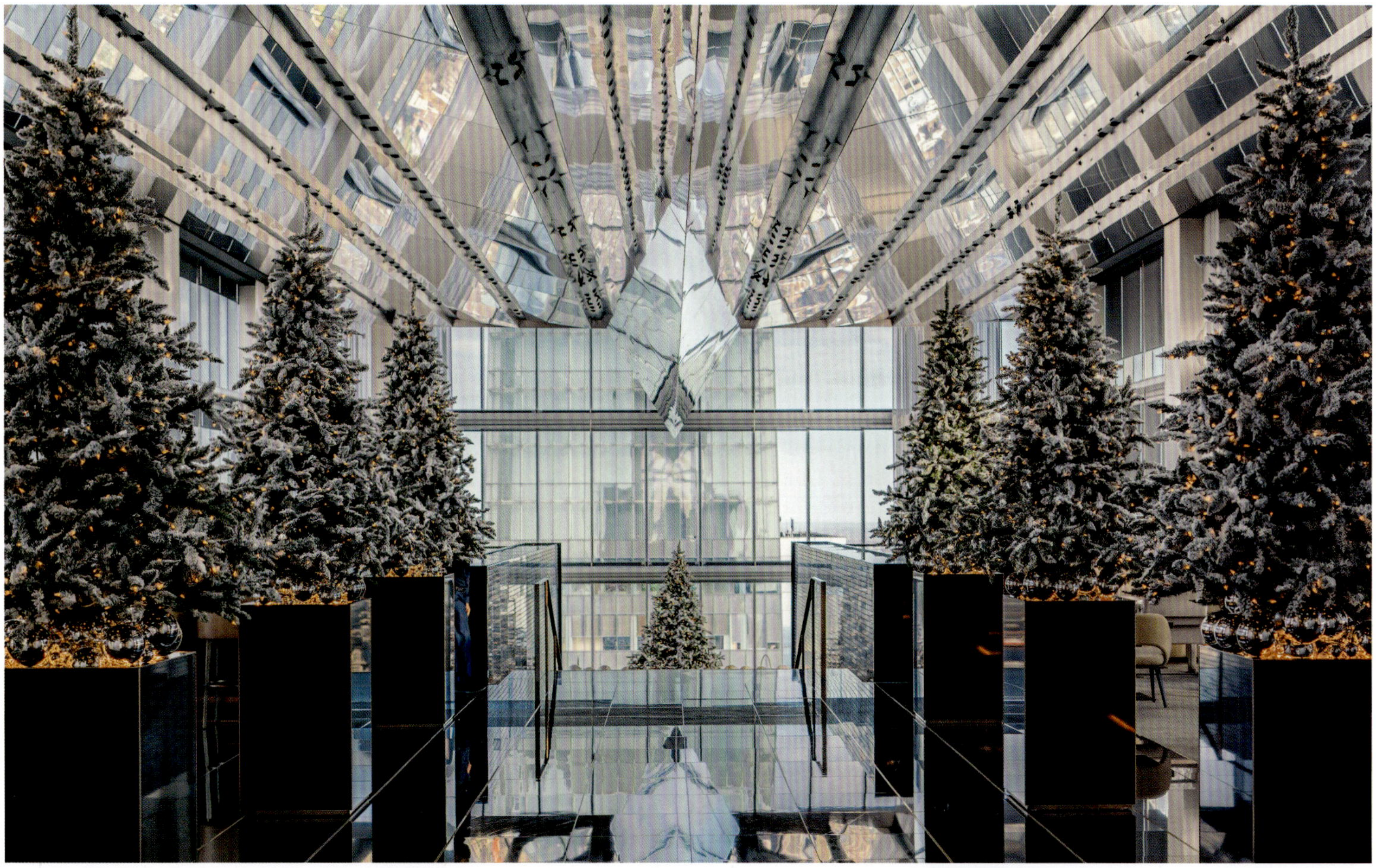

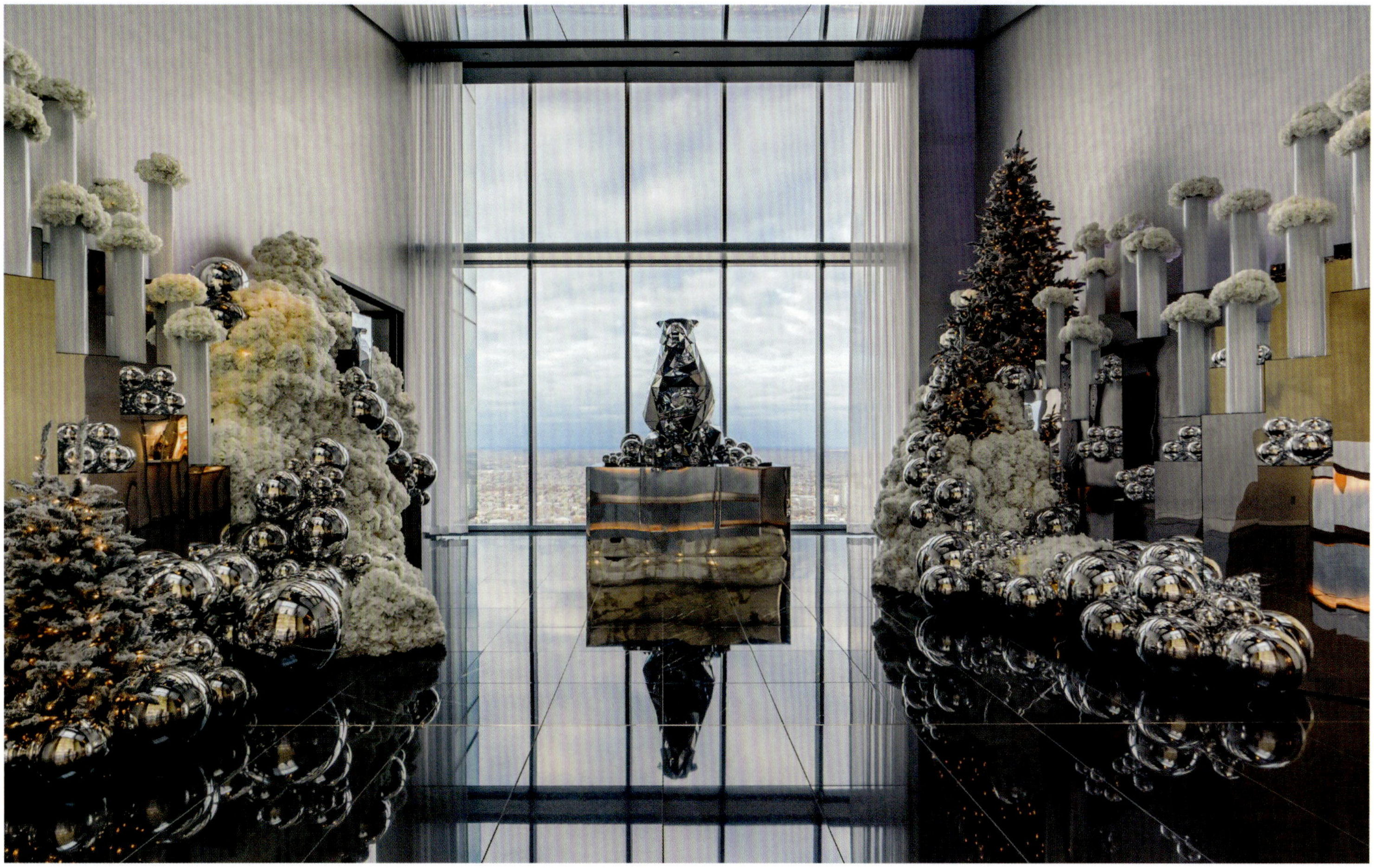

PREVIOUS: Four Seasons George V Lobby. White balls create dancing bears. ABOVE AND OPPOSITE: Four Seasons Philadelphia Lobby. Silver ornaments, hydrangeas, and silver acrylic bears. FOLLOWING: Four Seasons George V. Holiday lighting installations.

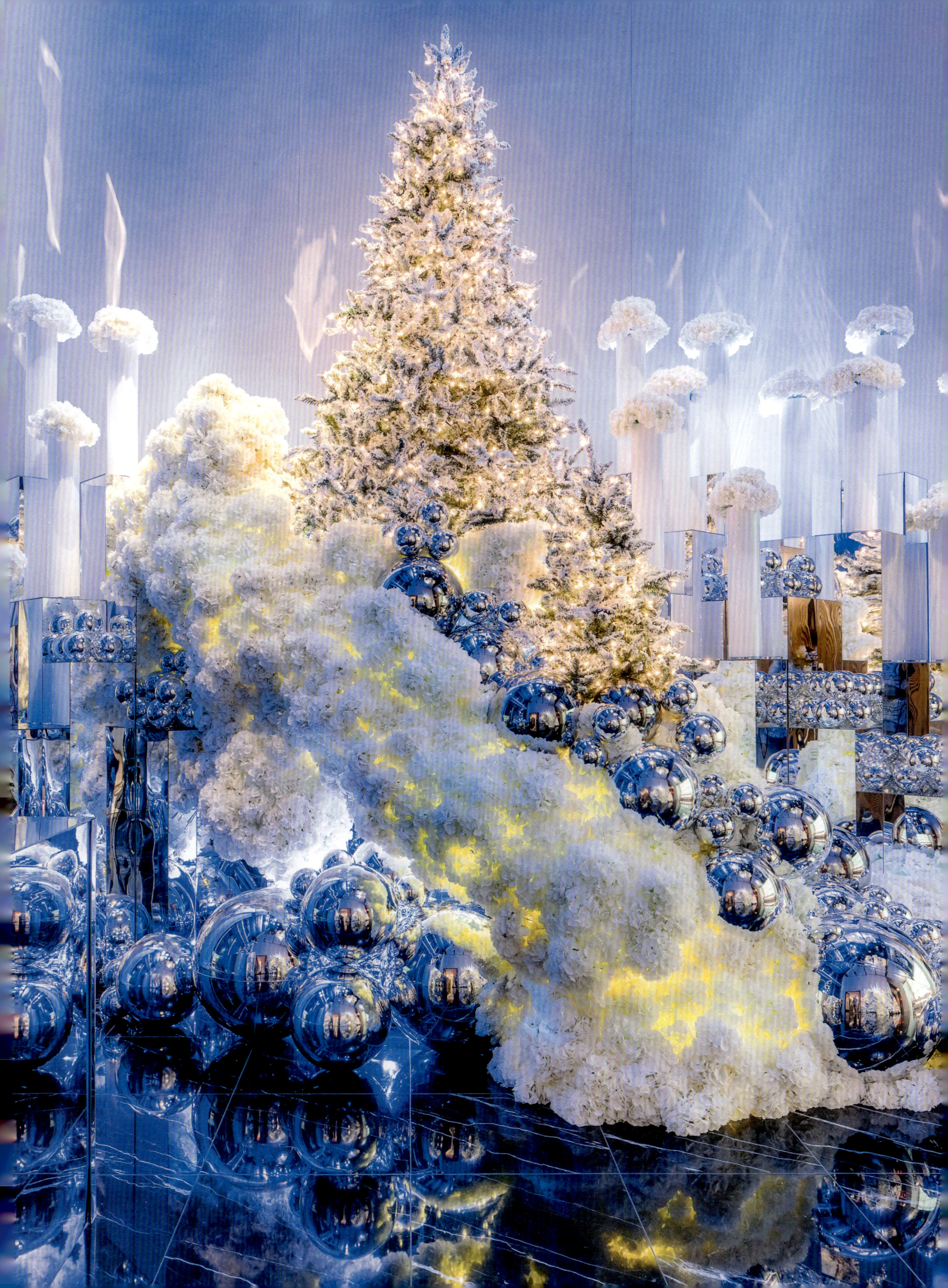

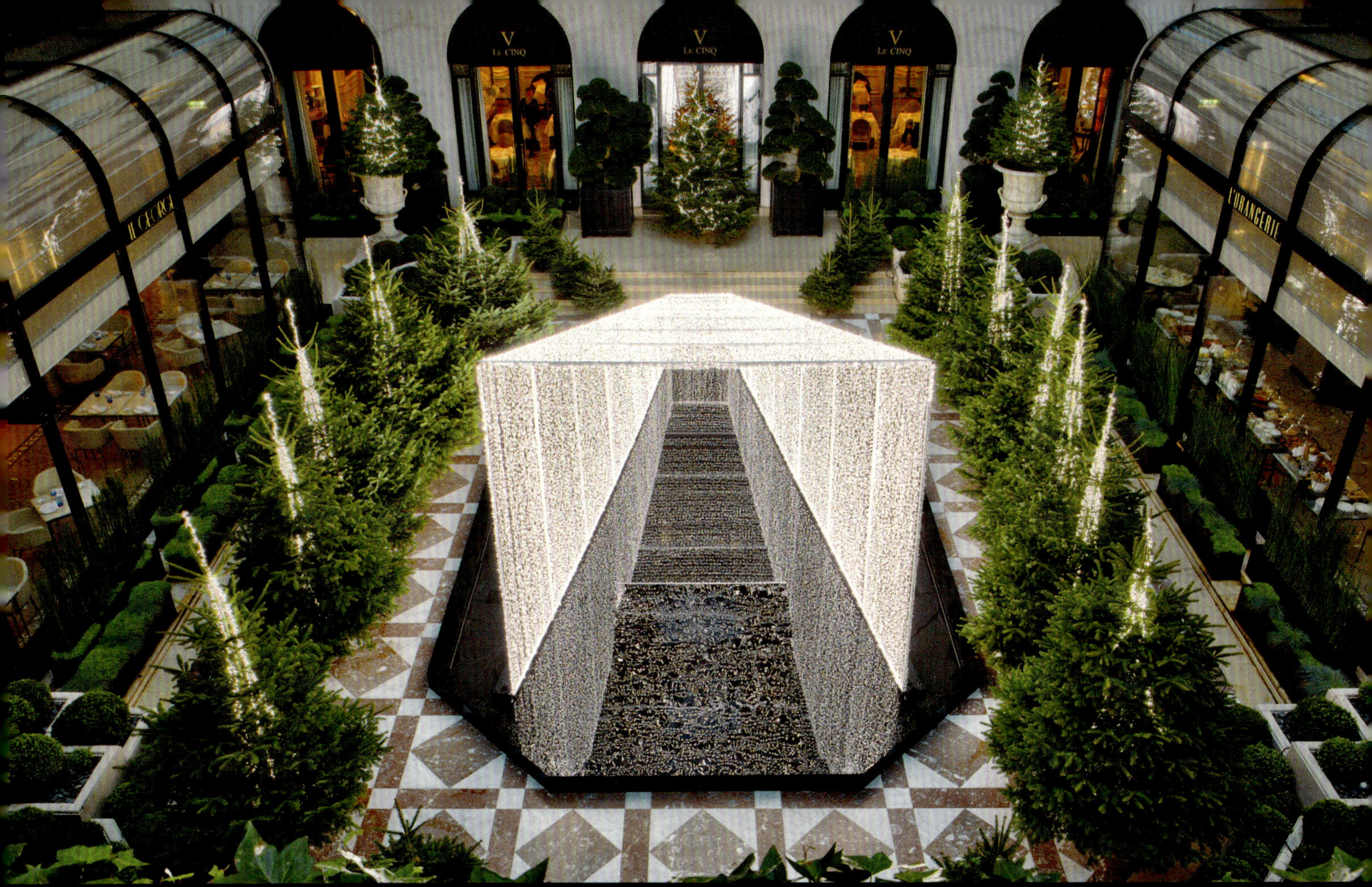
V
LE CINQ
V
LE CINQ
V
LE CINQ
L'ORANGERIE

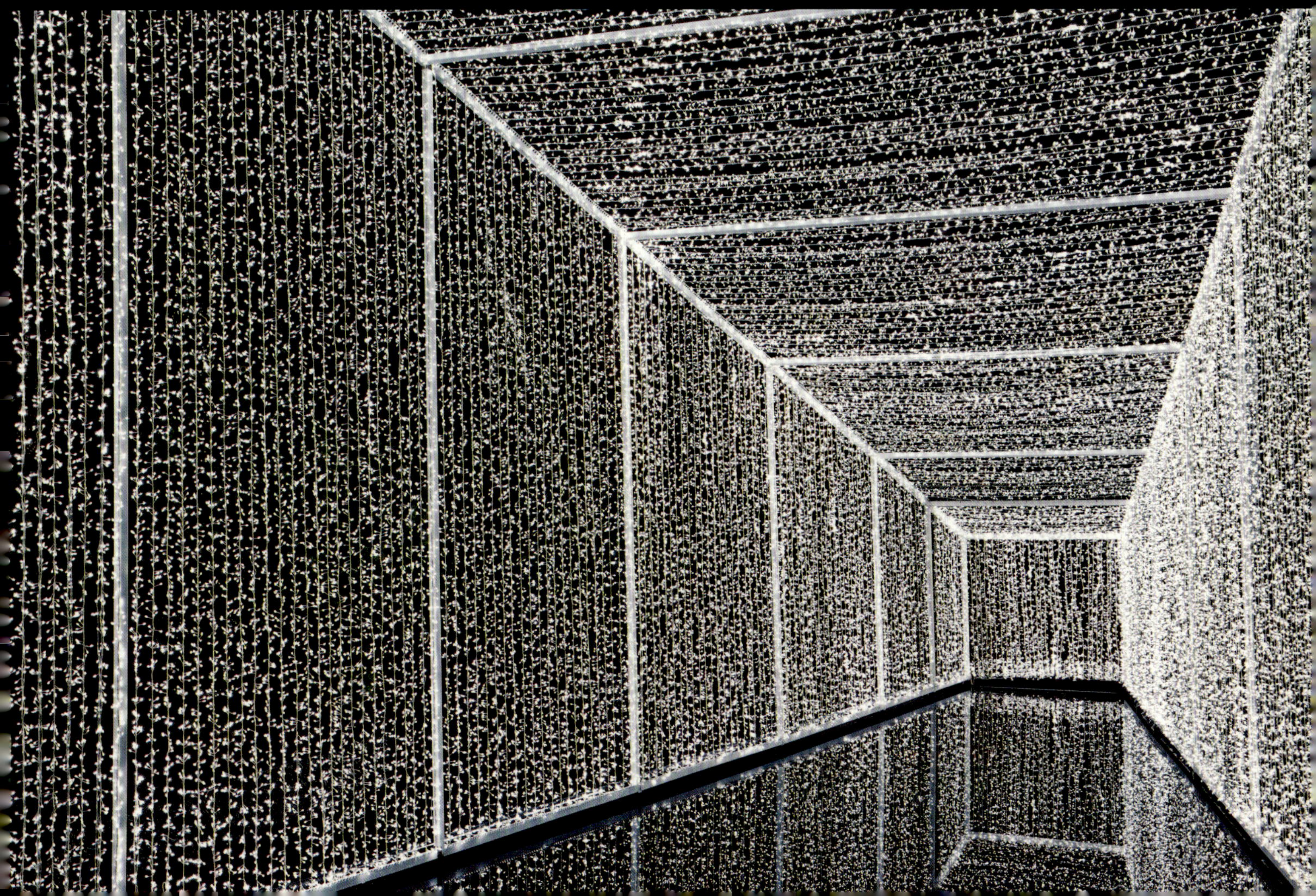

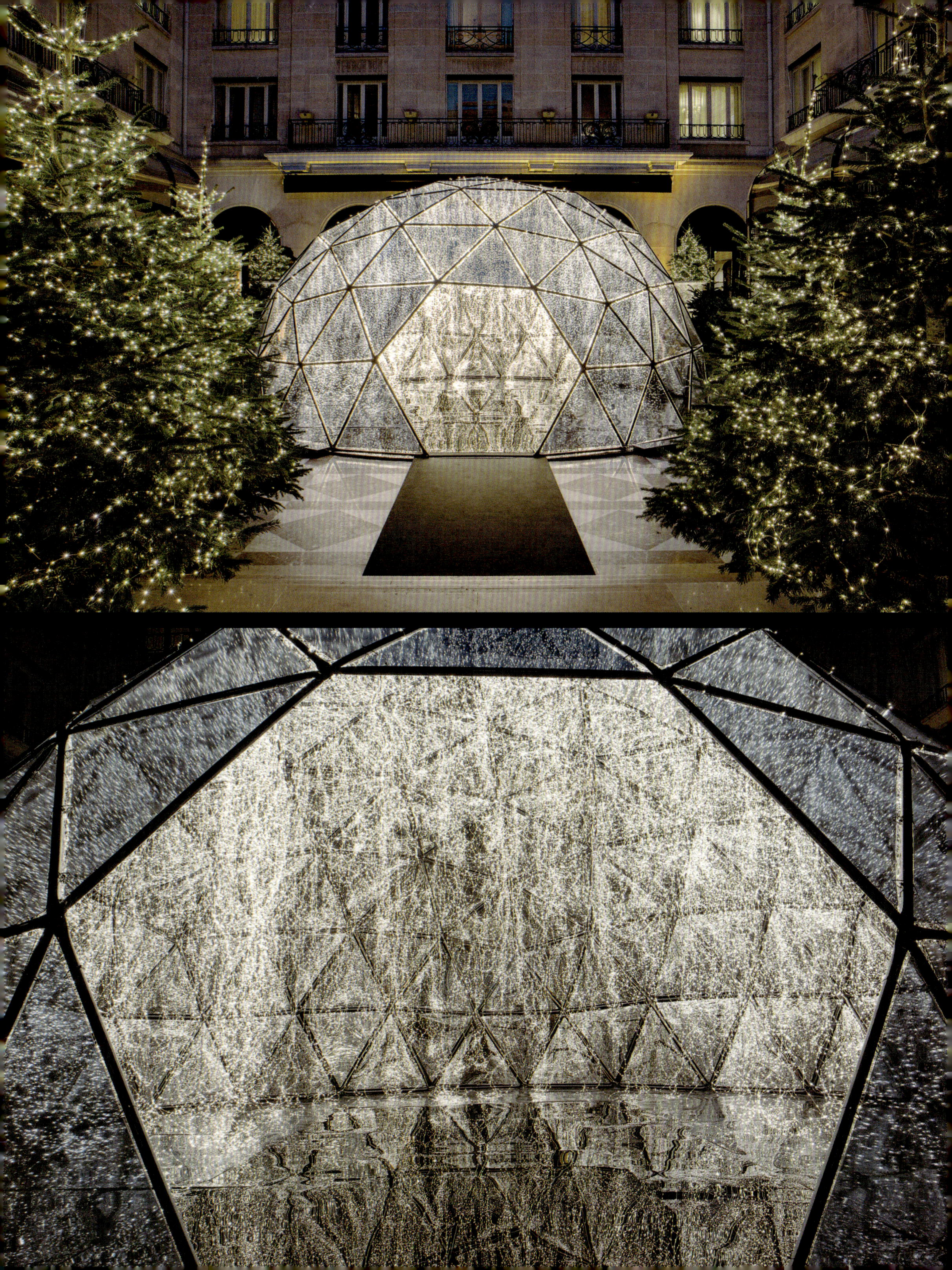

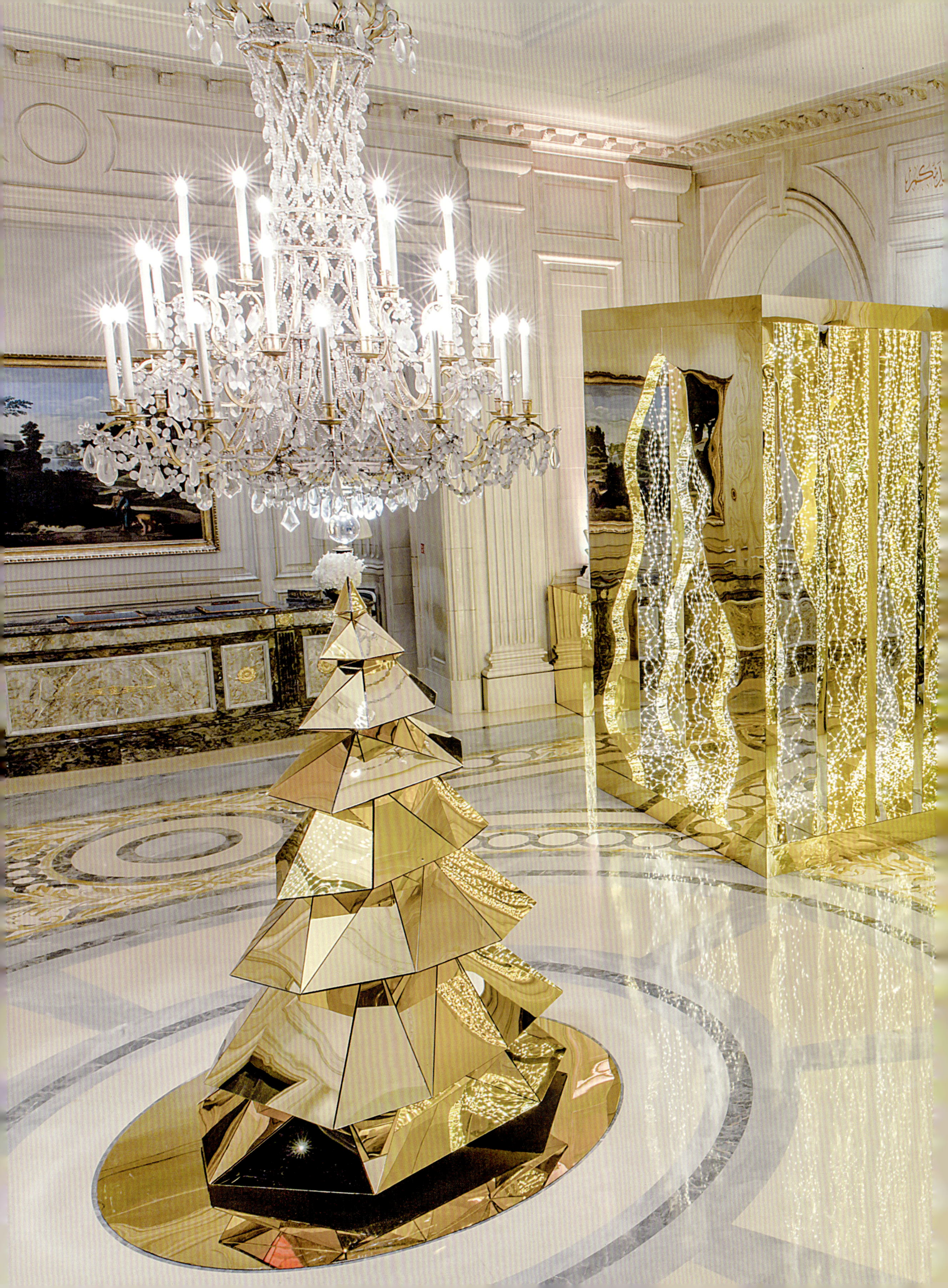

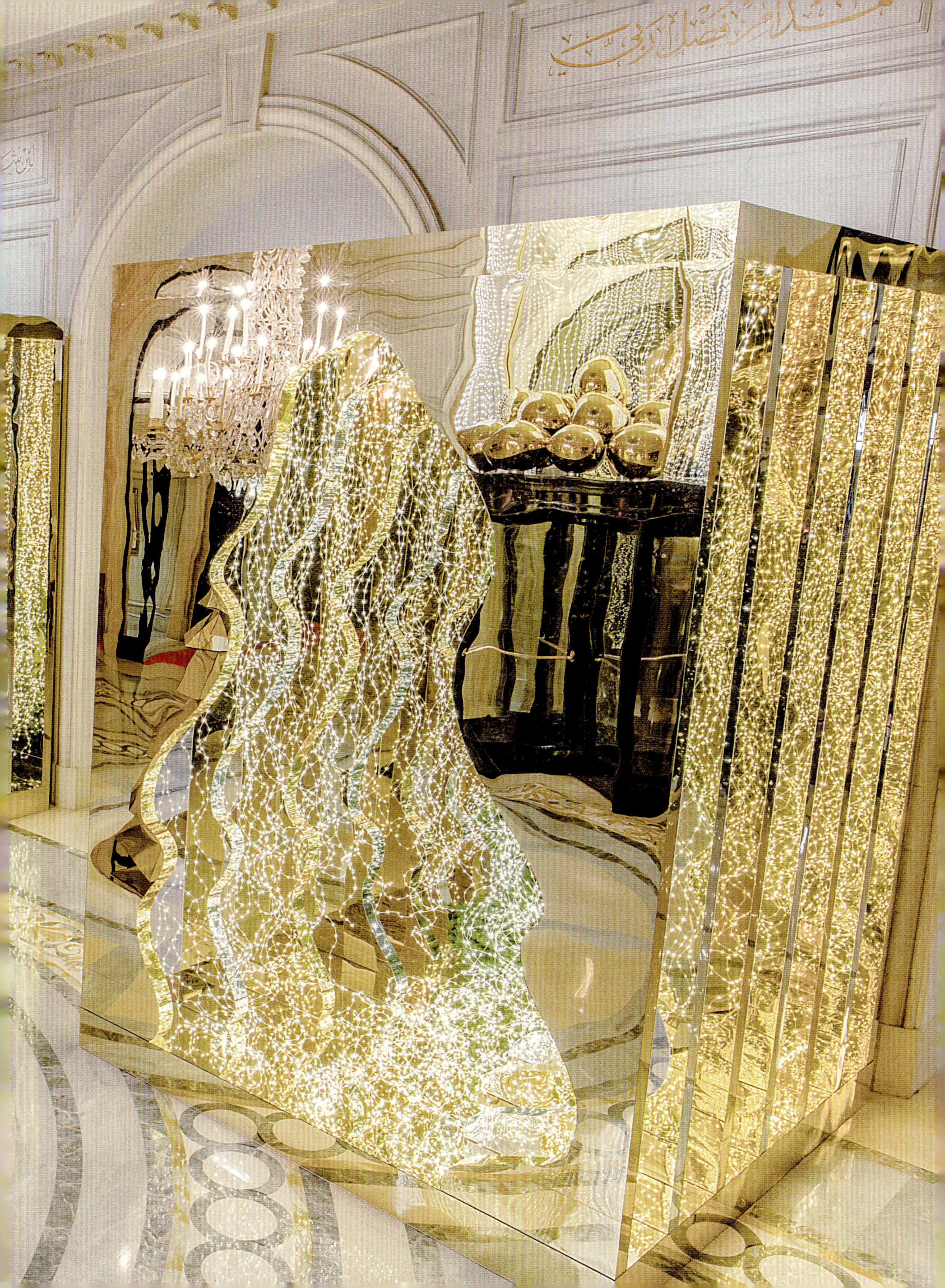

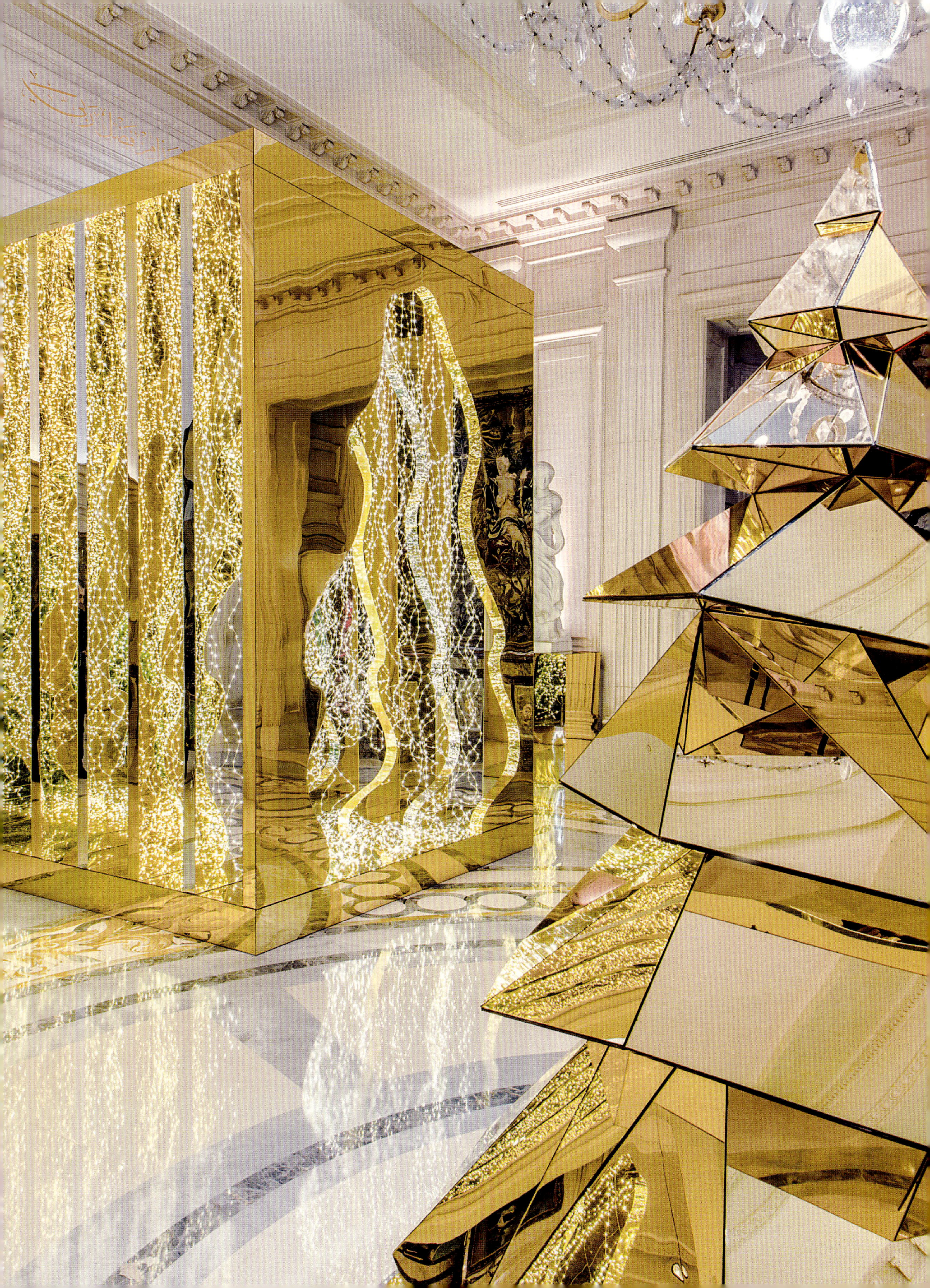

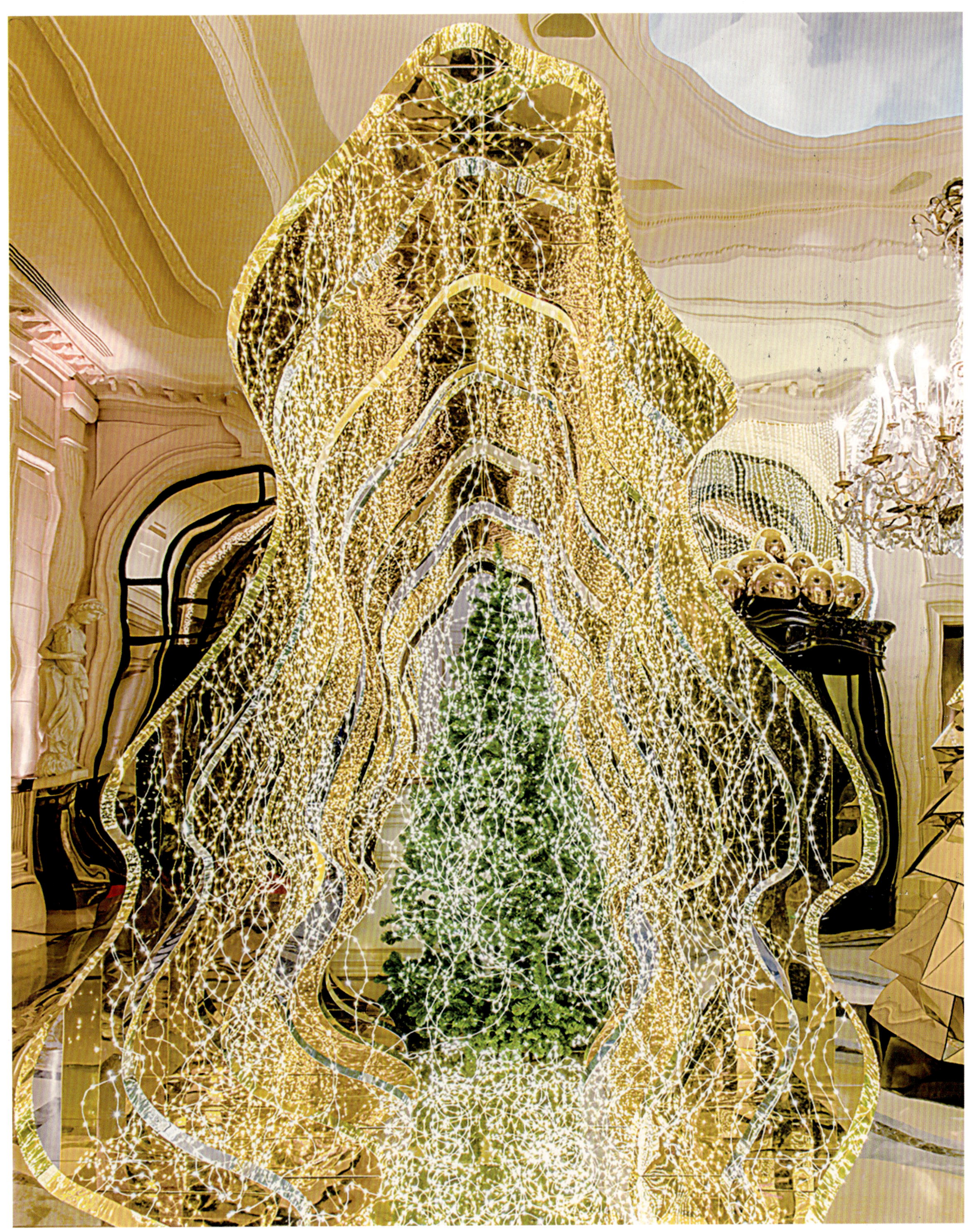

PAGES 234–237: Four Seasons George V Lobby. Lighting and acrylic glass installations.
PAGES 238–241: Four Seasons Philadelphia Lobby. Holiday lighting installations with acrylic glass, Ilex berries, and ornaments.

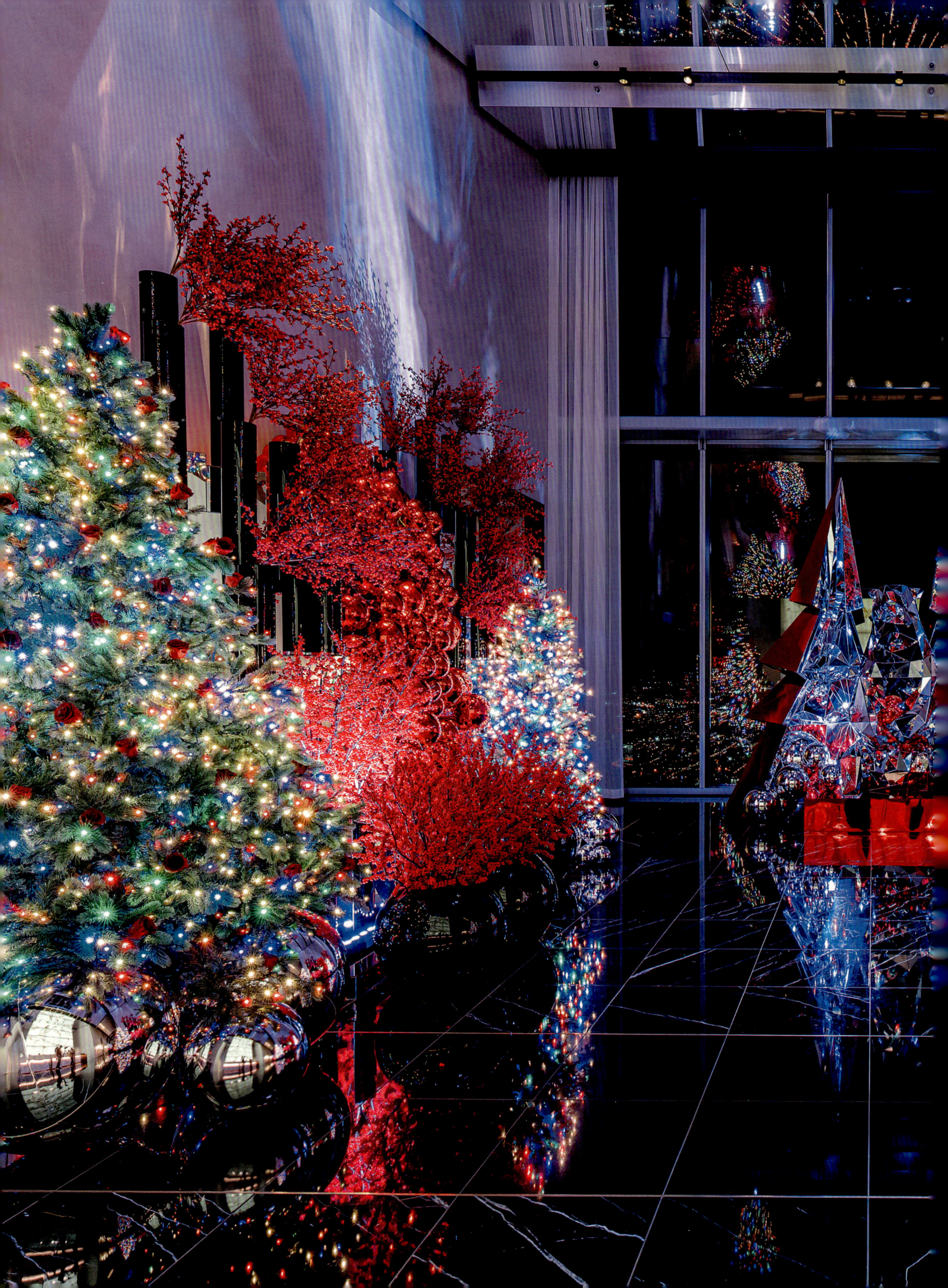

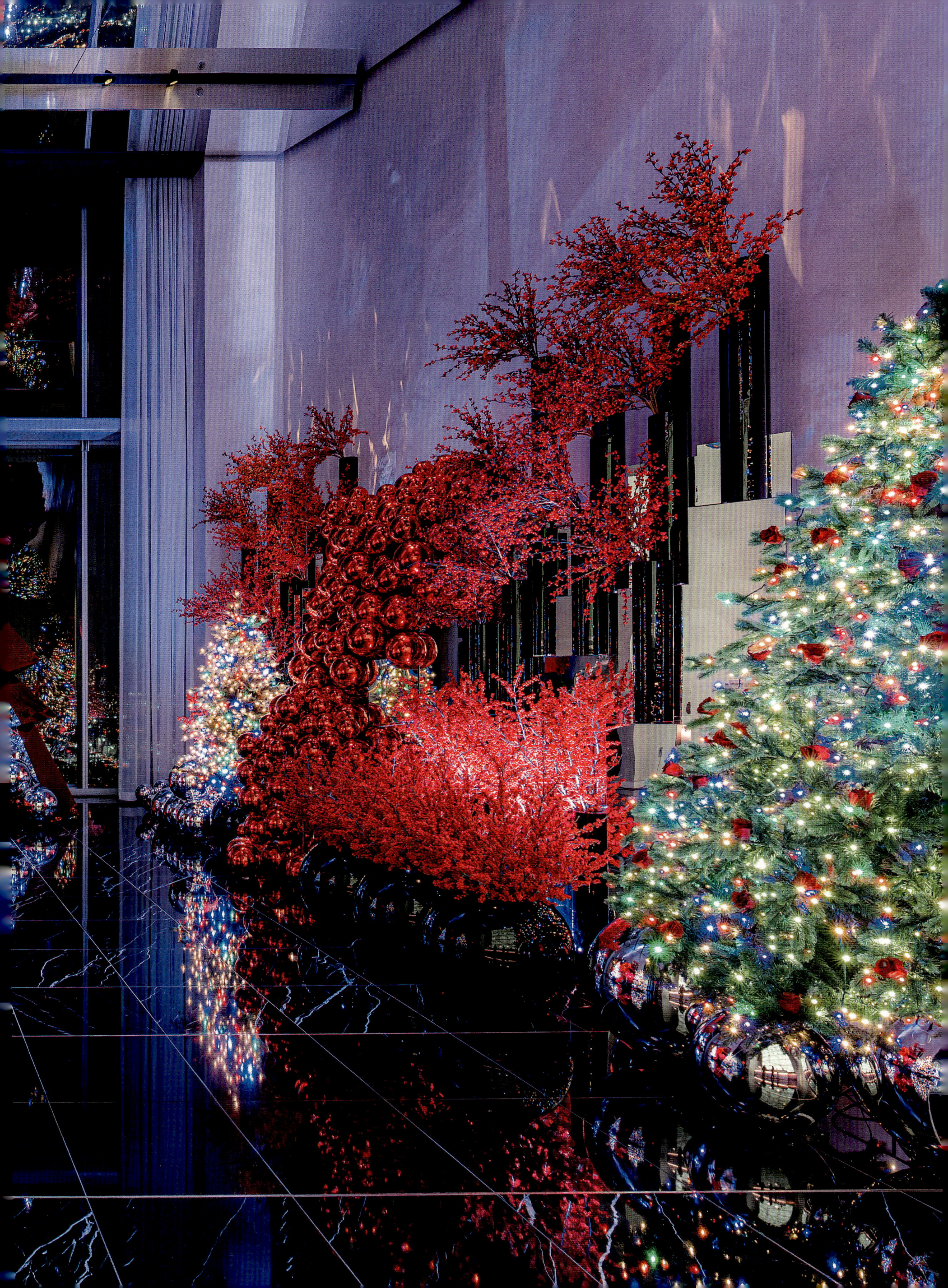

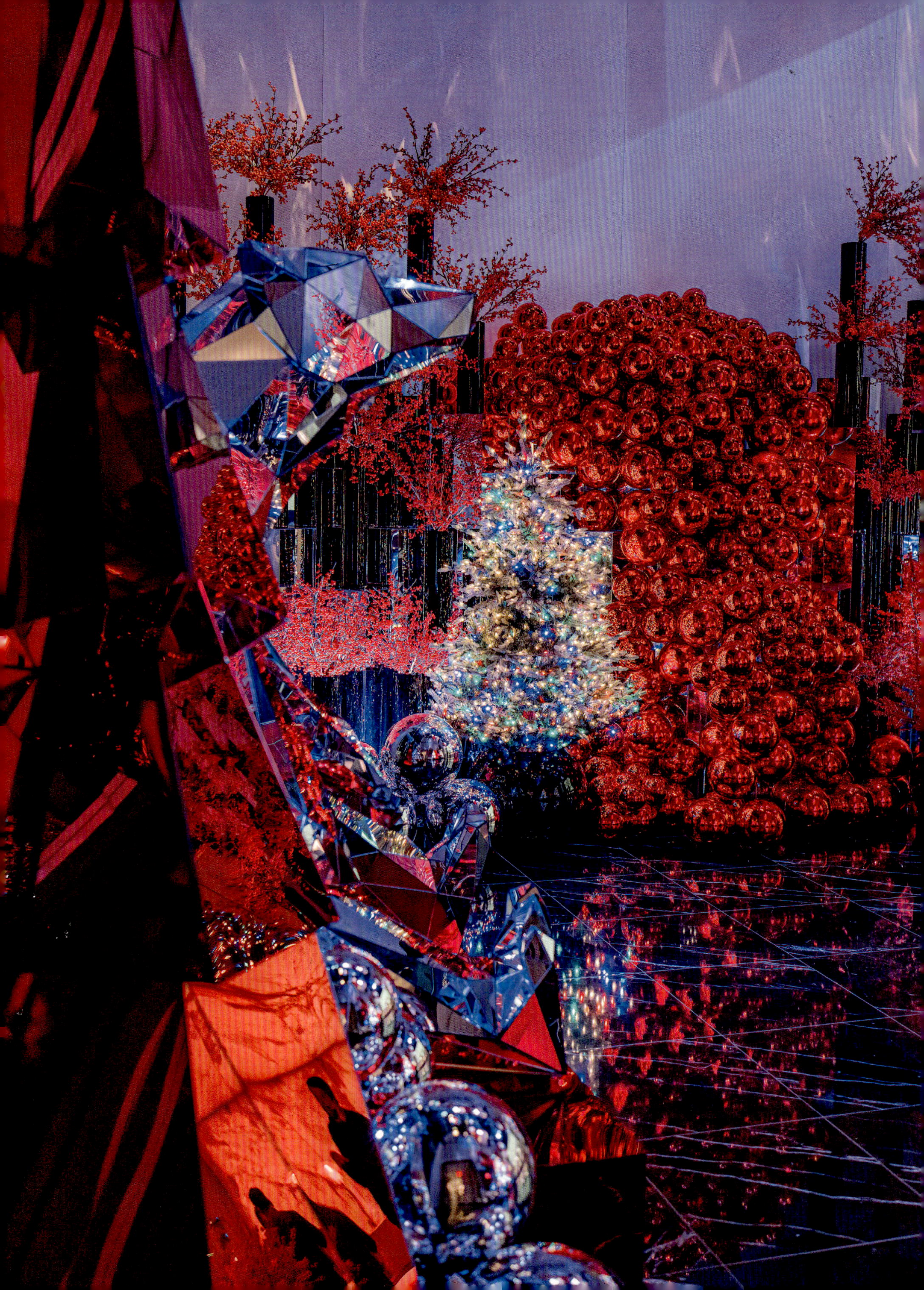

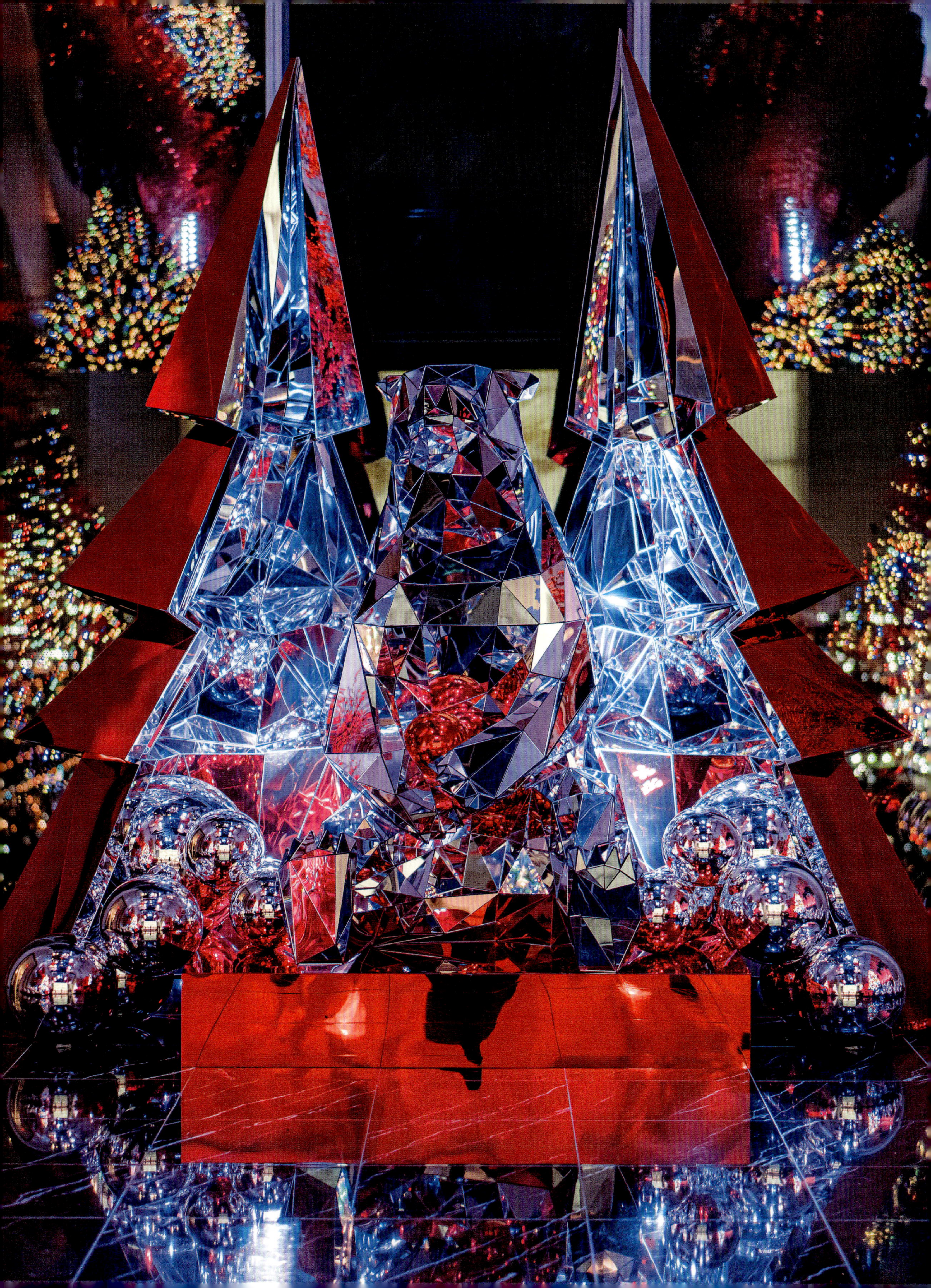

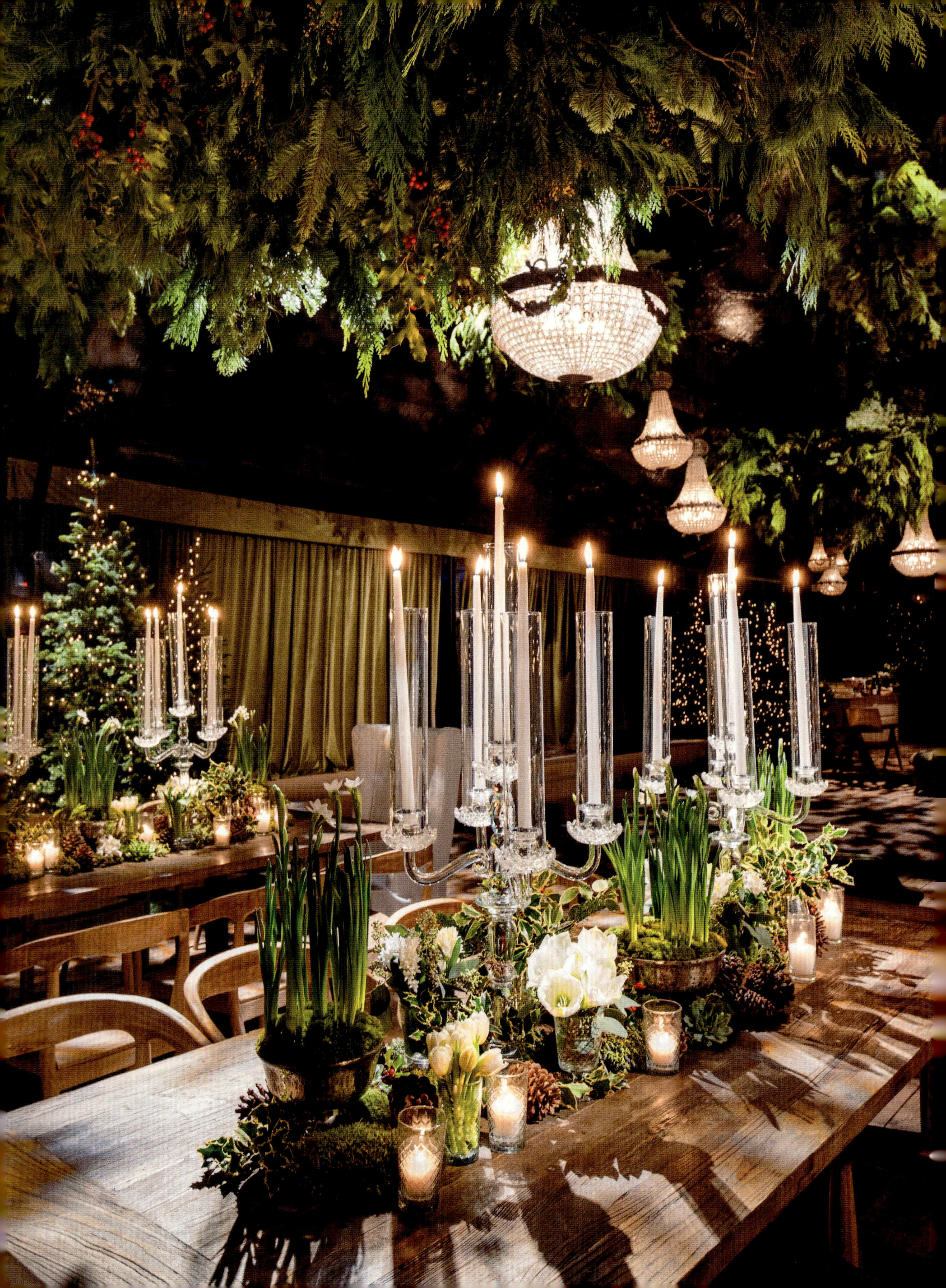

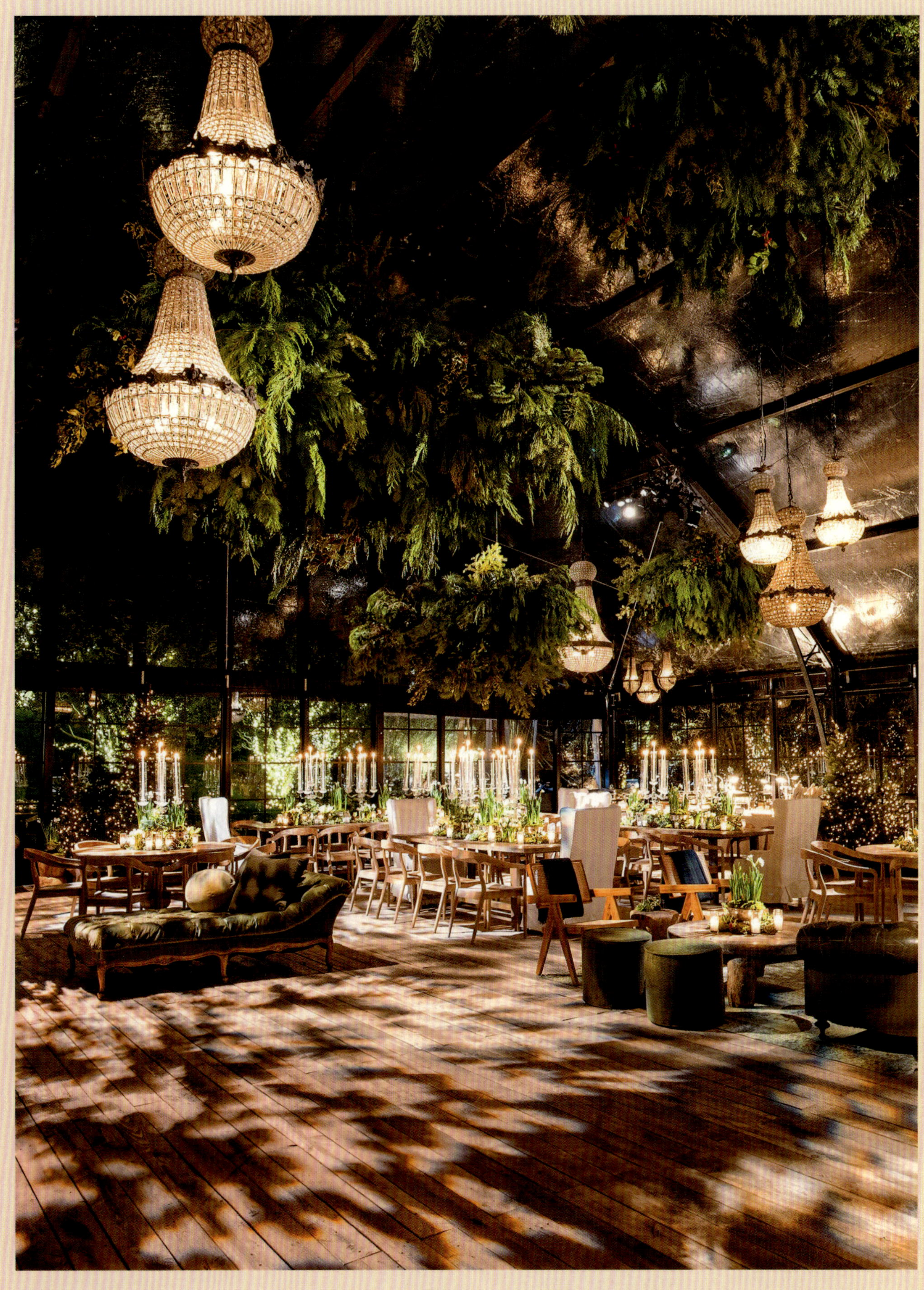

Private Event, Los Angeles. Paperwhites,
amaryllis, holly, and hyacinths. FOLLOWING:
Private Event, Los Angeles. Upside-down
pine trees and poinsettias.

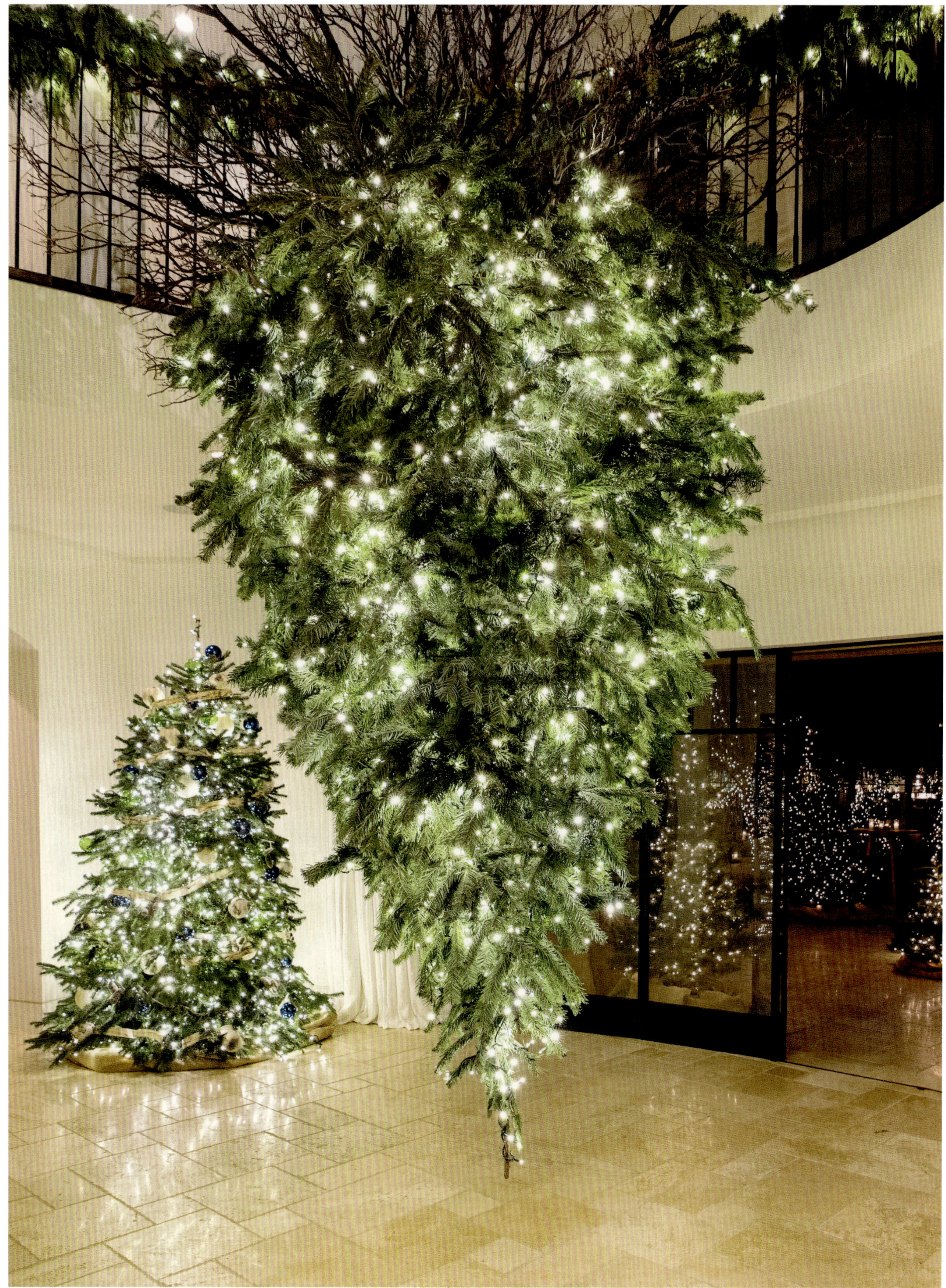

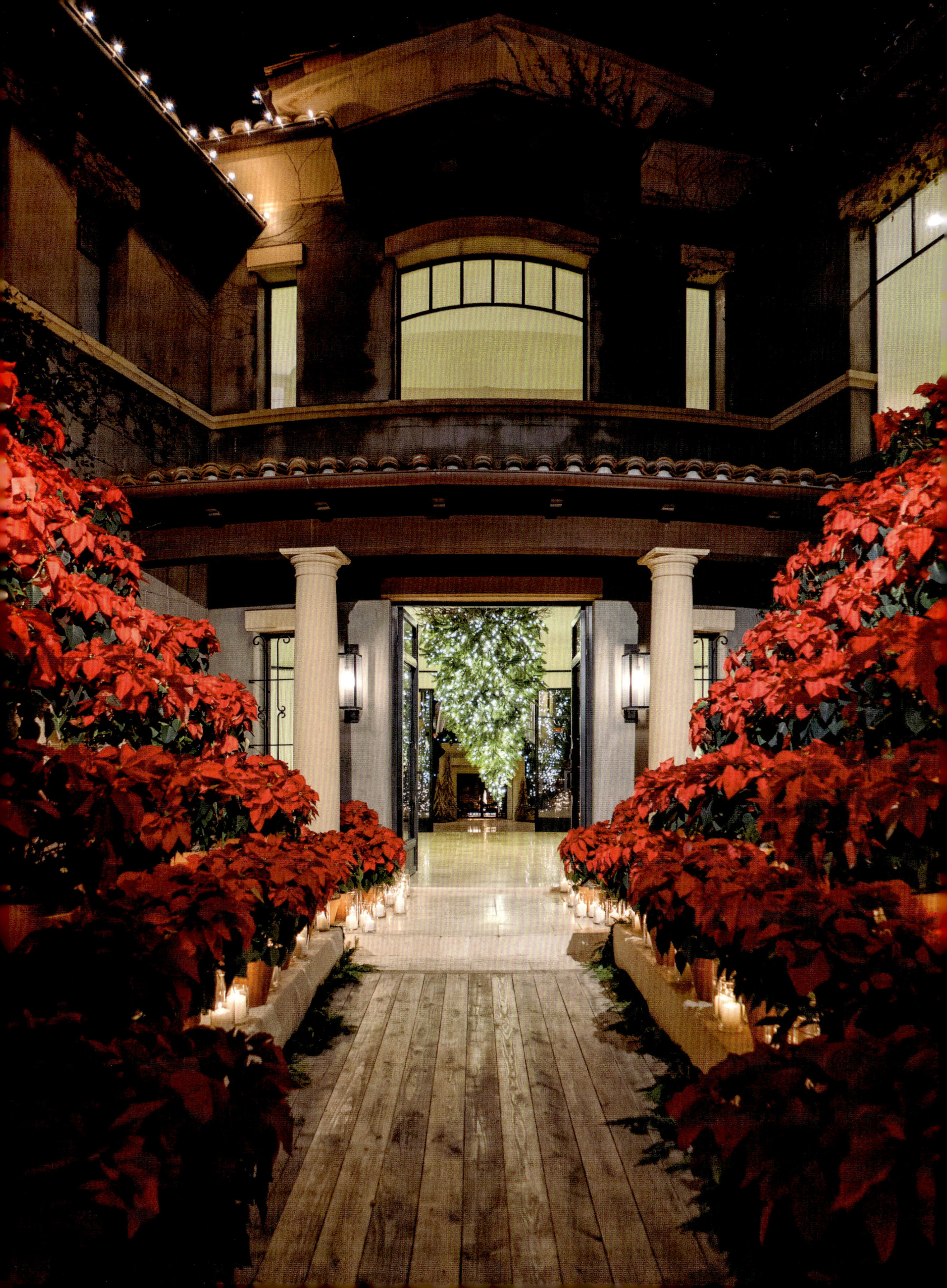

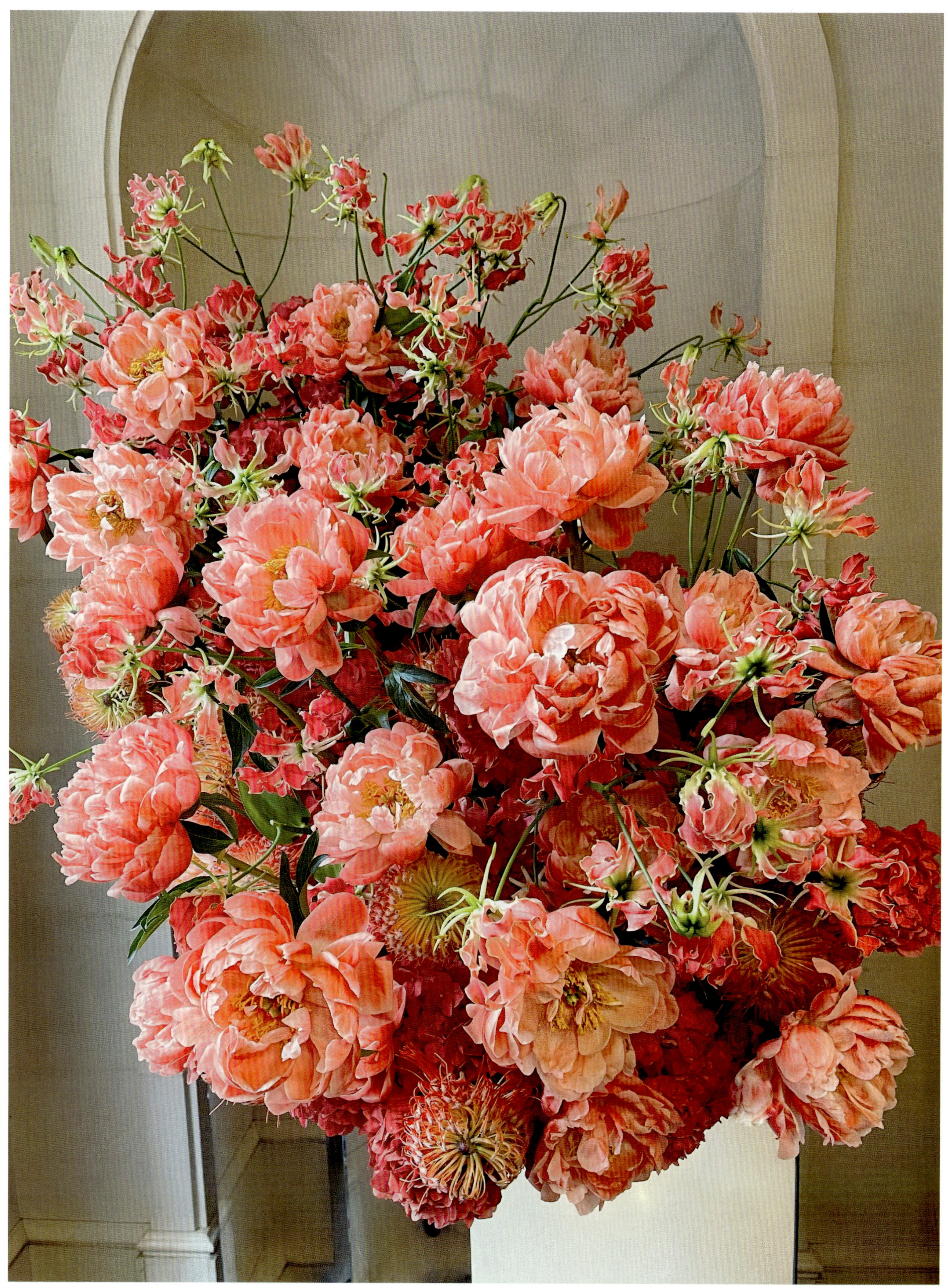

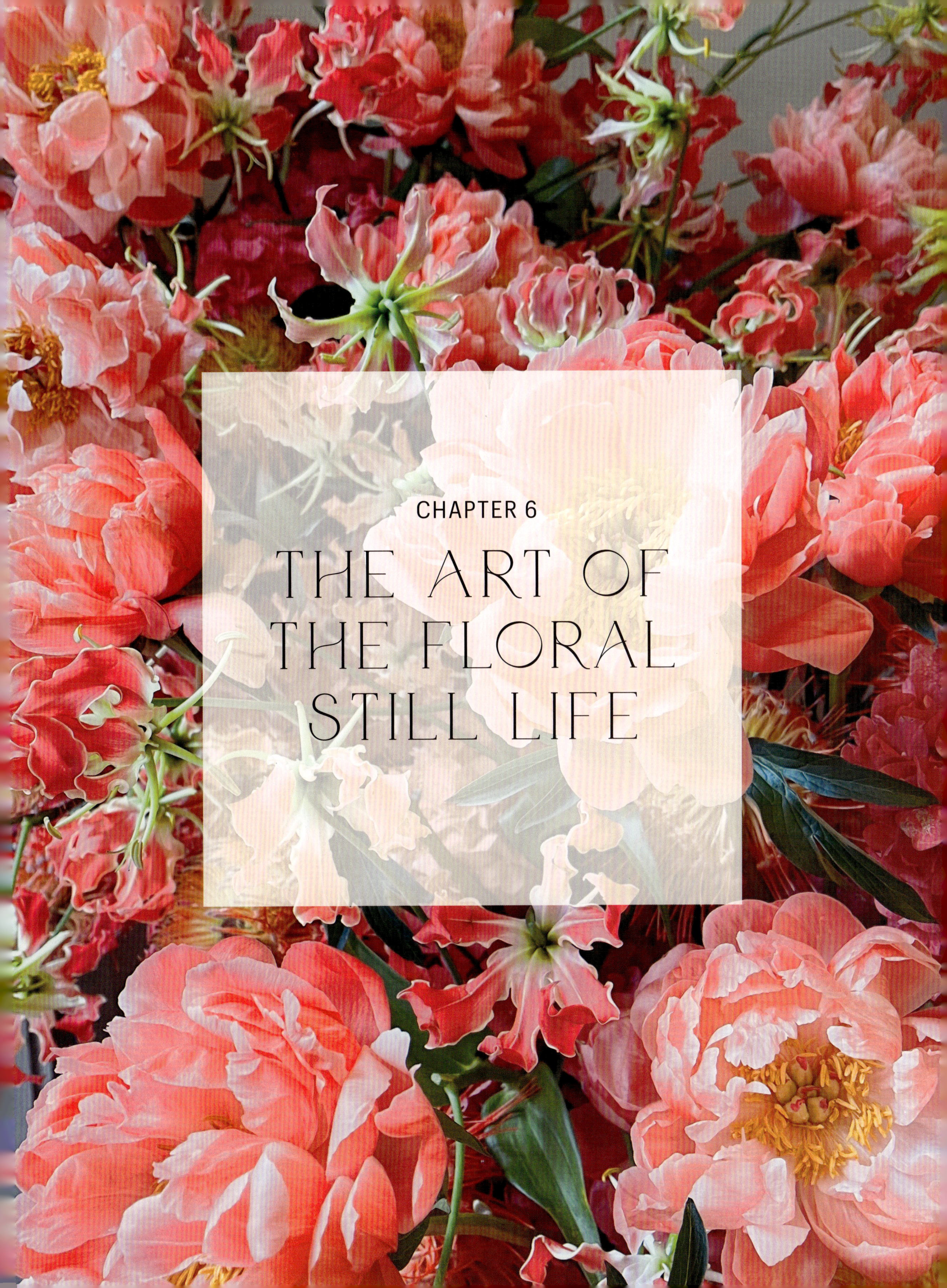

THE ART OF THE FLORAL STILL LIFE

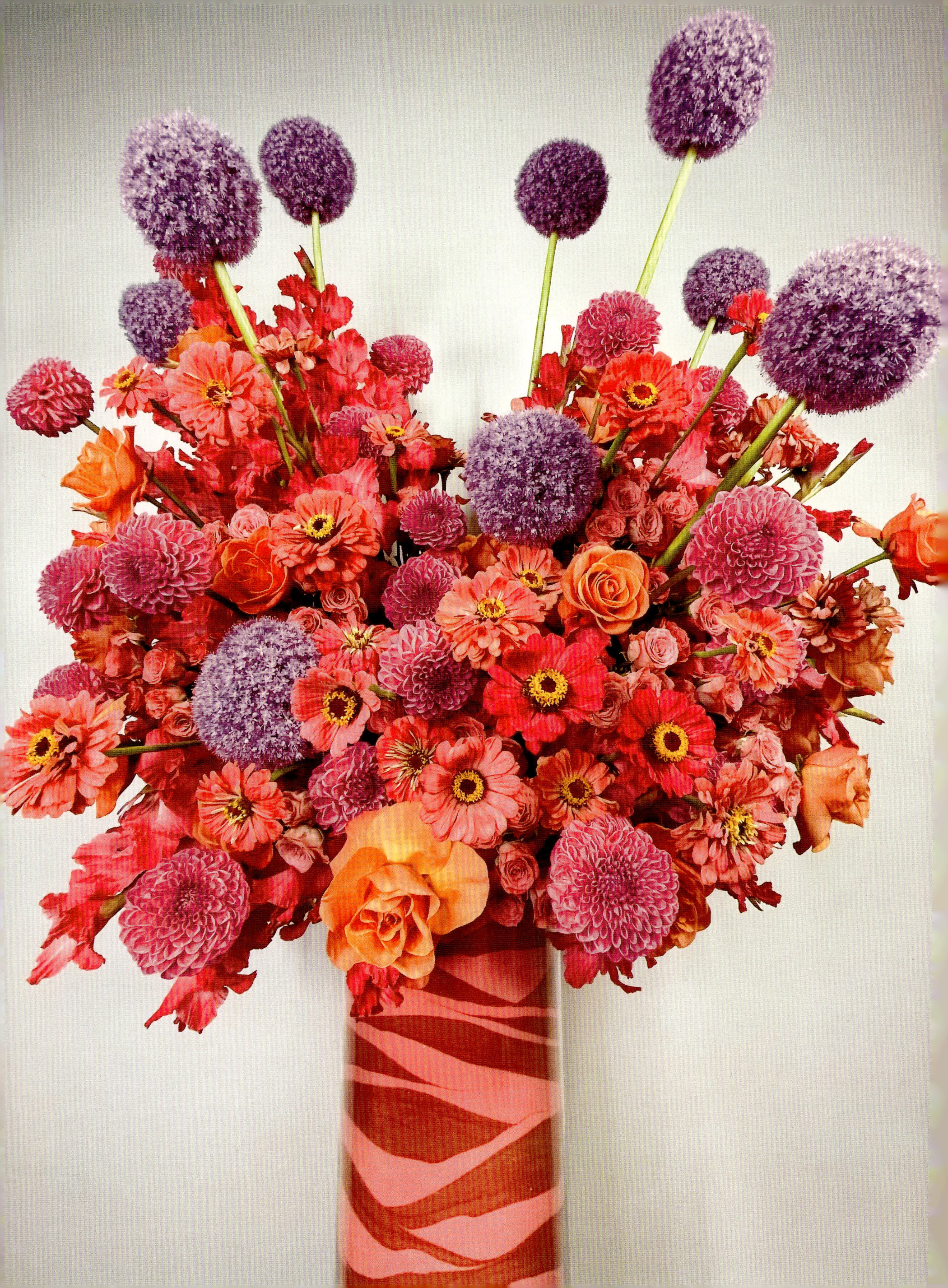

Creating floral still lifes is one of my most cherished activities. It's the one time I can let go of all my artistic obligations for which I'm known and be completely *free* to experiment, escape, and become fully immersed in my artwork without any time constraints or expectations placed on me by others. I love photography, and really admire photographer Robert Mapplethorpe, whose flower photographs simultaneously haunt and mesmerize. I am drawn to the way he captured the intensity, beauty, and simplicity of the flowers themselves. I love taking photos of flowers—pretending to be a movie director behind the camera—and playing with texture, color, shapes, and all kinds of flowers in countless combinations. Since I work with flowers every single day I like to see them from different angles and from alternative viewpoints. I want to photograph my still lifes through the lens of how *I* see them and as *I* made them. The only thing that should be missing is the fragrance.

In today's world of social media, photos dominate our cultural conversations and possess the power to inspire millions of viewers around the world. I love seeing talented designers from every imaginable country posting photos from their homes. Everyone has a different vision of flowers and a different method of using them in their works, which always inspires me. I enjoy sharing my experimental still lifes, too, so that others may be inspired to push their artistic abilities and boundaries.

As seen in the following pages, there are no rules to my still lifes; *everything* and *anything* is fair game. From more classic and traditional floral arrangements (which are experiencing a comeback these days) to modern and extravagant designs, I bounce around the floral design spectrum—and have the time of my life. However, a common thread they always share is that each still life is like a portrait on display in a home or a museum: it's just waiting to be looked at more closely, for a viewer to approach the piece and appreciate the minute details to be discovered within the frame. Always remember: be simple, be bold, and—most importantly—be yourself!

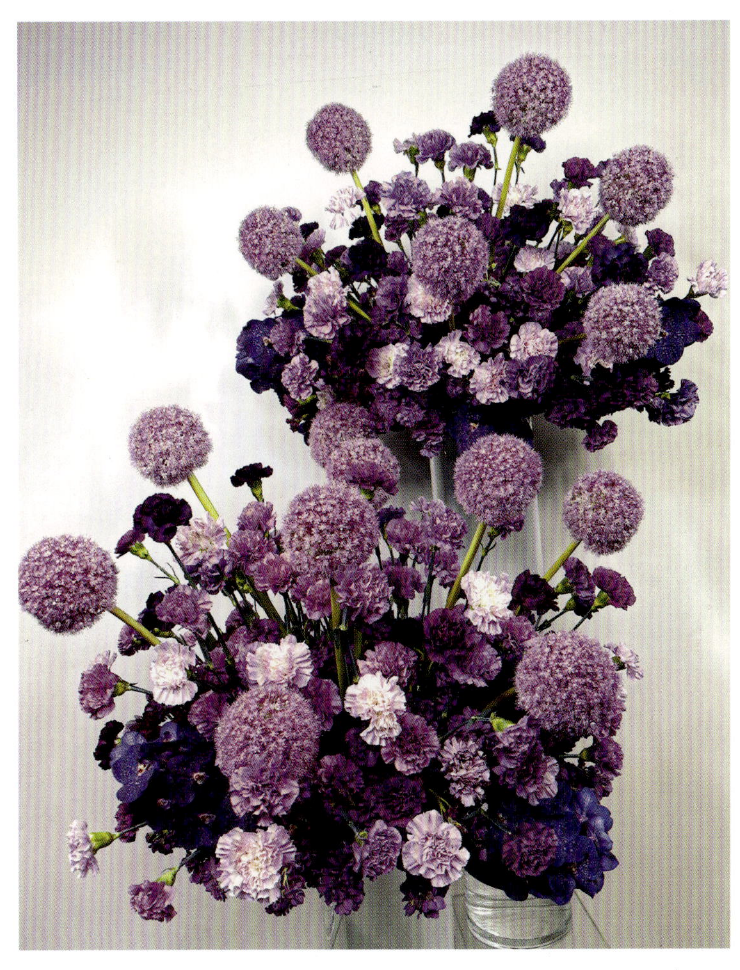

OPPOSITE: Purple alliums, orange crush roses, zinnias, and fuchsia dahlias. ABOVE: Purple alliums, carnations, and vanda orchids. FOLLOWING: Eremurus, roses, dahlias, gladiolas, zinnias, and alliums.

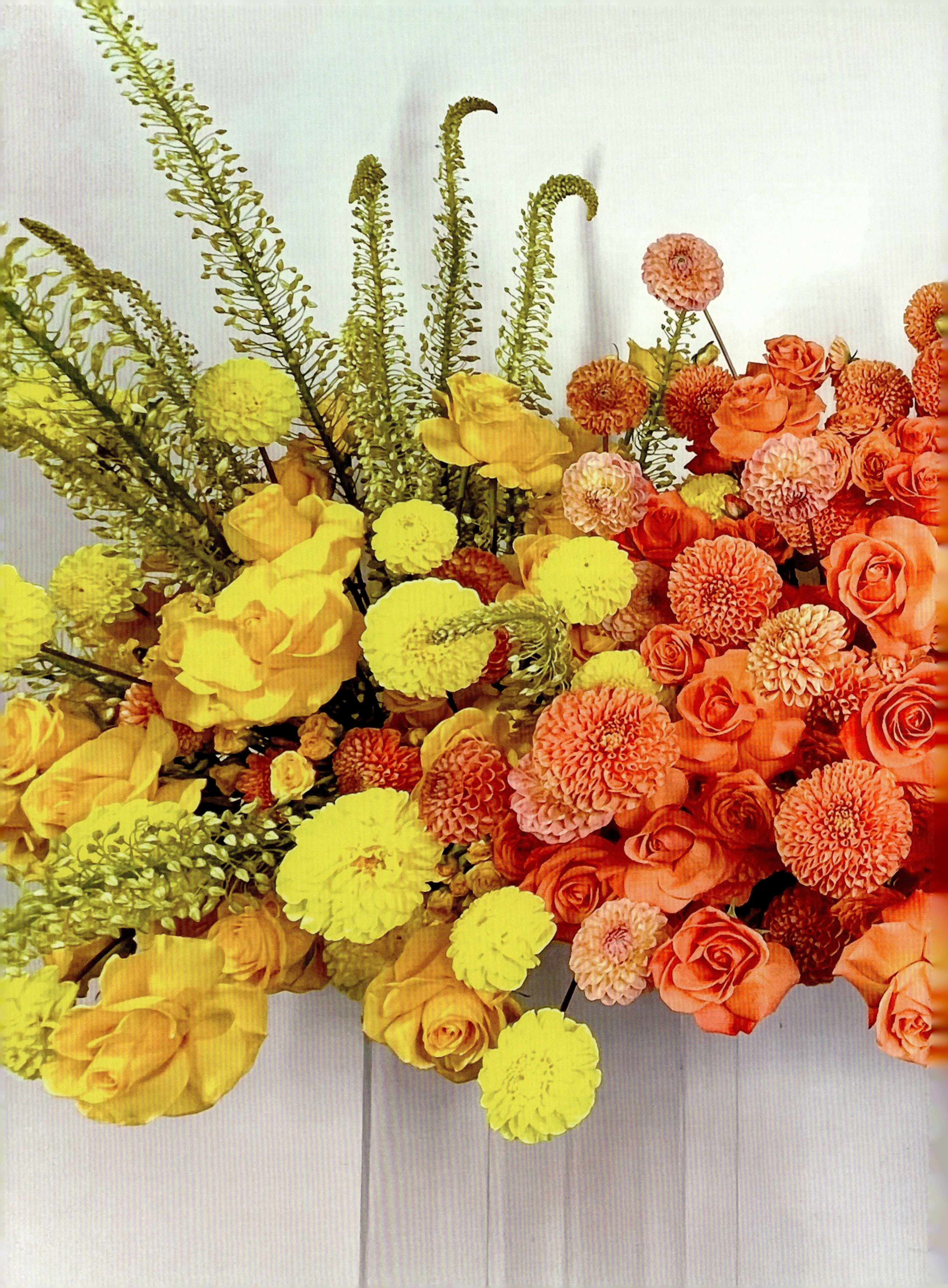

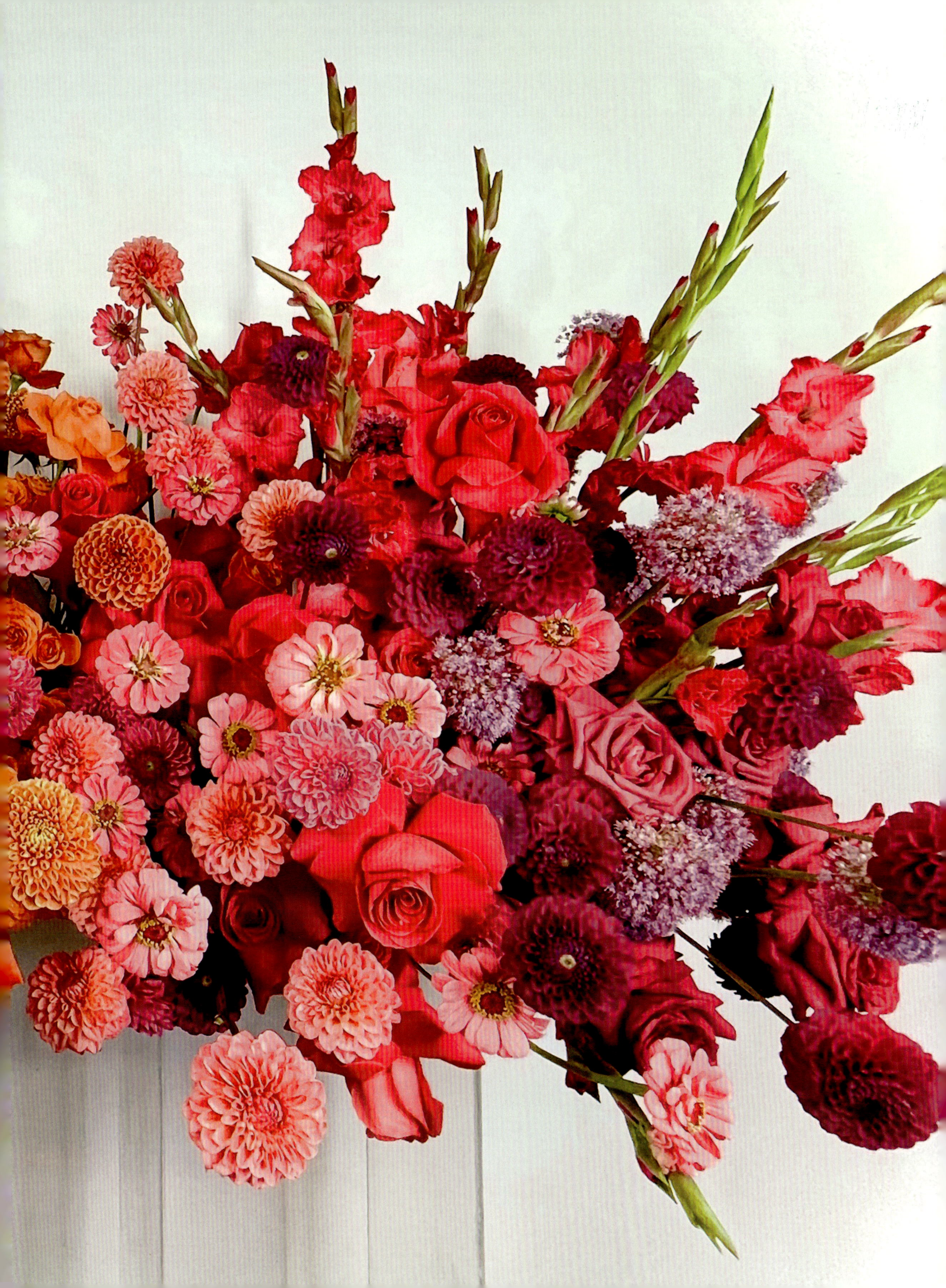

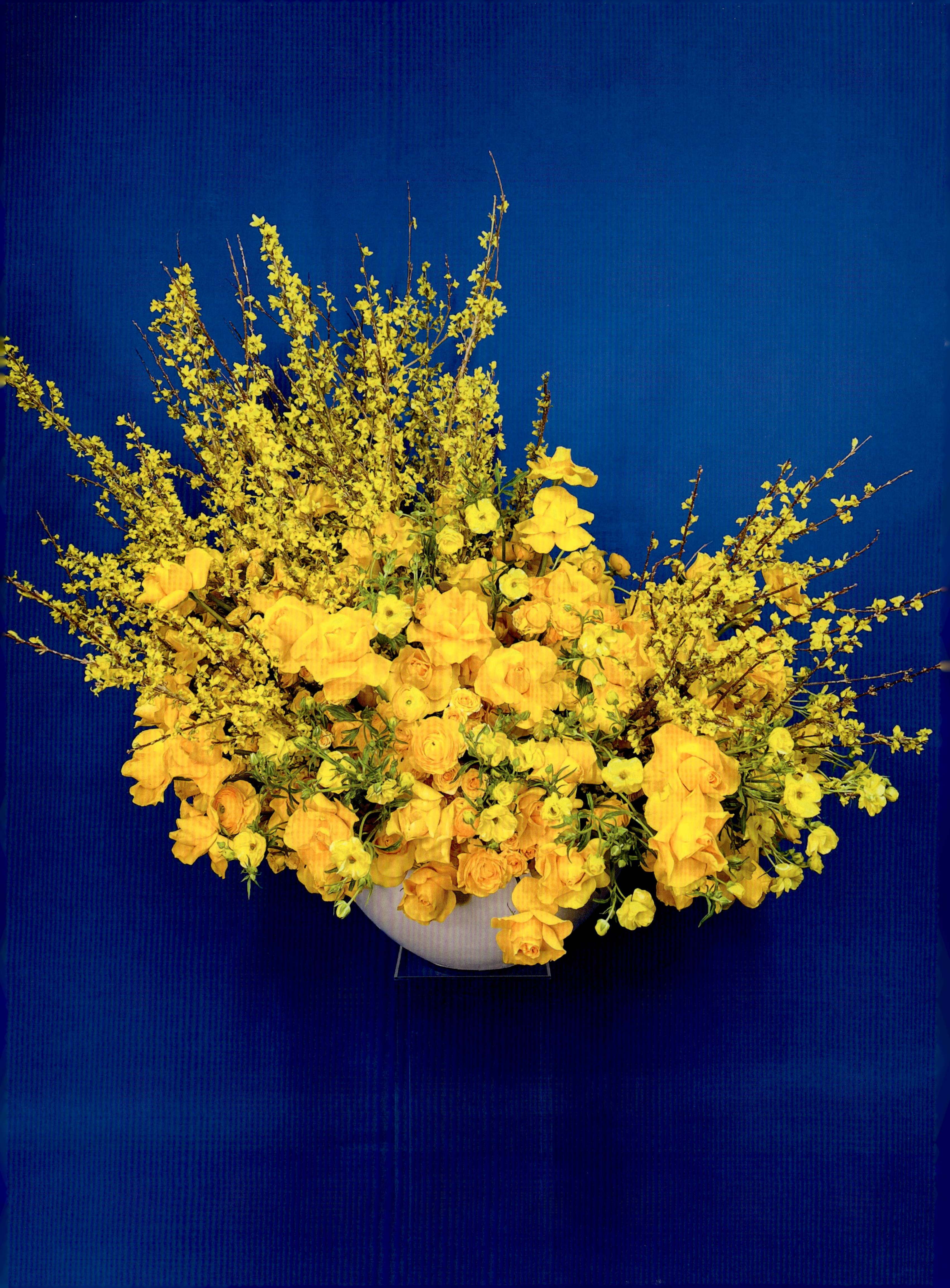

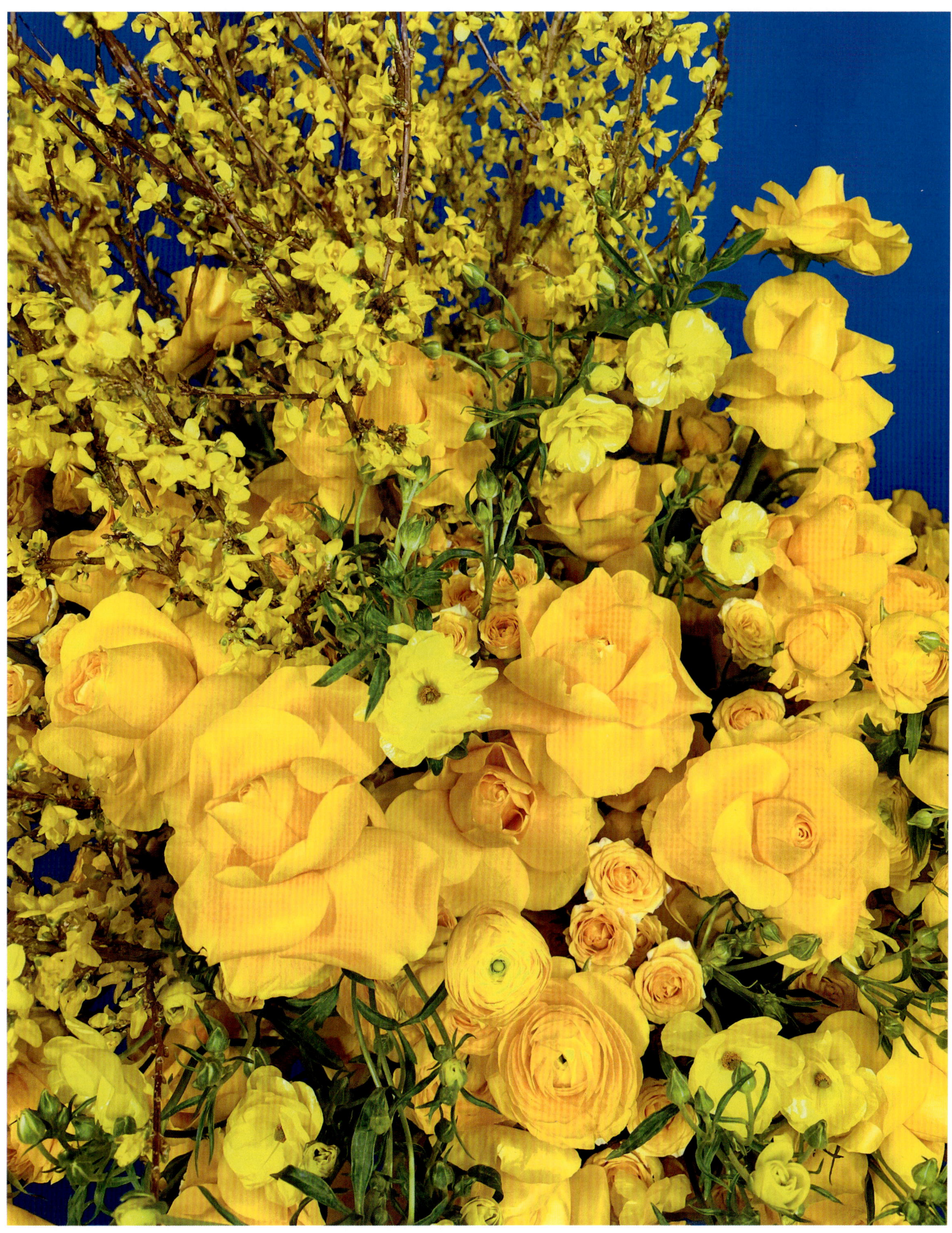

To bring awareness and support to the escalating situation in Ukraine,
forsythia, ranunculus, roses, and spray roses were used.

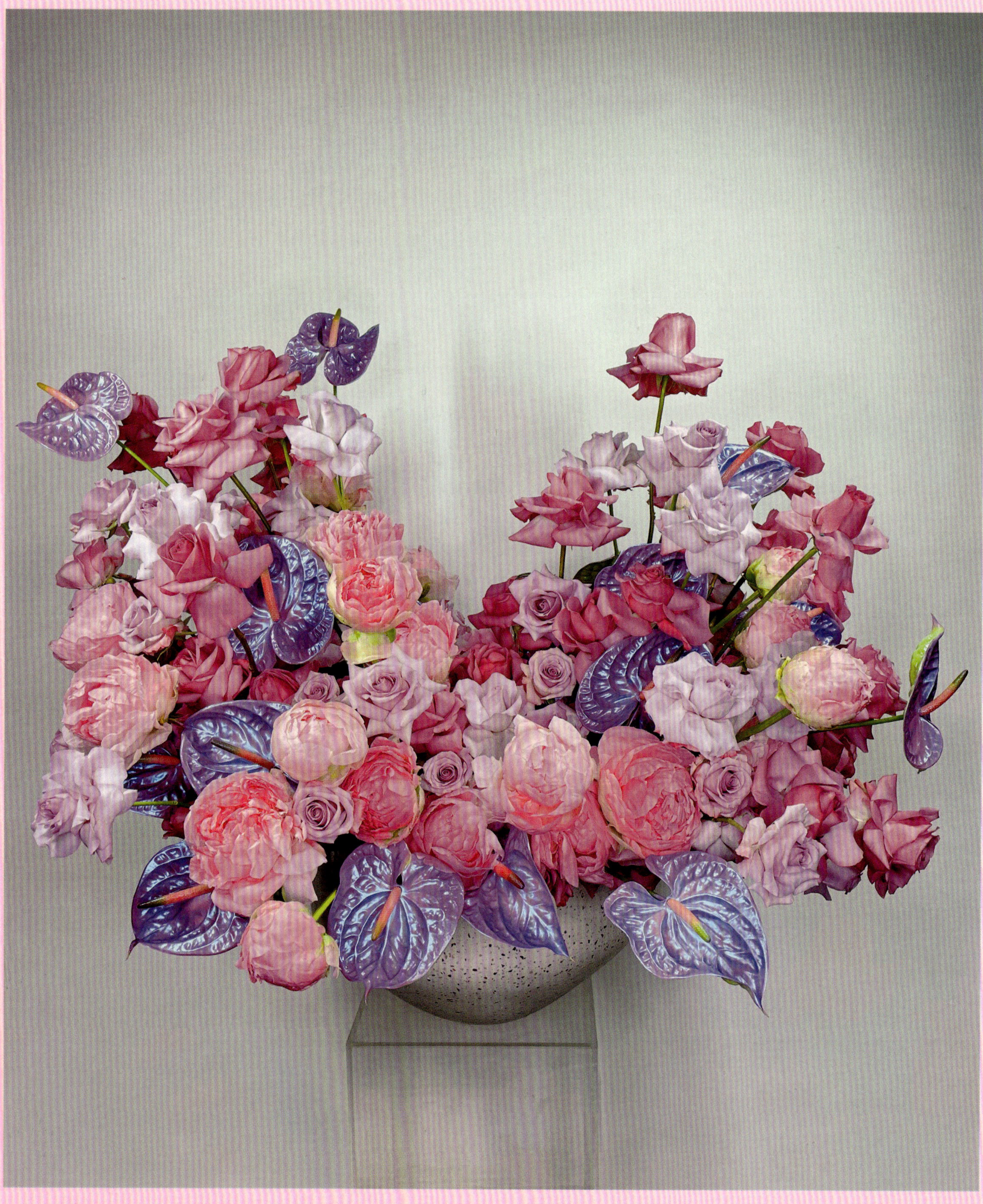

ABOVE: Anthurium, peonies, and roses.
OPPOSITE: Cherry blossoms, peonies, spray roses, and roses.

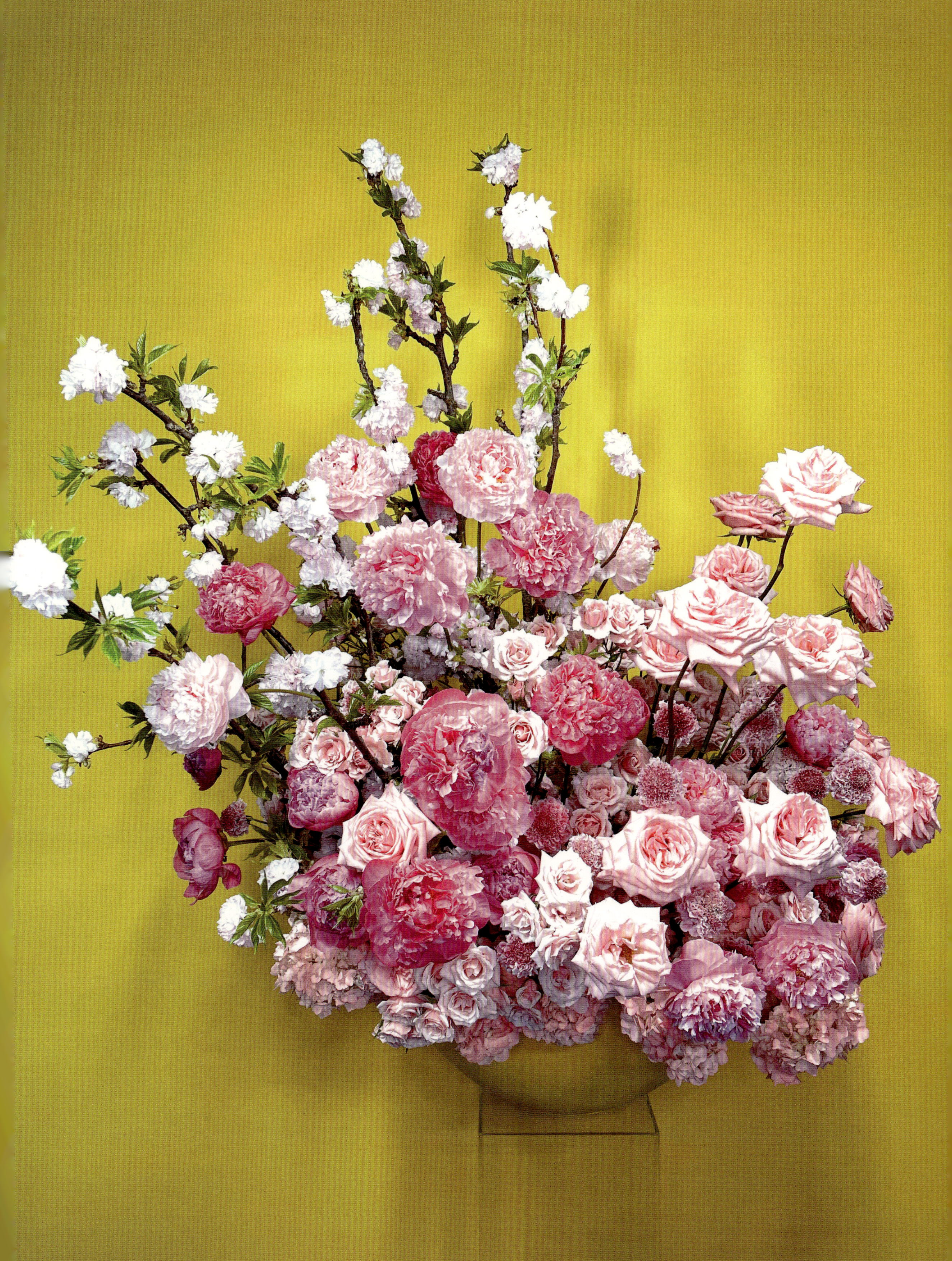

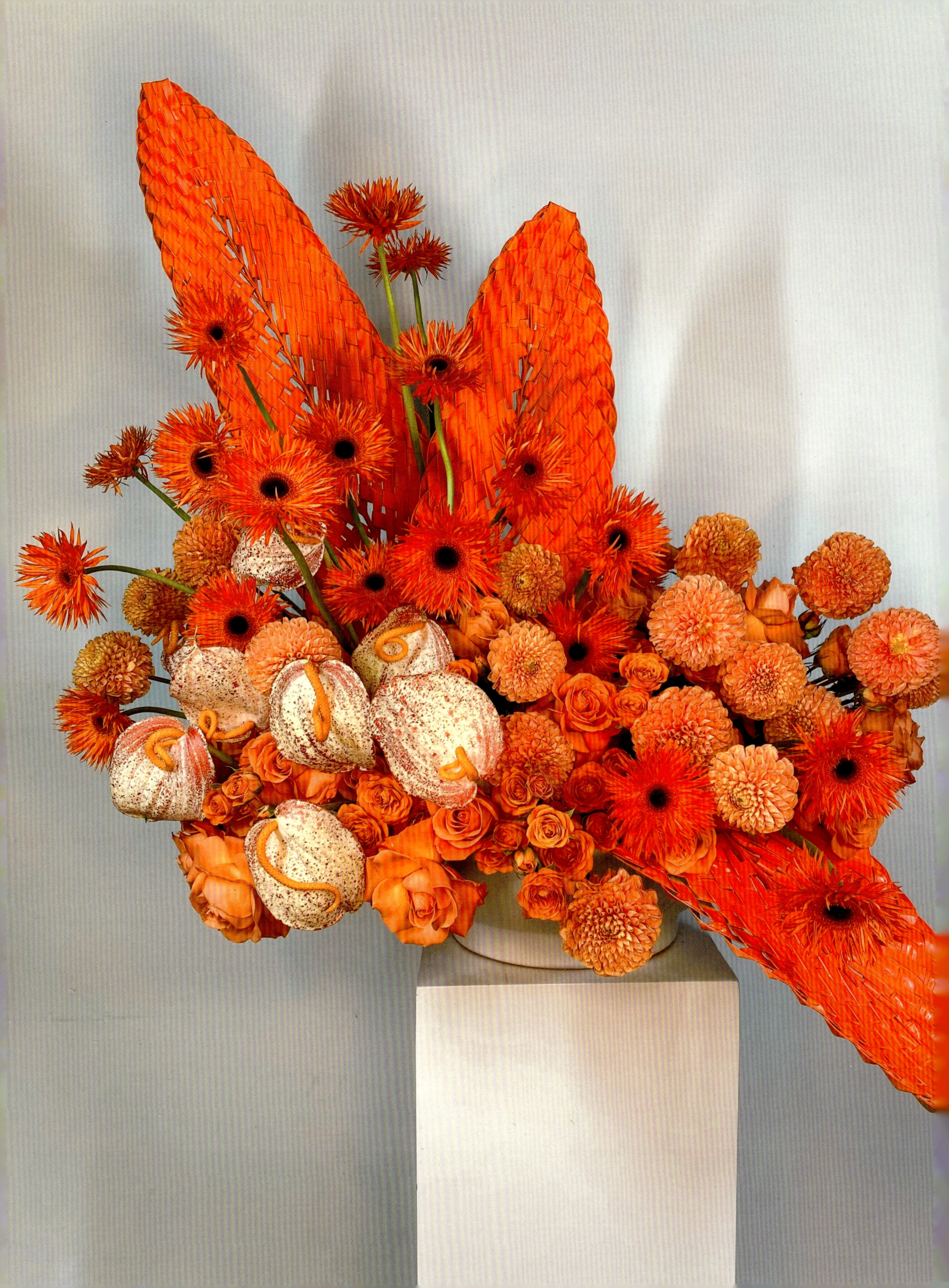

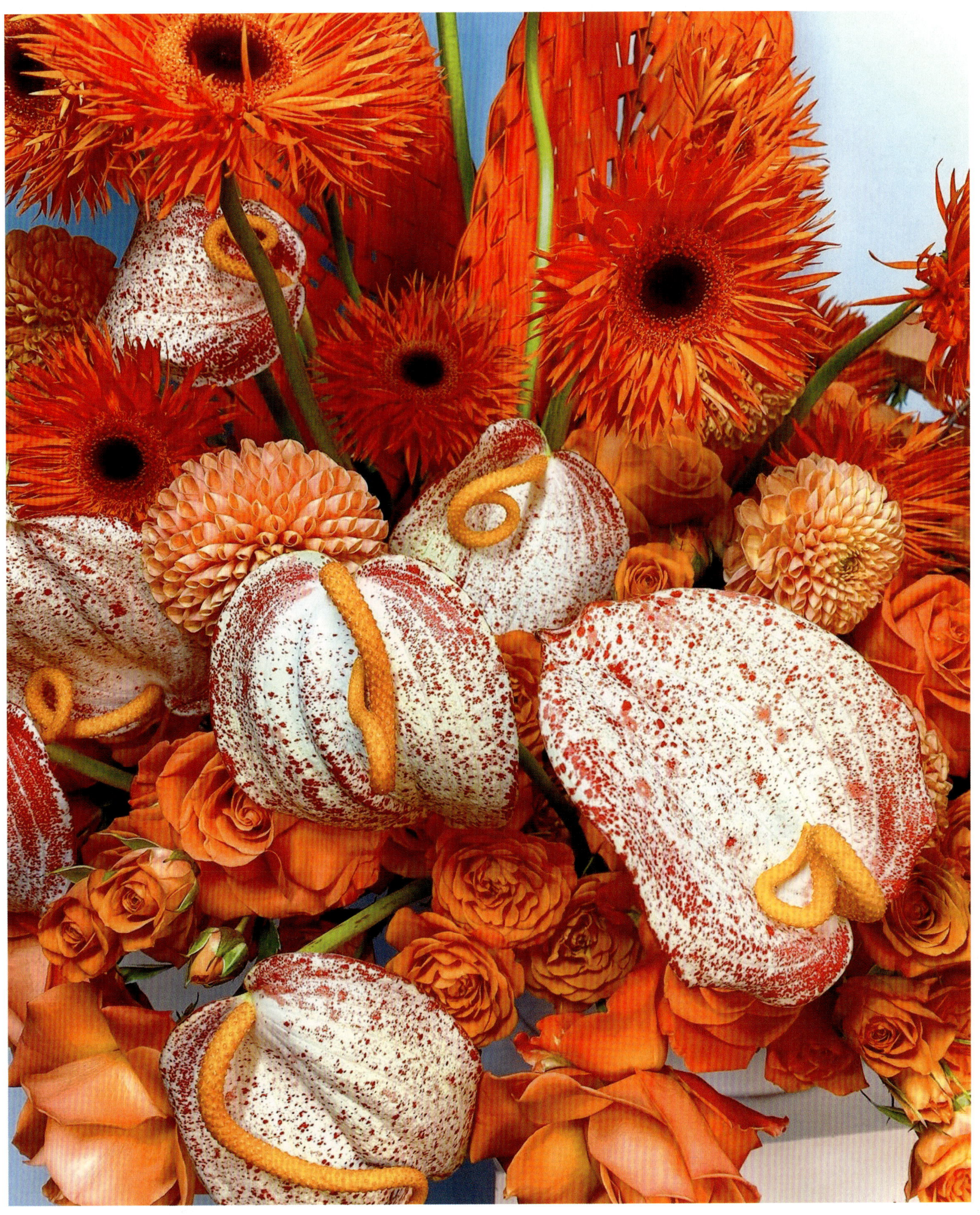

Anthurium, orange crush roses, orange babe spray roses, and orange dahlias.
FOLLOWING LEFT: Delphinium, Pink Floyd roses, and peonies.
FOLLOWING RIGHT: A bouquet of coral charm peonies and roses.

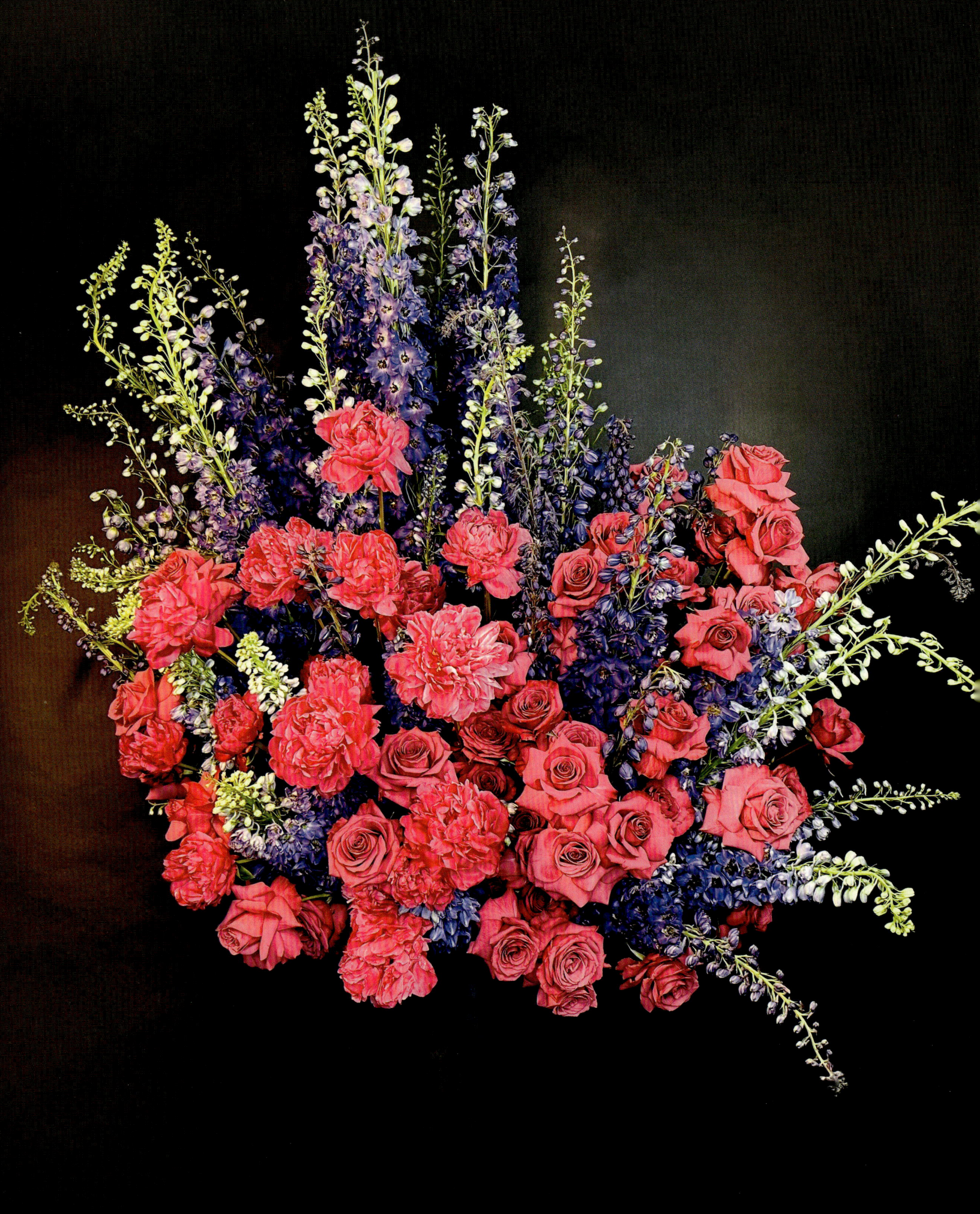

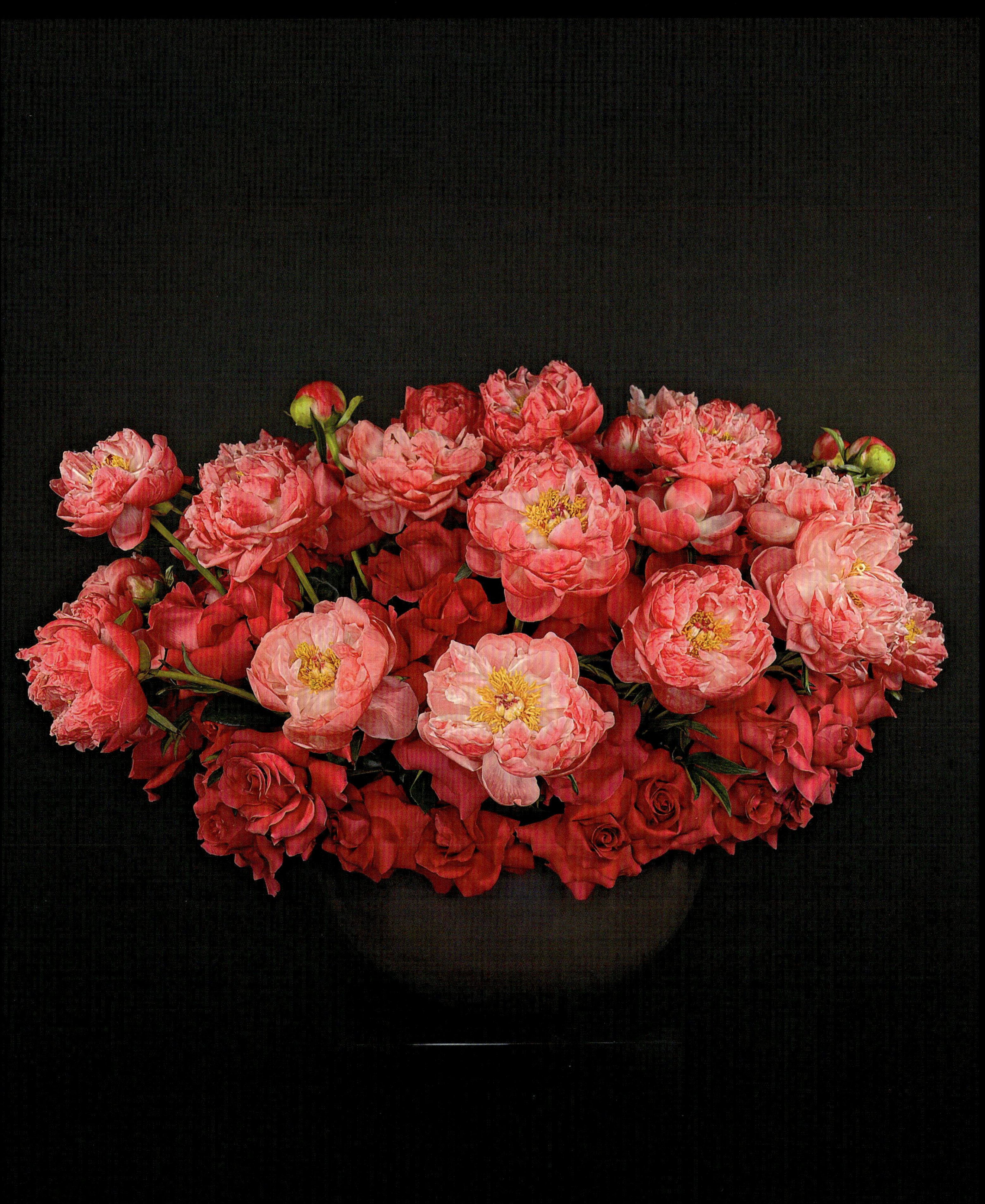

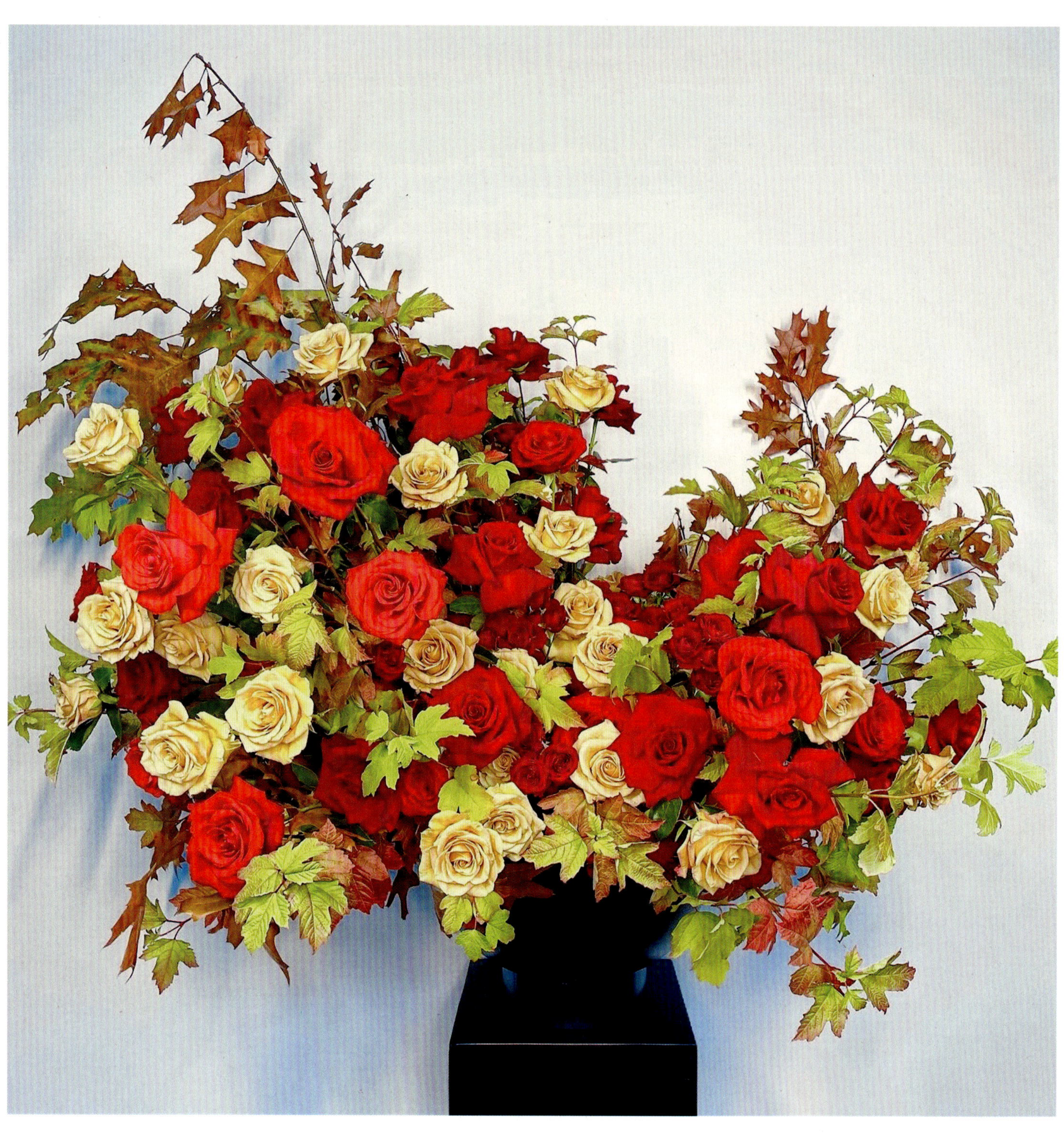

ABOVE: Roses and viburnum leaves.
OPPOSITE: A combination of roses.

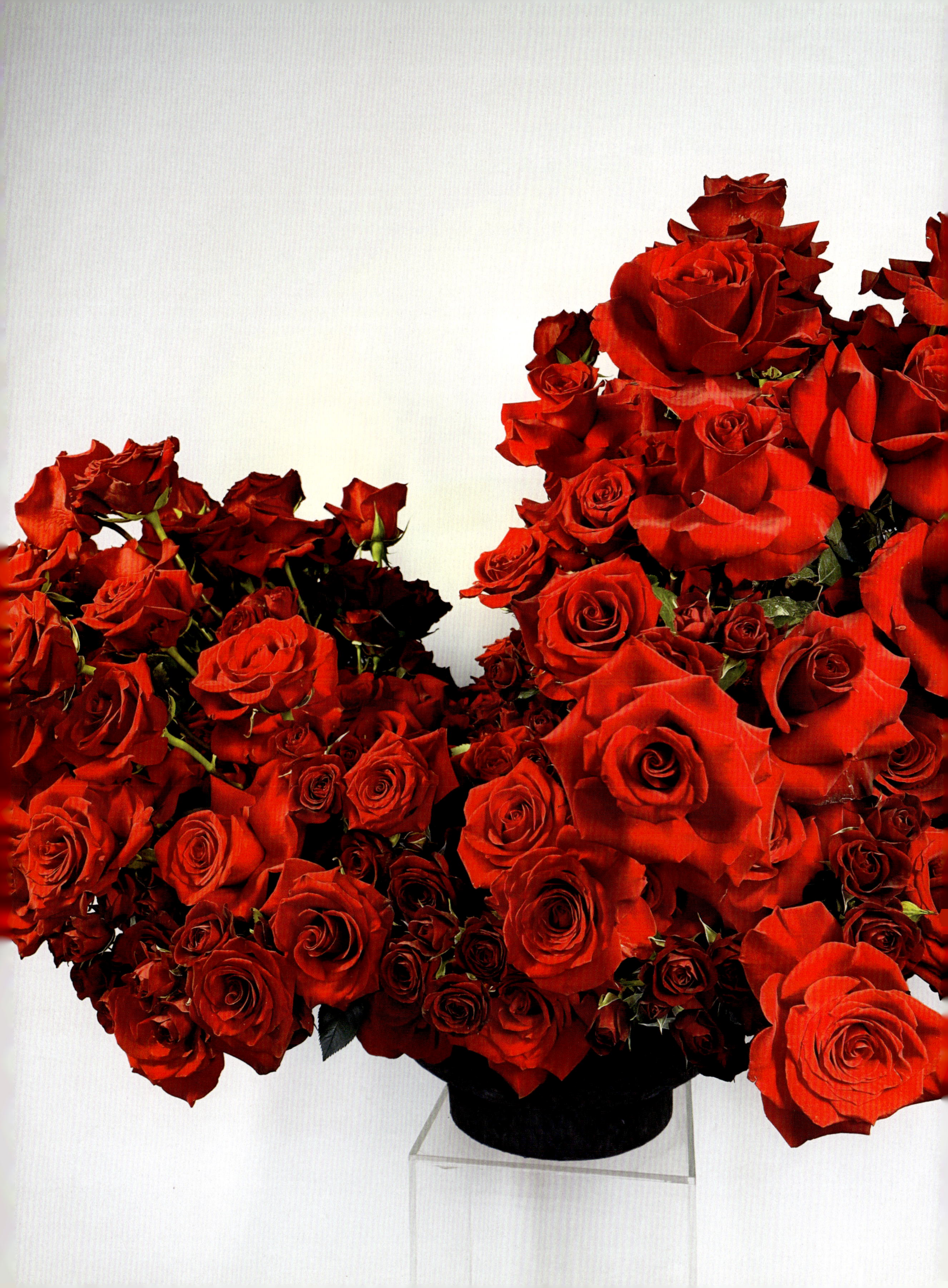

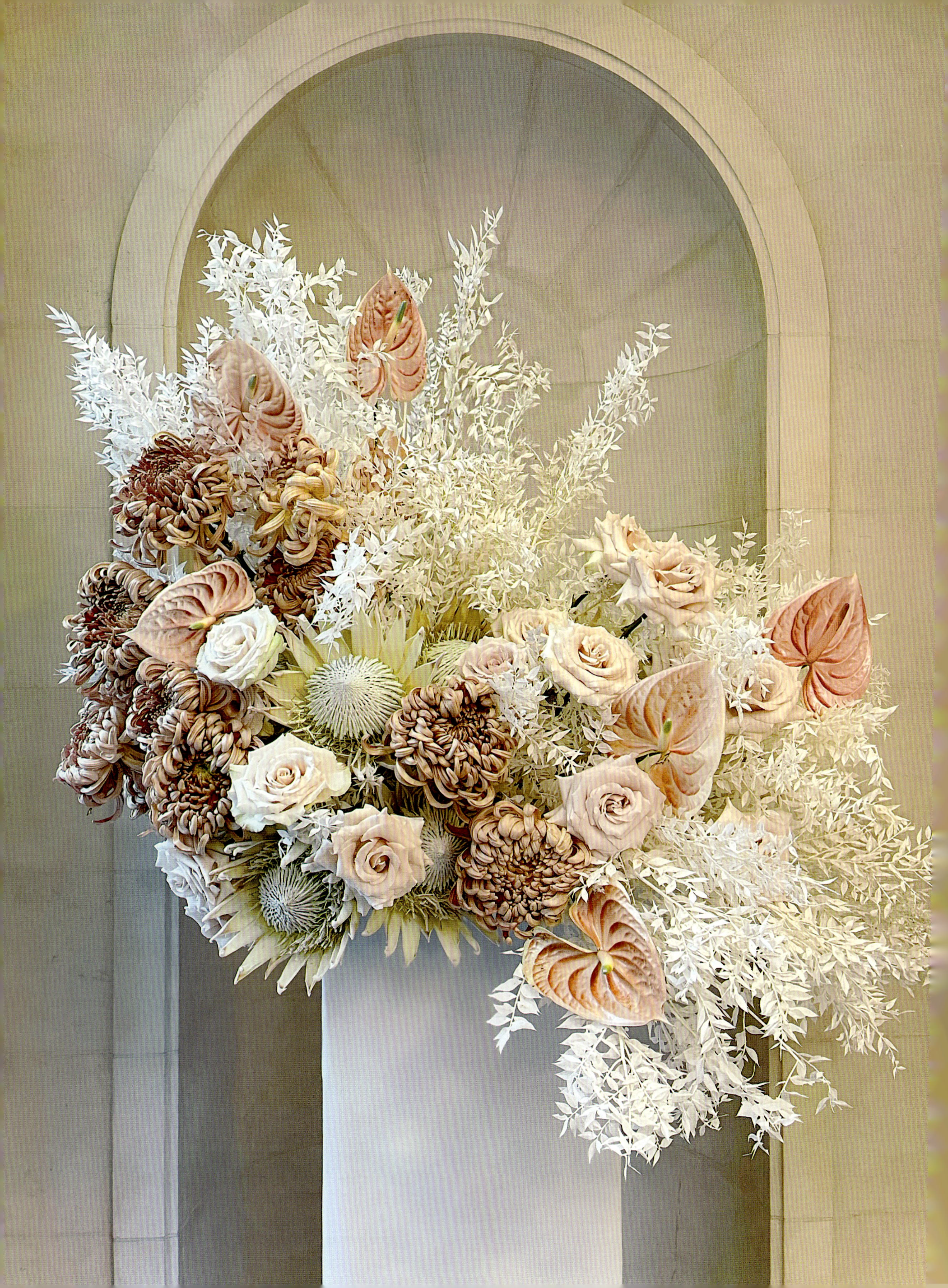

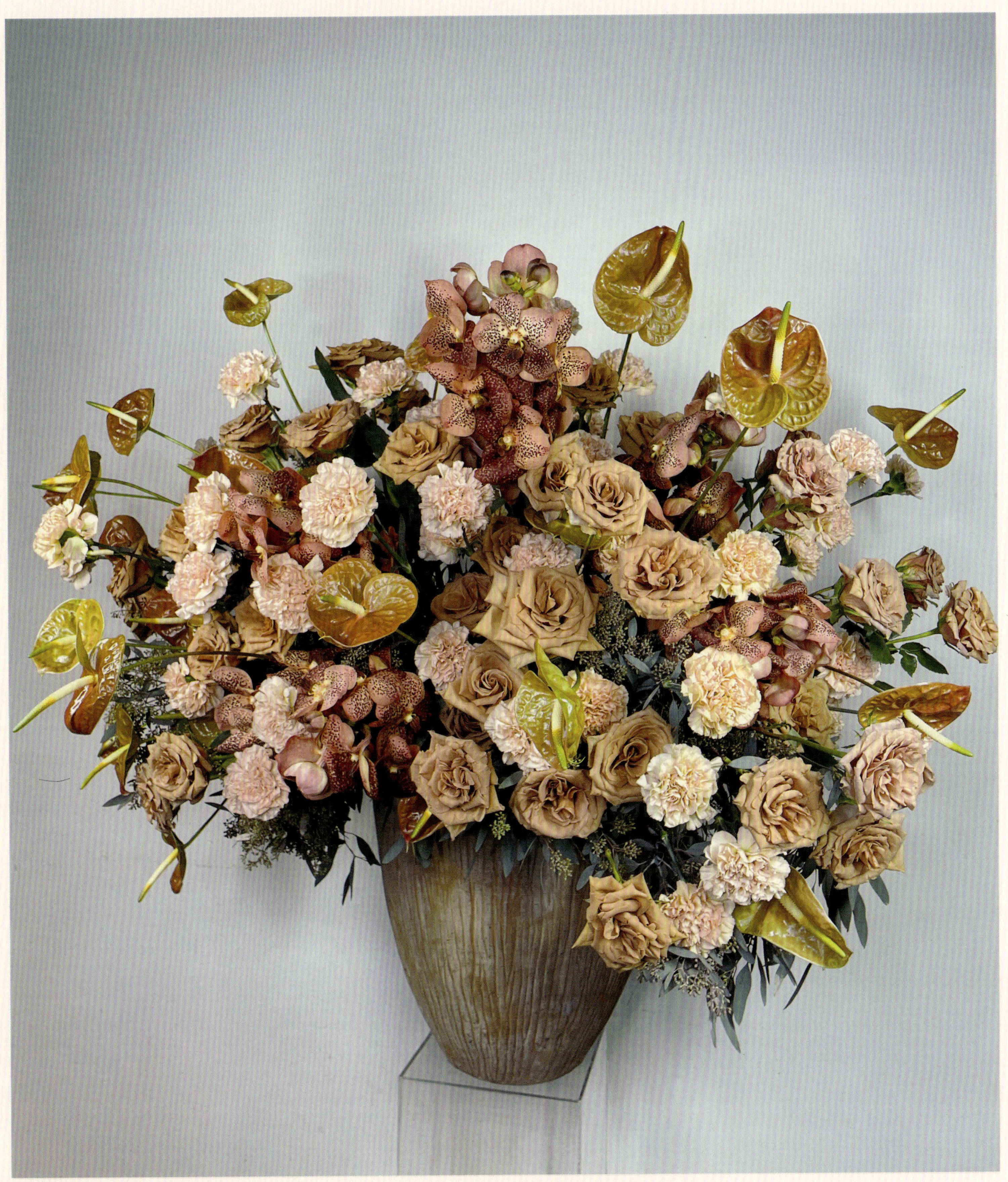

OPPOSITE: Anthurium, chrysanthemums, roses, and proteas.
ABOVE: Toffee roses, anthurium, vanda orchids, carnations, and
eucalyptus. PAGE 264: Eremurus, peonies, dahlias, and delphiniums.
PAGE 265: Cymbidium orchids, quicksand roses, and pink dahlias.
PAGE 266: Calla lilies, tuberose, hydrangeas, and roses.
PAGE 267: Black calla lilies and pumpkins.

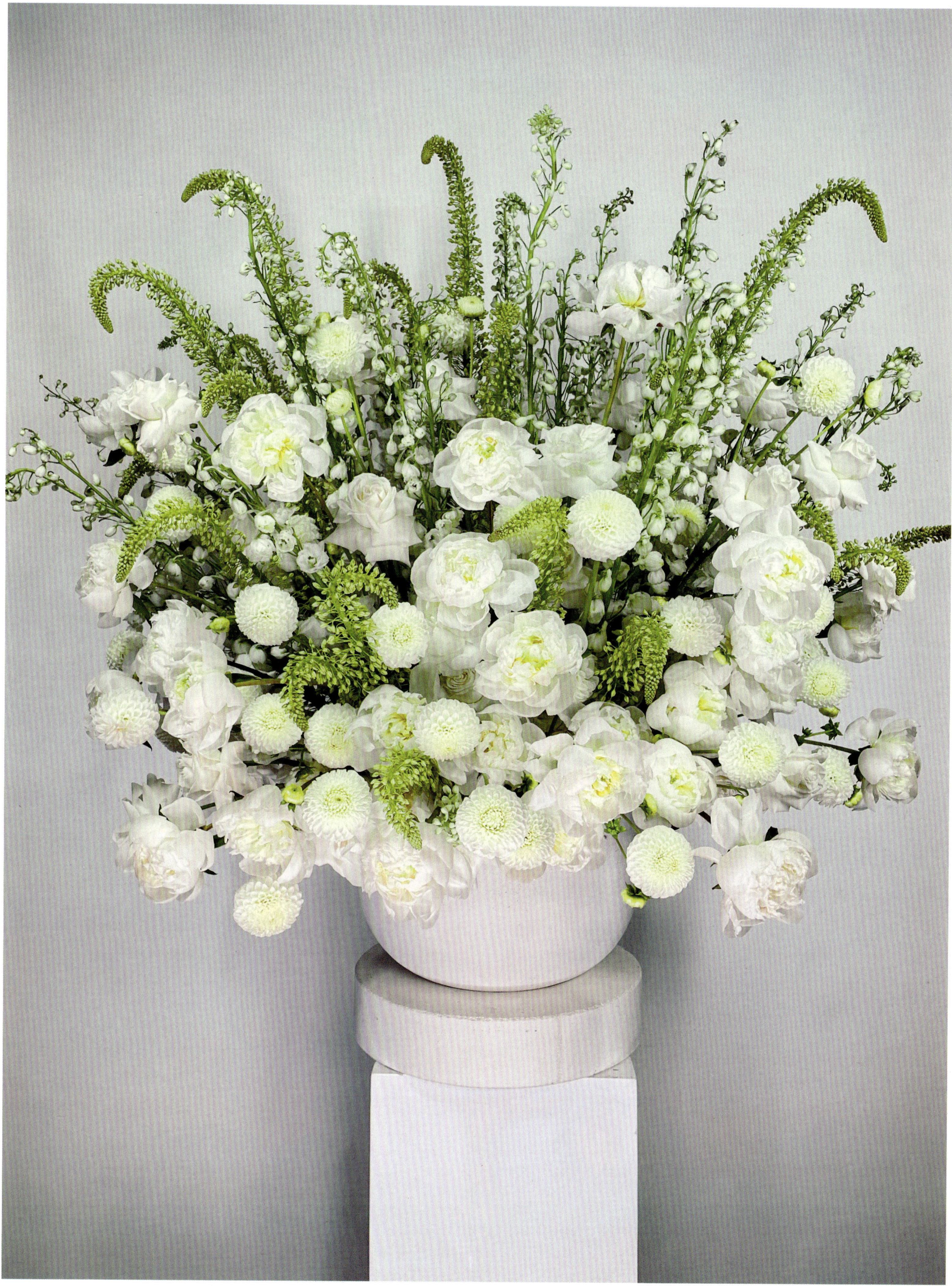

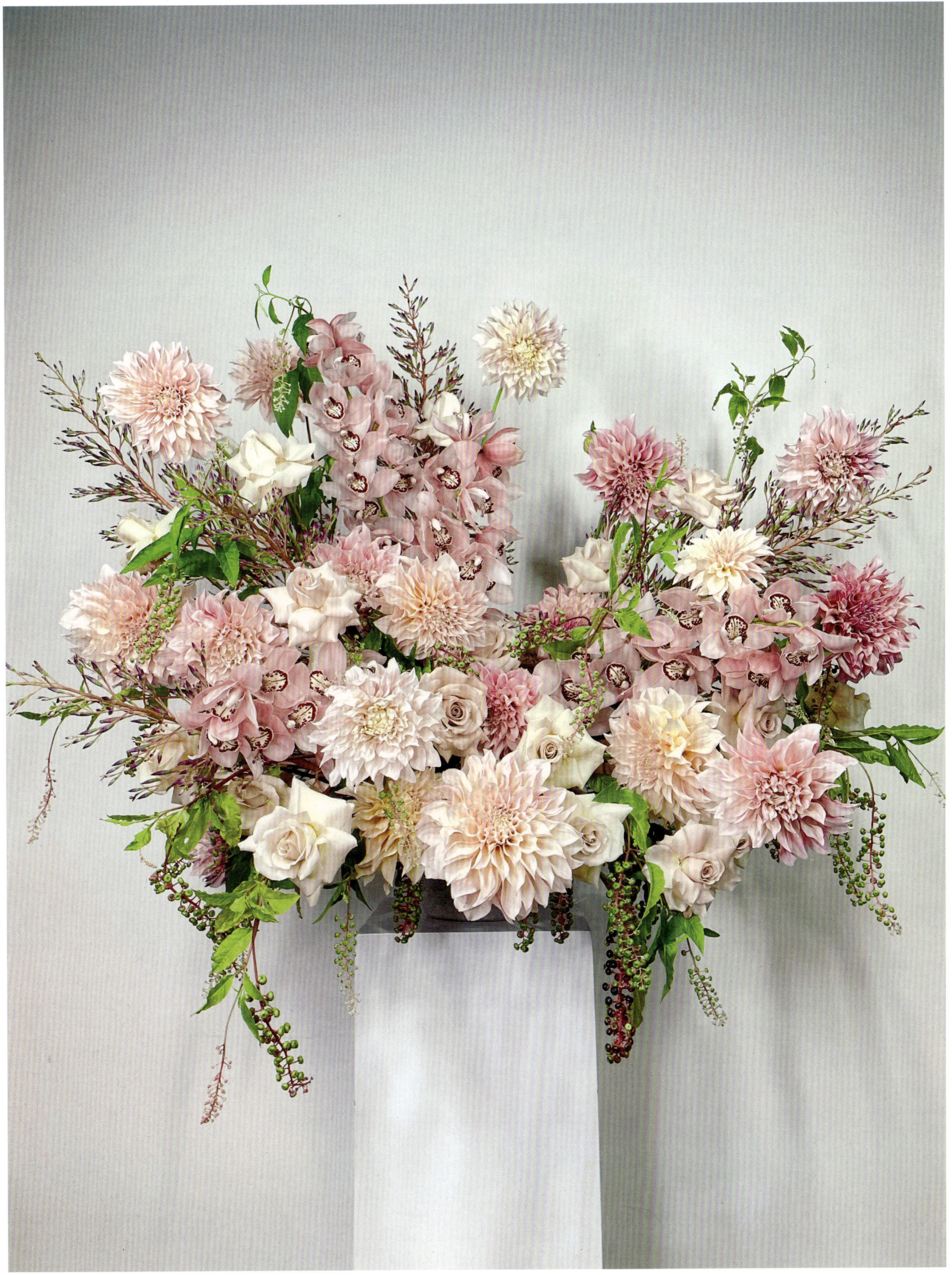

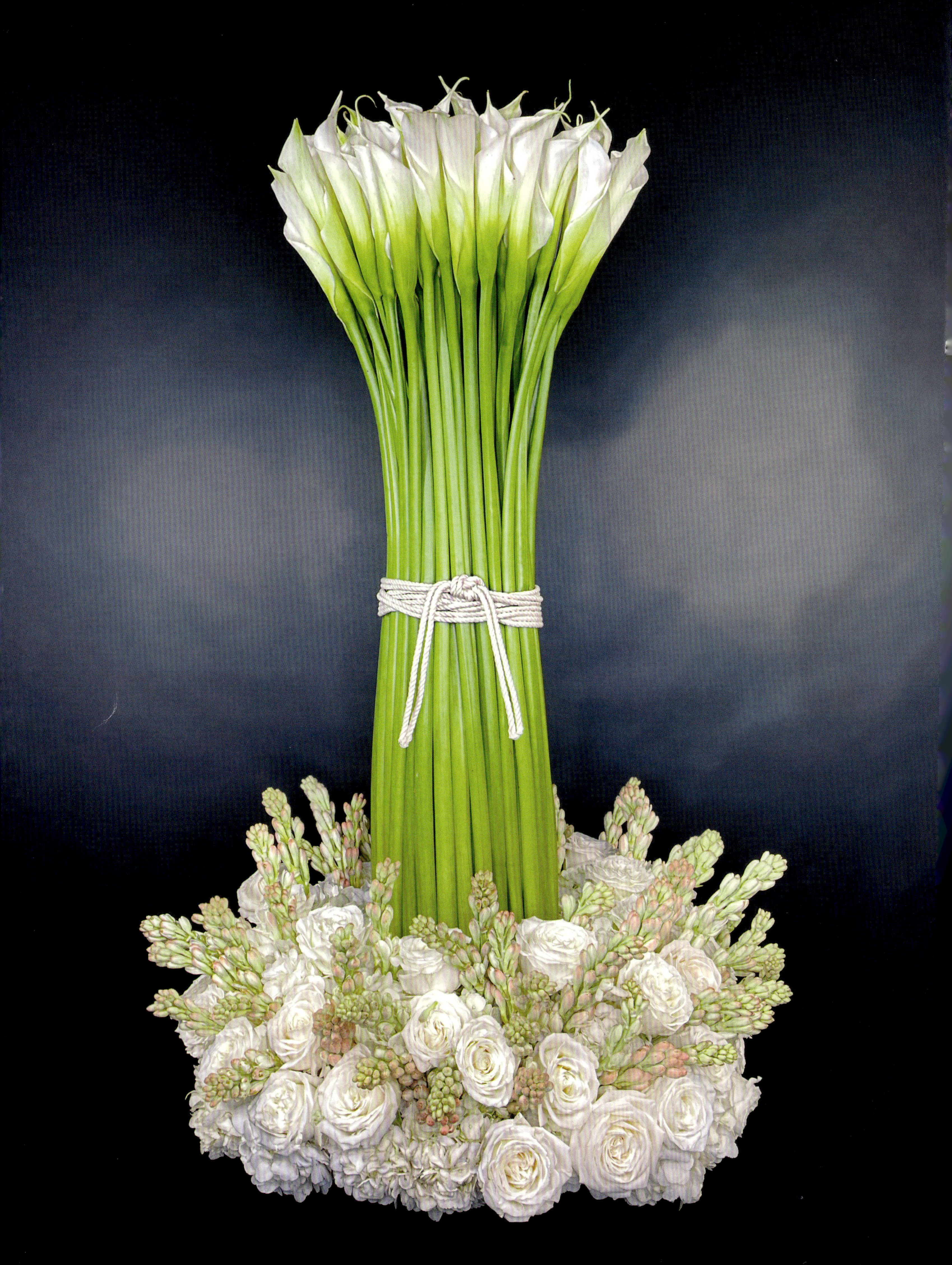

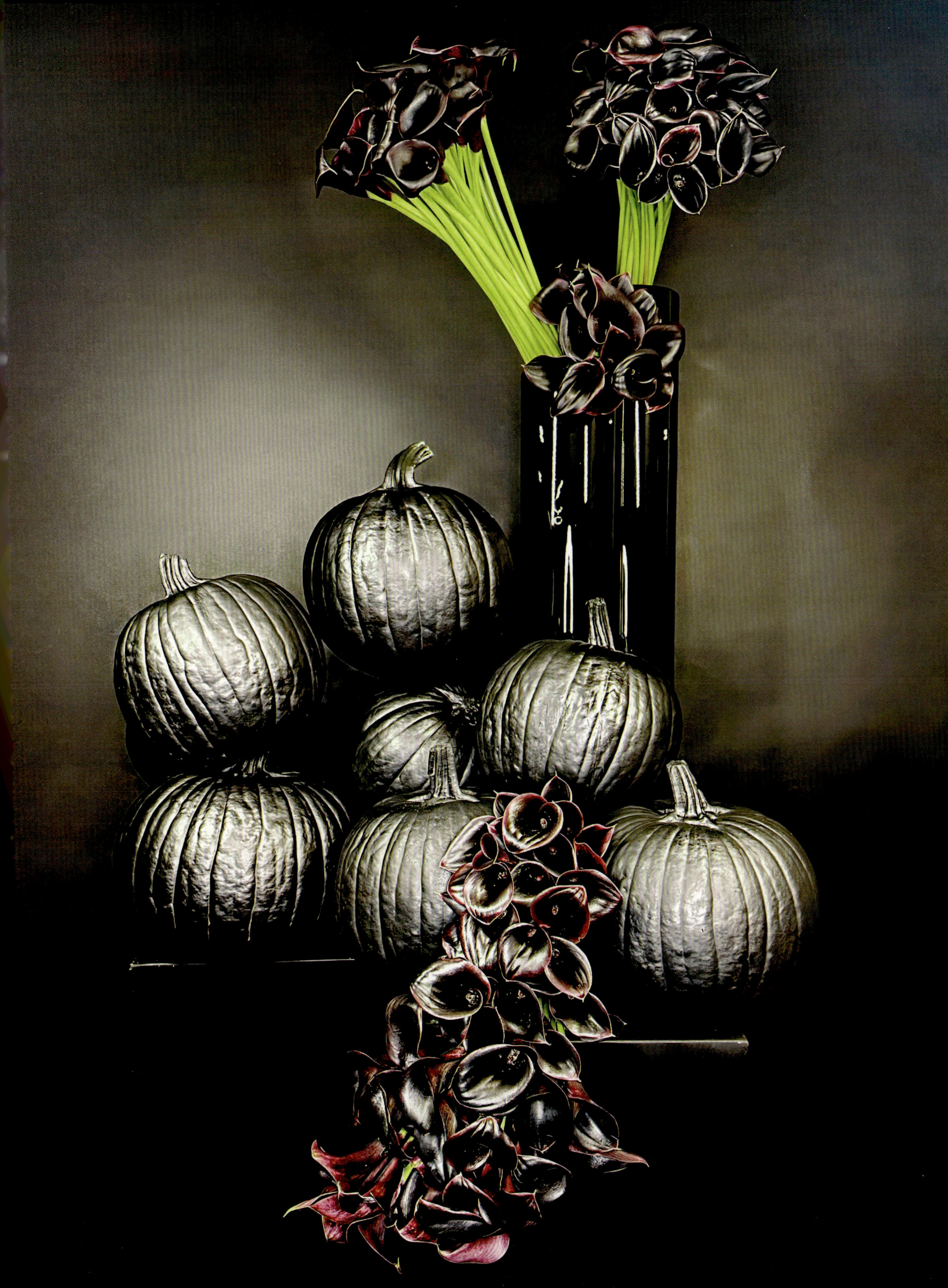

PHOTO CREDITS

Amir Mobin: pages 80–81

Andrew Boyle: pages 148–149, 223

Braedon Flynn: pages 116–117

Colin Vincent: pages 186–187

Corbin Gurkin: pages 4, 86, 94–99

Docuvitae: pages 8, 82–85

Donna Newman: pages 76–77, 110–111, 113, 198–199, 202–205

Elizabeth Messina: pages 100–101

Eric Kelley: pages 134–135

Four Seasons Hotel Los Angeles at Beverly Hills: pages 38–39, 42–43, 54–55, 226

Four Seasons Hotel Philadelphia: pages 40–41

Greg Swales: back cover, pages 2, 152–157, 176–177

Guillermo Aniel-Quiroga: pages 11, 15–29, 34–37, 44–47, 52, 56–57, 214–222, 224–225, 227–229, 232–237

Heather Kincaid: pages 72–75

Jeff Leatham: front cover, pages 6, 13–14, 114, 120–121, 138–141, 150–151, 159–161, 174–175, 178–179, 182–185, 192–197, 200–201, 206–208, 211, 246–267, 269

John & Joseph Photography, Inc.: pages 78–79, 158, 162, 164–173, 180–181, 188–191, 210, 242–245

Josh Pellegrini: pages 30–33, 48–51, 53, 58–61, 128–133, 209, 230–231, 238–241

KT Merry: pages 88–93

Raphe Wolfgang: page 12

Robert Fairer: pages 102–109

Ross Harvey Photography: pages 62–71

Stefanie M. Keenan: pages 136–137

The New York Botanical Garden: pages 142–147

Zuckermann Photography: pages 126–127

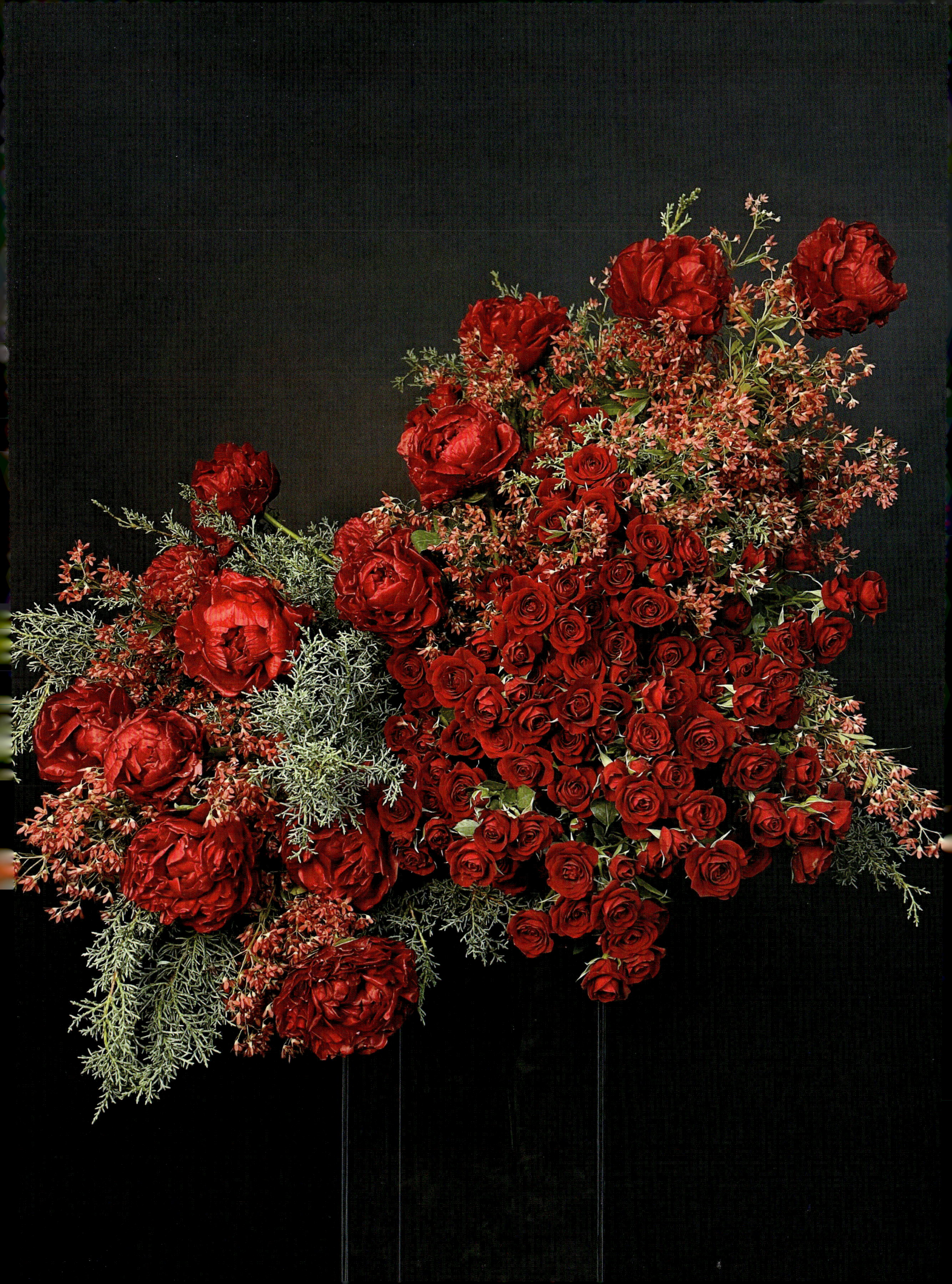

ACKNOWLEDGMENTS

I'd like to thank all of my family, friends, and clients for your love and support throughout the years. You are all dear to me, and I appreciate each, and every, one of you—as well as countless others.

In particular, I'd like to especially thank: Larry and Janet Leatham, and Jennifer Roush Leatham.

At the Four Seasons Hotels and Resorts: Isadore Sharp.

At the Four Seasons Hotel George V, Paris: Prince Alwaleed, Sarmad Zok, Jean Claude Wietzel, Jose Silva, Christian and Meg Clerc, Christopher and Brigitte Norton, Didier Le Calvez, Leah Marshall, Delphine Graness, Mathieu Miljavac, Michel Amann, and Team Leatham Paris.

At the Four Seasons Hotel Los Angeles at Beverly Hills: Michael Newcombe, the Cohen Family, Noah Wright, Montgomery Taylor, Sammy Nussdorf, Makenzie Kizis, Maggie Gastelum, Barrett Rouen, and Team Leatham LA.

At the Four Seasons Hotel Philadelphia: Brian Roberts, Karen Buchholz, Ben Shank, Cornelia Samara, Eduardo Spiller, Jenn Torpie, and Team Leatham Philly.

And the Wynn Palace Cotai.

The Kardashian and Jenner Family: Kris Jenner, Kourtney Kardashian, Kim Kardashian, Khloé Kardashian, Robert Kardashian, Kylie Jenner, Kendall Jenner, Travis Scott, and Tracy Romulus.

In addition, Evelyn Herrera, Tiandra Sharp, Kasanee Ortiz, Natalie Smith, Amanda and Gabe Watkins, Nori Bruno, Paige Dixon, Marc Boers, Sannie Boers, LM Flower Fashion, Amsterdam Growers, Mayesh LA, Maria Contreras at GM Floral Supply, LA Flower Market, Diego Ramirez, Flower Link, Liz Lauriello, Sunny Kim, Van Vliet NYC, NYBG, Revelry, Images by Lighting, Mindy Weiss, Debbie Geller, Andrew Haupt, Sharon Sacks, Claire Davis, Sade Awe, Emily Clark, Giannarelli International, Aytül Ayke Fıratoğlu, Naza Alakija, Pargol and Danial Aslanimehr, the Fertitta family, the Ambani family, the B. Carl family, the Kennedy family, the Gebert family, the McIngvale family, Cher, Tina Turner, Erwin Bach, Didier Ubersax, Eboni Nichols, Queen Latifah, Sofía Vergara, Joe Manganiello, Simon Huck, Phil Riportella, Mr. Chow, Vanessa Rano, Lauren Gaba, Brain Flanagan, and Martha Stewart.

Thank you to Publisher Roger Shaw, Art Director Ashley Quackenbush, Senior Production Manager Joshua Smith, and Senior Editor John Foster, and the entire Weldon Owen team.

And, finally, a special thanks to all you flower and design lovers: I love you. And always remember . . . love and beauty will always win!

ABOUT THE AUTHOR

Jeff Leatham, famed for his work at the Four Seasons Hotel George V, Paris; the Four Seasons Hotel Los Angeles at Beverly Hills; and the Four Seasons Hotel Philadelphia, has been creating sensations with his floral designs and installations since he first began working with flowers at the Four Seasons Hotel Los Angeles at Beverly Hills. One of Jeff's biggest honors to date is being awarded the prestigious Knighthood Chevalier of the Ordre des Arts et des Lettres, the French government's highest honor for artists who have made a significant contribution to French culture. Jeff's work is a combination of his love for flowers, people, and design. His creations are bold statements that use shape, color, and simplicity to produce a dramatic effect. His floral installations are often compared to contemporary art. Breathtaking and unforgettable, Jeff's signature designs are always integral to the setting, never merely a backdrop. He is known for pushing the boundaries of modern floral design and will continue to be a tastemaker in the industry for years to come.

Jeff's expertise attracts praise around the world, as seen in his previous books *Flowers by Jeff Leatham*, *Flowers by Design*, and *Jeff Leatham—Visionary Floral Art and Design*. Jeff starred in the docuseries *Flowers Uncut* and has been featured on the *Oprah Winfrey Show*. His continuous collaboration with international luxury brands has allowed Jeff to present his work in international design expositions around the world, which include luxury brands such as Dolce & Gabbana, Alexander McQueen, Chanel, Balenciaga, Bulgari, Swarovski Crystal, Givenchy, Elie Saab, Louis Vuitton, Goyard, Burberry, Waterford Crystal, Baccarat Crystal, Dom Pérignon, Lexus, Samsung, and the LEGO Group.

Jeff's floral design clientele is as impressive as his work, and includes Tina Turner, Oprah Winfrey, Cher, Beyoncé, and the Kardashian family. Jeff had the honor of designing the flowers for the weddings of Sofía Vergara, Eva Longoria, Tina Turner, and Chelsea Clinton.

Jeff's installations include the first major event since the time of Louis XIV and Marie Antoinette in the famed Galerie des Glaces at Château de Versailles and the reopening of the Museum of Modern Art in New York City. He designed the iconic holiday windows for Bloomingdale's New York City flagship store and two immersive art exhibits at Intersect by Lexus in New York City. In 2020 and 2022, Jeff was the featured artistic designer for the iconic Orchid Show at the New York Botanical Garden, and in 2021 he designed the main pavilion at Franklin Delano Roosevelt Park for the Philadelphia Flower Show's event "Habitat: Nature's Masterpiece." In 2021 and 2022, Jeff and Kim Kardashian launched two successful fragrance collections.

weldon**owen**

An imprint of Insight Editions
PO Box 3088
San Rafael, CA 94912
www.weldonowen.com

CEO Raoul Goff
VP Publisher Roger Shaw
Editorial Director Katie Killebrew
Senior Editor John Foster
Editorial Assistant Amanda Nelson
VP Creative Director Chrissy Kwasnik
Art Director Ashley Quackenbush
VP Manufacturing Alix Nicholaeff
Senior Production Manager Joshua Smith
Sr Production Manager, Subsidiary Rights Lina s Palma-Temena

Weldon Owen would like to thank Karen Levy for proofreading.

ISBN: 978-1-68188-923-8

Manufactured in China by Insight Editions
10 9 8 7 6 5 4 3 2 1

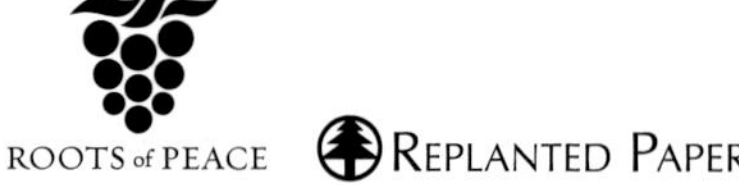